# Cognitive Limitations in Aging and Psychopathology

This book examines the major progress made in recent psychological science in understanding the cognitive control of thought, emotion, and behavior and what happens when that control is diminished as a result of aging, depression, developmental disabilities, or psychopathology. Each chapter of this volume reports the most recent research by a leading researcher on the international stage. Topics include the effects on thought, emotion, and behavior by limitations in working memory, cognitive control, attention, inhibition, and reasoning processes. Other chapters review standard and emerging research paradigms and new findings on limitations in cognitive functioning associated with aging and psychopathology. The explicit goal behind this volume was to facilitate cross-area research and training by familiarizing researchers with paradigms and findings in areas different from, but related to, their own.

Randall W. Engle is Professor and Chair in the School of Psychology at Georgia Institute of Technology. He received his M.A. and Ph.D. from Ohio State University. His research over the past 20 years has evolved from that regarding the nature of individual differences in working memory capacity (WMC) to the role of WMC in higher-order cognition.

Grzegorz Sedek is Director of the Institute of Social Psychology at Warsaw School of Social Psychology in Poland and professor at the Institute of Psychology, Polish Academy of Sciences. He received his M.A. and Ph.D. from the University of Warsaw in Poland. His main areas of research involve cognitive limitations in depression, aging, after uncontrollability pre-exposure, and dual-process models in social cognition.

Ulrich von Hecker is Lecturer at the School of Psychology at Cardiff University. His current research involves social cognition, cognitive limitations in depression, and the nature and the dynamic character of emotion. He has written many articles and has published in the *Journal of Experimental Psychology, European Journal of Social Psychology,* and *Social Cognition.*

Daniel N. McIntosh is Associate Professor of Psychology at the University of Denver. His research focuses on emotions and coping using survey, laboratory, and psychophysiological methods. In particular, he investigates the role of religion in coping, stress and coping in low control contexts, and cognitive deficits emerging from situations of uncontrollability and depression.

# Cognitive Limitations in Aging and Psychopathology

Edited by

**RANDALL W. ENGLE**
*Georgia Institute of Technology*

**GRZEGORZ SEDEK**
*Warsaw School of Social Psychology and
Polish Academy of Sciences*

**ULRICH VON HECKER**
*Cardiff University*

**DANIEL N. MCINTOSH**
*University of Denver*

**CAMBRIDGE**
UNIVERSITY PRESS

CAMBRIDGE UNIVERSITY PRESS
Cambridge, New York, Melbourne, Madrid, Cape Town, Singapore, São Paulo

Cambridge University Press
40 West 20th Street, New York, NY 10011-4211, USA

www.cambridge.org
Information on this title: www.cambridge.org/9780521834070

First published 2005

Printed in the United States of America

*A catalog record for this book is available from the British Library*

*Library of Congress Cataloging-in-Publication Data*
Cognitive limitations in aging and psychopathology / edited by Randall W.
Engle . . . [et al.].
 p.   cm.
Includes bibliographical references and indexes.
ISBN 0-521-83407-4 (hardback) – ISBN 0-521-54195-6 (pbk.)
1. Cognition disorders.   2. Cognition disorders in old age.   3. Developmental disabilities.
4. Psychology, Pathological.   5. Cognition in old age.   6. Cognitive psychology.
7. Cognition.   I. Engle, Randall W.
RC553.C64C635   2005
618.97'68 – dc22       2005000124

ISBN-13   978-0-521-83407-0 hardback
ISBN-10   0-521-83407-4 hardback

ISBN-13   978-0-521-54195-4 paperback
ISBN-10   0-521-54195-6 paperback

# Contents

# Contributors

**Deanna M. Barch**
Department of Psychology
Washington University
Campus Box 1125
One Brookings Drive
St. Louis, MO 63130
e-mail: dbarch@artsci.wustl.edu

**Chandramallika Basak**
Department of Psychology and
    Center for Health and Behavior
Syracuse University
430 Huntington Hall
Syracuse NY 13210
e-mail: cbasak@syr.edu

**Sylwia Bedynska**
Warsaw School of Social
Psychology
Chodakowska 19/31
03-815 Warsaw
Poland
e-mail: bedynska@pro.onet.pl

**Albina Bondar**
Max Planck Institute for Human
    Development
Center for Lifespan Psychology
Lentzeallee 94 D-14195 Berlin
Germany
e-mail:
    bondar@mpib-berlin.mpg.de

**Kara L. Bopp**
Department of Psychology
Hamilton College
198 College Hill Road
Clinton, NY 13323
kbopp@hamilton.edu

**Ritvij Bowry**
118 Haggar Hall
University of Notre Dame
Notre Dame, IN 46556
e-mail: Ritvij.Bowry.1@nd.edu

**Todd S. Braver**
Department of Psychology
Washington University
Campus Box 1125
One Brookings Drive
St. Louis, MO 63130
e-mail: tbraver@artsci.wustl.edu

**Aneta Brzezicka-Rotkiewicz**
Warsaw School of Social
Psychology
Chodakowska 19/31
03–815 Warsaw
Poland
e-mail: abrzezi2@swps.edu.pl

**John Cerella**
Department of Psychology and
    Center for Health and Behavior
Syracuse University
430 Huntington Hall
Syracuse NY 13210
e-mail: jcerella@psych.syr.edu

**Randall W. Engle**
School of Psychology
Georgia Institute of Technology
654 Cherry St.
Atlanta, GA 30332-0170
e-mail:
    randall.engle@psych.gatech.edu

**Susan Fojas**
Department of Psychology
University of Denver
Denver, CO 80208
e-mail: fojass@jccany.org

**Elaine Fox**
Department of Psychology,
University of Essex,
Wivenhoe Park,
Colchester CO4 3SQ
United Kingdom
e-mail: efox@essex.ac.uk

**George A. Georgiou**
School of Humanities and Social
    Sciences
Intercollege
46 Makedonitissas Ave.,
P.O. Box 24005,
1700 Nicosia,
Cyprus
georgiou.g@intercollege.ac.cy

**Richard P. Heitz**
School of Psychology
Georgia Institute of Technology
654 Cherry St.
Atlanta, GA 30332-0170
e-mail: gte016z@prism.gatech.edu

**Jutta Joormann**
Department of Psychology
Bldg. 420 Jordan Hall, Room 160
Stanford University, Stanford,
    CA 94305
e-mail:
    joormann@psych.stanford.edu

**Miroslaw Kofta**
Faculty of Psychology
University of Warsaw
Stawki 5/7 Warsaw
Poland
e-mail:
    kofta@engram.psych.uw.edu.pl

**Ralf Th. Krampe**
Max Planck Institute for Human
    Development
Center for Lifespan Psychology
Lentzeallee 94 D-14195 Berlin
Germany
e-mail:
    krampe@mpib-berlin.mpg.de

**Karen Z. H. Li**
Centre for Research in Human
    Development
Department of Psychology
Concordia University
7141 Sherbrooke Street West
Montreal, Quebec
Canada H4B 1R6
e-mail: kli@vax2.concordia.ca

**Elizabeth A. Maylor**
Department of Psychology
University of Warwick
Coventry CV4 7AL
United Kingdom
e-mail:
    Elizabeth.Maylor@warwick.ac.uk

**Daniel N. McIntosh**
Department of Psychology
University of Denver

Denver, CO 80208
e-mail: dmcintos@du.edu

**Klaus Oberauer**
University of Potsdam
Allgemeine Psychologie I
Postfach 60 15 53
14415 Potsdam
Germany
e-mail: ko@rz.uni-potsdam.de

**Kinga Piber-Dabrowska**
Warsaw School of Social
    Psychology
Chodakowska 19/31
03-815 Warsaw
Poland
e-mail: kinga.piber-
    dabrowska@swps.edu.pl

**Friederike Schlaghecken**
Department of Psychology
University of Warwick
Coventry CV4 7AL
United Kingdom
e-mail:
    F.Schlaghecken@warwick.ac.uk

**Grzegorz Sedek**
Warsaw School of Social
    Psychology and Polish
Academy of Sciences
Chodakowska 19/31
03-815 Warsaw
Poland
e-mail:
    Grzegorz.Sedek@swps.edu.pl

**Martin Sliwinski**
Department of Psychology
Huntington Hall 430
Syracuse University
Syracuse, NY 13244
e-mail: mjsliwin@psych.syr.edu

**Joshua Smyth**
Department of Psychology
Huntington Hall 430
Syracuse University
Syracuse, NY 13244
e-mail: jmsmyth@psych.syr.edu

**Robert S. Stawski**
Department of Psychology
Huntington Hall 430
Syracuse University
Syracuse, NY 13244
e-mail: rsstawski@syr.edu

**Nash Unsworth**
School of Psychology
Georgia Institute of Technology
654 Cherry St.
Atlanta, GA 30332-0170
e-mail: gtg039d@prism.gatech.edu

**Paul Verhaeghen**
Department of Psychology and
    Center for Health and Behavior
Syracuse University
430 Huntington Hall
Syracuse NY 13210
e-mail: pverhaeg@psych.syr.edu

**Ulrich von Hecker**
School of Psychology
Cardiff University
PO Box 901
Cardiff, CF10 3YG
United Kingdom
e-mail: vonheckeru@cardiff.ac.uk

**James A. Waltz**
University of Maryland School of
    Medicine
Maryland Psychiatric Research
    Center
P. O. Box 21247
Baltimore, MD 21228
e-mail:
    jwaltz@mprc.umaryland.edu

**Christina Wasylyshyn**
Dept. of Psychology
Huntington Hall 430
Syracuse University
Syracuse, NY 13244
e-mail: cwasylys@syr.edu

**Derrick G. Watson**
Department of Psychology
University of Warwick

Coventry CV4 7AL
United Kingdom
e-mail:
    D.G.Watson@warwick.ac.uk

**Robert West**
118 Haggar Hall
University of Notre Dame
Notre Dame, IN 46556
e-mail: west.19@nd.edu

# Preface

As technological advances lead to more understanding of the brain, or the "hardware" of human thought, the importance of understanding the "software" that is, cognitive functions, has become even more important. There has been progress in the cognitive sciences in understanding the basic processes of cognition and how these processes relate to the operations and behaviors of the organism in the environment. Among the most intensely studied processes are those relating to attention and working memory (e.g., inhibition, updating, and coordination) and higher level cognitive abilities such as planning, reasoning, comprehension, and problem solving, which are attributed to circuits associated with the brain's frontal lobe. One reason for this accelerating interest is the rapid progress in those areas of cognitive psychology and cognitive neuroscience that focus on *working memory* and *neuroimaging* research (Andrade, 2001; Cabeza & Nyberg, 2000; Davidson, Pizzagalli, Nitschke, & Putnam, 2002; Gazzaniga, Ivry, & Mangum, 1998; Logie & Gilhooly, 1999; Miyake & Shah, 1999; Richardson et al., 1996). Another reason for this surge of interest is that many populations, such as older adults (Craik & Salthouse, 2000; Perfect & Maylor, 2000; Rabbitt, 1997), persons with emotional disorders (Hertel, 1997; von Hecker & Sedek, 1999; Williams, Watts, MacLeod, & Mathews, 1997), and individuals with brain injuries (Waltz et al., 1999), have demonstrated cognitive limitations with respect to attention, working memory, and other so-called executive functions.

The significance of these functions is underscored by the wide range of populations in which such impairments have been found and by the areas of specialization within the cognitive sciences in which they have become increasingly important. In this broad interdisciplinary research domain, one might distinguish, on the one hand, basic research fostering the understanding of cognitive processes, and, on the other hand, research fields that combine those recent advances in cognitive psychology with the investigation into individual or group differences. Such individual differences might be associated with developmental changes such as aging, developmental problems such as reading disability, and psychopathology such as depression and schizophrenia. For example, *cognitive aging* links the research lines on aging to those on cognitive processes. Similarly, studies in *cognitive psychopathology* examine emotional, mental, and brain disorders in terms of the underlying basic cognitive mechanisms that are affected in these states. Unfortunately, the literatures in these affiliated fields tend to evolve and progress largely separate from each other, although they share common concepts and objectives and are tightly linked by their central objective to obtain insights into cognitive functions. Explanations of the effects of aging and psychopathology on cognitive performance often make use of concepts from the basic cognitive literature; however, contributors to the two literatures do not often communicate directly with one another. This lack of communication means that insights and information gained from scientists working with one population, or with a particular paradigm, often do little to advance understanding in other closely related areas.

Our experience is that discussions across disciplines provide inspiration that help focus and develop our own understanding and research. The goal of the present volume is to provide such stimulation to others working in the large area of the cognitive sciences. This volume is unique in that it is an original attempt to combine a range of recent research achievements of North American and European teams fostering innovative experimental investigations in the previously mentioned fields. The publication of the volume was motivated by an international, interdisciplinary conference in Kazimierz Dolny, Poland in autumn 2002, during which most of the chapter authors presented and discussed their work. Unlike larger conferences during which scientists communicate primarily with those working in their own areas of specialization, this conference focused on the presentation and discussion of cutting-edge paradigms and findings from each others' areas, and listening to the thoughts of "outsiders" regarding one's own work. The presenters came from different backgrounds with substantial overlap, such as the emotion–cognition link (Elaine Fox, Jutta Joormann, Edward Necka, Grzegorz Sedek), working memory (Randall Engle, Akira Miyake, Klaus Oberauer, James Waltz), social cognition (Miroslaw Kofta, Daniel McIntosh, Ulrich von Hecker), and cognitive aging (Elizabeth Maylor, Ralf Krampe, Paul Verhaeghen, Patrick Rabbitt).

The aim of the conference was to bring together scholars from different but intersecting fields in an environment that engendered dialogue and understanding of problems common to the intersecting areas. The beautiful Polish countryside and wonderful Polish food and vodka served to lubricate and stimulate the easy flow of ideas across the participants. In terms of this dialogue, for example, cognitive functioning and adaptation were addressed in the context of basic research on working memory and in various attempts to understand specific psychological states. Anxiety, depression, older age, or the experience of social stigmatization, to name just a few examples, can change the way we memorize, reason, or make judgments. Conversely, knowledge about these functional changes might again inform theories about working memory and social cognition in general. The speakers at the conference, and mostly the authors of the present volume, focused their contributions on the relation between the allocated amount of attentional resources and particular modes of processing and on how certain patterns of executive functioning may directly characterize certain states, such as anxiety, depression (dysphoria), or activated stereotypes. They also talked about different candidate functions within current models of working memory, such as attention, maintenance, or inhibition, to better understand the mechanisms of how psychological states might affect thinking and judgment.

In an attempt to further strengthen the theoretical and empirical scope of the volume along the lines discussed at the conference, we invited a number of further authors who are leading experts on related fields, but had not been part of our meetings, to share their views and contribute chapters. We are especially delighted to have received enthusiastic feedback to this invitation and thus be able to include Barch and Braver's chapter on impairments of cognitive control in schizophrenia; Sliwinski, Smyth, Stawski, and Wasylyshyn's chapter on the relation between stress experience and working memory performance; and West and Bowry's chapter on cognitive neuroscience methodologies applied to cognitive aging.

Our aim was to produce a work with chapters that meet the highest demands of accuracy and currency within specializations, but that is accessible to scientists and students outside the authors' specialties. To accomplish this aim, all chapters were reviewed not only by the external reviewers (professionals from the same research field) but also by graduate students who were specialists in areas other than the chapter they reviewed. We believe that those currently working in one area will find the chapters from researchers both inside and outside their area relevant and stimulating. We also believe that students of any of the cognitive sciences will benefit from exposure to both "hot cognition" and "cold cognition" perspectives represented here. We hope readers will find this volume as informative, stimulating, and generative as we found both the conference and the reading of these chapters.

Autumn 2004
Randall W. Engle
(Georgia Institute of Technology, USA)

Grzegorz Sedek
(Warsaw School of Social Psychology
and Polish Academy of Sciences, Poland)

Ulrich von Hecker
(Cardiff University, UK)
Daniel N. McIntosh
(University of Denver, USA)

## References

Andrade, J. (Ed.). (2001). *Working memory in perspective*. Hove, UK: Psychology Press.

Cabeza, R., & Nyberg, L. (2000). Imaging cognition II: An empirical review of 275 PET and fMRI studies. *Journal of Cognitive Neuroscience, 12*, 1–47.

Craik, F. I. M., & Salthouse, T. A. (2000). *The handbook of aging and cognition*. Mahwah, NJ: Lawrence Erlbaum Associates.

Davidson, R. J., Pizzagalli, D., Nitschke, J. B., & Putnam, K. (2002). Depression: Perspective from affective neuroscience. *Annual Review of Psychology, 53*, 545–574.

Hertel, P. T. (1997). On the contributions of deficient cognitive control to memory impairments in depression. *Cognition and Emotion, 11*, 569–583.

Logie, R. H., & Gilhooly, K. J. (Eds.). (1999). *Working memory and thinking*. Hove, UK: Psychology Press.

Miyake, A., & Shah, P. (Eds.) (1999). *Models of working memory: Mechanism of active maintenance and executive control*. New York: Cambridge University Press.

Perfect, T. J., & Maylor, E. A. (2000). *Models of cognitive aging*. New York: Oxford University Press.

Rabbitt, P. M. A. (1997). *Methodologies for frontal and executive function*. Hove, UK: Lawrence Erlbaum Associates.

Richardson, J. T. E., Engle, R. W., Hasher, L., Logie, R., Stolzfus, E., & Zacks, R. (Eds.). (1996). *Working memory and human cognition*. New York: Oxford University Press.

von Hecker, U., & Sedek, G. (1999). Uncontrollability, depression, and mental models in the social domain. *Journal of Personality and Social Psychology, 77*, 833–850.

Waltz, J. A., Knowlton, B. J., Holyoak, K. J., Boone, K. B., Mishkin, F. S., de Menezes Santos, M., Thomas, C. R., & Miller, B. L. (1999). A system for relational reasoning in human prefrontal cortex. *Psychological Science, 10*, 119–125.

Williams, J. M. G., Watts, F. N., MacLeod, C., & Mathews, A. (1997). *Cognitive psychology and emotional disorders*. Chichester: Wiley.

# Acknowledgments

The editors owe thanks to a number of people, organizations, and institutions. Without their help and support, it would not have been possible to complete this book.

First, we express our thanks to various granting agencies that supported our research and indeed the completion of our editing work. Randall Engle was supported by Grant F49620-00-1-131 from the Air Force Office of Scientific Research. Grzegorz Sedek was supported by the Polish Committee for Scientific Research (grant 5 H01F 013 21). Ulrich von Hecker was supported by the German National Research Foundation (grant He 2225) and by the Economic and Social Research Council (grant RES-000-23-0496). Daniel McIntosh was supported by the Walter Rosenberry Fund and Office of Internationalization at the University of Denver. The Warsaw School of Social Psychology provided financial and logistic help in organizing and running our conference in Kazimierz Dolny. Very obviously, much expertise and enthusiasm went into selecting and preparing such a wonderful, stimulating location for our meeting. In this respect, we thank all members of the local organizing committee, especially Aneta Brzezicka-Rotkiewicz, Sylwia Bedynska, Izabela Krejtz and Kinga Piber-Dabrowska.

Akira Miyake, Edward Necka, and Patrick Rabbitt gave presentations at the conference and shared highly stimulating ideas in the discussions. They did not contribute to the present volume, but we highly appreciated their input and company.

We would also like to express thanks to all those who read, reviewed, and commented on draft papers that led to the final chapters published in this book. This includes not only peers and colleagues but also graduate students at several universities. We feel that the book as a whole has hugely benefited from the expertise and the feedback of these early readers, the communication among authors and readers, and among author groups from different chapters. All of these communications have in fact sparked many ideas for innovative research. Communication was made easy and enjoyable by a website that was opened specifically for the purpose of exchanging views and arguments about the chapters and their draft versions during the time of writing. This website was professionally set up and managed by Tomasz Grzelka, whom we to thank wholeheartedly. And, of course, our thanks go to the authors of all chapters, all of whom cooperated in a constructive way, preparing two or three drafts upon receiving editorial comments and collegial criticism.

We sincerely thank Philip Laughlin from Cambridge University Press for smoothly guiding the whole book project and for many helpful suggestions during the editorial process. Rhiannon Buck language-edited and commented on drafts of various parts of the book. Wiola Wisniewska, Ewa Lipiec, and Rafal Albinski provided valuable help with technical issues of editing.

1

# Cognitive Limitations in Aging and Psychopathology:

## An Introduction and a Brief Tutorial to Research Paradigms

Randall W. Engle, Grzegorz Sedek, Ulrich von Hecker, and Daniel N. McIntosh

After a brief presentation of this book's structure and the questions that served to organize the material, we describe the basic research paradigms used in the research from the various chapters. The essence of the theoretical models and the value of empirical evidence is best articulated by the authors of thematic chapters, so we do not summarize them here. However, we do not want arcane terminology or a lack of knowledge of the specific methods on the reader's part to prevent researchers outside of the area from understanding the ideas presented here. Therefore, to make the material more accessible to students and to researchers outside mainstream cognitive psychology, we offer a brief tutorial on the various methods.

At the outset of this project, we tried to preserve an integrative approach by explicitly asking each author to address the same questions. The following set of issues and questions was proposed to be addressed by all authors:

Question 1: *Which cognitive functions are the focus of your research?* In response to this question, authors either provided a description of their own original models of working memory or executive functions, or they elaborated on more specialized executive functions or processes such as inhibition, attention control, or reasoning that they investigated. Authors were asked to review in the general introduction of their chapter the most important theoretical approaches related to their own field before presenting their approach in detail.

Question 2: *Which processing limitations and/or sources of individual differences in cognitive functions are most important in your research?* This was the core question for the genesis of this volume. We were interested in a deeper understanding of the similarities and differences in mechanisms of such limitations among populations studied in cognitive aging and cognitive psychopathology areas.

Question 3: *What are your specific methods and findings?* Authors were asked to describe in some detail the classical, new, or modified research methods applied or developed in their recent studies.

Question 4: *What are the implications of your research for other related research domains?* Authors were asked to formulate implications and new research questions relevant to more general models of working memory or for neighboring fields of cognitive impairment or limitation.

The 13 thematic chapters of this volume are organized in three separate but inherently interrelated sections, concerning: (a) working memory and cognitive functions; (b) cognitive control; and (c) attention, inhibition, and reasoning processes. Each section includes chapters that analyze cognitive processes in either aging or psychopathology. We hope this organization will stimulate collaboration between "cognitive agers" and "cognitive psychopathologists" on functioning across group and individual differences.

The opening thematic chapter (Unsworth, Heitz, & Engle, Chapter 2) and the final thematic chapter (von Hecker, Sedek, Piber-Dabrowska, & Bedynska, Chapter 14) exemplify well the main message of this volume. Namely, there is value in cross-talk among compartmentalized cognitive sciences, such as cognitive psychology, cognitive aging, cognitive psychopathology, and social cognition. Unsworth et al. (Chapter 2) demonstrate the broad view on working memory capacity, its role as a strong predictor of intelligence level and other higher order cognition, and its role in various real-world phenomena such as aging, stress, prejudice, and even alcohol consumption. On the other hand, von Hecker et al. (Chapter 14) crossed the traditional borders among cognitive disciplines and presented the research on the generative reasoning as influenced by depression, aging, stereotype threat, and prejudice.

When one compares the content of the chapters in this book, considerable support is given for the argument that such interdisciplinary attempts substantially add to the understanding of the issues in both literatures. We think that the most beneficial way to read this volume is to compare research strategies across different domains. Subsequently, we offer several examples of such possible broader views across different literatures.

As one example, considerable knowledge about attention processes might be achieved by analyzing the concept of executive attention (Unsworth et al., Chapter 2), comparing that with the role of attention in the studies on aging of cognitive control (West & Bowry, Chapter 5; Verhaeghen, Cerella, Bopp, & Basak, Chapter 7), and then comparing that with studies on the role of attention processes in cognitive psychopathology (attentional bias in anxiety, Fox & Georgiou, Chapter 10; context processing in schizophrenia, Barch & Braver, Chapter 6). As another example, understanding the basic research on working memory and its applications can be achieved by first reading a general overview from the perspective of cognitive psychology (Unsworth et al., Chapter 2), by next reading perspectives based on cognitive aging (Oberauer, Chapter 3), and then by reading cognitive psychopathology perspectives (Sliwinsky, Smyth, Stawski, & Wasylyshyn, Chapter 4; Waltz, Chapter 13). For yet another example, the best way to understand the research frontiers in inhibition processes may be to study chapters about inhibitory control in general cognitive psychology (Unsworth, et al., Chapter 2), then to compare that with chapters about aging of inhibitory processes (Oberauer, Chapter 3; Verhaeghen, Cerella, Bopp, & Basak, Chapter 7; Maylor, Schlaghecken, & Watson, Chapter 12), and finally to compare those with chapters about psychopathology of inhibitory processes (McIntosh, Sedek, Fojas, Brzezicka-Rotkiewicz, & Kofta, Chapter 9; Joormannn, Chapter 11).

Our final general example, indicating a *signum temporis* of modern technological advances, emphasizes that neuroimaging paradigms described in several chapters of our volume are important for understanding the mind/brain mechanisms of aging (West & Bowry, Chapter 5) and different forms of psychopathology (schizophrenia, Barch & Braver, Chapter 6; Alzheimer's disease, Waltz, Chapter 13).

One barrier to reading and integrating research outside one's own area of expertise is a lack of familiarity with paradigms common in research on other topics. An important goal of this volume is to facilitate cross-area research by familiarizing researchers with paradigms and findings in other areas. Thus, subsequently we present a brief tutorial on the basic research paradigms described in the book. Understanding those paradigms is crucial for understanding the questions addressed in the chapters, how the questions were addressed, and how the findings answer those questions. In that sense, the present volume offers an impressive collection of experimental tools for new research. For example, the researchers in the domain of emotional disorders might easily construct emotionally valenced versions of the cognitive procedures, as was done in the case of classical and emotional Stroop task, and as evidenced here in a chapter using an emotional version of negative priming (Joormann, Chapter 11) and an emotional version of a modified version of Oberauer's task (McIntosh, et al., Chapter 9). Understanding the theoretical and empirical nature of cognitive paradigms can also facilitate the applications of such tasks (e.g., spans of working memory capacity; see Unsworth, et al., Chapter 2 and Sliwinsky et al., Chapter 4) as mediators or moderators of real-life phenomena such as stereotypes, stress, or alcohol consumption.

A BRIEF TUTORIAL TO RESEARCH PARADIGMS

In this tutorial we describe the basic elements of the research paradigms. The chapters in parentheses are those that made use of the paradigms. In each description, we provide a reference to the paradigm, often a classic reference or a reference to a recent review of findings using the paradigm, and a concrete example of how the paradigm would be used. Our goal is to give the reader a basic understanding of the methods this distinguished group of researchers used to make inferences about mental functions and the limitations affecting those functions.

1. Stroop and Emotional Stroop (Unsworth et al., Chapter 2; West & Bowry, Chapter 6; Barch & Braver, Chapter 7; Fox & Georgiou, Chapter 10)
2. Span Tasks of Working Memory: Reading Span, Operation Span, and Counting Span (Unsworth et al., Chapter 2; Sliwinski et al., Chapter 4; von Hecker, et al., Chapter 14)
3. Task Set Switching (Oberauer, Chapter 3; Verhaeghen et al., Chapter 7)
4. Keep Track (Sliwinski et al., Chapter 4; Verhaeghen et al., Chapter 7; Li et al., Chapter 8)
5. Go–No Go Task (Verhaeghen et al., Chapter 7; West & Bowry, Chapter 6)
6. Negative Priming (Oberauer, Chapter 3; Maylor et al., Chapter 10; Joormann, Chapter 11)
7. N-back Task (Sliwinski et al., Chapter 4; Barch & Braver, Chapter 6; Verhaeghen et al., Chapter 7)
8. Dot-probe Task (Fox & Georgiou, Chapter 10; Joormann, Chapter 11)
9. Directed Forgetting (Oberauer, Chapter 3; Maylor et al., Chapter 10; Joormann, Chapter 11)
10. Flanker Task (West & Bowry, Chapter 5; Barch & Braver, Chapter 6; Fox & Georgiou, Chapter 10)
11. Linear Order Problems (Waltz, Chapter 13; von Hecker et al., Chapter 14)

For each research paradigm, we include a good reference to a classic use of this paradigm, a concrete example to walk the reader through, and some notes on the consensus of interpretation and/or debates about what inferences can be drawn. Thus, the reader will know where each given research paradigm came from, what is commonly made of it, and sources for getting more detail.

**Stroop and Emotional Stroop**

The Stroop task has been an important part of the psychologists tool chest for much of the past century but particularly so over the past 20 years. The reader is referred to a review by Colin M. MacLeod (1991) for a survey of important variables for this task, findings, and theoretical explanations. A more recent review of findings from studies using the emotional Stroop is by Williams, Mathews, and Colin MacLeod (1996). (The two MacLeods are different people, one from Canada and one from Australia.)

The Stroop task is performed in several different ways. One common technique is to do the task pretty much the same way John Ridley Stroop did it for his dissertation in 1935. Namely, words that reflect color names are printed in an ink that is incompatible with the word. The subject is to name the color of the ink in which the word is printed. Different control conditions are used but a common one is to also have the subject name the ink color in which nonsense words or strings of random letters are printed. A large number of the incompatible words are printed on one sheet and control items on another sheet. The dependent variable is the time to name the ink color of each item on the sheet. This technique is often used in clinical or group settings. The technique used more commonly in laboratory settings is to present a single color word or control item, typically on a computer screen, and to measure time to indicate the ink color of that item by key press or vocal response. The common finding with both techniques is that it takes longer to name the ink color if it is in the form of an incompatible color name (e.g., the word RED printed in green ink) than if it is in the form of a neutral word or random letters. It is more difficult to manipulate the nature of the Stroop task in the "sheet of items" procedure than in the "item at a time" technique. One such important technique is the presentation of compatible words such as RED printed in the color red intermixed with the incompatible words. The critical dependent variable remains the time to name the color of ink for incompatible words but the interference effect is generally larger and more robust when some of the items are color names compatible with the color of the ink. This manipulation appears to give a more reliable and robust group difference than the "sheet of items" approach or the "item at a time" technique with only incompatible items.

The emotional Stroop task also involves presenting words in various colors and having the subject name the color of the ink. However, the words in the experimental condition are not incompatible color words but words with emotional connotation (MacLeod, 1991). The assumption is that words associated with a particular psychopathology will cause more interference for a subject suffering from that psychopathology than for a control subject. Recently, there has been active debate of whether emotional Stroop and classical Stroop task capture similar cognitive phenomena (Algom, Chajut, & Lev, 2004).

## Span Tasks of Working Memory

The most popular span tasks in the cognitive literature are reading span, operation span, and counting span.

## Reading Span

The Reading span or Rspan was the complex working memory task used in the Daneman and Carpenter (1980, 1983) papers that started the search for the impact and nature of individual differences in working memory capacity. Many variants of the task have been used over the years, and we discuss those later. In the original version, subjects see a series of sentences and read each one aloud. Each succeeding sentence occurs immediately after the last word of the previous sentence has been vocalized. After a variable number of sentences, the subject sees a cue to recall and tries to recall the last word of each sentence, generally in the order in which they occurred. It is common, after recall is completed, to then ask the subject a question about one of the sentences to ensure that comprehension occurred. Another feature of the original version is that the number of sentences presented before recall increases from two to five or six, consecutively.

A variety of scoring procedures have been used with complex WMC tasks. Daneman and Carpenter (1980) used a strict span scoring procedure in which subjects received a single number for the task: the highest sentence set size recalled perfectly on two out of three presentations. This scoring method has some undesirable psychometric properties, however. First, it leads to rather severe restriction of range and reduced reliability. Second, the distributions of such scores are generally not normal. This method of scoring fits with the notion from Miller (1956) of the limit on immediate memory being based on some number of slots or bins, namely $7 \pm 2$.

Because Rspan and all the other complex WMC measures are typically used to study individual differences, such psychometric problems can be important. This is particularly true when a researcher would like to accept the null hypothesis about group differences and to have that nondifference be meaningful. The problems have been dealt with in several ways (Turner and Engle, 1989). The Engle lab compared a variety of scoring techniques and settled on what is called the absolute span. The score consists of the sum of the number of individual words from all perfectly recalled sets. Thus, if a subject recalls all the words from one set of five sentences and one set of six sentences, those contribute to the absolute span score. This method provides a much wider range of scores than does the Daneman & Carpenter span technique, and the reliability is better.[1]

Another feature of the Rspan task that has changed from the original version is the order of set size. Daneman and Carpenter started with three sets of two sentences each and progressively increased the set size to five or six. This assumes that each subject encodes and rehearses each sentence

---

[1] The reader should consult a paper by Conway, et al. (in press) for a full discussion of scoring such tasks and recommendations for a new and different scoring procedure.

equally, but another possibility is that there are individual differences in the effect of progressively larger set sizes that have little or nothing to do with differences in WMC. Cantor, Engle, and Hamilton (1991) initiated the idea of presenting the set sizes randomly so that subjects would be unable to predict the length of a set. Another innovation is to use unrelated items printed after the end of the sentence as the recall items. This allows much greater control over the nature of the items, and unrelated words, digits, and letters all have been successfully used. This precludes the possibility that the person does not actually recall the sentence-final word but reconstructs it from memory of the rest of the sentence. Kane et al. (2004), for example, used individual letters following each sentence. The correlations with other complex WMC tasks and with criterion tasks such as reading comprehension and Raven do not seem to depend on the specific form of Rspan.

## Operation Span

The Operation span or Ospan was first used by Turner and Engle (1986) to test the notion that the correlation between Rspan and reading comprehension was simply a result of the Rspan being a proxy for reading comprehension. If that were true, then the operation span should not predict reading comprehension. However, in fact, Ospan predicted reading comprehension at least as well as Rspan, and the two tasks account for considerable common variance in higher order tasks regardless of whether those tasks are verbal or spatial (Kane et al., 2004). The Engle lab has performed Ospan in a variety of ways and with a variety of to-be-remembered items. The most common version is to present the subject with a sentence including an arithmetic string such as "Is $6/3 + 2 = 7$ ? show" The subjects must respond yes or no, generally orally, as to whether the equation is correct and attempt to commit the word to memory. The tester then presses a key on the computer keyboard to progress to the item to be recalled. After some random number of operation–word strings, the subject sees a cue to recall such as ??? and tries to recall the words in the correct order (La Pointe & Engle, 1990). As with Rspan, the specific form of the operation span or the nature of the items to be recalled does not seem to materially affect the relationship with other WMC tasks or with criterion tasks (Engle, Tuholski, Laughlin, & Conway, 1999; Kane et al., 2004). The Engle lab recently developed an automated version of Ospan that can be administered with little or no supervision by the tester. That version is written in and therefore requires Eprime (Schneider, Eschman, & Zuccolotto, 2002) for administration. The program initially tests the time each subject requires to perform a series of arithmetic operations without a requirement to recall anything. That time per arithmetic string is passed through to the next stage of the program, which administers Ospan with the presentation time of the arithmetic string adjusted for that particular subject. The to-be-remembered items are letters, and recall is made with a mouse and button presses. This task has acceptable reliability and stability as indicated by alpha scores and by test–retest and has acceptable validity as indicated by the relationship with Raven and other WMC tasks. It can be downloaded from http://psychology.gatech.edu/renglelab/.

*Counting Span*

This task, also called Cspan, was developed by Robbie Case and his colleagues (Case, Kurland, & Goldberg, 1982) to study the neo-Piagetian concept of M-space in children and was first used as a WMC task by Baddeley, Logie, & Nimmo-Smith (1985). Case et al. showed children a series of pictures of circles that were two different colors, and each child counted the circles of a given color. After a series of such pictures, the child was to recall the digit string corresponding to the sums of the counted circles. Thus, the task is functionally a digit span task interleaved with counting. Engle et al. (1999) modified Cspan to require more attention control to count the objects. Circles and squares were displayed with the circles being in two different colors, one the same as the squares, and subjects counted the circles in that color. After a series of such displays, they recalled the digits corresponding to the sum of the circles on each display. This task loads well on the same latent variable as Rspan and Ospan and accounts for similar variance in criterion tasks such as Raven (Engle et al., 1999; Kane et al., 2004). One advantage of this task is that difficulty is easily manipulated via similarity of color of the objects and number of objects to be counted and distractors. Thus, the task is a good one for studies comparing different ages and developmental levels.

**Task Set Switching**

A wide variety of tasks are used to study task set switching, and we will only speak of them generally here. The seminal paper on such tasks appears to be Jersild (1927) but most modern literature can be traced back to studies by Allport, Styles, and Hsieh (1994) and Rogers and Monsell (1995). A prototypical task presents subjects with a string of symbols or events, and two or more different operations can be performed on the string. For example, a string of numbers may be shown to subjects, and they either add two to a number or subtract one. Which operation must be performed either is cued in some way such as the color of the number or a given operation is performed on some number of trials in a row before switching to the other operation for the same number of trials. Thus, subjects may add two to each number for three trials and then subtract one from each number for three trials. The cost of making a task switch can be calculated by comparing the time to perform an operation on a trial following a switch with the time to perform that operation in a block of pure trials in which only that operation is performed. This type of switch cost is called a local switch cost. If the time to do an operation on trials later than the first in that run (e.g., trials 2 and 3 in the run) is compared with time to do the operation in blocks of pure trials, a global switching cost can be calculated.

## Keep Track

This task, first described by Garavan (1998), is similar to task set switching paradigms but running counts of events must be maintained. For instance, subjects may be shown a long sequence of circles and triangles and must keep track of the number of each since the last query. Because subjects press a key to present each object, we can measure the time to increase the counter of a circle if it follows in another circle compared to the time to increase the counter if the circle follows a triangle. Generally, the time to increase the counter is faster if the circle follows another circle than if it follows a triangle. Thus, there is the equivalent of a task switch cost, which Garavan (1998) attributed to shifting information in the focus of attention.

## Go–No Go Task

This represents a response mode more than a particular task (e.g., Bates, Kiehl, Laurens, & Liddle 2002 and Logan 1994). In other words, a Go–No Go procedure could be used with nearly any cognitive task. Subjects are to make a response to some events and to withhold the response to other events. A common procedure is to present a string of two different letters (e.g., X and K) with one of the letters occurring much more frequently than does the other (e.g., $p(X) = .8$, $p(K) = .2$). In this case, the subject is to press a key as soon as possible when the X occurs but to do nothing when the K occurs. Critical comparisons across groups are the number of false alarms (i.e., making a response to a K) and the reaction time when a target (X) follows a distractor (K). This task is often used to study the ability to inhibit making a prepotent or predisposed response.

## Negative Priming

The term negative priming is often used as both a procedure and a phenomenon. For example, Tipper (1985) showed that a stimulus that has to be explicitly ignored as a distractor in one trial, a so-called *prime trial*, leads to slowed responding when it becomes a target in an immediately succeeding *probe trial*. In a typical procedure, pairs of partly superimposed letters of two different colours are presented, and participants are to name the letter that is presented in one of the colours, e.g., red, as quickly as possible. For example, the target in the prime trial may be a red "r," partly superimposed by a green "t." In the immediately succeeding probe trial, the red target is now a "t," superimposed by a different distractor, e.g., a green "d." The typical finding is that the subject is slower to name the "t" when it was presented as a distractor on the prime trial. In the classic version, a series of prime–probe trial sequences is presented as a column of letter pairs on a page, and reading time is taken for the page as a whole. In more recent computer-based versions, prime–probe trial sequences are presented individually on a screen, and response times are measured for those individual trials. Reading times of the prime versus probe trial in sequences of the described type are compared with the reading times from a series of control-trial sequences, which are designed such that, in the prime and probe trials, all four letters involved are different from each other. That is, in the control condition, there is no identity overlap between prime trial distractor and probe trial target. One widely discussed explanation for the negative priming effect is that as a to-be-ignored distractor, a letter is actively inhibited, and thus, either its activation in working memory is dampened, or its activation is decoupled from potential response effectors (May, Kane, & Hasher, 1995). The negative priming effect extends to situations in which to-be-ignored distractors and subsequent targets are not identical, but only related (Williams, Watts, MacLeod, & Mathews, 1997). Experiments have shown that the amount of negative priming (which is indicative of the assumed amount of active inhibition) diminishes as mental workload increases and that there is less negative priming observed in participants low (vs. high) in working memory capacity, as measured with the operation-word span task (Conway, Tuholski, Shisler, & Engle, 1999).

## N-back Task

This task has become quite popular because it lends itself to use in fMRI studies of working memory, even though we know relatively little about the experimental psychology of the task (Awh et al., 1996; Cohen et al., 1997; Smith & Jonides, 1997). Subjects are presented a string of events (e.g., letters, words, or pictures) and make a response as to whether the event is identical to the Nth item back. Thus, in a 2-back task, the response indicates whether the current event is identical to what was presented two items ago. Working memory demands of the task can be manipulated by varying N, and the specific component of the working memory system used for the task can be manipulated by varying the nature of the to-be-remembered events. Letters are likely to lead to use of speech-based–mechanisms and pictures more likely to require visual–spatial mechanisms.

## Dot-probe Task

This is a measure of visual attention that is often used in anxiety research (MacLeod, Mathews, & Tata, 1986). The participant is presented with word pairs on a computer screen. The two words are presented centrally on the screen, one above the other in a vertical distance of approximately 3 cm. The task is to always name the top word aloud. In some randomly specified trials, a dot appears for half a second on the screen, either at the position where the top word had been or where the bottom word had been. In such cases, the participant is supposed to hit a specified key as quickly as possible. Latencies associated with this type of dot detection can be interpreted as an indicator of visual attention (Navon & Margalit, 1983). In some trials, the word, presented either at the top or bottom, carries an emotional valence, for example, a threat-related word. A typical finding is that anxious participants respond more quickly to the dot when the dot replaces a threat-related word compared with when the dot replaces a neutral word. This result can be explained by assuming that anxious individuals direct their attention toward threat-related stimuli. Control participants often demonstrate an opposite pattern; that is, they tend to direct their attention away from threat-related information (see Williams et al., 1997).

## Directed Forgetting

In the standard version of this paradigm (see Bjork, 1989), participants are presented with a list of items to be memorized. After presentation of half this list, they receive an instruction that they should forget all items presented before this instruction and should remember only those that would follow. This way, the entire set of materials is divided into "to-be-forgotten" items (TBF) and "to-be-remembered" items (TBR). Subsequent to presentation of these stimuli, participants are given a recall test of all items, TBF and TBR. Typically, recall is at equal levels, sometimes even slightly elevated (Reitman, Malin, Bjork, & Higman, 1973) for TBR items, but is poor for TBF items, relative to a condition in which no "forget"-cue is given. The main interpretation of this finding is that there is strengthened inhibition at retrieval in the case of TBF items. The application of this paradigm to research on emotions has demonstrated that, for example, depressed participants showed better recall for TBF items that had negative valence relative to the neutral baseline, whereas nondepressed participants normally show even stronger directed-forgetting-effects for negative materials as compared to the neutral baseline (for a discussion of related effects see Dalgleish, Mathews, & Wood, 1999). The Directed Forgetting paradigm has been used in research on borderline personality disorder, obsessive–compulsive disorder, individual differences on the repressor–nonrepressor dimension, and autobiographical memory.

## Flanker Task

This elegantly simple task is used to study the effects of distraction on cognition (Eriksen & Eriksen, 1974). An example might be that subjects are presented with a five-letter string and the center letter is always an S or an H. The two letters are mapped to two different response keys on a keyboard. On compatible trials, the four letters surrounding the center letter are the same as the center letter. Thus, the strings would be SSSSS or HHHHH. On incompatible trials, the surrounding letters are distractors. Thus, incompatible trials would be HHSHH or SSHSS. If subjects are forced to respond quickly, they tend to make more errors in the incompatible condition. One interpretation is that it takes time to focus attention and, if a response is required early in processing the string, there will be more information available for the distractor than for the target.

## Linear Order Problems

This task addresses transitive reasoning, that is, if we learn that A is larger than B, and B is larger than C, then we can infer that A is also larger than C. Inferences such as this work "bottom up"; that is, they use given basis information to generate new information that itself was not part of the originally presented materials (Sedek & von Hecker, 2004). Separate, individualized pieces of knowledge are thus integrated into more abstract or comprehensive representations, such as mental images or mental models (Johnson-Laird, 1983). For example, ordered information, such as A > B, B > C, is integrated into a mental array, or linear order A – B – C (Huttenlocher, 1968), that can be later used as a device to retrieve the information from memory. In particular, participants who learn multiple pairs of transitive information such as the above (e.g., A-B, B-C, C-D, D-E, E-F) are found to be as accurate (or even more accurate) in responding to later queries on the relation between the end points of the hypothetical mental order (e.g., A-F) as they are in responding to the original pairs themselves (e.g., B-C or C-D; see for example Smith & Foos, 1975).

We hope this brief tour of the methods used by the researchers writing in this volume will help readers new to this field better understand and appreciate the work discussed in each chapter. The work presented here represents attempts to answer very fundamental questions about thought, emotion, and behavior – and it should not require a Ph.D. in psychology to understand those questions and how we go about answering them. Likewise, providing a brief description of the various methods to the experts in the field gives us hope that different researchers will use jargon terms to mean similar things. We hope this brief tutorial helps both types of reader get the full value from the book.

## Author Note

The works reported and preparation of this chapter were supported by Grant F49620-00-1-131 from the Air Force Office of Scientific Research, Polish Committee for Scientific Research grant 5 H01F 013 21, the Walter Rosenberry Fund, and the Office of Internationalization at the University of Denver.

## References

Algom, D., Chajut, E., & Lev, S. (2004). A rational look at the emotional Stroop phenomenon: A generic slowdown, not a Stroop effect. *Journal of Experimental Psychology: General, 133*, 323–338.

Allport, D. A., Styles, E. A., & Hsieh, S. (1994). *Shifting intentional set: Exploring the dynamic control of tasks.* In C. Umilta & M. Moscovitch (Eds.), Attention and performance XV (pp. 421–452). Cambridge, MA: MIT Press.

Awh, E., Jonides, J., Smith, E., Schumacher, E., Koeppe, R., & Katz, S. (1996). Dissociation of storage and rehearsal in verbal working memory: Evidence from PET. *Psychological Science, 7*, 25–31.

Baddeley, A., Logie, R., & Nimmo-Smith, I. (1985). Components of fluent reading. *Journal of Memory & Language, 24*, 119–131.

Bates, A. T., Kiehl, K. A., Laurens, K., & Liddle, P. F. (2002). Error-related negativity and correct response negativity in schizophrenia. *Clinical Neurophysiology, 113*, 1454–1463.

Bjork, R. A. (1989). Retrieval inhibition as an adaptive mechanism in human memory. In H. L. Roediger III & F. L. M. Craik (Eds.), *Varieties of memory and consciousness: Essays in memory of Endel Tulving* (pp. 309–330). Hillsdale, NJ: Lawrence Erlbaum Associates.

Cantor, J., Engle, R. W., & Hamilton, G. (1991). Short-term memory, working memory, and verbal abilities: How do they relate? *Intelligence, 15*, 229–246.

Case, R., Kurland, M. D., & Goldberg, J. (1982). Operational efficiency and the growth of short-term memory span. *Journal of Experimental Child Psychology, 33*, 386–404.

Cohen, J. D., Perlstein, W. M., Braver, T. S., Nystrom, L. E., Noll, D.C., Jonides, J., & Smith, E. E. (1997). Temporal dynamics of brain activation during a working memory task. *Nature, 386*, 604–608.

Conway, A. R. A., Tuholski, S. W., Shisler, R. J., & Engle, R. W. (1999). The effect of memory load on negative priming: An individual differences investigation. *Memory and Cognition, 27*, 1042–1050.

Conway, A. R. A., Kane, M. J., Bunting, M. F., Hambrick, D. Z., Wilhelm, O., Engle, R. W. (in press). Working Memory Span Tasks: A Methodological Review and User's Guide. *Behavior Research Methods.*

Dalgleish, T., Mathews, A., & Wood, J. (1999). Inhibition processes in cognition and emotion: A special case? In T. Dalgleish & M. J. Power (Eds.), *Handbook of cognition and emotion* (pp. 243–265). Chichester: Wiley.

Daneman, M., & Carpenter, P. A. (1980). Individual differences in working memory and reading. *Journal of Verbal Learning and Verbal Behavior, 19*, 450–466.

Daneman, M., & Carpenter, P. A. (1983). Individual differences in integrating information between and within sentences. *Journal of Experimental Psychology: Learning, Memory and Cognition, 9*, 561–583.

Engle, R. W., Tuholski, S. W., Laughlin, J. E., & Conway, A. R. R. (1999). Working memory, short-term memory and general fluid intelligence: A latent variable approach. *Journal of Experimental Psychology: General, 128*, 309–331.

Eriksen, B. A., & Eriksen, C. W. (1974). Effects of noise letters upon the identification of a target letter in a nonsearch task. *Perception & Psychophysics, 16*, 143–149.

Garavan, H. (1998). Serial attention within working memory. *Memory & Cognition, 26*, 263–276.

Huttenlocher, J. (1968). Constructing spatial images: A strategy in reasoning. *Psychological Review, 75*, 550–560.

Johnson-Laird, P. N. (1983). *Mental models: Towards a cognitive science of language, inference and consciousness.* Cambridge, UK: Cambridge University Press.

Jersild, A. T. (1927). Mental set and shift. *Archives of Psychology, 14*, 81.

Kane, M. J., Hambrick, D. Z., Tuholski, S. W., Wilhelm, O., Payne, T. W., Engle, R. W. (2004). The domain generality of working-memory capacity: A latent-variable approach to verbal and visuo-spatial memory and reasoning. *Journal of Experimental Psychology: General, 133*, 189–217.

La Pointe, L. B., & Engle, R. W. (1990). Simple and complex word spans as measures of working memory capacity. *Journal of Experimental Psychology: Learning, Memory and Cognition, 16*, 1118–1133.

Logan, G. D. (1994). *On the ability to inhibit thought and action: A users' guide to the stop signal paradigm.* In D. Dagenbach & T. H. Carr (Eds.), Inhibitory processes in attention, memory, and language (pp. 189–239). San Diego: Academic Press.

MacLeod, C., Mathews, A., & Tata, P. (1986). Attentional bias in emotional disorders. *Journal of Abnormal Psychology, 95*, 15–20.

MacLeod, C. M. (1991). Half a century of research on the Stroop effect: An integrative review. *Psychological Bulletin, 109*, 163–203.

May, C. P., Kane, M. J., & Hasher, L. (1995). Determinants of negative priming. *Psychological Bulletin, 118*, 35–54.

Miller, G. A. (1956). The magical number seven plus or minus two: Some limits on our capacity for processing information. *Psychological Review, 63*, 81–96.

Navon, D., & Margalit, B. (1983). Allocation of attention according to informativeness in visual recognition. *Quarterly Journal of Experimental Psychology, 35A*, 497–512.

Reitman, W., Malin, J. T., Bjork, R. A., & Higman, B. (1973). Strategy control and directed forgetting. *Journal of Verbal Learning and Verbal Behavior, 12*, 140–149.

Rogers, R. D., & Monsell, S. (1995). Costs of a predictable switch between simple cognitive tasks. *Journal of Experimental Psychology: General. 124*, 207–231.

Schneider, W., Eschman, A., & Zuccolotto, A. (2002). *E-Prime user's guide.* Pittsburgh, PA: Psychological Software Tools.

Sedek, G., & von Hecker, U. (2004). Effects of subclinical depression and aging on generative reasoning about linear orders: Same or different processing limitations? *Journal of Experimental Psychology: General, 133*, 237–260.

Smith K. H., & Foos, P. W. (1975). Effect of presentation order on the construction of linear orders. *Memory and Cognition, 3*, 614–618.

Smith, E. E., & Jonides, J. J. (1997). Working memory: A view from neuroimaging. *Cognitive Psychology, 33*, 5–42.

Tipper, S. P. (1985). The negative priming effect: Inhibitory priming of ignored objects. *The Quarterly Journal of Experimental Psychology, 37A*, 571–590.

Turner, M. L., & Engle, R. W. (1986). Working memory capacity. *Proceedings of the Human Factors Society, 30*, 1273–1277.

Turner, M. L., & Engle, R. W. (1989). Is working memory capacity task dependent? *Journal of Memory and Language, 28*, 127–154.

Williams, J. M. G., Matthews, A., & MacLeod, C. (1996). The emotional Stroop task and psychopathology. *Psychological Bulletin, 120*, 3–24.

Williams, J. M. G., Watts, F. N., MacLeod, C., & Mathews, A. M. (1997). *Cognitive psychology and emotional disorders* (2nd ed.). Chichester, UK: Wiley.

# WORKING MEMORY AND COGNITIVE FUNCTIONS

# 2

# Working Memory Capacity in Hot and Cold Cognition

## Nash Unsworth, Richard P. Heitz, and Randall W. Engle

Much has been said about the relationship between measures of Working Memory Capacity (WMC) and higher order cognition. Indeed, what exactly accounts for this relationship has been a major topic of inquiry in cognitive psychology for over 20 years (Engle & Oransky, 1999). Attempts to better understand this problem have shed considerable light on the role of WMC in a wide array of research domains. Specifically, research has shown that measures of WMC are related to complex learning (Kyllonen & Stephens, 1990), following directions (Engle, Carullo, & Collins, 1991), reasoning ability (Engle, Tuholski, Laughlin, & Conway, 1999; Kyllonen & Christal, 1990), and vocabulary learning (Daneman & Green, 1986). Additionally, not only has WMC been implicated in higher order cognition – indeed, these correlations point to the utility of such a concept in the first place – but also now WMC is being implicated in other research domains. Working memory measures not only predict reading comprehension scores (Daneman & Carpenter, 1980), performance on standard achievement tests (i.e., SAT: Engle et al., 1999), and reasoning, but also seem to predict early onset Alzheimer's (Rosen, Bergeson, Putnam, Harwell, & Sunderland, 2002), the effects of alcohol consumption (Finn, 2002), and one's ability to deal with life-event stress (Klein & Boals, 2001). Thus, the utility of WMC is not merely limited to performance on high-level cognitive tasks, but is also important in a variety of situations that impact people on a day-to-day basis. Working Memory Capacity is important in situations requiring both rational or cold cognition such as selective attention and reasoning (Engle et al., 1999; Kane & Engle, 2003) and is also important under conditions of emotional or hot cognition, such as stress and depression (Arnett et al., 1999; Klein & Boals, 2001). The present chapter will focus on the WMC's role in these situations in terms of our view that the basis for WMC is the ability to control attention.

## WORKING MEMORY CAPACITY, HIGHER ORDER COGNITION, AND ATTENTIONAL CONTROL

We view WMC as primarily reflecting the executive attentional component of a broader working memory (WM) system. Similar to Cowan's conception (1988, 1995), we think of working memory as consisting of memory units active above some threshold, which can be represented via a variety of different codes (phonological, visuospatial, semantic, etc.), and as an executive attention component. The executive attention component primarily deals with maintaining or suppressing activation of long-term memory units and task goals, conflict monitoring and resolution, and the flexible allocation of attentional resources. Thus, individual differences in WMC, and hence by our view executive attention, should be most apparent in situations in which active maintenance is needed, particularly in the face of potent environmental distractors or strong internal interference. That is, interference-rich situations make it more likely to temporarily lose novel task goals or for attention to be captured by environmental distractors and thus put a premium on the need for active maintenance. For example, consider a baggage screener at a busy international airport. The screener's task is to watch a monitor for several hours a day to make sure that unauthorized items are not brought onto the airplanes. Here, the screener must sustain attention on the task while simultaneously dealing with constant environmental distraction from crying babies, irritable passengers, and other events that capture one's attention away from the task. A temporary loss in goal maintenance (checking the monitor) can have detrimental consequences. It is in such situations that we believe WMC is of critical importance.

Furthermore, it is our belief that it is the executive attention component that drives the correlation between WM measures and higher order cognition. To investigate these claims, we have utilized quasi-experimental designs and large-scale correlation-based designs. Research reflecting the quasi-experimental methods is aimed primarily at determining what is the underlying primitive of individual differences in WMC. That is, what is the fundamental underlying cognitive mechanism that leads to covariation of the WMC tasks with tasks of higher order cognition? The correlation-based designs are aimed at determining the association and dissociation of various tasks and the domain-specific and domain-general nature of constructs identified by these methods. For both approaches, complex span measures modeled after the Daneman and Carpenter (1980) reading span task are used as the WMC measures. These tasks are essentially dual tasks in which the participant is required to engage in some process such as reading sentences (Daneman & Carpenter, 1980) or solving simple math operations (Turner & Engle, 1989) while simultaneously remembering stimuli (such as words, digits, or letters). These tasks have been shown to be reliable and valid. Specifically, previous research shows that measures of WMC have both good test-retest reliability and internal consistency (Conway, Cowan, Bunting, Therriault, & Minkoff, 2002; Engle et al., 1999; Klein & Fiss, 1999). Likewise, as noted previously, over the past 20 years, these complex span tasks have shown impressive correlations with a wide variety of higher order cognitive operations, which points to their validity.

### Complex Span Measures as Predictors of Higher Order Cognition

In our view, these complex WM span tasks measure a confluence of domain-specific skills and memory processes as well as a domain-general executive attention component. Although individuals will no doubt differ in their ability to utilize domain-specific processes such as verbal/ phonological skills, the domain-general executive attention component (central executive) is what is critical for the relationship between WMC measures and high-level cognition. For example, consider the operation span task (O-span; Turner & Engle, 1989). Here, the task is to solve simple math equations while simultaneously remembering unrelated words. Individual differences in math ability, and short-term storage skills, such as rehearsal and chunking, might contribute individual differences in overall task performance. That is, people will differ in both the processing component of the task and the storage component of the task. However, each of these abilities alone does not account for the correlation with higher order cognition. Rather, it is the executive attention component that coordinates the processing and storage components of the task that is important for higher order cognition.

Evidence for such a claim comes from several studies conducted by Engle and colleagues. First, Conway and Engle (1996) demonstrated that once participants are equated on math ability, the correlation between a WM measure (O-span) and reading comprehension (VSAT) does not diminish. Thus, individual differences in the processing component, in this case math skills, do not account for the relationship between WM and higher order cognition (see also Engle, Cantor, & Carullo, 1992). Second, Engle et al., (1999; see also Conway et al., 2002) showed, via structural equation modeling, that a latent variable made up of WM span tasks and a latent variable made up of simple short-term verbal memory span tasks were significantly correlated. However, the correlation between the STM measures and a gF composite was mediated by the WM span measures. Thus, simple storage alone cannot account for the relationship with higher order cognition, but rather it is the residual variance in WM span measures not indexed by storage that is important for higher order cognition. Engle et al. argued that the residual variance is an index of central executive processing and showed that this variance was highly correlated with gF (.49). The argument here is that both WMC and STM measures require simple storage of information and WM measures require additional attentional processes. Once the shared variance between the two constructs is accounted for, what is left over in the WM factor is essentially variance thought to be attributable to the executive attention component.

## Individual Differences in WMC and Attentional Control

By our rationale, then, individual differences in the efficacy of the executive attention component is critical for demonstrating correlations between WMC and tasks that measure higher order cognition. However, what evidence do we have that individual differences in WMC are primarily attentional differences? That is, what evidence is there that individual differences on measures of WMC correspond to individual differences in the ability to control attention? To test this claim, we used quasi-experimental, extreme groups designs in which participants were prescreened on a WM measure (typically operation span) and only those participants who scored in the top (high spans) and bottom (low spans) quartiles of the distribution were tested on a variety of classic selective attentional paradigms. If our logic is correct, we should see that high- and low-span individuals do not differ on relatively automatic forms of information processing, but that differences will emerge when controlled attention is necessary (Conway & Engle, 1994; Rosen & Engle, 1997; Tuholski, Engle, & Baylis, 2001).

As an elegant test of the claim that WMC is related to attentional control, Conway, Cowan, and Bunting (2001) tested high- and low-span individuals in the dichotic listening paradigm first popularized by Cherry (1953). Here, high- and low-span individuals were required to monitor a message presented to one ear while ignoring a message presented in the other ear. Moray (1959; see also Wood & Cowan, 1995) demonstrated that for the most part individuals have little difficulty in monitoring one channel at a time. However, Moray also found that when participants were presented with their own name in the irrelevant channel, roughly 33% of the participants reported detecting their own name. Conway et al. reasoned that if WMC is akin to attentional control capabilities, then WMC would be important for resisting particularly salient attentional capture (hearing your own name in the irrelevant channel). Thus, Conway et al. suggested that high-span individuals would be better at resisting the powerful attentional orienting cue of their own first name than would low-span individuals and thus would be less susceptible to the "cocktail party" effect. Indeed, this is what they found: 65% of participants classified as low spans reported hearing their name in the irrelevant ear, whereas only 20% of the high-span individuals reported hearing their name. These results suggest that individuals who differ on a WM span measure differ in their ability to resist a salient attention capturing cue when it conflicts with task goals.

Another striking example of individual differences in WMC being related to attentional control capabilities comes from a comprehensive analysis of the role of WMC in the Stroop task (Kane & Engle, 2003). The Stroop task has long been hailed as the "gold standard" of selective attention paradigms. On the face of it, the Stroop task is quite simple. Typically, participants are required to name the color in which color names are printed. When the color and the word match (e.g., red presented in red ink), the task is quite easy. However, when the color and the word conflict (e.g., blue presented in red ink), both reaction time and error rates increase. It is generally believed that the increase in latency and error reflect an inability to inhibit a prepotent response that conflicts with the task goal (e.g., "Say the color not the word"). Kane and Engle (2003) proposed that individual differences in WMC would arise in the Stroop when the need to maintain the task goal is high and that the differences would be differentially reflected in latency and errors. That is, based on the view that individual differences in WMC are due to differences in active maintenance and conflict monitoring and resolution, Kane and Engle argued for a dual-process view of Stroop performance in which span differences would arise in latency when response competition is highest and in errors when the demand for goal maintenance is greatest.

To test this claim, Kane and Engle (2003) manipulated the proportion of congruent and incongruent trials. In the 0% congruent condition, the color and word never matched and thus the task goal was consistently reinforced. In such trials, span differences mainly arose in RT reflecting a greater inability of low-span individuals to resolve competition between saying the color and not the word. In the 75% congruent condition in which the color and word matched most of the time, there is little response competition and thus little need for conflict resolution. In these trials, high- and low-span individuals did not differ on RT, but rather in error rates. Here, low-span participants tended to make more errors than high-span participants. Kane and Engle argued that these errors were an example of what Duncan (1990) has termed "goal neglect." Specifically, in the 75% congruent condition, subjects can respond correctly on most trials even if they don't work to keep active the goal ("say the color not the word"). However, on the rare occasion that the color and word do not match, then the response tendency to say the word is likely to be stronger and an error is more likely to occur.

## Individual Differences in WMC and the Antisaccade Task

The previous results provide compelling evidence that individuals differing in the number of items they recall while engaging in simultaneous online processing predict performance in two classic attentional control paradigms. Further evidence for this claim comes from several studies investigating the role of WM in the antisaccade task (Kane, Bleckley, Conway, & Engle, 2001; see also Roberts, Hager, & Heron, 1994; Larson & Perry, 1999). The antisaccade task, like dichotic listening and Stroop, is an attentional control paradigm that requires individuals to maintain task goals in the face of interference via the inhibition of a prepotent response in order to generate the correct response. The antisaccade task (Hallet, 1978; Hallet & Adams, 1980; see Everling & Fischer, 1998 for a review) requires participants to fixate on a central cue; after a variable amount of time, a flashing cue appears either to the right or left of fixation, and participants have to shift their attention and gaze to the opposite side of the screen as quickly and accurately as possible. Thus, in this task, there is good deal of conflict between the automatic orienting response and the task goal.

Given the reliance on inhibition of prepotent responses inherent within the antisaccade task, it is no surprise that the task has been used, much like Stroop, in a wide array of clinical and developmental research. For example, patients with lesions in the prefrontal cortex are more likely to make reflexive saccades, and even if they do make a correct saccade, they are slower to do so compared to healthy controls (e.g., Guitton, Buchtel, & Douglas, 1985). Additionally, these patients tend to show no decrements in the relatively automatic prosaccade task in which the goal is to simply shift your eyes and attention toward the exogenous cue. These same results also hold for schizophrenic and Parkinson patients, whose conditions are associated with disruptions in prefrontal cortex function (Everling & Fischer, 1998). For example, Fukushima et al. (1988) found that schizophrenic patients made more errors and had longer response latencies in an antisaccade but no differences on the prosaccade task compared to healthy controls.

Antisaccade task performance also tends to change as a function of age with young children and older adults making more reflexive saccades and having longer correct saccade latencies than young adults (e.g., Butler, Zacks, & Henderson, 1999; Fischer, Biscaldi, & Gezeck, 1997; Fukushima, Hatta, & Fukushima, 2000; Nieuwenhuis, Ridderinkhof, De Jong, Kok, & Van Der Molen, 2000). Accuracy and reaction times in the antisaccade task show a steady improvement with age, up to about 16 to 18 years old. Within the adult population, older adults show performance changes on the antisaccade task after their mid-30s, with error rates and reaction times increasing with age as compared to younger controls (Fischer et al., 1997; Butler et al., 1999). A similar decline in performance with age does not appear for the prosaccade task. These results demonstrate that suppression and voluntary control are critical for success on the antisaccade task and that these abilities seem to be reliant on prefrontal cortex (PFC) functioning. Additionally, given the strong link between WM and PFC functioning (see Kane and Engle, 2002 for a review), it seems logical to reason that individual differences in WM would correlate with performance on the antisaccade task.

Kane et al. (2001) reasoned that WMC would be important in the anti-saccade because it relies on the same domain-general executive attention component important in both dichotic listening and the Stroop task. Specif-ically, Kane et al. suggested that WMC would be important in the anti-saccade condition because of the need for active goal maintenance in the face of a powerful attention capturing cue. Roberts and Pennington (1996) advanced a similar view, noting: "the Antisaccade and Stroop tasks have strong prepotent responses but relatively light working memory demands: thus, even momentary lapses or slight deficiencies in working memory will affect the balance in favor of prepotency" (p. 112). That is, although the antisaccade task does not have a high memory load, it does carry a substantial executive load in order to resist prepotency and perform the correct behavior. Kane and colleagues, therefore, hypothesized that low-span individuals would be worse at maintaining the production in active memory ("if flash on the left – look right") than high-span individuals, and thus any lapse in attention (or intention) will result in the prepotent response guiding behavior and hence the occurrence of a fast error. Even if the first saccade is the correct direction, low spans should still be worse at controlling their attention, and thus differences in latency will occur when control is needed to resolve the conflict between the task goal and habit. However, in a prosaccade condition in which the subject is simply required to look at the flashing cue, Kane and colleagues (2001) argued that there should be no differences in WMC because both the task goal ("look at the flashing cue") and the automatic orienting response are the same and attentional control capabilities are not needed.

To test these claims, Kane et al. (2001) required participants to perform blocks of both prosaccade and antisaccade trials. Participants fixated on a central cue, and after a variable amount of time, a cue flashed either to the right or left of fixation. In the prosaccade condition, participants shifted their gaze to the same side of the screen and attempted to identify a briefly presented letter (B, P, or R) as quickly and accurately as possible via a key press. In the antisaccade condition, participants were also required to identify a briefly presented letter, but this time it appeared on the oppo-site side of the screen. The results supported the predictions. Specifically, there were no WM span differences in either RT or errors on prosaccade trials. In antisaccade trials, in contrast, lows spans were both slower to correctly identify the target letter and were less accurate. Additionally, in a second experiment in which eye movements were also recorded, Kane et al. demonstrated that the span differences in both accuracy and RT con-tinued to hold even over 360 antisaccade trials. These results suggest that high- and low-span individuals do not differ on relatively automatic forms of processing, but rather, differences emerge when attentional control is needed to maintain task goals in the face of potent environmental distractors. The finding that low spans were slower to correctly identify the target letter suggests, similar to Stroop's finding, that low spans are particularly deficient in their attentional control capabilities, especially when there is a conflict between task goals and habitual responses. Indeed, this argument was further bolstered by the fact that in addition to being slower at correctly identifying the target letter, low-span individuals were also slower to perform a correct saccade on antisaccade trials. In terms of the accuracy data, the eye movement results suggested that the reason low-span individuals made more errors at correctly identifying the target letter was due to the fact that they made more reflexive saccades to the flashing cue than did high spans. Thus, as predicted, low-span individuals were particularly deficient in their ability to maintain the task goal ("if flash on the left – look right") in active memory and thus were particularly susceptible to a salient environmental distractor. Additionally, even when the task goal was maintained, low spans were slower to implement control and thus resolve the conflict between the automatic orienting response and the task goal.

Although the above results are quite convincing, there is a possible problem that could limit the conclusions drawn from this study. Namely, it has been shown previously that adding a secondary task to the antisaccade task increases the number of reflexive errors (Roberts et al, 1994; Stuyven, Van der Goten, Vandierendonck, Claeys, & Crevits, 2000). It is therefore possible that low-span individuals made more reflexive errors in the Kane et al. study (2001) because the letter identification task acted as a secondary task that put low spans at a marked disadvantage. To alleviate this possible shortcoming, we (Unsworth, Schrock, & Engle, 2004) had high- and low-span individuals perform a simpler saccade paradigm in which the sole task requirement was an eye movement. When the flashing cue appeared, subjects had 600 ms to move their gaze to a target in the same location as the cue (prosaccade) or to a target on the opposite side of the screen (antisaccade). Unsworth et al. nicely replicated the basic findings of Kane et al. (2001) by demonstrating that high- and low-span individuals were equivalent in both RT and accuracy in the prosaccade condition, but that once again, as shown in Figure 2.1, low-span individuals made more reflexive saccades toward the flashing cue and were slower to make a correct saccade in the opposite direction. It seems that the span differences reported in Kane et al. were not solely a function of the secondary letter identification task.

In a second experiment, we questioned whether high- and low-span individuals would also differ on prosaccade trials if a premium was placed on active maintenance. Previous studies showed that in some situations, a secondary task can disrupt prosaccade trials (Pashler, Carrier, & Hoffman, 1993; Stuyven et al., 2000; but see Roberts et al., 1994). Additionally, several studies found that randomly intermixing prosaccade and antisaccade trials

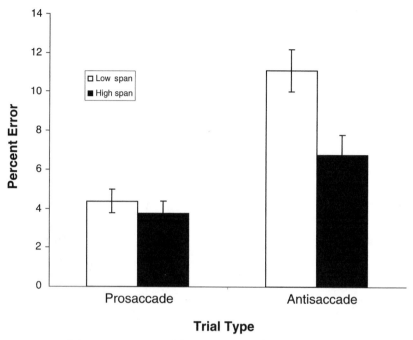

FIGURE 2.1. Mean percentage of direction errors for antisaccade and prosaccade trials for high- and low-span participants in Experiment 1. Error bars represent standard errors of the means.

can lead to disruptions in both antisaccade and prosaccade trials (Hallet & Adams, 1980; Weber, 1995). This suggests that increasing interference, and thus increasing the need for goal maintenance and strategic control, can affect performance on even prosaccade trials. We tested this idea by randomly intermixing prosaccade and antisaccade trials within the same block. In this task, as before, participants moved their eyes either toward or away from a flashing cue. However, unlike the previous studies, each trial began with a fixation symbol that remained on screen for 1,000 ms. The fixation symbol signaled to the participant whether the upcoming trial would be a prosaccade or antisaccade trial. Specifically, if a diamond symbol was presented, then the subject knew that the upcoming trial would be an antisaccade. If, however, the symbol was a circle, then this signaled to the subject that the upcoming trial would be a prosaccade. Strikingly, as can be seen in Figure 2.2, low spans made more eye movement errors and were marginally slower in making correct saccades on both antisaccades and prosaccades trials.

**Direction Errors: Experiment 2**

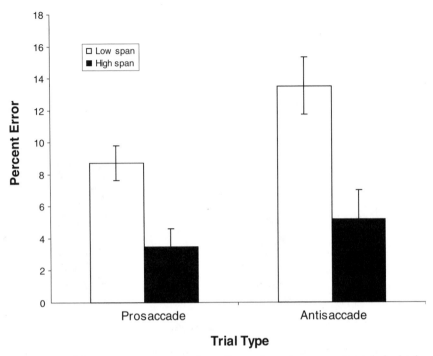

FIGURE 2.2. Mean error percentages for antisaccade and prosaccade trials for high- and low-span participants in Experiment 2. Error bars represent standard errors of the means.

Even in prosaccade trials in which both the automatic orienting response and the task goal coincide, low spans were more likely than high spans to look away from (and not toward) the flashing cue. These results suggest that low spans were unable to actively maintain the task goal long enough to perform the correct response. Thus, it seems that low spans were deficient in either interpreting the cue at the time of presentation (i.e., "What does diamond indicate again?") or even if they did correctly interpret the cue, they were unable to maintain the production in the period between the trial signal and the flashing cue. Either way, the results present a picture in which low spans are more susceptible to losses of goal maintenance (goal neglect) than high-span individuals, and these loses of goal maintenance impede low spans' ability to perform the task.

What can we conclude from the results of the antisaccade studies? It seems quite reasonable to conclude that individual differences in WMC correspond to attentional control abilities that are most apparent when active maintenance is needed in conditions of interference. Individuals scoring in the upper quartile on a WM span measure are better at inhibiting prepotent responses and maintaining task goals in memory than those scoring in the bottom quartile. Additionally, these results suggest that individual differences in WMC are probably not about the number of things that can be held in memory (e.g., Miller, 1956), but rather about the idea that individual differences in WMC seem to be related to the efficacy of the executive attention component of the broader WM system. The finding that low-span individuals are quite poor on tasks such as the antisaccade also suggests that individual differences in WMC are related to the broader issue of behavioral inhibition, which is important in a variety of real-world applications. It is these issues to which we now turn.

## ANTISACCADE AS A MODEL OF BEHAVIORAL INHIBITION

Performance on the antisaccade poses some interesting implications for day-to-day cognitive processing. According to our view, executive attention is necessary in situations in which task goals may be lost to potent environmental distractors (see also Roberts & Pennington, 1996). Within the antisaccade task, executive attention is needed to maintain the task goal ("look away from the flashing cue"), suppress the tendency to look toward the cue, and for the voluntary generation of a correct saccade in the opposite direction. A loss in maintenance will result in a fast reflexive saccade toward the cue, whereas a deficiency in control implementation will result in a correct, but slow, saccade in the opposite direction. These two functions of executive attention are needed in a host of other activities that people engage in on a routine basis. For instance, going back to the baggage screener example, as most of us know, airports are extremely busy environments with a plethora of distracting information. Keeping attention focused on the screen for a continuous amount of time and not letting attention be captured by attractive distractors requires considerable effort. Here the screener must constantly look for potentially dangerous material that passengers may be attempting to bring onboard. Any momentary lapse in attention, and hence a loss of goal maintenance, could result in a potentially serious error in detection.

It is easy to see how these basic concepts can be extrapolated to even broader issues in which a loss in goal maintenance or an inability to implement control can occur. This view is consistent with the work of Wegner (1989, 1994) who suggests that mental control is guided by the need to do one thing (A) while not doing another (B). However, making sure that you are doing A requires that you check and make sure you are not doing B. If B represents a sufficiently powerful construct (e.g., a flashing cue), then suppression will be needed to make sure that A is done and not B. However, like antisaccade and Stroop, any lapse in attention (or intention) will result in B being done instead. Wegner (1994) suggested that two processes are important for successful mental control. One is an automatic process that monitors for thoughts that are counter to the current goal-state and hence are unwanted. When such a thought is discovered, a second attentional process attempts to suppress the thought and maintain the current thought. This view is consistent with ours in that both internal and external distractors can automatically capture attention and therefore interfere with goal maintenance, in which case executive attention is needed to resolve the conflict between the unwanted thought and the current goal state in the form of active suppression.

## WMC and Thought Suppression

Klein and Boals (2001) have recently linked Wegner's theory of mental control (1994) with a view of WMC similar to ours. Klein and Boals argued that stressful thoughts are essentially internal distractors that need to be suppressed in order to maintain attention on the task at hand (e.g., Kahneman, 1973). The authors suggested that stress acts as a secondary load that disrupts attentional processing on a primary task, and thus, successful performance requires that stressful thoughts be suppressed. In order to test this hypothesis, participants were tested on a version of the operation span task and on a measure of overall life experience. Life-event stress was operationalized as the sum of events that were rated as negative life experiences. The authors reasoned that life-event stress effects should be most pronounced as a task becomes more demanding. In particular, as set size increases on the operation span (trying to remember seven instead of two words while solving math equations) the high stress levels should disrupt task performance. Indeed, this is precisely what Klein and Boals found. Specifically, the authors found that there was an almost linear increase in the correlation between the number of words recalled in each set size and life-event stress scores, with the largest correlation occurring at the largest set size ($r$ set size $7 = -.57$).

In a second study, the authors extended these findings by demonstrating that not only was an index of stress related to WMC, but also that the type of errors made on the WM span task was correlated with stress. Specifically, Klein and Boals (2001) recorded the number of intrusion errors made by subjects while performing the operation span task. Remember that in this task, subjects are required to verify whether or not math equations are correct while simultaneously remembering words. At the end of one set, subjects are required to recall the words in that set and only in that set. However, sometimes, subjects will recall words that were presented in earlier sets or even recall the words "true" and "false" (verification of the answer on the math equation). These intrusion errors are taken as an inability to deal with proactive interference from the previous trials (e.g., Chiappe, Hasher, & Siegal, 2000). Thus, Klein and Boals reasoned that if WM resources are needed to deal with proactive interference on the previous trial and to deal with possible intrusive thoughts brought about by heightened stress, then individuals with higher stress levels should also have more intrusive thoughts. Indeed, the correlation between an index of negative life-event stress and intrusion errors was moderate ($r = .33$). Taken together, these two studies suggest that WM span measures are related to the ability to deal with intrusive thoughts brought about by stress. Klein and Boals argued that intrusive thoughts brought about by increased levels of stress compete with WM resources, and this results in deficits in the ability to effectively inhibit these unwanted thoughts.

Brewin and Beaton (2001) also linked the concepts of thought suppression and WMC via the "white bear" paradigm, made popular by Wegner and colleagues (Wegner, Schneider, Carter, & White, 1987). In this study, Brewin and Beaton tested 64 participants on a measure of WMC (operation span), measures of both general fluid and crystallized intelligence, and the "white bear" paradigm. In the "white bear" paradigm, participants are instructed to verbalize their streams of consciousness while suppressing thoughts of a white bear. Each time a participant thinks of a white bear, they are instructed to ring a bell. Thus, like the antisaccade task, successful performance requires participants to maintain the task goal ("don't look at the flashing box," "don't think of a white bear") by suppressing the competing response ("looking at the flashing box," "thinking of a white bear"). The authors found that the number of intrusions was negatively correlated with both the WM measure and the gF measure. Thus, the ability to effectively deal with intrusive thoughts is related to measures of both WM and intelligence. Once again, these results suggest the importance of WMC in suppressing unwanted behaviors.

Recall that by our view, WMC is needed in situations in which attention must be devoted to a primary task while inhibiting possible internal and external distractors. This form of attentional control is typically found in many low-level attentional paradigms as demonstrated previously with both the Stroop and antisaccade. However, the above studies further demonstrate that executive attention is also needed to inhibit unwanted thoughts brought about by stress and task manipulations in order to perform the correct behavioral response, and that individuals who differ in WMC will differ in their ability to suppress unwanted thoughts. We take these results to suggest that the utility of WMC is not merely apparent in low-level tasks and higher order cognition such as reasoning and reading comprehension, but also apparent in tasks and constructs typically found within the social psychological literature.

In further support of this notion, consider a study by Schmader and Johns (2003) in which the role of WMC in stereotype threat was examined. Stereotype threat occurs when individuals perform poorly on a given task if a relevant stereotype is associated with performance on that task.

For example, saying that African Americans score more poorly on intelligence tests than Caucasians would result in poorer scores for the African American participants than would be obtained otherwise, with little to no change in the scores of Caucasians. Schmader and Johns (2003) reasoned that stereotype threat reduces WMC and thus results in poorer performance on a given task. Across three studies, Schmader and Johns found that stereotype threat lead to lower scores on a measure of WMC. Furthermore, in their Experiment 3, the authors found that the effects of stereotype threat on a measure of higher order cognition were mediated WMC. Thus, the authors argued that stereotype threat lead to reduced scores because stereotype information interfered with the individual's attentional control abilities and thus reduced the WMC.

## Executive Attention and Prejudice

A recent set of studies by Richeson and colleagues has further demonstrated the importance of executive attention in a dynamic social situation. In particular, one study (Richeson & Shelton, 2003) examined the effects of interracial interaction on executive control. Richeson and Shelton argued that interracial interaction can be an especially taxing exercise for individuals who are prejudiced against the person with whom they are interacting. Additionally, drawing on the work of Baumeister and colleagues (Baumeister, Muraven, & Tice, 2000), Richeson and Shelton suggested that interracial interaction for high prejudiced individuals would deplete executive attentional resources, and therefore, performance on a subsequent task requiring executive attention would be diminished. Richeson and Shelton (2003) first tested fifty White undergraduate participants on a version of the Implicit Association Test (IAT; Greenwald, McGhee, & Schwartz, 1998) to assess participants' implicit attitudes toward Whites and Blacks. Next, participants interacted with either a White or a Black experimenter on an unrelated task. Finally, participants performed a typical Stroop task. Richeson and Shelton reasoned that interacting with a Black experimenter for a person rated high in prejudice would tax executive attention and thus according to Baumeister and colleagues would diminish performance on a subsequent task relying on executive attention. As expected, the results showed that the amount of prejudice, as indexed by the IAT, predicted the amount of interference observed in the Stroop task only when participants interacted with the Black experimenter. Additionally, high prejudiced individuals experienced greater Stroop interference than did low prejudiced individuals after the interracial interaction. Thus, Richeson and Shelton argued that interracial interaction required a degree of executive control in the form of self-regulation and inhibition and that this engagement of executive control led to a subsequent disruption on another task requiring executive control.

Richeson et al. (2003) recently replicated and extended these findings via an fMRI study. Here, White undergraduates again completed the IAT to assess implicit attitudes; they then interacted with a Black confederate and finally performed the Stroop task. Additionally, in a separate session, the same subjects came back and participated in an fMRI session. In this session, participants were required to indicate whether a face appeared to the right or left of fixation. The faces were of either Black or White young adults. Richeson and colleagues reasoned that those individuals higher in implicit prejudice should show greater activation in areas thought to be important for behavioral inhibition (i.e., frontal gyrus; dorso-lateral prefrontal cortex, DLPFC; and anterior cingulate cortex). Additionally, the authors reasoned that the amount of activation in the DLPFC should also be related to the amount of interference observed in the Stroop task. That is, if behavioral inhibition is needed during interracial interaction, then areas associated with this inhibition should be related to areas involved in the inhibition of prepotent responses such as those in Stroop.

Strikingly, this is precisely what Richeson et al. (2003) found. Specifically, in addition to replicating the basic finding that engaging in behavioral inhibition actually hurt performance on the Stroop task for high prejudiced individuals, results suggest that the activation in the frontal gyrus and DLPFC, upon seeing Black faces, was significantly correlated to IAT scores. For White faces, however, no significant correlations were obtained. Thus, the amount of prejudice, as indexed by the IAT, was related to the amount of activation in areas thought to be important for behavioral inhibition. The results further demonstrated that the amount of interference observed in Stroop was significantly related to the amount of activity for Black faces in the frontal gyrus. Finally, the authors regressed the interference scores from the Stroop task on IAT scores and on activation from the frontal gyrus. The regression revealed that frontal gyrus activity was the only significant predictor of Stroop interference, suggesting that the relation between IAT scores and Stroop interference is mediated by activity in the frontal gyrus. Richeson et al. argued that this was due to the fact that interacting with a Black individual required relatively high prejudiced individuals to engage in behavioral inhibition; this need for behavioral inhibition resulted in a increase in activity in the frontal gyrus. This increased behavioral inhibition depleted executive attentional capacity, which diminished subsequent performance on the Stroop task.

These results and conclusions are intriguing. They suggest that the need for an executive attention mechanism is important for inhibition not only in low-level processing tasks, but also in situations in which social schemas and emotional attitudes are activated. According to the view outlined here, the executive attention mechanism responsible for the results of Richeson and colleagues findings is the same mechanism found to differentiate high and low working memory individuals. That is, despite the fact that WMC was not directly measured in these studies, the results do suggest a common link between our experiments and the findings of Richeson and colleagues. Specifically, goal maintenance in the face of interference or distraction and the resolution of the interference (conflict) are needed to generate the correct response. People who are prejudiced against a particular racial group, yet wish to maintain some degree of civility, then must attempt to act in accordance with the civility despite their prejudicial beliefs. Thus, the goal here is to act civil, not letting the prejudicial beliefs slip out. Similar to the antisaccade, in order to maintain the task goal and generate the correct response, you must inhibit the prepotent response, and in a sense, "block" your prejudicial views from becoming apparent. Richeson and colleagues (2003) further suggested that engaging in this form of behavioral inhibition is extremely effortful and can deplete executive attentional resources to the point that a subsequent task requiring these resources is hurt as well (see also Baumeister et al., 2000).

**The Effect of Alcohol on WMC**

The work relating stress (Klein & Boals, 2001) and prejudice (Richeson & Shelton, 2003) to executive attention suggested that these constructs work much like a cognitive load in the sense that they disrupt ongoing processing. Furthermore, these studies showed that successful performance is diminished when the need for conflict resolution between the task goal and a prepotent response is high. Work on the effects of alcohol on cognition has demonstrated that alcohol works similar to a cognitive load. Work by Finn and colleagues demonstrated a link among WM, behavioral inhibition, and alcohol consumption. Finn, Justus, Mazas, and Steinmetz (1999) had participants perform a Go/No-Go task with a contingency reversal halfway through the task while under the influence of alcohol and while sober. The Go/No-Go task required participants to learn when to hit the space bar (Go) and when not to hit the space bar (No-Go) based on rewards and punishments imposed after each trial. That is, after a response, a screen would appear indicating whether the participant had won or lost money during that trial. Participants performed 20 blocks of trials with a contingency reversal occurring at the eleventh block. At the onset of the 11th block, those stimuli and responses that had previously indicated a Go trial were now considered a No-Go trial and vice versa. Thus, contingency reversal created a response incompatibility in order to increase the need for behavioral inhibition. In addition, each participant completed a backward digit span task to assess WMC.

Finn et al. (1999) hypothesized that alcohol ingestion would lead to a deficiency in the ability to inhibit, and that these deficits in inhibition would be greatest for low WMC individuals. Furthermore, these inabilities should manifest themselves both in false alarms on the Go/No-Go task and in poorer performance after the contingency reversal. In support of these hypotheses, Finn et al. found that low WMC individuals, but not high WMC individuals (based on a median split), showed increased false alarm rates as a result of alcohol ingestion. Additionally, low WMC scores were related to inhibitory deficits after contingency reversal. Thus, low WMC individuals had a more difficult time inhibiting responses after the contingency reversal. These same low WMC individuals also demonstrated diminished performance because of alcohol ingestion. These results suggest that alcohol essentially places a load on WM and results in reduced ability to do the work required to inhibit. This deficiency in goal maintenance biased responding in favor of prepotent behavior and led to the incorrect response. Furthermore, these effects are most pronounced for individuals with low WMC scores. That is, those individuals hypothesized to be poorer at actively maintaining task goals demonstrated greater impulsive behavior brought about by a physiological load. This led Finn et al. to conclude that WM modulates behavioral inhibition and that alcohol consumption reduces the ability to effectively control impulsive behavior.

Taken together, the previous studies demonstrate the importance of WMC in wide array of real-world issues. Not only is WMC related to many real-world cognitive tasks such as reading comprehension (e.g., Daneman & Carpenter, 1980), reasoning (e.g., Kyllonen & Christal, 1990; Engle et al., 1999), and complex learning (Kyllonen & Stephens, 1990), but also these studies demonstrate the utility of executive attention in issues such as stress, prejudice, and alcohol consumption. The work has further demonstrated that executive attention is important in these areas because of a need to maintain task goals in the face of interference via behavioral inhibition. We have argued that our work with the antisaccade paradigm provides a clear and simple parallel between low-level attention tasks and these real-world issues via the need for active maintenance and inhibition. That is, the processes required in the antisaccade task can be extrapolated to other areas as a means of explaining the need for executive attention. When goal maintenance is threatened by heightened internal and external interference, executive attention works to keep task goals appropriately activated in order to deal with this interference. Our view, as well as the view of others (e.g., Roberts & Pennington, 1996), suggests that behavioral inhibition of intrusive thoughts and/or environmental distractors can only occur when the goal to do so is actively maintained.

## DIFFERENCES IN WMC AS A CAUSE OR A RESULT IN COGNITIVE FUNCTIONING

So far, we have discussed the role of WMC on a variety of tasks with relatively healthy, young adults. The results of our own studies suggest that individuals differing in WMC also differ on low-level attention paradigms in which goal maintenance and inhibition are important for successful task performance. In particular, both the Stroop and antisaccade task require that participants maintain a task goal (e.g., "say the color not the word," "don't look at the flashing box") in the face of a powerful pre-potent response. When task goals are actively maintained, inhibition of the prepotent response occurs and appropriate action is generated. However, if for any reason goal maintenance is lost, then habitual responding will guide behavior and errors or inappropriate responding will occur. Furthermore, we have argued that these executive control capabilities share common variance with tasks of higher order cognition. In several studies, we demonstrated that the same WM span measures that differentiated participants in the attentional tasks are highly predictive of higher order cognition. In particular, we argued that WMC is an important component of general-fluid intelligence. Thus, the results from normal, healthy adults suggest that WMC is a relative primitive in terms of cognitive functioning.

In addition, the results of the preceding section on behavioral inhibition have demonstrated that executive control is diminished under conditions of load brought about by stress, prejudice, and alcohol. We argued in the preceding section that the results of these studies could be interpreted in a framework similar to the antisaccade in that these loads introduced interference into the task in the form of unwanted thoughts that had to be suppressed. The loads imposed by these tasks make it more likely to temporarily lose task goals, and thus any loss in attention will result in the inappropriate behavior and subsequent decrements in performance.

In these cases, reductions in WMC and subsequent diminished cognitive functioning are a result of the load imposed by the relevant phenomena. That is, it is not that low WMC causes stress or alcohol consumption (although cyclic effects may occur in which low WMC may lead to more stress, which then leads to decrements in WMC, etc.), but rather these act as a secondary load that leads to disinhibited behavior and poor performance on tasks that require sustained and focused attention. Furthermore, these effects are similar to those brought about by normal aging and even psychopathology. In this view, tasks and situations that rely on WMC can be affected independently or interactively by both individual differences in WMC and secondary loads, stress, schizophrenia, depression, and alcohol consumption. As shown in Figure 2.3, performance on tasks such as Stroop and antisaccade is dependent on WMC, which in turn is affected by individual differences and also by secondary task loads, normal aging, and psychopathology. Additionally, some of these same factors (e.g., alcohol/prejudice) may work more as a moderator variable whereby the relationship between WMC and higher order cognition is affected only for those participants low in WMC. In this case, low WMC can be seen as a

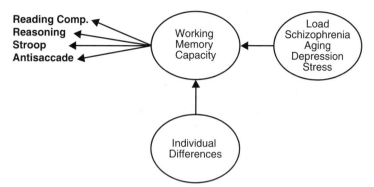

FIGURE 2.3. Schematic demonstrating the role of WMC to task performance as a function of individual differences and/or secondary loads, psychopathology, etc. Reading comp. = reading comprehension.

risk factor.[i] Therefore, performance deficits can occur as a result of abiding differences among individuals or because of other phenomena that tax WMC such psychopathology or a combination thereof.

## Aging

Extensive work has linked cognitive decrements in normal aging with deficits in WMC (e.g., see Oberaurer, this volume). It is our view that differences typically observed between older and younger adults are similar to those seen by low- and high-span individuals. That is, low WM span individuals and older adults tend to act similarly on many of the tasks discussed previously. Indeed, as noted earlier, research has shown performance differences on both Stroop (see West & Bowry, this volume) and the antisaccade task (Butler et al., 1999; Nieuwenhuis et al., 2000) between older and younger adults. Although the reasons for performance decrements for older adults and young adults who are low spans may be quite different (e.g., Engle, 1996).

Hasher, Zacks, and colleagues (1988; Stoltzfus, Hasher, & Zacks, 1996) advanced a theory similar to ours to explain cognitive declines in aging. Specifically, they (1988; Stoltzfus et al., 1996) argued that cognitive functioning declines in older adults because of a loss in efficient inhibitory ability. Thus, like our view, inhibition of irrelevant thoughts and distractors is needed to maintain task goals in the face of interference. However, the views differ slightly in regard to the underlying primitive responsible. We assume that difficulty in inhibiting task-irrelevant items is a function of attentional control (e.g., see Engle, Conway, Tuholski, & Shisler, 1995;

---

[i] We would like to thank Greg Sedek for suggesting this to us.

Engle, 1996), whereas Hasher, Zacks, and colleagues (1988; Stoltzfus et al., 1996) argued that the underlying primitive is individual differences, specifically in the ability to inhibit.

Regardless, difficulty in dealing with interference seems to result in performance decrements on many higher order tasks. Furthermore, for older adults, the declines in WMC are a result of a normal process, and thus subsequent disruption in higher order cognition is ultimately a result of normal aging of the neural circuitry involved in goal maintenance and conflict resolution (see West & Bowry, this volume). That is, in this case, processes involved in normal aging result in declines in WMC, which in turn results in declines in normal cognitive functioning. Thus, WMC acts as a mediator between normal cognitive aging and declines in higher order cognition.

### Psychopathology

In addition, cognitive declines in psychopathology (e.g., schizophrenia, depression, Alzheimer's disease, etc.) can often be seen as declines in goal maintenance and conflict resolution, which result in subsequent declines in higher order cognition. In these cases, it is not that WMC causes psychopathology, but rather that psychopathology results in declines in WMC. Then, to the extent to which WMC can be seen as a relative primitive in cognitive functioning, these declines in WMC result in subsequent declines in higher order functioning. The work of Cohen and colleagues (e.g., Cohen, Braver, & O'Reilly, 1996; see also Barch & Braver, this volume) suggested that the control deficits observed in schizophrenia are a result of deficits in active maintenance and inhibition, whereby disruptions in active maintenance result in a failure to inhibit prepotent responses. Indeed, Roberts and Pennington (1996) advanced a similar view of frontal dysfunction noting: "Frontal dysfunction could create two types of inhibitory deficits: a more global inhibitory deficit from tonic disinhibition, which would lower thresholds for prepotent responding generally, and a more specific form of response disinhibition that results from weaker working memory activations" (p. 112). Thus, like the view presented here, deficits as a result of psychopathology can be seen as disrupting the executive attention capabilities of the WM system in which active maintenance is lost and prepotent responses guide behavior.

Likewise, work in the realm of depression has suggested that depressed individuals show more interference than control subjects when attentional control is necessary, but little to no differences when relatively automatic processing is necessary (e.g., Hartlage, Alloy, Vázquez, & Dykman, 1993; Hasher & Zacks, 1979). Similarly, Arnett et al. (1999) demonstrated that depressed individuals performed worse on a measure of WMC (reading span), but there were no differences on a simple short-term memory measure (word span). Arnett et al. suggested that depression reduces the capacity of the executive attention component of the WM system. Additionally, work by Wegner and colleagues (Wenzlaff, Wegner, & Roper, 1988) showed that depressive individuals are worse at suppressing unwanted thoughts than are control subjects, specifically when the unwanted thoughts are negative in nature. Like the effects brought about by stress, depression results in a loss of goal maintenance, which in turn leads to an inability to effectively deal with interference and hence more intrusive thoughts. Thus, the rumination of negative thoughts associated with depression make it more difficult to focus attention on the task at hand, and thus performance decrements are observed.

In our view, individual differences in WMC, as measured by complex span tasks in healthy, normal, young adults provide a fruitful arena in which to investigate the possible mechanisms and consequences of these issues. That is, although it is possible that the underlying mechanisms responsible for individual differences in a "normal" population are not the same as those observed in normal aging and psychopathology, we believe that work within a "normal" population can shed light on these issues via a framework that relies on executive attentional capabilities in terms of active maintenance and inhibition (e.g., Roberts & Pennington, 1996).

CONCLUSION

We have presented a view of working memory capacity in which the executive attention component of the broader WM system is important in a diverse array of real-world phenomena including lower level attention tasks, measures of higher order cognition, as well as stress, prejudice, and alcohol consumption. Furthermore, we argued that the results from the antisaccade paradigm provide a simple framework in thinking about the possible role of WMC in many tasks. That is, we argued that the antisaccade task requires the inhibition of prepotent responses and that the inhibition of these responses can only occur when the intention to do so is actively maintained in WM. Furthermore, individual differences in WMC are most apparent in situations in which active maintenance is needed to generate the correct response in the face of potentially distracting information. We argued that these two functions of executive attention – active maintenance and conflict resolution, and hence WMC – are needed in many real-world situations. Whether or not the views outlined here will ultimately prove to be accurate, we believe that research in the next 20 years will not only provide more evidence about the ultimate link between measures of WM and higher order cognition, but will also provide evidence on the role of WMC in many other research domains.

## Author Note

We are grateful to Andy Conway and Tom Redick for helpful comments on a draft of the article. This research was supported by Grants F49620-97-1 and F49620-93-1-0336 from the Air Force Office of Scientific Research.

## References

Arnett, P. A., Higginson, C. H., Voss, W. D., Bender, W. I., Wurst, J. M., & Tippin, J. M. (1999). Depression in multiple sclerosis: Relationship to working memory capacity. *Neuropsychology, 13*, 546–556.

Baumeister, R. F., Muraven, M., & Tice, D. M. (2000). Ego depletion: A resource model of volition, self-regulation, and controlled processing. *Social Cognition, 18*, 130–150.

Brewin, C. R., & Beaton, A. (2002). Thought suppression, intelligence, and working memory capacity. *Behavior Research and Therapy, 40*, 923–930.

Butler, K. M., Zacks, R. T., & Henderson, J. M. (1999). Suppression of reflexive saccades in younger and older adults: Age comparisons on an antisaccade task. *Memory & Cognition, 27*, 584–591.

Cherry, C. E. (1953). Some experiments on the recognition of speech, with one and with two ears. *Journal of Acoustical Society of America, 25*, 975–979.

Chiappe, P., Hasher, L., & Siegal, L. S. (2000). Working memory, inhibitory control, and reading disability. *Memory and Cognition, 28*, 8–17.

Cohen, J. D., Braver, T. S., & O'Reilly, R. C. (1996). A computational approach to prefrontal cortex, cognitive control, and schizophrenia: Recent developments and current challenges. *Philosophical Transactions of the Royal Society of London Series B, 351*, 1515–1527.

Conway, A. R. A., & Engle, R. W. (1994). Working memory and retrieval: A resource-dependent inhibition model. *Journal of Experimental Psychology: General, 123*, 354–373.

Conway, A. R. A., & Engle, R. W. (1996). Individual differences in working memory capacity: More evidence for a general capacity theory. *Memory, 4*, 577–590.

Conway, A. R. A., Cowan, N., & Bunting, M. F. (2001). The cocktail party phenomenon revisited: The importance of working memory capacity. *Psychonomic Bulletin and Review Special Issue, 8*, 331–335.

Conway, A. R. A., Cowan, N., Bunting, M. F., Therriault, D. J., & Minkoff, S. R. B. (2002). A latent variable analysis of working memory capacity, short-term memory capacity, processing speed, and general fluid intelligence. *Intelligence, 30*, 163–183.

Cowan, N. (1988). Evolving conceptions of memory storage, selective attention, and their mutual constraints within the human information-processing system. *Psychological Bulletin, 104*, 163–191.

Cowan N. (1995). *Attention and memory: An integrated framework*. Oxford, England: Oxford University Press.

Daneman, M., & Carpenter, P. A. (1980). Individual differences in working memory and reading. *Journal of Verbal Learning and Verbal Behavior, 19*, 450–466.

Daneman, M., & Green, I. (1986). Individual differences in comprehending and producing words in context. *Journal of Memory and Language, 25,* 1–18.

Duncan, J. (1990). Goal weighting and the choice of behavior in a complex world. *Ergonomics, 33,* 1265–1279.

Engle, R. W. (1996). Working memory and retrieval: An inhibition-resource approach. In J. T. E. Richardson, R. W. Engle, L. Hasher, R. H. Logie, E. R. Stoltz-fus, & R. T. Zacks (Eds.), *Working memory and human cognition* (pp. 89–117). New York: Oxford University Press.

Engle, R. W., Cantor, J., & Carullo, J. J. (1992). Individual differences in working memory and comprehension: A test of four hypotheses. *Journal of Experimental Psychology: Learning, Memory, and Cognition, 18,* 972–992.

Engle, R. W., Carullo, J. J., & Collins, K. W. (1991). Individual differences in working memory for comprehension and following directions. *Journal of Educational Research, 84,* 253–262.

Engle, R. W., Conway, A. R. A., Tuholski, S. W., & Shisler, R. J. (1995). A resource account of inhibition. *Psychological Science, 6,* 19–23.

Engle, R. W., & Oransky, N. (1999). The evolution from short-term to working memory: Multi-store to dynamic models of temporary storage. In R. J. Sternberg (Ed.), *The Nature of Cognition* (pp. 515–555). Cambridge, MA: MIT Press.

Engle, R. W., Tuholski, S. W., Laughlin, J. E., & Conway, A. R. A. (1999). Working memory, short-term memory and general fluid intelligence: A latent-variable approach. *Journal of Experimental Psychology: General, 128,* 309–331.

Everling, S., & Fischer, B. (1998). The antisaccade: A review of basic research and clinical studies. *Neuropsychologia, 36,* 885–899.

Finn, P. R. (2002). Motivation, working memory, and decision making: A cognitive-motivational theory of personality vulnerability to alcoholism. *Behavioral and Cognitive Neuroscience Reviews, 1,* 183–205.

Finn, P. R., Justus, A., Mazas, C., & Steinmetz, J. E. (1999). Working memory, executive processes and the effects of alcohol on Go/No-Go learning: Testing a model of behavioral regulation and impulsivity. *Psychopharmacology, 146,* 465–472.

Fischer, B., Biscaldi, M., & Gezeck, S. (1997). On the development of voluntary and reflexive components in human saccade generation. *Brain Research, 754,* 285–297.

Fukushima, J., Fukushima, K., Chiba, T., Tanaka, S., Yamashita, I., & Kato, M. (1988). Disturbances of voluntary control of saccadic eye movements in schizophrenic patients. *Biological Psychiatry, 23,* 670–677.

Fukushima, J., Hatta, T., & Fukushima, K. (2000). Development of voluntary control of saccadic eye movements I. Age-related changes in normal children. *Brain & Development, 22,* 173–180.

Greenwald, A. G., McGhee, D. E., & Schwartz, J. L. K. (1998). Measuring individual differences in implicit cognition: The implicit association task. *Journal of Personality and Social Psychology, 74,* 1464–1480.

Guitton, D., Buchtel, H. A., & Douglas, R. M. (1985). Frontal lobe lesions in man cause difficulties in suppressing reflexive glances and in generating goal-directed saccades. *Experimental Brain Research, 58,* 455–472.

Hallet, P. E. (1978). Primary and secondary saccades to goals defined by instructions. *Vision Research, 18,* 1279–1296.

Hallet, P. E., & Adams, B. D. (1980). The predictability of saccadic latency in a novel voluntary oculomotor task. *Vision Research, 20*, 329–339.

Hartlage, S., Alloy, L. B., Vazquez, C., & Dykman, B. (1993). Automatic and effortful processing in depression. *Psychological Bulletin, 113*, 247–278.

Hasher, L., & Zacks, R. T. (1979). Automatic and effortful processes in memory. *Journal of Experimental Psychology: General, 108*, 356–388.

Hasher, L., & Zacks, R. T. (1988). Working memory, comprehension, and aging: A review and a new view. In G. H. Bower (Ed.), *The psychology of learning and motivation* (Vol. 22, pp. 193–225). San Diego, CA: Academic Press.

Kahneman, D. (1973). *Attention and effort*. Englewood Cliffs, NJ: Prentice-Hall.

Kane, M. J., Bleckley, M. K., Conway, A. R. A., & Engle, R. W. (2001). A controlled-attention view of working-memory capacity. *Journal of Experimental Psychology: General, 130*, 169–183.

Kane, M. J., & Engle, R. W. (2002). The role of prefrontal cortex in working-memory capacity, executive attention, and general fluid intelligence: An individual differences perspective. *Psychonomic Bulletin & Review, 9*, 637–671.

Kane, M. J., & Engle, R. W. (2003). Working-memory capacity and the control of attention: The contributions of goal neglect, response competition, and task set to Stroop interference. *Journal of Experimental Psychology: General, 132*, 47–70.

Klein, K., & Boals, A. (2001). The relationship of life event stress and working memory capacity. *Applied Cognitive Psychology, 15*, 565–579.

Klein, K., & Fiss, W. H. (1999). The reliability and stability of the Turner and Engle working memory task. *Behavioral Research Methods, Instruments, & Computers, 31*, 429–432.

Kyllonen, P. C., & Christal, R. E. (1990). Reasoning ability is (little more than) working-memory capacity?! *Intelligence, 14*, 389–433.

Kyllonen, P. C., & Stephens, D. L. (1990). Cognitive abilities as determinants of success in acquiring logic skill. *Learning and Individual Differences, 2*, 129–160.

Larson, G. E., & Perry, Z. A. (1999). Visual capture and human error. *Applied Cognitive Psychology, 13*, 227–236.

Miller, G. A. (1956). The magical number seven plus or minus two: Some limits on our capacity for processing information. *Psychological Review, 63*, 81–96.

Moray, N. (1959). Attention in dichotic listening: Affective cues and the influence of instructions. *Quarterly Journal of Experimental Psychology, 11*, 56–60.

Nieuwenhuis, S., Ridderinkhof, K. R., De Jong, R., Kok, A., & van der Molen, M. W. (2000). Inhibitory inefficiency and failures of intention activation: Age-related decline in the control of saccadic eye movements. *Psychology and Aging, 15*, 635–647.

Pashler, H., Carrier, M., & Hoffman, J. (1993). Saccadic eye movements and dual-task interference. *The Quarterly Journal of Experimental Psychology, 46A*, 51–82.

Richeson, J. A., Baird, A. A., Gordon, H. L., Heatherton, T. F, Wyland, C. L., Trawalter, S., et al. (2003). An fMRI examination of the impact of interracial contact on executive function. *Nature Neuroscience, 6*, 1323–1328.

Richeson, J. A., & Shelton, J. N. (2003). When prejudice does not pay: Effects of interracial contact on executive function. *Psychological Science, 14*, 287–291.

Roberts, R. J., & Pennington, B. F. (1996). An integrative framework for examining prefrontal cognitive processes. *Developmental Neuropsychology, 12,* 105–126.

Roberts, R. J., Hager, L. D., & Heron, C. (1994). Prefrontal cognitive processes: Working memory and inhibition in the antisaccade task. *Journal of Experimental Psychology: General, 123,* 374–393.

Rosen, V. M., Bergeson, J. L., Putnam, K., Harwell, A., & Sunderland, T. (2002). Working memory and *apolipoprotein* E: What's the connection? *Neuropsycholgia, 40,* 2226–2233.

Rosen, V. M., & Engle, R. W. (1997). The role of working memory capacity in retrieval. *Journal of Experimental Psychology: General, 126,* 211–227.

Stoltzfus, E. R., Hasher, L., & Zacks, R. T. (1996). Working memory and aging: Current status of the inhibitory view. In J. T. E. Richardson, R. W. Engle, L. Hasher, R. H. Logie, E. R. Stoltzfus, & R. T. Zacks (Eds.), *Working memory and human cognition* (pp. 66–88). New York: Oxford University Press.

Stuyven, E., Van der Goten, K., Vandierendonck, A., Claeys, K., & Crevits, L. (2000). The effect of cognitive load on saccadic eye movements. *Acta Psychologica, 104,* 69–85.

Tuholski, S. W., Engle, R. W., & Baylis, G. C. (2001). Individual differences in working memory capacity and enumeration. *Memory & Cognition, 29,* 484–492.

Turner, M. L., & Engle, R. W. (1989). Is working memory capacity task dependent? *Journal of Memory and Language, 28,* 127–154.

Unsworth, N., Schrock, J. C., & Engle, R. W. (2004). Working memory capacity and the antisaccade task: Individual differences in voluntary saccade control. *Journal of Experimental Psychology: Learning, Memory & Cognition, 30,* 1302–1321.

Weber, H. (1995). Presaccadic processes in the generation of pro and anti saccades in human subject – A reaction-time study. *Perception, 24,* 1265–1280.

Wegner, D. M. (1989). *White bears and other unwanted thoughts.* New York: Viking/Penquin.

Wegner, D. M. (1994). Ironic processes of mental control. *Psychological Review, 101,* 34–52.

Wegner, D. M., Schneider, D., Carter, S., & White, T. (1987). Paradoxical effects of thought suppression. *Journal of Personality and Social Psychology, 53,* 5–13.

Wenzlaff, R. M., Wegner, D. M., & Ropper, D. W. (1988). Depression and mental control: The resurgence of unwanted negative thoughts. *Journal of Personality and Social Psychology, 55,* 882–892.

Wood, N., & Cowan, N. (1995). The cocktail party phenomenon revisited: How frequent are attention shifts to one's name in an irrelevant auditory channel? *Journal of Experimental Psychology: Learning, Memory, and Cognition, 21,* 255–260.

# 3

# Age Differences and Individual Differences in Cognitive Functions

## Klaus Oberauer

Here is a pair of very simplistic hypotheses: (1) Differences among groups or individuals in cognitive performance can all be reduced to a single source, for instance, general intelligence. (2) This source is the same for all comparisons among groups of individuals that differ in broad cognitive functioning (e.g., children vs. adults, younger vs. older adults, healthy vs. cognitively impaired populations) such that the pattern of differences across various indicators of cognitive performance will be the same for every such group contrast.

In their plain form, these statements are certainly wrong. In a moderated version, however, they both have considerable merit. Cross-sectional comparisons of young adults (around 20 years of age) and older adults (age 60 and above), for instance, show that older age is associated with reduced cognitive performance across a wide variety of tasks, and a large portion of the age variance can be accounted for by a single factor in structural equation models (Salthouse, 1996; Lindenberger, Mayr, & Kliegl, 1993). Likewise, individual differences in cognitive abilities can to a large degree be captured by the $g$ factor of intelligence (Jensen, 1998), which in turn is strongly associated with working memory capacity (Engle, Tuholski, Laughlin, & Conway, 1999; Kyllonen, 1996; Süß, Oberauer, Wittmann, Wilhelm, & Schulze, 2002). Research on the aging of cognition has also shown that the pattern of age differences across a broad set of speeded tasks can often be described by a simple linear function: older adults' latencies equal younger adults' latencies on the same tasks or conditions, multiplied by a constant slowing factor (Cerella, 1985) or incremented by a constant (Verhaeghen & Cerella, 2002). Groups of individuals of the same age, distinguished by their general processing speed, can also be related to each other by a proportional factor across various experimental conditions (Hale & Jansen, 1994; Zheng, Myerson, & Hale, 2000).

Within each group comparison, the presence of a strong general factor raises the issue of whether a particular observation of performance differences among groups is a reflection of the general factor separating these groups or of an additional, more specific factor. In cognitive aging research, for example, the hypothesis of general proportional slowing is used as a baseline against which assumptions of more specific age-related deficits are tested (e.g., Mayr & Kliegl, 1993; Verhaeghen & Cerella, 2002). For example, if older adults show larger interference effects in the Stroop task than do younger adults, this could be interpreted as manifestation of a specific problem of older adults with inhibiting the inadequate word-reading process. An alternative interpretation, however, is that all cognitive processes are slowed in old age by a constant proportion, which would also increase all differences in reaction times among experimental conditions by the same proportional factor (Verhaeghen & De Meersman, 1998).

When we consider several group comparisons together, as it is done in the present volume, a couple of issues arise. Is the general factor that separates groups in one contrast the same as the general factor characterizing another group contrast? And are the specific factors the same for all group contrasts? For example, is aging equivalent to a loss in general (or fluid) intelligence? Can the cognitive effects of depression be described as a mild form of cognitive aging? In general, can we take the pattern of group differences over various cognitive functions observed in one group contrast as a model for another group contrast?

It is probably safe to say that the answer will in most cases be negative. Nonetheless, I regard the two simplistic hypotheses introduced above as useful, because we can learn about group differences in cognitive functions by falsifying these hypotheses in a theoretically interesting way. This means, first, identifying instances in which the performance of one group (e.g., older adults) differs from that of another group (e.g., younger adults) to a larger or a smaller degree than would be expected by a general factor (e.g., proportional slowing). Second, these instances should be interpretable as indicators of theoretical concepts that form part of causal models of cognition. Finding a task or experimental condition in which older adults perform much worse (or better) than would be expected from general slowing is a first step (e.g., Kliegl, Mayr, & Krampe, 1994; Mayr, Kliegl, & Krampe, 1996; Sliwinski & Hall, 1998), and it is sufficient for rejecting reductionist versions of the speed theory of cognitive aging. More is gained if this task or condition can be identified as reflecting a cognitive mechanism or a feature figuring in a theory of the cognitive system. We could then conclude that this mechanism or feature is specifically impaired (or spared) in the process of aging. Ideally, we should be able to map the specific performance difference between two groups onto a parameter in a formal model of the experimental task (Oberauer & Kliegl, 2001).

Progress in this direction requires that we construct task paradigms to measure theoretically postulated cognitive mechanisms, such as the inhibition of irrelevant information in long-term memory or the access to a representational unit in working memory. When the measures extracted from these paradigms can be validated as indicators of the theoretical construct in question, they can be applied to multiple group contrasts. Comparison across different group contrasts on the same indicators will eventually allow us to compare the profiles of selective impairments and sparings in cognitive functions of various groups relative to a control group (usually healthy young adults) and relative to each other.

In this chapter, I will illustrate this approach with three examples from cross-sectional comparisons between younger and older adults: Task-set switching, inhibition of irrelevant information in memory, and access to working memory. Where available, I will discuss corresponding data comparing groups of young adults differing in working memory capacity, so that we can ask to what degree differences between groups of high versus low capacity can be used as a model for the corresponding differences between age groups.

## TASK-SET SWITCHING

Many researchers assume that aging is associated with a deficit in executive functions that goes beyond the effect of general slowing (Mayr, Spieler, & Kliegl, 2001; West, 1996). The term executive control is often used in a broad, hardly constrained fashion. In an attempt to systematize the aspects of meaning it has acquired over the years, Smith and Jonides (1999) listed five functions they call executive: (1) Focusing attention on relevant information while inhibiting irrelevant information, (2) scheduling of processes, including switching of attention among tasks, (3) planning, (4) updating and checking working memory contents, and (5) coding representation in working memory. Miyake and his colleagues performed the first factor analysis on various indicators of executive function, extracting three factors that they identified as updating of working memory, inhibition of prepotent responses, and shifting among task sets (Miyake et al., 2000).

Here I will focus on one representative executive function, task-set switching. Since the studies of Allport, Styles, and Hsieh (1994), the task-set switching paradigm originally introduced by Jersild (1927) has become the most intensely studied experimental setting used to operationalize executive functions. Task-set switching falls under the scheduling function in the taxonomy of Smith and Jonides (1999), and it loaded on the shifting factor in the study of Miyake et al. (2000). Task sets are representations of the person's currently operative goal, together with an associated rule or a set of parameters that determine which stimuli are relevant and how to respond to them (Logan & Gordon, 2001). In a typical switching experiment, participants are asked to process a sequence of stimuli, alternating between two task rules, both of which can be applied to the same category of stimuli. For example, a list of numbers is given, and participants have to work through the list, switching between addition of two and subtraction of one. The cost of switching between the two rules is computed as the difference in response latency between mixed blocks and pure blocks of tasks. Mixed blocks are the ones in which participants switch between two tasks from trial to trial. In the pure blocks, participants work on the same kind of stimuli according to either of the two task rules exclusively. The baseline for the computation of switch costs is the average latency of the two pure blocks, one for each task (e.g., one block in which 2 is added to all numbers, and another block in which 1 is subtracted).

Rogers and Monsell (1995) introduced a variant of the paradigm that allows to distinguish between *general* and *specific* switch costs. They used mixed blocks in which participants switched among task sets every $n$ trials. The specific cost of switching among task sets from trial to trial within a mixed block is reflected by the elevated reaction time of the first trial in each run of length $n$ relative to those occurring later in the run. Reaction times on these later trials are still higher than those in pure blocks, however. This difference reflects the general increase of latencies in the mixed block relative to the pure blocks.

Kray and Lindenberger (2000) used the paradigm of Rogers and Monsell (1995) with run lengths $n = 2$ in a study comparing younger and older adults. They constructed three versions of the basic paradigm, one with numerical, one with verbal, and one with spatial content. Older adults were slower overall, and they had larger general and specific switch costs than did the younger group. The age difference in specific switch costs was not reliably different from what would be expected from the proportional slowing factor extracted from the older–younger ratio of latencies in pure blocks. Older adults' general switch costs, however, were disproportionally larger than those of younger adults in two out of three versions of the paradigm.[1] Thus, older adults seem to have a specific deficit, which goes beyond general slowing, in general switch costs but not in specific switch costs. This pattern was recently confirmed by a meta-analysis of age differences in task-set switching (Verhaeghen & Cerella, 2002; for more recent deviating results see Kray, Li, & Lindenberger, 2002).

In a study on individual differences in working memory capacity (WMC) and intelligence (Oberauer, Süß, Wilhelm, & Wittmann, 2003), my colleagues and I included four versions of the task-set switching paradigm of Rogers and Monsell (1995), one with numerical content, one with verbal content, and two with spatial–figural stimuli. From each version, we computed individual indicators of specific switch costs and of general switch

---

[1] Kray and Lindenberger (2000) defined general switch costs as the difference between the mean reaction time of all trials in the mixed block (including switch trials) and the mean of reaction times in the corresponding pure blocks, in order to obtain independent estimates of general and specific switch costs.

costs. Through structural equation modeling, we were able to separate three factors, one representing overall speed in both the pure and the mixed blocks, the second one representing the residual variance associated with all trials in the mixed blocks, and a third one representing the residual variance of only the switch trials (i.e., trials immediately following a task-set switch) in the mixed blocks. This factor analysis showed that there was common variance across the four versions of the task-set switching paradigm associated with general switch costs (i.e., the factor representing the residual of all mixed-block trials), and common variance associated with specific switch costs (i.e., the factor representing the residuals of only the switch trials). Thus, both general and specific switch costs can be measured reliably and can be generalized across versions of the paradigm using tasks and stimuli from different content domains (see also Kray & Lindenberger, 2000; Ward, Roberts, & Phillips, 2001).

Neither general nor specific switch costs, however, correlated substantially with WMC. With regard to general switch costs, this stands in contrast to the reliable age effect. To make the data from Oberauer, Süß et al. (2003) more comparable to studies of age differences in switching, I split the sample (N = 137) at the median of a composite measure of WMC. The composite was obtained by averaging the z-scores from 18 working memory tasks. The contrast between high- and low-capacity groups can be summarized in the form of a *Brinley plot*, which plots the mean reaction time of one group over the mean reaction time of the other group in the same task condition (Brinley, 1965). Brinley plots have become a common tool in cognitive aging research, because they graphically illustrate the proportional slowing factor relating one group to the other by the slope of the regression line fit to the data points. Deviations from general proportional slowing can be identified through a subgroup of data points that requires a separate regression line with a different slope or intercept. In that case, one can argue that the conditions associated with these data points do not fit into the general slowing pattern (c.f. Mayr & Kliegl, 1993; Verhaeghen, Cerella, Bopp, & Basak, this volume).

A Brinley plot of the contrast between groups of high and of low WMC is shown in Figure 3.1. It summarizes the means from the pure blocks and the means of nonswitch trials and of switch trials from the mixed blocks. A single regression line captures all 12 data points well, and none of the three conditions deviates systematically from it. Thus, the comparison of group means complements the correlational analysis: People with low WMC react slower in task-set switching settings than people with high capacity, but not more than can be expected from their performance in pure blocks. To the degree that task-set switching costs reflect the efficiency of an executive function, this finding questions the assumption that executive functions are strongly associated with working memory (e.g., Kane & Engle, 2002; Smith & Jonides, 1999).

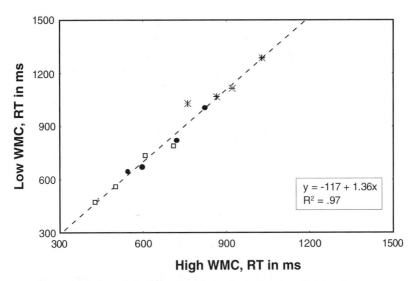

FIGURE 3.1. Brinley plot of reaction times in task-set switching for a group with low and a group with high working memory capacity (data from Oberauer, Süß et al., 2003). Data points represent mean reaction times from pure blocks (unfilled squares), from nonswitch trials in mixed blocks (filled circles), and from switch-trials in mixed blocks (crosses) of four versions of the task-set switching paradigm.

Comparing the age contrast and the WMC contrast with regard to general and specific switching costs reveals that these contrasts differ. This implies that the effects of aging on task-set switching cannot be reduced to older adults' reduction in WMC. Older adults' disproportionally large general switch costs point to a specific factor of cognitive differences among age groups beyond general slowing and loss of WMC. The next step would have to be finding out what this factor is.

One obvious hypothesis is that general switch costs reflect the extra load on working memory from two task sets instead of one (Kray & Lindenberger, 2000). The finding that general switch costs are not reduced for people with high working memory capacity questions this account. Additional evidence against the working memory load hypothesis comes from a study by Mayr (2001). He defined general switch costs (called "global selection costs") as the difference between the mixed block with ambiguous stimuli and a mixed block with unambiguous stimuli. Ambiguous stimuli were bars with two features: color and orientation (horizontal vs. vertical), one of which was relevant for each task set. Unambiguous stimuli were colored crosses (only color) or white bars (only orientation). The two conditions are equal with regard to the number of task sets to be held in working memory, but the unambiguous stimuli could be processed only

by one of the task sets. Mayr (2001) showed that older adults had disproportionally increased reaction times in ambiguous mixed blocks relative to
the unambiguous mixed block as baseline. This effect cannot be explained
by differences in working memory load. Instead, general switch costs seem
to arise because the irrelevant feature of the ambiguous stimuli is inadver-
tently processed according to the inappropriate task set, thereby generating
a conflict that slows down the response.

Such an inappropriate process can only occur if both the irrelevant stimulus feature and the irrelevant task set are available above baseline. An
executive system could prevent the inappropriate S-R translation by either
dampening the representation of the irrelevant feature or the representation of the irrelevant task set, or both. One hypothesis to account for
the age differences in general switch costs therefore could be that older
adults are less efficient in attending selectively to only the relevant stimulus feature (e.g., suppressing the form representation when the task is
to classify by color, and vice versa). However, Mayr (2001) also showed
that disproportional age differences in general switch costs were limited to
conditions in which the two task sets involved the same response buttons.
This demonstrates that not only stimulus ambiguity but also the overlap
of the responses (or response ambiguity) is necessary to generate particular difficulties for older adults. Hence, general switch costs probably arise
from an inability to completely neutralize the representation of the currently irrelevant task set while working on a mixed block (see also Mayr &
Liebscher, 2001). Older adults have a specific impairment in the efficiency
to shut down or inhibit temporarily irrelevant task sets, but this ability is
unrelated to working memory capacity.

Meanwhile, specific switch costs have been broken down into several
components (Meiran, Chorev, & Sapir, 2000), and there are several theoretical interpretations for them. Specific switch costs could result from *task-set
inertia* (Allport et al., 1994), the residual activation of the previous, no-
longer-relevant task set. Others interpret specific switch costs as reflecting
the time needed for *task-set reconfiguration* (Monsell, 2003). One could see
these two accounts as emphasizing two sides of the same phenomenon:
Task-set reconfiguration is the process needed to overcome task-set inertia.
Individual differences in specific switch costs can arise from larger task-
set inertia or weaker task-set reconfiguration processes. One speculation
arising from this analysis is that older and younger adults, or people with
high versus low WMC, could differ in both factors, such that the net effect
is no difference, as was observed in the studies reviewed here. Imagine,
for example, that older adults have more difficulty in selecting the relevant
task-set exclusively and in suppressing the operation of the irrelevant task
set. This would generate larger general switch costs, as discussed above.
In addition, it would generate larger task-set inertia. However, it would
also facilitate task-set reconfiguration, because the task set switched to has

not been suppressed very strongly in the first place. For the time being this account remains purely speculative.[2]

## INHIBITION OF IRRELEVANT INFORMATION IN MEMORY

The inhibition of irrelevant information is perhaps the most widely discussed factor proposed to account for age-related differences in cognition besides general slowing and reduced working memory capacity (Hasher & Zacks, 1988; Hasher, Zacks, & May, 1999). Hasher et al. (1999) proposed three inhibitory functions: The removal from working memory of information that is no longer relevant, the blocking of admission into working memory of irrelevant information, and the suppression of inappropriate actions.

A large amount of research has provided evidence that older adults have problems with the inhibition of representations in long-term memory. For example, in an implicit memory test older adults more than younger adults showed evidence of memory for sentence endings that were previously declared as irrelevant (Hartman & Hasher, 1991; Hasher, Quig, & May, 1997). In directed forgetting experiments, older adults were impaired relative to the younger group in memory for the items that were to be remembered, but they showed equivalent memory for items to be forgotten (Zacks, Radvansky, & Hasher, 1996).

Kliegl and Lindenberger (1993) compared younger and older adults on a paired associates memory task in which consecutive trials required learning new pairings of the old words (a so-called A-B, A-Br paradigm, where *r* stands for re-paired). Older adults showed an increased level of intrusion errors (i.e., wrongly recalling the associate from the previous instead of the current list), even after controlling for overall performance by adapting the list length to each individual's ability. This can be interpreted as showing a lack of inhibition for associations from previous, no longer relevant lists.

---

[2] Mayr (2001) argued against an account of age differences in terms of task-set inhibition, based on his finding that the backward-inhibition effect was larger in older than in younger adults. The backward-inhibition effect refers to the longer RT to the last trial in a sequence using task-sets A, B, A, compared to a sequence C, B, A. The explanation for this effect is that each task-set switch involves inhibition of the previous set, and inhibition gradually fades. When task-set A has to be used again immediately after it has been inhibited (through the switch to B), as in the ABA sequence, this is more difficult than when the inhibition of task-set A dates back longer, as in the CBA sequence. The backward-inhibition effect, however, does not reflect the absolute amount of inhibition of a currently not relevant task set, but the difference in degrees of inhibition between recently inhibited and less recently inhibited task sets, that is, the degree of inhibition, fading over a sequence of trials. Therefore, Mayr's (2001) finding does not rule out an inhibition account of age differences in switch costs.

In retrieval of arbitrary relational statements (e.g., "The lawyer is in the bank") older adults showed a larger *fan effect* than did younger adults (Gerard, Zacks, Hasher, & Radvansky, 1991). The fan effect (Anderson, 1974) is the increase of recognition times with the number of other facts learned that share one argument with the fact to be recognized (e.g., "The lawyer is in the church" or "The teacher is in the bank"). The increased fan effect can be interpreted as a result of reduced inhibition of memories for facts that are closely associated to the one currently probed, but nonetheless irrelevant and potentially misleading for the decision whether the probe has been learned before.

A reduced ability to inhibit irrelevant representations has also been assumed to be a source or a symptom of low WMC (Engle, 1996; Roberts, Hager, & Heron, 1994). In the more recent theorizing of Engle and his coworkers (Engle, Kane, & Tuholski, 1999; Unsworth, Heitz, & Engle, this volume), inhibition is regarded as one aspect of the efficiency of controlled attention, which they equate with WMC. Some of the findings reviewed above, which suggest an inhibition deficit in old age, are paralleled by comparisons of groups with high versus low WMC using very similar experimental paradigms. Rosen and Engle (1998) found that low-capacity individuals made more intrusion errors in a paired-associates learning task where the same cues were associated with different words in consecutive trials. Cantor and Engle (1993) reported a larger fan effect in low-capacity people compared to those with high capacity. Hence, there is some evidence that aging has a similar effect as low WMC with respect to the inhibition of irrelevant memory representations.

Hasher and Zacks (1988) proposed that older adults have more problems with working memory tasks than do younger adults because, as a consequence of their inhibition deficit, they cannot remove no-longer-relevant information from working memory or restrain entry of irrelevant information into working memory. In order to test this hypothesis, I designed a modified version of the Sternberg (1969) recognition task (Oberauer, 2001). In each trial of this task, participants first memorize two lists of words (see Figure 3.2). The lists were displayed in different locations of the computer screen, one in blue, the other in red. Each list could be either one or three words long. After the lists disappeared from the screen, a colored frame was displayed as a cue indicating which list is relevant for the memory task. The other list was thereby declared as irrelevant and could be forgotten. After a variable cue–stimulus interval (CSI), a probe appeared, and participants had to decide by a speeded key-press whether the probe was in the relevant list.

Following dual-process models of recognition (Mandler, 1980; McElree & Dosher, 1989; Yonelinas, 2002), I assume that responses to a probe depend on two sources of evidence in the cognitive system. One is a quickly available *familiarity* signal, which reflects the degree to which a representation

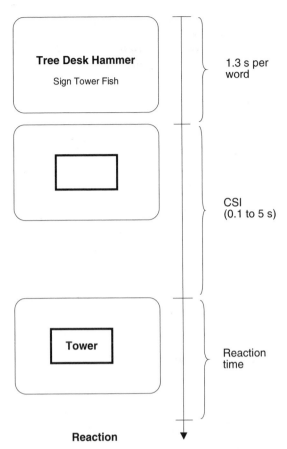

FIGURE 3.2. Sequence of events in a trial of the modified Sternberg task (Oberauer, 2001). Two lists of words are presented simultaneously as two lines, one in blue and one in red (illustrated here through different fonts). This is followed by a frame colored red or blue, indicating which list is relevant for this trial. After a variable cue–stimulus interval (CSI), the probe appears, and reaction time is measured until the participant decides through a key-press whether the probe was in the relevant list. The example shows an intrusion trial.

of the probe word in long-term memory (LTM) has been activated above baseline by its recent use. The other is evidence coming from *recollection* of an episode of having experienced a word in a particular context (e.g., in the last trial in the red list), which accumulates more slowly over the process of recognition (see Table 3.1).

The dual-process framework can be mapped onto a model of working memory I developed as an extension of the model proposed by Cowan (1995; 1999). The architecture of the model is illustrated in Figure 3.3

TABLE 3.1. *Features of Familiarity and Recollection in Recognition and How They Can Be Mapped Onto a Model of Working Memory*

|  | Familiarity | Recollection |
|---|---|---|
| Controllability | Automatic (can't be stopped even when misleading) | Controlled |
| Speed | Fast | Relatively slow |
| Comparison | Parallel matching with activated representations in memory | Parallel or serial comparison with individual episodes in memory |
| Evidential basis | Strength or activation of matching representations | Temporary binding between probe item and context (e.g., current relevant list) |
| Locus in WM model (Fig. 3.3) | Activated part of LTM | Direct access region |

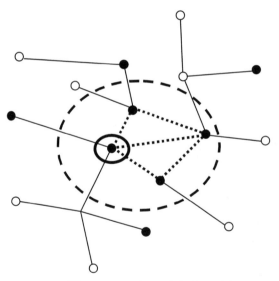

FIGURE 3.3. The concentric model of working memory (Oberauer, 2002). Nodes connected by continuous lines represent the network of associated representations in long-term memory; activated representations are highlighted in black. The large, broken circle delineates the region of direct access, in which new, temporary bindings (dotted lines) can be established and held for a brief period of time. The small, continuous circle represents the focus of attention that selects one element as the object of a cognitive operation.

(Oberauer, 2002). In line with Cowan, I assume that working memory representations are a subset of representations in long-term memory (LTM). Working memory is regarded as an attentional system that serves to provide selective access to memory representations.

The model identifies three levels of access. On a first level, potentially relevant LTM representations are activated above baseline. On a second level, a subset of representations is selected for which the system sets up and holds temporary bindings – for example, bindings among the representations of words in a recently read list and their colors, and their spatial positions, in the modified Sternberg task. Temporary bindings differ from associations in LTM in that they are quickly set up and quickly dissolved, such that they can change from trial to trial in an experimental task, always keeping the content–context association of the most recent event (e.g., the current list, as opposed to the list of previous trials). The representations linked together by temporary bindings constitute the content of the direct access region. The capacity limit of working memory is a limit on the amount of information that can be held in the direct access region, bound together into a coherent structure. A third level of access is constituted by the focus of attention, which selects a single representational unit (a chunk) as object of a cognitive operation.

I assume that in an immediate recognition task, such as the Sternberg task and its modifications, familiarity results from activation of representations of the list words in LTM. Recollection, on the other hand, relies on the temporary bindings between the current list words and their contexts (i.e., their color or position) in the direct access region (Oberauer, 2001). Therefore, we can ask two questions regarding the efficiency of removing irrelevant information from memory in the modified Sternberg task: How quickly can the activation of words from a list declared as irrelevant be dampened in LTM? And how quickly can a list be removed from the capacity-limited part of the working memory system, that is, the direct access region, once it has been declared as irrelevant?

The efficiency with which irrelevant list words are inhibited in the activated part of LTM can be assessed in the modified Sternberg task through *intrusion probes*, that is, words that had appeared in the irrelevant list (but not the relevant list). These are probes for which the two sources of evidence in the cognitive system come into conflict: They elicit a familiarity signal that is equally strong as that from a positive probe, but accurate recollection can provide evidence that the word had not been in the relevant list or that it had been in the irrelevant list. This conflict is mirrored in the longer times to reject intrusion probes, compared to negative probes (i.e., probes not present in either list and also not presented in other recent trials). The misleading high familiarity of intrusion probes results from the activation of irrelevant list words in LTM. Quickly inhibiting the irrelevant list words after the cue therefore should help to reject intrusion probes efficiently. We can use the intrusion cost, that is, the increase in reaction times to intrusion probes relative to negative probes, as an indicator for the residual activation of a word from the irrelevant list in LTM. If older adults have an inhibition deficit, they should find rejection of intrusion probes particularly difficult, resulting in enlarged intrusion costs relative to a younger group.

As an indicator for the removal of the irrelevant list from the direct access region of working memory, I used the list-length or set-size effect usually observed in the Sternberg task. The increase of recognition latencies with list length is to be expected if the list is held in the capacity limited part of working memory and if the capacity limit affects the speed of processing the contents of working memory. When the irrelevant list is removed from the direct access region, its length should not affect reaction times any more. Therefore, we can use the size of the irrelevant list-length effect to indicate the depletion of working memory capacity by the irrelevant list. If older adults have problems with working memory tasks because irrelevant information consumes part of the system's limited capacity (Hasher & Zacks, 1988), we should find that they show an effect of the irrelevant list length for a longer period of time.

Figure 3.4 shows the irrelevant list-length effects of 24 younger and 23 older adults over six levels of CSI (Oberauer, 2001, Experiment 1). The irrelevant list-length effect is defined as the difference between reaction times to long (three words) minus short (one word) irrelevant lists, averaging over the other conditions. Measuring the irrelevant list-length effect over a succession of CSIs allows tracing the gradual removal of the irrelevant list from working memory. Both groups show a significant list-length effect of the irrelevant list at the shortest CSI, consistent with the assumption that initially both lists are encoded into capacity limited working memory. For younger adults, there was a smooth decline of the irrelevant list length over increasing CSI, suggesting that they removed the irrelevant list from working memory after about one second. The data of older adults are noisier, but they too showed no significant effect of the irrelevant list length at most of the longer CSIs. This suggests that older adults are as efficient as younger adults in removing the irrelevant list from working memory.[3]

---

[3] The noise in the older adults' data, together with a tendency for positive irrelevant list length effects on the long CSIs in their data, could indicate that there is a lack of power to detect these effects. Meanwhile, I conducted two further experiments with older adults working on the modified Sternberg task. In both experiments, older adults showed a positive irrelevant list length effect after a moderately long CSI (1 and 2 s, respectively), which was numerically larger than that of the younger adults, but in both cases the age difference was not statistically significant. In a further unpublished experiment using digits as material instead of words and varying list length continuously from 1 to 4, both younger and older adults reduced the irrelevant list length to zero within a CSI of 1 second. Taken together, the data are not entirely conclusive, but if there is an age-related deficit in removing irrelevant information from the capacity limited part of working memory, it must be very small.

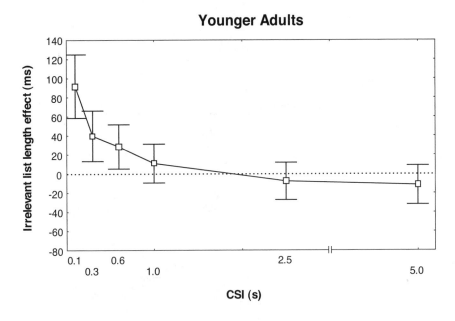

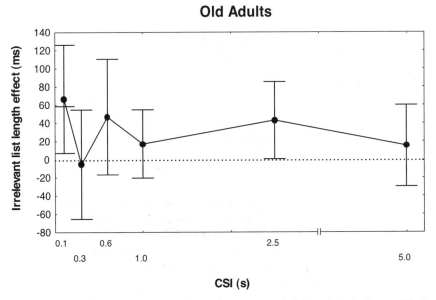

FIGURE 3.4. Irrelevant list length effects of younger and older adults in the modified Sternberg task (data from Oberauer, 2001, Experiment 1) as a function of cue–stimulus interval (CSI). Error bars represent two standard errors, such that means are significantly different from zero if their error bars do not include the dotted zero-line.

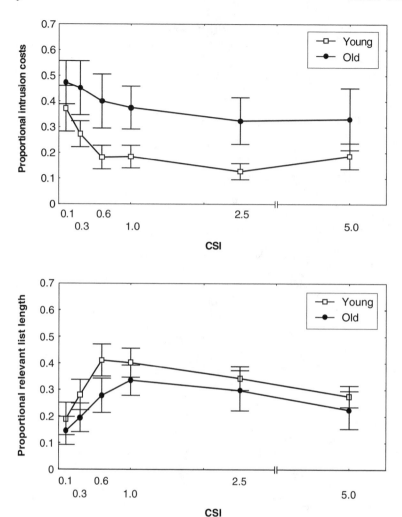

FIGURE 3.5. Top panel: Proportional intrusion costs of younger and older adults as a function of CSI. Intrusion costs are calculated as (RT intrusion − RT negative)/RT negative. Bottom panel: Proportional list-length effects of the relevant list of younger and older adults as a function of CSI. Data are from Oberauer (2001, Experiment 1). Error bars represent two standard errors.

The proportional intrusion costs of younger and older adults are plotted in the top panel of Figure 3.5. Intrusion costs remain substantial over all CSIs, indicating that the activation of irrelevant words in LTM does not cease for at least five seconds after they are known to be irrelevant. Inhibition of activated representations in LTM therefore seems to be a much slower process than removal of representations from the direct access region. More important in the present context is the finding that older adults show markedly increased intrusion costs compared to younger adults. Because this is an age difference in the proportional increase of reaction times to intrusion probes relative to reaction times to negative probes, the effect cannot be explained by a simple proportional slowing model.

Nonetheless, one could try to reconcile the disproportional intrusion costs of older adults with a more sophisticated general slowing account (Cerella, 1985). Reaction times consist of variance resulting from cognitive processes (e.g., comparison of the probe to memory representations) and sensorimotor processes (e.g., pressing the appropriate key). If age-related slowing affects cognitive processes more than sensorimotor ones, the intrusion cost, which can be assumed to reflect purely cognitive processes, would be expected to be inflated in old age to a larger degree than the baseline (i.e., reaction times to negative probes), which consists of a mixture of cognitive and sensorimotor processes. If this reasoning is accurate, we should find disproportional slowing on all reaction time *differences* that reflect different degrees of cognitive processing in different conditions.

One such difference that has been extensively studied in the context of the Sternberg task is the increase of reaction times with list length. I therefore computed the proportional list-length effect of the relevant list for younger and older adults by dividing the difference between reaction times to three-word lists and to one-word lists by the reaction time to one-word lists. The proportional list-length effect should reflect only cognitive processes involved in comparing a probe to a longer, as opposed to a shorter, list in working memory. If the sophisticated general slowing account is correct, older adults should show a disproportionally larger relevant list-length effect. This was ostensibly not the case, as can be seen in the bottom panel of Figure 3.5. If anything, the proportional list-length effects of older adults were smaller than those of younger adults.

A further way to demonstrate that the age effect on intrusion costs goes beyond general slowing is by analyzing Brinley plots. For both age groups, I computed means of reaction times to positive, negative, and intrusion probes for the six CSI conditions. The Brinley plot of these 18 data points is shown as Figure 3.6. An attempt to fit all data points by a single regression line yielded an $R^2$ of .87. A model with two slopes, one for the positive and the negative probes and one for the intrusion probes, provided a much better fit, $R^2 = .97$, and the improvement was statistically significant.[4] Thus, we can safely conclude that the increased intrusion effects of older

---

[4] Technically, the two-slope model was realized by introducing an interaction term, which is the product of the main predictor (younger adults' mean RT) and a dummy variable coding condition (0 for positive and negative probes, 1 for intrusion probes). The interaction term received a significant beta weight of .47, $t = 7.7$, $p < .001$.

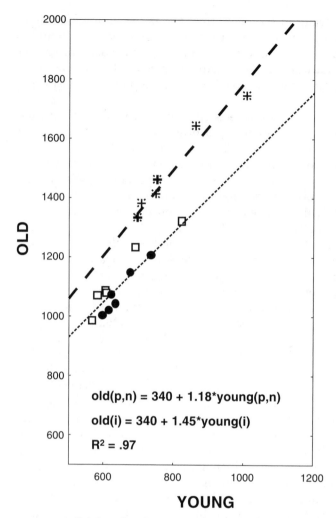

FIGURE 3.6. Brinley plot of older over younger reaction times in the modified Stern-berg task (Oberauer, 2001, Experiment 1). Open squares are reaction times to positive probes at six levels of CSI; filled circles represent negative probes, and stars represent intrusion probes. The broken line is the regression line for positive and negative probes, indexed as (p,n) in the equations. The dotted line is the regression line for intrusion probes, indexed (i).

adults reflect a specific factor of age-related cognitive decline that cannot be reduced to a general loss in the speed of cognitive processing.

But can it be reduced to a loss in working memory capacity? This question can be answered by investigating intrusion costs in groups of high versus low WMC within the same age level. In an as yet unpublished study, I tested 120 high school students with four working memory tests. In addition, they worked on the modified Sternberg task in exactly the same design and procedure as the participants in Experiment 1 of Oberauer (2001), described previously. The working memory tests were validated in a comprehensive factor-analytic study of working memory (Oberauer, Süß, Schulze, Wilhelm, & Wittmann, 2000). Two of them measured verbal working memory, the other two spatial working memory. I computed a composite score by averaging the $z$-scores on the four tasks and split the sample into two groups at the median of the composite.

The contrast of high versus low WMC groups yielded the same pattern of results as the age group contrast. Both groups were equally efficient in reducing the list-length effect of the irrelevant list to zero after about one second. The low-capacity group, however, showed larger proportional intrusion costs than did the high-capacity group for all levels of CSI, and the difference was significant overall in an analysis of log-transformed reaction times.[5] The differences were not as dramatic as that between age groups (on average over all CSIs, the high-capacity group had a proportional intrusion cost of 19%, whereas it was 24% for the low-capacity group). In the capacity group contrast, however, differences emerged not only in reaction times but also in errors: Specifically on the intrusion trials the low-capacity group committed substantially more errors than did the high-capacity group. Again, comparing high- and low-capacity groups on trials with different list lengths of the relevant list yielded no comparable group differences, confirming that the low-capacity group had a specific deficit in the suppression of intrusions.

To summarize, a similar pattern was obtained in contrasts of younger versus older adults and of high versus low WMC groups: In addition to being slower overall, the lower functioning group had a specific impairment in rejecting intrusion probes quickly and accurately. In the age contrast, this impairment was observed predominantly in reaction times, whereas, in the capacity contrast, it was more pronounced in error rates. The shift from reaction times to errors might simply reflect a difference in setting the speed–accuracy trade-off between older adults and low-capacity younger adults.

The comparison of two group contrasts on the same experimental paradigm serves to establish a strong link between the enlarged intrusion costs in old age and reduced working memory capacity. One interpretation could be, in line with Hasher and Zacks (1988), that the inability to inhibit irrelevant representations in LTM is a *cause* for impaired

---

[5] The log-transformation serves to move data into a proportional measurement space. Thus, testing for group differences in log-transformed reaction times is equivalent to testing for group differences in proportions of reaction times, instead of absolute differences (c.f. Verhaeghen et al., this volume).

performance in working memory tasks. The reduced ability to inhibit irrelevant information in the activated part of LTM could make these representations intrude back into the capacity-limited part of working memory
(i.e., the direct access region) even after they have been removed from it
and thereby reduce available capacity for relevant information. This interpretation happens to fit the trace of older adults' irrelevant list-length effect
over CSIs (Figure 3.4): The irrelevant list can quickly be removed from the
direct access region, such that the list-length effect drops toward zero, but
elements from the irrelevant list tend to intrude back occasionally, such
that over the whole range of CSIs the irrelevant list-length effect can pop
up again for some participants. In terms of the differentiation of inhibition functions proposed by Hasher et al. (1999), this interpretation means
that older adults have difficulty with restraining access of irrelevant information to working memory, whereas the function of removing irrelevant
information from working memory is unimpaired.

Alternatively, one could argue that a problem with rejecting the intrusion probes is a *consequence* of reduced working memory capacity. This
interpretation would attribute enlarged intrusion costs not to a deficit in
inhibitory power per se, but to a reduced ability to apply inhibition to the
right target. Working memory capacity is needed to hold available the temporary bindings between words and their list context, and this information
is necessary to discriminate between LTM representations to be inhibited
and others to be kept activated. It could be, therefore, that the ultimate
source of intrusion costs is a lack of robust context memory (c.f. Hedden &
Park, 2003; Oberauer, Süß, Wilhelm, & Sander, in press).

Finally, it is worth pointing out that the results reported here seem to
generalize over different experimental paradigms. Disproportional difficulty of older adults with rejecting intrusions in short-term recognition
paradigms was also reported by Zacks et al. (1996, Experiment 3) in a
variant of the Sternberg task in which the irrelevant list is always presented before the relevant list. Hedden and Park (2001, 2003), on the other
hand, found an increased error rate in older adults for rejecting intrusions
from an irrelevant list presented after the relevant list. Finally, De Beni
and her colleagues (De Beni, Palladino, Pazzaglia, & Cornoldi, 1998; De
Beni & Palladino, 2000) investigated intrusion effects in still another group
contrast – children differing in their reading ability. These researchers used
a dual-task paradigm in which participants had to recall one list of words
while detecting animal words in another list. Children with low reading
ability made more recall errors that were intrusions from the secondary-
task list than did children with high reading ability. Future research might
use this paradigm to compare younger and older adults, or groups with
high and low WMC, to determine whether the different susceptibility to
intrusion in people with low reading ability have the same source as the
intrusion difficulties of other low functioning groups.

## ACCESS TO WORKING MEMORY CONTENTS

In the previous section, I mapped two dependent variables extracted from the modified Sternberg task onto parameters of two components in my working memory model (see Figure 3.3), the activated part of long-term memory and the direct access region. The third component of the model, the focus of attention, has the function to access one mental object or chunk at a time from the set of objects in the direct access region and submit it to a cognitive operation. This last section describes my attempts to measure the efficiency of access to contents of working memory in younger and older adults.

To illustrate the role of the focus of attention in working memory, consider the task to add two three-digit numbers without the help of paper and pencil. Working memory is needed to remember the six given digits while we perform the computations on them and to remember the intermediate results. The digits must be bound to their roles (e.g., to represent the tens in the first number, or the carry after adding the ones), which can be accomplished by binding them temporarily to locations on an imagined blackboard. According to my model, this is the function of the direct access region. For each step in the computation, the system has to pick out one digit and increment it by the amount specified by another digit, while at the same time keeping the remaining digits available but unchanged. Picking out the digit that is manipulated by the arithmetic operation is the function of the focus of attention.

Mental arithmetic is a task domain particularly suited for age-comparative research because older adults show very little deficit relative to younger adults in both speed and accuracy of simple arithmetic operations (i.e., addition or subtraction of single digits). Simple arithmetic tasks therefore provide a particularly useful baseline for assessment of performance in more complex task versions. Verhaeghen, Kliegl, and Mayr (1997), for example, measured time-accuracy functions of younger and older participants on arithmetic chain tasks with and without brackets. No differences between the age groups were obtained for the tasks without brackets. On the tasks with brackets, however, older adults were slower and reached lower asymptotic performance than did the younger adults. This hints at a deficit beyond general slowing, because the basic arithmetic operations were not slowed at all in the older relative to the younger group.

In a recent experiment (Oberauer, Wendland, & Kliegl, 2003), we tried to narrow down the source of older adults' difficulty in the complex arithmetic tasks. Arithmetic tasks with brackets differ from tasks without brackets by the requirement to hold intermediate results available during computation of other results. For example, in order to obtain the result for $(7 + 2) - [(3 - 2) + 4]$, one must keep the result of $7 + 2$ in mind while solving the brackets. In addition to this load on working memory, the task also requires selective access to the right digit at the right time. For example, after computing 3 − 2, one has two intermediate results in working memory, and one has to pick the right one to add 4 to it. After this has been accomplished, the other intermediate result must be accessed as the basis for subtraction.

We used a numerical memory-updating task to disentangle working memory load from access to a new element in working memory. Participants first memorized a set of digits, each one presented in a separate frame on the screen. After the digits disappeared, arithmetic operations were displayed, one at a time, in individual frames. The participants' task was to update the memorized digit in the respective frame by the operation, working through a sequence of 13 operations in a self-paced fashion. Memory load was varied through the number of frames (1–4), which determines effectively the "list length" of digits to be held in WM at any moment. Access was varied by contrasting operations displayed in a new frame with operations displayed in the same frame as the one immediately before. Operations displayed in a new frame require the focus of attention to switch from one digit to another within the memory set, whereas operations in the same frame as before can directly be applied to the result of the previous computation, which is still in the focus of attention (c.f. Garavan, 1998; Oberauer, 2003; Verhaeghen et al., this volume).

The memory-updating task was particularly suited for our purposes for two other reasons. One is that a version of this task was shown to load strongly on a factor of verbal–numerical WMC (Oberauer et al., 2000). Therefore, an interpretation of age differences in this tasks in terms of WMC would be plausible, and the pattern of age differences obtained in an experimental version of the memory updating task can in turn be used as a hypothesis for what distinguishes groups with high and low WMC. The other reason is that experimental work with the numerical memory-updating task (Oberauer, 2002) provides the best available evidence so far for the distinction of the three components of the working memory model sketched in Figure 3.3. This makes the mapping of observations with this task onto concepts in the model more straightforward.

The most important results from this experiment are displayed in Figure 3.7. Latencies of individual arithmetic operations were equivalent for younger and older adults when the memory load was just one digit. This condition corresponds to the arithmetic chain tasks without brackets in the experiment of Verhaeghen et al. (1997), in that only the last result of each computation has to be remembered and no focus switch is ever required. Latencies increased with memory load for operations following a switch and for operations without a switch to a new mental object. With memory loads larger than one, older adults were slightly, but significantly, slower than younger adults. This finding matches the dissociation between simple and complex arithmetic tasks in the Verhaeghen et al. (1997) study. It also

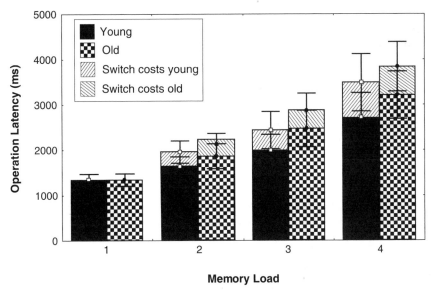

FIGURE 3.7. Latencies for individual operations in numerical memory updating (data from Oberauer, Wendland et al., 2003). Latencies of operations without object switch are represented by solid bars, and additional time costs for switch latencies are depicted by hatched bars. Error bars represent two standard errors.

matches previous studies with the memory-updating task (Oberauer & Kliegl, 2001), in which older adults were increasingly slowed and reached lower asymptotic performance, when memory load increased. Different from these previous studies, however, we observed no age differences in accuracy in the present study. This could be due to a particularly proficient sample of older adults or to the self-paced nature of the task that gave participants more leeway to adapt to the task demands.

The most interesting finding regards the switching costs. Latencies following an object switch were reliably larger than when no switch was required. The switch costs increased with working memory load, but they were not larger for older than for younger participants. If anything, there was a trend for older adults to show smaller object switch costs than for younger adults. This trend, although not statistically significant, was observed on all three levels of memory load.

We conclude that older adults had a reduced capacity to hold several digits in the direct access region – although the age-related decline at higher memory load levels was relatively modest in this experiment compared to previous studies with the same or similar tasks. Converging evidence that older adults have difficulties with the storage aspect of working memory comes from Belleville, Rouleau, and Caza (1998). There was no evidence in our study that older persons have specific problems with selective access to elements in working memory. This is consistent with the results of a previous study on mental arithmetic (Oberauer, Demmrich, Mayr, & Kliegl, 2001) using a different experimental paradigm.

Currently, we have no data for a contrast between high- and low-capacity younger adults on memory updating that can be compared to the ones reviewed above. We know from correlational studies (Oberauer et al., 2000) that there are overall performance differences in numerical memory updating between high- and low-capacity groups, but at the moment we cannot locate their source. Here lies a desideratum for future work.

## CONCLUSION

Our picture of general and specific factors responsible for cognitive differences between age groups, and between groups of high versus low WMC, is still largely incomplete. In this chapter, I tried to illustrate that investigating different group contrasts with the same, theoretically founded experimental paradigms can help to carve out which factors characterize cognitive deficits in general and which are specific to a particular contrast of high-versus low-functioning groups. For example, studies on task-set switching revealed that older adults and people with low working memory capacity are characterized by longer reaction times overall, but only older adults have, in addition, a specific difficulty with the mixed blocks (i.e., enlarged general switch costs). On the other hand, the difficulty with inhibiting no-longer-relevant information in working memory, as revealed by the modified Sternberg task, seems to be shared by older persons and persons with low WMC. Whether it is also shared by other groups with reduced cognitive performance remains an open question for future research.

Use of the same experimental paradigms is critical for the comparison across different group contrasts, because otherwise we cannot be certain whether suggested commonalities are real or arise only from the use of the same labels for different empirical indicators. As long as there is no positive evidence that two tasks, or two experimental effects, reflect the same construct, we should not generalize from one to the other. For example, different tasks presumed to measure executive functions seem to have little variance in common (Duncan, Johnson, Swales, & Freer, 1997; Kramer, Humphrey, Larish, Logan, & Strayer, 1994; Shilling, Chetwynd, & Rabbitt, 2002; Ward et al., 2001), so any conclusion that older adults suffer from an executive deficit just as people with low WMC do is a premature simplification as long as we cannot show that the same profile of selective deficits is shown by both groups on the same tasks. The investigation of task-set switching costs above already presents one counterexample to such a generalization.

A second important concern is that we use indicators of cognitive difficulties that can be linked to theories of cognitive processes. Therefore,

TABLE 3.2. *Summary of Findings and Their Relationship to Theoretical Constructs*

| Experimental Effect | Theoretical Construct | Difference in Younger-Older Contrast | Difference in WMC Contrast | Validation/Converging Evidence |
|---|---|---|---|---|
| General task-set switching costs | Suppressing operation of irrelevant task-set | yes | no | |
| Specific task-set switching costs | Task-set inertia and task-set reconfiguration | no | no | |
| List-length effect of irrelevant list | Removing irrelevant information from WM | no (?) | no | |
| Intrusion costs in recognition | Inhibition of irrelevant information in LTM or availability of context memory | yes | yes | Zacks et al. (1996); Hedden & Park (2001, 2003) |
| List-length effect on recall from WM | Holding information in WM | yes | yes (?) | Belleville et al. (1998); Oberauer & Kliegl (2001) |
| Object switch costs in WM | Access to new elements in WM | no | | Oberauer et al. (2001) |

Legend: WM = working memory

experimental tasks that were constructed to operationalize a specific theoretical construct, such as the control of task sets or the inhibition of irrelevant information in LTM, are much better suited to identify the underlying sources of a group's cognitive deficit than, for instance, intelligence test tasks that usually draw upon a complex, unknown mix of cognitive functions (see, for example, Piccinin & Rabbitt, 1999). Group differences observed in experimental effects such as task-set switching costs, object switching costs, or intrusion costs can be used to test hypotheses about which component or mechanism in the cognitive system is different in the groups under investigation. Table 3.2 gives a summary of the hypotheses tested by the research reviewed here and also indicates some of the gaps in the current picture.

A third consideration is that no single task can unambiguously represent a theoretical construct. All conclusions about the underlying sources of cognitive deficits in old age, or in individuals with low WMC, are tentative so far, because they must be validated by generalization across different task paradigms. Validation should come from three sources. One source is the experimental test of hypotheses derived from the theoretical framework associated with a task paradigm or an effect. Another needed form of validation comes from factor-analytic research, showing that several suggested indicators of a construct are substantially correlated. Finally, validation should come from converging findings from group contrasts using different paradigms designed to tap into the same theoretically defined cognitive function. The last column of Table 3.2 contains what little evidence we have so far that goes some way toward validation of the results reviewed here by providing convergent evidence. The many empty cells in that column are but one illustration of the long way we still have to go.

## Author Note

Parts of the research reviewed in this chapter were supported by Deutsche Forschungsgemeinschaft (DFG), grants WI 1390/1, INK 12 (project C), KL 955/4, and OB 121/3. I thank the many people who contributed to this work in various ways, in particular Petra Grüttner, Reinhold Kliegl, Ralf Schulze, Heinz-Martin Süß, Mirko Wendland, Oliver Wilhelm, and Werner W. Wittmann.

## References

Allport, A., Styles, E. A., & Hsieh, S. (1994). Shifting intentional set: Exploring the dynamic control of tasks. In C. Umiltá & M. Moscovitch (Eds.), *Attention & Performance* (Vol. XV, pp. 421–452). Cambridge, MA: MIT Press.

Anderson, J. R. (1974). Retrieval of propositional information from long-term memory. *Cognitive Psychology, 5*, 457–474.

Belleville, S., Rouleau, N., & Caza, N. (1998). Effect of normal aging on the manipulation of information in working memory. *Memory & Cognition, 26*, 572–583.

Brinley, J. F. (1965). Cognitive sets, speed and accuracy of performance in the elderly. In A. T. Welford & J. E. Birren (Eds.), *Behavior, aging, and the nervous system* (pp. 114–149). Springfield, IL: Mason.

Cantor, J., & Engle, R. W. (1993). Working-memory capacity as long-term memory activation: An individual-differences approach. *Journal of Experimental Psychology: Learning, Memory, and Cognition, 19*, 1101–1114.

Cerella, J. (1985). Information processing rates in the elderly. *Psychological Bulletin, 107*, 260–273.

Cowan, N. (1995). *Attention and memory: An integrated framework.* New York: Oxford University Press.

Cowan, N. (1999). An embedded-process model of working memory. In A. Miyake & P. Shah (Eds.), *Models of working memory. Mechanisms of active maintenance and executive control* (pp. 62–101). Cambridge, UK: Cambridge University Press.

De Beni, R., & Palladino, P. (2000). Intrusion errors in working memory tasks. Are they related to reading comprehension ability? *Learning and Individual Differences, 12*, 131–143.

De Beni, R., Palladino, P., Pazzaglia, P., & Cornoldi, C. (1998). Increases in intrusion errors and working memory deficit of poor comprehenders. *Quarterly Journal of Experimental Psychology, 51A*, 305–320.

Duncan, J., Johnson, R., Swales, M., & Freer, C. (1997). Frontal lobe deficits after head injury: Unity and diversity of function. *Cognitive Neuropsychology, 14*, 713–741.

Engle, R. W. (1996). Working memory and retrieval: An inhibition-resource approach. In J. T. E. Richardson, R. W. Engle, L. Hasher, R. H. Logie, E. R. Stoltzfus, & R. T. Zacks (Eds.), *Working memory and human cognition* (pp. 89–119). New York: Oxford University Press.

Engle, R. W., Kane, M. J., & Tuholski, S. W. (1999). Individual differences in working memory capacity and what they tell us about controlled attention, general fluid intelligence, and functions of the prefrontal cortex. In A. Miyake & P. Shah (Eds.), *Models of working memory. Mechanisms of active maintenance and executive control* (pp. 102–134). Cambridge, UK: Cambridge University Press.

Engle, R. W., Tuholski, S. W., Laughlin, J. E., & Conway, A. R. A. (1999). Working memory, short term memory and general fluid intelligence: A latent variable approach. *Journal of Experimental Psychology: General, 128*, 309–331.

Garavan, H. (1998). Serial attention within working memory. *Memory & Cognition, 26*, 263–276.

Gerard, L., Zacks, R. T., Hasher, L., & Radvansky, G. A. (1991). Age deficits in retrieval: The fan effect. *Journal of Gerontology: Psychological Sciences, 43*, 27–33.

Hale, S., & Jansen, J. (1994). Global processing-time coefficients characterize individual and group differences in cognitive speed. *Psychological Science, 5*, 384–389.

Hartman, M., & Hasher, L. (1991). Aging and suppression: Memory for previously relevant information. *Psychology & Aging, 6*, 587–594.

Hasher, L., Quig, M. B., & May, C. P. (1997). Inhibitory control over no-longer-relevant information: Adult age differences. *Memory & Cognition, 25*, 286–295.

Hasher, L., & Zacks, R. T. (1988). Working memory, comprehension, and aging: A review and a new view. In G. H. Bower (Ed.), *The psychology of learning and motivation* (Vol. 22, pp. 193–225). New York: Academic Press.

Hasher, L., Zacks, R. T., & May, C. P. (1999). Inhibitory control, circadian arousal, and age. In D. Gopher & A. Koriat (Eds.), *Attention and Performance* (pp. 653–675). Cambridge, MA: MIT Press.

Hedden, T., & Park, D. (2001). Aging and interference in verbal working memory. *Psychology & Aging, 16*, 666–681.

Hedden, T., & Park, D. C. (2003). Contributions of source and inhibitory mechanisms to age-related retroactive interference in verbal working memory. *Journal of Experimental Psychology: General, 132*, 93–112.

Jensen, A. R. (1998). *The g factor*. Westport: Praeger.

Jersild, A. T. (1927). Mental set and shift. *Archives of Psychology, 89*.

Kane, M. J., & Engle, R. W. (2002). The role of prefrontal cortex in working-memory capacity, executive attention, and general fluid intelligence: An individual-differences perspective. *Psychonomic Bulletin and Review, 9*, 637–671.

Kliegl, R., & Lindenberger, U. (1993). Modeling intrusions and correct recall in episodic memory: Adult age differences in encoding of list context. *Journal of Experimental Psychology: Learning, Memory, & Cognition, 19*, 617–637.

Kliegl, R., Mayr, U., & Krampe, R. T. (1994). Time-accuracy functions for determining process and person differences: An application to cognitive aging. *Cognitive Psychology, 26*, 134–164.

Kramer, A. F., Humphrey, D. G., Larish, J. F., Logan, G. D., & Strayer, D. L. (1994). Aging and inhibition: Beyond a unitary view of inhibitory processing in attention. *Psychology & Aging, 9*, 491–512.

Kray, J., Li, K. Z. H., & Lindenberger, U. (2002). Age differences in executive functioning: The search for sources of age-differential decline in task-switching components. *Brain & Cognition, 49*, 363–381.

Kray, J., & Lindenberger, U. (2000). Adult age differences in task switching. *Psychology and Aging, 15*, 126–147.

Kyllonen, P. C. (1996). Is working memory capacity Spearman's g? In I. Dennis & P. Tapsfield (Eds.), *Human abilities: Their nature and measurement* (pp. 49–75). Mahwah, NJ: Lawrence Erlbaum Associates.

Lindenberger, U., Mayr, U., & Kliegl, R. (1993). Speed and intelligence in old age. *Psychology and Aging, 8*, 207–220.

Logan, G. D., & Gordon, R. D. (2001). Executive control of visual attention in dual-task situations. *Psychological Review, 108*, 393–434.

Mandler, G. (1980). Recognizing: The judgment of previous occurrence. *Psychological Review, 87*, 252–271.

Mayr, U. (2001). Age differences in the selection of mental sets: The role of inhibition, stimulus ambiguity, and response-set overlap. *Psychology & Aging, 16*, 96–109.

Mayr, U., & Kliegl, R. (1993). Sequential and coordinative complexity: Age-based processing limitations in figural transformations. *Journal of Experimental Psychology: Learning, Memory and Cognition, 19*, 1297–1320.

Mayr, U., Kliegl, R., & Krampe, R. T. (1996). Sequential and coordinative processing dynamics in figural transformation across the life span. *Cognition, 59*, 61–90.

Mayr, U., & Liebscher, T. (2001). Is there an age deficit in the selection of mental sets? In U. Mayr, D. H. Spieler & R. Kliegl (Eds.), *Ageing and executive control* (pp. 47–70). Hove: Psychology Press.

Mayr, U., Spieler, D. H., & Kliegl, R. (Eds.). (2001). *Ageing and executive control*. Hove: Psychology Press.

McElree, B., & Dosher, B. A. (1989). Serial position and set size in short-term memory: The time course of recognition. *Journal of Experimental Psychology: General, 118*, 346–373.

Meiran, N., Chorev, Z., & Sapir, A. (2000). Component processes in task-switching. *Cognitive Psychology, 41*, 211–253.

Miyake, A., Friedman, N. P., Emerson, M. J., Witzki, A. H., Howerter, A., & Wager, T. D. (2000). The unity and diversity of executive functions and their contributions to complex "frontal lobe" tasks: A latent variable analysis. *Cognitive Psychology, 41*, 49–100.

Monsell, S. (2003). Task switching. *Trends in Cognitive Science, 7*, 134–140.

Oberauer, K. (2001). Removing irrelevant information from working memory. A cognitive aging study with the modified Sternberg task. *Journal of Experimental Psychology: Learning, Memory, and Cognition, 27*, 948–957.

Oberauer, K. (2002). Access to information in working memory: Exploring the focus of attention. *Journal of Experimental Psychology: Learning, Memory, and Cognition, 28*, 411–421.

Oberauer, K. (2003). Selective attention to elements in working memory. *Experimental Psychology, 50*, 257–269.

Oberauer, K., Demmrich, A., Mayr, U., & Kliegl, R. (2001). Dissociating retention and access in working memory: An age-comparative study of mental arithmetic. *Memory & Cognition, 29*, 18–33.

Oberauer, K., & Kliegl, R. (2001). Beyond resources: Formal models of complexity effects and age differences in working memory. *European Journal of Cognitive Psychology, 13*, 187–215.

Oberauer, K., Süß, H. M., Schulze, R., Wilhelm, O., & Wittmann, W. W. (2000). Working memory capacity – Facets of a cognitive ability construct. *Personality and Individual Differences, 29*, 1017–1045.

Oberauer, K., Süß, H.-M., Wilhelm, O., & Sander, N. (in press). Individual differences in working memory capacity and reasoning ability. In J. N. Towse (Ed.), *Variation in working memory*. New York: Oxford University Press.

Oberauer, K., Süß, H. M., Wilhelm, O., & Wittmann, W. W. (2003). The multiple faces of working memory – storage, processing, supervision, and coordination. *Intelligence, 31*, 167–193.

Oberauer, K., Wendland, M., & Kliegl, R. (2003). Age differences in working memory: The roles of storage and selective access. *Memory & Cognition, 31*, 563–569.

Piccinin, A. M., & Rabbitt, P. M. A. (1999). Contribution of cognitive abilities to performance and improvement on a substitution coding tast. *Psychology & Aging, 14*, 539–551.

Roberts, R. J., Jr., Hager, L. D., & Heron, C. (1994). Prefrontal cognitive processes: Working memory and inhibition in the antisaccade task. *Journal of Experimental Psychology: General, 123*, 374–393.

Rogers, R. D., & Monsell, S. (1995). Costs of a predictable switch between simple cognitive tasks. *Journal of Experimental Psychology: General, 124*, 207–231.

Rosen, V. M., & Engle, R. W. (1998). Working memory capacity and suppression. *Journal of Memory and Language, 39*, 418–436.

Salthouse, T. A. (1996). The processing speed theory of adult age differences in cognition. *Psychological Review, 103*, 403–428.

Shilling, V. M., Chetwynd, A., & Rabbitt, P. M. A. (2002). Individual inconsistency across measures of inhibition: an investigation of the construct validity of inhibition in older adults. *Neuropsychologia, 40,* 605–619.

Sliwinski, M. J., & Hall, C. B. (1998). Constraints on general slowing: A meta-analysis using hierarchical linear models with random coefficients. *Psychology and Aging, 13,* 164–175.

Smith, E. E., & Jonides, J. (1999). Storage and executive processes in the frontal lobes. *Science, 283,* 1657–1661.

Sternberg, S. (1969). Memory scanning: Mental processes revealed by reaction-time experiments. *American Scientist, 57,* 421–457.

Süß, H. M., Oberauer, K., Wittmann, W. W., Wilhelm, O., & Schulze, R. (2002). Working memory capacity explains reasoning ability – and a little bit more. *Intelligence, 30,* 261–288.

Verhaeghen, P., & Cerella, J. (2002). Aging, executive control, and attention: a review of meta-analyses. *Neuroscience and Biobehavioral Reviews, 26,* 849–857.

Verhaeghen, P., & De Meersman, L. (1998). Aging and the Stroop effect: A meta-analysis. *Psychology and Aging, 13,* 120–126.

Verhaeghen, P., Kliegl, R., & Mayr, U. (1997). Sequential and coordinative complexity in time-accuracy functions for mental arithmetic. *Psychology and Aging, 12,* 555–564.

Ward, G., Roberts, M. J., & Phillips, L. H. (2001). Task-switching costs, Stroop-costs, and executive control: A correlational study. *Quarterly Journal of Experimental Psychology, 54A,* 491–511.

West, R. L. (1996). An application of prefrontal cortex function theory to cognitive aging. *Psychological Bulletin, 120,* 272–292.

Yonelinas, A. P. (2002). The nature of recollection and familiarity: A review of 30 years of research. *Journal of Memory and Language, 46,* 441–517.

Zacks, R. T., Radvansky, G., & Hasher, L. (1996). Studies of directed forgetting in older adults. *Journal of Experimental Psychology: Learning, Memory, and Cognition, 22,* 143–156.

Zheng, Y., Myerson, J., & Hale, S. (2000). Age and individual differences in visuospatial processing speed: Testing the magnification hypothesis. *Psychonomic Bulletin & Review, 7,* 113–120.

# 4

## Stress and Working Memory

*Between-Person and Within-Person Relationships*

Martin Sliwinski, Joshua Smyth, Robert S. Stawski, and
Christina Wasylyshyn

The individual differences construct of working memory capacity (WMC) is a topic of increasing interest in cognitive psychology. The primary reason for this interest stems from research that demonstrates consistently strong relationships between measures of WMC and higher order cognitive function, such as fluid intelligence (Engle, Tuholski, Laughlin, & Conway, 1999). In addition to being an important predictor of psychometric measures of intellectual ability, WMC predicts performance on standardized achievement tests and grade point average (Cantor, Engle, & Hamilton, 1991; Engle et al., 1999). According to Engle et al. (1999) and Engle (2002), WMC reflects the ability to maintain relevant information in the focus of attention in the face of irrelevant and distracting stimuli. Engle and colleagues (Engle et al., 1999; Unsworth, Heitz, & Engle, this volume) argued that WMC is a central component of fluid intelligence and, hence, is a cognitive primitive.

Although WMC is often viewed as a stable trait, some theorists have argued that changes in arousal, motivation, and the experience of stress can produce fluctuations in attentional reserve (Eysenck & Calvo, 1992; Kahneman, 1973; Hasher & Zacks, 1988). Consistent with this view, recent research suggests that the experience of even mild life-event stress might impair working memory performance (Klein & Boals, 2001a) and that interventions that ameliorate the effects of stress can improve working memory (Klein & Boals, 2001b). One theoretical account of this relationship proposes that the experience of stress leads to the subsequent experience of intrusive or worrisome thoughts. Attempts to control these unwanted thoughts draw from the same pool of attentional resources that is required to perform working memory tasks, such as the operation span task (O-span; Turner & Engle, 1989).

Although results from individual-differences studies (e.g., Klein & Boals, 2001a) are suggestive, we do not believe that they address the fundamental question of whether or not stress is related to working memory *within individuals.* The primary aim of this chapter is to argue for the necessity of translating individual-differences research to designs that allow for an intraindividual level of analysis. The examination of stress effects on working memory provides one example of how to execute this translation. We will make the case that analyses of individual differences do not provide statistical support for inferences regarding psychological and cognitive processes that transpire within individuals and that further assumptions are required to support the leap from between-person analyses to within-person inferences.

This chapter is organized into three sections. In the first, we review research regarding the relationship between stress and working memory and several of the theoretical accounts of this relationship. In the second section, we argue that the between-person analysis of individual differences does not convey any information regarding the association of psychological processes that occur within individuals. Finally, in the third section, we present some research from our lab that extends the study of stress and working memory to the analysis of the intraindividual relationship between the experience of stress and working memory performance. Specifically, we describe results from a measurement-burst design (see Nesselroade, 1991) indicating that both younger and older adults exhibit significantly lower performance on a high attentional-demand task (i.e., a variant of the N-Back task) on days on which they experience stress compared to days on which they do not experience stress.

## THE RELATIONSHIP(S) BETWEEN STRESS AND COGNITION

There are a number of ways that stress has been operationally defined, including objective events (e.g., life-event checklists), subjective responses (e.g., self-report of stress), and physiological responses (e.g., sympathetic activation, cortisol secretion). Although each of these processes have unique strengths (and weaknesses), using objective events to measure stress is the least sensitive to individual differences and provides the least capacity to examine within-person changes. In contrast, both subjective reports of stress (or even reports of stressor occurrence) and physiological measures of stress response are desirable when one wants to examine both between- and within-person relationships.

Clinical research and a number of experimental studies on individuals with post-traumatic stress disorder (PTSD) have established a strong link between stress and impaired cognitive function. Experimentally induced stress can impair declarative memory, and this impairment correlates with elevations in cortisol (Kirschbaum, Wolf, May, Wippich, & Hellhammer, 1996). Acute administration of (synthetic corticosteroids) cortisol impairs both working memory (Lupien, Gillin, & Hauger, 1999; Lupien & Lapage, 2001) and declarative memory (Newcomer et al., 1999). Interestingly, there are some data to suggest that working memory may be more sensitive than declarative memory to cortisol treatment (Lupien et al., 1999) and that prolonged administration of cortisol may be required to produce evidence of declarative memory impairment (Newcomer et al., 1999). Clinical correlational studies in patients with PTSD have produced results consistent with experimental outcomes. For example, PTSD patients show impairments in attention (Vasterling, Brailey, Constans, & Sutker, 1998; Vasterling et al., 2002), learning (Vasterling et al., 2002), and working memory (Vasterling et al., 2002).

The physiological mechanism underlying stress-related cognitive impairment involves how the stress-induced release of glucocorticoids (GC) damages the hippocampus (Lupien & McEwen, 1997) and frontal-limbic neural circuits (Bremner, Southwick, & Charney, 1999). Exposure to stress activates a sequence of physiological events along the hypothalamic-pituitary-adrenal axis (Kemeny, 2003). The hypothalamus triggers the release of hormones that promotes the synthesis of glucocorticoids (i.e., cortisol). Elevated levels of cortisol can play an adaptive function in the short term by reducing inflammation, increasing arterial blood pressure, and elevating blood glucose levels. However, over longer periods of time, chronic exposure to stress, and hence elevated levels of cortisol, can have severe negative health consequences (see McEwen, 2000, for review). In the short term, elevated cortisol levels can also impair neuronal excitability in the hippocampus, cause reversible atrophy of hippocampal neurons, and inhibit neurogensis in the dentate gyrus. If exposure to elevated cortisol levels is sufficiently prolonged, permanent hippocampal cell loss can result. Although less clear, there is some research to suggest that the hippocampus is not the only brain structure adversely affected by chronic exposure to stress. Studies of individuals with PTSD and depression have reported atrophy of the amygdala and prefrontal cortex (Bremner et al., 1999; Devrets et al., 1997) in addition to damage to the hippocampus. The physiological impact of stress on brain function can be so pronounced that some theories postulate that age-related hippocampal atrophy and resulting memory impairment derive, at least in part, from prolonged exposure to GCs (e.g., Seeman, McEwen, Rowe, & Singer, 2001).

Cortisol-related damage to the hippocampus provides a physiological mechanism that can account for the chronic and possibly for the acute effects of stress on cognition. A complementary account posits a psychological mechanism by which the experience of stress can impair cognition. One such account is the processing efficiency theory of Eysenck and Calvo (1992). This theory states that worry about task performance detracts from available attentional resources for task-relevant performance, especially in individuals with high levels of trait anxiety. An important feature of processing efficiency theory is the clear distinction between components of the model that apply to within-person processes (e.g., worry) and between-person differences (e.g., trait anxiety). For example, this theory specifies that "internal processing and performance are determined by state anxiety rather than by trait anxiety" (Eysenck & Calvo, 1992, p. 425). This theory also predicts that between-person differences in trait anxiety moderate the effects of state anxiety on cognitive performance, especially in tasks that place heavy demands on the central executive component of working memory (e.g., Eysenck, 1989). For example, an increase in state anxiety should have a more detrimental effect on performance in individuals who have higher levels of trait anxiety than in those with lower trait anxiety. Thus, the causal processes transpire within persons, although these processes might operate differently in different individuals.

A recent series of experiments by Ashcraft and Kirk (2001) showed that individuals high in math anxiety exhibited impairments on tasks requiring mathematical and even simple counting operations. Ashcraft and Kirk (2001) examined how individual differences in math anxiety related to individual differences on two working memory tasks: one that required mathematical operations (the counting span task) and one that did not (the listening span task). An interesting finding, not predicted by processing efficiency theory, was that there were roughly comparable correlations between math anxiety and both the computation span ($r = -.44$) and listening span performance ($r = -.36$). These results suggest that anxiety need not be specific to the task at hand to produce impaired performance. In fact, between-person measures of general anxiety and math anxiety are positively correlated (we have noted a correlation of .29 in our lab). Ashcraft and Kirk concluded that the effect of anxiety on cognition is a result of worry about performance disrupting working memory functioning. However, their results and those from other labs suggest that worry-related depletion of attentional resources may not be limited to worry specific to performing the task at hand.

Several studies have shown that general life event stress may correlate with impaired performance on tasks that place high demands on working memory. Klein and Boals (2001a) examined how individual differences on measures of life events stress were related to individual differences on the Turner and Engle operation span (O-span) task. In their first study, they administered the O-span, as well as the Life Experiences Scale (LES; Sarason, Johnson, & Siegel, 1978) and the state anxiety component of the State-Trait Anxiety Inventory (STAI; Spielberger, Gorsuch, & Lushene, 1969) to 22 college students. The LES requires individuals to answer which of 47 possibly stressful events they have experienced within the past six months. The STAI assesses the level of participants' anxiety at the time of the study. Klein and Boals (2001a) found that the LES and state anxiety measure correlated $-.46$ and $-.32$ with O-span, respectively. Given their relatively small sample size, only the LES/O-span correlation was statistically significant (at the .05 level). Similarly, we have recently reported that experiencing various adverse childhood experiences (e.g., divorce of parents, major academic problems) is differentially related to working memory (O-span scores) among healthy college students (Smyth, Gaudy, & Sliwinski, in review). These studies relating life-event stress to cognition, however, provide less information on the mechanism of this relationship.

Klein and Boals' (2001a) explanation of their results derives from Wegner's theory of thought control, the theory of ironic mental processes (Wegner, 1994). Essentially, Wegner's theory states that individuals rely on two processes to control their thoughts. One process operates automatically to detect unwanted (or off-task) thoughts. When this automatic monitoring process detects an unwanted thought, a second process activates to redirect thoughts to more appropriate or task-relevant goals. This second process requires attentional resources and, when operating, leaves available fewer resources for performing other attention-demanding activities. Klein and Boals (2001a) argued that individuals under high levels of life stress would be more likely to experience unwanted or intrusive thoughts and consequently have to expend limited attentional resources in attempts to suppress unwanted stressful thoughts. These individuals would thus have fewer available attentional resources and would perform worse on working memory tasks than those not attempting to suppress stressful thoughts.

Follow-up studies by Klein and Boals (2001a) more directly tested this intrusion-suppression hypothesis of the effects of stress on working memory. Individuals were asked to write a brief description about a negative stressful event and then were given the Impact of Events Scale (IES; Horowitz, Wilner, & Alvarez, 1979). The IES consists of 15 items that ask about the frequency of experiencing undesired thoughts regarding the stressful experience or how frequently individuals attempted to avoid thinking about the experience. Klein and Boals found that individuals who reported having more frequent intrusive thoughts scored lower on the O-span than those who reported having fewer intrusive thoughts ($r = -.22$).

A subsequent intervention study (Klein & Boals, 2001b) demonstrated that college students who underwent a stress-management intervention improved their O-span scores significantly more than a control group. Their results also showed that the improvement in working memory performance was mediated by an intervention-related reduction in intrusive/avoidant thinking (as measured by the IES).

We recently conducted a number of studies to further explore the relationship between stress and cognition. If the hypothesis that intrusive or avoidant thinking is the key source of stress-related working memory impairment, then measures of thought control (e.g., intrusive thinking, avoidant thinking) should better predict working memory performance than measures of perceived stress. Before examining whether thought control and stress differentially predict cognition, we examined whether they formed distinguishable constructs. Stawski, Wasylyshyn, Sliwinski, Smyth, and Hofer (in review) examined whether measures of life stress and thought control formed distinguishable factors. In this study, 148 undergraduate students completed a series of questionnaires that included instruments thought to tap negative psychological life stress and instruments we hypothesized would reflect thought control. In addition to using the LES as an indicator of life stress, we administered a brief adjective checklist to measure the amount of psychological distress experienced over the week previous to testing and the Perceived Stress Scale (PSS; Cohen, Kamarck, & Mermelstein, 1983). For indicators of thought control, the IES avoidance and intrusion subscales were used, as were the White-Bear Suppression Inventory (WBSI; Wegner & Zanakos, 1994) and the Thought Control Questionnaire (TCQ; Wells & Davies, 1994). Unlike the IES, which targets avoidant and intrusive thinking related to a specific event, both the WBSI and TCQ ask about a person's general tendencies to ruminate, to engage in avoidant thinking, and to experience worrisome thoughts. Confirmatory factor analysis yielded a two-factor solution with distinguishable factors of life stress and thought control. Although these two factors were highly correlated (.77), a two-factor solution yielded significantly better fit than did a one-factor solution, and the correlation between stress and thought control was significantly less than 1.0. Thus, it appears that the life event stress and the tendency to control one's thoughts reflect distinguishable, though strongly related, constructs. Given that subjective stress and thought control form distinct constructs, we proceeded to examine how well each construct could predict cognitive performance.

In a second study, Wasylyshyn, Stawski, & Sliwinski (in preparation) examined the correlations among life stress, thought control, and cognition. Two-hundred-thirty-five undergraduates completed a battery of stress and thought control questionnaires similar to those previously described (Stawski et al., in review). In addition, participants performed a series of cognitive tasks that measured fluid intelligence (e.g., processing speed, verbal fluency, episodic memory). Participants were tested in groups of 8 to 15, and the cognitive tests were adapted for group administration. Confirmatory factor analyses again revealed evidence of distinct but correlated stress and thought control factors (correlation = .67). The thought control factor correlated (−.27) with a latent variable representing fluid intelligence, but the stress factor did not (.05).

Wasylyshyn et al. (in preparation) conducted a follow-up study in which participants were tested individually, and multiple indicators were used to assess working memory. One-hundred-nineteen undergraduates performed several tasks measuring working memory: the O-span (Turner & Engle, 1989), the counting span (Engle et al., 1999), and a 2-back version of the N-Back task (Awh et al., 1996). The 2-back task is a continuous performance task in which each trial consists of displaying a single digit and requiring the participant to determine whether the displayed digit matched the $n$th-digit back. Participants also completed a category task and a letter fluency task and a word list–learning task. The correlation between the stress and thought control factors was .76 and was significantly different from unity. Therefore, we retained distinct stress and thought control factors for correlating with our working memory factor. The working memory factor was correlated $-.52$ with the thought control factor and $-.22$ with the negative psychological stress factor. These results indicated that, on average, poorer working memory performance was observed for individuals who reported greater tendencies to engage in thought control. However, the relationship between the negative psychological stress factor and the working memory factor failed to reach statistical significance.

Because the experience of stress is thought to impair working memory performance by reducing available attentional resources, one might predict amplified stress effects in older adults. The rationale behind this prediction derives from theoretical accounts of cognitive aging effects, which propose older adults have diminished attentional resources and are less able to suppress or inhibit off-task thoughts. Stawski, Wasylyshyn, and Sliwinski (2004) examined the relationship between intrusive/avoidant thinking and perceived stress in a sample of older adults. One-hundred-six older adults (ages 66–90) completed the IES and PSS and a battery of cognitive tests that assessed controlled attention and processing speed performance. Analysis of the first-order correlations revealed significant relationships between the IES and all of the cognitive tests, while the correlations between the PSS and cognitive tests failed to reach statistical significance. The correlations between IES and speed measures ranged from .19 to .30, whereas the correlations between IES and controlled attention measures ranged from $-.21$ to .31. Next, a structural equation model was estimated, with IES and PSS each predicting performance on latent factors that represented controlled attention and processing speed. Only the IES reliably predicted performance on both the controlled attention factor (Standardized beta $= -.32$) and processing speed factor (Standardized beta $= .51$). The findings of Stawski et al. (2004) extend the results of Klein and Boals (2001a) to a sample of older adults and demonstrate that cognitive performance is not comparably predicted by measures of perceived stress and cognitive reactivity to stress. These findings provide further evidence that the need to control or inhibit stress-induced thoughts depletes attentional and processing resources, suggesting that cognitive reactivity is a more important predictor than emotional reactivity to stress. Distinguishing between these two types of stress reactivity may provide further clues regarding the mechanisms that underlie the negative stress–cognition relationship.

Our findings supported the results of Klein and Boals (2001a, 2001b) that high levels of life stress and poor thought control correlate with lower-than-average working memory performance. In addition, these studies demonstrated that stress and thought control not only predict individual differences on working memory measures, but they also predict individual differences on measures that tap other aspects of fluid intelligence (e.g., verbal fluency, processing speed). These results are also consistent with the claim of Engle et al. (1999; Engle, 2002) that both working memory and fluid intelligence reflect the ability of individuals to keep mental representations active in the focus of attention, especially in the face of distraction. One implication of this theory is that a person's effective working memory capacity, and hence fluid intelligence, is not a fixed quantity, but rather can vary as a function of factors that constrain available attentional resources, such as life stress. A difficulty in extending the empirical evidence to address this possibility is that the individual differences research we have reported described between-person relationships between stress and cognition, whereas a key issue is whether there is a relationship between stress and cognition at the within-person level.

## DISTINGUISHING BETWEEN-PERSON AND
## WITHIN-PERSON RELATIONSHIPS

Although the relationship between the physiology of the stress response and aspects of cognitive function is relatively well established, it is not clear whether stress plays an important role in affecting cognitive function in our daily lives, other than in extreme or pathologic cases (e.g., PTSD). Studies along the lines of Klein and Boals (2001a, 2001b) are important because they suggest that the experience of relatively mild, subclinical stress might impair a very basic and important component of cognitive functioning. These results raise the seldom considered possibility that there may be important dynamic and transient determinants of an individual's cognitive function that are not best examined by individual differences or a conventional experimental approach.

A significant limitation of much of the research (including the research from this lab) on stress and working memory comes from its emphasis on between-person differences in stress and cognition. Correlational research demonstrating that individual differences in stress covary with individual differences in working memory does not map onto the theories that specify the mechanisms by which stress influences cognition (e.g., intrusive/avoidant thought tendencies). Before describing our research on the intraindividual association between stress and cognition, we present an argument to justify the necessity of translating designs and analytic approaches from the between-person to the within-person level of analysis. The central claim of this argument is that demonstrating an association between two variables (e.g., stress and working memory) at the between-person level does not provide any information regarding the relationship of these two variables within persons.

This claim is rather strong, but it is not unique. Robinson (1950) identified the "ecological fallacy" as one that involves that assuming relationships among variables observed at the group level apply to individuals. Those who conduct research on aging routinely acknowledge a related limitation of cross-sectional research that makes the assumption that age difference among individuals provides a good approximation of age changes that occur within individuals. Yet another simple example involves the relationship between amount of exercise and blood pressure. Individuals who engage in higher levels of exercise exhibit lower blood pressure than those who do not exercise (i.e., the between-person relationship). In contrast, when an individual exercises, her blood pressure will be higher than when she is sedentary.

Lamiell (1981) presented an argument demonstrating that a correlation coefficient describing the relationship between two individual differences variables provides no information regarding the behavioral proclivities of any individual. The context of Lamiell's argument was the study of human personality and reflects tensions that were articulated 40 years before the publication of his article (e.g., Allport, 1940). Recently, Borsboom, Mellenbergh, and van Heerden (2003) presented a more general analysis of the theoretical status of latent variables, and their conclusions are the same as Lamiell's. Specifically, the analysis of between-person covariation (i.e., individual differences) between two variables does not provide information regarding the within-person relationships between those variables. Not all psychological theorizing demands that the relationships obtained at the between-person level also be found at the within-person level, although much theorizing does presuppose such "ergodicity" (Nesselroade & Molenaar, 1999; Sliwinski & Hofer, 1999).

The methodology under the heading of "multilevel modeling" embraces the inherent distinction of between-person- versus within-person-level analyses. Snidjers and Bosker (1999) provided a formal demonstration that relationships at these two levels need not be the same (i.e., are formally independent) and, in fact, can be opposite in direction (pp. 52–56, section 4.5). This point can be illustrated with an intuitive example: Suppose a psychologist were interested in the direction of the relationship between the speed of performing a simple perceptual comparison task and the accuracy with which the task is performed. Cognizant of speed-accuracy trade-offs, the psychologist makes the following prediction: The relationship between speed and accuracy is negative. Also, mindful of good sampling practices, a random sample of five individuals from the population is selected to perform this task. Figure 4.1 displays a plot showing the relationship between each person's mean speed and accuracy

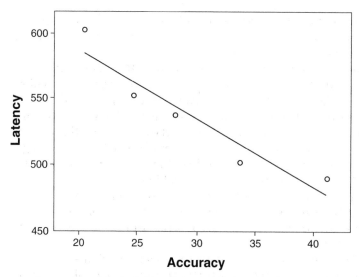

FIGURE 4.1. Hypothetical data showing the between-person relationship between the speed and accuracy of performing a simple cognitive task.

(averaged across five blocks of trials). The relationship is nearly perfectly positive, indicating that fast performance is associated with accurate performance. This example illustrates the individual-differences approach to establishing a relationship between two variables. We have intentionally used imprecise language thus far in describing the psychologist's prediction and interpretation of the results. However, we will now begin to use appropriate language to illustrate the *real* question that was answered by the analysis described in Figure 4.1. This analysis indicates that individuals who are faster than average are also more accurate than average, which is a correct interpretation for any positive correlation involving the analysis of individual differences. Thus, the question this analysis answers is: "Are individuals who are faster than average also more accurate than average?" This question is appropriately framed at the between-person level, because the only sources of variability in the data are the differences among persons.

Unfortunately, this was not the question that the psychologist really wanted to answer. Instead, the psychologist's interest lay in whether individuals respond more slowly when they increase their accuracy. This interest demands a within-person analysis, such as the one graphically depicted in Figure 4.2, which shows the performances of each of the five individuals on each of five blocks of trials. Clearly, the relationship is strongly negative for each individual. In contrast to the strongly negative within-person relationship, the between-person relationship was strongly positive. One could easily imagine such a configuration of results if individuals differed

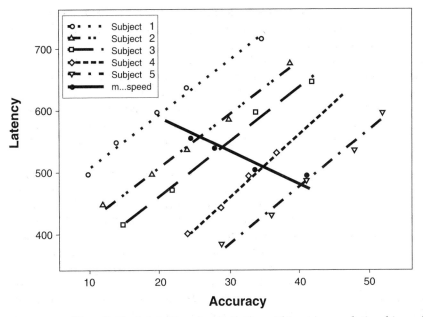

FIGURE 4.2. Hypothetical data showing both the within-person relationship and the between-person relationship of performing a simple cognitive task.

in terms of age, with younger individuals being both more accurate and faster than older participants and if the relative emphasis on speed or accuracy was experimentally manipulated across blocks of trials. This is a within-person analysis because the source of variability is variability that exists within, and not between, individuals.

This example conveys a very important and rarely recognized point that applies to much of psychological research. Specifically, demonstrating a relationship between two variables at the between-person level of analysis provides no information regarding the relationship between those two variables for individuals at the within-person level of analysis. Molenaar (1999) provided yet another formal demonstration of this point by showing that obtaining good model fits in a population (i.e., between-person analysis) does not imply that the same model fits any person in that population (i.e., within-person analysis). Because most psychological theorizing is intended to explain the behavior and cognitions of individuals, we are compelled to assume that our statistical models of individual differences in some way apply to individuals (e.g., the local homogeneity assumption; Ellis & Van den Wollenberg, 1993). However, there is nothing in our statistical results of individual-differences analyses that can speak to this assumption. Borshboom et al. (2003) provided a trenchant analysis that demonstrated why one cannot draw causal inferences at the individual level from analysis conducted at the between-person level. The key reason one cannot use relationships observed at the between-person level of analysis to substantiate claims of causality is that one cannot be sure (or even in the least bit confident) that between-person relationships exist at the within-person level. A demonstration of a very strong positive relationship between two variables at the between-person level of analysis does not in any way imply that the within-person relationship between those variables is positive. The within-person relationship could just as likely be positive, negative, or nonexistent. Figures 4.1 and 4.2 graphically illustrate this point.

To the extent that our theoretical accounts posit processes and operations that exist and transpire within individuals, between-person analyses may be of questionable theoretical utility. In fact, this argument implies that the theoretical utility of between-person analyses depends on how successfully theorists can connect between-person models to models of processes that transpire at the level of individuals. Fortunately, much of the individual-differences research on working memory provides this conceptual linkage of within-person processes to between-person individual differences (e.g., Kane & Engle, 2002; Miyake, Friedman, Rettinger, Shah, & Hegarty, 2001; Oberauer, this volume; Unsworth et al., this volume). Essentially, this approach requires a theoretical analysis of how individual-level cognitive processes can produce specific patterns of between-person covariations (e.g., latent variables). However, one must recognize that patterns of between-person covariation are emergent properties (Borsboom et al., 2003) of individual-level processes, and consequently they cannot inform as to what type of intraindividual patterns of variability and covariability produced them. Therefore, if the central research hypothesis specifies relationships that must exist for individuals, the between-person individual-differences approach must be supplemented by a within-person intraindividual-level analysis. This is especially the case regarding the relationship between stress and working memory; this relationship is primarily interesting, on both theoretical and practical grounds, only if it exists at the within-person level.

## WITHIN-PERSON COUPLING OF DAILY STRESS AND WORKING MEMORY

The explanation for the stress–working memory relationship advanced by Klein and Boals (2001a, 2001b) is one that describes a sequence of processes and events that transpire within the minds of individuals. The occurrence of an event that an individual appraises as being stressful initiates this sequence. At some point after the stressor, the individual is faced with having to suppress stress-related thoughts in order to focus on daily tasks, or to focus on performing an experimental cognitive task if he or she happens to be a research participant. Attempts to suppress such thoughts, whether or not they are successful, occupy attentional resources, leaving fewer resources available for performing high-attention-demanding tasks. The key prediction of this account is that when individuals experience stress and the resulting need to control their thoughts, they should be impaired on high-attention-demanding tasks compared to times when they do not experience stress and have less of a need to control their thoughts. However, this prediction has not been directly tested yet. Rather, evidence in support of this account comes from demonstrations that individuals who engage in more than average avoidant and suppressive thinking score lower than average on a variety of cognitive tasks.

This prediction is intraindividual in nature because it specifies how an individual's cognitive performance should vary from one occasion to the next. To test this prediction directly requires a repeated-measures design in which individuals' cognition and level of stress are measured on multiple occasions. We conducted such a study as part of a larger longitudinal project (Sliwinski, Smyth, Hofer, & Stawski, in review). In this study, individuals were assessed on six occasions over a 14-day period. Each assessment involved the individual performing a brief battery of cognitive tasks and completing a brief questionnaire to assess their experience of stressors over the previous 24 hours. We predicted that, on average, an individual's performance should be impaired on high-stress occasions relative to low-stress occasions. Note how this prediction is framed at the within-person level and differs from the conventional individual-differences (between-person) prediction. The between-person-level prediction would be that individuals with higher than average stress would score lower than average on cognitive testing.

One-hundred-four older adults (aged 66–90) and 65 younger adults (aged 18–22) participated in this study. The older adults were screened for dementia and major health problems that might interfere with cognitive performance (e.g., history of stroke). The cognitive tasks measured processing speed, working memory, and attention switching. A number-string comparison (NC) task, a computerized variant of common psychometric comparison speed tasks, was used to measure processing speed (Salthouse, 1996). Participants had to decide as quickly as possible whether two random strings of numbers contained the same numbers, regardless of their order. A variant of the N-Back task (Awh et al., 1996; Cohen et al., 1997; Smith & Jonides, 1997) was used to assess working memory. We report the results from the 2-back condition. This condition has a high attentional demand because it requires active and continuous shunting of information between short-term memory and the focus of attention. A variant of a serial-attention task developed by Garavan (1998) was used to assess the speed of shifting attentional focus from distinct representations in working memory. For this task (Keep-Track), participants had to maintain a running count of two different geometric shapes by shifting their focus of attention from one item to another. In this case, the "items" held in memory are the two running counts. The dependent measure for all cognitive tasks was response time (RT). Daily stress was assessed using a variant of the semistructured Daily Inventory of Stressful Events (DISE; Almeida, Wethington, & Kessler, 2002). The version of this instrument used in this study consisted of five stem questions that ask if certain stressors (e.g., interpersonal conflict, health problems) have occurred in the past 24 hours. Severity ratings for each stressor were also obtained, but we will describe only the results from examining the effect of the number of reported stressors on performance.

All data were detrended by fitting a quadratic function to model practice effects on the cognitive tasks. This detrending was performed before comparison between stressor-absent and stressor-present performance to avoid spurious association among variables that might arise because of mean changes across occasions (e.g., retest effects). Multilevel modeling was used to test the within-person hypothesis that RT would be higher on stressor days compared to days on which no stressor was reported. Figure 4.3 shows the within-person stress effects on RT for younger and older adults on the three cognitive tasks as a function of the number of stressors reported on a given day. As is common in comparisons of older and younger adults, the older adults were significantly slower than the younger adults on all tasks. Neither younger nor older adults showed a within-person stress effect on the measure of processing speed. Both younger and older adults showed a statistically significant within-person stress effect on the 2-Back task, indicating slower performance on days where stressors were reported. The magnitude of the stressor effect on 2-Back performance was roughly equivalent for younger and older adults, with the former showing a slowing of 45 msec per stressor, and the latter showing a slowing of 63 msec per stressor. If stressor days are compared to nonstressor days, then the stress effect for the older and younger adults was 119 msec and 65 msec, respectively. It is useful to compare the magnitude of the stressor effect to the effect of age in the older adults. The age slope in the older adults showed a slowing on the 2-Back task of 16 msec/year. This implies that the daily within-person stress effect impaired performance to a magnitude equivalent to aging about four years.

There was an age-by-stress interaction on the Keep-Track attention-switching task indicating a significant stressor effect of 25 msec/stressor in the older, but no effect in the younger (−3 msec/stressor). One reason for discrepancy in stress effects between the 2-Back and Keep-Track for the younger group might simply be that the Keep-Track task was not sufficiently demanding to be sensitive to stress effects. That is, the younger

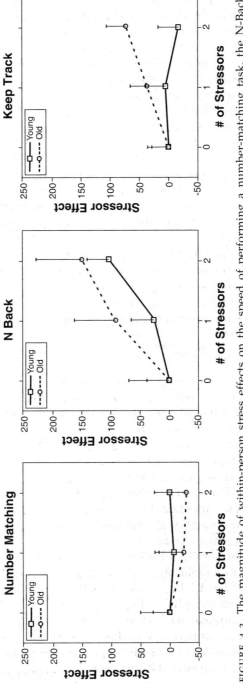

FIGURE 4.3. The magnitude of within-person stress effects on the speed of performing a number-matching task, the N-Back task, and the Keep-Track task.

adults might have sufficient attentional resources to compensate for influence of daily stressors by increasing effort during task performance. The other difference between the 2-Back task and the Keep-Track task is that the former requires continuous encoding of new information that must be held in short-term memory, whereas the Keep-Track task does not require such encoding. Finally, there was no evidence of a stressor effect for either younger or older adults on the simple processing speed task.

These results are unique in at least two respects. First, they demonstrate that intraindividual cognitive variability is, at least to some extent, systematic and predictable. Recent interest in intraindividual cognitive variability has mainly emphasized between-person or between–age group comparisons of the magnitude of intraindividual variability (e.g., Hultsch, MacDonald, & Dixon, 2002). In contrast, these results show that intraindividual deviations from a person's average performance can be modeled at the within-person level and that they convey important information about dynamic events and processes that transpire within individuals. Second, these results demonstrate that the stress–working memory relationship exists within individuals. This is an important translational step in moving from the between-person analysis of individual differences to a level of analysis that can directly support theoretical claims regarding the covariation of psychological processes within individuals.

CONCLUSIONS AND IMPLICATIONS

This chapter reviewed evidence relating the experience of stress to cognitive impairment, in particular to impaired working memory performance. Individual-differences research has shown that people with higher-than-average levels of stress exhibit lower-than-average performance on working memory tasks. One theoretical account of this relationship proposes that individuals who are in the process of coping with a stressor need to suppress stress-related thoughts while engaged in other attention-demanding tasks. Whether or not this attempt to suppress off-task thoughts succeeds, it occupies attentional resources and consequently can impair performance in high attentionally demanding tasks, such as the O-span or N-Back working memory tasks. This account postulates the relationship among mental processes that transpires within individuals, and the predicted impairments should also be conceptualized at the within-person or intraindividual level. That is, this hypothesis predicts that a person will be impaired while coping with a stressor(s) compared to when coping demands are minimal (e.g., when stressors are not present). Although intriguing, individual-differences studies of the between-person relationship between stress and working memory cannot support such theoretical claims regarding the relationship between stress and working memory within individuals. In fact, it is possible that those with lower WMC are less able to cope with environmental demands and thus are more affected by stress.

We reviewed research from our lab that extended the study of stress and working memory to the intraindividual level of analysis. We demonstrated that the experience of stress and working memory are coupled within individuals, such that both older adults and college-aged individuals exhibit worse performance on high-stress days than on low-stress days. The within-person stress effect was relatively large: A stressful day can impair performance by a magnitude equivalent to an age difference of about four years in older adults. Because the reported stressors occurred prior to assessment of working memory, these findings suggest that stress leads to impaired working memory, not vice versa.

Although this research is a promising first step, there are some significant limitations. For example, one would expect that the time between the experience of a stressor and cognitive assessment would influence the magnitude of the resulting impairment. Unfortunately, our temporal resolution of the occurrence of a given stressor is rather poor (i.e., a 24-hour period). A useful approach might be to combine Ecological Momentary Assessments (EMA; e.g., Stone & Shiffman, 1994) of daily experiences of stress with laboratory (or even reliable ambulatory) assessments of cognitive function to get a better handle on the temporal relationship among stress, coping, and cognitive impairment. Although use of EMA techniques would improve the validity and precision of assessing a person's subjective experience of stress, self-reports of stress should also be supplemented with ambulatory physiological measurements of stress reactivity. Laboratory studies have shown correlations between experimentally induced elevation in cortisol and cognitive impairment. However, there is only a weak concordance between results of cortisol responses to laboratory and real-life stressors (Dimsdale, 1984; van Eck, Nicolson, Berkhof, & Sulon, 1996). Therefore, a potentially fruitful line of research would be to examine the relationship among *in vivo* stress, cortisol measurements, and cognitive function. For example, to our knowledge there is no research examining how the diurnal cortisol slope relates to cognition.

Finally, we should comment more generally on the limitations of between-person analysis of individual differences for supporting theoretical claims that are framed at the intraindividual level. We agree with the position advanced by others (e.g., Borsboom et al., 2003; Lamiell, 1981; Molenaar, 1999) that information about between-person patterns of covariation among variables provides no information regarding the association of those variables within individuals. This is the case whether the variables in question are stress and working memory or working memory and fluid intelligence. We hope that recognizing this limitation of the individual-differences approach will motivate researchers to translate their research questions from the between-person level to the within-person level.

## Author Note

This research was supported in part by a grant from the National Institute on Aging (AG-12448).

## References

Allport, G. W. (1940). The psychologist's frame of reference. *Psychological Bulletin, 37*, 1–28.

Almeida, D., Wethington, E., & Kessler, R. (2002). The Daily Inventory of Stressful Experiences (DISE): An interview-based approach for measuring daily stressors. *Assessment, 9*, 41–55.

Ashcraft, M. H., & Kirk, E. P. (2001). The relationships among working memory, math anxiety, and performance. *Journal of Experimental Psychology: General, 130*, 224–237.

Awh, E., Jonides, J., Smith, E., Schumacher, E., Koeppe, R., & Katz, S., (1996). Dissociation of storage and rehearsal in verbal working memory: Evidence from PET, *Psychological Science, 7*, 25–31.

Borsboom, D., Mellenbergh, G., & van Heerden, J. (2003). The theoretical status of latent variables? *Psychological Review, 130*, 208–218.

Bremner, J. D., Southwick, S. M., & Charney, D. S. (1999). The neurobiology of posttraumatic stress disorder: An integration of animal and human research. In P. A. Saigh & J. D. Bremner (Eds.), *Posttraumatic stress disorder: A comprehensive text (pp. 103–143).* Needham Heights, MA: Allyn & Bacon.

Cantor, J., Engle, R. W., & Hamilton, G. (1991). Short-term memory, working memory, and verbal abilities: How do they relate? *Intelligence, 15*, 229–246.

Cohen, J. D., Perlstein, W. M., Braver, T. S., Nystrom, L. E., Noll, D. C., Jonides, J., & Smith, E. E. (1997). Temporal dynamics of brain activation during a working memory task. *Nature, 386*, 604–608.

Cohen, S., Kamarck, T., & Mermelstein, R. (1983). A global measure of perceived stress. *Journal of Health and Social Behavior, 24*, 385–396.

Devrets, W., Price, J., Simpson, T., Todd, R., Reich, T., Vannier, M., & Raichle, F. (1997). Subgenual prefrontal cortext abnormalities in mood disorders. *Nature, 386*, 824–827.

Dimsdale, J. E. (1984). Generalizing from laboratory studies to field studies of human stress physiology. *Psychosomatic Medicine, 46*, 463–469.

Ellis, J. L., & Van den Wollenberg, A. L. (1993). Local homogeneity in latent trait models: A characterization of the homogeneous monotone IRT model. *Psychometrika, 58*, 417–429.

Engle, R. W. (2002). Working memory capacity as executive attention. *Current Directions in Psychological Science, 11*, 19–23.

Engle, R. W., Tuholski, S. W., Laughlin, J. E., & Conway, A. R. A. (1999). Working memory, short-term memory and general fluid intelligence: A latent variable approach. *Journal of Experimental Psychology: General, 128*, 309–331.

Eysenck, M. W. (1989). Anxiety and cognition: Theory and research. In T. Archer & L-G. Nillson (Eds.), *Aversion, avoidance, and anxiety: Perspectives on aversively motivated behavior* (pp. 323–334). Hillsdale, NJ: Lawrence Erlbaum Associates.

Eysenck, M. W., & Calvo, M. G. (1992). Anxiety and performance: The processing efficiency theory. *Cognition and Emotion, 6*, 409–434.

Garavan, H. (1998). Serial attention within working memory. *Memory & Cognition, 26*, 263–276.

Hasher, L., & Zacks, R. (1988). Working memory, comprehension, and aging: A review and a new view. In G. Bower (Ed.), *The psychology of learning and motivation* (pp. 193–225). San Diego: Academic Press.

Horowitz, M. J., Wilner, N., & Alvarez, W. (1979). Impact of Event Scale: A measure of subjective stress. *Psychosomatic Medicine, 41*(3), 209–218.

Hultsch, D. F., MacDonald, S. W. S., & Dixon, R. A. (2002). Variability of reaction time performance of younger and older adults. *Journal of Gerontology: Psychological Sciences, 57B*, P101–P115.

Kahneman, D. (1973) *Attention and effort*. Englewood Cliffs, NJ: Prentice-Hall.

Kane, M. J., & Engle, R. W. (2002). The role of prefrontal cortex in working-memory capacity, executive attention, and general fluid intelligence: An individual differences perspective. *Psychonomic Bulletin & Review, 9*, 637–671.

Kemeny, M. E. (2003). The psychobiology of stress. *Current Directions in Psychological Science, 12*, 124–129.

Kirschbaum, C., Wolf, O., May, M., Wippich, W., & Hellhammer, D. (1996). Stress- and treatment-induced elevations of cortisol levels associated with impaired declarative memory in healthy adults. *Life Sciences, 58*, 1475–1483.

Klein, K., & Boals, A. (2001a). Expressive writing can increase working memory capacity. *Journal of Experimental Psychology: General, 130*, 520–533.

Klein, K., & Boals, A. (2001b). The relationship of life stress and working memory. *Journal of Applied Cognitive Psychology, 15*, 565–579.

Lamiell, J. T. (1981). Toward an idiothetic psychology of personality. *American Psychologist, 36*, 276–289.

Lupien, S., Gillin, C., & Hauger, R. (1999). Working memory is more sensitive than declarative memory to acute effects of corticosteroids: A dose-response study in humans. *Behavioral Neuroscience 113*, 420–430.

Lupien, S. J., & Lapage, M. (2001). Stress, memory, and the hippocampus: Can't live with it, can't live without it. *Behavioural Brain Research, 127*, 137–158.

Lupien, S., & McEwen, B. (1997). The acute effects of corticosteroids on cognition: Integration of animal and human model studies. *Brain Research Reviews, 24*, 1–27.

McEwen, B. (2000). Allostasis and allostatic load: Implications for neuropsychopharmacology. *Neuropsychopharmacology, 22*, 108–124.

Miyake, A., Friedman, N. P., Rettinger, D. A., Shah, P., & Hegarty, M. (2001). How are visuospatial working memory, executive functioning, and spatial abilities related? A latent variable analysis. *Journal of Experimental Psychology: General, 130*, 621–640.

Molenaar, P. (1999). Longitudinal analysis. In H. J. Ader & G. J. Mellenbergh (Eds.), *Research methodology in the life, behavioral and social sciences*. Thousand Oaks, CA: Sage.

Nesselroade, J. R. (1991). The warp and woof of the developmental fabric. In R. Downs, L. Liben, & D. S. Palermo (Eds.), *Visions of aesthetics, the environment, and development: The legacy of Joachim F. Wohwill* (pp. 213–240). Hillsdale, NJ: Lawrence Erlbaum Associates.

Nesselroade, J. R. & Molenaar, P. C. (1999). Pooling lagged covariance structures based on short, multivariate time-series for dynamic factor analysis. In R. H. Hoyle (Ed.), *Statistical strategies for small sample research*. Newbury Park, CA: Sage.

Newcomer J., Selke, G., Melson, A., Kershey, T., Craft, S., Richards, K., & Alderson, A. (1999). Decreased memory performance in healthy humans induced by stress-level cortisol treatment. *Archives of General Psychiatry, 56*, 527–533.

Robinson, W. S. (1950). Ecological correlations and the behavior of individuals. *American Sociological Review, 15*, 569–583.

Salthouse, T. A. (1996). The processing speed theory of adult age differences in cognition. *Psychological Review, 103*, 403–428.

Sarason, I. G., Johnson, J. H., & Siegel, J. M. (1978). Assessing the impact of life changes: Development of the life experiences survey. *Journal of Consulting and Clinical Psychology, 46*, 932–946.

Seeman, T. E., McEwen, B. S., Rowe, J. W., & Singer, B. H. (2001). Allostatic load as a marker of cumulative biological risk: MacArthur studies of successful aging. *Proceedings of National Academy of Sciences, 98*, 4770–4775.

Sliwinski, M., & Hofer, S. (1999). How strong is the evidence for mediators of age-related memory loss? *Gerontology, 45*, 351–354.

Sliwinski, M., Smyth, J., Hofer, S., & Stawski, R. S. (in review). Intraindividual coupling of daily stress and cognition.

Smith, E. E., & Jonides, J. J. (1997). Working memory: A view from neuroimaging. *Cognitive Psychology, 33*, 5–42.

Smyth, J., Gaudy, J., & Sliwinski, M. (in review). The relation of reported past trauma to working memory. *Cognition & Emotion*.

Snidjers, T., & Bosker, R. (1999). *Multilevel Analysis: An introduction to basic and advanced multilevel modeling*. London: Sage.

Spielberger, C. D., Gorsuch, R. L., & Lushene, R. E. (1969). *The State Trait Anxiety Inventory manual*. Palo Alto, CA: Consulting Psychologists Press.

Stawski, R. S., Wasylyshyn, C., & Sliwinski, M. J. (2004, April). *The relationship between stress and cognitive performance in older adults*. Poster session presented at the biannual Cognitive Aging Conference, Atlanta, GA.

Stawski, R. S., Wasylyshyn, C., Sliwinski, M. J., Smyth, J. M., & Hofer, S. M. Negative psychological stress and intentional thought control: Two separate but related constructs. Manuscript under review.

Stone, A. A., & Shiffman, S. (1994). Ecological momentary assessment (EMA) in behavorial medicine. *Annals of Behavioral Medicine, 16*, 199–202.

Turner, M. L., & Engle, R. W. (1989). Working memory capacity: An individual differences approach. *Journal of Memory and Language, 28*, 127–154.

Van Eck, M. M. M., Nicolson, N. A., Berkhof, H., & Sulon, J. (1996). Individual differences in cortisol responses to a laboratory speech task and their relationship to responses to stressful daily events. *Biological Psychology, 43*, 69–84.

Vasterling, J. J., Brailey, K., Constans, J. I., & Sutker, P. B. (1998). Attention and memory dysfunction in posttraumatic stress disorder. *Neuropsychology, 12*, 125–133.

Vasterling, J. J., Duke, L. M., Brailey, K., Constans, J. I., Allain, A. N. Jr., & Sutker, P. B. (2002). Attention, learning, and memory performance and intellectual resources in Vietnam veterans: PTSD and no disorder comparisons. *Neuropsychology*, *16*, 5–14.

Wasylyshyn, C., Stawski, R. S., & Sliwinski, M. J. A latent variable analysis of the relationship between stress, intentional thought control and cognitive performance. Manuscript in preparation.

Wegner, D. M. (1994). Ironic processes of mental control. *Psychological Review*, *101*, 34–52.

Wegner, D. M., & Zanakos, S. (1994). Chronic thought suppression. *Journal of Personality*, *62*, 615–640.

Wells, A., & Davies, M. I. (1994). The thought control questionnaire: A measure of individual differences in the control of unwanted thoughts. *Behaviour Research and Therapy*, *32*, 871–878.

# AGING AND PSYCHOPATHOLOGY OF COGNITIVE CONTROL

# 5

## The Aging of Cognitive Control

*Studies of Conflict Processing, Goal Neglect, and Error Monitoring*

Robert West and Ritvij Bowry

Over the past two decades, constructs bearing a strong conceptual resemblance to currently popular ideas related to cognitive control or the ability to regulate the information processing system in accordance with the goals of the individual have dominated models of cognitive aging. Hasher and Zacks (1979) argued that age-related declines across various domains of cognition result from reductions in the efficiency of effortful or controlled processes. More recently, these authors refined their position, arguing that age-related declines in the efficiency of inhibitory processes that allow one to modulate the influence of task irrelevant information were one of the primary causes of age-related disruptions in higher order cognition (Hasher & Zacks, 1988). Craik and Byrd (1982) argued that age-related declines in processing resources (i.e., working memory capacity or speed of processing) are largely responsible for age-related declines in cognition. The early paper of Hasher and Zacks (1979) and that of Craik and Byrd (1982) provided the foundation for extensive work during the 1980s and 1990s, demonstrating that many of the effects of age on higher order cognition are mediated by age-related variance in processing resource variables (see Park & Schwartz, 2000; Salthouse, 1996). During the same period, other investigators demonstrated that individual differences in processing resources, such as working memory capacity, were also good predictors of complex cognitive activity including reading and language comprehension in college-aged individuals (for a review see Engle, 1996). They also demonstrated that the influence of individual differences in working memory capacity is most pronounced in task conditions demanding inhibitory control (Conway & Engle, 1994; Kane, Bleckley, Conway, & Engle, 2001).

Paralleling the rise of cognitive neuroscience, investigators have become increasingly interested in the neural basis of age-related declines in cognition. Early work in this line of inquiry tended to take the form of studies examining age-related differences on neuropsychological tests sensitive to various forms of brain damage (e.g., Daigneault, Braun, & Whitaker, 1992) or of studies examining correlations between age-related variance in neuropsychological measures and performance on various cognitive tasks (e.g., Craik, Morris, Morris, & Loewen, 1990). With advances in neuroimaging techniques, i.e., positron emission tomography (PET) and functional magnetic resonance imaging (fMRI), and the increased availability of electrophysiological techniques, i.e., event-related brain potentials (ERPs), much of the emphasis has shifted from examining age-related differences on neuropsychological test performance to identifying the neural correlates of age-related declines in cognition (Ford, Roth, Mohs, Hopkins, & Kopell, 1979; Grady et al., 1995; for a review see Cabeza, 2001). Complementing advances in our understanding of the neural correlates of cognitive aging derived from the areas of functional neuroimaging and electrophysiology, recent advances have also been made in computational neuroscience (e.g., Braver et al., 2001; Li, 2002). This work resulted in the development of integrated models of the effects of cognitive aging at behavioral and neurobiological levels.

Our own work examined the effects of aging on aspects of cognitive control and working memory within the context of cognitive (West & Baylis, 1998), neuropsychological (West, Ergis, Winocur, & Saint-Cyr, 1998), and cognitive neuroscience (West & Alain, 2000b) models using behavioral and electrophysiological methods. Our behavioral studies sought to define the conditions under which age-related declines in conflict processing (e.g., West & Baylis, 1998) and goal-neglect (West, 1999) emerge. Complementing this behavioral work, other studies have used ERPs to identify the neural correlates of conflict processing (West & Alain, 2000b) and goal-neglect (West & Alain, 2000c) and to examine the effects of aging on the neural correlates of cognitive control (West & Alain, 2000a; West, 2004). In providing an overview of our work in this area, we first provide a summary of current neurobiologically constrained models of cognitive aging and then turn to a limited consideration of evidence related to the structural and functional effects of aging on the brain. This information is designed to provide the reader a general context within which to place the discussion of particular ideas related to the effects of aging on the neural correlates of cognitive control. With this foundational information in place, we proceed with a comprehensive review of our work related to the effects of aging on aspects of cognitive control that support performance of the Stroop task. Following the review of our work in the area of cognitive control, we provide an overview of recent work related to the neural correlates of error processing. Where applicable, we highlight parallels between the effects of aging and schizophrenia on behavioral and electrophysiological indices of cognitive control.

NEURAL AGING: MODELS AND DATA

## Neuropsychological Models of Cognitive Aging

A common theme throughout much of the neuropsychological literature related to the effects of aging is that aspects of cognition that are dependent upon the functional integrity of the prefrontal cortex are more sensitive to the effects of aging than are aspects of cognition that are dependent upon the functional integrity of posterior cortical structures (Albert & Kaplin, 1980; Dempster, 1992; West, 1996). This supposition represents the foundation of the frontal lobe hypothesis of aging (West, 1996). Evidence for the frontal lobe hypothesis is found in large-scale studies that reveal stronger effects of aging on neuropsychological measures sensitive to frontal lobe damage than damage to other cortical and subcortical structures (Ardila & Rosselli, 1989; Whelihan & Lesher, 1985). An additional assumption of the frontal lobe hypothesis is that the effects of age should begin earlier on frontal functions than on nonfrontal functions. Consistent with this idea, Shimamura and Jurica (1994) found age-related differences in the frequency of pointing errors in the self-ordered pointing task in a group with a mean age of 61 years whereas age-related differences in item recognition were not observed until 71 years of age. More recent work has led to the suggestion that there are differential effects of aging within subregions of the prefrontal cortex. As an example, MacPherson, Phillips, and Della Sala (2002) observed significant effects of aging on measures of dorsolateral prefrontal function but not on measures of ventromedial frontal function (Phillips & Della Sala, 1998).

Although the frontal lobe hypothesis of aging has been widely embraced, it is not universally accepted (Greenwood, 2000; Rubin, 1999). Greenwood (2000) reviewed evidence demonstrating significant age-related differences in cognitive tasks thought to be dependent upon frontal, temporal, parietal, and occipital cortices and argued that there is relatively little evidence to support the proposal of greater or earlier decline of the prefrontal cortex. Rubin (1999) took a somewhat different approach, arguing that age-related decline in the caudate nucleus, rather than the prefrontal cortex, may be a primary cause of cognitive decrement observed in later adulthood. The argument of Rubin is interesting in that it would account for the strong relationships observed among age, speed of processing, and higher order cognition (Salthouse, 1996), given that one of the hallmarks of basal ganglia dysfunction is perceptual-motor slowing (Kaasinen & Rinne, 2002).

Rubin's proposal (1999) raised the interesting question of whether the neuropsychological effects of aging are more accurately characterized as resulting from a decrease in the efficiency of the brain's dopamine systems or are the effects attributed to loss within one or more specific brain structures (Braver et al., 2001; Li, 2002). Braver et al. (2001) argued that age-related declines in the modulatory effects of dopamine produce a fundamental deficit in context processing in older adults, which gives rise to age-related declines in working memory and selective attention. Supporting this proposal, this group demonstrated that the reduction of the strength of a model parameter associated with the maintenance of contextual information captures age-related differences in both response time and accuracy in a computational model of the AX version of the continuous performance task (AX-CPT). The role of the dopamine system in cognitive control is interesting within the broader context of this book, because other work by this group demonstrated that similar computational mechanisms can account for disrupted context processing in individuals with schizophrenia (Braver & Cohen, 1999; chapter 7).

Complementing the work of Braver et al. (2001), Li and colleagues (Li & Lindenberger, 1999; Li & Sikström, 2002) demonstrated that reductions in the modulatory effects of dopamine can account for age-related declines in performance across a variety of tasks that tap working memory and associative learning (Li & Lindenberger, 1999). The locus of this effect is a loss of the distinctiveness of representations or items held in memory (Li & Sikström, 2002). An interesting aspect of this work is that reductions in the modulatory effects of dopamine result in increased intra-subject variability (Li & Lindenberger, 1999) and also capture age-related declines in mean levels of performance. This finding is consistent with recent behavioral data demonstrating age-related increases in performance variability when task performance demands high levels of cognitive control (West, Murphy, Armilio, Craik, & Stuss, 2002).

### Anatomical and Functional Correlates of Brain Aging

Studies using PET and fMRI have consistently revealed activation of lateral and medial frontal cortex and the anterior cingulate in a variety of tasks that require cognitive control. These findings are in agreement with the neuropsychological models reviewed in previous paragraphs wherein age-related decline in cognitive control is thought to arise from changes in the structural (i.e., reductions in brain volume) and functional (i.e., changes in neurotransmitter or metabolic efficacy) integrity of the prefrontal cortex and basal ganglia. The prominent place of the anterior cingulate in recent neurobiolologically constrained models of cognitive control (Botvinick, Braver, Barch, Carter, & Cohen, 2001) may also have implications for the effects of aging (West & Moore, 2003). In light of these models, it seems beneficial to briefly review recent evidence related to the structural and functional effects of aging on prefrontal cortex, basal ganglia, and anterior cingulate before embarking on a consideration of the relationship between aging and specific aspects of cognitive control.

The effects of aging on gross neuroanatomy have been extensively explored in studies using volumetric measures derived from structural magnetic resonance images (MRI; for a review see Raz, 2000). In those studies reviewed by Raz, the effects of aging were considerably greater on the frontal cortex and basal ganglia than on the anterior cingulate. Volume reductions appear to be more strongly related to changes in cell size and loss of dendritic arborization than to cell loss in healthy individuals (West, 1996). Age-related reductions in brain volume in the frontal cortex and putamen are moderately correlated with performance on neuropsychological measures of working memory and executive functions (Raz, Gunning-Dixon, Head, Dupuis, & Acker, 1998; Raz, Williamson, Gunning-Dixon, Head, & Acker, 2000), indicating that volume reductions account for some age-related declines in cognitive function. The effects of aging and schizophrenia on frontal lobe volume appear to be quite similar. Convit et al. (2001) observed similar volume reductions in the superior frontal gyrus and orbital frontal cortex in older adults and in individuals with schizophrenia relative to healthy younger adults. In contrast, there were no differences among these three groups in middle or inferior frontal gyrus or anterior cingulate volume.

Significant reductions in pre- and postsynaptic markers of dopamine function have been observed in later adulthood in studies using postmortem and functional imaging methods. Postmortem studies revealed age-related reductions in the numbers of dopamine D1 and D2 receptors in the frontal cortex, caudate, and putamen (de Keyser, De Backer, Vauquelin, & Ebinger, 1990; Rinne, 1987). Similar rates of receptor loss were observed *in vivo* in studies using PET (Suhara et al., 1991). In contrast to data from studies of brain volume, aging is associated with a loss in the concentration of D2/D3 receptors in the anterior cingulate (Kaasinen et al., 2000). Consistent with the hypothesis that declines in the efficiency of the dopamine system contribute to age-related declines in cognitive control, Volkow et al. (1998) demonstrated that age-related reduction in the concentration of dopamine receptors was correlated with performance on the Stroop task. Expanding upon this finding, Bäckman et al. (2000) demonstrated that age-related differences in the concentration of D2 receptors in the caudate and putamen accounted for 85 to 97% of the age-related variance in tests of perceptual speed and episodic memory.

COGNITIVE CONTROL AND THE STROOP TASK

**Behavioral and Electrophysiological Correlates of Conflict Processing**

The Stroop task (Stroop, 1935) has been used extensively to explore the effects of aging (Verhaeghen & De Meersman, 1998), of schizophrenia (Perlstein, Carter, Barch, & Baird, 1998) and more recently of individual differences in working memory (Kane & Engle, 2003) on aspects of cognitive control. In the Stroop task, individuals are typically required to identify the color of a color–word pair when color and word are congruent (e.g., RED presented in red), neutral (e.g., DOG or XXX presented in red), or incongruent (e.g., RED presented in blue). When color naming is required, response time is faster for congruent than neutral trials (i.e., Stroop facilitation) and slower for incongruent than neutral trials (i.e., Stroop interference). Error rates can also vary across the three conditions and are greater for incongruent trials than for neutral or congruent trials (MacLeod, 1991). The interference effect for response accuracy results from the presence of intrusion errors, in which individuals read the word instead of naming the color (West, 1999).

Over the past several years, our research group has been engaged in a line of work using ERPs to examine the neural correlates of cognitive control in the Stroop and related tasks. ERPs reflect event-locked electrical activity generated by neural ensembles; they consist of a series of positive and negative deflections above some prestimulus baseline level of activity that peaks at particular intervals following stimulus onset. For instance, the third positive deflection following the onset of a target stimulus is generally labeled the P3, and a negative deflection occurring at 400 ms could be labeled N400. In this research, we have sought to understand the functional characteristics of modulations of the ERPs elicited during performance of the Stroop task (West & Alain, 2000b; West, 2003). The presentation of a color–word stimulus is consistently associated with two modulations of the ERPs, i.e., N450 and conflict sustained potential (SP), that differentiate incongruent trials from congruent and neutral trials (Liotti, Woldorff, Perez, & Mayberg, 1999; Rebai, Bernard, & Lannou, 1997; West & Alain, 2000b). The N450 reflects a phasic negativity that peaks between 400 and 500 ms after stimulus onset over the frontal–central region of the scalp (Figure 5.1). Source analysis indicates that the N450 arises from the activity of a neural generator in the anterior cingulate (Liotti et al., 1999) or from a pair of neural generators in the anterior cingulate and anterior frontal cortex (West, 2003). The N450 is elicited in a number of stimulus–response compatibility tasks (West, Jakubek, Wymbs, & Perry, 2002) and is elicited in the Stroop task when either color or word identification is required (West, 2003). The amplitude of the N450 is modulated by attentional allocation and is greater when trials are mostly congruent relative to when trials are mostly incongruent (West & Alain, 2000b). The conflict SP reflects a sustained potential that emerges around 500 ms after stimulus onset and persists for several hundred milliseconds (Figure 5.1). The conflict SP reflects greater positivity over the parietal region of the scalp and reflects negativity over the lateral frontal regions of the scalp for incongruent trials relative to congruent trials. The amplitude of the conflict SP covaries with response accuracy and is greater for correct responses than

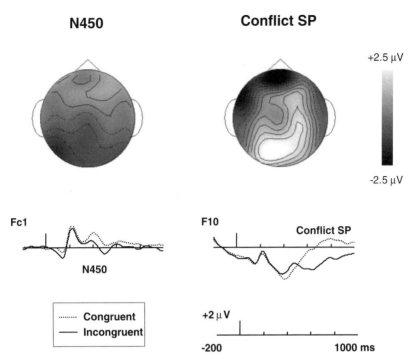

FIGURE 5.1. The N450 that reflects greater negativity for incongruent than for congruent trials in the Stroop task and is associated with conflict detection and the conflict SP that reflects greater lateral frontal negativity for incongruent than congruent trials and is associated with conflict resolution.

for intrusion errors in which individuals read the word instead of naming the color (West, 2003). This finding led to the suggestion that the conflict SP is associated with conflict resolution in the Stroop task and that the left and right hemispheres may be differentially involved in conflict resolution processes (for a similar argument, see Jonides, Badre, Curtis, Thompson-Schill, & Smith, 2002).

### Aging and Conflict Processing

When measured using response time, the Stroop interference effect is consistently larger in older than in younger adults, whereas the effect of age on the Stroop facilitation effect is more variable across studies (Spieler, Balota, & Faust, 1996; West & Baylis, 1998). The age-related increase in the Stroop interference effect has been attributed to a number of different causes including general slowing (Salthouse & Meinz, 1995; Verhaeghen & DeMeersman, 1998, chapter 13), an inhibitory deficit (Spieler et al., 1996), disruption of the anterior attention system (Hartley, 1993), and a disruption of context processing (West & Baylis, 1998). The influence of general slowing on age-related differences in the Stroop interference effect was examined in studies using both correlational and meta-analytic methods. Salthouse and Meinz (1995) demonstrated that age-related variance in the Stroop effect was virtually eliminated when variance shared with measures of processing speed was controlled. Consistent with this finding, evidence from a meta-analytic study demonstrated that age-related differences in neutral and incongruent trials were well fit by a single slowing function (Verhaeghen & De Meersman, 1998). The proposal that disruption of the anterior attention system contributes to age-related differences in the Stroop interference effect is supported by studies demonstrating that the interference effect is greater in older than in younger adults when color and word information are *integrated* and is equivalent for younger and older adults when color and word information are *separated* (Hartley, 1993; West & Bell, 1997). This later effect is thought to result from the relative immunity of the posterior attention system to the effects of aging (Hartley, 1993). Complementing their behavioral data, West and Bell (1997) also observed age-related differences in the degree of alpha suppression (i.e., the decrease in power in the alpha frequency band of the EEG associated with task performance) in the electroencephalogram over the lateral and medial frontal regions of the scalp when color and word were integrated and similar levels of alpha suppression in younger and older adults when color and word were separated. Together the findings reviewed in this paragraph demonstrate that both general (i.e., slowing) and task specific factors (i.e., task context) may contribute to age-related differences in the Stroop task.

The influence of age-related declines in the efficiency of context processing upon performance of the Stroop task was examined in studies in which the proportion of congruent and incongruent trials was manipulated (West & Baylis, 1998) and in which a constant or variable task set was used across trials (West, 2004). In the study by West and Baylis (1998), one half of the participants performed a Stroop task where trials were mostly congruent, and the remaining participants performed a Stroop task where trials were mostly incongruent. Evidence from a number of studies demonstrated that the interference effect is larger when trials are mostly congruent relative to when trials are mostly incongruent (Lowe & Mitterer, 1982), with the difference thought to result from variation in the allocation of cognitive control across task contexts (Botvinick et al., 2001; Lindsay & Jacoby, 1994). West and Baylis (1998) reasoned that if aging is associated with a decline in the efficiency of context processing, then there should be differences in the expression of the proportion congruent effect in younger and older adults. Consistent with this prediction, the Stroop effect was larger in older than in younger adults in the mostly incongruent condition when demands for cognitive control were greatest; likewise, there was no difference in the size of the interference effect between older and younger adults in the mostly congruent condition when demands for cognitive control were minimal.

A second study, examining the effect of age-related declines in context processing, used blocked and trial-by-trial cueing versions of the Stroop task (West, 2004). For the blocked condition, individuals were required to identify either the color or the word on each trial; in the trial-by-trial cueing condition, individuals were required to switch between color and word identification based upon the identity of a cue that was presented before the onset of the Stroop stimuli. If aging is associated with a decline in the efficiency of context processing, age-related differences in the Stroop interference effect were expected to be greater for the trial-by-trial than blocked cueing condition. The data from this experiment revealed that age-related differences in response accuracy for incongruent trials were much greater for the trial-by-trial cueing condition than for the blocked cueing condition (Figure 5.2a). In contrast, the response time data revealed similar age-related differences in the Stroop interference effect across cueing conditions. This difference in the effect of cueing for response accuracy and response time is consistent with a recent proposal that distinct processes supporting goal maintenance and conflict resolution underlie performance of the Stroop task (Kane & Engle, 2003).

The findings of West (2004) are interesting within the context of recent work examining the effects of schizophrenia in a trial-by-trial cueing Stroop task (Cohen, Barch, Carter, & Servan-Schreiber, 1999). In this study, the interference effect was much greater for patients than for controls in color naming trials and only slightly greater for patients than controls for word reading trials. A comparison of the error rates across the color naming and word reading conditions reveals almost identical performance in patients and older adults relative to controls and younger adults, indicating that aging and schizophrenia may be associated with functionally similar impairments of cognitive control in the Stroop task.

The response time data from West (2004) revealed one other interesting pattern. In this study, significant interference was observed for incongruent trials requiring both color and word identification (Figure 5.2b; MacDonald, Cohen, Stenger, & Carter, 2000; West, 2003). The interference effect was greater for color than for word blocks, with response time being greater for color incongruent trials than for word incongruent trials, and there being no difference among congruent trials across conditions. As is often the case, interference was greater for older than for younger adults for color trials; in contrast, interference was similar for younger and older adults for word trials. This finding indicates that age-related differences in the Stroop effect are modulated by task context (Hartley, 1993; West & Bell, 1997). This seems difficult to reconcile with general slowing accounts of the effects of aging on the Stroop task when a single rate of slowing

a)

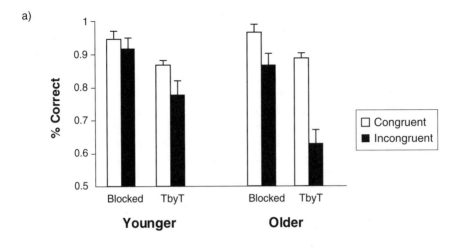

b)

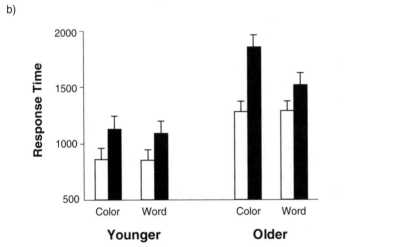

FIGURE 5.2. (a) Mean proportion of errors for younger and older adults in blocked and trial-by-trial cueing conditions in the Stroop task. Note the greater effect of aging for trial-by-trial relative to blocked cueing in the probability of making an intrusion error. (b) Mean response time for younger and older adults for color and word identification trial. Note the similar interference for younger and older adults for word trials and the greater interference for older than younger adults for color trials.

is assumed across task conditions, given that there were no differences in response time for congruent trials between the color and word blocks.

In addition to the age-related increase in the Stroop interference effect, aging is associated with alterations of the ERPs associated with conflict processing. The amplitude of the N450 is greatly attenuated in older adults relative to younger adults (West & Alain, 2000a; West, 2004) and has only been reliably measured in one of five task conditions that we examined (i.e., color identification with trial-by-trial cueing; Figure 5.3a; West, 2004). This finding is consistent with evidence from a recent study using fMRI revealing altered patterns of anterior cingulate activation in older adults during performance of the Stroop task (Milhan el al., 2002). The effects of aging on the conflict SP are somewhat more complex (Figure 5.3b). When word identification is required, the amplitude and topography of the conflict SP is similar in younger and older adults; in contrast, when color identification is required, the amplitude of the conflict SP is attenuated and has not been reliably measured (West, 2004). In addition to the attenuated conflict SP observed in older adults for color identification trials, a parietal negative-frontal positive sustained potential is observed in older adults, but not in younger adults, which differentiates color-incongruent from color-congruent trials (West, 2004). Differences in the effects of aging on the conflict SP and the Stroop interference effect in the response time data when color or word identification are required may indicate that similar neural generators are recruited by younger and older adults in task conditions associated with age equivalent Stroop interference effects (i.e., when word identification is required). This may also indicate that different neural generators are recruited by younger and older adults in task conditions associated with age-related increases in the Stroop interference effect. This proposal is consistent with the findings of Milhan et al. (2002) who observed different patterns of prefrontal and anterior cingulate activation in older and younger adults when color identification was required.

The effects of schizophrenia on the N450 and conflict SP when color identification is required are highly similar to the effects of aging on these ERP modulations. The N450 is attenuated and the conflict SP is dramatically attenuated or absent in individuals with schizophrenia (McNeely, West, Christensen, & Alain, 2003). These findings complement other data indicating that schizophrenia is associated with a disruption of anterior cingulate and prefrontal systems supporting aspects of conflict detection and resolution (Carter, Mintun, Nichols, & Cohen, 1997). In the study by McNeely et al. (2003), there were relatively modest differences between patients and controls in the behavioral data, aside from a substantial degree of general slowing, indicating that robust pathology related alterations of modulations of the ERPs may emerge either before or in the absence of pronounced behavioral deficits.

## Aging and Goal Neglect

In addition to providing insight into the effects of aging on those processes supporting conflict processing, studies using the Stroop task were also valuable in characterizing the behavioral and physiological correlates

a)

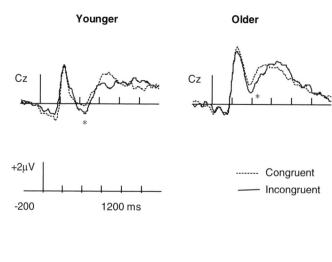

b)

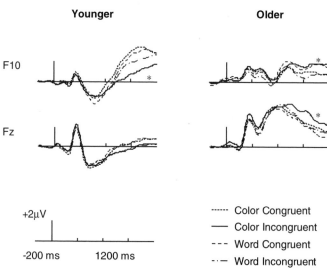

FIGURE 5.3. (a) The N450 marked by the asterisk in younger and older adults for color identification in the trial-by-trial cueing condition. (b) The conflict SP and frontal-parietal slow wave marked by the asterisk in younger and older adults for color and word identification trials. Note that the conflict SP is similar for younger and older adults for the word trials and that the frontal-parietal slow wave is only observed for older adults for color trials.

of goal neglect (West, 1999; West & Alain, 2000c). Goal neglect is observed when the goals of an individual become dissociated from her immediate actions (Duncan, Emslie, Williams, Johnson, & Freer, 1996; Reason, 1979). In the Stroop task, intrusion errors can be considered as instances of goal neglect as individuals most often have the intention to name the color of the stimulus in mind while in fact reading the word (West, 1999). In studies from our laboratory, the frequency of intrusion errors is consistently higher in older than in younger adults (West, 1999; West, 2004).

West (1999) performed a detailed analysis of patterns of intrusion errors in younger and older adults in an effort to characterize the nature of age-related differences in goal neglect. One goal of this study was to determine whether age-related differences resulted from an increase in the frequency or duration of goal neglect in a Stroop task that only included incongruent trials. The frequency of goal neglect was determined by counting the number of intrusion errors preceded by a correct response, and the duration of each episode of goal neglect was determined by counting the number of consecutive intrusion errors. The data from this experiment revealed that instances of goal neglect were more frequent and tended to last longer in older than in younger adults, although most instances of goal neglect lasted only a single trial in either younger (94%) or older (85%) adults. The number of instances of goal neglect lasting a single trial was stable across the 35 to 45 minutes required to complete the task, and response time for trials preceding intrusion errors and intrusion errors were slower than were other trials in the task. Together these findings led to the suggestion that instances of goal neglect arise from transient fluctuations of an attentional process that both supports goal-directed action and is susceptible to the effects of aging (Bunce, Warr, & Cochrane, 1993; West, 2001). The slowing of response time for trials preceding and including intrusion errors observed by West (1999) is particularly interesting when considered within the context of recent work examining the effects of individual differences in working memory capacity on response time for intrusion errors (Kane & Engle, 2003). Kane and Engle observed that response time for intrusion errors was significantly faster than response time for correct incongruent trials and nearly as fast as correct congruent trials. The reason for the difference in the findings of West (1999) and Kane and Engle (2003) is unclear, although there were substantial differences among the tasks used in the two studies. Kane and Engle (2003) reported response time data for error trials from a mostly congruent condition; in contrast, West's (1999) study included only incongruent trials. This difference in task context might produce fast intrusion errors resulting from instances in which attentional control was only weakly allocated in support of task performance, allowing the word to capture the response on error trials (Kane & Engle, 2003). The difference might also produce slow intrusion errors resulting from instances of waning cognitive control in a task that consistently requires high levels of control in order to maintain efficient task performance (West & Alain, 2000b).

In addition to examining the behavioral characteristics of goal neglect, we have also used ERPs to explore the neural correlates of goal neglect in younger and older adults. In the first study in this line of research, we sought to identify a neural correlate of the slowing of response time preceding intrusion errors (West, 1999). To accomplish this, we time-locked the ERPs to several hundred milliseconds before intrusion errors and correct incongruent trials. In two experiments, a slow wave was observed over the anterior frontal and central regions of the scalp that emerged 400 to 800 ms before onset of the Stroop stimuli and differentiated intrusion errors from correct incongruent trials (West & Alain, 2000c). Experiment 2 of this study demonstrated that the amplitude of the slow wave was greater when trials were mostly congruent relative to when trials were mostly incongruent. This finding is consistent with the idea that variations in the proportion of congruent trials serve to modulate the allocation of cognitive control in the Stroop task (Kane & Engle, 2003; West & Alain, 2000b; West & Baylis, 1998).

One limitation of the findings of West and Alain (2000c) related to the neural correlates of goal neglect is that it is difficult to know whether the frontal slow wave was associated with a general disruption of goal maintenance or was more specifically related to the loss of an attentional set supporting color identification. This issue has been addressed in two recent studies using the trial-by-trial cueing version of the Stroop task. By considering modulations of the ERPs associated with presentation of the cues, one can distinguish between these two alternatives. If the slow wave activity is associated with general goal maintenance, this activity should differentiate intrusion errors from correct trials regardless of the relevant stimulus dimension (i.e., color vs. word) or type of Stroop stimulus (i.e., congruent vs. incongruent); in contrast, if slow wave activity is associated with the establishment of a particular task set, it should differentiate preparation for one attribute from another and be independent of stimulus type. Modulations of the ERPs consistent with both of these alternatives have been observed. West (2003) observed a slow wave between the presentation of the dimension cue and onset of the Stroop stimulus. This slow wave reflected greater frontal positivity and occipital-parietal negativity for intrusion errors relative to correct congruent and incongruent trials when either color or word identification was required, consistent with the activity of a neural generator associated with goal maintenance (Figure 5.4a). In contrast, West and Moore (2003) observed a left frontal positive slow wave for trials requiring a switch from word to color identification, but not a switch from color to word identification, consistent with the activity of a neural generator supporting processing of the non-dominant stimulus attribute (Figure 5.4b). This finding is similar to data

a)

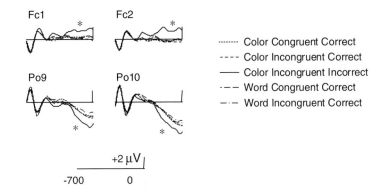

Fc1        Fc2

Po9        Po10

∙∙∙∙∙∙∙ Color Congruent Correct
- - - - Color Incongruent Correct
——— Color Incongruent Incorrect
∙— — Word Congruent Correct
—∙— Word Incongruent Correct

+2 μV

-700        0

b)

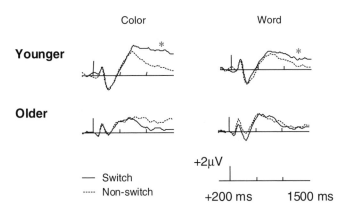

Color        Word

**Younger**

**Older**

+2μV

——— Switch
∙∙∙∙∙ Non-switch

+200 ms        1500 ms

FIGURE 5.4. (a) The frontal negative occipital-parietal positive slow wave marked by the asterisk differentiating intrusion errors from correct trials in younger adults providing a neural index of goal maintenance. (b) Anterior frontal slow wave marked by the asterisk associated with a switch from word to color identification.

reported by MacDonald et al. (2000), who observed greater activation in left dorsolateral prefrontal cortex for color than for word cues in a study using event-related fMRI.

Aging is associated with a disruption in the efficiency of those neural mechanisms supporting both goal maintenance and the establishment of a task set that facilitates color processing. The effects of aging on modulations of the ERPs related to goal maintenance were explored in our study comparing blocked and trial-by-trial cueing in the Stroop task (West, 2004). In this study, cues were associated with a frontal positive-occipital negative

slow wave that differentiated the trial-by-trial and blocked cueing conditions (West, 2003). Between 500 and 1000 ms after onset of the cue, the
amplitude of this slow wave was similar for younger and older adults; in
contrast, between 1,000 ms after presentation of the cue and onset of the
Stroop stimuli, the slow wave persisted in younger adults but was attenuated or absent in older adults. The frontal slow wave related to switching
from word to color identification is also greatly attenuated or absent in
older adults (West & Moore, 2003). This finding indicates that older adults
have difficulty establishing a nondominant task set. Furthermore, it may
be the case that reductions in the ability to maintain an accurate representation of the goal state and to switch among relevant stimulus dimensions contributes to the high frequency of intrusion errors observed in both
older adults and in patients with schizophrenia in the trial-by-trial cueing
version of the Stroop task (Cohen et al., 1999; West, 2004).

ERROR PROCESSING

The discovery of the error-related negativity (ERN; Gehring, Goss, Coles,
Meyer, & Donchin, 1993) or error negativity (Falkenstein, Hohnsbein,
Hoorman, & Blanke, 1991) in the early 1990s led to a renewed interest
in the neurocognitive processes underlying error detection and compensation in choice response tasks. The ERN is a phasic negativity that peaks
between 50 and 100 ms after an errant response in choice response and
stimulus–response compatibility tasks (Falkenstein et al., 1991; Gehring
et al., 1993). The ERN is maximal in amplitude over the frontal-central
region and is thought to reflect the activity of a neural generator, which
is involved in a comparator process between actual and intended actions
(Gehring et al., 1993; Falkenstein, Hoorman, Christ, & Hohnsbein, 2000)
or response conflict (Botvinick et al., 2001). Generation of the ERN arises
from the activity of a distributed network including the anterior cingulate, lateral frontal cortex, and basal ganglia (Falkenstein, Hielscher et al.,
2001; Gehring & Knight, 2000; Swick & Turken, 2002) and may be elicited
when a negative feedback signal from the basal ganglia arrives at the anterior cingulate (Holroyd & Coles, 2002). In addition to the ERN, a correct
response negativity (CRN) was observed in some studies that may be similar in topography to the ERN (Coles, Scheffers, & Holroyd, 2001). The
functional significance of the CRN has been debated in recent empirical
reports and commentaries with theorists suggesting that it may reflect a
stimulus locked artifact, the processing of partial errors on correct trials,
or conflict processing on correct trials (Coles et al., 2001; Falkenstein et al.,
2000).

The amplitude of the ERN is attenuated in older adults across a variety
of tasks including mental rotation (Band & Kok, 2000), four alternative
forced choice (Falkenstein, Hoorman, & Hohnsbein, 2001), probabilistic

learning (Nieuwenhuis et al., 2002), the flanker task (Falkenstein, Hoorman et al., 2001; Nieuwenhuis et al., 2002), and the Stroop task (West, 2004), indicating that aging is associated with a rather general decline in the neural processes underlying error processing. Falkenstein, Hoorman et al. (2001) have demonstrated that the effect of aging does not result from increased latency jitter of the ERN or a failure of the ERN to be elicited on some trials in older adults. Recent computational work led to the suggestion that the age-related decrease in the amplitude of the ERN may arise from the attenuation of a negative reinforcement signal transmitted from the basal ganglia to the anterior cingulate (Nieuwenhuis et al., 2002). The amplitude of the CRN appears to be similar in younger and older adults (Band & Kok, 2000; Falkenstein, Hoorman et al., 2001; West, 2004), although only weak CRNs were observed in studies examining the effects of aging on the ERN. Therefore, it is possible that the presence of a small age-related difference in the amplitude of the CRN was obscured.

Similar to the effects of aging, schizophrenia is associated with a reduction in the amplitude of the ERN across a variety of tasks including the flanker task (Kopp & Rist, 1999), the picture-word naming task (Mathalon et al., 2002), the Go/No-Go task (Bates, Kiehl, Laurens, & Liddle, 2002), and the Stroop task (Alain, McNeely, Yu, Christensen, & West, 2002). Schizophrenia is also associated with a reduction in the amplitude of the BOLD signal in the anterior cingulate that is elicited by errors (Carter, MacDonald, Ross, & Stenger, 2001). Some evidence indicates that the reduction in the amplitude of the ERN is greatest in individuals with schizophrenia who exhibit paranoid symptoms (Kopp & Rist, 1999; Mathalon et al., 2002). However, other studies have failed to find a significant relationship between ratings of patients' symptoms and amplitude of the ERN (Alain et al., 2002). Variation in the relationship between the amplitude of the ERN and symptom severity may arise from the tendency to use relatively healthy, community dwelling individuals who present only mild positive symptoms at the time of testing (Alain et al., 2002; Bates et al., 2002).

In addition to the reduction in the amplitude of the ERN, schizophrenia is associated with an increase in the amplitude of the CRN. Those studies that reported data for both the CRN and ERN failed to reveal significant differences in the amplitude of these two modulations of the ERPs (Alain et al., 2002; Mathalon et al., 2002). The increase in the amplitude of the CRN in patients with schizophrenia relative to controls may differentiate the effects of schizophrenia from those of normal aging because age-related differences in the amplitude of the CRN were not observed in at least some studies (Band & Kok, 2000; Falkenstein, Hoorman et al., 2001; West, 2004). The effects of a number of other neurological and psychiatric disorders on the ERN have been explored in recent studies. Focal damage to the anterior cingulate is associated with a reduction in the amplitude of the ERN, but not the CRN (Swick & Turken, 2002), while damage to the lateral prefrontal cortex has little effect on the amplitude of the ERN and results in an increase in the amplitude of the CRN (Gehring & Knight, 2000). Complementing the findings of these studies, neurological disorders associated with more diffuse neuropathology can also produce alterations of the ERN. As an example, Falkenstein, Hielscher et al. (2001) observed that the amplitude of the ERN, but not the CRN, was reduced in patients with Parkinson's disease (PD) in the flanker, Simon, and Go/No-Go tasks. However, the findings of a second study revealed ERNs of similar amplitudes in individuals with PD and controls (Holroyd, Praamstra, Plat, & Coles, 2003). The reason for the difference between the findings of these two studies is unclear, but may be related to the effects of medication. Falkenstein, Hielscher et al. (2001) tested patients on medications, while Holroyd et al. (2003) tested patients following the overnight withdrawal of medications, so it may be the case that medication served to disrupt the functioning of the basal ganglia–anterior cingulate dopaminergic pathway, which is generally less dramatically affected than the basal ganglia motor pathway during the early stages of the disease (Kaasinen & Rinne, 2002). In contrast to the reduction in the amplitude of the ERN associated with normal aging, schizophrenia, PD, and focal damage to the anterior cingulate, other disorders are associated with an increase in the amplitude of the ERN. For example, larger ERNs, but not CRNs, were observed in adults with obsessive-compulsive disorder (Gehring, Himle, & Nisenson, 2000) and in children with attention deficit-hyperactivity disorder (Burgio-Murphy, 2002).

## SUMMARY AND CONCLUSIONS

In this review, we have sought to provide an overview of work related to the effects of aging on various aspects of cognitive control including conflict and error processing and goal neglect. The evidence considered in this chapter demonstrates that there are both structural and functional declines in the neural systems that support cognitive control. Data from studies using structural MRI reveal greater age-related volume reduction in the frontal cortex and basal ganglia than in the anterior cingulate (Raz, 2000). However, the anterior cingulate is clearly not immune to the effects of aging because there are significant reductions in dopamine receptor binding in the anterior cingulate in later adulthood (Kaasinen et al., 2000). Age-related volume reductions are moderately correlated with age-related declines in cognition (Raz, 2000), while age-related declines in receptor binding account for nearly all of the age-related variance in measures of cognition (Bäckman et al., 2000). This finding leads to the suggestion that changes in transmitter efficacy are one of the primary determinants of age-related declines in cognitive control and general cognition in later adulthood.

Aging has negative effects on multiple processes supporting cognitive control including conflict and error processing, goal maintenance, and set switching. The effects of aging on those processes supporting conflict processing and goal maintenance interact with the demands of the task. Aging has no effect on the Stroop interference effect measured in response time or modulations of the ERPs when word identification is required or when color and word are spatially separated. However, the interference effect is greater and modulations of the ERPs are altered in older adults when color identification is required and when color and word are integrated (West, 2004; West & Bell, 1997). These findings indicate that general slowing may not provide a full account of the effects of aging on those processes supporting conflict processing in the Stroop task.

Aging is also associated with declines in the efficiency of those processes supporting goal maintenance. Evidence from behavioral studies demonstrates that instances of goal neglect result from transient fluctuations of cognitive control and that older adults are more susceptible to goal neglect than are younger adults (West, 1999). Evidence from ERP studies indicates that aging is associated with slowed encoding of contextual information and an inability to maintain this information in order to guide task performance (West, 2004). Older adults also appear to have difficulty establishing a task set that supports color identification, which results in the exaggerated number of intrusion errors observed for color trials when trial-by-trial cueing is used (West & Moore, 2003). Patients with schizophrenia also demonstrate high levels of intrusion errors for color trials under trial-by-trial cueing (Cohen et al., 1999), indicating that aging and schizophrenia may result in similar impairments of cognitive control associated with both structural and functional changes in the integrity of the prefrontal dopamine systems.

**Author Note**

Preparation of this chapter was supported by grants from the American Foundation for Aging and the Faculty Research Program of the University of Notre Dame.

**References**

Alain, C., McNeely, H. E., Yu, H., Christensen, B. K., & West, R. (2002). Neurophysiological evidence of error monitoring deficits in patients with Schizophrenia. *Cerebral Cortex, 12*, 840–846.

Albert, M., & Kaplin, E. (1980). Organic implications of neuropsycholgical deficits in the elderly. In L. W. Poon (Ed.), *New directions in memory and aging: Proceedings of the George A. Talland Memorial Conference* (pp. 403–432). Hillsdale, NJ: Lawrence Erlbaum Associates.

Ardila, A., & Rosselli, M. (1989). Neuropsychological characteristics of normal aging. *Developmental Neuropsychology, 5*, 307–320.

Band, G., & Kok, A. (2000). Age effects on response monitoring in a mental rotation task. *Biological Psychology, 51*, 201–221.

Bates, A. T., Kiehl, K. A., Laurens, K., & Liddle, P. F. (2002). Error-related negativity and correct response negativity in schizophrenia. *Clinical Neurophysiology, 113*, 1454–1463.

Bäckman, L., Ginovart, N., Dixon, R. A., Wahlin, T.-B. R., Whalin, A., Halldin, C., & Farde, L. (2000). Age-related cognitive deficits mediated by changes in the striatal dopamine system. *American Journal of Psychiatry, 157*, 635–637.

Botvinick, M. M., Braver, T. S., Barch, D. M., Carter, C. S., & Cohen, J. D. (2001). Conflict monitoring and cognitive control. *Psychological Review, 108*, 624–652.

Braver, T. S., Barch, D. M., Keys, B. A., Carter, C. S., Cohen, J. D., Kaye, J. A., Janowsky, J. S., Taylor, S. F., Yesavage, J. A., Mumenthaler, M. S., Jaguest, W. J., & Reed, B. R. (2001). Context processing in older adults: Evidence for a theory relating cognitive control to neurobiology in healthy aging. *Journal of Experimental Psychology: General, 130*, 746–763.

Braver, T. S., & Cohen, J. D. (1999). Dopamine, cognitive control, and schizophrenia: The gating model. *Progress in Brain Research, 121*, 327–349.

Bunce, D. J., Warr, P. B., & Cochrane, T. (1993). Blocks in choice responding as a function of age and physical fitness. *Psychology and Aging, 8*, 26–33.

Burgio-Murphy, A. (2002). Error monitoring in children with attention-deficit hyperactivity disorder: ERPs and reaction time slowing. *Dissertation Abstracts International, 62(8-B)*, 3794.

Cabeza, R. (2001). Functional neuroimaging of cognitive aging. In R. Cabeza & A. Kingstone (Eds.), *Handbook of Functional Neuroimaging of Cognition* (pp. 331–377). Cambridge, MA: MIT Press.

Carter, C. S., MacDonald 3rd, A. W., Ross, L. L., & Stenger, V. A. (2001). Anterior cingulate cortex activity and impaired self-monitoring of performance in patients with schizophrenia: An event-related fMRI study. *American Journal of Psychiatry, 158*, 1423–1428.

Carter, C. S., Mintun, M., Nichols, T., & Cohen, J. D. (1997). Anterior cingulate gyrus dysfunction and selective attention deficits in schizophrenia: an [$^{15}$O]H$_2$O PET study during single trial Stroop task performance. *American Journal of Psychiatry, 154*, 1670–1675.

Cohen, J. D., Barch, D. M., Carter, C., & Servan-Schreiber, D. (1999). Context-processing deficits in schizophrenia: Converging evidence from three theoretically motivated cognitive tasks. *Journal of Abnormal Psychology, 108*, 120–133.

Coles, M. G. H., Scheffers, M. K., & Holroyd, C. B. (2001). Why is there an ERN/Ne on correct trials? Response representations, stimulus-related components, and the theory of error-processing. *Biological Psychology, 56*, 173–189.

Convit, A., Wolf, O. T., de Leon, M. J., Patalinjug, M., Kandil, E., Caraos, C., Scherer, A., Saint Louis, L. A., & Cancro, R. (2001). Volumetric analysis of the pre-frontal regions: findings in aging and schizophrenia. *Psychiatry Research: Neuroimaging Section, 48*, 61–73.

Conway, A. R. A., & Engle, R. W. (1994). Working memory and retrieval: A resource-dependent inhibition model. *Journal of Experimental Psychology: General, 123*, 354–373.

Craik, F. I. M., & Byrd, M. (1982). Aging and cognitive deficits: The role of attentional resources. In F. I. M. Craik & S. Trehub (Eds.), *Aging and cognitive processes* (pp. 191–211). New York: Plenum.

Craik, F. I. M., Morris, L. W., Morris, R. G., & Loewen, E. R. (1990). Aging, source amnesia, and frontal lobe functioning. *Psychology and Aging, 5*, 148–151.

Daigneault, S., Braun, C. M. J., & Whitaker, H. A. (1992). Early effects of normal aging on perseverative and non-perseverative prefrontal measures. *Developmental Neuropsychology, 8*, 99–114.

de Keyser, M. J., De Backer, J.-P., Vauquelin, G., & Ebinger, G. (1990). The effect of aging on the D1 dopamine receptors in human frontal cortex. *Brain Research, 528*, 309–310.

Dempster, F. N. (1992). The rise and fall of inhibitory mechanisms: Toward a unified theory of cognitive development and aging. *Developmental Review, 12*, 45–75.

Duncan, J., Emslie, H., Williams, P., Johnson, R., & Freer, C. (1996). Intelligence and frontal lobe: The organization of goal-directed behavior. *Cognitive Psychology, 30*, 257–303.

Engle, R. W. (1996). Working memory and retrieval: An inhibition-resource approach. In J. T. E. Richardson, R. E. Engle, L. Hasher, R. H. Logie, E. R. Stoltzfus, & R. T. Zacks (Eds.), *Working memory and human cognition* (pp. 89–119). New York: Oxford University Press.

Falkenstein, M., Hielscher, H., Dziobek, I., Schwarzenau, P., Hoorman, J., Sundermann, B., & Hohnsbein, J. (2001). Action monitoring, error detection, and the basal ganglia: An ERP study. *Neuroreport, 12*, 157–161.

Falkenstein, M., Hohnsbein, J., Hoorman, J., & Blanke, L. (1991). Effects of crossmodal divided attention on late ERP components: II. Error processing in choice reaction tasks. *Electroencephalography and Clinical Neurophysiology, 78*, 447–455.

Falkenstein, M., Hoorman, J., Christ, S., & Hohnsbein, J. (2000). ERP components on reaction errors and their functional significance: a tutorial. *Biological Psychology, 51*, 87–107.

Falkenstein, M., Hoorman, J., & Hohnbein, J. (2001). Changes of error-related ERPs with age. *Experimental Brain Research, 138*, 258–262.

Ford, J. M., Roth, W. T., Mohs, R. C., Hopkins, W. F., Kopell, B. S. (1979). Event-related potentials recorded from young and old adults during a memory retrieval task. *Electroencephalography and Clinical Neurophysiology, 47*, 450–459.

Gehring, W. J., Goss, B., Coles, M. G. H., Meyer, D. E., & Donchin, E. (1993). A neural system for error detection and compensation. *Psychological Science, 4*, 385–390.

Gehring, W. J., Himle, J., & Nisenson, L. G. (2000). Action-monitoring dysfunction in obsessive-compulsive disorder. *Psychological Science, 11*, 1–6.

Gehring, W. J., & Knight, R. T. (2000). Prefrontal-cingulate interactions in action monitoring. *Nature Neuroscience, 3*, 516–520.

Grady, C. L., McIntosh, A. R., Horwitz, B., Maisog, J., Ungerleider, L. G., Mentis, M. J., Pietrini, P., Schapiro, M. B., & Haxby, J. V. (1995). Age-related reductions in human recognition memory due to impaired encoding. *Science, 269*, 218–221.

Greenwood, P. M. (2000). The frontal aging hypothesis evaluated. *Journal of the International Neuropsychological Society, 6*, 705–726.

Hartley, A. A. (1993). Evidence for the selective preservation of spatial selective attention in old age. *Psychology and Aging, 8*, 371–379.

Hasher, L., & Zacks, R. T. (1979). Automatic and effortful processes in memory. *Journal of Experimental Psychology: General, 108,* 356–388.

Hasher, L., & Zacks, R. T. (1988). Working memory, comprehension, and aging: A review and new view. In G. H. Bower (Ed.), *The psychology of learning and motivation* (Vol. 22, pp. 193–225). New York: Academic Press.

Holroyd, C. B., & Coles, M. G. H. (2002). The neural basis of human error processing: Reinforcement learning, dopamine, and the error-related negativity. *Psychological Review, 109,* 679–709.

Holroyd, C. B., Praamstra, P., Plat, E., & Coles, M. G. H. (2002). Spared error-related potentials in mild to moderate Parkinson's disease. *Neuropsychologia, 40,* 2116–2124.

Jonides, J., Badre, D., Curtis, C., Thompson-Schill, S. L., & Smith, E. E. (2002). Mechanisms of conflict resolution in prefrontal cortex. In D. T. Stuss & R. T. Knight (Eds.), *Principles of frontal lobe function* (pp. 233–245). Oxford, UK: Oxford University Press.

Kane, M. J., Bleckley, M. K., Conway, A. R. A., & Engle, R. W. (2001). A controlled-attention view of working memory capacity. *Journal of Experimental Psychology: General, 130,* 169–183.

Kane, M. J., & Engle, R. W. (2003). Working-memory capacity and the control of attention: The contribution of goal neglect, response competition, and task set to Stroop interference. *Journal of Experimental Psychology: General, 132,* 47–70.

Kaasinen, V., & Rinne, J. O. (2002). Functional imaging studies of dopamine system and cognition in normal aging and Parkinson's disease. *Neuroscience & Biobehavioral Reviews, 26,* 785–793.

Kaasinen, V., Vilkman, H., Hietala, J., Någren, K., Helenius, H., Olsson, H., Farde, L., & Rinne, J. O. (2000). Age-related dopamine D2/D3 receptor loss in extrastriatal regions of the human brain. *Neurobiology of Aging, 21,* 683–688.

Kopp, B., & Rist, F. (1999). An event-related brain potential substrate of disturbed response monitoring in paranoid schizophrenia patients. *Journal of Abnormal Psychology, 108,* 337–346.

Li, S-C. (2002). Connecting the many levels and facets of cognitive aging. *Current Directions in Psychological Science, 11,* 38–43.

Li, S-C., & Lindenberger, U. (1999). Cross-level unification: A computational exploration of the link between deterioration of neurotransmitter systems and dedifferentiation of cognitive abilities in old age. In L.-G. Nilsson & H. J. Markowitsch (Eds.), *Cognitive Neuroscience of Memory* (pp. 103–146). Seattle: Hogrefe & Huber.

Li, S-C., & Sikström, S. (2002). Integrative neurocomputational perspectives on cognitive aging, neuromodulation, and representation. *Neuroscience & Biobehavioral Reviews, 25,* 795–808.

Lindsay, D. S., & Jacoby, L. L. (1994). Stroop process dissociations: The relationship between facilitation and interference. *Journal of Experimental Psychology: Human Perception and Performance, 20,* 219–234.

Liotti, M., Woldorff, M. G., Perez III, R., & Mayberg, H. S. (1999). An ERP study of the temporal course of the Stroop color-word interference effect. *Neuropsychologia, 38,* 701–711.

Lowe, D. G., & Mitterer, J. O. (1982). Selective and divided attention in a Stroop task. *Canadian Journal of Psychology, 36,* 684–700.

MacDonald, A. W. 3ʳᵈ., Cohen, J. D., Stenger, V. A., & Carter, C. S. (2000). Dissociating the role of the dorsolateral prefrontal and anterior cingulate cortex in cognitive control. *Science, 288,* 1835–1838.

MacLeod, P. M. (1991). Half a century of research on the Stroop effect: An integrative review. *Psychological Bulletin, 109,* 163–203.

MacPherson, S. E., Phillips, L. H., & Della Sala, S. (2002). Age, executive function, and social decision making: A dorsolateral prefrontal theory of cognitive aging. *Psychology and Aging, 17,* 598–609.

Mathalon, D. H., Fedor, M., Faustman, W. O., Gray, M., Askari, N., & Ford, J. M. (2002). Response-monitoring dysfunction in schizophrenia: An event-related brain potential study. *Journal of Abnormal Psychology, 111,* 22–41.

McNeely, H. E., West, R., Christensen, B. K., & Alain, C. (2003). Neurophysiological evidence for disturbances of conflict processing in patients with schizophrenia. *Journal of Abnormal Psychology, 112,* 679–688.

Milhan, M. P., Erickson, K. I., Banich, M. T., Kramer, A. F., Webb, A., Wszalek, T., & Cohen, N. J. (2002). Attentional control in the aging brain: Insights from an fMRI study of the Stroop task. *Brain and Cognition, 49,* 277–296.

Nieuwenhuis, S., Ridderinkhof, K. R., Talsma, D., Coles, M. G. H., Holroyd, C. B., Kok, A., & van der Molen, M. W. (2002). A computational account of altered error processing in older age: Dopamine and the error-related negativity. *Cognitive, Affective, & Behavioral Neuroscience, 2,* 19–36.

Park, D. C., & Schwarz, N. (2000). *Aging and cognition: A student primer.* Philadelphia: Psychology Press.

Perlstein, W. M., Carter, C. S., Barch, D. M., & Baird, J. W. (1998). The Stroop task and attention deficits in schizophrenia: A critical evaluation of card and single-trial Stroop methodologies. *Neuropsychology, 12,* 414–425.

Phillips, L. H., & Della Sala, S. (1998). Aging, intelligence, and anatomical segregation in the frontal lobes. *Learning and Individual Differences, 10,* 217–243.

Raz, N. (2000). Aging of the brain and its impact on cognitive performance: Integration of structural and functional findings. In F. I. M. Craik & T. A. Salthouse (Eds.), *The handbook of aging and cognition* (2ⁿᵈ ed., pp. 1–90). Mahwah, NJ: Lawrence Erlbaum Associates.

Raz, N., Gunning-Dixon, F. M., Head, D. P., Dupuis, J. H., & Acker, J. D. (1998). Neuroanatomical correlates of cognitive aging: Evidence from structural MRI. *Neuropsychology, 12,* 95–114.

Raz, N., Williamson, A., Gunning-Dixon, F., Head, D., & Acker, J. D. (2000). Neuroanatomical and cognitive correlates of adult age differences in acquisition of a perceptual-motor skill. *Microscopy Research and Technique, 51,* 85–93.

Reason, J. (1979). Actions not as planned: The price of automatization. In G. Underwood & R. Stevens (Eds.), *Aspects of consciousness* (pp. 67–89). London, UK: Academic Press.

Rebai, M., Bernard, C., & Lannou, J. (1997). The Stroop's test evokes a negative brain potential, the N400. *International Journal of Neuroscience, 91,* 85–94.

Rinne, J. O. (1987). Muscarinic and dopaminergic receptors in the aging human brain. *Brain Research, 404,* 162–168.

Rubin, D. C. (1999). Frontal-striatal circuits in cognitive aging: Evidence for caudate involvement. *Aging, Neuropsychology, and Cognition, 6,* 241–259.

Salthouse, T. (1996). The processing-speed theory of adult age differences in cognition. *Psychological Review*, *103*, 403–428.

Salthouse, T. A., & Meinz, E. J. (1995). Aging, inhibition, working memory, and speed. *Journal of Gerontology: Psychological Sciences*, *50B*, P297–P306.

Shimamura, A. P., & Jurica, P. J. (1994). Memory interference effects and aging: Findings from a test of frontal lobe function. *Neuropsychology*, *8*, 408–412.

Spieler, D. H., Balota, D. A., & Faust, M. E. (1996). Stroop performance in healthy younger and older adults and in individuals with Dementia of the Alzheimer's Type. *Journal of Experimental Psychology: Human Perception and Performance*, *22*, 461–479.

Stroop, J. R. (1935). Studies of interference in serial verbal reactions. *Journal of Experimental Psychology*, *18*, 643–663.

Suhara, T., Fukuda, H., Inoue, O., Itoh, T., Suzuki, K., Yamasaki, T., & Tateno, Y. (1991). Age-related changes in human $D_1$ dopamine receptors measured by positron emission tomography. *Psychopharmacology*, *103*, 41–45.

Swick, D., & Turken, A. U. (2002). Dissociation between conflict detection and error monitoring in the human anterior cingulate cortex. *Proceeding of the National Academy of Science*, *99*, 16354–16359.

Verhaeghen, P., & De Meersman, L. (1998). Aging and the Stroop effect: A meta-analysis. *Psychology and Aging*, *13*, 120–126.

Volkow, N. D., Gur, R. C., Wang, G. J., Pappas, N., Logan, J., MacGregor, R., Alexoff, D., Wolf, A. P., Warner, D., Cilento, R., & Zezulkova, I. (1998). Association between decline in brain dopamine activity with age and cognitive and motor impairment in healthy individuals. *American Journal of Psychiatry*, *155*, 344–349.

West, R. (1999). Age differences in lapses of intention in the Stroop task. *Journal of Gerontology: Psychological Sciences*, *54B*, P34–P43.

West, R. (2001). The transient nature of executive control processes in younger and older adults. *European Journal of Cognitive Psychology*, *13*, 91–105.

West, R. (2003). Neural correlates of cognitive control and conflict detection in the Stroop and digit-location tasks. *Neuropsychologia*, *41*, 1122–1135.

West, R. (2004). The effects of aging on controlled attention and conflict processing in the Stroop task. *Journal of Cognitive Neuroscience*, *16*, 103–113.

West, R., & Alain, C. (2000a). Age-related decline in inhibitory control contributes to the increased Stroop effect observed in older adults. *Psychophysiology*, *37*, 179–189.

West, R., & Alain, C. (2000b). Effect of task context and fluctuations of attention on neural activity supporting performance of the Stroop task. *Brain Research*, *873*, 102–111.

West, R., & Alain, C. (2000c). Evidence for the transient nature of a neural system supporting goal-directed action. *Cerebral Cortex*, *8*, 748–752.

West, R. & Baylis, G. C. (1998). Effects of increased response dominance and contextual disintegration on the Stroop interference effect in older adults. *Psychology and Aging*, *13*, 206–217.

West, R., & Bell, M. A. (1997). Stroop color-word interference and EEG activation: Evidence for age-related decline in prefrontal functioning. *Neuropsychology*, *11*, 421–427.

West, R., Ergis, A-M., Winocur, G., & Saint-Cyr, J. (1998). The contribution of impaired working memory monitoring to performance of the Self Ordered Pointing task in normal aging and Parkinson's disease. *Neuropsychology, 12,* 546–554.

West, R., Jakubek, K., Wymbs, N., & Perry, M. (2002, April). Neural correlates of conflict processing in the Stroop and Stoop-like tasks. *Journal of Cognitive Neuroscience: Supplement, 24.*

West, R., & Moore, K. (in press). Adjustments of cognitive control in younger and older adults. Cortex.

West, R., Murphy, K. J., Armilio, M. L., Craik, F. I. M., & Stuss, D. T. (2002). Lapses of intention and performance variability reveal age-related increases in fluctuations of executive control. *Brain and Cognition, 49,* 402–419.

West, R. L. (1996). An application of prefrontal cortex function theory to cognitive aging. *Psychological Bulletin, 120,* 272–292.

Whelihan, W. M., & Lesher, E. L. (1985). Neuropsychological changes in frontal functions with aging. *Developmental Neuropsychology, 1,* 371–380.

# 6

## Cognitive Control and Schizophrenia
*Psychological and Neural Mechanisms*

Deanna M. Barch and Todd S. Braver

Schizophrenia is a complex and debilitating psychiatric disorder that affects approximately one percent of the population. Lay conceptions of schizophrenia typically focus on symptoms such as hallucinations, delusions, and disorganized speech, which are often considered the hallmark features of this disorder. However, clinicians, researchers, and theorists have long noted that individuals with schizophrenia also commonly suffer from disturbances in memory and cognition, often severely so. Interestingly, recent research suggests that disturbances in social and occupational functioning in individuals with schizophrenia may be more influenced by the severity of their cognitive deficits than the severity of symptoms such as hallucinations and delusions (Green, Kern, Braff, & Mintz, 2000). Such findings have led to a resurgence of interest in identifying the nature of cognitive abnormalities in schizophrenia. A close examination of the types of symptoms and cognitive disturbances displayed by individuals suggests that many of these disturbances appear to reflect an inability to control or regulate their cognitive and emotional states. In this chapter, we review the evidence that one of the core cognitive disturbances in schizophrenia is a deficit in one or more components of executive function, which leads to disturbances in the ability to appropriately regulate thoughts and behavior in accordance with internal goals. More specifically, we suggest that individuals with schizophrenia suffer from a disturbance in a specific type of executive control process that we refer to as a deficit in the ability to represent and maintain context.

Researchers have long recognized that individuals with schizophrenia appear to show profound deficits on cognitive tasks that are thought to require what is collectively referred to as "executive functions" or cognitive control functions. For example, numerous studies have shown that individuals with schizophrenia are impaired on tasks, such as the Wisconsin Card Sorting Task, that require a number of different components of executive function, including problem solving, set switching, and working memory (Weinberger, Berman, & Zec, 1986). At the same time, individuals with schizophrenia also display deficits in a number of other cognitive domains, including selective attention, inhibition, working memory, perceptual integration (Silverstein, Kovacs, Corry, & Valone, 2000), and sustained attention (Carter, Robertson, & Nordahl, 1992; Chapman & McGhie, 1962; Cornblatt & Keilp, 1994; Gold, Carpenter, Randolph, Goldberg, & Weinberger, 1997; Gold, Randolph, Carpenter, Goldberg, & Weinberger, 1992; Nuechterlein & Dawson, 1984; Park & Holzman, 1992). These findings of deficits in a broad array of task domains raised the question of whether individuals with schizophrenia have a number of independent (or at least semi-independent) cognitive deficits, or whether there is some fundamental or basic component of cognitive control that is impaired in this disorder, which in turn contributes to disturbances on tasks thought to measure many different cognitive domains. In prior work, we and our colleagues have put forth the hypothesis that one of the fundamental disturbances in cognitive control present in schizophrenia is a deficit in the ability to represent and maintain context information (Barch et al., 2001; Braver, Barch, & Cohen, 1999a; Braver & Cohen, 1999; Cohen & Servan-Schreiber, 1992) because of a disturbance in the function of dopamine in dorsolateral prefrontal cortex.

To develop more explicit theories and testable predictions about context processing deficits in schizophrenia, we have drawn upon computational modeling as a tool for specifying the neural mechanisms that support context processing (e.g., dorsolateral prefrontal cortex and the dopamine system) and how specific disturbances to these mechanisms lead to cognitive impairments (Braver, 1997; Braver et al., 1999a; Braver, Barch, & Cohen, 1999b; Braver & Cohen, 1999; Braver, Cohen, & McClelland, 1997; Braver, Cohen, & Servan-Schreiber, 1995; Cohen & Servan-Schreiber, 1992). These models were constructed within the parallel distributed processing (PDP), or "neural network" framework, allowing the quantitative simulation of human performance in cognitive tasks using principles of processing that are similar to those believed to apply in the brain (McClelland, 1993; Rumelhart & McClelland, 1986). The nature of these models and the results of simulations are discussed in detail elsewhere (Braver, 1997; Braver et al., 1999a, 1999b; Braver & Cohen, 1999; Braver et al., 1997; Braver et al., 1995).

## CONTEXT PROCESSING

As discussed in many of the other chapters in this volume, such as that by West and Bowry, cognitive control requires the ability to detect, adjust, and respond to changing contingencies and feedback in the environment and no doubt requires a number of different functions and mechanisms. In our own work, we focused on several such mechanisms that we think are important for cognitive control, including context representation, context

maintenance, context updating, conflict detection, and subgoal processing (Barch et al., 2001; Barch et al., 2001; Botvinick, Braver, Barch, Carter, &
Cohen, 2001; Braver et al., 1999a; Braver & Bongiolatti, 2002; Braver, Cohen,
& Barch, 2002; O'Reilly, Noelle, Braver, & Cohen, 2002). In regards to understanding cognitive control deficits in schizophrenia, we argued that deficits
in the representation, maintenance, and updating of context may be central
to this disorder. By context information, we mean information that must
be "actively" held in mind in a form that allows it to be used to mediate
task appropriate behavior. In our models, representations of context are
used specifically to support task-relevant information against sources of
interference that can occur simply as a function of time (e.g., noise accumulating in the system) or because of specific competing processes (e.g.,
the need to process other stimuli, distractions). Context representations
can comprise a variety of different types of information, such as a specific
prior stimulus, the result of processing a sequence of prior stimuli, or more
abstract information such as task instructions. As an example, take the following sentence: "In order to keep pigs, you need a pen." In this sentence,
the first clause serves as context that biases you toward the appropriate
meaning of the word "pen" (a fenced enclosure) for this sentence, rather
than the more common meaning of the word "pen" (a writing instrument).
This is a case in which the result of processing the first part of the sentence
(e.g., a sequence of prior stimuli) creates a contextual representation that
can bias future behavior (e.g., semantic interpretation of the word "pen").
As another example, take the well-known Stroop task. In one condition
of this task, participants are shown color words written in different colors
(e.g., the word "RED" written in blue). In the absence of any other information, a participant's natural response is to read the word rather than
to name the color, as this is what one typically does when presented with
verbal stimuli. In other words, reading the word rather than naming the
color is the prepotent response. However, in the Stroop task, participants
are given the instruction to ignore the word and instead read the color. We
would argue that in this situation, the task instructions serve as context that
allows the participant to inhibit the prepotent response tendency to read the
word.

In many ways, one might argue that such a definition of context could
be overly broad or inclusive, as almost any type of stimulus could be seen
as forming a context representation. However, we would argue that context information or representations can be distinguished, both theoretically and empirically, from other related concepts in important ways. As
an example, we argued that the representation and maintenance of context can be distinguished from both the constructs of short-term memory and working memory (Barch, Carter, & Cohen, 2003; Cohen, Barch,
Carter, & Servan-Schreiber, 1999; Cohen & Servan-Schreiber, 1992). Short-
term memory is often used to refer to processes necessary to temporarily

store recently presented information in a form somewhat close to the form in which it was presented (e.g., without conceptual transformation). Such information held in short-term memory may or may not have implications for how one should respond in a future situation. In contrast, our definition of context information is that it must be information that has relevance for later behavior, but it may not correspond to the actual identity of previously presented information. In fact, our assumption is that context representations are almost always transformations of the identity of specific stimuli into their meaning for behavior, which often may no longer include the initial identify of the stimulus. We do think context processing is much more closely aligned with conceptions of working memory, which is commonly defined as the collection of processes responsible for the on-line maintenance and manipulation of information necessary to perform a cognitive task (Baddeley, 1994). However, we do not believe that context processing and working memory are interchangeable constructs. Instead, we view context representations as a subset of representations within working memory, which govern how other representation held within either working memory or long-term memory are used.

An important insight that has emerged from our work is that the context processing functions of our model demonstrate how a single underlying mechanism, operating under different task conditions, might subserve three cognitive functions that are often treated as independent: attention (selection and support of task-relevant information for processing), active memory (on-line maintenance of such information), and inhibition (suppression of task-irrelevant information). When a task involves competing, task-irrelevant processes (as in the Stroop task), it is often assumed that a dedicated inhibitory function is responsible for suppressing, or overriding, these irrelevant processes. However, in our model, there is no dedicated mechanism for inhibition. Rather, context representations accomplish the same effect by providing top-down support for task-relevant processes, allowing these to compete effectively against irrelevant ones. In contrast, when a task involves a delay between a cue and a later contingent response, it is usually assumed that a working memory function is involved. Once again, there is no dedicated mechanism for this function in our model. Rather, the mechanism used to represent context information is used to maintain task relevant information against the interfering and cumulative effects of noise over time. Thus, both for tasks that tap "inhibition" and for those that tap "working memory," the same mechanism is involved; it is simply a matter of the behavioral conditions under which it operates (i.e., the source of interference) that lead us to label it as having an "inhibitory" or a "working memory" function. Furthermore, under both types of conditions, context representations serve an attentional function by selecting task-relevant information for processing over other potentially competing sources of information. Thus, in all circumstances, the same context processing mechanism is involved. We hypothesize that this context processing mechanism is impaired in schizophrenia. Consequently, we suggest that disturbances in context processing may form a common basis for many of the deficits observed across multiple cognitive domains in schizophrenia, including attention, inhibition, working memory, and language processing.

In many ways, this notion of deficits in the representation of context is related to the notion of goal neglect discussed by West and Bowry in another chapter in this volume and in previous work (West, 1999; West & Alain, 2000). It is also related to similar ideas put forth by Duncan (Duncan, Emslie, Williams, Johnson, & Freer, 1996). For example, one can think of context information as representations of goals that are held in memory to guide and constrain ongoing processing. Difficulties in the sustained active maintenance of such representations can lead to a number of behavioral deficits on cognitive control tasks as described by West. As discussed in greater detail later, our model of context processing and the associated neurobiological mechanisms provides some hypotheses as to disturbances that might contribute to deficits in context processing and/or goal neglect.

Further, our hypotheses regarding the role of context processing in cognitive control (and the influence of such maintained context representations to overcome the negative influences of interference and conflict) are consistent with the role of "executive attention" in the working memory model put forth by Engle and colleagues (Engle & Kane, 2004). Specifically, Engle suggests the term executive attention refers to the ability to maintain even a single bit of information (e.g., a goal) in working memory in the face of a variety of sources of conflict. As with our theory, Engle and colleagues do not draw a strong line between mechanisms involved in the maintenance of information and those involved in the control and manipulation of ongoing processing. For example, Engle argues that although there may be multiple components of working memory capacity, the component most closely linked to success in a number of real-world outcomes (e.g., new vocabulary learning) is the ability to use attentional control to maintain goal-relevant information when there is interference or competition for other processes or stimuli. This is in contrast to the type of working memory model put forth by Baddeley, which does postulate a stricter segregation of storage/maintenance processes and central executive processes (Baddeley, 1996; Baddeley, 1986, 2000; Baddeley & Hitch, 1994), although more recently Baddeley emphasized the importance of attention control for working memory function (Baddeley, 1993; Baddeley & Logie, 1999). Thus, our model can be thought of as being highly compatible with that of Engle and colleagues. The primary differences between the models are ones of emphasis and the experimental domains upon which they have focused. Engle and colleagues have primarily focused on studies of healthy young adults, using both an individual differences approach and standard cognitive psychology methodology. In contrast, our own model focused as heavily on special populations (i.e., schizophrenia, older adults) as on healthy young adults and integrated computational and cognitive neuroscience methodologies with cognitive experimental ones.

## CONTEXT PROCESSING IN SCHIZOPHRENIA

In many ways, our hypotheses about context processing deficits in schizophrenia are very similar to earlier suggestions about the nature of cognitive deficits in this disorder put forth by researchers such as Shakow (Shakow, 1962). For example, Shakow suggested that "we see particularly the various difficulties created by context . . . It is as if, in the scanning process which takes place before the response to a stimulus is made, the schizophrenic is unable to select out the material relevant for optimal response (p. 4)" (Shakow, 1962). There is now a growing body of evidence from a variety of different task domains that supports the idea that individuals with schizophrenia have a deficit in the ability to represent and maintain context information, including tasks drawn from the domains of working memory, selective attention, inhibition, and language processing.

## AX-CPT Task

One task that we used in numerous studies is a version of the classic Continuous Performance Test (Rosvold, Mirsky, Sarason, Bransome, & Beck, 1956) known as the AX-CPT (Cohen et al., 1999; Servan-Schreiber, Cohen, & Steingard, 1996). This test was specifically designed as a measure of context representation and maintenance. As shown in Figure 6.1a, in this task, participants are presented with cue–probe pairs and told to make a target response to an "X" (probe) but only when it follows an "A" (cue), and a nontarget response otherwise. A correct response to "X" depends upon maintaining the "context" provided by the cue ("A" or not-"A"). One change to the standard AX-CPT was to increase the frequency of target ("AX") trials so that they occur with a high frequency (70%, see Figure 6.1b), with the remaining 30% of trials distributed across three types of nontarget trials ("BX", "AY", and "BY" where "B" refers to any non-"A" cue and "Y" refers to any non-"X" probe). This creates two types of biases that can be used to probe the integrity of context processing. The first bias, or prepotent response, is that participants expect to make a target response when they see an "X" probe, because this is the correct response on most of the trials (87.5% of trials in which an X is presented). On "BX" trials, participants have to use to the context provided by the "B" cue to inhibit this bias to respond target to an "X" (which would lead to a false alarm). Thus, impaired context representations will lead to poor performance on "BX" trials, because the context provided by the "B" cue would not be available

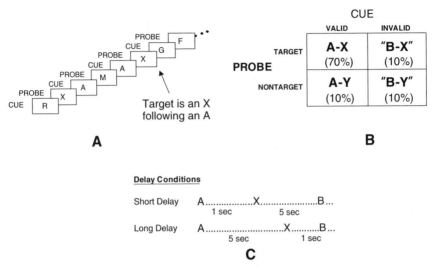

FIGURE 6.1. Panel A: Schematic of stimuli presentation across time in the AX-CPT. Panel B: Illustration of relative frequencies of different trial types in the AX-CPT. Panel C: Illustration of the timing of the stimuli in task conditions of the AX-CPT with either a short or a long delay between the cue and the probe.

to override the tendency to want to response target to the "X." The second bias is that participants expect to make a target response after they see an "A" cue, because most of the time an "X" follows the "A" cue (87.5% of "A" cue trials). However, on trials in which the "A" is not followed by an "X", this predictive aspect of context actually *creates* the tendency to false alarm. Thus, intact representations of context will hurt performance on "AY" trials, because context induces an invalid expectancy, leading to worse "AY" than "BX" performance. In contrast, individuals with impaired context representations should show worse "BX" than "AY" performance. In other words, individuals with impaired context representations (such as individuals with schizophrenia) should show worse "BX" performance, but *better* "AY" performance, than individuals with intact context representations.

A second manipulation included in the AX-CPT task is to examine maintenance of context information and the initial representation of context by manipulating the delay between the cue and probe (see Figure 6.1c). When the interval or delay between the cue and the probe is lengthened from, for example, 1 second to 5 or 10 seconds, context must be actively maintained within *working memory* (supported by prefrontal cortex in this and other theories of working memory function; see below). One prediction of the context processing theory is that performance on "AY" and "BX" trials will vary as a function of delay (Braver et al., 1999a; Braver et al., 2002; Braver et al., 1995). When context can be maintained, then the strength of context representations should stay the same or increase with delay. If so, then "BX" performance should stay the same or even get better with longer delays because there is more time for context information to prepare the person to inhibit an incorrect response to the "X". In contrast, "AY" performance should stay the same or get worse with delay because there is more time for context representations to induce the participant to prepare for a target response, which must be inhibited when a "Y" rather than an "X" occurs. In contrast, if context maintenance is impaired, then "BX" performance should get worse with delay, but "AY" performance should actually *improve*.

A number of prior studies found results with this AX-CPT task that provide evidence consistent with an impairment in context processing in schizophrenia (Barch et al., 2001; Barch et al., 2003; Cohen et al., 1999; Javitt, Shelley, Silipo, & Lieberman, 2000; Servan-Schreiber et al., 1996; Stratta, Daneluzzo, Bustini, Casacchia, & Rossi, 1998; Stratta, Daneluzzo, Bustini, Prosperini, & Rossi, 2000). For example, earlier work in our lab (Barch et al., 2001) demonstrated that as predicted, individuals with schizophrenia (first episode, neuroleptic naïve; see Figure 6.2a) made significantly more "BX" errors than did healthy controls, but significantly *fewer* "AY" errors, particularly at the longer delay. This pattern of both impaired and improved performance suggests that context representations are less available or less able to influence processing in individuals with schizophrenia, leading to an inability to override the incorrect tendency to respond target to the "X" on "BX" trials. In addition, such impairments in the processing of context lead to less predictive use of context on "AY" trials (which normally leads to errors on "AY" trials). In addition, the individuals with schizophrenia were significantly slower than controls on correct "BX" trials (suggesting increased interference from the "X" cue when there is a need to override a prepotent response tendency). However, the individuals with schizophrenia were not significantly slower than controls on "AY" trials, despite the fact that patients are typically overall slower on all tasks (see Figure 6.2b). This lack of an RT difference on AY trials again suggests that patients did not use context in a predictive fashion, leading them to actually experience less of a context-induced interference effect.

Across a number of different studies, results with the AX-CPT have consistently demonstrated that individuals with schizophrenia have deficits in the representation of context, in that they show the predicted patterns of increased BX errors and RTs, but not increased AY errors (or even decreased) and RTs. However, the answer to the question of whether patients with schizophrenia have a deficit in the maintenance of context

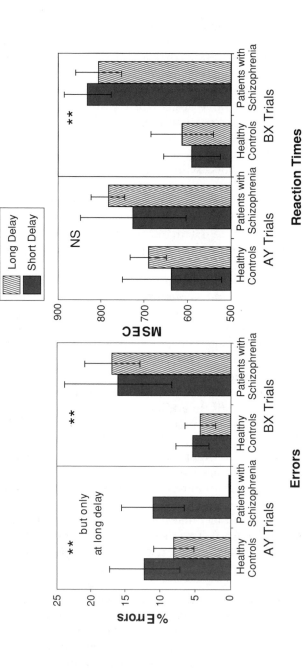

FIGURE 6.2. The graph on the left depicts "BX" and "AY" errors in the AX-CPT task in participants from (Barch, Carter et al., 2001); the graph on the right depicts "BX" and AY RTs from the same participants.

(e.g., effects exacerbated at the longer delay) and a deficit in the initial representation of context (e.g., deficits at short delay) is unclear. If patients with schizophrenia were primarily experiencing deficits in the representation of context, but not in maintenance, then performance deficits should be equal across the short and long delay. In contrast, if patients had deficits in representation and maintenance, then deficits should be worse at the long as compared to short delay. Some studies have shown that individuals with schizophrenia show an increase in context processing deficits at the long as compared to short delay (Cohen et al., 1999; Elvevag, Duncan, & McKenna, 2000; Javitt et al., 2000; Servan-Schreiber et al., 1996; Stratta et al., 1998; Stratta et al., 2000), whereas other studies have not (Barch et al., 2001; Barch et al., 2003; MacDonald et al., in submission; Perlstein, Dixit, Carter, Noll, & Cohen, 2003). However, close examination of the patterns of data across these different studies suggests that two different factors may be influencing whether context processing deficits are significantly greater at the long as compared to short delay in patients with schizophrenia as compared to controls. The first factor is whether the patients are early in the course of illness (e.g., first episode) or more chronic. To date, the studies with first episodic patients have not, for example, found significant increases in "BX" errors or RTs at the long as compared to the short delay (Barch et al., 2001; Barch et al., 2003; MacDonald et al., in submission) or have at least found smaller increases as a function of delay than in studies with chronic patients (Javitt et al., 2000). This suggests that early in the course of illness, patients with schizophrenia experience deficits in the initial representation of context but not further deficits in the maintenance of context. In contrast, studies with chronic patients do indicate that "BX" errors and RTs are significantly increased at the long as compared short delay (Cohen et al., 1999; Elvevag et al., 2000; Javitt et al., 2000; Servan-Schreiber et al., 1996; Stratta et al., 1998; Stratta et al., 2000), suggesting that chronic patients may have deficits in context maintenance and in initial context representation. A second factor is the performance of controls. In some studies with chronic patients, the controls also showed an increase in "BX" errors or RTs from the short to long delay, making it difficult to detect a differentially greater increase in patients (Cohen et al., 1999; Javitt et al., 2000). At this point, it is not entirely clear why some healthy controls show reductions in context processing at the long versus short delay, though it is possible that this may be related to some changes in the ability to represent and/or maintain context that occurs with age (see below for further discussion of aging and context processing) (Braver et al., 2001) or that can vary as a function of factors such as fluid intelligence (Burgess & Braver,). Additional studies more directly examining stage of illness effects or longitudinal changes in context processing among both patients with schizophrenia and healthy controls will help to clarify the magnitude of deficits in

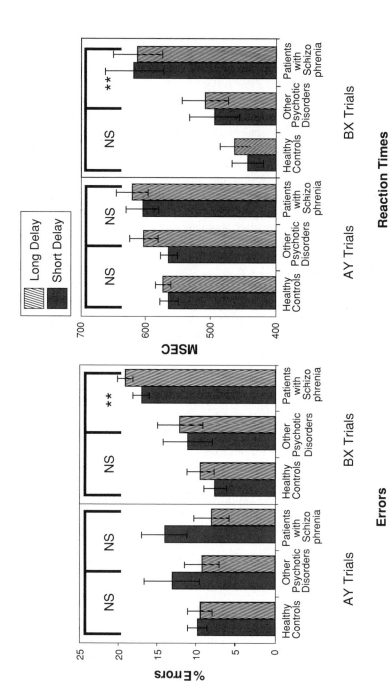

FIGURE 6.3. The graph on the left depicts "BX" and "AY" errors in the AX-CPT task in participants from (Barch et al., 2003); the graph on the right depicts "BX" and "AY" RTs from the same participants.

the initial representation of context versus the maintenance of context in schizophrenia.

In other work, we also examined the degree to which such context processing deficits are specific to individuals with schizophrenia as compared to other psychiatric disorders. For example, one study compared chronic individuals with schizophrenia to individuals with nonpsychotic major depression and found that unlike individuals with schizophrenia, individuals with major depression did not show any evidence of impairments in context processing (Cohen et al., 1999). In more recent work (Barch et al., 2003), we compared the specificity of context processing deficits to individuals with schizophrenia versus individuals with other psychotic disorders (e.g., major depression with psychotic features, bipolar disorder, delusional disorder, psychotic disorder NOS). In this study, participants were entered into the study upon their first contact with psychiatric services and tested before they were ever administered antipsychotic medications. Participants were then followed longitudinally, with repeat testing after four weeks and a confirmation of their diagnostic status at six months. At study admission, the individuals with psychotic disorders other than schizophrenia demonstrated a very similar pattern of deficits in context processing to that shown by individuals with schizophrenia. This included more "BX" errors and slower "BX" RTs as compared to controls, but *the same or "AY"* errors and no difference in "AY" RTs. Again, this suggests that both the individuals with schizophrenia and the individuals with other psychotic disorders were less able to use context representations to inhibit an incorrect target response on "BX" trials and less able to use context to predict potential targets on "AY" trials.

However, at four weeks, the individuals with other psychotic disorders, but not the individuals with schizophrenia, began to show improvements in context processing. As shown in Figure 6.3, by four weeks, the individuals with other psychotic disorders no longer differed from controls in "BX" performance (either errors or RT), but they did show significantly performance differences when compared to individuals with schizophrenia. Taken together, we argued that such results suggest that context processing deficits are a more stable component of schizophrenia, perhaps forming part of the vulnerability to this disorder. In contrast, context processing deficits may be more state-related in other psychotic disorders (Barch et al., 2003).

Others research found that individuals at risk for schizophrenia, and who presumably share liability for this disorder, also display deficits in context processing on the AX-CPT task. For example, MacDonald and colleagues showed that nonpsychotic siblings of patients with schizophrenia show a similar performance pattern on the AX-CPT to that found with schizophrenia patients, demonstrating increased "BX" errors and RTs and decreased "AY" errors and no difference in "AY" RTs (MacDonald,

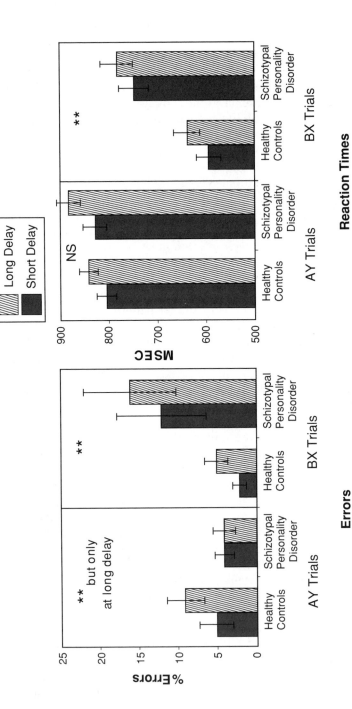

FIGURE 6.4. The graph on the left depicts "BX" and "AY" errors in the AX-CPT task in controls and individuals with schizotypal personality disorder (SPD) from (Barch, Mitropoulou et al., in press); the graph on the right depicts "BX" and "AY" RTs from the same participants.

Pogue-Geile, Johnson, & Carter, 2003). In our own work, we examined context processing deficits in individuals with schizotypal personality disorder, a disorder thought to share genetic liability with schizophrenia. As shown in Figure 6.4, we also found a pattern of deficits on the AX-CPT among individuals with schizotypal personality disorder that is indicative of a disturbance in context processing (Barch et al., in press). Like individuals with schizophrenia, the individuals with schizotypal personality disorder displayed increased "BX" errors, but not "AY" errors, combined with increased "BX" RTs, but not "AY" RTs. However, none of these effects were significantly exacerbated with delay in the individuals with schizotypal personality disorder. Taken together, these results suggest that individuals with schizotypal personality disorder also have difficulty utilizing contextual information to govern behavioral responding, but that this deficit is not worsened by increasing the delay over which such information must be maintained.

## Other Measures of Context Processing

A number of studies using tasks other than the AX-CPT also provided evidence for deficits in context processing in schizophrenia. For example, a growing number of studies suggest that deficits in context processing can be observed in the domain of language comprehension and production. Very interesting evidence for context processing deficits in schizophrenia comes from a number of studies examining an ERP component called the N400, which is thought to index the degree of consistency or relatedness between a stimulus (e.g., word) and the preceding context (which could be a single word, a sentence, or an entire discourse; Brown & Hagoort, 1993; Kutas & Hillyard, 1980). The N400 is a negative going component of an ERP waveform that occurs approximately 400 msec after the onset of the stimulus of interest. In cognitively intact individuals, words that are not consistent with the preceding context elicit a larger N400 than words that are consistent with the preceding context.

A number of such N400 studies using different types of paradigms have provided evidence for context processing deficits in schizophrenia. For example, Condray used a lexical decision task in which pairs of words were presented that were either semantically related or semantically unrelated (Condray, Steinhauer, Cohen, van Kammen, & Kasparek, 1999; for related studies, see Grillon, Ameli, & Glzer, 1991). Controls demonstrated a significant priming effect in N400s (larger N400s to unrelated as compared to related words), whereas drug-free individuals with schizophrenia did not show an N400 priming effect. This suggests that patients were unable to use the context provided the first word to bias processing of the second word. Salisbury (Salisbury, O'Donnell, McCarley, Nestor, & Shenton, 2000) used a paradigm in which he presented four-word sentences to participants, of the form "THE *NOUN* WAS *ADJECTIVE/VERB.*" In this paradigm, the adjective or verb was always congruent with the noun. Controls showed significantly reduced N400s to the sentence final adjective/verbs as compared to the nouns presented earlier in the sentence, consistent with the idea that the controls use the noun to generate contextual representations that can help facilitate processing of consistent semantic information. However, the patients with schizophrenia did not show any reduction in N400 to the sentence final words as compared to the nouns, suggesting that patients were unable to either develop or use such contextual representations.

In more recent work, Sitnikova and colleagues (Sitnikova, Salisbury, Kuperberg, & Holcomb, 2002) examined N400s in a paradigm involving two clause sentences. The first clause ended with a homograph that had asymmetrical meanings (a dominant meaning and a subordinate meaning), and the second clause started with a strong semantic associate of the dominant meaning of the homograph. On half the trials, the first clause biased the dominant meaning of the homograph (so that the second clause should be consistent and not elicit an N400). On the other half of the trials, the first clause biased the subordinate meaning of the homograph (so that the second clause should be inconsistent and should elicit an N400). The control participants demonstrated reliably larger N400s in the inconsistent second-clause condition as compared to the consistent second-clause condition. This suggests that controls were able to use the context in the first clause to facilitate processing of the subordinate meaning of the homograph and suppress the dominant meaning. In contrast, the patients with schizophrenia showed a significantly smaller N400 than controls to the dominant meaning of the homograph when it followed a context that should have biased the subordinate meaning, and in fact showed no differences in N400 to consistent and inconsistent second clauses (for related studies, see (Adams et al., 1993; Niznikiewicz et al., 1997; Ohta, Uchiyama, Matsushima, & Toru, 1999; Olichney, Iragui, Kutas, Nowacki, & Jeste, 1997; Strandburgh et al., 1997; Titone, Holzman, & Levy, 2002; Titone, Levy, & Holzman, 2000)). Again, such results suggest that the patients with schizophrenia were less able to use the context provided by the first part of the sentence to bias ongoing processing. Of note, we do not mean to imply that we think the N400 itself is necessarily generated by the same context representation and maintenance processes that support AX-CPT task performance. However, variations in the N400 (and the cognitive processes generating this ERP component) may be influenced by the integrity of such context representation mechanisms. If so, then examining variations in the N400 may allow one to make inference about context representation and maintenance processes that modulate the types of integration or semantic process that give rise to the N400.

Studies in the domain of selective attention have also been used as evidence for deficits in context processing. For example, a number of studies using the color–word Stroop task found that individuals with schizophrenia are less able to inhibit the prepotent response to read the word, as evidenced by increased errors in the incongruent condition (color and word conflict) or by an increase in the total Stroop effect in RT (Barch et al., 1999; Barch, Carter, Hachten, & Cohen, 1999; Carter et al., 1992; Chen, Wong, Chen, & Au, 2001; Cohen et al., 1999; Elvevåg et al., 2000; Henik et al., 2002; Taylor, Kornblum, & Tandon, 1996). Further, in recent work, we used the process dissociation techniques developed by Jacoby to estimate the contributions of both word naming and color reading to Stroop performance in schizophrenia and found that color reading estimates are reduced whereas word reading estimates increased (Barch, Carter, & Cohen, in press). As described previously, our theory posits that task instructions to attend to color and ignore words serve as context representations in the Stroop tasks that normally allow one to inhibit the tendency to read words. Thus, we argued that Stroop task deficits in schizophrenia are consistent with a deficit in context processing.

Silverstein and colleagues suggested that deficits in context processing and contextual integration among individuals with schizophrenia extend even to the level of basic perceptual processing. (Silverstein et al., 2000). It is not yet clear whether the type of contextual processing measured in these paradigms is the same as that measured in tasks such as AX-CPT. However, such results raise the intriguing possibility that deficits in context processing account for deficits among individuals with schizophrenia both on high-level cognitive tasks and in more basic sensory and perceptual domains.

## INTERRELATIONSHIP OF CONTEXT PROCESSING AND OTHER COGNITIVE CONSTRUCTS

As noted earlier, one of our hypotheses is that deficits in context processing serve as a common underlying impairment across a wide variety of cognitive domains, including working memory, inhibition/selective attention, and language processing. To test this hypothesis, we conducted a study in which we administered several different tasks to individuals with schizophrenia, along with healthy controls and depressed individuals (see Figure 6.5) (Cohen et al., 1999). We picked tasks that had traditionally been associated with different cognitive domains: (a) working memory with the AX-CPT; (b) inhibition/selective attention with the color–word Stroop; and (c) language processing with a lexical disambiguation task. However, each of the tasks included similar manipulations designed to increase their reliance on context representation and maintenance. As shown in Figure 6.5, each task included some type of contextual cue, a prepotency manipulation (either naturally occurring or induced in the task), and a delay manipulation (between the context and the need to use the context). The AX-CPT task was administered as described earlier. The Stroop task was modified to be a "switching" Stroop in which trials randomly

## Context Tasks

In each task, there was:
1) a delay between the cue (context) and response
2) an asymmetry in the relative prepotency of competing responses

| Task | Context | Prepotency | Delay |
|------|---------|------------|-------|
| AX-CPT | "A" or "Not-A" cue | 70% Target (A-X) Sequences | 1 or 5 sec cue-probe interval |
| Stroop | Word Reading or Color Naming Instruction | Word Reading more prepotent than color naming | 1 or 5 sec cue-stimulus interval |
| Lexical Disambig-uation | Sentence that biases a dominant or subordinate completion **Example:** race/rage ("ra_e") **Race:** Fred and Bob dashed to the finish line in a tie. **Rage:** Fred and Bob had bad tempers and often became quite angry. | One completion of an item ("ra_e") more frequent (race) in the absence of context than other completion (rage) | Sentence order, either: neutral -> Bias or bias -> Neutral |

FIGURE 6.5. Description of the tasks and manipulations of context representation and delay (Cohen et al., 1999).

alternated from color-naming to word-reading, with the type of trial indicated by a cue (i.e., context) that occurred at the start of each trial. Thus, participants needed to use the context provided by this cue to inhibit the tendency to read the word on color naming trials and needed to update this context information on a trial-by-trial basis. In addition, we manipulated the delay between the cue and the onset of the stimulus in order to assess maintenance of context. In the lexical disambiguation task, participants were presented with words missing one letter that could be completed in one of two ways, with one completion occurring more frequently than another (in the general population). These "missing letter" stimuli were preceded by sentences that could bias the participant toward the more dominant completion or toward the less frequent completion. As such, participants needed to use the context provided by the preceding sentences to modulate the tendency to complete the letter strings with the dominant versus subordinate completion. As with the other two tasks, we also manipulated the delay between this contextual information and the occurrence of the missing letter stimuli to assess context maintenance.

The results of this study indicated that, for the most part, individuals with schizophrenia were impaired across all three cognitive domains and tasks in the conditions that we would argue most strongly tap the need to represent and maintain context information. For example, the patients with schizophrenia again demonstrated increased "BX" errors as compared to the controls, but no increased AY errors, as well as no increased "AX" errors, especially with a long delay. On the Stroop task, the patients with schizophrenia demonstrated significantly more errors than did the controls, particularly in the incongruent condition of the color naming task, the condition we argue is most dependent on context processing. On the lexical disambiguation task, the individuals with schizophrenia demonstrated a clear pattern indicative of impaired context processing, which included: (a) demonstrating the same asymmetry in production of the dominant versus subordinate completions as the controls in the absence of any biasing context; (b) the production of fewer subordinate completions, particularly with a long delay, when the sentence context should have biased such completions; and (c) the production of fewer dominant completions than controls when the sentence context should have biased them toward such completions (ruling out the possibility that patients simply had a dominant response bias). More importantly, however, were the results of the analyses examining cross-task relationships. We found that among the total sample and just within the individuals with schizophrenia, performance on each of the three tasks in conditions dependent on context processing were strongly and selectively interrelated, whereas performance on conditions not dependent on context (but psychometrically matched) were not related. Such results provide support for the hypothesis that deficits in a wide variety of cognitive domains in schizophrenia may result from disturbances in contextual processing.

In other studies, we also found that performance on tasks specifically designed to measure context processing, such as the AX-CPT, are strongly correlated with performance on tasks measuring other cognitive processes, which we would argue are also dependent on context processing. For example, in a large sample of healthy younger and older adults, we found that performance on the AX-CPT was correlated with performance on a number of standard measures of working memory, including the reading span, a highly demanding digit span, and an "N-back" task (Keys, Barch, Braver, & Janowsky, submitted). In the study described previously with individuals who have schizotypal personality disorder, we found that AX-CPT performance was strongly correlated with performance on an "N-Back" task, which measures working memory, and on an Eriksson Flanker task, which measures selective attention (Barch et al., in press). Again, such findings are consistent with the hypothesis that deficits in context processing may contribute to disturbances in a variety of related cognitive domains.

THE NEUROBIOLOGY OF CONTEXT PROCESSING

We hypothesized that the representation and maintenance of context processing are subserved by a specific set of neural mechanisms. In particular, we postulate that representations of context information are housed within the dorsolateral portion of the prefrontal cortex (DL-PFC) and actively maintained there when task demands require such active maintenance (O'Reilly, Braver, & Cohen, 1999). Further, we hypothesize that the dopamine (DA) projections to DL-PFC regulate the access to such context information, insulating this information from the interfering effects of noise over intervals in which the information must be sustained, while at the same time allowing for the appropriate updating of such context information when needed (Braver & Cohen, 2000). These hypotheses are consistent with the broader neuroscience literature, in which active maintenance in the service of control is a commonly ascribed function to PFC (Fuster, 1989; Goldman-Rakic, 1987; Miller & Cohen, 2001), and the DA system is widely held to modulate the active maintenance properties of PFC (Cohen, Braver, & Brown, 2002; Luciana, Collins, & Depue, 1998; Sawaguchi, Matsumura, & Kubota, 1990; Williams & Goldman-Rakic, 1995). In our model, the context processing functions of cognitive control critically depend upon DL-PFC and DA system interactions. As a consequence, the model predicts that individuals and populations with impairments in either or both DL-PFC or the DA system should demonstrate specific patterns of impaired cognitive control related to the processing of context.

## ROLE OF PREFRONTAL CORTEX

As noted above, a large number of functional neuroimaging studies have demonstrated that prefrontal cortex is activated when individuals have to maintain information in working memory (Cabeza & Nyberg, 2000). However, the majority of these studies used tasks that may or may not tap context processing, and they were not specifically designed to selectively measure context processing. However, we and our colleagues conducted a number of neuroimaging studies using tasks, such as the AX-CPT and the switching Stroop, that were specifically designed to measure context processing. For example, our early research with the AX-CPT demonstrated that dorsolateral PFC and ventrolateral PFC showed selective increases in activity when context representations had to be maintained over a long delay as compared to short delay (Barch et al., 1997; Braver & Cohen, 2001). In contrast, these same PFC regions did not show increased activity when the AX-CPT task was made more difficult by degrading the stimuli (but not changing maintenance demands). This suggests that dorsolateral PFC regions are not simply activated whenever the task gets more challenging, although the anterior cingulate did respond to this difficulty manipulation, leading to subsequent research on the role of the anterior cingulate in conflict detection (Botvinick et al., 2001). Such findings dissociating the control processes subserved by the dorsolateral PFC relative to other brain regions (such as the anterior cingulate) have been replicated by other studies as well (MacDonald, Cohen, Stenger, & Carter, 2000). Of interest, the only brain regions to show a sustained increase in activity when required to maintain context information were the dorsolateral and ventrolateral PFC regions. This is in contrast to the patterns of brain activity often found during working memory tasks, which is typically much more widespread, including regions such as the parietal cortex, frontomedial motor regions, and other subcortical regions (e.g., cerebellum, basal ganglia). We argued that this selective responsivity of PFC regions to the context maintenance manipulation provides strong support for their central role in supporting this particular component of cognitive control.

We also examined how challenging context processing in healthy individuals alters task-related PFC activity. For example, we developed a version of the AX-CPT in which participants are presented with distractor items during the delay between the cue and the probe. Our hypothesis was that if deficits on the AX-CPT among individuals with schizophrenia were due to disturbances in the ability to maintain context information, disturbing the ability to maintain context information in healthy adults should elicit the same types of task deficits as found in individuals with schizophrenia. Consistent with this hypothesis, we found that adding distractors during the delay between the cue and the probe in the long-delay conditions of the AX-CPT increased the number of "BX" errors (and slowed "BX" RTs) that healthy participants made, but *decreased* the number of "AY" errors, consistent with a reduced ability to use context information. In a subsequent functional neuroimaging study using the same task design, we found that the addition of distractions and impairments in task performance was accompanied by a selective decrease in dorsolateral PFC activity but no change or even an increase in ventrolateral PFC activity (Braver & Cohen, 2001). The results of this study and others have provided some clues about the different contributions that dorsolateral versus ventrolateral PFC play in context processing. More specifically, we argued that ventrolateral regions of PFC may serve a more general role in phonological processing or rehearsal that may in no way be selective or specific to context representations, an idea put forth by many other researchers as well. In contrast, it may be that dorsolateral PFC (particularly in the left hemisphere) may be more specifically involved in the development and/or maintenance of context representations.

We also examined the patterns of brain activity found in individuals with schizophrenia during the performance of tasks such as the AX-CPT. In one such study, medication naïve first episode individuals with schizophrenia and controls were presented with trials that had either a short- or a long-delay period between the cue and the probe (Barch et al., 2001). The trials were designed so that four images of the brain were acquired during each trial, allowing us to glean some rough information about the time course

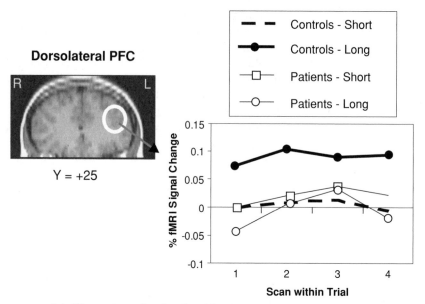

FIGURE 6.6. Illustration of task-related brain activity in dorsolateral PFC during the AX-CPT. The image displays a coronal slice through the brain 25 mm anterior to the anterior commissure plane. The graph illustrated percent fMRI signal change during each scan of the trial, relative to the first scan of the short delay condition, for each group in each condition.

of brain activity during context maintenance. As shown in Figure 6.6, the healthy controls once again demonstrated a sustained increase in dorsolateral PFC activity during the long as compared to short-delay condition. However, the medication naïve individuals with schizophrenia did not show any significant increased in dorsolateral PFC activity in response to the context maintenance demand. In contrast, as shown in Figure 6.7, the individuals with schizophrenia did show increased delay related activity in ventrolateral PFC regions, activity that did not differ in magnitude from controls. Again, this provides evidence for the fact that dorsolateral and ventrolateral regions of PFC play different roles in context processing and are differentially impaired in schizophrenia.

Such findings of impaired dorsolateral PFC activity during the performance of context processing tasks have now been replicated several times, in chronic and in first episode patients (MacDonald, in press; Perlstein, Dixit, Carter, Noll, & Cohen, 2003). Further, recent research suggests that such dorsolateral PFC deficits are specific to individuals with schizophrenia as compared to individuals with other psychotic disorders, who show a different pattern of potentially increased dorsolateral PFC activity (MacDonald et al., in submission).

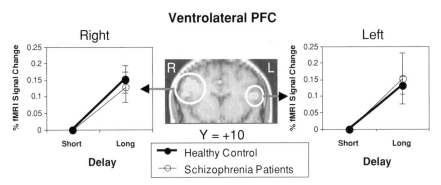

FIGURE 6.7. Illustration of task-related brain activity in ventrolateral PFC during the AX-CPT. The image displays a coronal slice through the brain 10 mm anterior to the anterior commissure plane. The graphs for both the left and right ventrolateral regions display the increase in task-related brain activity from the short- to the long-delay condition.

ROLE OF DOPAMINE

As described above, our models also postulate a central role for dopamine in context processing and hypothesize that impaired dopamine function in dorsolateral PFC contributes to context processing deficits. There is a large body of evidence in nonhuman primates and humans suggesting that dopamine plays an important role in working memory more generally (Arnsten, Cai, Murphy, & Goldman-Rakic, 1994; Barch, in press; Brozoski, Brown, Rosvold, & Goldman, 1979; Cai & Arnsten, 1997; Castner, Williams, & Goldman-Rakic, 2000; de Sonneville, Njiokiktjien, & Bos, 1994; Goldman-Rakic, 1995; Kimberg & D'Esposito, 2003; Kimberg, D'Esposito, & Farah, 1997; Luciana & Collins, 1997; Luciana, Collins, & Depue, 1995; Luciana et al., 1998; Luciana, Depue, Arbisi, & Leon, 1992; Mattay et al., 1996; Mattay et al., 2000; Mattay et al., 2003; Mehta et al., 2000; Mehta, Swainson, Gogilvie, Sahakian, & Robbins, 2001; Mintzer & Griffiths, 2003; Muller, von Cramon, & Pollmann, 1998; Sawaguchi & Goldman-Rakic, 1994; Williams & Goldman-Rakic, 1995). This includes evidence that non-specific dopamine agonists, such as amphetamine, can improve working memory in medicated patients with schizophrenia (Barch & Carter, in preparation; Daniel et al., 1991; Goldberg, Bigelow, Weinberger, Daniel, & Kleinman, 1991) and that changes in $D_1$ receptor availability in DLPFC are associated with working memory impairment in schizophrenia (Abi-Dargham et al., 2002). Unfortunately, however, there is little direct evidence yet for a role for dopamine specifically in context processing in humans, as compared to working memory more generally. However, we have recently completed a double-blind placebo controlled study examining the influence of d-amphetamine on AX-CPT performance in healthy individuals.

In this study we used both our standard version of the AX-CPT and the "interference" version described previously, in which distractors appeared between the cue and the probe. As noted earlier, including such distractors normally elicits a pattern of performance in controls analogous to that found in schizophrenia (e.g., increased "BX" errors and RT; decreased "AY" errors). Participants were 12 healthy controls who participated in two experimental sessions spaced no more than one week apart. In each session, participants performed both the baseline and interference conditions. At each session, participants were orally administered either placebo or D-AMP, at a dosage of 0.25 mg/kg of body weight, at the beginning of the session. The drug on each day was administered in a double-blind manner (with an unlabeled opaque capsule), and drug order was randomly counterbalanced across participants. Because D-AMP effects peak after one to two hours, and are stable over the following one to two hours (Angrist, Corwin, Barlett, & Cooper, 1987) participants were tested approximately two hours postingestion. To analyze the data, we examined a measure of context sensitivity that we refer to as d'-context, a signal-to-noise measure comparing hits to "AX" trials and false alarms to "BX" trials. As shown in Figure 6.8, we found that under placebo, the addition of distractors during the cue-probe period of long-delay trials reduced sensitivity to context, as indexed by a reduced d'-context (e.g., increased "AX" misses and "BX" false alarms). However, this effect was significantly reduced with d-amphetamine. More specifically, there was a significant main effect of d-amphetamine on d'-context ($F(1,11) = 6.41$, $p < .05$) and a significant drug $\times$ condition interaction ($F(1,11) = 6.31$, $p < .05$). Planned contrasts revealed that under placebo, context sensitivity was reduced in the interference condition ($F(1,11) = 18.39$, $p < .01$), but that there was no significant difference between the two conditions under D-AMP ($F(1,11) = 0.32$, $p > .10$) (see Figure 6.8). Results of studies such as this provide some more specific evidence for a relationship between dopamine function and context processing, at least in healthy individuals.

On a related note, the finding that dopaminergic agents can influence context processing may help to shed light on the mechanisms that by which stress influences working memory. In another chapter in this book, Sliwinski and colleagues review evidence that higher perceived levels of stress are associated with cognitive impairment, particularly impaired working memory, on both a between-person basis (i.e., comparing individuals with high and low levels of perceived stress) and a within-person basis (i.e., comparing times with high and low perceived stress within the same person). Sliwinski and colleagues put forth the hypothesis that this relationship may reflect that fact that individuals coping with a stressor may use cognitive resources to suppress stress-related thoughts, leaving fewer resources available for other cognitive tasks. However, stress is also known to alter dopamine function, at least acutely, and some animal research has shown a

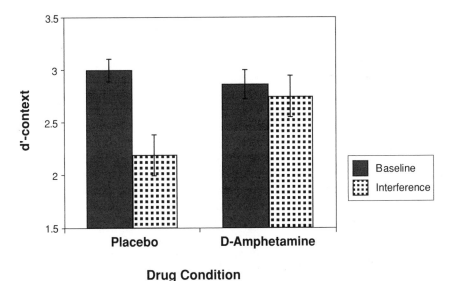

FIGURE 6.8. Graph illustrating change in d'-context as a function of adding interfering distractors, both under placebo and under d-amphetamine.

detrimental impact of stress on working memory via dopaminergic mechanisms in prefrontal cortex (Arnsten & Goldman-Rakic, 1998). As such, it is possible that stress influences working memory, and potentially context processing, via disruption of the dopamine system. This hypothesis is not meant to be an alternative to the one put forth by Sliwinski, but rather may provide a different level of explanation for the same mechanism.

## RELATIONSHIP OF CONTEXT PROCESSING TO CLINICAL SYMPTOMS IN SCHIZOPHRENIA

One important question that arises when discussing context processing deficits in schizophrenia is whether such disturbances are present in all individuals with schizophrenia with equal severity, or whether the severity of such context processing deficits are related to the severity of specific symptoms. We and others found that context processing deficits in schizophrenia appear to be strongly related to the severity of a constellation of behaviors referred to as disorganization symptoms, which include disorganized behavior (dressing in an unusual manner, behaving oddly in public), attentional problems, and difficulties in producing goal directed speech (e.g., loose associations (Barch et al., 1999; Barch & Carter, 1998; Barch et al., 2003; Cohen et al., 1999; MacDonald et al., in submission; Perlstein, Carter, Noll, & Cohen, 2001; Perlstein et al., 2003; Stratta et al., 2000). Such findings are interesting in light of research suggesting that representations of context information are important for guiding coherent ongoing language production (Levelt, 1989). Further, such associations are consistent with the research reviewed above, suggesting that impairments in language comprehension, homograph interpretation/meaning selection, and semantic priming may be related to impairments in the ability to use or maintain contextual information.

More recently, we also found some evidence that deficits in context processing may also be related to disturbances in the ability to regulate the influence of emotion on cognitive processing in schizophrenia. More specifically, we found that individuals with impaired context processing show greater language production disruptions (in the form of unclear references) when discussing affectively negative as compared to affective neutral topics (Burbridge & Barch, 2002). There is a growing literature in affective neuroscience examining the role that different cognitive control functions play in emotional regulation and the role that dorsolateral PFC plays in emotional regulation (Gray, 2001; Gray, Braver, & Raichle, 2002; Ochsner, Bunge, Gross, & Gabrieli, 2002). One hypothesis is that intact representations of context are also important for the regulation of emotionbecause such information provides clues as to what emotional responses are appropriate in given situations and a means by which to alter emotional responses that are not compatible with current task demands. As such, it will be interesting in future research to examine the role that the representation and maintenance of context plays in successful emotional regulation and the potential influence of disordered context processing on disturbed emotional functioning in disorders such as schizophrenia.

## CONTEXT PROCESSING IN OTHER POPULATIONS

Individuals with schizophrenia are not the only population thought to experience changes in prefrontal function that may be associated with changes in dopamine function. For example, individuals with Parkinson's disease are known to have disturbances in dopamine function and disturbances in tasks designed to measure working memory and other aspects of cognitive control (Zgaljardic, Borod, Foldi, & Mattis, 2003). In addition, individuals with attention deficit hyperactivity disorder are thought to suffer from disturbances in dopamine function and prefrontal function and again show deficits on a range of cognitive control tasks (Casey et al., 1997; Aron, Dowson, Sahakian, & Robbins, 2003; Nigg, 2003). Of interest, healthy older adults represent a nonpathological population that also experiences cognitive control problems that may be related to changes in prefrontal and dopamine function. For example, a growing body of work suggests that healthy aging involves systematic changes in prefrontal function as measured by functional imaging techniques (Cabeza, 2001; Grady, 1998) and involves changes in cognitive functions thought to be associated with prefrontal function (Balota, Dolan, & Duchek, 2000; Jacoby, Debner, & Hay, 2001), both of which may be associated with changes in dopamine function with aging (Arnsten et al., 1994; Arnsten, Cai, Steere, & Goldman-Rakic, 1995; de Keyser, De Backer, Vauquelin, & Ebinger, 1990; Goldman-Rakic & Brown, 1981; Suhara et al., 1991; Volkow et al., 1998)). Further, in many ways, the types of cognitive deficits shown by healthy older individuals are very similar to those found in individuals with schizophrenia. The chapter by West and Bowry in this volume nicely articulates many of the types of cognitive deficits shown by healthy older adults, which are similar to deficits seen in individuals with schizophrenia, For example, both individuals with schizophrenia and healthy older adults show increased incongruent errors in the Stroop and an increased total Stroop effect in RT (Spieler, Balota, & Faust, 1996; Verhaeghen & De Meersman, 1998; West & Baylis, 1998), and both populations have more difficulties with color naming in a switching Stroop that varies the task to be performed on a trial-by-trial basis, as compared to blocked trials of color naming (Cohen et al., 1999; West, in press). Similar to our interpretations of the source of these deficits in schizophrenia, West attributed such Stroop task deficit in healthy older adults to disturbances in context processing.

We directly studied context processing and related functions in healthy aging (e.g., working memory, inhibition) and also found evidence that healthy older adults show deficits in context processing (Braver et al., 2001), which are strongly correlated with deficits in measures of working memory and inhibition (Keys et al., submitted). For example, in recent work, we found that healthy young-older adults (ages 65 to 75) show deficits in context representation, in the form of increased "BX" RTs as compared to younger adults, but not increased "AY" RTS (Braver, Satpute, Keys, & Racine, in press). Further, healthy much older adults (76+) demonstrated additional deficits in context maintenance, in that their "BX" worsened as a function of delay, while "AY" performance improved.

RELATIONSHIPS AMONG ANTERIOR CINGULATE, DOPAMINE FUNCTION, AND COGNITIVE CONTROL

In addition, West and others examined additional components of cognitive control in healthy aging, such as error processing as indexed by an ERP component referred to as the error related negativity (ERN). The ERN is thought to index either error monitoring and/or correction (Falkenstein, Hohnsbein, Hoorman, & Blanke, 1991; Falkenstein, Hoorman, Christ, & Hohnsbein, 2000; Gehring, Goss, Coles, Meyer, & Donchin, 1993) or conflict processing (Botvinick et al., 2001), critical components of cognitive control. A number of researchers believe that one of the main generators of the ERN is the anterior cingulate, and that alterations in the ERN may also reflect changes in dopamine function in the anterior cingulate (Botvinick et al., 2001; Holroyd & Coles, 2002). As reviewed by West, the amplitude of the ERN is reduced in healthy older adults across a wide range of task paradigms (Band & Kok, 2000; Falkenstein, Hoorman, & Hohnbein, 2001; Nieuwenhuis et al., 2002; West, in press), a finding consistent with the research on reduced dopamine function in healthy aging. Similarly, a growing number of studies also suggest reduced ERNs in individuals with schizophrenia, even when there are no behavioral differences in conditions thought to be associated with increased conflict (Alain, McNeely, Yu, Christensen, & West, 2002; Bates, Kiehl, Laurens, & Liddle, 2002; Carter, MacDonald III, Ross, & Stenger, 2001; Kopp & Rist, 1999) and decreased anterior cingulate activity, a potential generator of the ERN (Carter et al., 2001). Again, such results in schizophrenia may reflect abnormalities in dopamine function, which influences anterior cingulate and dorsolateral PFC function. Such results suggest that both individuals with schizophrenia and healthy older adults may experience deficits in error monitoring/ conflict processing and deficits in context processing.

Despite the many similarities in the profiles of cognitive disturbances shown by individuals with schizophrenia and healthy older adults, there are also intriguing differences. For example, in studies of context processing in healthy older adults using the AX-CPT task, deficits in at least the young-older adults are apparent primarily in RTs rather than errors. In contrast, individuals with schizophrenia manifest context-processing deficits in both errors and RTs on the AX-CPT. In the Stroop task, research examining process-dissociation estimates of color naming and word reading has found increased word reading estimates in older adults, but no changes in color naming estimates (Spieler et al., 1996). In contrast, in schizophrenia, we have found both increased word reading and decreased color naming estimates (Barch et al., in press). In addition, as noted by West, studies of healthy aging populations have not found increased correct trial related negativities in ERP studies (referred to as the CRN; Band & Kok, 2000; Falkenstein et al., 2001; West, in press), whereas studies of schizophrenia have reported such increased CRNs (Alain et al., 2002; Mathalon et al., 2002). One argument is that increased CRNs reflect additional conflict because of inadequate goal representations or context representations that normally serve to reduce conflict in information processing. These differences in the performance of individuals with schizophrenia and healthy older adults suggest that although these two populations may share some common cognitive and neurobiological disturbances, there are also important differences. For example, one possibility is that the severity of context processing deficits is simply worse in individuals with schizophrenia as compared to healthy adults. Such a hypotheses would be consistent with the fact that individuals with schizophrenia show problems in both errors and RTs and alterations in both color and word processing estimates (alterations in only word processing estimates among older adults might reflect a less severe disturbance). However, it is somewhat less clear why a less severe context processing deficit would lead to reductions only in the ERN and not the CRN, as compared to the concurrent reductions in the ERN and the CRN found in schizophrenia. Future research more directly comparing the performance of individuals with schizophrenia and healthy older adults in the same exact paradigms may help clarify some of these issues and better delineate the similarities and differences in the profiles of cognitive disturbances found in these two populations.

It is not necessarily surprising that both individuals with schizophrenia and healthy older individuals show similar patterns of cognitive deficits if both populations experience changes in prefrontal function associated with dopamine changes. Although the source of the prefrontal cortex and dopamine changes in schizophrenia and healthy aging may be very different, it may still be the case that a final common pathway of changes in prefrontal function leads to somewhat similar cognitive deficits in schizophrenia and healthy aging. However, at the same time, it also clear that there are many differences between individuals with schizophrenia and healthy older adults, both in the severity of their cognitive deficits and the associated symptoms and phenomenology found in schizophrenia. Such differences may reflect several factors. First, many researchers believe that at least some aspects of the neurobiological pathology found in schizophrenia are neurodevelopmental in origin and are thus present throughout the life span. In contrast, changes in prefrontal function in healthy older adults may begin to occur much later in life, with intact prefrontal function early in life. The eventual outcome of neurodevelopmental changes in prefrontal function may be very different than changes that occur only later in life, because such prefrontal changes could then influence the course of learning, skill acquisition, and cognitive development in individuals with schizophrenia, which may have additional contributions to the profile of cognitive disturbances found in schizophrenia. Second, it is unlikely that changes in prefrontal cortex and dopamine function are the only neurobiological disturbances found in schizophrenia. As such, the interaction of multiple sources of neurobiological and cognitive abnormalities in schizophrenia may contribute to many of the cognitive deficits/symptoms found in schizophrenia that are not present in healthy aging (although healthy aging also may involves changes in brain regions other than prefrontal cortex).

## SUMMARY

In this chapter, we described our theory regarding one component of cognitive control, the representation and maintenance of context, that we argue is important for the ongoing control of thoughts, behaviors, and emotion. We argued that this particular component of cognitive control is supported by dopamine function in dorsolateral prefrontal cortex. As described in more detail above, this theory regarding cognitive control is highly consistent with the theories put forth by a number of authors of other chapters in this volume, including the ideas put forth by Engle, West, Sliwinski and their colleagues. Further, we argued that populations that experience disturbances in either or both dopamine function and dorsolateral prefrontal cortex function experience deficits in the processing of context, and we reviewed empirical data supporting this assertion. One important area for future research will be to better delineate the similarities and difference in the profiles of cognitive and neurobiological disturbances across populations thought to suffer from disturbances in prefrontal and dopamine function. By better understanding the relationships between specific types of cognitive control deficits and particular kinds of neurobiological disturbances, we can better validate, modify, and/or expand theories regarding the neurobiology of cognitive control. We have also suggested that the processes involved in the representation and maintenance of context may play a critical role in emotion regulation, though considerably more empirical and theoretical work is needed to examine this hypothesis.

## Author Note

Research was supported by grants from the National Alliance for Research on Schizophrenia and Depression, the Dana Foundation, and the National Institute of Mental Health.

## References

Abi-Dargham, A., Mawlawi, O., Lombardo, I., Gil, R., Martinez, D., Huang, Y., et al. (2002). Prefrontal dopamine D1 receptors and working memory in schizophrenia. *Journal of Neuroscience, 22,* 3708–3719.

Adams, J., Fauz, S. F., Nestor, P. G., Shenton, M. E., Marcy, B., Smith, S. R., et al. (1993). ERP abnormalities during semantic processing in schizophrenia. *Schizophrenia Research, 10,* 247–257.

Alain, C., McNeely, H. E., Yu, H., Christensen, B. K., & West, R. (2002). Neurophysiological evidence of error monitoring deficits in patients with schizophrenia. *Cerebral Cortex, 12,* 840–846.

Angrist, B., Corwin, J., Barlett, B., & Cooper, T. (1987). Early pharmacokinetics and clinical effects of oral d-amphetamine in normal subjects. *Biological Psychiatry, 22,* 1357–1368.

Arnsten, A. F., Cai, J. X., Murphy, B. L., & Goldman-Rakic, P. S. (1994). Dopamine D1 receptor mechanisms in the cognitive performance of young adult and aged monkeys. *Psychopharmacology, 116,* 143–151.

Arnsten, A. F., Cai, J. X., Steere, J. C., & Goldman-Rakic, P. S. (1995). Dopamine D2 receptor mechanisms contribute to age-related cognitive decline: the effects of quinpirole on memory and motor function in monkeys. *Journal of Neuroscience, 15*, 3429–3439.

Arnsten, A. F., & Goldman-Rakic, P. S. (1998). Noise stress impairs prefrontal cortical cognitive function in monkeys: Evidence for a hyperdopaminergic mechanism. *Archives of General Psychiatry, 55*, 362–368.

Aron, A. R., Dowson, J. H., Sahakian, B. J., & Robbins, T. W. (2003). Methylphenidate improves response inhibition in adults with attention-deficit/hyperactivity disorder. *Biological Psychiatry, 54*, 1465–1468.

Baddeley, A. (1994). The magical number seven: Still magic after all these years. *Psychological Review, 101*, 353–356.

Baddeley, A. (1996). Exploring the central executive. *Quarterly Journal of Experimental Psychology, 49*, 5–28.

Baddeley, A. D. (1986). *Working memory*. New York: Oxford University Press.

Baddeley, A. D. (1993). Working memory or working attention? In A. D. Baddeley & L. Weiskrantz (Eds.), *Attention: Selection, awareness, and control: A tribute to Donald Broadbent* (pp. 152–170). Oxford: Clarendon Press.

Baddeley, A. D. (2000). The episodic buffer: A new component of working memory? *Trends in Cognitive Science, 4*, 417–423.

Baddeley, A. D., & Hitch, G. J. (1994). Developments in the concept of working memory. *Neuropsychology, 8*, 485–493.

Baddeley, A. D., & Logie, R. H. (1999). Working memory: The multiple-component model. In A. Miyake & P. Shah (Eds.), *Models of working memory: Mechanisms of active maintenance and executive control* (pp. 28–61). Cambridge: Cambridge University Press.

Balota, D. A., Dolan, P. O., & Duchek, J. M. (2000). Memory changes in healthy older adults. In E. Tulving & F. I. M. Craik (Eds.), *The Oxford handbook of memory* (pp. 395–409). New York: Oxford University Press.

Band, G., & Kok, A. (2000). Age effects on response monitoring in a mental rotation task. *Biological Psychology, 51*, 201–221.

Barch, D. M. (in press). Pharmacological manipulations of human working memory. *Psychopharmacology*.

Barch, D. M., Braver, T. S., Akbudak, E., Conturo, T., Ollinger, J., & Snyder, A. V. (2001). Anterior cingulate cortex and response conflict: Effects of response modality and processing domain. *Cerebral Cortex, 11*, 837–848.

Barch, D. M., Braver, T. S., Nystom, L. E., Forman, S. D., Noll, D. C., & Cohen, J. D. (1997). Dissociating working memory from task difficulty in human prefrontal cortex. *Neuropsychologia, 35*, 1373–1380.

Barch, D. M., & Carter, C. S. (1998). Selective attention in schizophrenia: Relationship to verbal working memory. *Schizophrenia Research, 33*, 53–61.

Barch, D. M., & Carter, C. S. (in preparation). *The influence of d-amphetamine on cognition and language in medicated patients with schizophrenia*. Manuscript in preparation.

Barch, D. M., Carter, C. S., Braver, T. S., McDonald, A., Sabb, F. W., Noll, D. C., et al. (2001). Selective deficits in prefrontal cortex regions in medication naive schizophrenia patients. *Archives of General Psychiatry, 50*, 280–288.

Barch, D. M., Carter, C. S., & Cohen, J. D. (2003). Context processing deficit in schizophrenia: Diagnostic specificity, 4-week course, and relationships to clinical symptoms. *Journal of Abnormal Psychology, 112*, 132–143.

Barch, D. M., Carter, C. S., & Cohen, J. D. (in press). Process dissociation analyses of Stroop performance in schizophrenia. *Neuropsychology.*

Barch, D. M., Carter, C. S., Hachten, P. C., & Cohen (1999). The "benefits" of distractibility: The mechanisms underlying increased Stroop effects in schizophrenia. *Schizophrenia Bulletin, 24*, 749–762.

Barch, D. M., Carter, C., Perlstein, W., Baird, J., Cohen, J., & Schooler, N. (1999). Increased Stroop facilitation effects in schizophrenia are not due to increased automatic spreading activation. *Schizophrenia Research, 39*, 51–64.

Barch, D. M., Mitropoulou, V., Harvey, P. D., New, A. S., Silverman, J. M., & Siever, L. J. (in press). Context processing deficits in schizotypal personality disorder. *Journal of Abnormal Psychology.*

Bates, A. T., Kiehl, K. A., Laurens, K. R., & Liddle, P. F. (2002). Error-related negativity and correct response negativity in schizophrenia. *Clinical Neurophysiology, 113*, 1454–1463.

Botvinick, M. M., Braver, T. S., Barch, D. M., Carter, C. S., & Cohen, J. C. (2001). Conflict monitoring and cognitive control. *Psychological Review, 108*, 624–652.

Braver, T. S. (1997). *Mechanisms of cognitive control: A neurocomputational model.* Unpublished doctoral disseration, Carnegie Mellon University, Pittsburgh, PA.

Braver, T. S., Barch, D. M., & Cohen, J. D. (1999a). Cognition and control in schizophrenia: A computational model of dopamine and prefrontal function. *Biological Psychiatry, 46*, 312–328.

Braver, T. S., Barch, D. M., & Cohen, J. D. (1999b). *Mechanisms of cognitive control: Active memory, inhibition, and the prefrontal cortex* (Technical Report No. PDP.CNS.99.1). Pittsburgh PA: Carnegie Mellon University.

Braver, T. S., Barch, D. M., Keys, B. A., Carter, C. S., Cohen, J. D., Kaye, J. A., et al. (2001). Context processing in older adults: Evidence for a theory relating cognitive control to neurobiology in healthy aging. *Journal of Experimental Psychology: General, 130*, 746–763.

Braver, T. S., & Bongiolatti, S. R. (2002). The role of the frontopolar prefrontal cortex in subgoal processing during working memory. *NeuroImage, 15*, 523–536.

Braver, T. S., & Cohen, J. D. (1999). Dopamine, cognitive control, and schizophrenia: The gating model. *Progress in Brain Research, 121*, 327–349.

Braver, T. S., & Cohen, J. D. (2000). On the control of control: The role of dopamine in regulating prefrontal function and working memory. In S. Monsell & J. Driver (Eds.), *Attention and performance XVIII* (pp. 713–738). Cambridge, MA: MIT Press.

Braver, T. S., & Cohen, J. D. (2001). Working memory, cognitive control, and the prefrontal cortex: Computational and empirical studies. *Cognitive Processing, 2*, 25–55.

Braver, T. S., Cohen, J. D., & Barch, D. M. (2002). The role of the prefrontal cortex in normal and disordered cognitive control: A cognitive neuroscience perspective. In D. T. Stuss & R. T. Knight (Eds.), *Principles of Frontal Lobe Function* (pp. 428–448). Oxford: Oxford University Press.

Braver, T. S., Cohen, J. D., & McClelland, J. L. (1997). *An integrated computational model of dopamine function in reinforcement learning and working memory.* Paper presented at the Society for Neuroscience Abstracts, New Orleans.

Braver, T. S., Cohen, J. D., & Servan-Schreiber, D. (1995). Neural network simulations of schizophrenic performance in a variant of the CPT-AX: A predicted double dissociation. *Schizophrenia Research, 15,* 110.

Braver, T. S., Satpute, A. B., Keys, B. A., & Racine, C. A. (in press). Context processing and context maintenance in healthy aging and early-stage dementia of the Alzheimer's type. *Psychology and Aging.*

Brown, C., & Hagoort, P. (1993). The processing nature of the N400: evidence from masked priming. *Journal of Cognitive Neuroscience, 5,* 34–44.

Brozoski, T. J., Brown, R. M., Rosvold, H. E., & Goldman, P. S. (1979). Cognitive deficit caused by regional depletion of dopamine in prefrontal cortex of rhesus monkey. *Science, 205,* 929–931.

Burbridge, J., & Barch, D. M. (2002). Emotional valence and reference disturbance in schizophrenia. *Journal of Abnormal Psychology, 111,* 186–191.

Burgess, G. C., & Braver, T. S. (submitted). *Proactive interference effects on working memory can be modulated by expectancy: Evidence for dual mechanisms of cognitive control.* Manuscript submitted for publication.

Cabeza, R. (2001). Functional neuroimaging of cognitive aging. In R. Cabeza & A. Kingstone (Eds.), *Handbook of functional neuroimaging of cognition.* Cambridge, MA: MIT Press.

Cabeza, R., & Nyberg, L. (2000). Imaging cognition II: An empirical review of 275 PET and fMRI studies. *Journal of Cognitive Neuroscience, 12,* 1–47.

Cai, J. X., & Arnsten, A. F. T. (1997). Dose-dependent effects of the dopamine D1 receptor agonists A77636 or SKF81297 on spatial working memory in aged monkeys. *The journal of pharmacology and experimental therapeutics, 283,* 183–189.

Carter, C. S., MacDonald III, A. W., Ross, L. L., & Stenger, V. A. (2001). Anterior cingulate cortex activity and impaired self-monitoring of performance in patients with schizophrenia: an event-related fMRI study. *American Journal of Psychiatry, 158,* 1423–1428.

Carter, C. S., Robertson, L. C., & Nordahl, T. E. (1992). Abnormal processing of irrelevant information in schizophrenia: Selective enhancement of Stroop facilitation. *Psychiatry Research, 41,* 137–146.

Casey, B. J., Castellanos, F. X., Giedd, J. N., Marsh, W. L., Hamburger, S. D., Schubert, A. B., et al. (1997). Implication of right frontostrial circuitry in response inhibition an attention-deficit/hyperactivity disorder. *Journal of the American Academy of Child & Adolescent Psychiatry, 36,*

Castner, S. A., Williams, G. V., & Goldman-Rakic, P. S. (2000). Reversal of antiphychotic induced working memory deficits by short term dopamine D1 receptor stimulation. *Science, 287,* 2020–2022.

Chapman, J., & McGhie, A. (1962). A comparative study of disordered attention in schizophrenia. In *Depression and personality* (pp. 487–500). Missing info

Chen, E. Y. H., Wong, A. W. S., Chen, R. Y. L., & Au, J. W. Y. (2001). Stroop interference and facilitation effects in first-episode schizophrenia patients. *Schizophrenia Research, 48,* 29–44.

Cohen, J. D., Barch, D. M., Carter, C., & Servan-Schreiber, D. (1999). Context-processing deficits in schizophrenia: Converging evidence from three theoretically motivated cognitive tasks. *Journal of Abnormal Psychology, 108,* 120–133.

Cohen, J. D., Braver, T. S., & Brown, J. W. (2002). Computational perspectives on dopamine function in prefrontal cortex. *Current Opinion in Neurobiology, 12,* 223–229.

Cohen, J. D., & Servan-Schreiber, D. (1992). Context, cortex and dopamine: A connectionist approach to behavior and biology in schizophrenia. *Psychological Review, 99,* 45–77.

Condray, R., Steinhauer, S. R., Cohen, J. D., van Kammen, D. P., & Kasparek, A. (1999). Modulation of language processing in schizophrenia: effects of context and haloperidol on the event-relate potential. *Biological Psychiatry, 45,* 1336–1355.

Cornblatt, B. A., & Keilp, J. G. (1994). Impaired attention, genetics, and the pathophysiology of schizophrenia. *Schizophrenia Bulletin, 20,* 31–62.

Daniel, D. G., Weinberger, D. R., Jones, D. W., Zigur, J. R., Coppola, R., Handel, S., et al. (1991). The effect of amphetamine on regional cerebral blood flow during cognitive activation in schizophrenia. *The Journal of Neuroscience, 11,* 1907–1917.

de Keyser, J., De Backer, J.-P., Vauquelin, G., & Ebinger, G. (1990). The effect of aging on the D1 dopamine receptors in human frontal cortex. *Brain Research, 528,* 308–310.

de Sonneville, L. M., Njiokiktjien, C., & Bos, H. (1994). Methylphenidate and information processing: Part 1: Differentiation between responders and non-responders; Part 2: Efficacy in responders. *Journal of Clinical and Experimental Neuropsychology, 16,* 877–897.

Duncan, J., Emslie, H., Williams, P., Johnson, R., & Freer, C. (1996). Intelligence and the frontal lobe: The organization of goal-directed behavior. *Cognitive Psychology, 30,* 257–303.

Elvevåg, B., Duncan, J., & McKenna, P. J. (2000). The use of cognitive context in schizophrenia: An investigation. *Psychological Medicine, 30,* 885–897.

Engle, R. W., & Kane, M. J. (2004). Executive attention, working memory capacity and a two-factor theory of cognitive control. In B. Ross (Ed.), *The psychology of learning and motivation* (Vol. 44). New York: Elsevier.

Falkenstein, M., Hohnsbein, J., Hoorman, J., & Blanke, L. (1991). Effects of cross-modal divided attention on late ERP components: II. Error processing in choice reaction tasks. *Electroencephalography and Clinical Neurophysiology, 78,* 447–455.

Falkenstein, M., Hoorman, J., Christ, S., & Hohnsbein, J. (2000). ERP components on reaction errors and their functional significance: a tutorial. *Biological Psychology, 51,* 87–107.

Falkenstein, M., Hoorman, J., & Hohnbein, J. (2001). Changes in error-related ERPS with age. *Experimental Brain Research, 138,* 258–262.

Fuster, J. M. (1989). *The prefrontal cortex* (2nd ed.). New York: Raven Press.

Gehring, W. J., Goss, B., Coles, M. G. H., Meyer, D. E., & Donchin, E. (1993). A neural system for error detection and compensation. *Psychological Science, 4,* 385–390.

Gold, J. M., Carpenter, C., Randolph, C., Goldberg, T. E., & Weinberger, D. R. (1997). Auditory working memory and Wisconsin Card Sorting Test performance in schizophrenia. *Archives of General Psychiatry, 54,* 159–165.

Gold, J. M., Randolph, C., Carpenter, C. J., Goldberg, T. E., & Weinberger, D. R. (1992). Forms of memory failure in schizophrenia. *Journal of Abnormal Psychology, 101,* 487–494.

Goldberg, T. E., Bigelow, L. B., Weinberger, D. R., Daniel, D. G., & Kleinman, J. E. (1991). Cognitive and behavioral effects of the coadministratino of dextroamphetamine and haloperidol in schizophrenia. *American Journal of Psychiatry, 148,* 78–84.

Goldman-Rakic, P. S. (1987). Circuitry of primate prefrontal cortex and regulation of behavior by representational memory. In F. Plum & V. Mountcastle (Eds.), *Handbook of Physiology – The Nervous System V* (Vol. 5, pp. 373–417). Bethesda, MD: American Physiological Society.

Goldman-Rakic, P. S. (1995). Cellular basis of working memory. *Neuron, 14,* 477–485.

Goldman-Rakic, P. S., & Brown, R. M. (1981). Regional changes of monoamines in cerebral cortex and subcortical structures of aging rhesus monkeys. *Neuroscience, 6,* 177–187.

Grady, C. L. (1998). Brain imaging and age-related changes in cognition. *Experimental Gerontology, 33,* 661–673.

Gray, J. R. (2001). Emotional modulation of cognitive control: Approach-withdrawal states double-dissociate spatial from verbal two-back task performance. *Journal of Experimental Psychology: General, 130,* 436–452.

Gray, J. R., Braver, T. S., & Raichle, M. E. (2002). Integration of emotion and cognition in the lateral prefrontal cortex. *Proceedings of the National Academy of Sciences USA, 99,* 4115–4120.

Green, M. F., Kern, R. S., Braff, D. L., & Mintz, J. (2000). Neurocognitive deficits and functional outcome in schizophrenia: are we measuring the "right stuff"? *Schizophrenia Bulletin Special Issue: Psychosocial treatment for schizophrenia, 26,* 119–136.

Grillon, C., Ameli, R., & Glzer, W. M. (1991). N400 and semantic categorizaton in schizophrenia. *Biological Psychiatry, 29,* 467–480.

Henik, A., Carter, C. S., Salo, R., Chaderjian, M., Kraft, L., Nordahl, T. E., et al. (2002). Attentional control and word inhibition in schizophrenia. *Psychiatry Research, 110,* 137–149.

Holroyd, C. B., & Coles, M. G. (2002). The neural basis of human error processing: reinforcement learning, dopamine, and the error-related negativity. *Psychological Review, 109,* 679–709.

Jacoby, L. L., Debner, J. A., & Hay, J. F. (2001). Proactive interference, accessability bias, and process dissociations: Valid subjective reports of memory. *Journal of Experimental Psychology: Learning, Memory, and Cognition, 27,* 686–700.

Javitt, D. C., Shelley, A., Silipo, G., & Lieberman, J. A. (2000). Deficits in auditory and visual context-dependent processing in schizophrenia. *Archives of General Psychiatry, 57,* 1131–1137.

Keys, B. A., Barch, D. M., Braver, T. S., & Janowsky, J. S. (submitted). *Task sensitivity to age differences in working memory: Relative superiority of the N-back paradigm.* Manuscript submitted for publication.

Kimberg, D. Y., & D'Esposito, M. (2003). Cognitive effects of the dopamine receptor agonist pergolide. *Neuropsychologica, 41,* 1020–1027.

Kimberg, D. Y., D'Esposito, M., & Farah, M. J. (1997). Effects of bromocriptine on human subjects depend on working memory capacity. *Neuroreport, 8,* 381–385.

Kopp, B., & Rist, F. (1999). An event-related brain potential substrate of disturbed response monitoring in paranoid schizophrenia patients. *Journal of Abnormal Psychology, 108,* 337–346.

Kutas, M., & Hillyard, S. A. (1980). Reading senseless sentences: Brain potentials reflect semantic incongruity. *Science, 207,* 203–205.

Levelt, W. J. M. (1989). *Speaking: From intention to articulation.* Cambridge, Mass: MIT Press.

Luciana, M., & Collins, P. F. (1997). Dopamine modulates working memory for spatial but not object cues in normal humans. *Journal of Cognitive Neuroscience, 4,* 58–68.

Luciana, M., Collins, P. F., & Depue, R. A. (1995). *DA and 5-HT influences on spatial working memory functions of prefrontal cortex.* Paper presented at the Cognitive Neuroscience Society Second Annual Meeting, San Francisco, CA.

Luciana, M., Collins, P. F., & Depue, R. A. (1998). Opposing roles for dopamine and serotonin in the modulation of human spatial working memory functions. *Cerebral Cortex, 8,* 218–226.

Luciana, M., Depue, R. A., Arbisi, P., & Leon, A. (1992). Facilitation of working memory in humans by a $D_2$ dopamine receptor agonist. *Journal of Cognitive Neuroscience, 4,* 58–68.

MacDonald, A., Carter, C. S., Kerns, J. G., Ursu, S., Barch, D. M., Holmes, A. J., et al. (in submission). *Specificity of prefrontal dysfunction and context processing deficts to schizophrenia in a never medicated first-episode psychotic sample.* Manuscript submitted for publication.

MacDonald, A. W. (in press). Event-related fMRI study of context processing in dorsolateral prefrontal cortex of patients with schizophrenia. *Journal of Abnormal Psychology.*

MacDonald, A. W., Cohen, J. D., Stenger, V. A., & Carter, C. S. (2000). Dissociating the role of the dorsolateral prefrontal cortex and anterior cingulate cortex in cognitive control. *Science, 288,* 1835–1838.

MacDonald, A. W., Pogue-Geile, M. F., Johnson, M. K., & Carter, C. S. (2003). A specific deficit in context processing in the unaffected siblings of patients with schizophrenia. *Archives of General Psychiatry, 60,* 57–65.

Mathalon, D. H., Dedor, M., Faustman, W. O., Gray, M., Askari, N., & Ford, J. M. (2002). Response-monitoring dysfucntion in schizophrenia: An event-related brain potential study. *Journal of Abnormal Psychology, 111,* 22–41.

Mattay, V. S., Berman, K. F., Ostrem, J. L., Esposito, G., Van Horn, J. D., Bigelow, L. B., et al. (1996). Dextroamphetamine enhances "neural network-specific" physiological signals: A positron-emission tomography rCBF study. *Journal of Neuroscience, 15*(August), 4816–4822.

Mattay, V. S., Callicott, J. H., Bertolino, A., Heaton, I., Frank, J. A., Coppola, R., et al. (2000). Effects of dextroamphetamine on cognitive performance and cortical activation. *Neuroimage, 12,* 268–275.

Mattay, V. S., Goldberg, T. E., Fera, F., Hariri, A. R., Tessitore, A., Egan, M. F., et al. (2003). Catechol O-methyltransferase val158-met genotype and individual variation in the brain response to amphetamine. *Proceedings of the National Academy of Sciences, 100,* 6186–6191.

McClelland, J. L. (1993). Toward a theory of information processing in graded, random, and interactive networks. In D. E. Meyer & S. Kornblum (Eds.), *Attention and Performance XIV: Synergies in experimental psychology, artificial intelligence, and cognitive neuroscience* (pp. 655–688). Cambridge, MA: MIT Press.

Mehta, M. A., Owen, A. M., Sahakian, B. J., Mavaddat, N., Pickard, J. D., & Robbins, T. W. (2000). Methylphenidate enhances working memory by modulating discrete frontal and parietal lobe regions in the human brain. *The Journal of Neuroscience, 20,* 1–6.

Mehta, M. A., Swainson, R., Gogilvie, A. D., Sahakian, B. J., & Robbins, T. W. (2001). Improved short-term spaital memory but impaired reversal learning following the dopamine D2 agonist bromocriptime in human volunteers. *Psychopharmacology, 159,* 10–20.

Miller, E. K., & Cohen, J. D. (2001). An integrative theory of prefrontal cortex function. *Annual Review of Neuroscience, 21,* 167–202.

Mintzer, M., & Griffiths, R. R. (2003). Triazolam-amphetamine interaction: disociation of effects of memory versus arousal. *Journal of Pharmacology, 17,* 17–29.

Muller, U., von Cramon, Y., & Pollmann, S. (1998). D1- versus D2-receptor modulation of visuospatial working memory in humans. *The Journal of Neuroscience, 18,* 2720–2728.

Nieuwenhuis, S., Ridderinkhof, K. R., Talsma, D., Coles, M. G. H., Hoyroyd, C. B., Koki, A., et al. (2002). A computational account of altered error processing in older age: Dopamine and error-related negativity. *Cognitive, Affective and Behavioral Neuroscience, 2,* 19–36.

Nigg, J. T. (2003). Response inhibition and disruptive behaviors: toward a multi-process conception of etiological heterogeneity for ADHD combined type and conduct disorder early-onset type. *Annals of the New York Academy of Sciences, 1008,* 170–182.

Niznikiewicz, M. A., O'Donnell, B. F., Nestor, P. G., Smith, L., Law, S., Karapelou, M., et al. (1997). ERP assessment of visual and auditory language processing in schizophrenia. *Journal of Abnormal Psychology, 106,* 85–94.

Nuechterlein, K. H., & Dawson, M. E. (1984). Information processing and attentional functioning in the developmental course of schizophrenia disorders. *Schizophrenia Bulletin, 10,* 160–203.

O'Reilly, R. C., Braver, T. S., & Cohen, J. D. (1999). A biologically-based computational model of working memory. In A. Miyake & P. Shah (Eds.), *Models of Working Memory: Mechanisms of Active Maintenance and Executive Control.* New York: Cambridge University Press.

O'Reilly, R. C., Noelle, D. C., Braver, T. S., & Cohen, J. D. (2002). Prefrontal cortex and dynamic categorization tasks: representational organization and neuromodulatory control. *Cerebral Cortex, 12,* 246–257.

Ochsner, K. N., Bunge, S. A., Gross, J. J., & Gabrieli, J. D. (2002). Rethinking feelings: an FMRI study of the cognitive regulation of emotion. *Journal of Cognitive Neuroscience, 14,* 1215–1229.

Ohta, K., Uchiyama, M., Matsushima, E., & Toru, M. (1999). An event-related potential study in schizophrenia using japanese sentences. *Schizophrenia Research, 40,* 159–170.

Olichney, J. M., Iragui, V. J., Kutas, M., Nowacki, R., & Jeste, D. V. (1997). N400 abnormalities in late life schizophrenia and related psychoses. *Biological Psychiatry, 42*, 13–23.

Park, S., & Holzman, P. S. (1992). Schizophrenics show spatial working memory deficits. *Archives of General Psychiatry, 49*, 975–982.

Perlstein, W. H., Carter, C. S., Noll, D. C., & Cohen, J. D. (2001). Relation of prefrontal cortex dysfunction to working memory and symptoms in schizophrenia. *American Journal of Psychiatry, 158*, 1105–1113.

Perlstein, W. M., Dixit, N. K., Carter, C. S., Noll, D. C., & Cohen, J. D. (2003). Prefrontal cortex dysfunction mediates deficits in working memory and prepotent responding in schizophrenia. *Biological Psychiatry, 53*, 25–38.

Rosvold, H. E., Mirsky, A. F., Sarason, I., Bransome, E. D. Jr., Beck, L. H. (1956). A continous performance test of brain damage. *Journal of Consulting Psychology, 20*, 343–350.

Rumelhart, D. E., & McClelland, J. L. (1986). *Parallel distributed processing: Explorations in the microstructure of cognition* (Vols. 1 and 2). Cambridge, MA: MIT Press.

Salisbury, D., O'Donnell, B. F., McCarley, R. W., Nestor, P. G., & Shenton, M. E. (2000). Event-related potentials elicitd during a context-free homograph task in normal versus schizophrenic subjects. *Psychophysiology, 37*, 456–463.

Sawaguchi, T., & Goldman-Rakic, P. S. (1994). The role of D1-dopamine receptor in working memory: Local injections of dopamine antagonists into the prefrontal cortex of rhesus monkeys performing an oculomotor delayed-response task. *Journal of Neurophysiology, 71*, 515–528.

Sawaguchi, T., Matsumura, M., & Kubota, K. (1990). Effects of dopamine antagonists on neuronal activity related to a delayed response task in monkey prefrontal cortex. *Journal of Neurophysiology, 63*, 1401–1410.

Servan-Schreiber, D., Cohen, J. D., & Steingard, S. (1996). Schizophrenic deficits in the processing of context: A test of a theoretical model. *Archives of General Psychiatry, 53*(Dec), 1105–1113.

Shakow, D. (1962). Segmental set: A theory of the formal psychological deficit in schizophrenia. *Archives of General Psychiatry, 6*, 1–17.

Silverstein, S. M., Kovacs, I., Corry, R., & Valone, C. (2000). Perceptual organization, the disorganization syndrome, and context processing in chronic schizophrenia. *Schizophrenia Research, 43*, 11–20.

Sitnikova, T., Salisbury, D. F., Kuperberg, G., & Holcomb, P. J. (2002). Electrophysiological insights into language processing in schizohprenia. *Psychophysiology, 39*, 851–860.

Spieler, D. H., Balota, D. A., & Faust, M. E. (1996). Stroop performance in healthy younger and older adults and in individuals with dementia of the Alzheimer's type. *Journal of Experimental Psychology: Human Perception and Performance, 22*, 461–479.

Strandburgh, R. J., Marsh, J. T., Brown, W. S., Asarnow, R. F., Guthrie, D., Harper, R., et al. (1997). Event-related potential correlates of linguistic information processing in schizophrenics. *Biological Psychiatry, 42*, 596–608.

Stratta, P., Daneluzzo, E., Bustini, M., Casacchia, M., & Rossi, A. (1998). Schizophrenic deficits in the processing of context. *Archives of General Psychiatry, 55*, 186–187.

Stratta, P., Daneluzzo, E., Bustini, M., Prosperini, P., & Rossi, A. (2000). Processing of context information in schizophrenia: relation to clinical symptoms and WCST performance. *Schizophrenia Research, 44,* 57–67.

Suhara, T., Fukuda, H., Inoue, O., Itoh, T., Suzuki, K., Yamasaki, T., et al. (1991). Age-related changes in human D1 dopamine receptors measured by positron emission tomography. *Psychopharmacology, 103,* 41–45.

Taylor, S. F., Kornblum, S., & Tandon, R. (1996). Facilitation and interference of selective attention in schizophrenia. *Journal of Psychiatric Research, 30,* 251–259.

Titone, D., Holzman, P. S., & Levy, D. L. (2002). Idiom processing in schizophrenia: literal implausibility saves the day for idiom priming. *Journal of Abnormal Psychology, 111,* 313–320.

Titone, D., Levy, D. L., & Holzman, P. S. (2000). Contextual insensitivity in schizophrenic language processing: evidence from lexical ambiguity. *Journal of Abnormal Psychology, 109,* 761–767.

Verhaeghen, P., & De Meersman, L. (1998). Aging and the Stroop effect: a meta-analysis. *Psychology and Aging, 13,* 120–126.

Volkow, N. D., Gur, R. C., Wang, G.-J., Fowler, J. S., Moberg, P. J., Ding, Y.-S. et al. (1998). Association between decline in brain dopamine activity with age and cognitive and motor impairment in healthy individuals. *American Journal of Psychiatry, 155,* 344–349.

Weinberger, D. R., Berman, K. F., & Zec, R. F. (1986). Physiological dysfunction of dorsolateral prefrontal cortex in schizophrenia: I. Regional cerebral blood flow evidence. *Archives of General Psychiatry, 43,* 114–125.

West, R. (1999). Age differences in lapses of intention in the stroop task. *Journal of Gerontology: Psychological Sciences, 54B,* P34-P43.

West, R. (in press). The effect of aging on controlled attention and conflict processing in the Stroop task. *Journal of Cognitive Neurosocience.*

West, R., & Alain, C. (2000). Effects of task context and fluctuations of attention on neural activity supporting performance of the Stroop task. *Brain Research, 873,* 102–111.

West, R., & Baylis, G. C. (1998). Effects of increased response dominance and contextual disintegration on the Stroop interference effect in older adults. *Psychology & Aging, 13,* 206–217.

Williams, G. V., & Goldman-Rakic, P. S. (1995). Modulation of memory fields by dopamine D1 receptors in prefrontal cortex. *Nature, 376* (August), 572–575.

Zgaljardic, D. J., Borod, J. C., Foldi, N. S., & Mattis, P. (2003). A review of the cognitive and behavioral sequelae of Parkinson's disease: relationship to frontostriatal circuitry. *Cognitive and Behavioral Neurology, 16,* 193–210.

# 7

## Aging and Varieties of Cognitive Control

*A Review of Meta-Analyses on Resistance to Interference,
Coordination, and Task Switching, and an Experimental
Exploration of Age-Sensitivity in the Newly Identified
Process of Focus Switching*

Paul Verhaeghen, John Cerella, Kara L. Bopp, and
Chandramallika Basak

Adult age differences favoring the young have been demonstrated in a
wide variety of tasks of fluid intelligence. Such age-sensitive tasks include
(among many others): simple reaction times and choice reaction times,
working memory tasks, tests of episodic memory, tests of spatial and
reasoning abilities, mental rotation, and visual search performance (for
exhaustive reviews, see e.g., Kausler, 1991; Salthouse, 1985, 1991; note that
performance on other tasks, such as vocabulary measures, does not show
negative age effects; e.g., Salthouse, 1991; Verhaeghen, 2003). The challenge
for cognitive aging as a field is to identify the basic changes responsible
for these declines. Given that the deficits are so widespread across the cognitive system, it is reasonable to assume that a limited number of basic
mechanisms may explain a large number of the deficits.

It is no surprise, then, that much of the research on cognitive aging
has centered on the investigation of the age effects of so-called cognitive
primitives, that is, variables that influence the cognitive system without
themselves being reducible to other psychological constructs. For a long
time, the dominant theory in the field pertained to the influence of *processing speed* (Salthouse, 1991, 1996; for a meta-analysis, see Verhaeghen &
Salthouse, 1997). This hypothesis views cognition as being driven by a
processing rate and asserts that this rate is slower in older adults than in
younger adults. More recently, the attention of the field has been drawn
toward more process-specific accounts. The currently active theories of
this sort postulate age-related deficits that are specific to particular basic
control processes in working memory.

More specifically, three types of control processes have been researched
extensively in the field of cognitive aging (see Miyake, Friedman,
Emerson, Witzki, & Howerter, 2000 for a classification of control processes). First, *resistance to interference*, also known as inhibitory control, was

a central explanatory construct in aging theories throughout the 1990s (e.g., Hasher & Zacks, 1988; Hasher, Zacks, & May, 1999; for a computational approach, see Braver & Barch, 2002). Inhibition theory casts resistance to interference as a true cognitive primitive and posits an age-related breakdown in this resistance. A breakdown with aging would lead to mental clutter in an older adult's working memory, thereby limiting its functional capacity and perhaps also its speed of operation. Second, age-related deficits have been posited in the ability to *coordinate* distinct tasks or distinct processing streams. Some of the attendant literature pertains to dual-task performance (e.g., Hartley & Little, 1999; McDowd & Shaw, 2000), but the concept has also received some attention in the working memory literature (e.g., Mayr & Kliegl, 1993; Verhaeghen, Kliegl, & Mayr, 1997). This theory typically sees age differences in coordination as independent of age differences in speed; that is, coordination is considered a mechanism that operates over and beyond the effects of mere slowing and is presumably necessary to explain age-related differences in more complex tasks. Third, in the late 1990s and early 2000s, there has seen a surge in the number of publications devoted to aging and *task switching* (e.g., Mayr, Spieler, & Kliegl, 2001). Much like the coordination theory, this work considers age differences in task switching as in addition to other age-related deficits that might exist in the cognitive system. A fourth factor, working memory *updating*, has been investigated relatively rarely in an aging context (e.g., Van der Linden, Brédart, & Beerten, 1994). We therefore touch on this process very briefly here. Claims for these process-specific deficits are mainly based on experimental evidence; that is, studies in which performance on conditions with a high demand for control processes is contrasted with performance on baseline conditions with a low demand for control, and the researcher tests whether this contrast is larger in older than in younger adults.

These different views on the major causes of aging have been developed largely in independence from one other. Therefore, the experimental work pertaining to these several theories remains to a large extent compartmentalized. Broad overviews of the aging-and-cognitive-control literature are rare, and quantitative overviews, in which the available data are pooled and conclusions are reached based on statistical analysis on the total corpus of data, are even rarer.

The present chapter aims at remediating this situation. In the first part, we bring together the available data on aging and executive control processes in a series of meta-analyses on the three types of processes mentioned above, namely: (a) resistance to interference (using the sample cases of Stroop interference and negative priming; Verhaeghen & De Meersman, 1998a, 1998b); (b) coordination ability (using the sample case of dual-task performance; Verhaeghen, Steitz, Sliwinski, & Cerella, 2003); and (c) task switching (investigating both local and global switch costs;

Washylyshyn, Verhaeghen, & Sliwinski, 2003). Meta-analysis (the particular method used is explained in more detail below) allows us to objectively evaluate evidence gathered over a variety of tasks, experimental paradigms, and imputed processes.

The second part of this chapter is dedicated to a brief review of our own efforts to investigate a control process that until recently has received only scant attention, namely the *focus-switching* process (Garavan, 1998; McElree, 2001; McElree & Dosher, 1989; Oberauer, 2002). Recent theories (e.g., Cowan, 1995) have claimed that the true workplace of working memory coincides with the focus of attention. The focus-switching process is the process that is responsible for shunting items from the storage space of working memory into the focus of attention and vice versa. We will present some experimental evidence that this process may well be a cognitive primitive in its own right (that is, that it cannot be reduced to any of the other known processes), and we will show that it is indeed age-sensitive.

AGING AND "GENERAL SLOWING": THE NULL HYPOTHESIS

First and foremost, it must be pointed out that older adults are found to be slower than younger adults very generally, even in tasks that are extremely simple and place little or no demands on control processes (e.g., simple reaction times or tests of perceptual speed). This is one of the basic findings in the field of cognitive aging (for overviews, see Cerella, 1990; Salthouse, 1996; for meta-analyses, see, e.g., Cerella, Poon, & Williams, 1980; Myerson, Hale, Wagstaff, Poon & Smith, 1990). The phenomenon is so ubiquitous that age-related slowing has become the basic expectation in any type of cognitive aging research involving response times or latencies of some sort. Exceptions to this pattern exist, but they are rare (the subitizing and counting processes might present one such exception; Basak & Verhaeghen, 2003; and lexical processes are also relatively, but not completely, spared with aging; Lima, Hale, & Myerson, 1991; other exceptions have been noted as well; Verhaeghen et al., 2003).

More interesting than the mere fact of slowing is the finding that this slowing takes a particular form and that it can be quantified. The main tool of investigation is the so-called *Brinley plot* (after Brinley, 1965). In a Brinley plot, performance of a group or groups of older adults (typically, performance in a set of different conditions within an experiment or in a meta-analytic study of different conditions or types of tasks across studies) is displayed as a function of average performance of a group or groups of younger adults who completed the same tasks or conditions. For example, if a group of younger adults in a particular study needed 200 ms on average for a simple reaction time and 350 ms for a choice reaction time, and the corresponding values of older adults were 400 ms and 700 ms, the Brinley plot would contain the pairs (200, 400) and (350, 750). The locus of points in the plot is called the *Brinley function*. In meta-analyses collected over tens and even hundreds of studies, Brinley functions have been found to be linear or near-linear, with slopes (in nonlexical tasks) typically ranging between 1.5 and 2.0; the intercept is (typically) small and negative (see Cerella, 1990, for more details; for an alternative model, see Myerson et al., 1990). The current explanation for this finding is that the slope reflects age-related slowing in central processes, as opposed to peripheral, input/output processes (Cerella, 1990; for further debate on theses issues, see Perfect, 1994 and the rebuttal by Myerson, Adams, Hale, & Jenkins, 2003, of criticisms voiced by Ratcliff, Spieler, & McKoon, 2000).

This regularity – older adults are slower than younger adults, and the relation is captured adequately by a linear function with a slope larger than unity – is what cognitive aging researchers have labeled "general slowing." General slowing implies that, whatever time it takes a young adult to complete a certain central process, an older adult will need about 1.5 to 2 times longer. This immediately implies that, in any single experiment, the age difference in response time is not expected to be constant across conditions. Rather, the age difference is expected to grow larger with increasing latency of the task, by virtue of this general slowing of central processes. We stress here that general slowing is not a theory, but an empirical generalization that holds across a broad range of tasks. Therefore, the field has considered it wise to adopt this expectation as the null hypothesis for any statistical testing involving age effects in response times (e.g., Perfect & Maylor, 2000). In other words, before it can be stated that there is true age-sensitivity in some process tapped by a critical condition, it needs to be demonstrated that the shift in the age difference from the baseline to the critical condition is reliably larger than the age effect predicted from general slowing alone.

The phenomenon of age-related general slowing, then, has consequences for the way age-related effects on specific processes should be assessed. More specifically, the traditional workhorse of experimental psychology, namely analysis of variance, cannot be applied blindly (e.g., Cerella, 1985, 1990; Verhaeghen, 2000) because ANOVA tests for constancy of absolute differences between groups or conditions. There are, fortunately, relatively easy ways to overcome this problem. One method is to revert to a different experimental methodology, such as deriving complete time-accuracy functions (the technique was pioneered in aging research by Mayr and Kliegl and associates, e.g., Kliegl, Mayr, & Krampe, 1994; see Verhaeghen, 2000, for an overview on the methodology), so that the age-related slowing factors can be assessed directly for each of the conditions. Another solution is to apply statistical control techniques to the data (an excellent overview of statistical control techniques is provided in Faust, Balota, Spieler, & Ferraro, 1999). The easiest of these statistical control techniques is to apply logarithmic transformations to response times before applying traditional analysis of variance, if the focus is on age by condition interactions. Logarithmic transformation reverts the traditional test for additive effects into a test for multiplicative effects. The reasoning is that if age differences can be approximated by: $RT_{old} = \alpha\ RT_{young}$, with $\alpha$ being the multiplicative age-related slowing factor (in actual data, the linear intercept is typically very close to zero and may be justifiably neglected in a first approximation), then $\log(RT_{old}) = \log(\alpha\ RT_{young}) = \log(\alpha) + \log(RT_{young})$. Thus, logarithmic transformation isolates the originally multiplicative age deficit $\alpha$ in an additive factor. Therefore, testing for age by condition interactions in an ANOVA on log-transformed data will be a direct test for the hypothesis that age-related slowing factors are equal across conditions. A third method is to explicitly estimate age-related slowing factors over a wide variety of tasks or task conditions in a graphical meta-analysis, much as the original discovery of age-related slowing has been made (Cerella et al., 1980).

AGING OF COGNITIVE CONTROL PROCESSES: BEYOND
THE NULL HYPOTHESIS

The age-related decline in speed explains a large proportion of the age-related variance in tasks of higher-order cognition. For instance, in a large meta-analysis, Verhaeghen and Salthouse (1997) found that perceptual speed was a reliable mediator between age and more complex cognitive constructs such as short-term and working memory span, spatial ability, reasoning ability, and episodic memory; perceptual speed explained 65% of the age-related variance or more. This indicates, first, that speed is a powerful predictor of performance on higher-order cognitive tests and, second, that it is a major factor in explaining age-related differences in cognition.

However, although speed differences clearly explain a large amount of the relevant variance (at least in cross-sectional studies), evidence is accumulating that other factors besides speed are needed for a full account of age differences in complex cognitive tasks. Evidence of this sort comes from several studies (e.g., Verhaeghen et al., 1997; Verhaeghen et al., 2002) that have shown that age differences in processing time can be obtained for tasks requiring a high degree of cognitive control, even in the complete absence of age differences in low-control baseline versions of the same tasks. For instance, in a time-accuracy study, Verhaeghen et al. (1997) found no age differences whatsoever in the speed of executing simple mental arithmetic operations that were chained in a sequence (e.g., $5 + 2 - 3 - 2 + 6 - 3$); clear age differences emerged, however, when the inclusion of brackets necessitated control processes such as swapping of elements in and out of storage, updating stored elements, and scheduling of operations (e.g., $[5 - (1 + 2)] + [(2 + 6) - 3]$). In this case, the age differences in the bracket condition could not be reduced to age-related speed differences in the basic operations of the task, because there were none. This suggests that there is a specific age-related deficit in at least some aspect of cognitive control, in addition to and independent of any age-related difference in speed.

This brings us to the question raised in our chapter: Do all control processes suffer from age-related decline? And, if they do not, which processes are spared in aging and which are not?

### Graphical Meta-Analysis: A Brief Tutorial

We attempted to answer this question by pooling all of the available research literature on (a) aging and the Stroop effect and aging and negative priming (both tasks tap resistance to interference); (b) aging and dual-task performance (tapping coordination); and (c) aging and task switching. These pooled data were subjected to meta-analysis. The methods of our meta-analyses were graphical. Latency data that were compiled from each of the literature surveys were used to construct a related pair of scatter plots that exposed (a) age effects within and across conditions (a Brinley plot) and (b) complexity effects within and across age groups (state space).

*Brinley plots* were introduced above. They display the response times of older adults across several conditions as a function of the response times of younger adults over the same conditions. As stated, the slope of the *Brinley function* can be identified as the age-related slowing factor for the particular task under study (Cerella, 1990). To test whether there are age differences in a particular contrast of interest (in our case: in baseline conditions with low control requirements versus critical conditions with high control requirements), the data points are separated along the relevant dimension, and regression analysis is applied. More specifically, a test is made to determine whether a single line suffices to explain the data, or whether two different lines (one for baseline conditions, one for critical conditions) are needed to adequately describe the relation between the performance of younger and older adults. If two lines are needed, this would be direct evidence for age-sensitivity of the processes involved in the critical conditions.

In *state space* (Mayr, Kliegl, & Krampe, 1996), performance in the critical conditions is plotted as a function of performance in the corresponding baseline conditions. Thus, the response times of one age group across several low-control conditions are shown as a function of the response times of the same age group over the corresponding high-control conditions. The resulting locus of points is the *state trace*. In the regression analysis, the data points are separated by age group. Again, the question is whether a single line suffices to explain the data, or whether two different lines (one for younger adults, one for older adults) are needed to adequately describe the relation between critical and baseline conditions. If a single line were to fit the data, it would imply that there was no age difference in the

## Additive complexity effect

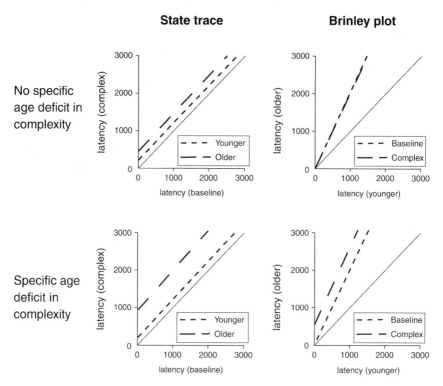

FIGURE 7.1. Expected patterns in state traces and Brinley plots under four scenarios: (A) an additive complexity effect (i.e., the complexity manipulation adds a stage or multiple stages to the stages in the baseline task) without and with specific age differences resulting from the complexity manipulation, and (B) a multiplicative complexity effect (i.e., the complexity manipulation interferes with central processing in the baseline task) without and with specific age differences resulting from the complexity manipulation.). When the complexity manipulation does not yield specific age differences, the two lines in the Brinley plot coincide. The diagonal is indicated by a thin full line.

relation between critical and baseline performance. If two lines appear (one for young, one for older adults), the interpretation depends on the form the complexity cost takes (see the next paragraph). Note that state trace analysis is a more sensitive test for group differences than the more traditional Brinley analysis (an observation made by Perfect, 1994) when sampling variance is large in comparison to the experimental effect (Verhaeghen & De Meersman, 1998a). This is because state traces involve within-subject comparisons, and Brinley functions involve between-subject comparisons.

# Multiplicative complexity effect

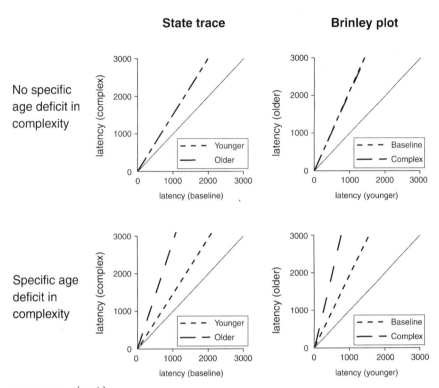

FIGURE 7.1. (*cont.*)

Compared to Brinley functions, state traces reduce the amount of variance as a result of sampling or individual differences.

Many configurations of Brinley functions and state traces are possible. We have constructed a framework (Verhaeghen et al., 2003), within which several of these configurations lead to straightforward interpretation. Figure 7.1. shows four of those possibilities, obtained by crossing two types of control costs (see the subsequent example) with the presence or absence of specific age differences in those costs. Our framework rests on several assumptions. The first is that response time can be decomposed into two independent components: peripheral processes (i.e., input/output processes), and central or computational processes. For example, in order to solve the arithmetic problem 73 + 91, time is needed to encode the numbers and the plus sign, to access their meaning, and, once the answer is known, to key in the result or utter a verbal response – these are all treated as peripheral processes. The central process here is the computation that produces the answer. The second assumption is that within each of the divisions examined (baseline tasks versus critical tasks), the general slowing principle is valid; that is, we assume that within the baseline tasks and within the task requiring cognitive control, the duration of central processes in elderly adults will be prolonged by a fixed, multiplicative slowing factor.

Increasing the need for executive control in a task will presumably lead to a latency increase in the central component. (We henceforth assume that peripheral processing is unaltered.) The increase may take several forms. Verhaeghen et al. (2003) offer a formal mathematical treatment of the Brinley and state-trace functions for younger and older adults under two cases: additive complexity effects and multiplicative complexity effects. We summarize the mathematical development here.

First, it is possible that the cognitive control manipulation either adds an extra processing stage to the baseline task or that it prolongs an existing stage in the baseline task, perhaps by imposing a fixed overhead cost or "set-up charge." We label this type of cost *additive*, because the manipulation will induce additive effects between the baseline and critical conditions: Latencies in the high-control conditions will be equal to latencies in the baseline conditions plus a constant. This constant is the cost that is due to the presence of the control process. The resulting state trace will be a line elevated above and parallel to the diagonal. The control cost or set-up charge is then given directly by the intercept value of the state trace, that is, the distance from the diagonal. The general slowing assumption stipulates that the cost for older adults will be equal to the cost for younger adults times the slowing constant (which is itself given by the slope of the Brinley function for the baseline task). This means that the state trace for older adults will be elevated above and parallel to the state trace for younger adults. The Brinley plot will show either one line or two parallel lines. If two lines are present, this carries with it the implication that the overhead component of a complex task is slowed by a larger factor than the central component, in contrast to the general slowing prediction (see Verhaeghen et al., 2003, for more details).

Alternately, a cognitive control manipulation may modulate all of the central processing of a task by prolonging or "inflating" each step in the chain of baseline computation. We label this type of complexity *multiplicative*, because it will induce multiplicative effects: Central-processing latencies in the high-control conditions will be a fixed ratio (larger than one) of central-processing latencies in the simpler conditions. In state space, this will lead to a line with a slope greater than unity; the inflation factor is given directly by the slope of the state trace. The state trace for older adults will either overlay the state trace for younger adults or it will diverge from it, depending on whether the control deficit is greater than the baseline deficit or not. The Brinley functions follow the state traces, with slopes greater than unity. Like the state traces, the critical function will either overlap or diverge from the baseline function, depending on whether the control deficit exceeds the central deficit.

To summarize, this framework provides clear signatures for two types of control effects. An additive effect leads to a pair of lines in state space, one for the young and one for the old, that are parallel to the diagonal. The Brinley plot shows either a single line or a pair of parallel lines; the slope of the baseline line gives the amount of slowing in the central processes of the baseline task; an offset in the critical line signals that the age-related control deficit is greater than the baseline slowing. A multiplicative effect leads to slopes greater than unity in both of the scatter plots. Either one line or two lines may be seen, depending on the magnitude of the control deficit relative to the central deficit. The following paragraphs describe the application of this meta-analytic framework to each of the four surveys (i.e., Stroop, negative priming, dual-task performance, and task switching).

## Age Effects in Resistance to Interference: The Stroop Task and Negative Priming

The Stroop task and negative priming are the procedures most often used to test for age differences in resistance of interference. In the Stroop task, participants are presented with colored stimuli and have to report the stimulus' color. One compares reaction time in a baseline condition where the stimulus is neutral, for instance a patch of color or a series of Xs, with a critical condition in which the stimulus is itself a word denoting a color (e.g., the word "yellow" printed in red). Response times are typically slower in this condition because of interference from the meaning of the word. In the negative priming task, participants are shown two stimuli simultaneously, one of which is the stimulus to be reported on (the target), the other stimulus is to be ignored (the distractor). For example, the participant can be asked to name a red letter in a display that also contains a superimposed green letter. If the distractor on one trial becomes the target on the next (the critical, negative priming condition), reaction time is typically slower than in a neutral condition in which none of the stimuli are ever repeated (the baseline condition). Note that this effect is counterintuitive: Higher levels of selective attention are associated with larger costs.

Results from the two meta-analyses (Verhaeghen & De Meersman, 1998a, 1998b) are presented in Figure 7.2 (the total number of studies was 20 for Stroop and 21 for negative priming). The regression lines in the plots were obtained using weighted least squares. Each data point represents a result obtained at the study level and was weighted using the sample size of the original study.

Both Stroop interference and negative priming induced multiplicative control effects, signaled by slopes greater than unity in the state traces.

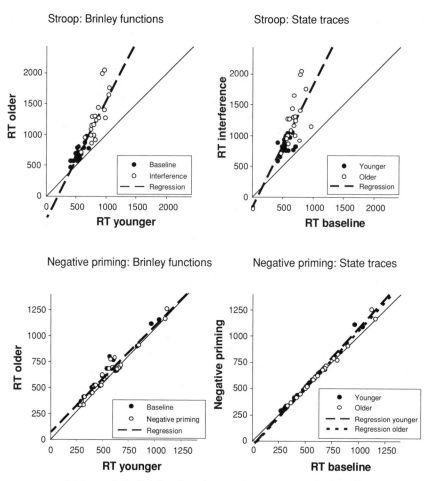

FIGURE 7.2. Meta-analytic Brinley functions and state traces, along with regression lines, for two tasks measuring resistance to interference (the Stroop color–word task, and negative priming); each of the data points plotted in the figures represents data from a single study. Adapted from Verhaeghen and De Meersman (1998a, 1998b). The diagonal is indicated by a thin full line. A single regression line suffices to capture the data in both the Brinley plots and state spaces for the Stroop task indicating that Stroop is not age-sensitive; the age-sensitivity in negative priming, indicated by the presence of two lines in the state trace, is slight.

This indicates that the need to resist interference inflates central processing. Although both effects were multiplicative, they differed in magnitude. The inflation factor in the Stroop tasks (a slope of 1.9, indicating 90% inflation) was much larger than in the negative priming tasks (a slope of 1.1, indicating 10% inflation). The difference may be due to the temporal dynamics of the two tasks. The Stroop task involves selection of one of two information sources that are present simultaneously; negative priming involves reactivating a stimulus that was deactivated on the previous trial. The time delay alone may explain the smaller effect in negative priming.

The second result to observe in Figure 7.2 is the absence of age deficits specific to the interference effects. A single line sufficed to capture the inflation of central processes in both young and old state traces; so too, a single line was sufficient to capture both baseline and critical conditions in the Brinley plot. (Note that our data did show a very slight age difference in the state trace for negative priming, 10% inflation in the younger versus 8% inflation in the older; a recent update of this meta-analysis, however, showed completely equivalent control effects in younger and older adults; Gamboz, Russo, & Fox, 2002).

Like the inflation factor, the age-related slowing factor was larger for color naming (with or without interference, the slope of the Brinley function was 1.8) than it was for negative priming (with or without priming, the slope of the Brinley function was 1.04). This difference may be due to the fact that the typical task involved in negative priming is the naming of letters or of depicted objects, whereas the color naming required by the Stroop task may be a spatial process. The different degrees of slowing then probably reflect the often-replicated dissociation, mentioned previously, between lexical and nonlexical age effects – lexical processes are relatively spared by aging, nonlexical processes clearly are not (Hale & Myerson, 1996).

## Aging and Coordination: Dual-Task Performance

One test of coordinative ability is to compare baseline performance on a single task with a critical "dual-task" condition in which performance on the same task is measured when another task has to be performed concurrently (e.g., a visual reaction time task with or without a concurrent auditory reaction time task). The results of our meta-analyses of dual-task studies are summarized in Figure 7.3 (based on a total of 33 studies; Verhaeghen et al., 2003). The analysis of these data differed from the two previous analyses in that the regression technique used was multilevel modeling rather than standard least-squares analysis. This change in method was possible because, unlike the two previous analyses, dual-task studies often report multiple manipulations within the baseline and executive control conditions. Multilevel modeling takes the nested structure of conditions within studies into consideration and provides information about the state-trace function for any single study; it also leads to less biased coefficients than least-squares analysis (Sliwinski & Hall, 1998).

The regression lines in the Figure 7.3 are those obtained at the study-level, that is, a weighted average of the regression lines found within studies. The results are very different from those obtained for resistance to interference. First, the state traces, having positive intercepts and slopes of unity, show an additive effect. This indicates a set-up cost that does

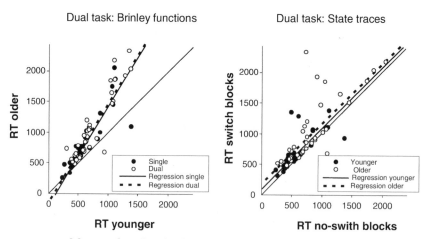

FIGURE 7.3. Meta-analytic Brinley functions and state traces, along with regression lines, for one task measuring coordinative ability (viz., dual-task performance); each of the data points plotted in the figures represents data from a single study. Adapted from Verhaeghen et al. (2002). The diagonal is indicated by a thin full line. Two regression lines are necessary to capture the data in both the Brinley plot and state space, indicating that dual-task performance is age-sensitive.

not permeate the computational processes involved in the baseline task. Second, the results suggest age-sensitivity in the control processes involved in task coordination: the lines for single and dual separate out in the Brinley plot, indicating that the control process is slowed by a larger amount than the central computational process.

It should be noted that we examined several moderators of the effect (e.g., the lexical versus nonlexical nature of the primary task; its modality – visual versus auditory – and the matching of its modality with that of the secondary task; and the more peripheral or more central nature of the primary task) and found that none interacted reliably with age. Therefore, the age-sensitivity of coordination seems to be primarily the result of the control process itself and not to how the control process is implemented under different task conditions. We should note, however, that the effect does not appear to be very large. The age-related slowing factor in the baseline task (i.e., the slope of the Brinley function) was 1.6. The corresponding age-related slowing factor in the average dual-task effect would be the old/young ratio of the absolute difference between dual-task conditions and baseline conditions. This slowing factor had a value of 1.8.

## Aging and Task Switching: Local and Global Effects

A more recent paradigm, called task switching (e.g., Allport, Styles, & Hsieh, 1994), requires the maintenance and scheduling of two mental task sets. In task-switching research, the participant is shown a series of stimuli and has to perform one of two tasks on each, the required task being indicated by the experimenter (e.g., a series of numbers is shown, if the number is printed in red, the participant must indicate whether it is odd or even; if the number is printed in blue, the participant must indicate whether it is smaller or larger than 5); the switch can be predictable or not; in the former case, it can be explicitly cued (e.g., by the color coding just described) or not.

Two types of task-switching costs can be calculated. First, one can compare reaction times in blocks with only single tasks with reaction times in blocks when the participant has to switch between tasks. This is the "global" task-switching cost and is thought to indicate the set-up cost associated with maintaining and scheduling two mental task sets. This cost, then, is calculated similarly to a dual-task cost in which performance on a block of dual-task trials is compared to performance on a block of single-task trials. In fact, the two paradigms, dual-task performance and global task switching, differ mainly in their temporal dynamics: In task switching, task A and task B are performed in succession; in dual tasking, they are performed concurrently.

A second type of task-switching cost involves the comparison, within a block of task-switching trials, between trials in which task switching is actually required with trials in which the task did not switch. This "local" task-switching cost is an indication of the control process associated with the actual switching.

The results of our meta-analysis of task switching (based on a total of 10 studies for global switching and 15 studies for local; Wasylyshyn et al., 2003) are presented in Figure 7.4. The regression lines were obtained using multilevel modeling.

For global task switching, we found an additive complexity effect; for local task switching, a multiplicative effect was obtained. Global task switching was clearly age-sensitive. In state space, the lines for younger and older adults separate out reliably, as do the lines for switch and nonswitch blocks in the Brinley plot. The age-related slowing factor in the global task-switching cost (i.e., the old/young ratio of the average difference between global task-switching trials and single-task trials) was 2.2, compared to an age-related slowing factor of 1.6 in the baseline task. Local task switching was found to be age-constant. One line described the data adequately in both state space and the Brinley plot. Again, several moderator variables were examined, but none yielded reliable interactions with age.

## Aging and Executive Control: An Interim Conclusion

It should be noted that meta-analysis considers the data at a fairly high level of aggregation: the forest, rather than the trees. Nuances within studies, or the effects of particular manipulations that are relatively rather rare,

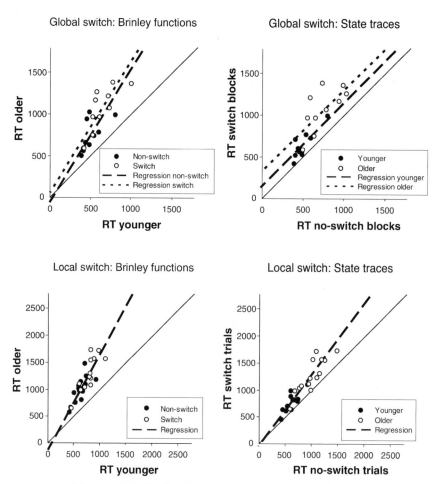

FIGURE 7.4. Meta-analytic Brinley functions and state traces, along with regression lines, for studies investigating local and global task switching; each of the data points plotted in the figures represents data from a single study. Adapted from Wasylyshyn, Verhaeghen, & Sliwinski (2003). The diagonal is indicated by a thin full line. Two regression lines are needed for global switching in both the Brinley plot and state space, indicating that global task switching is age-sensitive. A single regression line suffices to capture the data for local switching, indicating that this process is not age-sensitive.

are likely to get lost because of a lack of statistical power or to the effects of data averaging. (One example of this is the recent finding that global task-switch costs, which are generally assumed to increase with age, might disappear when switching becomes both predictable and cued; Kray, Li, & Lindenberger, 2002; Verhaeghen & Basak, 2005) This is a clear drawback of the method. The advantage is that any signal strong enough to be picked up by a meta-analysis is likely to be important and true.

What are those signals? The first and most important conclusion that emerges from the several analyses is that no one age-related deficit is associated with all and every demand for cognitive control, over and beyond the general-slowing deficit common to all computational processes. Not all control processes decline with age. Age effects were absent in tasks measuring resistance to interference and in local task-switching costs; this is apparent from both the state traces and the Brinley functions. In contrast, age effects were seen in dual-task performance and global task switching: In the state space, separate (and parallel) lines were required for the two age groups; in Brinley space, separate (and parallel) lines were required for the two condition levels. As noted in our analytical framework, distinct lines are to be expected in the state space if the control cost is additive, on the basis of general slowing alone. From the dissociation found in the Brinley plots, we can infer further that the age deficit specific to the set-up charge exceeded the general-slowing deficit. In both the dual-task studies and the global task-switching studies, the age-related slowing factor in the baseline condition was 1.6. Dual tasking inflated this age-related slowing factor to 1.8, global task switching to 2.2. Although the differences between baseline and critical conditions appear to be rather modest, they are reliable, partially because they were obtained under a strong experimental design, that is, as within-subject effects. A key theoretical question is whether or not the age-related slowing factors obtained under dual-task and global task-switching conditions are different or are random variations around a value of about 2. Because these slowing factors stem from between-subject comparisons, it would be imprudent to compare them directly, and careful experimental work using a within-subject design is needed to assess whether they are, in fact, identical or not.

Considering all meta-analyses together, a pattern in the age outcomes becomes apparent. It can be formulated at two levels. At an abstract mathematical level, we can state that no specific attention-related age deficits were observed whenever control costs were multiplicative, that is, when central processes were inflated. Whenever costs were additive, that is, when a processing stage was added or extended, age deficits did emerge, and these deficits were larger than those extrapolated from the baseline tasks. At a more concrete level, closer to the tasks, another regularity emerges. We note that specific age deficits did not emerge in tasks that involved active selection of relevant information, such as determining the ink color of words (Stroop), in tasks that involved actively ignoring or inhibiting a stimulus (negative priming), or tasks that involved relinquishing attention from one aspect of the stimulus to reattach it to a different aspect (local task switching). In those cases, the selection requirement inflated central processing, but the degree of inflation was not greater in older adults than in younger adults. Age differences did emerge in tasks that involved the maintenance of two distinct mental task sets, as in dual-task performance or global task switching. The costs of maintaining such dual states of mind were additive – a stage was added to processing, or it was prolonged. This processing penalty led to an increase in age differences over and beyond the slowing that was present in the baseline tasks.

From these meta-analyses, then, we conclude that there is no age-related deficit specific to processes of selective attention, but that dual task-set maintenance does involve a deficit over and beyond the effects of general slowing. If we are correct, this implies, on the one hand, that a simple, one-parameter slowing theory is insufficient, even though a single parameter would account for a large proportion of the variance in the data assembled in Figures 7.2 through 7.4. On the other hand, theories that have proposed either specific age-related deficits in resistance to interference or general age-related effects in executive control are in excess.

## AGING AND FOCUS SWITCHING: A NEW AGE-SENSITIVE COGNITIVE PRIMITIVE?

### The Focus-Switching Process

Our survey points to the conclusion that dual (or multiple) task-set maintenance might be an important determinant of age differences in working memory functioning, a determinant that is not reducible to age-related slowing. Multiple task-set maintenance challenges the control system in many ways. We now describe a series of experimental studies aimed at identifying what we assumed may be a critical component of this complex demand.

We turned to a control process that has not been investigated in an aging context but that seems highly relevant to the demands of task maintenance, namely the process of focus switching (Garavan, 1998, McElree, 2001; McElree & Dosher, 1989; Oberauer, 2002). Focus switching pertains to moving elements residing in working memory in and out of the limited focus of attention. The focus-switching process has been shown to be time-consuming and the available evidence suggests it is all-or-none; that is, that the cost is dependent on the presence of a focus switch, but possibly independent of further increases of the working memory load (McElree, 2001). Focus switching may therefore be a fundamental process, implicated in any task that requires the processing of more than a single sequential stream of items, as is the case in global task switching and dual-task coordination.

The existence of a focus-switching process is a logical consequence of recent theories that view working memory as an embedded-process system. Cowan (e.g., 1995, 2001) proposed a hierarchical two-tier structure for working memory, distinguishing a zone of immediate access, labeled the focus of attention (typically considered to contain a magical number of about three to four items) from a larger, activated portion of long-term memory (not capacity-limited per se, but subject to interference and decay, processes that limit its functional capacity), which is available but not immediately accessible. In this view, working memory is seen not as a separate cognitive system but rather as an arena consisting of activated elements on which attentional processes operate.

More recent work, however, suggests that the focus of attention is much narrower than previously assumed and that perhaps only a single item can be held for processing without access costs. A concomitant of this view is that there must be a control process that enables, schedules, and regulates the shunting of items in and out of the focus of attention. In one study, Garavan (1998) asked participants to keep a separate running count of triangles and squares that appeared in random order on a computer screen. Presentation was self-paced, allowing for the recording of response times. Response times were about 500 ms slower when the stimulus shape was changed from the previous trial than when both stimuli had the same shape. The results were interpreted as showing that participants kept separate mental counters for each stimulus shape and that switching between counters, that is, focus switching, was a time-consuming process. Other evidence derives from access speed in a Sternberg recognition task, where McElree and Dosher (1989) found that the last item presented was much more accessible than the other list items, suggesting this item was still stored in the focus of attention and the items presented previously were not.

A third piece of evidence for the existence of focus switching comes from an identity judgment version of the N-Back task (a task used in our work). In this task, participants are presented with a running series of stimuli on a computer screen, shown one at a time. The task is to judge whether the item currently presented is identical to the item presented $N$ positions earlier or not. Using a speed-accuracy trade-off procedure, McElree (2001) found that access times were much faster for $N = 1$ than for either $N = 2$ or $N = 3$. Moreover, McElree also contrasted a standard 3-Back condition with a condition in which participants had to respond to a target occurring in any of the last three positions. The latter condition challenged participants to maintain three rather than a single item in an accessible state; speed of performance suffered accordingly, suggesting that only one item could be retained in the focus of attention with high probability.

McElree's observations were elaborated in a model that posits an interesting dissociation between response time and accuracy. In the model, response time measures the speed of access of items; this property of an item is called its "accessibility." Access times are cast as a step function of $N$. That is, it is assumed that the item in the $N = 1$ version of the task has privileged access because, unlike the items in the $N > 1$ versions, no retrieval process is needed prior to the comparison process. Access times are portrayed as not differing between further values of $N$ as long as $N$ is smaller than the functional working memory capacity, because items outside the focus of attention are, like items in long-term memory, directly content-addressable. Accuracy, on the other hand, is supposed to decrease monotonically and smoothly over $N$, because the probability that an item will be available for processing decreases over time, either because of item decay or item interference. This property of an item is called its "availability."

In sum, the model proposes that one and only one item can be kept in the focus of attention, where it is actively manipulated; the other items will be stored as passive representations outside the focus of attention. In the N-Back task, the duration of the focus-switching process can be estimated by subtracting the response time for the $N = 1$ version of the task from response times for items outside the focus of attention (i.e., when $N > 1$).

### Age Effects in Focus Switching in a Modified N-Back Task

We adapted McElree's identity judgment N-Back task for the collection of response times. In McElree's version of the N-back task, the participant is presented with a running series of stimuli, shown one at a time on a computer screen. She responds by evaluating whether the current digit is identical to the digit presented $N$ positions back in the stimulus series; in the baseline version of the task (1-Back), the comparison is between an item just viewed and one appearing on the screen. McElree collected time-accuracy functions. In our version of the task, participants executed a key press to indicate their answer ("Match" or "NonMatch"); this key press also advanced them to the next stimulus. To minimize the control demand of keeping track of the items, digits were projected on the computer screen in columns, the number of columns equaling $N$; additionally, each column received its own color code. Digits were presented one at a time, the first digit in column 1 row 1, the second in column 2 row 1 (if $N > 1$), and so forth. Therefore, the participant always compared the current digit with the digit presented previously just above it in the same column.

### Age Differences in Focus Switching Over Values of N of 1-to-5

In a first experiment, we varied $N$ over the range 1–5 (Verhaeghen & Basak, 2005; Experiment 1). Response times and accuracies as a function of $N$ are shown in Figure 7.5. The results for younger adults conform completely to McElree's predictions. Focus switching indeed entailed a cost in that accuracy dropped smoothly over $N$, and response time increased for the transition from $N = 1$ to $N = 2$. The response time curve stayed flat over the whole $N = 2$ to $N = 5$ range, suggesting, first, that working memory

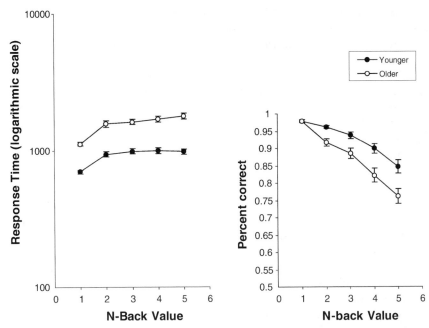

FIGURE 7.5. Latency (for correct responses only) and accuracy obtained in an identity judgment N-Back task. Adapted from Verhaeghen and Basak (2005). Focus-switching costs operate in the performance difference between $N = 1$ and $N = 2$. No age-sensitivity for focus switching was found in response time, but accuracy focus-switching costs were reliably larger for older adults than for younger adults. The error brackets in Figures 7.5–7.7 represent the standard error of the mean.

outside the focus of attention was content-addressable, and, second, that the focus-switching cost was not an artifact of memory load, but must be due to the focus-switching process itself.

How did the performance of older adults compare to that of younger adults on these control processes? First and foremost, after logarithmic transformation of the response time data,[1] no age by $N$ interaction was found for the critical comparison between $N = 1$ and $N = 2$, showing that the slowing factor operating in the $N = 1$ condition was sufficient to explain the $N = 2$ age outcome. This indicates that there was age stability in focus-switching costs in response time, once general slowing was

---

[1] As explained in the introduction, testing for age by condition interaction after logarithmic transformation of response times amounts to testing for a difference in the slowing ratio in the $N = 1$ and $N = 2$ conditions, as a way of controlling for general-slowing effects. If an age interaction emerged from the log-transformed response times, it would indicate a slowing factor in the critical condition that was greater than the baseline factor. This is equivalent to finding a dissociation in a Brinley plot, within the confines of a single experiment. (Note that the Y-axis in our plots of response times is logarithmic.)

taken into account. Thus, the first item stored outside the focus of attention was equally accessible for younger and older adults, compared to the baseline time needed for accessing the single item held inside the focus of attention.

Other aspects of task switching, however, evidenced clear age deficits. First, focus switching induced a differential cost in availability of items: There were no age differences in accuracy for the item in the focus of attention, but a clear age deficit emerged for the items residing outside the focus of attention. The effect appears to be tied to focus switching, because age differences did not further increase reliably over $N = 2$ to $N = 5$. Thus, even though items outside the focus of attention remained equally accessible in older participants (after taking general slowing into account), they were available with a lower probability than for younger adults. One implication of this finding is that interference, or decay, seemingly operates only on items stored outside the focus of attention.

Second, the slope of the response time by $N$ function for the items outside the focus of attention in older adults was not flat as in younger adults, but had a reliable 70 ms/$N$ slope. We argued (for more details, see Verhaeghen & Basak, 2005) that the most likely explanation for this is that the functional limit of working memory in older adults may be smaller than 5 in some individuals, leading to a further increase of response times at the limits of working memory. If there is individual variability in the size limit, then the slope may simply be an artifact of averaging across individuals.

Additionally, this experiment allowed us to examine age differences in the working memory updating process. That is, in half of the trials, the stimulus shown on the screen matched the stimulus held in the focus of attention, which bypasses the need to update the stored digit; in the other half of the trials, the current stimulus and the stored digit differ, and an updating manipulation is necessary. Focus switching interacted with updating (updating was more difficult when $N > 1$), but updating was not found to be age-sensitive. The age-related dissociation between the processes of focus switching and updating–focus switching is age-sensitive, updating is not – constitutes evidence for the independence or separability of the two processes.

### Age Differences in Focus Switching Compared to Task Switching

In a second experiment (Verhaeghen & Basak, 2005, Experiment 2), we combined the identity judgment N-Back task with a relative-size judgment task (i.e., Is the present stimulus larger or smaller than the item shown in the position $N$ back?) under three conditions: (a) identity judgment alone, (b) relative size judgment alone, and (c) predictable, cued, alternating switches between identity and relative size judgments. The values of $N$ used were 1 and 2. The results are presented in Figure 7.6, where we show the data as

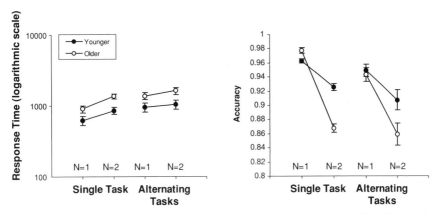

FIGURE 7.6. Latency (for correct responses only) and accuracy under baseline and task switching conditions in an identity judgment and relative size judgment N-Back task. Adapted from Verhaeghen and Basak (2005). Focus-switching costs (i.e., the difference in performance between $N = 1$ and $N = 2$) were identical for younger and older adults in response time, but older adults showed reliably larger costs for accuracy. Task-switching costs (i.e., the difference between single-task and alternating-task conditions) were identical across age groups and did not vary as a function of the presence or absence of a focus switch.

a function of single-task versus alternating-task conditions for both values of $N$.

The response time and accuracy data for focus switching were in complete accordance with the data from the identity N-Back task from the first experiment. With regard to response time, both younger and older adults evidenced a focus-switching cost (i.e., an increase in RT from $N = 1$ to $N = 2$), and this cost was identical across age groups (after logarithmic transformation of the data). This was true for both the single task and the task-switching conditions. With regard to accuracy, we did find reliable age differences in focus-switching cost, and the pattern of the data was identical to that of Experiment 1: No age difference was found in accuracy for $N = 1$, but a clear age difference emerged for $N = 2$. Again, this was true for both the single task and the task-switching conditions.

With regard to task switching, we found evidence for reliable global task-switching costs in both response time and accuracy for both younger and older adults. These task-switching costs were, however, not found to be age-sensitive, contrary to the results from our meta-analysis. This was probably due to the completely predictable and cued nature of the switching requirement; a similar result was obtained by Kray et al. (2002).

The main result of this second experiment is that there is an age-related dissociation between the two types of switching, at least as these two processes are measured in the present paradigm. That is, focus switching is age-sensitive, global task switching is not. This dissociation strongly suggests that focus switching is a process in its own right, and not, for instance, simply a different manifestation of a general switching ability that might be hypothesized to underlie both task switching and focus switching.

## Age Differences in Focus Switching Compared to Coordination

The N-Back task allowed us to investigate the independence of focus switching from task switching and updating. To investigate the independence of focus switching from coordination, we turned to a new paradigm, namely a repetition–detection task (Bopp, 2003). In this task, participants are presented with a series of stimuli, presented one at a time on a computer screen. Within each series, one of the stimuli is shown twice; the participant's task is to indicate the identity of the repeated stimulus. Progress through the series is self-paced, so that response times and accuracy can be measured.

Three conditions were included. One was the standard repetition detection task, using digits as stimuli. Each series presented to the participant was 10 digits long, and digits were shown alternatively in red and blue. For this baseline condition, the stimulus color carried no meaning. It did, however, for the two other conditions. In the focus-switch condition, there was a repeated stimulus within the blue digit series and within the red digit series; one across-series repeat was also included. The participant's task was to indicate the identity of the stimuli that repeated within each of the two colors (i.e., the blue repeat and the red repeat). For the coordination condition, the stimulus set had identical patterns as for the focus-switching condition, but now the participant's task was to indicate which stimulus repeated across the blue and red series (i.e., identify the one stimulus that occurred in both the red and the blue series). The latter condition necessitates coordination; that is, the two series need to be stored in separate registers (or receive some other form of source tag), and the information from these registers needs to be combined to derive the correct answer. In the focus-switching condition, the registers never need to be compared; there is no coordinative requirement.

The results are shown in Figure 7.7. As expected, focus switching incurred a large accuracy cost. So did coordination, and the costs were identical for both conditions. The costs were also (and surprisingly, given the results of our three previous experiments) identical across age groups. Additional to the accuracy costs, older adults also showed response time costs; younger adults did not. The age by condition interaction in response time was significant (and remained significant after logarithmic transformation); focus switching and coordination yielded larger age differences than the baseline condition, but the age differences for focus

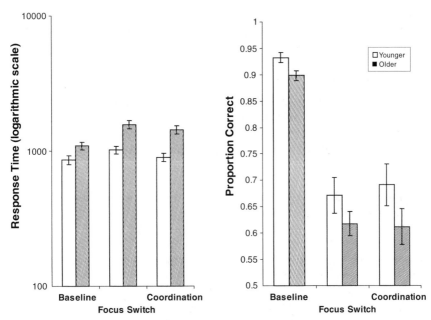

FIGURE 7.7. Latency (for correct responses only) and accuracy in a repetition–detection task, in a baseline condition, a focus-switching condition, and a coordinative condition. Adapted from Bopp (2003). Age differences in focus-switching costs emerged for response time, not accuracy. Age differences in response time did not further increase in the coordination condition.

switching and coordination were identical. The unexpected cross-over in the dependent variable that yielded the age effect may have been due to differential speed-accuracy trade-offs in the two age groups. Younger adults appear to have kept their response times constant across conditions, at the detriment of accuracy. Older adults apparently were willing to sacrifice speed in the focus-switching and coordination condition, thereby obtaining higher levels of accuracy than expected.

An important conclusion from this experiment is that the process of coordination did not lead to a greater increase in response time or a greater decrease in accuracy than did the focus-switch manipulation in either age group. Likewise, age differences were identical across the focus-switching and coordination conditions. This suggests that the performance decrements observed under typical coordinative conditions may actually be due to the focus-switching process that is integral to such conditions, rather than to the coordinative requirement per se. This is added evidence for the focus-switching process as a cognitive primitive. At the same time, it suggests that results from many experiments in the literature that have been interpreted as an age-related deficit specific to coordinative ability (e.g., Kliegl et al., 1994; Mayr & Kliegl, 1993; Mayr et al., 1996; Verhaeghen et al., 1997) may be reducible to an age difference in the focus-switching cost.

### Aging and Focus Switching: Interim Conclusions

Several of the findings described above suggest that the focus-switching process is a cognitive primitive not previously recognized in the literature on working memory and attentional control. First, focus switching was found experimentally to be distinct from (global) task switching. Second, focus switching was also found to be distinct from updating. Third, there was some evidence that focus switching may be the real driving force behind age differences in coordination, which would imply that it is a more basic process than coordination.

The focus-switching process also appears to be age-sensitive. In the N-Back task and in one of our repetition-detection experiments, accuracy costs resulting from the focus-switching process were reliably larger for older than for younger adults. In the other repetition–detection experiment, response time costs were larger for older adults than for younger adults. Although these findings clearly establish the age-sensitivity of the focus-switching process, the inconsistency of the affected performance measure (response time or accuracy) is in need of further clarification. The age-related effects were more often seen in the accuracy measure. This is a reason for both optimism and concern with regard to the usefulness of the focus-switching process as an explanatory primitive for age-related effects in more complex cognitive tasks. The accuracy effects set this process apart from the other primitives investigated in the meta-analyses, in which the age-related effects were expressed in response time (see the original papers for more details on accuracy costs). This opens up the possibility that the focus-switching process might be involved in shaping the age-related differences in more complex aspects of cognition that are measured exclusively or primarily in the accuracy domain, such as age differences in working memory span (see Bopp & Verhaeghen, 2002, for a meta-analysis) or reasoning ability (Verhaeghen & Salthouse, 1997). But there is a downside here: An age-related difference in accuracy might not invade response time at all. Hence, it might not serve to explain any of the variance in the response time differences between age groups so often examined by cognitive aging researchers, unless we can find out under which circumstances age differences in focus switching will express themselves in accuracy and under which in response time.

### AGING AND COGNITIVE CONTROL: A MANIFOLD

In this chapter, we considered age differences in six cognitive resources or control processes, namely, speed of processing, resistance to interference, coordination, local task switching, global task switching, and focus switching; and we touched briefly on a seventh process, updating. Several conclusions emerged clearly. Speed of processing unequivocally decreases with aging, seen, for example, in the larger-than-unity slopes of all the Brinley plots describing baseline conditions. Our meta-analyses strongly suggest that processes that are traditionally considered markers of selective attention (i.e. that is, resistance to interference and local task switching) are spared by aging, once baseline differences in speed are taken into account. On the other hand, processes that are traditionally associated with divided attention (i.e., coordination and global task switching) do decline with advancing age, over and beyond the expected effects of general slowing. We have shown some experimental evidence that a newly recognized process, namely focus switching, is age-sensitive and furthermore that it may be the basic process underlying both condition effects and age differences in coordinative tasks. The focus-switching process is, however, independent from global task switching. The latter result suggests that age differences in global task switching can probably not be traced back to focus switching, although more experimental evidence is needed before that conclusion can be accepted with certainty.

Our conclusions with regard to age differences have implications for general psychology. Age-related dissociations point up the independence, or modular nature, of the specific processes under study, and these conclusions could not have been reached by examining samples of college students only. Furthermore, our investigation of performance of older adults has uncovered a stronger divide between the focus of attention and the working memory region outside the focus of attention than previously assumed. Third, our work on aging has prompted us to carefully consider scaling issues (an issue rarely considered by experimental psychologists), leading to the uncovering of different types of complexity effects (additive and multiplicative) in different aspects of cognitive control. In these ways, aging research has proven itself useful for cognitive psychology in a broader sense.

Returning to age differences, the main conclusion from the evidence gathered here is that at least three primitives are needed for an adequate account of age differences in complex aspects of cognition, namely, processing speed, global task switching, and focus switching. The status of two other processes is less certain. We found that the coordination process could be reduced to focus switching and hence may not be an aging primitive. Similarly, we found that a working memory updating requirement engendered no deficit beyond that of focus switching and hence may not be an aging primitive. Both results, though, were single observations, and the final status of these two operations waits on further evidence.

The bottom line is that there is neither a global age-related deficit in cognitive control nor is there age-sparing in all cognitive control processes.

Identifying age-sensitivity, and possibly differential age-sensitivity, in basic processes is an important step forward in our understanding of cognitive aging deficits; a step that may have implications for a broader class of more complex tasks.

### Author Note

We thank William J. Hoyer, Marc Howard, Martin Sliwinski, and David Steitz for helpful discussions regarding this topic. This research was supported in part by a grant from the National Institute on Aging (AG-16201).

### References

Allport, A., Styles, E. A., & Hsieh, S. (1994). Shifting intentional set: Exploring the dynamic control of tasks. In C. Umilta & M. Moscovitch (Eds.), *Attention and performance IV* (pp. 421–452). Cambridge, MA: MIT Press.

Basak, C., & Verhaeghen, P. (2003). Subitizing speed, subitizing range, counting speed, the Stroop effect, and aging: Capacity differences, speed equivalence. *Psychology and Aging, 18,* 240–249.

Bopp, K. L. (2003). *Exploration of age-related differences in executive control processes of verbal and visuo-spatial working memory: Evidence from the repetition detection paradigm.* Unpublished doctoral dissertation, Syracuse University, Syracuse.

Bopp, K. L., & Verhaeghen, P. (2002). *Aging and verbal span tasks: A meta-analysis.* Manuscript submitted for publication.

Braver, T. S., & Barch, D. M. (2002). A theory of cognitive control, aging cognition, and neuromodulation. *Neuroscience and Biobehavioral Reviews, 26,* 809–817.

Brinley, J. F. (1965). Cognitive sets, speed and accuracy of performance in the elderly. In A. T. Welford & J. E. Birren (Eds.), *Behavior, aging and the nervous system* (pp. 114–149). Springfield, IL: Thomas.

Cerella, J. (1985). Information processing rates in the elderly. *Psychological Bulletin, 98,* 67–83.

Cerella, J. (1990). Aging and information processing rate. In J. E. Birren & K. W. Schaie (Eds.), *Handbook of the psychology of aging* (3rd. ed., pp. 201–221). San Diego, CA: Academic Press.

Cerella, J., Poon, L. W., & Williams, D. H. (1980). Age and the complexity hypothesis. In L. W. Poon (Ed.), *Aging in the 1980's* (pp. 332–340). Washington, DC: American Psychological Association.

Cowan, N. (1995). Attention and memory: An integrated framework. New York, NY: Oxford University Press.

Cowan, N. (2001). The magical number 4 in short-term memory: A reconsideration of mental storage capacity. *Behavioral and Brain Sciences, 24,* 87–185.

Faust, M. E., Balota, D. A., Spieler, D. H., & Ferraro, F. R. (1999). Individual differences in information-processing rate and amount: Implications for group differences in response latency. *Psychological Bulletin, 125,* 777–799.

Gamboz, N., Russo, R., & Fox, E. (2002). Age differences and the negative priming effect: An updated meta-analysis. *Psychology and Aging, 17,* 525–531.

Garavan, H. (1998). Serial attention within working memory. *Memory and Cognition, 26,* 263–276.

Hale, S., & Myerson, J. (1996). Experimental evidence for differential slowing in the lexical and nonlexical domains. *Aging, Neuropsychology, and Cognition, 3,* 154–165.

Hartley, A. A., & Little, D. M. (1999). Age-related differences and similarities in dual task interference. *Journal of Experimental Psychology: General, 128,* 416–449.

Hasher, L., & Zacks, R. T. (1988). Working memory, comprehension, and aging: a review and a new view. In G. H. Bower (Ed.), *The psychology of learning and motivation* (Vol. 22, pp. 193–225). San Diego, CA: Academic Press.

Hasher, L., Zacks, R. T., & May, C. P. (1999). Inhibitory control, circadian arousal, and age. In D. Gopher & A. Koriat (Eds.), *Attention & performance, XVII, Cognitive regulation of performance: Interaction of theory and application* (pp. 653–675). Cambridge, MA: MIT Press.

Kausler, D. H. (1991). *Experimental psychology, cognition, and human aging* (2nd ed.). New York: Springer-Verlag.

Kliegl, R., Mayr, U., & Krampe, R. T. (1994). Time-accuracy functions for determining process and person differences: An application to cognitive aging. *Cognitive Psychology, 26,* 134–164.

Kray, J., Li, K. Z. H., & Lindenberger, U. (2002). Age-related changes in task-switching components: The role of task uncertainty. *Brain and Cognition, 49,* 363–381.

Lima, S. D., Hale, S., & Myerson, J. (1991). How general is general slowing? Evidence from the lexical domain. *Psychology and Aging, 6,* 416–425.

Mayr, U., & Kliegl, R. (1993). Sequential and coordinative complexity: Age-based processing limitations in figural transformations. *Journal of Experimental Psychology: Learning, Memory, and Cognition, 19,* 1297–1320.

Mayr, U., Kliegl, R. & Krampe, R. T. (1996). Sequential and coordinative processing dynamics in figural transformations across the life span. *Cognition, 59,* 61–90.

Mayr, U., Spieler, D. H., & Kliegl, R. (2001). *Aging and executive control.* New York: Routledge.

McDowd, J. M., & Shaw, R. J. (2000). Attention and aging: A functional perspective. In F. I. M. Craik & T. A. Salthouse (Eds.), *The handbook of aging and cognition* (2nd ed., pp. 221–292). Mahwah, NJ: Erlbaum.

McElree, B. (2001). Working memory and focal attention. *Journal of Experimental Psychology: Learning, Memory, and Cognition, 27,* 817–835.

McElree, B. M., & Dosher, B. A. (1989). Serial position and set size in short term memory: The time course of recognition. *Journal of Experimental Psychology: General, 118,* 346–373.

Miyake, A., Friedman, N. P., Emerson, M. J., Witzki, A. H., & Howerter, A. (2000). The unity and diversity of executive functions and their contributions to complex "frontal lobe" tasks: A latent variable analysis. *Cognitive Psychology, 41,* 49–100.

Myerson, J., Adams, D. R., Hale, S., & Jenkins, L. (2003). Analysis of group differences in processing speed: Brinley plots, Q–Q plots, and other conspiracies. *Psychonomic Bulletin and Review, 10,* 224–237.

Myerson, J., Hale, S., Wagstaff, D., Poon, L. W., & Smith, G. A. (1990). The information-loss model: A mathematical theory of age-related cognitive slowing. *Psychological Review, 97*, 475–487.

Oberauer, K. (2002). Access to information in working memory: Exploring the focus of attention. *Journal of Experimental Psychology: Learning, Memory, and Cognition, 28*, 411–421.

Perfect, T. J. (1994). What can Brinley plots tell us about cognitive aging? Journal of Gerontology: *Psychological Sciences, 49*, 60–64.

Perfect, T. J., & Maylor, E. A. (2000). Rejecting the dull hypothesis: The relation between method and theory in cognitive aging research. In T. J. Perfect & E. A. Maylor (Eds.), *Models of cognitive aging* (pp. 1–18). Oxford, UK: Oxford University Press.

Ratcliff, R., Spieler, D., & McKoon, G. (2000). Explicitly modeling the effects of aging on response time. *Psychonomic Bulletin and Review, 7*, 1–25.

Salthouse, T. A. (1985). *A theory of cognitive aging*. Amsterdam: North-Holland.

Salthouse, T. A. (1991). *Theoretical perspectives on cognitive aging*. Hillsdale, NJ: Lawrence Erlbaum Associates.

Salthouse, T. A. (1996). The processing-speed theory of adult age differences in cognition. *Psychological Review, 103*, 403–428.

Sliwinski, M., & Hall, C. B. (1998). Constraints on general slowing: A meta-analysis using hierarchical linear models with random coefficients. *Psychology and Aging, 13*, 164–175.

Van der Linden, M., Brédart, S., & Beerten, A. (1994). Age-related differences in updating working memory. *British Journal of Psychology, 85*, 145–152.

Verhaeghen, P. (2000). The parallels in beauty's brow: Time-accuracy functions and their implications for cognitive aging theories. In T. J. Perfect and E. A. Maylor (Eds.), *Models of cognitive aging* (pp. 50–86). Oxford: Oxford University Press.

Verhaeghen, P. (2003). Aging and vocabulary scores: A meta-analysis. *Psychology and Aging, 18*, 332–339.

Verhaeghen, P., & Basak, C. (2005). Aging and switching of the focus of attention in working memory: Results from a modified N-Back task. *Quarterly Journal of Experimental* Psychology. (A),), *58*, 134–154.

Verhaeghen, P., & Cerella, J. (2002). Aging, executive control, and attention: A review of meta-analyses. *Neuroscience and Biobehavioral Reviews, 26*, 849–857.

Verhaeghen, P., Cerella, J., Semenec, S. C., Leo, M. E., Bopp, K. L., &. Steitz, D. W. (2002). Cognitive efficiency modes in old age: Performance on sequential and coordinative verbal and visuo-spatial tasks. *Psychology and Aging, 17*, 558–570.

Verhaeghen, P., & De Meersman, L. (1998a). Aging and negative priming: A meta-analysis. *Psychology and Aging, 13*, 435–444.

Verhaeghen, P., & De Meersman, L. (1998b). Aging and the Stroop effect: A meta-analysis. *Psychology and Aging, 13*, 120–126.

Verhaeghen, P., Kliegl, R., & Mayr, U. (1997). Sequential and coordinative complexity in time-accuracy function for mental arithmetic. *Psychology and Aging, 12*, 555–564.

Verhaeghen, P., & Salthouse, T. A. (1997). Meta-analyses of age-cognition relations in adulthood: Estimates of linear and non-linear age effects and structural models. *Psychological Bulletin, 122,* 231–249.

Verhaeghen, P., Steitz, D. W., Sliwinski, M. J., & Cerella, J. (2003). Aging and dual-task performance: A meta-analysis. *Psychology and Aging, 18,* 443–460.

Washylyshyn, C., Verhaeghen, P., & Sliwinski, M. J. (2003). *Aging and task switching: A meta-analysis.* Manuscript submitted for publication.

# 8

## An Ecological Approach to Studying Aging and Dual-Task Performance

### Karen Z. H. Li, Ralf Th. Krampe, and Albina Bondar

> "... cognitive aging researchers can accept the reality of declining cognitive powers stemming from the reduced efficiency of the brain but at the same time look for means by which older adults can best hold the negative effects of aging at bay and optimize the mental capacities they possess."
>
> – Salthouse and Craik (2000, p. 701)

A pervasive challenge of modern adult life is to satisfy numerous demands within a constrained period of time. The simultaneous performance of two or more tasks, such as driving and conversing (e.g., Strayer & Johnston, 2001), walking and talking (Kemper, Herman, & Lian, 2003), or listening while note-taking (Tun & Wingfield, 1995), constitutes a cognitive dual-task situation in which attention must be divided. Questionnaire data indicate that older adults rate the difficulty of everyday divided attention activities higher than do younger adults, whereas younger adults report a higher frequency of engaging in dual-task situations compared to older adults (Tun & Wingfield, 1995). The majority of age-comparative studies of divided attention performance concur with the subjective report data (for reviews, see Hartley, 1992; Kramer & Larish, 1996; McDowd, Vercruyssen, & Birren, 1991; McDowd & Shaw, 2000). Since the early 1960s, the importance of dual-task functioning for independent living in old age, coupled with the general trend of age-related declines in such performance, has prompted a steady output of empirical work on this topic (e.g., Broadbent & Heron, 1962).

As with many other areas of cognitive aging research (Craik & Salthouse, 2000), substantial efforts have been devoted to understanding how and why age-related loss in dual-task performance is observed, but less work has been done to understand how such age deficits can be ameliorated (but see Kramer, Larish, & Strayer, 1995). Further, little is known about the development of cognitive adaptations that may occur in midlife and beyond in response to normative cognitive declines. Our approach to cognitive aging research (loss-plus-compensation) acknowledges both the reduction of efficiency and the compensatory means, as alluded to in our opening quotation. In this context, we highlight the interacting effects of specific losses in cognitive ability on the one hand and compensatory resource allocation on the other. This perspective is informed by the Selection, Optimization, and Compensation (SOC) model of adaptive development advanced by Baltes and Baltes (1990), in which adaptation to losses can involve compensatory behaviors or a revision of goal or task priorities.

In this chapter, we first review central findings and theoretical models of aging and dual-task performance. We then discuss the importance of considering a more holistic or ecological approach to studying dual-task performance, illustrating with recent findings from the domain of concurrent cognitive and sensorimotor dual-task performance. Finally, we propose ways in which our loss-plus-compensation perspective might be applicable to models of individual and pathological differences in cognitive processing. There, we argue that taking a developmental approach to studying cognitive deficits associated with clinical conditions would help clarify debates concerning causality vis à vis symptomatology and cognitive status.

WHAT PROCESSING LIMITATIONS ARE KNOWN?

With few exceptions, investigations of aging and dual-task performance have been cross-sectional in design, with standard convenience samples of young adults in their second and third decades, and older adults in their sixth and seventh decades. The standard method of investigation involves measuring performance on each single task condition (Task A, Task B) and on the dual-task condition (Task A&B) to determine the degree to which Task A and B performance decreases under dual-task conditions compared to their respective single-task baseline levels (dual-task costs; DTCs). Figure 8.1 illustrates the derivation of absolute and proportional dual-task costs.

**Early Empirical Observations**

Broadbent and Heron (1962) tested concurrent visual search of specified digits and auditory detection of repeated letters, finding age-related deficits in the auditory task but age-equivalence in the visual task. Talland (1962) reported a similar pattern using concurrent motor tasks (bead manipulation and rapid button pressing) such that older adults showed DTCs only on the second task, relative to young adults. Two subsequent studies juxtaposed simultaneous auditory and visual presentations of digits (McGhie, Chapman, & Lawson, 1965) or alternating digits and letters (Broadbent & Gregory, 1965). Both studies reported substantial age-related decreases in

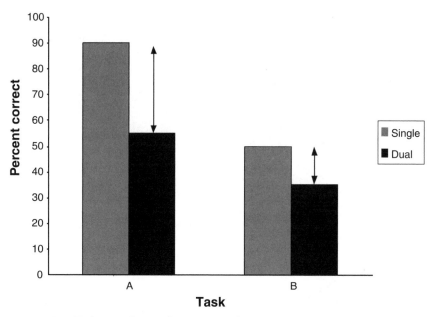

FIGURE 8.1. Task A and B performance under single- and dual-task conditions. Arrows indicate the magnitude of absolute dual-task costs (e.g., for Task A, $90 - 55 = 35$; for Task B, $50 - 35 = 15$). Proportional dual-task costs would be computed by dividing the computed absolute cost by single-task performance (e.g., for Task A, $[90 - 55]/90 = .39$; for Task B, $[50 - 35]/50 = .30$).

dual-task performance in both tasks. As noted by McDowd et al. (1991), older adults in these early studies appear to have shown some evidence of focusing on one task at the expense of the other. By modern standards, these studies lack the control of temporal parameters associated with some more recent work, allowing more opportunities for older adults to sequentialize or switch between tasks rather than concurrently perform both tasks.

### Processing Resource Explanations

Subsequent dual-task research focused more on specifying the processes responsible for age-related differences in dual-task performance. Wright's (1981) investigation of concurrent digit span and verbal reasoning showed increasing age effects as a function of task complexity, which she attributed to decreasing general processing resources.

A more specific resource reduction approach was taken by Salthouse and colleagues, who argued that reductions in general processing speed result in lower dual-task performance because of the added processing stages required to carry out two tasks instead of one. Somberg and Salthouse

(1982) prompted several important considerations by arguing that previous studies had not taken into account the age differences inherent under single-task conditions. In one experiment involving simultaneous visual target detection, they first calibrated single-task difficulty to ensure equivalent accuracy levels across individuals and age groups (Experiment 1). In a second experiment involving simultaneous tone detection and sequential digit keying, they computed relative, or proportional, DTCs by computing the absolute difference in single versus dual-task performance, then dividing by single-task performance. Using these two methods of controlling for variations in single-task performance, Somberg and Salthouse reported age-invariance in DTCs. A subsequent study (Salthouse, Rogan, & Prill, 1984) produced an important caveat: Using more complex tasks than before, Salthouse et al. (1984) reported greater DTCs in older than in younger participants, even when task difficulty was individually calibrated. As well, with these more controlled stimuli, Salthouse and colleagues demonstrated that younger and older adults were similar in their ability to shift their attentional emphasis across tasks when instructed to by using proportions or ratios as goals (e.g., 25:75, 50:50, 75:25; see also Crossley & Hiscock, 1992).

Salthouse's early dual-task findings provoked a more direct examination of the effects of task complexity (McDowd & Craik, 1988). Using auditory 2-choice reaction time (RT) and visual 4-choice RT tasks, McDowd and Craik manipulated the depth of processing (perceptual or semantic) required to make the decisions in each task (Experiment 1). These increases in complexity had interacting effects with age when calculated as absolute, but not relative, DTCs (see also Baron & Mattila, 1989). In a second experiment using different visual and auditory tasks, they found that manipulations of difficulty had comparable effects on younger and older adults. Taken together, these experiments yield mixed support for the complexity hypothesis, although they demonstrate a clear age-related decline in dual-task performance. Lorsbach and Simpson (1988) also introduced a manipulation of complexity by varying depth of processing. Participants made same-different judgments to letter pairs on the basis of physical (aa), name (Aa), or category (consonant-consonant/vowel-vowel) criteria. The secondary task was an auditory probe, presented at unpredictable times. In contrast to the McDowd and Craik (1988) study, older adults' RTs were disproportionately slowed as a function of increasing complexity, although older adults were *more* accurate than younger adults in some conditions (see also Wickens, Braune, & Stokes, 1987).

## Cross-Talk Between Tasks, Controlled Processing

Another issue addressed in several papers is whether the *relationship* between tasks interacts with age effects in dual-task performance. Ponds,

Brouwer, and van Wolffelaar (1988) paired two motor tasks, pursuit rotor and serial choice RT, adjusting single-task difficulty per individual. They reported age deficits in dual-task performance, which they attribute to age deficits in motor integration or coordination. Korteling (1991) compared age groups on similar motor tasks, using simultaneous manual tracking, after calibrating tracking difficulty per individual. Korteling noted that for older participants, increasing the similarity of the component tasks did not help dual-task performance, suggesting that they could not benefit from the opportunity to integrate their movements, while younger adults could.

Dual-task research has also focused on the effects of divided attention on encoding and retrieval processes (e.g., Anderson, Craik, & Naveh-Benjamin, 1998; Park, Smith, Dudley, & Lafronza, 1989). Across a variety of retrieval conditions (free recall, cued recall, recognition), younger and older adults' memory performance was comparably disrupted by divided attention during encoding processes, although older adults' secondary task performance was disrupted more so than was younger adults' (Anderson et al., 1998). Anderson and colleagues interpret the contrast between the attentional demands of encoding and retrieval to be a difference in the degree of controlled processing required in each phase. Fernandes and Moscovitch (2000) qualified these conclusions by demonstrating that in cases of high overlap between primary and secondary task stimuli, retrieval can be disrupted by a secondary task.

### Disuse Interpretations and Expertise

The extent to which single and dual-task performance is practiced has been investigated in the context of aging and disuse interpretations of cognitive decline. The general assumption is that older adults may show worse dual-task performance than do younger adults because of lack of practice. By this assumption, training programs should reduce the age differences observed in dual-task performance. McDowd's (1986) study of extended practice involved six sessions of single and dual-task performance pairing pursuit tracking and 3-choice tone identification. She reported a similar rate of improvement with training across age groups, such that age differences in DTCs remained at the end of training. Rogers, Bertus, and Gilbert (1994) examined age differences in concurrent visual search and memory probe performance. Participants underwent training on consistent and variable mapping conditions of visual search. Despite considerable practice (seven sessions), older participants were unable to reach a point of automaticity. Furthermore, the age groups showed equivalent proportional DTCs. Together, the Rogers et al. (1994) and McDowd (1986) studies suggest that the age differences in dual-task performance observed in single-session studies are not an overestimate of age differences, although absolute levels of performance will improve with training. Kramer et al. (1995) produced further results in a training study involving more complex component tasks: visual monitoring of multiple gauges and alphabet arithmetic. Notably, Kramer et al. devised a lengthy training regimen of fixed and variable priority training to examine optimal training protocols and transfer of training in younger and older adults. Continuous visual feedback was shown so participants could adjust their attentional allocation during each trial. In the variable priority conditions, participants were instructed on each trial to emphasize Task A and B at varying ratios. This training format proved more effective overall compared to the fixed priority training. Further, older adults benefited equally, if not more, from the variable priority training format in comparison to younger adults.

A different method of examining disuse is to study expertise in dual-task abilities. Tsang and Shaner (1998) tested younger, middle-aged, and older adults who were either expert or novice pilots. Their critical dependent measures were time sharing ability (as measured by DTCs) and resource allocation adjustment to varying emphasis instructions. Pairs of concurrent tasks varied in terms of structural similarity (spatial tracking, mental rotation, and short-term recognition of consonants). Clear effects of age and expertise were found in terms of time sharing ability, resource allocation, and adherence to task priority instructions, in favor of younger adults and expert pilots. As well, expertise seemed to attenuate some age deficits in dual-task performance, although it did not reduce age differences dramatically, thus concurring with the aforementioned training studies.

### Attentional Bottleneck Models

Although the vast majority of aging and dual-task findings account for age deficits using resource reduction models (e.g., processing resources, speed, coordination ability), others implicate age deficits in task swapping or task alternation to account for the findings. Anderson et al. (1998) tentatively consider an alternative explanation for their findings using Pashler's (1994) bottleneck model of dual-task performance. In this model, retrieval processes might "shut out" secondary task processes until primary task processes, such as item retrieval, are near completion. Whereas Anderson's experiments were not designed to directly investigate Pashler's model, others have employed the psychological refractory period (PRP) procedure to do so. The PRP procedure involves the performance of two tasks on each trial, with the priority directed to Task A and a varying delay (SOA: stimulus onset asynchrony) before Task B can be initiated. Allen, Smith, Vires-Collins, and Sperry (1998) employed this procedure in comparing younger and older adults' time-sharing ability while performing dot location and tone discrimination (letter matching in Experiment 2) tasks. Older adults showed significantly greater PRP effects in both studies, suggesting age deficits in time-sharing ability. Hartley and Little (1999) extended these findings in seven experiments, adding the qualification that age differences in PRP effects are more pronounced when response modalities compete across the two tasks (see also Hartley, 2001). As with Allen et al. (1998), Hartley and Little (1999) reported that older adults adopted a more conservative response strategy, withholding Task A responses until Task B processes were complete. Similarly, Glass et al. (2000) compared younger and older adults in two PRP experiments to explore a computational model of multiple-task performance (Meyer & Kieras, 1997) in relation to cognitive aging. In two experiments, Glass et al. (2000) found significant, but not sizeable, age differences in dual-task performance. Their interpretation underscores the flexible variation of task prioritization strategies that are preserved in old age, but that might lead to apparent age-related deficits in dual-task performance.

## Summary

To summarize the extant body of aging and dual-task research, several observations are notable. First, with only a few exceptions, dual-task costs appear to be greater in older adults than in younger adults, as measured by both absolute and proportional DTCs. Second, explanatory models, such as declining processing speed, attentional resources, or processing resources, do not account fully for all of the findings. Third, methodological considerations, such as practice, task similarity, temporal constraints on Task A and B onset, and response competition, modulate the size of observed age effects. Fourth, whereas the precision of task priority and attentional allocation appears to be maintained in older adults, given adequate practice and feedback, studies in which task priority is leniently enforced, *and* in which task initiation is more explicitly defined (e.g., the PRP procedure), have shown age-related differences in dual-task emphasis (but see Anderson et al., 1998; Crossley & Hiscock, 1992; Salthouse et al., 1984).

Our point of departure from the foregoing literature review is this fourth general observation: That older, compared to younger, adults may be more flexible in terms of dual-task priority than originally thought (e.g., Glass et al., 2000). Salthouse, Fristoe, Lineweaver, and Coon (1995) tackled the issue of attentional trade-offs among tasks, recommending that composite measures of DTCs (e.g., summing DTCs across each task domain) may be more appropriate than considering DTCs separately for each task. Using this method in two experiments, they reported age-invariance in composite DTCs, suggesting that processing speed, rather than simple attentional decrements, could account for the observed performance. We agree that a closer look at differences in attentional allocation is warranted, but disagree that such trade-offs are in all cases undesirable (cf. Hartley & Little, 1999).

## DUAL-TASK PERFORMANCE AND ECOLOGICAL CONSTRAINTS: CONCEPTUAL FRAMEWORK AND METHODS

The vast majority of studies reviewed thus far employed rather artificial laboratory tasks to assess age differences in divided attention or multitasking. Additionally, researchers were for the most part interested in participants' resource demands (or the degree of automatization) for a primary task (mostly complex cognition). Secondary task performances (such as tapping or tracking) had to be maintained only at a certain level and the focus of data analyses in most papers was on the performance decrements in the primary task. Different from this perspective, the ecological approach we pursue in this chapter emphasizes resource allocation processes and related interindividual differences as they result from normative age-graded change or abnormal cognitive status. As we detail below, four methodological concerns distinguish the ecological approach from previous research: (a) the use of laboratory tasks that mimic everyday processing demands in multitasking; (b) the comparison of coordination costs and their interrelations for all tasks involved; (c) a systematic variation of task difficulties that challenge individuals' potentials at an age-appropriate or individual level (adaptive testing, testing-the-limits approach); and (d) the use of manipulations that challenge participants' control over their resource allocation operations.

The ecological approach to multitasking is conceptually inspired by the model of selection, optimization, and compensation (SOC), which was originally proposed by Paul and Margret Baltes (1990). Since then it has been developed into a framework of lifespan development that attempts to define universal processes of developmental regulation, i.e., the adaptive mastery of life (Freund & Baltes, 2000). The fundamental approach to developmental regulation is that individuals must continuously adapt to opportunities and constraints, both of which take different forms or change throughout the life-course. Selection involves goals or outcomes such as prioritizing commitment to the family over pursuing a professional career or prioritizing the maintenance of postural stability at the cost of excelling in cognitive performance in dual-task situations. Optimization relates to goal-relevant means such as practice (e.g., working on technical skills as a pianist). Finally, compensation denotes the use of alternative means to maintain performance in the face of losses of means, for example, the use of a wheelchair or walking aids to maintain mobility after a stroke or older chess experts' reliance on their superior move-selection strategies, presumably compensating for their slower search rates (for this hypothesis, see Charness, 1991).

A good example of SOC processes at work can be found in the area of cognitive and motor decline in old age. Age-graded changes in cognitive resources, as defined in terms of perceptual-motor speed, are a well-documented phenomenon in the literature (Li et al., 2004; Salthouse, 1996). The assumption that motor functions become increasingly "cognitive" in later adulthood is motivated by the idea that in old and very old age, the general integrity of the nervous system must be considered as a larger base of support for all kinds of adaptive behavior. Related correlational evidence (Lindenberger & Baltes, 1994; Lindenberger & Baltes, 1997) indeed points to a strong connection between bodily functioning and intellectual abilities during the third and the fourth ages.

The SOC-framework can be then applied to everyday situations including those in which younger and older adults must perform a sensorimotor task such as walking or maintaining a stable posture while simultaneously performing a cognitive task (Freund, Li, & Baltes, 1999; Krampe & Baltes, 2003). The emphasis on adaptive resource allocation warrants the specific consideration of three aspects that are by themselves subject to empirical test: (1) the age-related reduction in overall cognitive resources available; (2) the relative increase in cognitive resource demands for sensorimotor functions in older adults because of age-related biological decrements in motor functioning; and (3) the higher ecological relevance of walking or maintaining a stable posture for older compared to younger adults.

In the context of cognitive and sensorimotor aging, our ecological relevance argument refers to objective risks and subjective fear of falling and the higher costs in terms of resulting physical impairment for older adults. More generally, we consider evaluations of dual-task performance to be more ecologically relevant when task emphasis instructions are less constrained. That is, although it is informative to know that in highly controlled situations, younger and older adults are able to flexibly allocate their attention between two tasks, in everyday dual-task situations, task priority is more likely to be determined by the individual.

The SOC-Model's adaptive resource allocation perspective permits specific predictions with regard to performance in dual-task situations. First, the relative increase in cognitive resource demands for sensorimotor functions in older adults should induce higher costs if walking or balance are combined with cognitive task demands. If older adults must already invest cognitive resources into their balance or gait under normal conditions, we would expect negative age effects in DTCs to be pronounced under conditions of increased sensorimotor challenges. At the same time, the SOC-Model predicts that when facing potentially threatening challenges (such as heavy sway or obstacles), older adults invest most of their cognitive resources into maintaining their stability; that is, they prioritize sensorimotor functions at the cost of cognitive performance.

Our assumptions about resource availability or resource allocation in dual-task contexts outlined so far are underspecified with respect to the nature of the cognitive resources involved and regarding the underlying cognitive or neural mechanisms controlling their allocation. Response scheduling and resource allocation, both arguably processes potentially relevant to dual-tasking, have been linked to executive control processes; and notably Baddeley (1992) and, more recently, Engle (2002) argued that dual-task performance indeed requires executive functions. The executive control concept is itself a matter of debate, however. In the context of the task-set switching paradigm, Rogers and Monsell (1995) emphasized the unique role of task sets or abstract plans, the representations of which must be maintained, updated, and executed during performance. Using latent-variable analyses on a large-scale sample of participants, Miyake, Friedman, Rettinger, Shah, and Hegarty (2001) found that, in the visuospatial domain, processing-and-storage WM tasks and storage-oriented STM tasks equally implicate executive functioning and are not clearly distinguishable. These findings are in contrast to results from the verbal domain. In addition, the authors showed that spatial ability factors differ with respect to their degree of executive involvement. The bottom line is that the involvement of executive functions might depend to some degree on the combination of tasks under consideration in a dual-task experiment.

To evaluate the scope of these different proposals, we need comparisons of dual-task performances in individuals differing in cognitive capacities such as processing speed or levels of executive functioning. A central question related to the specifics of underlying control mechanisms is to what degree resource allocation in dual-task contexts is under individuals' deliberate control in the first place. The SOC-Model emphasizes the importance of long-term adaptations such as response tendencies that were acquired and overlearned in everyday settings. This proposal may well turn out to be commensurable with executive control accounts; however, it implicates experimental approaches guided by the ecological validity of dual-task settings and systematic variations of challenges and their salience for different individuals. We now turn to our review of studies that have addressed these issues.

## BALANCE AND COGNITIVE FUNCTION IN NORMAL AND PATHOLOGICAL AGING

Somberg and Salthouse (1982) advocated that more experimental paradigms are needed to fully understand the potentials and limits of an aging system in the situations of divided attention. In contrast to standard laboratory cognitive tasks, "real-world" dual-task situations often comprise sensorimotor components such as keeping upright posture or walking. During normative aging, the efficiency of sensorimotor abilities becomes impaired alongside the emerging cognitive deficits. The question arises whether age-related differences in performance of dual tasks exist when cognitive tasks are paired with tasks that are highly relevant to everyday functioning. Everyday observations suggest that, in comparison with younger individuals, older adults prioritize sensorimotor activities, particularly in divided attention situations. For example, while standing in a bus, they focus primarily on keeping balance at the expense of carrying on a conversation. Why do older adults set their priorities this way?

Research on falling indicates that 30 to 50% of adults 65 years of age and older and 40% of adults over the age of 80 experience one or more falls annually (e.g., Sattin, 1992). The majority of falls in elderly adults occur during their usual daily life activities, such as walking or changing position (Tinetti, Speechley, & Ginter, 1988). Moreover, falls may have dramatic consequences in old age (Tinetti, 1995), such as injury, fear, decreased mobility, and morbidity (Simoneau & Leibowitz, 1996). Further evidence for a linkage between cognitive functioning and risk of falling comes from research on pathological aging. Nakamura et al. (1997) found that reduced frontal blood flow correlated with gait and postural disturbances in patients with diagnosed Alzheimer's dementia. The rate of falls increases with progressive dementia (Wolfson, 1991), and a threefold increase in incidence of falls has been found for individuals diagnosed with Alzheimer's dementia relative to the general population (Buchner & Larson, 1987).

## Postural Control is Cognitively Demanding

Empirical evidence shows that posture control, which is often viewed as a highly practiced automatized skill, becomes increasingly difficult in old age and that this deficit is especially apparent in dual-task situations in which individuals are given an attentional load (see Woollacott & Shumway-Cook, 2002 for review). To demonstrate that cognitive involvement in posture control increases in old age, several investigations have adopted a classical dual-task paradigm from cognitive psychology and computed DTCs similarly. In these studies, postural control is typically measured during either static or dynamic balance tests. Static balance is the ability to remain upright over a fixed base of support (e.g., quiet standing). Dynamic balance is the ability to continuously adjust the center of gravity over a moving base of support (e.g., keeping equilibrium during perturbations or walking). For both types of balance task, force platforms are used to assess the center of pressure (COP) displacement (see Figure 8.2).

The most frequently used measures are COP path, velocity, area, and stabilization time. It has been proposed that the body is less stable, the longer the path or the stabilization time, the higher the velocity, or the larger the COP area (Means, Rodell, O'Sullivan, & Winger, 1998; Thapa, Gideon, Brockman, Fought, & Ray, 1996). Figure 8.3 illustrates age-group differences in the COP area under single-task conditions.

Stelmach, Zelaznik, and Lowe (1990) investigated the effects of a cognitive (i.e., mental counting of the number of correct addition problems)

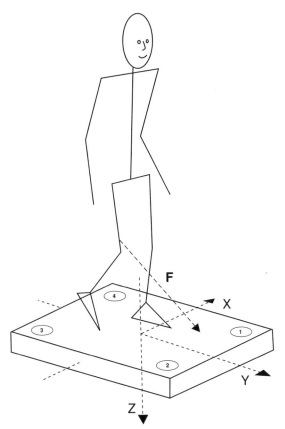

FIGURE 8.2. Schematic diagram of a force platform. By collecting the components of the ground reaction force (force X – medial-lateral component, force Y – anterior-posterior component, and force Z – vertical component) and corresponding moments the force platform quantifies the center of pressure (COP) position within the coordinate system.

and a motor (i.e., bimanual squeezing) task on the recovery of younger and older adults from minor postural disturbances caused by arm swinging. When attention was occupied by a more demanding cognitive task, older adults required a greater amount of time to regain postural stability. Maylor and Wing (1996) investigated the differential influence of five cognitive tasks on stability as measured by variability in weight distribution during standing in two age groups. They found significant decrements in postural stability when older adults were performing secondary memory tasks (Brooks' spatial memory and backward digit recall) in comparison with other cognitive tasks (random digit generation, silently counting, and counting aloud backward in threes). Similarly, Maylor, Allison, and

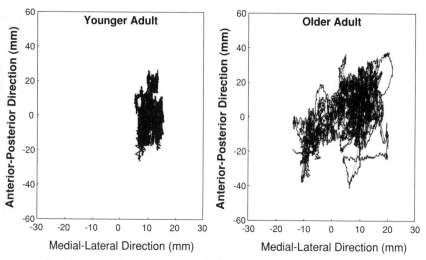

FIGURE 8.3. An example of age-group differences in COP area under single-task conditions. The area within which the COP moves reflects the amount of shifts in the forces applied on the platform by the body in its effort to maintain its upright stance during dynamic balance. Adapted from Bondar et al. (2003).

Wing (2001) demonstrated that postural stability, as measured by variability in weight distribution during standing, declined with age, and that this decline was greatest when performing a spatial memory task. Shumway-Cook, Woollacott, Kerns, and Baldwin (1997) examined effects of two types of secondary cognitive tasks (sentence completion and visual perceptual matching) on stability (COP displacement) during quiet stance on firm versus compliant surfaces in younger and older adults with and without a history of falls. When task complexity was increased (either through the introduction of a cognitive task or a more challenging postural condition such as standing on the compliant surface), significant age-group differences in stability emerged and were particularly pronounced in those older adults with a history of falls.

Together, the reviewed studies demonstrate an age-related increase of cognitive involvement in posture control. However, these findings contradict the theoretical considerations of the SOC model that, in old age, allocation of resources is directed toward a task of higher survival value, that is, toward sensorimotor functioning at the expense of cognitive performance. Note that the sensorimotor tasks used in these studies were low in difficulty. Some have argued that the inability to allocate sufficient attention to postural control under multitask conditions might be a contributing factor to imbalance in older adults (e.g., Teasdale et al., 1992). Others have emphasized, however, the complexity of resource allocation during concurrent performances of sensorimotor and cognitive tasks. Task priority depends on many factors including the nature of both the cognitive and postural task, the goal of an individual, and the task emphasis instructions (Shumway-Cook et al., 1997). The prioritization of postural control may also depend on environmental factors that alter the level of postural threat. In other words, the prioritization or "posture first" hypothesis (Shumway-Cook et al., 1997) might be confirmed with increasing ecological validity of a sensorimotor task. Several investigations have examined this possibility.

### Prioritization of Postural Control

Lajoie, Teasdale, Bard, and Fleury (1996) measured stance under two difficulty conditions (i.e., on a broad and narrow support surface) and performance on a concurrent verbal RT task. They found that increasing the difficulty of the balance task significantly increased RTs in older, but not in younger, adults. Teasdale and colleagues obtained similar findings (Teasdale et al., 1992; Teasdale, Bard, LaRue, & Fleury, 1993). In addition, the authors found that in old age RTs changed as a function of the position of the COP. The closer the COP was to the edge of the support surface, the longer were the reaction times. Similarly, Brown and colleagues (Brown, Sleik, Polych, & Gage, 2002) examined whether the prioritization of postural control over secondary task performance was altered in younger and older adults during several levels of postural threat (i.e., standing in the middle of the platform at ground level, standing at the edge of the platform at ground level, standing in the middle of the elevated platform, and standing at the edge of the elevated platform). Standing balance was paired with a concurrent mental imagery task. Moreover, a prioritization index was used to quantify changes in the relationship between postural control and secondary task performance under conditions of postural threat. Generally, the results revealed that in comparison to younger adults, more older individuals prioritized postural control by significantly reducing COP area in the most threatening stance condition.

In sum, the findings by Teasdale and colleagues (Lajoie et al., 1996; Teasdale et al., 1992; Teasdale et al., 1993) and Brown and collaborators (Brown et al., 2002) indicate that, in dual-task situations, older participants give preference to balance control as opposed to cognitive functioning, especially under more challenging postural conditions. Given the cognitive aging and dual-task research, a possibility remains that this pronounced prioritization toward stability appeared because of several reasons: (a) lack of control of age-group differences inherent under baseline conditions; (b) insufficient task familiarity, which is particularly critical for performances of older adults; (c) insufficient ecological relevance of cognitive components of dual tasks; and (d) failure to measure divided attention independent of resource allocation strategies (cf. Glass et al., 2000; Rabbitt, Lowe, & Shilling, 2001; Somberg & Salthouse, 1982). Several recent studies have taken these methodological considerations into account.

Lindenberger, Marsiske, and Baltes (2000) investigated the simultaneous execution of a challenging locomotion task and an episodic memory task in younger, middle-aged, and older adults. Skilled walking on a narrow track was paired with memory encoding using mental imagery. After participants were equated on single-task performances through training to criterion in the mnemonic technique and extensive walking practice, they were instructed to perform the two tasks concurrently with equal emphasis. In both domains, age-group differences were observed in DTCs. Li and collaborators (Li, Lindenberger, Freund, & Baltes, 2001) extended this paradigm by giving more extensive training and by estimating task difficulty levels on an individual basis. The authors systematically manipulated task difficulty in the dual-task condition by using faster presentation rates for words and placing obstacles on the track. Moreover, younger and older participants were provided with compensatory walking and memory aids (access to a handrail and a pause button for word presentation, respectively). In dual-task blocks, participants were instructed to perform both tasks with equal emphasis. In comparison to younger individuals, the dual-task performance of older adults was generally on a lower level. However, the age-related difference in dual-task costs was especially pronounced in the memory domain. Figure 8.4 reveals that, within each difficulty condition, the distance between data points of younger and older adults is larger in the vertical (memory DTCs) than in the horizontal (walking DTCs) dimension. Moreover, in the condition in which both tasks were made more difficult, and both compensatory aids were available, older adults benefited from handrail use, whereas younger participants successfully compensated by using the memory aid. According to Li et al. (2001) and consistent with the SOC-model and the "posture first" hypothesis, the findings indicate that older adults selected the domain that was more important to them, that is, walking.

Note that in the studies by Lindenberger et al. (2000) and Li et al. (2001) participants were explicitly instructed to optimize both tasks equally. Given the findings on reduced resources and flexibility with which older adults can shift their attentional emphasis across two cognitive tasks, a possibility remains that the observed pattern could be due to age-related differences in the ability to adjust performances according to experimental instructions. To rule out this possibility and to investigate whether prioritization of a sensorimotor component of dual tasks is a robust behavior inherent in old age, Bondar, Krampe, and Baltes (2004) systematically varied task priorities via instructions (cf. Kramer et al., 1995; Salthouse et al., 1984; Somberg & Salthouse, 1982; Tsang & Shaner, 1998).

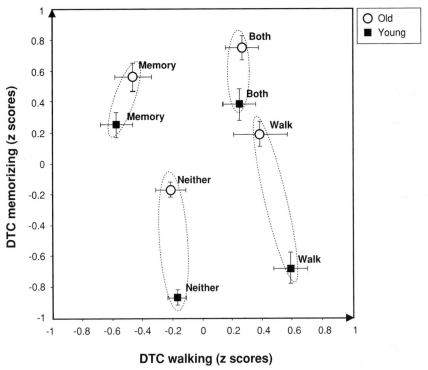

FIGURE 8.4. Dual-task costs (DTCs) for walking speed as a function of DTCs for memorizing, for each age group and difficulty condition (i.e., when task difficulty was increased in both, walking, memorizing, or neither task). DTCs for all participants and conditions were pooled, then standardized. Task difficulty for memory, walking, or both tasks was increased by 25% for each individual. Dotted ovals highlight the young–old pair for each difficulty condition. Positive values indicate high DTCs. Error bars depict standard errors of mean DTCs. Adapted with permission of the Blackwell Publishing from Li, Lindenberger, Freund, and Baltes (2001, p. 235, Figure 3). Copyright © 2001 by the Blackwell Publishing.

Bondar et al. (2004) conducted an experiment in which younger and older adults performed a sensorimotor (balance) and a cognitive (RT) task separately and concurrently. The balance task involved maintaining upright stability despite unpredictable platform perturbations. Postural stability was expressed in terms of COP area. The RT task involved making manual responses to acoustic stimuli. Correct response latencies and accuracy were measured for the RT task. To challenge the available resources, task difficulty was manipulated in each domain: perturbation size (large, small) varied on the force platform, and response complexity (one versus two choices) varied on RT task. To address the issue of age differences in attentional flexibility, participants were asked to focus either primarily on balance, cognition, or to perform both tasks equally well. To ensure stable performance levels, both tasks were practiced extensively prior to the experimental assessment, both singly and concurrently.

Dual-task costs were greater in the cognitive than in the balance domain and were greater in older than in younger adults. Whereas younger adults had zero or negative DTCs in the balance domain, older participants had significant costs in both domains. However, the DTCs of older adults were greater in the cognitive than in the balance domain. The poorer cognitive performance of older adults was observed in terms of accuracy, response latency, and frequency of omissions. The DTCs of both age groups were sensitive to task-priority instructions. However, this sensitivity was more pronounced in the easy than in the difficult condition. Within the easy condition, DTCs were the highest under the instruction "Focus on Balance" and the lowest under the instruction "Focus on RT." Under the instruction "Equal Emphasis," DTCs were on the intermediate level in comparison to the two other instructional conditions. In the difficult condition, the instructions "Focus on RT" and "Equal Emphasis" influenced DTCs similarly. Additionally, DTCs were more sensitive to instructions in the cognitive than in the balance domain. Whereas cognitive performance of both age groups varied smoothly according to task-priority instructions, the balance performance of older adults remained stable under all instructional conditions. Younger adults showed a strong tendency to follow the instruction "Focus on RT" and to sway more under this instruction in the difficult condition.

In line with previous research, the findings of this study strongly suggest that there is an age-related deficit in concurrent performance of a sensorimotor and a cognitive task beyond that of a general decline, and that there is a domain-specific asymmetry in resource allocation. That is, individuals invest more resources into the sensorimotor than into the cognitive domain (cf. Li et al., 2001; Lindenberger et al., 2000). Moreover, the results rule out the possibility that older adults prioritize a sensorimotor component of a dual-task situation because of their reduced ability to follow experimental instructions. Similar to findings from cognitive research (cf. Salthouse et al., 1984; Somberg & Salthouse, 1982), both age groups demonstrated smooth resource allocation adjustment to varying emphasis instructions. However, this flexibility was reduced in the sensorimotor domain and when resource limitations were more pronounced. Higher DTCs in the cognitive than in the balance domain, frequent omission of responses in dual-task contexts, and reduced ability to adjust balance behavior to experimental demands particularly in the difficult condition were taken to mean that age-related resource limitations and the ecological relevance of sensorimotor tasks force older adults to prioritize postural control at the expense of cognitive performance. By contrast, younger adults were able to sacrifice the low-priority sensorimotor performance in order to optimize the high-priority cognitive task when instructed to do so.

This study validates the previous findings that, in older adults, dual-task performances in general and motor control in particular are resource demanding (e.g., Maylor et al., 2001; McDowd, 1986; Salthouse et al., 1984; Shumway-Cook et al., 1997). By manipulating the task emphasis instructions, Bondar et al. (2004) elaborated on previous research on age-group specific patterns of prioritization behavior in dual-task situations (e.g., Brown et al., 2002; Li et al., 2001) and demonstrated that older adults prioritize balance even after individuals' relative emphases were controlled for. The mismatch between the performance of older adults and the experimental requirements is interpreted as a consistent prioritization of the sensorimotor component of dual tasks. From a developmental perspective, it is an example of adaptive behavior. Taking into account the theoretical considerations of the SOC-model and the empirical evidence, we conclude that internal constraints force older individuals toward "intelligent" resource management, that is, prioritization of sensorimotor activities in multitask situations.

Extending this work into the field of non-normative aging, Rapp, Krampe, and Baltes (2003) investigated dual-task performance in younger and older adults and an age-matched (to older adults) sample of individuals with early Alzheimer's dementia (AD-patients) with dysexecutive syndrome diagnoses. To disambiguate the effects of age, dementia, and perceptual-motor speed, a fourth age-matched group of older adults with low scores on the Digit Symbol Substitution test (DSS: Wechsler, 1981) was included. The authors assessed participants' sway using the area of center of pressure movement (COP area) under single-task conditions and also while they were simultaneously performing a working memory task (N-Back: Dobbs & Rule, 1989). To challenge their sensorimotor functioning, participants had to perform while standing on the stable platform and under conditions of continuous platform movement. Single-task performance in cognitive and sensorimotor tasks was assessed before and after dual-task trials. COP areas under single-task conditions were similar for the four groups when the platform was stable.

Platform movement induced stronger sway in older compared to younger adults and this effect was pronounced in AD-patients. Rapp et al. (2003) hypothesized that older adults and AD-patients should already invest cognitive resources into their balance under single-task conditions. This assumption was indeed borne out in the group differences in DTCs: Whereas younger adults showed virtually no costs in either balance or cognition under stable platform conditions, DTCs in both domains were significant in older adults and this was even more true for AD-patients. A different picture emerged for the moving platform condition. DTCs for balance

in younger adults increased relative to the stable platform condition; however, older adults and even more so AD-patients showed increased costs
in cognition, but surprisingly low costs in balance. Put differently, all three
age groups maintained dual-task balance at levels similar to single-task
performance (i.e., they prioritized) at the cost of cognitive performance.
Note that low DSS older adults for the most part showed similar levels of
performance to normal older adults.

The pronounced DTC's in both cognition and balance that (Rapp
et al., 2003) observed in older adults and Alzheimer's patients on the stable
platform suggest that executive functioning is involved in multitasking as
long as the challenge to postural stability is low. Under potentially threatening conditions, however, the prioritization skill typical of older adults
remains effective even in AD-patients. This prioritization of sensorimotor
over cognitive performance in older adults was already observed in the
Li et al. (2001) study, in which participants walked a parcours with obstacles. More recently, Krampe, Schaefer, and Baltes (2003) found that older
adults showed reductions in walking speed that were similar to 9-year-
olds (and markedly higher than in younger adults) when simultaneously
performing a word-fluency task. Different from the Li et al. study, older
adults maintained their cognitive performance at single-task levels during
walking. The critical difference between the Li et al. experiment and this
latter investigation was that participants did not have to master obstacles
and were hardly at a risk of stumbling.

Presumably, prioritization of postural stability and walking under challenging conditions reflects an adaptive capacity resulting from long-term
learning in everyday settings that can override executive control functions
operating in situations with little sensorimotor demands. Different from a
more general perspective, the ecological approach to aging and dual-task
performance holds potential to clarify the explanatory scope of executive
control accounts and their limitations.

## IMPLICATIONS REGARDING THE CONCEPTUALIZATION OF INTELLECTUAL DEVELOPMENT

The reviewed evidence supports a certain role of executive functions in
the coordination of multiple task demands. At the same time, these functions can probably be "overruled" by learned, adaptive mechanisms that
have a high protective value for individuals at risk of falling. Krampe
and Baltes (2003) argued that mental capacity as measured by extant
psychometric tests has only limited value as a measure of individuals'
cognitive resources. The capability to coordinate simultaneous processing demands (executive control) and the potential for SOC-like protective
mechanisms clearly deserve more consideration when predicting multitask
behavior.

Likewise, older adults' increased demands for cognitive resources to support their sensorimotor functioning are not captured by psychometric IQ-tests, which are typically administered in settings with small sensorimotor demands. Our knowledge about the cognitive-resource demands for bodily functions in older adults is quite limited, however. As an example, it is feasible that digestion exerts costs on older adults performances even in standard testing situations. Another example would be an incontinent older adult's intrusive worries about where to find the next restroom. There is also evidence accumulating that the interplay between cognitive and sensorimotor functions in children differs from that in younger adults. In a recent study, Krampe et al. (2003) found that decrements in walking speed through simultaneous performances of a verbal fluency task decreased systematically from ages 9 and 11 to younger adulthood. In fact, related dual-task costs were similar in 9-year-olds and older adults in their 60s. Studies with children diagnosed with developmental dyslexia (e.g., Nicolson & Fawcett, 1993; Smiley-Oyen, Subbot, & Gallagher, 2001) or attentional deficit syndrome (e.g., Kroes et al., 2002; Sheppard, Bradshaw, Georgiou, Bradshaw, & Lee, 2000) also point to a tighter coupling of sensorimotor functions and cognition in these groups. Based on this and related evidence, Krampe and Baltes (2003) argued that ecologically relevant assessments of intellectual potential must comprise measures of sensorimotor functioning in addition to psychometric IQ-tests.

## IMPLICATIONS FOR MODELS OF NORMATIVE AND NONNORMATIVE COGNITION

From a life-span developmental perspective on cognitive change, a broader implication for models of attentional control and working memory such as those advanced by Engle (2002), Unsworth, Heitz, and Engle (this volume), and Miyake et al. (2000) concerns the phenomenon of *plasticity*. A major theme of our work is that over time, behavioral plasticity, or adaptation to weakness in the cognitive system, is likely to occur (e.g., Li & Lindenberger, 2002). Such behavioral plasticity, in the form of compensatory attentional reallocation, or task prioritization, may be identifiable if one analyzes complex cognitive performance in terms of subtasks or components.

In the domain of working memory performance, language researchers (Waters & Caplan, 1996) have distinguished between independent processing and storage components within standard working memory span tasks (Daneman & Carpenter, 1980). Echoing this distinction, it has been demonstrated in cognitive aging research that older adults prioritize the processing (e.g., *sentence verification*) demands over the storage (*end-word recall*) demands to compensate for cognitive slowing, or for reductions in working memory capacity (Brébion, Smith, & Ehrlich, 1997). Given that working memory performance by definition requires simultaneous storage and processing (e.g., Baddeley, 1986; Engle, 2002), by extension it can be considered a situation requiring multiple-task coordination. A similar observation has been noted in studies of linear transitive reasoning (Sedek & von Hecker, 2004; von Hecker, Sedek, Piper-Dabrowska, & Bedynska, this volume), in which older adults performed well relative to younger adults on the mental operations, but performed more poorly with increased storage demands. The SOC framework predicts that older adults would reallocate their attentional resources to favor the task component they can more easily accomplish or that has more face validity.

Examinations of earlier stages of processing also suggest age-related compensatory adaptations: In several studies, older adults rely more on semantic context (sentence stems) to identify sentence-final words when compared to younger adults. This is particularly true when the signal-to-noise ratio is unfavorable, presumably taxing attentional resources (e.g., Pichora-Fuller, Schneider, & Daneman, 1995). Similar findings have emerged from studies of accelerated speech (Wingfield, Koh, Tun, & Rosen, 1999) and cluttered visual working memory (Speranza, Daneman, & Schneider, 2000), suggesting again that under difficult selection conditions, older adults may be flexibly utilizing more top-down processes than do younger adults, even when hearing conditions (dB levels) or viewing conditions are individually tailored and made comparable across participants.

In the context of executive functions and attentional control, again, a closer examination of cognitive performance yields interesting insights. For example, Mayr (2001, Experiment 1) recently demonstrated that older, compared to younger, adults displayed comparable residual switch costs during task-set switching, a paradigm that has become emblematic of executive functioning (for reviews, see Logan, 2003; Monsell & Driver, 2000). In contrast to widely hypothesized age-related declines in inhibitory functioning (e.g., Hasher & Zacks, 1988), and age-related declines in task-set switching (e.g., Kray, Li, & Lindenberger, 2002; Meiran, Gotler, & Perlman, 2001), Mayr reported age-related *increases* in the magnitude of backward inhibition, such that older adults were more efficient than were younger adults at suppressing a task set they had recently abandoned. Mayr's tentative interpretation was that older adults may have been utilizing backward inhibition processes to compensate for age-related difficulties in activating and maintaining relevant task sets. If so, this finding illustrates the flexible nature of the cognitive system in addressing weakened processes by utilizing others.

Extrapolating from the work on age differences and individual differences to special populations, our loss-plus-compensation perspective may be applicable to cases of anxiety disorders or depression, following the cognitive-attentional models recently proposed (Fox, Rabbitt, Waltz; von Hecker et al., this volume; Rokke, Arnell, Koch, & Andrews, 2002). Given the common theme of reduced attentional control or capacity, one could surmise that long-standing clinical conditions such as schizophrenia might bear a functional resemblance to normative cognitive aging or would be overlaid with normative age-related decline over time. From our developmental perspective, we speculate that cognitive adaptations may occur for individuals with such clinical conditions over time, as a means of compensating for reductions in cognitive or attentional processing efficiency.

Ultimately, individuals who develop normatively or nonnormatively must carry out basic information processing tasks on a daily basis. Beyond focusing on the faulty mechanisms or capacity reductions as observed in cross-sectional or group-comparative research, conceptualizing the observed deficits as a result of gradual loss and ameliorative adaptations would be a fruitful direction of research. Arguably, even cognitive functions that appear to remain intact may be carried out using different systems or strategies (see Karmiloff-Smith, 1998 for a similar argument regarding Williams syndrome).

A related issue concerns the causal direction between psychopathology and cognitive status. Ideally, developmental research incorporating longitudinal designs would shed light on this issue. For example, examination of lead-lag relationships using multivariate statistical techniques would indicate whether earlier cognitive status might be predictive of later pathology, whether the relationship should be characterized as more bidirectional (i.e., cognitive predisposition interacts with clinical predisposition) or if a clinical condition leads to a decline of cognitive functioning from normative levels. It may well be that across an extended duration, the directionality of influence changes such that psychopathology precedes cognitive limitations, but then as the individual adjusts, adaptive changes have affects on clinical symptomatology. Going beyond our mere speculations, we urge clinical researchers to consider the possibility that reductions of cognitive processing may be accompanied by adaptive compensatory strategies or changes in cognitive style.

## CONCLUSIONS AND OUTLOOK

In summary, we have briefly surveyed the extant work on normative aging and dual-task processes and have argued for a more ecological approach that takes into consideration individual priorities and strategies used to compensate for weaknesses in other processes. Our own work on cognitive-sensorimotor dual-task performance underscores the importance of identifying the strategic differences in attentional allocation that might arise from variations in task priority or from selective age-related decline in cognitive processes. In relation to research on individual differences and clinically mediated deficits in cognitive capacity, it remains to be seen whether a threshold of capacity reduction, or a state of chronic cognitive reduction, is necessary for compensatory changes to take effect. It also remains for future studies to determine whether such behavioral plasticity has a subsequent effect on neural reorganization or neural recruitment (Cabeza, 2002; Grady & Craik, 2000; Li & Lindenberger, 2002). Future cognitive aging research is also needed to explore whether task priorities change as a function of individual needs (e.g., frail versus physically fit older adults) or task demands (e.g., when the cognitive task is more imperative, such as remembering medications).

## Author Note

We acknowledge the funding support of the Natural Sciences and Engineering Research Council (NSERC) and the Fonds pour la Formation de Chercheurs et l'Aide a la recherche (FCAR) awarded to the first author. Thanks also to Sarah Fraser, Natalie Ebner, and Natalie Phillips for their helpful comments on previous drafts of this chapter.

## References

Allen, P. A., Smith, A. F., Vires-Collins, H., & Sperry, S. (1998). The psychological refractory period; Evidence for age differences in attentional time-sharing. *Psychology and Aging, 13,* 218–229.

Anderson, N. D., Craik, F. I. M., & Naveh-Benjamin, M. (1998). The attentional demands of encoding and retrieval in younger and older adults: 1. Evidence from divided attention costs. *Psychology and Aging, 13,* 405–423.

Baddeley, A. (1986). *Working memory.* Oxford: Oxford University Press.

Baddeley, A. (1992). Working memory. *Science, 255,* 556–559.

Baltes, P. B., & Baltes, M. M. (1990). Psychological perspectives on successful aging: The model of selective optimization with compensation. In P. B. Baltes & M. M. Baltes (Eds.), *Successful aging: Perspectives from the behavioral sciences* (pp. 1–34). Cambridge, NY: Cambridge University Press.

Baron, A., & Mattila, W. R. (1989). Response slowing of older adults: Effects of time-limit contingencies on single- and dual-task performances. *Psychology and Aging, 4,* 66–72.

Bondar, A., Krampe, R. T., & Baltes, P. B. (2004). *The dynamics between balance and cognition in young and older adults: Older adults maintain task-specific flexibility of resource allocation despite higher dual-task costs.* Berlin: Max Planck Institute for Human Development.

Brébion, G., Smith, M. J., & Ehrlich, M. F. (1997). Working memory and aging: Deficit or strategy differences? *Aging, Neuropsychology and Cognition, 4,* 58–57.

Broadbent, D. E., & Gregory, M. (1965). Some confirmatory results on age differences in memory for simultaneous stimulation. *British Journal of Psychology, 56,* 77–80.

Broadbent, D. E., & Heron, A. (1962). Effects of a subsidiary task on performance involving immediate memory by younger and older men. *British Journal of Psychology, 53,* 189–198.

Brown, L. A., Sleik, R. J., Polych, M. A., & Gage, W. H. (2002). Is the prioritization of postural control altered in conditions of postural threat in younger and older adults? *Journal of Gerontology: Medical Sciences, 57A*, M785–M792.

Buchner, D., & Larson, E. (1987). Falls and fractures in patients with Alzheimer-type dementia. *Journal of the American Medical Association, 257*, 1492–1495.

Cabeza, R. (2002). Hemispheric asymmetry reduction in older adults: The HAROLD model. *Psychology and Aging, 17*, 85–100.

Charness, N. (1991). Expertise in chess: The balance between knowledge and search. In K. A. Ericson & J. Smith (Eds.), *Toward a general theory of expertise: Prospects and limits* (pp. 39–63). Cambridge, England: Cambridge University Press.

Craik, F. I. M., & Salthouse, T. A. (Eds.). (2000). *The handbook of aging and cognition* (2nd ed.). Mahwah, NJ: Lawrence Erlbaum Associates.

Crossley, M., & Hiscock, M. (1992). Age-related differences in concurrent-task performance of normal adults: Evidence for a decline in processing resources. *Psychology and Aging, 7*, 499–506.

Daneman, M., & Carpenter, P. A. (1980). Individual differences in working memory and reading. *Journal of Verbal Learning and Verbal Behavior, 19*, 450–466.

Dobbs, A. R., & Rule, B. G. (1989). Adult age differences in working memory. *Psychology and Aging, 4*, 500–503.

Engle, R. W. (2002). Working memory capacity as executive attention. *Current Directions in Psychological Science, 11*, 19–23.

Fernandes, M. A., & Moscovitch, M. (2000). Divided attention and memory: Evidence of substantial interference effects of retrieval and encoding. *Journal of Experimental Psychology General, 129*, 155–176.

Freund, A. M., & Baltes, P. B. (2000). The orchestration of selection, optimization, and compensation: An action-theoretical conceptualization of a theory of developmental regulation. In W. J. Perrig & A. Grob (Eds.), *Control of human behavior, mental processes, and consciousness* (pp. 35–58). Mahwah, NJ: Lawrence Erlbaum Associates.

Freund, A. M., Li, K. Z. H., & Baltes, P. B. (1999). Successful development and aging: The role of selection, optimization, and compensation. In Brandtstädter, J., & Lerner, R. M. (Ed.), *Action and self-development: Theory and research throughout the life-span* (pp. 401–434). Thousand Oaks, CA: Sage.

Glass, J. M., Schumacher, E. H., Lauber, E. J., Zurbriggen, E. L., Gmeindl, L., Kieras, D. E., & Meyer, D. E. (2000). Aging and the psychological refractory period: Task-coordination strategies in young and old adults. *Psychology and Aging, 15*, 571–595.

Grady, C. L., & Craik, F. I. M. (2000). Changes in memory processing with age. *Current Opinion in Neurobiology, 10*, 224–231.

Hartley, A. (1992). Attention. In F. I. M. Craik & T. A. Salthouse (Eds.), *The handbook of aging and cognition* (2nd ed., pp. 3–49). Mahwah, NJ: Lawrence Erlbaum Associates.

Hartley, A. (2001). Age differences in dual-task interference are localized to response-generation processes. *Psychology and Aging, 16*, 47–54.

Hartley, A. A., & Little, D. M. (1999). Age-related differences and similarities in dual-task interference. *Journal of Experimental Psychology: General, 128*, 416–449.

Hasher, L., & Zacks, R. T. (1988). Working memory, comprehension, and aging: A review and a new view. In G. H. Bower (Ed.). *The psychology of learning and motivation: Advances in research and theory*, Vol. 22 (pp. 193–225). San Diego, CA: Academic Press, Inc.

Karmiloff-Smith, A. (1998). Development itself is the key to understanding developmental disorders. *Trends in Cognitive Sciences, 2*, 389–398.

Kemper, S., Herman, R. E., & Lian, C. H. T. (2003). The costs of doing two things at once for young and older adults: Talking while walking, finger tapping, and ignoring noise or speech. *Psychology and Aging, 18*, 181–192.

Korteling, J. E. (1991). Effects of skill integration and perceptual competition on age-related differences in dual-task performance. *Human Factors, 33*, 35–44.

Kramer, A. F., & Larish, J. F. (1996). Aging and dual-task performance. In Rogers, W. A., Fisk, A. D., & Walker, N. (Eds.), *Aging and skilled performance: Advances in theory and application* (pp. 83–112). Mahwah, NJ: Lawrence Erlbaum Associates.

Kramer, A. F., Larish, J. F., & Strayer, D. L. (1995). Training of attentional control in dual task settings: A comparison of young and old adults. *Journal of Experimental Psychology: Applied, 1*, 50–76.

Krampe, R. T., & Baltes, P. B. (2003). Intelligence as adaptive resource development and resource allocation: A new look through the lenses of SOC and expertise. In R. J. Sternberg & E. L. Grigorenko (Eds.), *Perspectives on the psychology of abilities, competencies, and expertise* (pp. 31–69). New York: Cambridge University Press.

Krampe, R. T., Schaefer, S., & Baltes, P. B. (2003). *Walking and long-term-memory retrieval: Dual-task performance in children, young, and older adults*. Berlin, Germany: Max-Planck Institute for Human Development.

Kray, J., Li, K. Z. H., & Lindenberger, U. (2002). Age-specific changes in task-switching components: The role of task uncertainty. *Brain and Cognition, 49*, 363–381.

Kroes, M., Kessels, A. G. H., Kalff, A. C., Feron, F. F. M., Vissers, Y. L. J., Jolles, J., & Vles, J. S. H. (2002). Quality of movement as predictor of ADHD: results from a prospective population study in 5- and 6-year-old children. *Developmental Medicine & Child Neurology, 44*, 753–760.

Lajoie, Y., Teasdale, N., Bard, C., & Fleury, M. (1996). Attentional demands for walking: Age-related changes. In A.-M. Ferrandez & N. Teasdale (Eds.), *Changes in sensory motor behavior in aging* (pp. 235–256). Amsterdam: Elsevier Science.

Li, K. Z. H., & Lindenberger, U. (2002). Relations between aging sensory/sensorimotor and cognitive functions. *Neuroscience and Biobehavioral Reviews, 26*, 777–783.

Li, K. Z. H., Lindenberger, U., Freund, A. M., & Baltes, P. B. (2001). Walking while memorizing: Age-related differences in compensatory behavior. *Psychological Science, 12*, 230–237.

Li, S.-C., Lindenberger, U., Hommel, B., Aschersleben, G., Prinz, W., & Baltes, P. B. (2004). Transformations in the couplings among intellectual abilities and constituent cognitive processes across the life span. *Psychological Science, 15*, 155–163.

Lindenberger, U., & Baltes, P. B. (1994). Sensory functioning and intelligence in old age: A strong connection. *Psychology and Aging, 9,* 339–355.

Lindenberger, U., & Baltes, P. B. (1997). Intellectual functioning in old and very old age: Cross-sectional results from the Berlin Aging Study. *Psychology and Aging, 12,* 410–432.

Lindenberger, U., Marsiske, M., & Baltes, P. B. (2000). Memorizing while walking: Increase in dual-task costs from young adulthood to old age. *Psychology and Aging, 3,* 417–436.

Logan, G. D. (2003). Executive control of thought and action: In search of the wild homunculus. *Current Directions in Psychological Science, 12,* 45–48.

Lorsbach, T. C., & Simpson, G. B. (1988). Dual-task performance as a function of adult age and task complexity. *Psychology and Aging, 3,* 210–212.

Maylor, E. A., Allison, S., & Wing, A. M. (2001). Effects of spatial and nonspatial cognitive activity on postural stability. *British Journal of Psychology, 92,* 319–338.

Maylor, E. A., & Wing, A. M. (1996). Age differences in postural stability are increased by additional cognitive demands. *Journal of Gerontology: Psychological Sciences, 51B,* P143–P154.

Mayr, U. (2001). Age differences in the selection of mental sets: The role of inhibition, stimulus ambiguity, and response-set overlap. *Psychology and Aging, 16,* 96–109.

McDowd, J. M. (1986). The effects of age and extended practice on divided attention performance. *Journal of Gerontology, 41,* 764–769.

McDowd, J. M., & Craik, F. I. M. (1988). Effects of aging and task difficulty on divided attention performance. *Journal of Experimental Psychology: Human Perception and Performance, 14,* 267–280.

McDowd, J. M., & Shaw, R. J. (2000). Attention and aging: A functional perspective. In F. I. M. Craik & T. A. Salthouse (Eds.), *The handbook of aging and cognition* (2nd ed., pp. 221–292). Mahwah, NJ: Lawrence Erlbaum Associates.

McDowd, J., Vercruyssen, M., & Birren, J. E. (1991). Aging, divided attention, and dual task performance. In D. L. Damos (Ed.), *Multiple-task performance* (pp. 387–414). London: Taylor & Francis.

McGhie, A., Chapman, J., & Lawson, J. S. (1965). The effect of distraction on schizophrenic performance: I. Perception and immediate memory. *British Journal of Psychiatry, 111,* 383–390.

Means, K. M., Rodell, D. E., O'Sullivan, P. S., & Winger, R. M. (1998). Comparison of a functional obstacle course with an index of clinical gait and balance and postural sway. *Journal of Gerontology: Medical Sciences, 53A,* M331–M335.

Meiran, N., Gotler, A., & Perlman, A. (2001). Old age is associated with a pattern of relatively intact and relatively impaired task-set switching abilities. *Journals of Gerontology: Psychological Sciences, 56B,* P88–P102.

Meyer, D. E., & Kieras, D. E. (1997). A computational theory of executive cognitive processes and multiple-task performance: I. Basic mechanisms. *Psychological Review, 104,* 3–65.

Miyake, A., Friedman, N. P., Emerson, M. J., Witzki, A. H., & Howerter, A. (2000). The unity and diversity of executive functions and their contributions to complex "frontal lobe" tasks: A latent variable analysis. *Cognitive Psychology, 41,* 49–10.

Miyake, A., Friedman, N. P., Rettinger, D. A., Shah, P., & Hegarty, M. (2001). How are visuospatial working memory, executive functioning, and spatial abilities related? A latent-variable analysis. *Journal of Experimental Psychology: General, 130*, 621–640.

Monsell, S., & Driver, J. (Eds.). (2000). *Control of cognitive processes: Attention and performance XVIII.* Cambridge, MA: The MIT Press.

Nakamura, T., Meguro, K., Yamazaki, H., Okuzumi, H., Tanaka, A., Horikawa, A., Yamaguchi, K., Katsuyama, N., Nakano, M., Arai, H., & Sasaki, H. (1997). Postural and gait disturbance correlated with decreased frontal cerebral blood flow in Alzheimer disease. *Alzheimer Disease and Associated Disorders, 11*, 132–139.

Nicolson, R. I., & Fawcett, A. J. (1993). Children with dyslexia automatize temporal skills more slowly. *Annals of the New York Academy of Sciences, 682*, 390–393.

Park, D. C., Smith, A., Dudley, W. N., & Lafronza, V. N. (1989). Effects of age and a divided attention task presented during encoding and retrieval on memory. *Journal of Experimental Psychology: Learning, Memory and Cognition, 15*, 1185–1191.

Pashler, H. (1994). Dual-task interference in simple tasks: Data and theory. *Psychological Bulletin, 116*, 220–244.

Pichora-Fuller, M. K., Schneider, B. A., Daneman, M. (1995). How young and old adults listen to and remember speech in noise. *Journal of the Acoustical Society of America, 97*, 593–608.

Ponds, R. W., Brouwer, W. H., & van Wolffelaar, P. C. (1988). Age differences in divided attention in a simulated driving task. *Journal of Gerontology, 43*, 151–156.

Rabbitt, P., Lowe, C., & Shilling, V. (2001). Frontal tests and models for cognitive ageing. *European Journal of Cognitive Psychology, 13*, 5–28.

Rapp, M., Krampe, R. T., & Baltes, P. B. (2003). *Selective resource allocation to postural control is preserved in Alzheimer's Disease.* Berlin: Max Planck Institute for Human Development.

Rogers, R. D., & Monsell, S. (1995). The cost of a predictable switch between simple cognitive tasks. *Journal of Experimental Psychology: General, 124*, 207–231.

Rogers, W. A., Bertus, E. L., & Gilbert, D. K. (1994). Dual-task assessment of age differences in automatic process development. *Psychology and Aging, 9*, 398–413.

Rokke, P. D., Arnell. K. M., Koch, M. D., & Andrews, J. T. (2002). Dual-task attention deficits in dysphoric mood. *Journal of Abnormal Psychology, 111*, 370–379.

Salthouse, T. A. (1996). The processing-speed theory of adult age differences in cognition. *Psychological Review, 103*, 403–428.

Salthouse, T. A., & Craik, F. I. M. (2000). Closing comments. In F. I. M. Craik & T. A. Salthouse (Eds.), *The handbook of aging and cognition* (2nd ed., pp. 689–703). Mahwah, NJ: Lawrence Erlbaum Associates.

Salthouse, T. A., Fristoe, N. M., Lineweaver, T. T., & Coon, V. E. (1995). Aging of attention: Does the ability to divide decline? *Memory & Cognition, 23*, 59–71.

Salthouse, T. A., Rogan, J. D., & Prill, K. A. (1984). Division of attention: Age differences on a visually presented memory task. *Memory & Cognition, 12*, 613–620.

Sattin, R. W. (1992). Falls among older persons: A public health perspective. *Annual Reviews in Public Health, 13*, 489–508.

Sedek, G., & von Hecker, U. (2004). Effects of subclinical depression and aging on generative reasoning about linear orders: Same or different processing limitations? *Journal of Experimental Psychology: General, 133*, 237–260.

Sheppard, D. M., Bradshaw, J. L., Georgiou, N., Bradshaw, J. A., & Lee, P. (2000). Movement sequencing in children with Tourette's syndrome and attention deficit hyperactivity disorder. *Movement Disorder*, *15*, 1184–1193.

Shumway-Cook, A., Woollacott, M., Kerns, K. A., & Baldwin, M. (1997). The effects of two types of cognitive tasks on postural stability in older adults with and without a history of falls. *Journal of Gerontology: Medical Sciences*, *52A*, M232–M240.

Simoneau, G. G., & Leibowitz, H. W. (1996). Posture, gait, and falls. In J. E. Birren & K. W. Schaie (Eds.), *Handbook of the psychology of aging* (pp. 204–217). San Diego, CA: Academic Press.

Smiley-Oyen, A. L., Subbot, M. D., & Gallagher, J. D. (2001). Bimanual control and timing precision in children with developmental dyslexia. *Journal of Sport and Exercise Psychology*, *23*, S57–S57.

Somberg, B. L., & Salthouse, T. A. (1982). Divided attention abilities in young and old adults. *Journal of Experimental Psychology: Human Perception and Performance*, *8*, 651–663.

Speranza, F., Daneman, M., & Schneider, B. A. (2000). How aging affects the reading of words in noisy backgrounds. *Psychology and Aging*, *15*, 253–258.

Stelmach, G. E., Zelaznik, H. N., & Lowe, D. (1990). The influence of aging and attentional demands on recovery from postural instability. *Aging*, *2*, 155–161.

Strayer, D. L., & Johnston, W. A. (2001). Driven to distraction: Dual-task studies of simulated driving and conversing on a cellular telephone. *Psychological Science*, *12*, 462–466.

Talland, G. A. (1962). The effect of age on speed of simple manual skill. *Journal of Genetic Psychology*, *100*, 69–76.

Teasdale, N., Bard, C., Dadouchi, F., Fleury, M., LaRue, J., & Stelmach, G. E. (1992). Posture and elderly persons: Evidence for deficits in the central integrative mechanisms. In G. E. Stelmach & J. Requin (Eds.), *Tutorials in motor behavior II* (pp. 917–931). Amsterdam: Elsevier Science.

Teasdale, N., Bard, C., LaRue, J., & Fleury, M. (1993). On the cognitive penetrability of posture control. *Experimental Aging Research*, *19*, 1–13.

Thapa, P. B., Gideon, P., Brockman, K. G., Fought, R. L., & Ray, W. A. (1996). Clinical and biomechanical measures of balance as fall predictors in ambulatory nursing home residents. *Journal of Gerontology: Medical Sciences*, *51A*, M239–M246.

Tinetti, M. E. (1995). Falls. In W. R. Hazzard, E. L. Bierman, J. P. Blass, W. H. Ettinger, & J. B. Halter (Eds.), *Principles of geriatric medicine and gerontology* (3rd ed.). New York: McGraw-Hill.

Tinetti, M. E., Speechley, M., & Ginter, S. F. (1988). Risk factors for falls among elderly persons living in the community. *The New England Journal of Medicine*, *319*, 1701–1707.

Tsang, P. A., & Shaner, T. L. (1998). Age, attention, expertise, and time-sharing performance. *Psychology and Aging*, *13*, 323–347.

Tun, P. A., & Wingfield, A. (1995). Does dividing attention become harder with age? Findings from the divided attention questionnaire. *Aging and Cognition*, *2*, 39–66.

Waters, G. S., & Caplan, D. (1986). The measurement of verbal working memory capacity and its relation to reading comprehension. *Quarterly Journal of Experimental Psychology, 49A,* 51–79.

Wechsler, D. (1981). *WAIS-R manual.* New York: Psychological Corp.

Wickens, C. D., Braune, R., & Stokes, A. (1987). Age differences in the speed and capacity of information processing: 1. A dual-task approach. *Psychology and Aging, 2,* 70–78.

Wingfield, A., Tun, P. A., Koh, C. K., & Rosen, M. J. (1999). Regaining lost time: Adult aging and the effect of time restoration on recall of time-compressed speech. *Psychology and Aging, 14,* 380–389.

Wolfson, L. (1991). Falls and gait. In R. Katzman & J. W. Rowe (Eds.), *Principles of geriatric neurology* (pp. 281–299). Philadelphia: F. A. Davies.

Woollacott, M. H., & Shumway-Cook, A. (2002). Attention and the control of posture and gait: a review of an emerging area of research. *Gait and Posture, 16,* 1–14.

Wright, R. E. (1981). Aging, divided attention, and processing capacity. *Journal of Gerontology, 36,* 605–614.

# 9

## Cognitive Performance After Preexposure to Uncontrollability and in a Depressive State

*Going with a Simpler "Plan B"*

Daniel N. McIntosh, Grzegorz Sedek, Susan Fojas, Aneta Brzezicka-Rotkiewicz, and Miroslaw Kofta

What is a helpless mind to do? Extending previous work noting parallels between cognitive impairments in depression and after preexposure to uncontrollability (Cox, Enns, Borger, & Parker, 1999; Flett, Vredenburg, & Krames, 1997; Hartlage, Alloy, Vazquez, & Dykman, 1993; Healy & Williams, 1988; Seligman, 1978), we present in this chapter new evidence that the mind switches to a simpler, less effortful "Plan B." In examining the pattern of performance of complex cognitive tasks observed among helpless or depressed participants, we observe that this lowered level of performance is still clearly above the threshold of random or chaotic behavior. In our presentation of previous and new experimental evidence, we are guided by the view that the switch to the less efficient, but still not chaotic, performance (i.e., a switch to a *cognitive exhaustion state*, see Kofta & Sedek, 1998; von Hecker, Sedek, & McIntosh, 2000; von Hecker & Sedek, 1999) might represent an adaptive way of adjusting to prolonged uncontrollability and might also describe characteristic aspects of cognitive functioning in depression. In these states, there are not merely decrements across all measures, but instead there are impairments specifically in higher-order processes.

After we recall the origins of uncontrollability research, we unpack our perspective first by noting the similar pattern of cognitive deficits after exposure to uncontrollability among two very smart, although completely different, populations: laboratory rats and high school students. We then describe the cognitive exhaustion model of uncontrollability and depression and briefly summarize existing research evidence. Next, we describe our research examining cognitive functioning in complex task situations applying different experimental paradigms: syllogistic reasoning, dual-task performance, a modified Oberauer task, and a cognitive psychophysical approach to neurological tests (PASAT). The common denominator of these complex cognitive tasks is that they can be solved at various levels of efficiency, and different patterns of inefficiency can be attributed to specific dysfunctions. Our particular interest is to shed more light on the specificity of the "pathomechanism" of the inefficient performance of helpless or depressed participants across different cognitive tasks: What are the characteristic aspects of task demands that are preserved, which aspects are seriously impaired, and how might these behavioral patterns be explained by existing models of cognitive performance? In brief, we find that individuals who are in depressed or helpless states fall back from using the most effective strategies and instead use a simpler "Plan B" – they do the one thing that is clear and do it well.

BACKGROUND

## Origins of Uncontrollability Research

Since Seligman and colleagues (Seligman & Maier, 1967; Overmier & Seligman, 1967) described learning deficits in dogs exposed to uncontrollable shocks, psychologists have sought to understand the effects of uncontrollability on humans. Sustained exposure to uncontrollability leads to a syndrome of psychological disturbances (Wortman & Brehm, 1975). Three deficits are classically associated with such helplessness states: failure to initiate responses (motivational), emotional disturbances (affective), and failure to learn (cognitive; Maier & Seligman, 1976).

Motivating investigation into learned helplessness has been the observation that it may present a laboratory model of some mental dysfunctions associated with reactive depression (Miller & Seligman, 1975; Seligman, 1978). In 1975, Miller and Seligman suggested that the similar effects of helplessness training and depression appear primarily cognitive in nature. Despite this view of cognitive deficits as a key link between helplessness and depression, since the late 1970s, the most influential theoretical approaches in human uncontrollability research have highlighted the role of beliefs and negative emotions as the primary motivational aspects of performance deficits. One approach follows the attributions individuals make in uncontrollable circumstances (Abramson, Seligman, & Teasdale, 1978; Sweeney, Anderson, & Bailey, 1986). A second view focuses on the negative emotional concomitants of failure (e.g., Benson & Kennelly, 1976; Frankel & Snyder, 1978), holding motivation as the primary deficit. Linking to the early proposal that the cognitive deficit in helplessness is crucial in understanding performance deficits associated with depression, our work has instead focused on understanding the nature of the relatively neglected cognitive dysfunctions caused by exposure to uncontrollable circumstances.

## Animal and Human Studies on Complex Learning After Preexposure to Uncontrollability

To illustrate the similarities among cognitive deficits in animals and humans, we succinctly present studies on cognitive deficits among rats after inescapable shocks (Jackson, Alexander, & Maier, 1980; Minor, Jackson, & Maier, 1984; Maier & Minor, 1993) and compare the results with our previous research on uncontrollability deficits among students (Kofta & Sedek, 1989b; Sedek & Kofta, 1990).

Jackson et al. (1980) used a Y-maze response choice task in which the rat must choose between two response alternatives (turning left or turning right). Because of the Y shape of the maze, the rat could be in any of the arms at the start of a given block of trials, and the correct avoidance response was defined as the systematic turning in relation to the rat's actual position (e.g., go to the right). Rats previously exposed to inescapable shocks learned this rule more poorly than did rats from the control group. In fact, the performance of rats from the uncontrollability exposed group did not improve above chance (50% errors) during half of the experimental session, and the difference in accuracy between the two groups remained substantial through the end of the experimental session. Of particular interest is that the accuracy index was not correlated with response latency. This pattern of dissociation of simple response performance and loss of complex functions is one we will see also in later research.

The researchers replicated these results with the extended triadic design. Rats from the first control group were merely restrained in their wheel-turn boxes and did not receive any shocks in the first phase of the study. The second control group (escape) was first trained to escape shocks by turning a wheel. The third (yoked) group had experimentally induced uncontrollability; rats in this condition received inescapable shocks yoked to the shocks received by the second control group. Therefore, rats from both the escape control group and the yoked experimental group received the same number and durations of shocks; however, only the rats from the yoked group had no control over the shocks. All groups were examined on the Y-maze avoidance learning task 24 hours later. Rats from the yoked group were significantly slower to learn the escape rule than the rats from the both control groups.

Minor et al. (1984) replicated these findings and demonstrated that the uncontrollability-related impairment was especially pronounced when irrelevant external cues were presented (a light appeared randomly in one of the three arms). Therefore, the poor learning was attributed to the deficits in selective attention.

An alternative explanation is that the results are due to the inescapable shocks producing excessive fear (perhaps inescapable shocks produce more fear than the same, but escapable shocks), which is activated in the next escape tasks. In fact, the model assuming intensive overactivation of critical neurons in frontal cortex resulting from pretreatment fear, leading to sensitization and neural exhaustion, is intensively examined in the animal helplessness and escape performance literature (Hunter, Balleine, & Minor, 2003; Minor, Chang, & Winslow, 1994; Minor & Hunter, 2002). However, Maier and Minor (1993) demonstrated that the deficits in the Y-maze choice learning could not be attributed to induced fear. Selected rats from each condition received fear-reducing drugs (e.g., diazepam) before the pretreatment sessions. The drugs eliminated the standard motivational deficit between the groups in simple escape response speed (implying that the motivational deficit is emotion-related), but they had no effect on the interference in escape learning observable in the group preexposed to uncontrollability. These findings strongly suggest that uncontrollability in rats interferes with complex choice learning through a mechanism not involving fear/anxiety processes.

In our studies with high school students (Kofta & Sedek, 1989b) examining the relative role of uncontrollability and repeated failure on complex avoidance learning and response latency (response speed), we obtained a similar pattern of findings. The uncontrollability manipulation we applied was an unsolvable versus a solvable concept-formation task, frequently used in studies on learned helplessness in humans (e.g., Hiroto & Seligman, 1975). During the test phase, participants were presented with a series of trials with unpleasant noises. They had the opportunity to avoid the unpleasant noise by discovering a hidden rule (pressing the appropriate button when a green lamp was lit on a panel). If participants failed to avoid the noise, they could escape it by pressing another button (the escape response was simpler). Across two studies, we found interaction effects between experimental condition and block of trials. Specifically, for participants in the control group, the number of correct avoidance responses increased over time, whereas for participants in the uncontrollable condition they did not. However, helpless participants were not completely incapable of learning. As with the rats, reaction time and accuracy were not coupled. Data for the latency measure (primarily measuring speed of escape responding) showed that both control and helpless participants got faster over trials. This is the first demonstration in humans of the characteristic pattern that we scrutinize with subsequent experimental paradigms.

To summarize, for both animals and humans, preexposure to uncontrollability seems to impair more refined ways of solving complex tasks but preserves a capability to manage the tasks using simpler fallback strategies. As specified in the next section, our research is guided by the general idea of the evolutionary adaptive ability of higher organisms to switch to a cognitive exhaustion state after prolonged and futile mental activity. In this temporary Plan B state cognitive performance is less efficient but requires less mental effort. The ability to avoid a complete loss of problem-solving capabilities and to preserve even nonoptimal performance is an adaptive strategy in strained situations.

## Cognitive Exhaustion Background

The research described in this chapter is based on the cognitive exhaustion model of helplessness and depression. This model assumes that people are likely to engage in systematic mental activity when dealing with problem-solving situations. In controllable situations, these mental activities stimulate people to engage in more generative modes of thinking like the construction of integrative memory representations, such as mental models or elaborating complex cognitive strategies with a hierarchy of subgoals. However, in uncontrollable surroundings, such activity is futile because it cannot lead to real progress in problem solving. It is hypothesized that prolonged cognitive effort without "cognitive gain" results in an altered psychological state, which we term *cognitive exhaustion*.

The essential quality of this transitory state is a generalized impairment of constructive and integrative mental processing. In terms of general adaptive functions, cognitive exhaustion states seem especially disruptive to more complex problem solutions requiring multiple nonroutine, flexible steps of processing in either achievement or interpersonal realms.

There are a number of close parallels between some aspects of cognitive functioning in depression and the state resulting from preexposure to uncontrollability. We believe that some of the cognitive impairments observed in depression can be explained in terms of experienced uncontrollability. This experience may stem from past, irreversible life events, from subsequent ruminating, or from counterfactual thinking. We theorize that uncontrollability and, in particular, ruminating thoughts about uncontrollable conditions, lead to a depletion of those cognitive resources that support generative and flexible thinking. On the other hand, depressed persons' performance is seldom impaired in tasks dealing with more elementary cognitive strategies.

In another chapter (von Hecker, Sedek, Piber-Dabrowska & Bedynska, this volume), findings are reviewed that examine specifically how the cognitive deficits in depression and helplessness states might be characterized as dysfunctions in deploying higher-order strategies requiring coordinative processing of incoming piecemeal information into mental models (von Hecker & Sedek, 1999; Sedek & von Hecker, 2004). In the present chapter, we tested the predictions that in those states there are also decrements in other complex cognitive tasks.

In a number of studies over the past decade, we have used a laboratory paradigm that, as we argue later, is analogous to a crucial aspect of a depressive style of rumination, to investigate cognitive deficits associated with cognitive effort without cognitive gain (Kofta & Sedek, 1998; Sedek & Kofta, 1990). This *Informational Helplessness Training* (IHT) paradigm differs from behavioral learned helplessness approaches to depression in that it does not require ineffective behavior for the deficits to appear. In IHT, participants in each of four problems attempt to learn a rule based on five dimensions, each with two features: (a) size (large, small); (b) shape (circle, triangle); (c) pattern (dotted, plain); (d) line position (top, bottom); and (e) letter size (r, R). One figure at a time appears on a monitor with "yes" or "no," indicating the presence or absence of the target feature. In the control condition, "yes" and "no" each appear 50% of the time and are consistent across trials with a given feature. In the helpless condition, "yes" and "no" each appear 50% of the time, but each feature appears twice with "yes" and twice with "no," so that no hypothesis for the identity of the target feature is correct. Each participant indicates his or her final hypothesis at the end of the trial from a list that includes all the features. At no time is the participant given feedback on his or her performance.

In our first set of experiments (Sedek & Kofta, 1990), we confirmed the hypothesis that after preexposure to informational uncontrollability, performance in a more complex task (avoidance of unpleasant noise) is grossly impaired but performance in a simpler task (escape learning) remains intact. The more recent research indicates that among helpless participants and also among subclinically depressed students, subsequent constructive and integrative mental processing is impeded (von Hecker & Sedek, 1999). Participants in the helplessness condition show cognitive demobilization, lack of task involvement, inhibited generation of ideas, and difficulties with attentional focus (Sedek & Kofta, 1990; Sedek, Kofta, & Tyszka, 1993). This phenomenon may account for deficits such as impaired cognitive functioning in depression and intellectual helplessness in school settings (Kofta, 1993; Kofta & Sedek, 1998; Sedek & Kofta, 1990; Sedek & McIntosh, 1998). The primacy of the cognitive underpinnings of the phenomenon is supported by data showing that these deficits emerge in conditions that minimize the likelihood of effort withdrawal as an ego-protective tactic, in the absence of social performance feedback, when negative mood is statistically controlled, and for accuracy but not effort outcomes (Kofta & Sedek, 1989b; Ric & Scharnitzky, 2003; Sedek & Kofta, 1990; Sedek & McIntosh, 1998; for discussion, see Snyder & Frankel, 1989 and Kofta & Sedek, 1989a).

It is important to note that during IHT participants from both control and uncontrollable groups are not overtly responding and consequently there is no evaluative feedback concerning their responses. The essence of this procedure is exposure to inconsistent task information that does not enable formulation and support for any reasonable task solution, even when a considerable amount of cognitive effort is invested. As we discuss later, some persistent mental activities among depressed individuals, such as ruminations or counterfactual thinking, might be conceptualized as self-generated forms of informational helplessness training.

### Ruminations and Counterfactuals as Forms of Helplessness Training in Depression

Rumination may link helplessness and depression, as it may serve as a form of helplessness training after an aversive event and thus cause the cognitive deficit we have explored in the laboratory. Moreover, nonproductive rumination associated with depression may be part of the cause of cognitive deficits seen in depressed individuals.

After a negative event, individuals often experienced intrusive, recurrent thoughts about it; this rumination is considered part of the process of psychologically integrating the information of the experience (Horowitz, 1976; Janoff-Bulman, 1989). Although repeated thoughts of negative events may be necessary for assimilating such experiences, they are dysfunctional if they do not cause progress in understanding such events (Epstein, 1998). One type of reflection that differs from more general rumination is counterfactual thinking, which focuses not on the events as they actually occurred but rather on consideration of what did *not* happen – how the event may have been avoided (Davis, Lehman, Wortman, Silver, & Thompson, 1995). Counterfactuals may be constructive when they enable enhanced control over future events; however, in situations in which future control is not possible (e.g., a singular traumatic event), counterfactual thinking is probably not adaptive (Davis et al., 1995; Markman & Weary, 1998). Consideration of alternative realities that are better than one's true situation is associated with less satisfaction in laboratory paradigms (Markman, Gavanski, Sherman, & McMullen, 1993) and higher levels of distress after traumatic life events (Bulman & Wortman, 1977; Davis et al., 1995). As we elaborated in more detail elsewhere (Kofta & Sedek, 1998), repeated engagement in mental undoing of a negative event means long-lasting cognitive investment in a futile problem-solving attempt, just as IHT provides exposure to long-lasting cognitive effort without any gain.

As Joormann (this volume) notes, there is an important difference between rumination that facilitates digestion of an event (see McIntosh, Silver, & Wortman, 1993) and rumination that is simply cognitive chewing. We believe this distinction between effective and ineffective cognitive processing is crucial and provides a window into understanding both the effects of counterfactual ruminations after aversive events and some cognitive deficits of depression. Rumination is a key cognitive characteristic of dysphoria and depression (Hertel, 2004; Papageorgiou & Siegle, 2003; see also Joormann, this volume); individuals who are depressed experience sustained cognitive load in the seconds following exposure to emotional information (Siegle, Steinhauer, Carter, Ramel, & Thase, 2003). Rumination in the presence of dysphoria is associated with reduced ability to solve problems (Nolen-Hoeksema, 1996). Indeed, it is rumination combined with dysphoria that appears detrimental, not mere rumination (Lyubomirsky, Kasri, & Zehm, 2003). Depressive rumination appears different from typical rumination in that it involves brooding about problems without taking action to solve those problems (Nolen-Hoeksema, 1996). This thinking without solution is reminiscent of counterfactual thinking and the cognitive effort combined with no cognitive gain that leads to cognitive exhaustion. Note that rumination after a stressful event seems particularly predictive of depressive episodes and their duration (Robinson & Alloy, 2003). In this sense "bad habits" (Hertel, 2004) of being involved in ineffective cognitive activities such as a depressive way of ruminating and counterfactual thinking might be understood as cognitive entrapments producing prolonged effects similar to a situation of endless informational helplessness training.

## NEW RESEARCH

In the following sections, we review studies based on the helplessness and cognitive exhaustion theories discussed above. The goal of this set of studies is to identify the nature of cognitive deficits in uncontrollability and depression. We start with a demonstration of how uncontrollability causes individuals to think more simply on syllogism tasks and then move to demonstrations of parallel deficits seen in clinical depression and helplessness on dual tasks. In both groups, the deficit in complex thinking is evident, yet there is a preservation of performance on simple, straightforward tasks. We next present work that conceptually replicates the dual-task findings and examines specifically the role of negatively valenced information. In the final paradigm, we use time–accuracy functions to more closely determine the mechanisms of cognitive inefficiency we see in helplessness and depression.

### IHT and Syllogisms

To examine complex thinking in helplessness, we had undergraduate participants solve a series of syllogistic reasoning tasks. They were randomly assigned in a yoked design to helpless and control conditions. IHT, as described previously, was used to manipulate helplessness. Participants completed a syllogisms task used by Channon and Baker (1994), which was adapted from Gilhooly, Logie, Wetherick, and Wynn (1993).

Each participant was presented serially with 20 syllogisms, each consisting of two premises from which a solution had to be deduced. There are three strategies of varying sophistication that participants could use to solve syllogisms. The most sophisticated strategy is logic, which leads to correct conclusions in every case. A less sophisticated strategy follows two atmosphere rules as summarized by Begg and Denny (1969). The rule of quality states that if at least one premise is negative, then the conclusion is negative; if neither premise is negative, then the conclusion is positive. The rule of quantity states that if at least one premise is particular, then the conclusion is particular; if neither premise is particular, then the conclusion is universal. A still simpler strategy is matching, in which the rule is to match the form of the solution to the most conservative form of the premises, where the forms from most to least conservative are "No," "Some not," "Some," and "All." Note that the less sophisticated strategies do not require keeping both premises in mind when determining the answer. A simple, but not completely ineffective, rule can be used.

Responses were compared to those produced by the three strategies. In cases in which more than one strategy could have been used to produce the answer given, participants received credit for using both (or all) strategies. The number of responses fitting each strategy category was totaled, and participants were categorized by the strategy type employed in at least 55% of their responses. If participants used multiple strategies equally and at least 55% of the time, they were categorized as using a mixed strategy (e.g., atmosphere/matching). If no strategy was used consistently, the participant was categorized as such. A score was created in which the strategies used consistently were ranked by level of sophistication (logic = 5, atmosphere = 4, atmosphere/matching = 3, matching = 2, and no consistent strategy = 1). Higher scores on this measure reflect the use of more sophisticated strategies.

Consistent with expectations, there was a significant difference between control and helplessness trained groups in the level of sophistication of the strategies used in solving syllogisms, with controls consistently using more sophisticated strategies than the helpless group. Helplessness appears to reduce complex thinking, but did not result in completely random performance. In the studies that follow, we use a variety of paradigms to determine what aspects of performance are reduced in helplessness and depression and what aspects are spared.

## Clinical Depression, IHT, and Dual-Task Performance

We adopted an analytical approach to understanding the mechanisms of lowered efficiency of depressed and helpless participants in cognitively demanding tasks. We begin from an analysis of similarities in the impairments in dual-task processing between clinically depressed patients and students who underwent IHT. An informative introduction to the history and goals of dual-task methodology is offered by Li, Krampe, & Bodnar (this volume). We share their perspective and the view of other authors in the present volume that it is important not only to look at general composite mean levels of performance of given task, but also to conduct more fine-grained analyses of the behavioral patterns responsible for the observable group difference in task performance (see the analytical approach of West and Bowry, this volume, to understand the pattern of Stroop test performance of older adults). In doing so, we first describe the dual-task problems applied in these studies and then present analytical predictions examined in a series of experiments.

In the first experiment on dual-task processing (McIntosh & Sedek, 2005), 24 clinically depressed patients participated; they were tested in the beginning of their stay in a psychiatric hospital and 1 month later after intensive pharmacotherapy. A control group was matched to the clinical group on age and education. The findings of this study are compared to results of a second experimental study in which 24 high school students underwent IHT and another 24 students were in the control group.

We examined participants' cognitive functioning using a modified version of the dual-task procedure developed by Necka (1996, 1997). In this task, participants first completed a series of a primary task, and then they engaged in a series of trials while also performing a secondary task. The single, primary task involved letter recognition. A computer program presented an uppercase letter in a central frame on a screen. The program then presented various lowercase letters in different surrounding frames. Participants were to press the left key of the computer mouse whenever the lowercase letter matching the uppercase target was presented. The matched letter was presented for 1 second. During the primary task two or four distracting letters were simultaneously visible. We recorded *hits* (the number of times the key was pressed when a letter matching the target was present), *false alarms* (the number of times the key was pressed when the matching lowercase letter was not on screen), and the *response time* (RT) for the correct responses, that is, RT of hits (how long after the matching letter appeared does the participant press the key).

During the dual-task segment, participants simultaneously completed both the primary task and a secondary task. For the secondary task, the computer program displayed a horizontal line in one of the rectangles next to the letter matrix used for the primary task. The line automatically drifted downward, and the participant used the right mouse key to raise the line. The task was to press the right mouse key to prevent the moving line from crossing two boundaries indicated by small spots. If the line fell too far or was raised too high, the computer made an unpleasant noise. As a measure of secondary task performance, we recorded the mean deviation from the middle points. These data addressed the question of whether performance on the primary task is sacrificed to enhance secondary task performance.

From the analytical, procedural perspective adopted here, the cognitive demands of this dual task can be understood as the flexible and orchestrated implementation of several (sub)goals. The first, relatively simple goal was to quickly press the appropriate key if the participant notices the correct letter. If we calculated the mean correct RT, we can assess the efficiency of this procedure, *independent* of whether the number of correct responses (hits) was relatively low or high. We expected that this goal would be executed relatively well by depressed or helpless participants because it is simple and clearly explicated in the instructions. However, there were three other goals that needed to be implemented to perform the dual-task requirements most effectively. To implement the second goal, participants needed to notice *all* matched elements (maximize number of hits over omissions). To implement the third goal, participants needed to inhibit the tendency of pressing the mouse key on not matched (distracting) letters, to avoid making false alarms. The fourth goal was to keep the performance of the secondary task at the demanded level.

From the cognitive exhaustion perspective that assumes worsening of cognitive efficiency during task performance, we predicted deeper impairments for the number of hits and false alarms (these procedures are more complex to implement, as they require contingent responses) than for correct RT measure (this goal is the easiest to implement, as it requires only attention to one stimulus state and motivation to perform a simple task).

For the clinical study, the methodological problem discussed in detail by Li, Krampe, and Bondar (this volume) in their chapter about dual-task approach in studying aging was immediately apparent. The clinically depressed participants differed from control participants not only on dual-task performance, but also on single-task performance. Therefore, to evaluate the specific demands created by adding the secondary task, we calculated dual-task costs [see detailed discussion of Li et al., this volume, about relative and proportional dual-task costs (DTC)]. For hits and correct RT, dual-task costs were calculated by computing the difference in single versus dual-task performance, then dividing by single-task performance.

The predicted pattern emerged (see Figure 9.1) concerning DTC for correct RT and hits. There were no significant differences for correct RT among clinically depressed patients, those patients after 1 month of pharmacotherapy, and control participants. However, a different pattern was revealed for the hits; there was a proportionally similar number of hits made by depressed participants before pharmacotherapy in comparison to the test after pharmacotherapy, and both pre- and post-pharmacotherapy depressed groups differed from control participants. This deficit was especially evident in the dual-task conditions. For the false alarms measure, there was an interesting pattern (see Figure 9.2), indicating that the number of false alarms did not change significantly after 1 month of pharmacotherapy and did differ significantly from the control group. In contrast to hits and correct RT measures, the number of false alarms was similar in single- and dual-task conditions.

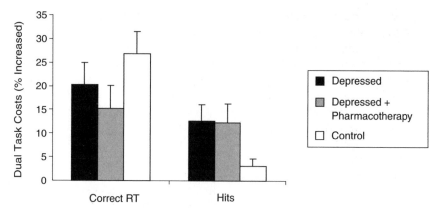

FIGURE 9.1. Dual-task related decline in performance in Correct RT and Hits on Necka task for depressed participants pre- and post-pharmacotherapy and for control participants. There are no group differences for correct RT. Regarding Hits, control participants showed significantly less dual-task costs than pre- and post-pharmacotherapy depressed groups.

Regarding the students in which IHT was used to induce helplessness, the pattern for DTC concerning correct RT and hits is quite similar to the depression data when comparing participants in the uncontrollable condition to control students (see Figure 9.3).

Again, there was no difference in correct RT, but there was a difference in number of hits. As with the depressed patients, the helpless students pressed the key button as quickly as the control participants *if they noticed*

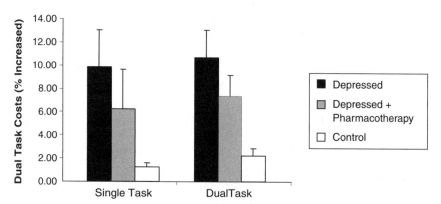

FIGURE 9.2. Number of false alarms during single and dual conditions on the Necka task for depressed participants pre- and post-pharmacotherapy and for control participants. False alarms did not change after 1 month of pharmacotherapy, and the control group showed fewer false alarms than did the other groups. The number of false alarms was similar in single- and dual-task conditions.

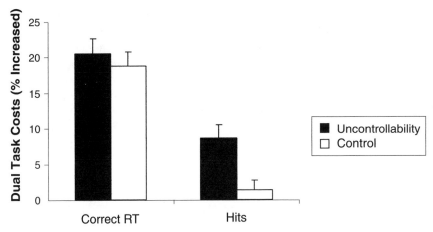

FIGURE 9.3. Dual-task related decline in performance in Correct RT and Hits on Necka task for participants in control and induced uncontrollability conditions. There are no group differences for correct RT. Control participants showed significantly less dual-task costs than did those in the uncontrollability group.

the correct element. However, similar to clinically depressed patients, helpless students made proportionally fewer correct responses in the more demanding dual-task condition. For the number of false alarms (see Figure 9.4), the pattern is slightly different than it was in the clinical study; the number of false alarms is significantly higher in the uncontrollable situation, but this difference is especially visible in the dual-task situation.

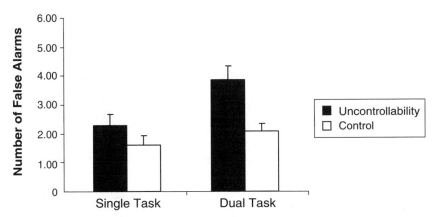

FIGURE 9.4. Number of false alarms during single and dual conditions on the Necka task for participants in control and induced uncontrollability conditions. Number of false alarms is significantly higher in the uncontrollable condition; this difference is especially visible in dual-task situation.

In both studies, performance on the secondary task (deviations from midpoint) was used to determine whether poorer performance on hits and false alarms was caused by compensatory improvement of secondary task performance. It was not. Secondary task performance of the depressed group was better after pharmacotherapy but still worse than for the control participants. For students, the uncontrollable group level of performance of the secondary task was similar to the control group.

To summarize, we found a similar pattern of results for the clinical and uncontrollability studies, indicating the predicted pattern of findings. The performance of the simplest goal was intact – when you notice the target element, press the key. However, more implicit and complex procedures that needed to be implemented in this task to solve it most effectively were substantially impaired both among depressed and helpless participants.

## Depression and Performance on Modified Oberauer Task

The next experiment sought to conceptually replicate, using a new paradigm, the above dual-task findings regarding preservation of performance on the simple rule but decrements in execution of a complex set of rules. In addition, we addressed the question of the specific role of negative self-relevant information in processing an executive task that demands coordination of several goals. We compared performance of subclinically depressed participants with control participants. Outcome predictions differ depending on whether one believes that negative self-information has attentional priority for depressed individuals. One prediction might be that the execution of a task demanding processing of negative information would be especially impaired because the attention of depressed participants would be especially distracted in this condition. Alternatively, another stance might be that there is a more general deficit in execution of multi-goal tasks (such as the previously studied dual-task problems) and thus the influence of negative information on processing might not be crucial here, and similar impairments would be observed for neutral and positive conditions. In either case, we are looking for the overall pattern seen in the dual task described earlier.

As existing literature shows (see review in Joormann, this volume), depression impairs performance of emotionally neutral memory and inhibitory tasks; however, sometimes deficits are more evident when there is negative emotional content. In this project, we examined the nature of cognitive deficits in depression using a modified Oberauer (2001) task, because neutral or highly emotional material can easily be implemented and produce strong interference in so-called intrusion probes.

Our modification of the Oberauer task (Oberauer, 2001; Oberauer, this volume) focuses on the intrusive character of the probes with the same word or phrases but different colors and thus removes the active forgetting aspect (we omit presentation of a color frame). Participants were instructed that after a short presentation of two words or two phrases with different colors, they would be presented with a single word or single phrase. They were instructed to press the YES key only if the second, single stimulus was an *already presented* word (or phrase) with the *same color*; this was the *positive probe*. They were instructed to press the NO key if the second stimulus was *a new* word (or phrase); this was the *negative probe*. They were also told to press the NO key if the second stimulus was *an already presented* word (or phrase) with *a different color*; this was the *intrusion probe*, as it includes an already presented stimulus, but with a negating characteristic. In addition, the stimuli varied on whether they were negative or positive in self-reference and emotional content. The participants were presented with four kinds of material in random order:

1. two nouns of different colors (e.g., pencil, house)
2. two self-referred phrases of positive meaning
3. two self-referred phrases of negative meaning
4. two self-refereed phrases of nonsense meaning

To illustrate this procedure a bit more, in condition (2) participants were presented with two sentences such as: "I'm wonderful" in green and "I'm excellent" in red. In the test phase only one sentence was presented. If it was, for example, "I'm excellent" in green (already presented phrase, but differing color – an intrusion probe), the participant should press NO.

In this study, the simple rule is to press NO when the second stimulus is a new word or phrase. The complication is that the participant also has to keep in mind that one must press NO when it is the same word or phrase presented in a different color. For this kind of task, we propose a general hypothesis for cognitive impairment of depressed persons similar to what we found for dual-task performance: larger differences in accuracy than in correct RT, especially for intrusive trials. That is, we do not expect a difference in how quickly individuals will perform the primary, simple goal – reaction time for correct NOs should be the same across conditions. However, we expect accuracy will be compromised because we theorize that the depressed group will have trouble maintaining the rule to press NO when the second stimulus is an old word (cuing YES) but a different color. The rationale is that it is more difficult to implement the goal to notice and carefully differentiate the cases in which the words were already presented but are dissimilar in colors. As already mentioned, another interesting question was whether these impairments would be especially evident for negatively valenced material.

There were highly significant main effects of probe type: The worst performance was for intrusion probes, the best was for negative probes, and performance on positive probes was in between. The results

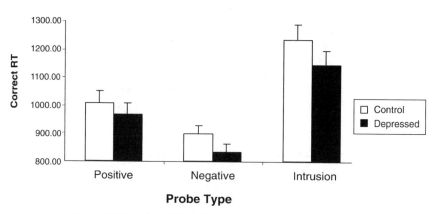

FIGURE 9.5. Correct RT on modified Oberauer task for each probe type for control and depressed participants. There was a significant main effect, with the worst performance for intrusion probes, the best for negative probes, and performance on positive probes was in between. There is no significant probe by group interaction.

were significant both for proportion correct (hits) and correct RT (see Figure 9.5).

As predicted, the significant interactions with depression emerged only for accuracy data, not response time. There was a general significant interaction effect of depression x probe type across all kinds of presented material (see Figure 9.6) and no interaction with the emotional content

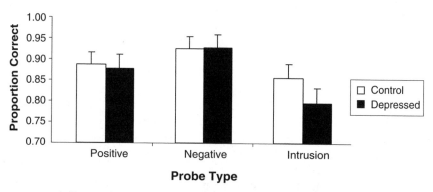

FIGURE 9.6. Proportion correct on modified Oberauer task for each probe type for control and depressed participants. The probe by group interaction is significant.

of material. However, subsequent analyses showed that this interaction is most significant for negative self-referred material. It seems then that similar to the findings for dual-task processing, there is a general impairment in performing more complex processing goals but the simpler goal is relatively intact. The negative valence aspect of the task increased the strength of observed interference, but it was not the necessary condition for the emerging of the depression-related impairment. Emotion appears neither necessary for the observed deficits, nor irrelevant to their presence.

## Subclinical Depression and Time Accuracy Functions: Studies With Modified PASAT

In this final section, we describe studies applying a new methodology – cognitive psychophysics – to capture more precisely the mechanisms of cognitive inefficiency in subclinical depression. We start with the recognition that previous results in dual tasks and modified Oberauer tasks may be described by two distinctive mechanisms.

One mechanism of the observed cognitive inefficiency can be described in terms of fluctuation of cognitive efficacy caused by individuals with depression being easily attentionally distracted. This account predicts that if those with depression were able to focus fully on the complex problems such as dual tasks for a long time, there would be no observable impairments. In line with this explanation, depressed individuals are constantly distracted by negative thoughts or task-irrelevant stimuli. Consequently, they might be able to carry out the simple processing goal but are too distracted to orchestrate implementing other important task goals included in the instructions.

An alternative mechanism can be described in terms of a persistently lowered cognitive efficiency in depressed individuals. Instead of the sudden and unpredictable "ups and downs" as described previously, they exhibit a continuously stable level of lowered efficiency in more cognitively demanding task situations. The important caveat is that we are not attempting here to describe the dynamic of mental activity on a longer period of time, but we are simply focused on the dynamics of mental efficiency during the limited time spent on performance of cognitively demanding tasks.

To compare the above two explanations of lowered cognitive efficiency in subclinical depression, we needed an experimental paradigm that both enabled reliable diagnosis of each individual's level of cognitive performance and enabled making intergroup comparisons.

In this section, we will describe the main results of two studies using *time accuracy functions* (TAF; for the detailed description of the paradigm, see Kliegl, Mayr, & Oberauer, 2000; Verhaeghen, 2000). The originators of this relatively new method describe it as a cognitive psychophysics, because

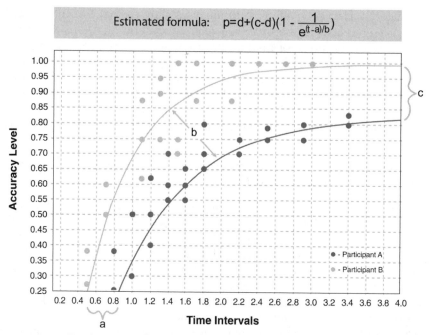

FIGURE 9.7. Description of estimating parameters of time accuracy function (TAF) from the accuracy points for different time intervals. In this paradigm presentation time (t) is converted into accuracy (p) according to a delayed exponential function. As a consequence of this procedure, for each individual the precise parameters of the function might be calculated instead of one average index of performance. Parameter *a* (location, chance level crossing) – time needed for processing information above chance level. Parameter *b* (slope or rate) – how fast performance is rising to the maximum (asymptotic) level. Parameter *c* (asymptote) – maximum level of performance under infinite amount of time.

they determine psychometric functions at the individual task-specific level using presentation time in the same way that stimulus as energy was used in psychophysics (e.g., manipulations of tone intensity to determine the ear sensitivity). The main assumption to apply TAF to a given cognitive task is that task accuracy is a monotonic function of presentation time. The data for each participant is based on an experimental procedure in which presentation-time demands are specified for some levels of target accuracy by decreasing or increasing presentation time (see Figure 9.7 for explanation of the approach). As a consequence of this procedure for each individual, the precise parameters of exponential functions can be calculated covering the range between chance and perfect performance for given individual. To our knowledge, this approach has never been used on studies concerning depression or other emotional disorders. Based on the findings from similar data on research concerning cognitive aging (Mayr, Kliegl, &

Krampe, 1996; Oberauer & Kliegl, 2001; Verhaeghen, Kliegl, & Mayr, 1997), we applied the following formula, where presentation time ($t$) is related to accuracy ($p$) according to a negatively accelerated exponential function:

$$p = d + (c - d)\left(1 - e^{(-t-a)/b}\right),$$

where $d$ is a parameter for chance performance, parameter $c$ represents the asymptotic accuracy reached when processing time is not externally limited, parameter $b$ is the slope of the function – the rate of approaching asymptote, and parameter $a$ the point in time ($t$) where accuracy rises above chance (see Figure 9.7). In our estimations of parameters, we fixed $d$ (parameter of chance performance) to 0.25 because, during task performance, the participants answered by selecting one of four keys. The maximum value of parameter $c$ is 1 (100% accuracy), for the other parameters, the larger the value, the worse the performance. That is, as illustrated at Figure 9.7, the participant with larger $a$ needed more time to respond above chance level, and the participant with larger $b$ achieved asymptotic level at slower rate.

As explained in detail by Verhaeghen (2000) the exact meaning of the parameters depends on the specificity of cognitive task; it is different when the TAF methodology is applied to a simple attentional task or, as in our case, to the complex working memory task known as Paced Auditory Serial Addition Test (PASAT; Gronwall, 1977). In general, parameters $a$ and $b$ describe the dynamic aspects of performance (speed and effectiveness), parameter $c$ refers more to the absolute limit of performance; it estimates the potential upper limit of accuracy in task performance when the task is solved without time restrictions.

We adapted time-accuracy functions to the PASAT (Gronwall, 1977). This popular neuropsychological test was devised by Gronwall and colleagues to provide an estimate of a participant's rate of processing (or the amount of information that can be handled at one time). The PASAT is thought to measure some central information processing capacity similar to that seen on divided attention tasks. According to many neuropsychological findings, PASAT is very sensitive to even very subtle deficits in information processing ability among postconcussion patients, those with mild and severe head injuries, and brain-injured patients with attention disorders.

PASAT requires that a participant continuously add pairs of heard randomized digits so that each digit is added to the digit immediately preceding it. For example, if the spoken digits were 5, 3, 7, 5, the appropriate answers should be: 8(5 + 3), 10(3 + 7), 12(7 + 5).

In our computerized procedure, the participant is required to comprehend the auditory input from the computer program and respond by pressing the correct key (selected from four options). It is important to note that this procedure contained the aspects of different executive functions of working memory, such as coordination, memory preserving of needed information, inhibition, and updating. To produce the correct answers 10 and 12 in the previous example, the participants first have to inhibit the previously selected answer 8, update from memory digit 3, add it to just heard digit 7, select 10 among four options and press the appropriate key, then inhibit this sum, update 7, and add to just heard digit 5, select 12 among four options, and so on.

As is clear from the previous example, the participants had to develop a system of internal commands to be able to perform this task correctly. In particular, they had to inhibit encoding their own response while attending to the next stimulus in a series, update instead the previous digit, and then perform selection of the correct response at an externally determined pace. In line with previous findings, we expected that this procedure would reveal some details of working memory limits among subclinically depressed students.

Participants were subclinically depressed participants and controls. We tested in two sessions. The first day was preliminary training with various time intervals. The next day, after a short training, there were two 25–35 minute sessions of continuous adding with eight time intervals, changing to a shorter or faster pace after a series of 12 presentations. One benefit of this procedure is that the precise parameters of the function can be calculated for each individual separately, instead of one overall group average index of performance. The first step in analyzing these data was examining if the accuracy data fit well the postulated exponential formula and then examining whether there were significant differences between groups. If the fit were poor or there were significant differences resulting from a more chaotic way of responding among depressed participants, the results of TAF might not be valid. It appeared, however, that the fit was perfect, and the mean the R-square in curvilinear regression analyzes was .96 in the control group and a similarly high .95 in the depressed group. The extremely good fit to the exponential function of the depressed participants is inconsistent with the first presented explanation provided earlier of subclinically depressed individuals having lowered cognitive performance because of fluctuations in performance. If the depressed participants had made a lot of unpredictable attentional lapses during performance of this task, then the fit to the function would be poor and significantly lower than among the nondepressed participants.

The pattern for the three estimated parameters is depicted in Figure 9.8. The analyses revealed no differences in the asymptotic level of performance (parameter $c$ in both groups was about .90). However, there were significant differences between subclinically depressed and control participants for both parameters $a$ and $b$ (recall that larger scores reflect worse performance). Interestingly, Channnon, Baker, and Robertson (1993) in their research on working memory impairments in clinical depression also

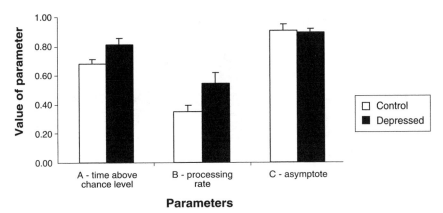

FIGURE 9.8. Time Accuracy Function parameters on Modified PASAT task for control and subclinically depressed participants. There are no differences in the asymptotic level of performance (parameter *c*). However, there were significant group differences for both parameters *a* and *b* (larger scores reflect worse performance).

included the classical version of PASAT, and they obtained marginally significant differences. It seems that the more sophisticated TAF methodology with the modified PASAT is able to identify some subtle differences in working memory functions, even among subclinically depressed participants. In the next study, we examined whether the complexity of the required set of internal commands is the key component of the observed deficit, or if the crucial component is the necessity to inhibit encoding the sum. If the latter explanation is correct, then we should observe a similar difference between depressed and control participants when the list of internal commands of this task is shortened, but the need to avoid encoding and adding next digit to the just calculated sum is retained. Again in two sessions, participants were first trained and then tested the next day on the two kinds of tasks. The first one was the same as before; participants had to add two randomly generated digits. The second task was to add 5 to continuously spoken digits and select the appropriate answer among four. In this version, the participants needed to encode the digit, add 5, select appropriate answer among four, then inhibit the sum, listen the next digit and again add 5, and so on. As is clear, the list of commands here is much shorter, but the inhibitory aspect of the task remains. Therefore, the question was whether this inhibitory aspect was sufficient to produce the significant differences between groups. It was not. As depicted in Figure 9.9, in the random digit task, requiring execution of the coordinated list of commands, there was a replication of the previous findings: significant differences in parameters *a* and *b*, no differences in parameter c. However, when participants performed the version of task with the constant adding to 5, there were no significant differences between depressed

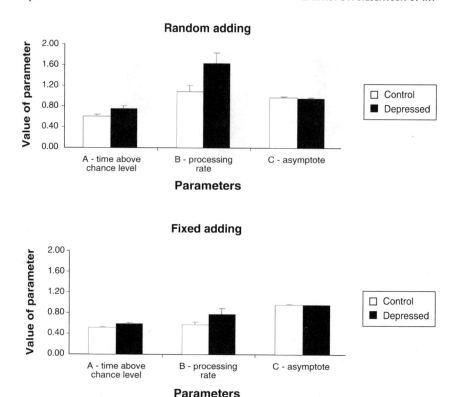

FIGURE 9.9. Time Accuracy Function parameters on random and fixed adding task for control and subclinically depressed participants. The top graph shows that in the random adding task there were significant differences in parameters *a* and *b* and no differences in parameter *c*. The bottom graph shows that in the constant adding task, there were no significant differences between depressed and control groups.

and control groups: The inhibition aspect of the task was not sufficient to produce reliable differences in estimated performance.

The integration of these two studies indicates that the critical aspect of impairments in depression in this modified PASAT procedure appears to be sequential coordination of different subgoals in a fast and efficient way, which could not be reduced solely to a deficit in inhibitory control.

## SUMMARY AND CONCLUSION

Building on the foundation of early learned helplessness work that pointed to the importance of similarities in the cognitive deficits in helplessness and depression, we here presented several studies aimed at identifying what it is that helpless and depressed minds do. We approach this question from a cognitive exhaustion perspective. That is, we believe that sustained cognitive effort (e.g., in our laboratory tasks or from unproductive ruminations common in reactive depression or dysphoria) can lead to a changed cognitive state in which complex thinking is abandoned in favor of more simple, less effortful thinking. We believe it is striking that the pattern of results is consistent across paradigms. The deficit does not seem tied to a particular method of assessment, and thus we believe it has good ecological validity. Indeed, underscoring the applicability of this approach is that it has been used successfully to account for difficulties in school performance (Sedek & McIntosh, 1998). Common to each study was a decrement in higher-order thinking involving coordination of premises (as in the syllogism task), subgoals (as the PASAT), or task requirements (as in dual-task paradigm and Oberauer tasks), with the simultaneous preservation of simple tasks, such as using simple reasoning rules in syllogisms and responding quickly when the proper target is perceived (dual tasks and Oberauer).

We also believe that the performance parallels between the induced helpless participants and the depressed participants (combined with the data indicating separable emotional and cognitive deficits in helpless rats; Maier & Minor, 1993) suggest that explanations of the deficits in depression (and dysphoria) should consider factors beyond the emotional. It is important to note that we are not arguing that cognitive exhaustion related to sustained cognitive effort with no gain explains depression. Our goal is not to propose a new model for depression, but instead to note that a fundamental aspect of depression, ruminations, can lead to some of the cognitive deficits evident in depression. Moreover, given that these deficits are present in subclinical populations, it would be imprudent to consider these deficits or the rumination as the cause of depression.

The next steps in this research program will include specifying the nature of the deficit; the final study using time accuracy functions in PASAT is a step in this direction. Further, additional work exploring the connections with depression and rumination (e.g., in processing a traumatic life event) are important in the application in this research. Determining if similar processes occur in other populations will help detect the parameters of this phenomenon (e.g., could ruminations regarding an activated stereotype explain cognitive deficits under conditions of stereotype threat, Steele & Aronson, 1995?).

Most broadly, we think it is worthwhile to note that the mind is adaptive. Humans and other animals inevitably face situations in which sustained cognitive effort does not lead to success. Although we see clear evidence for subsequent deficits in these situations, we also see evidence that thinking does not turn off or become chaotic. Any consideration of deficits (in depression and other psychopathologies, helplessness, aging, and the like) should simultaneously consider what functions are preserved. Generally speaking, our minds appear to move to a backup "Plan B" in which simple, but sustainable, strategies are employed to allow at least some level of performance in even quite difficult cognitive circumstances. Understanding what is lost and what is retained will enhance both basic understanding of the mind and behavior, and will also suggest compensatory strategies and interventions that may be helpful to individuals in these conditions.

## Author Note

The experiments reported and preparation of this chapter were supported by Polish Committee for Scientific Research grant 5 H01F 013 21 and the Walter Rosenberry Fund and Office of Internationalization at the University of Denver. We are grateful for Noemi Geller for helpful comments on a draft of this chapter.

## References

Abramson, L. Y., Seligman, M. E. P., & Teasdale, J. D. (1978). Learned helplessness in humans: Critique and reformulation. *Journal of Abnormal Psychology, 87,* 49–74.

Begg, I., & Denny, J. P. (1969). Empirical reconciliation of atmosphere and conversion interpretations of syllogistic reasoning errors. *Journal of Experimental Psychology, 81,* 351–354.

Benson, J. S., & Kennelly, K. J. (1976). Learned helplessness: The result of uncontrollable reinforcements or uncontrollable aversive stimuli? *Journal of Personality and Social Psychology, 34,* 138–145.

Bulman, R. J., & Wortman, C. B. (1977). Attributions of blame and coping in the "real world": Severe accident victims react to their lot. *Journal of Personality and Social Psychology, 35,* 351–363.

Channon, S., & Baker, J. (1994). Reasoning strategies in depression: Effects of depressed mood on a syllogism task. *Personality and Individual Differences, 17,* 707–711.

Channon, S., Baker, J. E., & Robertson, M. M. (1993). Effects of structure and clustering on recall and recognition memory in clinical depression. *Journal of Abnormal Psychology, 102,* 323–326.

Cox, B. J., Enns, M. W., Borger, S. C., & Parker, J. D. A. (1999). The nature of the depressive experience in analogue and clinically depressed samples. *Behaviour Research and Therapy, 37,* 15–24.

Davis, C. G., Lehman, D. R., Wortman, C. B., Silver, R. C., & Thompson, S. C. (1995). The undoing of traumatic life events. *Personality and Social Psychology Bulletin, 21,* 109–124.

Epstein, S. (1998). Personal control from the perspective of cognitive-experiential self-theory. In M. Kofta, G. Weary, & G. Sedek (Eds.), *Personal control in action: Cognitive and motivational mechanisms* (pp. 5–26). New York: Plenum.

Flett, G. L., Vredenburg, K., & Krames, L. (1997). The continuity of depression in clinical and nonclinical samples. *Psychological Bulletin, 121,* 395–416.

Frankel, A., & Snyder, M. L. (1978). Poor performance following unsolvable problems: Learned helplessness or egotism? *Journal of Personality and Social Psychology, 36*, 1415–1424.

Gilhooly, K. J., Logie, R. H., Wetherick, N. E., & Wynn, V. (1993). Working memory and strategies in syllogistic reasoning tasks. *Memory and Cognition, 21*, 115–124.

Gronwall, D. (1977). Paced auditory serial addition task: A measure of recovery from concussion. *Perceptual and Motor Skills, 44*, 367–373.

Hartlage, S., Alloy, L. B., Vazquez, C., & Dykman, D. (1993). Automatic and effortful processing in depression. *Psychological Bulletin, 113*, 247–278.

Healy, D., & Williams, J. M. G. (1988). Dysrythmia, dysphoria, and depression: The interaction of learned helplessness and circadian dysrythmia in the pathogenesis of depression. *Psychological Bulletin, 103*, 163–178.

Hiroto, D. S., & Seligman, M. E. (1975). Generality of learned helplessness in man. *Journal of Personality and Social Psychology, 31*, 311–327.

Horowitz, M. (1976). *Stress response syndromes*. New York: J. Aronson.

Hertel, P. T. (2004). Memory for emotional and nonemotional events in depression: A question of habit? In D. Reisberg & P. Hertel (Eds.), *Memory and emotion* (pp. 186–216). New York: Oxford University Press.

Hunter, A. M., Balleine, B. W., & Minor, T. R. (2003). Helplessness and escape performance: Glutamate-adenosine interactions in the frontal cortex. *Behavioral Neuroscience, 117*, 123–135.

Jackson, R. L., Alexander, J. H., & Maier, S. F. (1980). Learned helplessness, inactivity, and associative deficits: Effects of inescapable shock on response choice escape learning. *Journal of Experimental Psychology: Animal Behavior Processes, 6*, 1–20.

Janoff-Bulman, R. (1989). Assumptive worlds and the stress of traumatic events: Applications of the schema construct. *Social Cognition, 7*, 113–136.

Kliegl, R., Mayr, O., & Oberauer, K. (2000). Resource limitations and process dissociations in individual differences research, In U. von Hecker, S. Dutke, & G. Sedek (Eds.), *Generative mental processes and cognitive resources: Integrative research on adaptation and control* (pp. 337–366). Dordrecht: Kluwer.

Kofta., M. (1993). Uncertainty, mental models, and learned helplessness: An anatomy of control loss. In G. Weary, F. Gleicher, & K. L. Marsh (Eds.), *Control motivation and social cognition* (pp. 122–153). New York: Springer.

Kofta, M., & Sedek, G. (1989a). Egotism versus generalization-of-uncontrollability explanations of helplessness: Reply to Frankel & Snyder. *Journal of Experimental Psychology: General, 118*, 413–416.

Kofta, M., & Sedek, G. (1989b). Repeated failure: A source of helplessness, or a factor irrelevant to its emergence? *Journal of Experimental Psychology: General, 118*, 3–12.

Kofta, M., & Sedek, G. (1998). Uncontrollability as a source of cognitive exhaustion: Implications for helplessness and depression. In M. Kofta, G. Weary, and G. Sedek (Eds.), *Personal control in action: Cognitive and motivational mechanisms* (pp. 391–418). New York: Plenum Press.

Lyubomirsky, S., Kasri, F., & Zehm, K. (2003). Dysphoric rumination impairs concentration on academic tasks. *Cognitive Therapy and Research, 27*, 309–330.

Maier, S. F., & Minor, T. R. (1993). Dissociation of interference with the speed and accuracy of escape produced by inescapable shock. *Behavioral Neuroscience, 107,* 139–146.

Maier, S. F., & Seligman, M. E. P. (1976). Learned helplessness: Theory and evidence. *Journal of Experimental Psychology: General, 105,* 3–46.

Markman, K. D., Gavanski, I., Sherman, S. J., & McMullen, M. N. (1993). The mental simulation of better and worse possible worlds. *Journal of Experimental Social Psychology, 29,* 87–109.

Markman, K. D., & Weary, G. (1998). Control motivation, depression, and counterfactual thought. In M. Kofta, G. Weary, & G. Sedek (Eds.), *Personal control in action: Cognitive and motivational mechanisms* (pp. 363–390). New York: Plenum.

Mayr, U., Kliegl, R., & Krampe, R. T. (1996). Sequential and coordinative processing dynamics in figural transformations across the life span. *Cognition. International Journal of Cognitive Science, 59,* 61–90.

McIntosh, D. N., & Sedek, G. (2005). *Uncontrollability, clinical depression and dual task performance.* Manuscript in preparation.

McIntosh, D. N., Silver, R. C., & Wortman, C. B. (1993). Religion's role in adjustment to a negative life event: Coping with the loss of a child. *Journal of Personality and Social Psychology, 65,* 812–821.

Miller, W. R., & Seligman, M. E. P. (1975). Depression and learned helplessness in man. *Journal of Abnormal Psychology, 84,* 228–238.

Minor, T. R., Chang, W. C., & Winslow, J. L. (1994). Stress and adenosine: I. Effect of methylxanthine and amphetamine stimulants on learned helplessness in rats. *Behavioral Neuroscience, 108,* 254–264.

Minor, T. R., & Hunter, A. M. (2002). Stressor controllability and learned helplessness research in the United States: Sensitization and fatigue processes. *Integrative Physiological & Behavioral Science, 37,* 44–58.

Minor, T. R., Jackson, R. L., & Maier, S. F. (1984). Effects of tasks irrelevant cues and reinforcement delay on choice escape learning following inescapable shock: Evidence for deficit in selective attention. *Journal of Experimental Psychology: Animal Behavior Processes, 10,* 543–556.

Necka, E. (1996). Attentive mind: Intelligence in relation to selective attention, sustained attention, and dual task performance. *Polish Psychological Bulletin, 27,* 3–24.

Necka, E. (1997). Attention, working memory, and arousal: Concepts apt to account for the "process of intelligence." In G. Matthews (Ed.), *Cognitive science perspectives on personality and emotion* (pp. 503–554). Amsterdam: Elsevier Science.

Nolen-Hoeksema, S. (1996). Chewing the cud and other ruminations. In R. S. Wyer, Jr. (Ed.), *Ruminative thoughts* (pp. 135–144). Mahwah, NJ: Lawrence Erlbaum Associates.

Oberauer, K. (2001). Removing irrelevant information from working memory: A cognitive aging study with the modified Sternberg task. *Journal of Experimental Psychology: Learning, Memory and Cognition, 27,* 948–957.

Oberauer, K., & Kliegl, R. (2001). Beyond resources: Formal models of complexity effects and age differences in working memory. *European Journal of Cognitive Psychology, 13,* 187–215.

Overmier, J. B., & Seligman, M. E. P. (1967). Effects of inescapable shock upon subsequent escape and avoidance learning. *Journal of Comparative and Physiological Psychology, 63,* 23–33.

Papageorgiou, C., & Siegle, G. J. (2003). Rumination and Depression: Advances in Theory and Research. *Cognitive Therapy and Research, 27,* 243–245.

Ric, F., & Scharnitzky, P. (2003). Effects of control deprivation on effort expenditure and accuracy performance. *European Journal of Social Psychology, 33,* 103–118.

Robinson M. S., & Alloy, L. B. (2003). Negative cognitive styles and stress-reactive rumination interact to predict depression: A prospective study. *Cognitive Therapy and Research, 27,* 275–292.

Sedek, G., & Kofta, M. (1990). When cognitive exertion does not yield cognitive gain: Toward an informational explanation of learned helplessness. *Journal of Personality and Social Psychology, 58,* 729–743.

Sedek, G., Kofta, M., & Tyszka, T. (1993). Effects of uncontrollability on subsequent decision making: Testing the cognitive exhaustion hypothesis. *Journal of Personality and Social Psychology, 65,* 1270–1281.

Sedek, G., & McIntosh, D. N. (1998). Intellectual helplessness: Domain specificity, teaching styles, and school achievement. In M. Kofta, G. Weary, & G. Sedek (Eds.), *Personal control in action: Cognitive and motivational mechanisms* (pp. 391–418). New York: Plenum Press.

Sedek, G., & von Hecker, U. (2004). Effects of subclinical depression and aging on generative reasoning about linear orders: Same or different processing limitations? *Journal of Experimental Psychology: General, 133,* 237–260.

Seligman, M. E. P. (1978). Comment and integration. *Journal of Abnormal Psychology, 87,* 165–179.

Seligman, M. E. P., & Maier, S. F. (1967). Failure to escape traumatic shock. *Journal of Experimental Psychology, 74,* 1–9.

Siegle, G. J., Steinhauer, S. R., Carter, C. S., Ramel, W., & Thase, M. E. (2003). Do the seconds turn into hours? Relationships between sustained pupil dilation in response to emotional information and self-reported rumination. *Cognitive Therapy and Research, 27,* 365–382.

Snyder, M. L., & Frankel, A. (1989). Egotism versus learned helplessness as an explanation fort he unsolvable problem effect: Comment on Kofta and Sedek (1989). *Journal of Experimental Psychology: General, 118,* 409–412.

Steele, C. M., & Aronson, J. (1995). Stereotype threat and the intellectual test performance of African Americans. *Journal of Personality and Social Psychology, 69,* 797–811.

Sweeney, P. D., Anderson, K., & Bailey, S. (1986). Attributional style in depression: A meta-analytic review. *Journal of Personality and Social Psychology, 50,* 974–991.

Verhaeghen, P. (2000). The parallels in beauty's brow: Time accuracy functions and their implications for cognitive aging theories, In T. J. Perfect, & E. A. Maylor (Eds.), *Models of cognitive aging* (pp. 50–86). Oxford, UK: Oxford University Press.

Verhaeghen, P., Kliegl, R., & Mayr, U. (1997). Sequential and coordinative complexity in time-accuracy functions for mental arithmetic. *Psychology and Aging, 12,* 555–564.

von Hecker, U., & Sedek, G. (1999). Uncontrollability, depression, and the construction of mental models. *Journal of Personality and Social Psychology, 77,* 833–850.

von Hecker, U., Sedek, G., & McIntosh, D. N. (2000). Impaired systematic, higher order strategies in depression and helplessness: Testing implications of the cognitive exhaustion model. In U. von Hecker, S. Dutke, & G. Sedek (Eds.), *Generative mental processes and cognitive resources: Integrative research on adaptation and control* (pp. 245–276). Dordrecht: Kluwer.

Wortman, C. B., & Brehm, J. W. (1975). Responses to uncontrollable outcomes: An integration of reactance theory and the learned helplessness model. In L. Berkowitz (Ed.), *Advances in experimental social psychology, 8,* 277–336. New York: Academic Press.

# ATTENTION, INHIBITION, AND REASONING PROCESSES

# 10

# The Nature of Attentional Bias in Human Anxiety

Elaine Fox and George A. Georgiou

The nature of the world in which mammals have evolved has resulted in an attentional system that is highly *selective*. It is obvious that natural environments consist of multiple objects, most of which also contain many different attributes. For example, a walk down a typical high street bombards us with a variety of sounds, colours, and odours. In addition to these external objects, there may also be a range of competing internal thoughts that occupy our minds. Because of this huge variety of stimuli, it seems clear that the ability to efficiently select and focus on *currently* relevant information is critical for coherent behaviour. In addition, it would also seem to be adaptive to rapidly notice stimuli that may pose a danger. For instance, it is important to notice the predator or potential mugger lurking in the nearby bushes. Therefore, in addition to the necessity for selection of relevant objects and thoughts, an efficient attentional system must also be open and flexible to stimuli that may represent a threat. Thus, there may well be a subset of stimuli that has privileged access to the attentional system. In addition to certain classes of stimuli that may be especially salient in terms of attracting attentional resources (e.g., snakes, spiders, angry facial expressions, etc.), there may be groups of individuals who are particularly sensitive to threat-related stimuli. Indeed, anxiety has often been characterized as the quintessential example of a hypervigilant attentional system. To illustrate, a large empirical literature shows that the attentional system of anxious people does indeed seem to be biased toward threat-related information (see Eysenck, 1992; Power & Dalgleish, 1991, 1997 Williams, Watts, MacLeod, & Mathews, 1988, 1997 for reviews). Our own work has built on this literature and has attempted to determine the particular component of attention that may be biased by individual differences in anxiety (e.g., Fox, Russo, Bowles, & Dutton, 2001; Fox, Russo, & Dutton, 2002; Georgiou et al., in press.

The aim of the present chapter is to provide a brief overview of some traditional theoretical models of attention, with a particular emphasis on *visual selective attention.* We will then consider some of the more common paradigms used to address the question of whether there are subsets of threat-related stimuli that may be especially salient to anxious people. Recent work has tried to elucidate the precise nature of attentional processing in anxious people. These issues will be addressed in relation to the four main questions underlying the aims of this book.

*First, which cognitive functions are of special interest to our research programme?* Although memory and reasoning biases are undoubtedly important elements in the understanding of emotional disorders such as depression and anxiety, it is *attentional* processes that seem to be the cognitive functions of most relevance in anxiety disorders.

*Second, what are the processing limitations and/or sources of individual differences in cognitive functions that are most important to our research?* Our work has been driven by the consistent differences that have been observed between anxious and nonanxious people on tasks involving selection between a threat-related and a neutral stimulus. For example, if a threatening word (e.g., attack) is presented alongside a neutral word (e.g., house), then the attentional resources of an anxious person seem to be captured by the threat-related word; this does not happen for the low-anxious person. This seems to be the case for both clinically anxious people and for those who report high levels of anxiety on a standardized questionnaire but who have not been diagnosed as having a clinical anxiety disorder. This difference in attentional bias between anxious and nonanxious people has been found in many different paradigms, and our research is focused on determining what particular attentional processes are most affected by this individual difference.

*Third, what are our specific methods and findings?* Our recent research used visual stimuli, and threat was indicated by means of facial expressions (e.g., anger, fear) and compared with neutral or happy facial expressions. We designed tasks that attempt to determine whether the nature of attentional bias in anxiety is associated with a faster shift toward threatening information *or* whether anxiety is characterized by an increased dwelling on threatening information once it has been noticed. To date, our results suggest the latter possibility. It seems that anxiety may be associated with a delay in disengaging attentional resources from threat-related stimuli.

*Fourth, what are the implications of our research for other related research domains?* One implication of our work is that when studying cognitive processes, we need to be very careful about drawing theoretical conclusions from empirical demonstrations. For example, our work has shown that enhanced processing of threat in selective tasks does *not* necessarily imply that attention shifts more rapidly toward the threat-related information in anxious people. We need to use a variety of different paradigms to determine what particular cognitive function is affected by a particular individual difference. In addition, our work has shown that individual differences in anxiety at subclinical levels can have profound effects on how threat-related information is processed. Although work is ongoing, it seems that a relatively small attentional effect (of the order of milliseconds) may lead to increases in negative rumination and worry. Thus, depending on the nature of the stimuli being used, a self-report measure of anxiety may be a useful addition in studies of cognitive aging, for example. It is not beyond the bounds of possibility that older adults may be more anxious than younger adults, especially if they have suffered a decline in physical capability. This may result in a delay in disengaging from negative newspaper stories (e.g., increased burglaries in their area) relative to positive stories, which in turn may lead to more rumination and worry with a consequent overloading of cognitive resources.

## SELECTIVE ATTENTION

As mentioned previously, selective attention is the cognitive function of most relevance to our research. Much of the early research on selective attention focused on the question of *when* an object was identified or analysed at a semantic level. For example, Broadbent (1958) argued that all stimuli that reach the sensory system are analysed in terms of physical attributes (e.g., location, pitch, colour, orientation). However, the part of the attentional system responsible for identifying the meaning of an object or word was considered to be strictly limited in capacity and therefore only one item could be processed to the point of semantic analysis at a time. This *filter* or *early selection* theory was highly influential and suggested that attention was a necessary prerequisite of semantic analysis. However, alternative so-called *late-selection* theories were also proposed and postulated that there were no capacity limits on semantic identification and that an object could be processed to a semantic level without being directly attended (Deutsch & Deutsch, 1963; Norman, 1968). Treisman (1960) suggested a compromise between these theories by suggesting that the selective filter attenuates rather than completely blocks unattended information. Under this model, information that is attended gets a boost relative to unattended information, but the unattended information does get processed to some extent depending on its personal relevance or danger significance. Although this theory appears elegant and adequately explained much of the empirical data at the time, subsequent researchers tended to polarize the argument around the question of whether attentional selection is early or late. More recently, research has shown that the answer is probably sometimes early, sometimes late. For example, when the perceptual load of a visual task is relatively low (e.g., one or two objects), then an irrelevant distractor produces strong interference effects (i.e., response competition). However, when the display is more crowded and load is high (about six objects), then there is little evidence for interference (Lavie, 1995). Lavie and her colleagues argued that attentional selectivity is "early" when perceptual load is high because perceptual capacity is exhausted. However, when perceptual load is very low, then there are spare perceptual resources that will be unable to prevent analysing all stimuli that are present and hence a "late" selection pattern of results (Lavie & Tsal, 1994; Lavie, 1995; Lavie & Fox, 2000). In other words, the nature of the visual scene has a profound effect on whether attentional selection occurs early or late in the stream of information processing.

Although early- and late-selection theorists argued about the point at which an item was selected for semantic analysis, both theories assumed that the main processing activity took place on the attended item. In other words, attended information was given a processing boost through some excitatory mechanism, whereas unattended information either was not processed to a high level (early selection) or was processed to a semantic level and hence was boosted to some extent with a consequent fading of excitation back to some baseline level (late selection). More recently, the case was made that selection takes place through a dual mechanism of activation of the attended information alongside the active suppression of the unattended information (Houghton & Tipper, 1994). Tipper (1985) demonstrated what he termed the *negative priming effect*, which was considered to be evidence for an active inhibitory process in visual selection (see also Neill, 1977). Negative priming is the demonstration that ignoring an item on trial $n$ leads to slower responses to that item if it is presented as a target on trial $n + 1$. This effect is robust and has been shown with a range of stimuli such as words, pictures, letters, and shapes. Although there is some dispute about the mechanisms underlying negative priming, many investigators assume that the effect is a good index of inhibitory processes in attentional selection (see Fox, 1995; May, Kane, & Hasher, 1995 for review). Therefore, negative priming has been widely used to examine variations in inhibitory functioning in groups of people such as older adults (Hasher, Stoltzfus, Zacks, & Rympa, 1991), people diagnosed with schizophrenia (Beech, Powell, McWilliams, & Claridge, 1989), and people with high levels of self-reported trait-anxiety (Fox, 1994). Joorman (this volume) used a negative priming paradigm with positive and negative words and found that dysphoric participants did not show as much negative priming with negative distractors as with positive distractors. This suggests that these participants may have problems in inhibiting negative material at an attentional level.

Research on selective attention is pertinent to our research on the nature of attentional processing in anxiety for a number of reasons. First, several tasks have been developed to investigate how easy or difficult it is to ignore distracting information (e.g., dichotic listening, Stroop, flanker task), and these can be modified to present the to-be-ignored information as being threat-related or nonthreat-related. This allows for an examination of whether anxious people find it more difficult to ignore threatening information. Moreover, negative priming tasks may also be helpful in terms of attempting to understand the nature of the mechanisms underlying any selection differences between anxious and nonanxious participants. These selective attention paradigms will be described later in this chapter.

ORIENTING OF ATTENTION

In addition to the selectivity of attention, the way in which attention can be oriented in the visual field is fundamentally important to our work on attentional biases in anxiety. Posner (1980) developed a simple technique in which participants are required to detect the onset of a light in either a box on the left or the right side of a computer screen. Just before the onset of the target (light), participants are given a cue in the form of one of the peripheral boxes being illuminated for a brief period (50 msec). The validity of these cues, in terms of indicating the location of the target, can be varied to investigate the way in which such *exogenous* cues can be used to draw or direct attention. The results showed that when the cue was valid (e.g., left box illuminated, target in left box), participants were much faster and more accurate in detecting the target than they were when the cue was invalid (e.g., right box illuminated, target in left box). Moreover, people were unable to ignore the cue so that even when they believed that the cue was invalid, there was still a pattern of benefits and costs related to the validity of the cue. This facilitated visual processing by means of an exogenous cue led Posner to suggest that "attention can be likened to a spotlight that enhances the efficiency of the detection of events within its beam" (Posner, 1980, p. 172). Subsequent research has indicated that there are a number of brain regions called the *posterior attentional system* (parietal lobe, superior colliculus, and parts of the pulvinar), which seem to be specialized for covert orienting of attention to a location or object (Posner & Petersen, 1990). This system can be broken down into three separate components of visual–spatial attention: shifting, engaging, and disengaging. In other words, a shift of attention from one object to another (e.g., from a book to a friend who has just entered the room) involves the disengaging of attention from the current focus (the book), the movement of attention through space to the relevant object (your friend), and the re-engaging of attention on the new object. The output of this posterior system feeds forward to the *anterior attentional system*, which is concerned primarily with the identification of an object. The nature of the patterns of neuronal connectivity between the anterior system in the prefrontal cortex and the posterior system suggests that the anterior system may have a role in controlling the posterior system (Posner & Petersen, 1990). The distinction among disengage, move, and engage components of attention is central to our work, which is designed to determine what component might be most involved in anxiety-related attentional biases (Fox et al., 2001). However, before we discuss our own work, we will briefly review the evidence that there are indeed selective attentional biases toward threat-related information in anxious people.

## ARE THERE ATTENTIONAL BIASES TOWARD THREAT IN ANXIOUS PEOPLE?

Research investigating information processing biases in anxiety can be divided into those employing clinically diagnosed anxious patients and those individuals reporting high self-reported trait-anxiety on a standard-ised scale. With regard to the latter, the most common scale used is the State-Trait Anxiety Scale (STAI: Spielberger, Gorsch, Lushene, Vagg, & Jacobs, 1983), which independently assesses the state (transient mood state indexed by how the individual feels at the present moment in time) and trait (enduring personality characteristic indexed by how the individual generally feels) components of anxiety. Investigations into nonclinical anxiety are considered important as many have argued that high trait-anxiety represents a good model for clinical anxiety (Rapee, 1991).

Early theories predicted general cognitive biases for threatening stimuli in relation to both general mood and emotional disorders. For example, a number of studies demonstrated that induced sad or happy moods led to a tendency to recall negative and positive information, respectively (Bower, 1981). Bower developed a theory based on the notion of semantic net-works, which predict general mood congruency effects in both attentional and memory tasks. From a more clinical perspective, Beck (e.g., Beck & Emery, 1985) proposed high-level cognitive schemata that were supposed to bias cognitive processing in a mood-congruent way. For example, anx-ious people would possess schemata related to future threat and harm, and this would mean that threat-related stimuli would be particularly salient for anxious individuals. Eysenck (1992) suggested that because attention has to do with rapidly detecting potential danger in the environment, it would be expected that anxiety should be characterized by a hypervigilant attentional system. He reviewed a range of evidence consistent with this notion (Eysenck, 1992, 1997). A more general model of cognitive processing in emotional disorders was proposed and argues that anxiety and depres-sion are actually characterized by different types of processing (Williams et al., 1988, 1997). Their information processing model suggests that anx-iety is associated with processes that integrate a mental representation of a stimulus (e.g., a spider) by rendering it more *accessible*. In contrast, depression is characterized by elaborative processing that increases the number of associations among mental representations. Thus, anxiety should be associated with attentional biases, whereas depression should be associated with memory biases. Williams et al. (1988, 1997) reviewed a large body of empirical evidence consistent with this approach.

Mogg and Bradley (1998) highlighted potential problems for models, like that of Williams et al. (1988, 1997), which rely heavily on the use of single word stimuli. They point out that threat words almost certainly have a higher frequency of usage in highly anxious people compared to low-anxious people. Therefore, the attentional bias effects typically found for threat words may have more to do with its disproportionate usage in anxious individuals than with the actual valence of the word. Secondly, it was argued that some threat words may be low in subjective threat value in low-anxious people. Again, this can pose a major problem when it comes to interpreting the results as some threat words may not be particularly threatening for low-anxious individuals (e.g., *alone, inquest*). Therefore, it is important to demonstrate an attentional bias with stimuli that both high- and low-anxious participants consider to be threatening (e.g., threatening faces). In addressing these issues, Mogg and Bradley (1998) proposed a cognitive-motivational view of anxiety that proposes the existence of two functionally distinct systems. The Valence Evaluation System is primarily involved in the appraisal of a stimulus' threat value. The results from the Valence Evaluation System are fed into the Goal Engagement System, which determines whether there is subsequent engagement or disengagement of external goals. It is argued that these mechanisms may be able to account for a lack of an attentional bias in patients diagnosed with depression while currently experiencing high levels of self-reported anxiety (an issue not theoretically accounted for by Williams et al.'s model). For example, a lack of attentional bias toward threat (i.e., negative valence) transpires when external goal engagement is low (i.e., disengagement from external environment) as is the case with clinically diagnosed depression with or without concurrent anxiety. In line with an evolutionary perspective, the cognitive–motivational model predicts that once a stimulus' threat value exceeds a certain threshold, then vigilant behaviour typically found in highly anxious individuals will also transpire in low-anxious individuals. This is in contrast to the prediction made by the *interaction hypothesis*, which states that low-anxious individuals would become increasingly more avoidant of threatening material as the threat value of such material increases (e.g., Williams et al., 1988, 1997). Therefore, attentional biases can also be found in low-anxious individuals when encountering material of a sufficient threat severity. As a consequence, the model does not assign the biases in attention a critical role in the causation of anxiety, but its influence in maintaining anxiety states is nevertheless not discounted.

Below, we present a brief overview of some of the major paradigms used in this area of research and a selective review of some typical experimental studies. Following this, we present a rationale and a description of the methods used in our own research.

## TRADITIONAL PARADIGMS

### Dichotic Listening Studies

The dichotic listening task involves the simultaneous auditory presentation of stimuli to both ears. Participants are typically required to ignore information presented to a designated channel (i.e., the unattended ear) while shadowing (i.e., repeating loud) information from the attended ear. Of special interest is whether the individual is able to detect information presented to the unattended channel. The earliest studies of this kind found that participants had very little memory for unattended material, although there were reports that some sounds could be heard (Cherry, 1953). With regard to the information presented to the unattended channel, participants were typically not aware if the unattended voice was played backward or whether the language changed from English to German. However, it was later found that pertinent information (e.g., participant's name) presented to the unattended ear could break through into conscious awareness in some cases (Moray, 1959).

The idea that unattended information (in theory anyway) could break through into conscious awareness was intriguing to later researchers. For example, Mathews and MacLeod (1986) asked a group of generalised anxiety disordered (GAD) patients to shadow a neutral story presented to the attended ear while simultaneously ignoring threat-related or nonthreat-related words presented to the unattended ear. While carrying out this task, patients were required to detect the occasional presentation of a visual probe. The findings revealed that GAD patients were slower in detecting the visual probe when threat-related words were simultaneously presented in the unattended channel. This occurred despite participants maintaining that they were not aware of hearing any words presented in the unattended channel. This was empirically confirmed when an unexpected recognition test showed no increased memory for unattended words previously presented. Similar results were found in a nonclinical study conducted by Eysenck, MacLeod, and Mathews (1987) using an auditory tone rather than a visual probe. The findings revealed that high trait-anxiety participants responded more quickly to the tone when it was presented to the same ear as the threat-related words, whereas slower responses to the tone were observed when it was presented to the opposite ear to the threat word. Again, low trait-anxiety participants tended to avoid orienting their attention to the same ear previously occupied by threat-related words.

This study illustrates a selective attentional bias in high trait-anxiety participants toward threat and an avoidance of threat in the low trait-anxiety group.

## Stroop Studies

Most of the empirical studies examining selective processing of threat in anxiety have used the Stroop task (Stroop, 1935). This task requires people to simply name the colours in which words are presented. During critical trials, naming the ink colour of an incompatible colour word (e.g., the word BLUE presented in red ink) is required. This incongruence between the two dimensions (i.e., colour word and ink colour) reliably leads to slower colour-naming latencies compared to when the two dimensions are congruent (e.g., the word BLUE presented in blue ink) or when a row of Xs are presented instead of a word. The emotional Stroop task differs from the original task in that participants are required to name the ink colour of words differing in emotional connotation (e.g., threat-related, neutral, or positive).

A comprehensive review of the emotional Stroop studies in clinical and nonclinical anxiety is available (Williams, Mathews, & MacLeod, 1996). One reported study was that of Mathews and MacLeod (1985), who found that patients diagnosed with GAD displayed slower colour-naming latencies for threat-related words (i.e., physical and social threat words) compared to nonthreatening words. Although all anxious patients showed colour-naming interference effects for social threat words (compared to matched control stimuli), specificity effects were found in anxious patients characterised as physical worriers with longer colour-naming latencies for physical threat words (again compared to matched control stimuli). This finding is in contrast to the performance of the control group, who displayed similar ink colour-naming latencies for the threat and nonthreat words. Likewise, Mogg, Mathews, and Weinman (1989) found that anxious patients exhibited longer colour-naming latencies for specific threat-related words that matched their current predominant concern (e.g., social or physical concerns).

The majority of nonclinical investigations have shown that participants high in trait-anxiety display longer colour-naming latencies for threat-related words (e.g., *cancer*) compared to neutral words (e.g., *table*; Dalgleish, 1995; Fox, 1993; Richards & French, 1990; Richards & Millwood, 1989). However, some evidence was found for an "emotionality hypothesis," which predicts that high trait-anxious participants will show interference effects for all emotional words (i.e., positive and negative) and not just threat-related words per se (Mogg & Marden, 1990). In Martin, Williams, and Clark's (1991) study, physical threat, social threat, and neutral and positive adjectives were presented in one of four different colours to a group of GAD patients and nonanxious controls (matched for age, sex, and occupation). The findings showed that GAD patients displayed similar colour-naming interference effects for the threat (i.e., physical and social threat) and positive adjectives, such that there was no significant difference in performance between the two, while both were slower than neutral words. In contrast, the nonanxious control group displayed similar colour-naming latencies across threat, positive, and neutral words. An absence of Stroop interference in the nonclinically anxious group prompted speculations that this effect may be confined to clinical anxiety, even though previous research had demonstrated such a bias in high trait-anxious individuals (Mogg & Marden, 1990; Richards & Millwood, 1989). Mathews and Klug (1993) set out to determine the potential impact of both the emotionality (i.e., positive, negative) and the relatedness (related or unrelated to the individual's current anxiety symptoms) of a word on Stroop interference. They found that anxious patients displayed longer colour-naming latencies for words related to their anxiety irrespective of whether they were positive (e.g., *confident*) or negative (e.g., *nervous*). This suggests that the relatedness of a word to the anxious person's current concern is central to the manifestation of Stroop interference. Similar results were found in a study carried out by Riemann and McNally (1995), who also found colour-naming interference effects for words (both negative and positive) preselected on the basis of an individual's current preoccupation. However, others have argued that in clinical anxiety, it is indeed the negative aspect of the word and not just the matching of the word to an individual's current concern that is the main driving force behind colour interference effects (McNally et al., 1994). On the basis of the available evidence, Williams et al. (1996) concluded that in nonclinical anxiety, stimuli related to an individual's current preoccupation is a necessary factor in the manifestation of Stroop interference. However, the relatedness of the word in addition to the word having a negative connotation seems to be equally important in the manifestation of colour-naming interference in clinical patients (see Williams et al. 1996 for more details).

Studies have also been carried out showing that Stroop interference is a good predictor of subsequent stress. For instance, in an innovative longitudinal study, MacLeod and Hagan (1992) administered the emotional Stroop task, which comprised masked trials (i.e., following stimulus presentation, a random string of letters is presented) and unmasked trials to highly stressed participants waiting for a colposcopy diagnosis for cervical pathology. The best predictor in determining vulnerability to a future stressful event (i.e., a later positive screening for cervical pathology after 2 months) was the magnitude of the interference effect found during masked threat trials. The greater the Stroop interference, the greater the reported level of emotional distress measured in a postdiagnostic mood questionnaire when diagnosed with cervical pathology. In a replication study, van den Hout, Tenney, Huygens, Merckelbach, and Kindt (1995) reported the same key pattern of results with a sample not currently experiencing high levels of stress at the time of the initial assessment. These findings suggest a causal role of selective processing biases and subsequent emotional adjustment.

There have been reported instances in which Stroop interference effects have not been found for highly anxious participants. For example, Mathews and Sebastian (1993) failed to find colour-naming interference effects for snake-related words or threatening words of a general nature, compared to neutral words in snake-avoidant participants. The absence of the Stroop interference effect coincided with the presence of either a snake (related to the words used in the Stroop task) or, in a later experiment, a large tarantula spider (unrelated to the words used in the Stroop task) in the testing room. However, when the threatening item (the snake or the spider) was removed from the testing area, colour-naming interference was found for snake-related words in snake-avoidant people. These findings are counterintuitivebecause previous studies have tended to show that elevations in stress have usually led to enhanced Stroop interference effects. It is possible that participants were so distracted by the presence of their feared animal that this nullified the Stroop interference.

In summary, Stroop studies tend to support the hypothesis that in most cases highly anxious individuals find it difficult to ignore the content of threat words despite attempting to attend solely to the word's colour. These Stroop interference effects are assumed to be the direct consequence of the preferential processing of threat-related words over neutral words in highly anxious individuals.

## Dot-Probe Studies

Another paradigm widely used in the study of selective processing for threat is the dot-probe task. This visual analogue of the dichotic listening task was originally employed in mainstream cognitive psychology and later modified by MacLeod, Mathews, and Tata (1986). A key problem was identified with the use of the emotional Stroop task, which allows an alternative and equally plausible explanation for the Stroop interference effect. MacLeod et al. (1986) suggest that the processing of threat-related words may elevate the participant's current emotional state leading to subsequent disruption in ink colour-naming performance. This may occur because the threat material is always focally attended in the Stroop, and constant processing of threat may result in increased anxiety and arousal. Indeed, any task that infers an attentional bias when performance is impaired (e.g., slower reaction times) when processing threatening material is susceptible to this criticism (MacLeod & Mathews, 1988). Importantly, this potential confound is eliminated in the dot-probe task because both the response (i.e., button press) and the probe (i.e., dot) to be detected are both neutral. Therefore, it seems reasonable to argue that the dot-probe task, compared to the emotional Stroop, is better placed to investigate attentional bias associated with anxiety.

In MacLeod et al.'s (1986) study, the distribution of attention was directly measured by presenting word pairs for 500 ms, one above and the other below the computer screen's point of fixation. Participants were required to read out loud the upper word of each pair and the termination of the word display; 25% of trials involved the presentation of a visual probe in one of the spatial locations previously occupied by one of the words. The participant's task was to detect the spatial location of the dot-probe as quickly as possible. During critical trials, word pairs consisted of a threat-related word and a neutral word. GAD patients showed a selective attentional bias for threat indicated by their faster detection of probes occurring in spatial locations previously occupied by a threat-related word. In normal controls, the tendency was to shift their attention away from the threatening stimuli. A problem with the original task was that only 25% of trials were used in the data analysis because of the number of irrelevant trials, thus reducing the statistical power of the study. Furthermore, although the probability of a dot appearing after a threat or a neutral word was the same, the presentation of a threat word did signal to the participants the increased possibility that it would be followed by a probe. To overcome these problems Mogg, Bradley, and Williams (1995) presented a probe on each trial thus eliminating any potential random relationship between the presentation of a negative word and the occurrence of a probe. There was also increased statistical power as participants had to categorise a probe on every trial. This forced- choice version of the dot-probe task demonstrated an attentional bias for threat words across both masked and unmasked conditions in a clinically anxious group.

Mogg, Bradley, de Bono, and Painter (1997) investigated the time course of attentional bias in the dot-probe task by examining the relative influences of automatic (i.e., unconscious) and controlled (i.e., conscious) facets of attentional orientation. Time intervals of 100 msec, 500 msec, and 1500 msec between the word pairs and the onset of the dot probe were employed. An attentional bias toward threat-related words was evident across all three time intervals in high state-anxious individuals, suggesting that both early automatic and late controlled processes may both be playing an integral role in the manifestation of attentional bias in anxiety.

Other studies have employed a pictorial version of the dot-probe task using more ecologically valid stimuli, such as fearful and angry faces (Bradley, Mogg, Falla, & Hamilton, 1998; Fox, 2002; Mogg & Bradley, 1999). Fox (2002) presented pairs of photographed faces (Ekman & Friesen, 1975) consisting of an emotional face (fearful or happy) and a neutral face for 500 ms on the left and the right side of the computer's point of fixation. On the immediate offset of the face pair, one of two types of probes (i.e., : or.) were presented in one of the two locations previously occupied by one of the facial expressions. Participants were required to determine which of the two probes was presented as quickly and accurately as possible. The study revealed that high trait-anxious individuals displayed faster reaction times for probes occupying spatial locations previously occupied by a fearful face compared to a happy or neutral facial expression. Interestingly, the fastest probe detection times were for fearful faces that were presented in the left visual field. This not only illustrates that highly anxious individuals were more likely to direct their attentional resources toward fearful faces but also suggests that the right hemisphere may play a key role in the processing of negative facial expressions. Furthermore, this bias was found to be especially strong when the fearful facial expression was masked, suggesting that the bias may operate outside of conscious awareness. This study replicated the key results of Mogg and Bradley (1999) in which the high trait-anxiety group was found to display faster discrimination responses for angry faces in the LVF when presented under masked conditions. In contrast, the low trait-anxiety group was found to selectively orientate their attention away from angry faces. The orientation of attention away from threat in low trait-anxious individuals is consistent with a number of previous findings (Bradley et al., 1998; MacLeod & Mathews, 1988;) and with predictions from various cognitive models of anxiety (Eysenck, 1992, 1997; Williams et al., 1988, 1997).

A recent study by Wilson and MacLeod (2003) demonstrated that the level of intensity of a stimulus may play a far more decisive role in the orientation of attention in anxiety than previously suspected. A variant of the attentional probe task was employed in which a probe (i.e., white line) was presented in the spatial location of one of the pair of faces. Participants were required to determine whether the probe was pointing either to the top left or the top right side of the computer screen. Using computer morphing technology a series of angry faces was created that differed in threat intensity. The results revealed that all participants, irrespective of whether they were high or low in trait-anxiety, were found to orientate their attention away from faces classified as *mildly* threatening and toward faces designated as *extremely* threatening. However, the high trait-anxiety group showed greater orientation of attention toward angry faces when the level of intensity was at an intermediate level. Subjective threat ratings of the photographs were carried out and were not found to differ statistically between the high and low trait-anxious groups. This suggests that the high trait-anxiety group did not appraise such photographs as more threatening did than the low trait-anxiety group. Wilson and MacLeod (2003) propose that only when the level of threat intensity reaches a fairly high level do we observe attentional vigilance for threat in the low-anxious group. In contrast, vigilance for threat is observed in the high trait-anxious group at an intermediate level of threat intensity. This is consistent with recent models that suggest that the threat appraisal mechanism may play a key role in differentiating performance between the high and the low trait-anxiety groups (Mathews & Mackintosh, 1998; Mogg & Bradley, 1998).

## Does Trait- or State-Anxiety Drive Attentional Bias?

Early cognitive models of emotional disorders theorised that either high trait-anxiety (Beck & Emery, 1985) or elevated levels of current anxious mood state (Bower, 1981) represented the main impetus behind the attentional bias toward threatening material in nonclinical anxiety. A notable feature of Williams et al.'s (1988, 1997) model is the "state-anxiety X trait-anxiety" interaction hypothesis. This model hypothesises that when state-anxiety is low, differences between high and low trait-anxious in terms of attentional orientation are minimal. However, differences in attentional orientation begin to surface when state-anxiety levels begin to rise, resulting in increased vigilance for threat in high trait-anxious individuals and increased avoidance of threat in low trait-anxiety individuals.

Capitalising on a naturalistic stressor (i.e., impending examinations), MacLeod and Mathews (1988) employed the dot-probe detection task in order to investigate the interactive role of trait- and state-anxiety and the potential impact it may have on the deployment of attentional resources when encountering threat-related stimuli. Medical students characterised as high or low trait-anxious were recruited and tested across two test sessions: 12 weeks before their annual examination (when state-anxiety was low) and retested 1 week before the start of the examination (when state-anxiety was high). During the first testing session, probe detection performances were similar across the two groups when examination-related threat words were presented. On the second testing session, however, the high trait-anxiety group showed increased vigilance for examination-threat. Although not reaching statistical significance, the low trait-anxious group showed a numerical tendency to avoid threatening stimuli. In a similar study, MacLeod and Rutherford (1992) employed masked and unmasked examination-related and examination-unrelated stimuli. The testing of participants was conducted in two separate sessions. The first was carried out 1 week before examinations (i.e., high-stress condition: HSC) and the second was carried out approximately 6 weeks after the exams (i.e., low-stress condition: LSC). In the LSC, both high and low trait-anxiety groups performed similarly across threat and neutral stimuli. However, in the HSC, the high trait-anxious group displayed colour-naming interference effects for masked exam-related threat stimuli compared with non-threat words. It may be the case that once highly anxious individuals become aware of the presence of threat, they are able to avoid it. This strategy may not be available during the presentation of masked trials, as highly anxious individuals seem unable to avoid the automatic processing of threat.

Some investigators have attempted to artificially elevate current stress levels under laboratory conditions. For instance, Mogg, Mathews, Bird, and MacGregor-Morris (1990) found that individuals randomly assigned to a high-stress condition (solving difficult anagrams coupled with false negative feedback) compared to the low-stress condition (solving easy anagrams coupled with false positive feedback) exhibited an attentional bias toward threat on a dot-probe task. The manifestation of the bias toward threat was independent of whether the individual belonged to the high or low trait-anxiety group, thus emphasising the role of state-anxiety. In light of these conflicting findings, Mogg, Bradley, and Hallowell (1994) aimed to disentangle the differential impact that laboratory induced and examination induced stress may have on attentional bias. The most relevant finding of their dot-probe study revealed that high trait-anxious individuals demonstrated an attentional bias toward unmasked threatening material when assigned to the examination stress but not the laboratory-induced stress condition. This study successfully replicates the state-anxiety X trait-anxiety interaction reported in MacLeod and Mathews' (1988) study. Furthermore, it is also in line with Mogg et al.'s (1990) study, in failing to document such an interaction when stress was elevated artificially in the laboratory. In the masked condition, high trait-anxious individuals demonstrated an attentional bias toward threat but only in the unstressed condition. The authors acknowledged that the two studies differed on a number of methodological dimensions (e.g., different experimental design, different types of stressors used) and concluded that the use of an examination-induced stressor may produce more reliable results as it can be considered to be more ecologically valid and is experienced for a longer time period.

## Our Own Research

The review above indicates that threat-related stimuli do indeed affect attentional processing in anxious people in a way that does not happen with nonanxious people. In summary, anxiety is associated with delayed responses when threat-related words are presented on an unattended channel in the dichotic listening task; with delayed colour- naming time when Stroop words are threat related; and with facilitated probe-detection when probes are presented in the same location previously occupied by a threat-related word or face. All of this evidence is consistent with the notion that anxious people rapidly detect the presence of threat in their environment and quickly shift their attention toward this location. However, there is another possibility. It may be the case that anxious people do not notice threat any faster than nonanxious people, but that once threat has been detected they "get stuck" or cannot rapidly move on from the threat stimuli. In other words, anxiety may be associated with biases in the *disengage* component of attention, rather than with the shift or engage component. Early work presented several versions of the Stroop task in which the critical words (threat-related, positive, or neutral) were separated from the primary task (Fox, 1993, 1994). To illustrate, using a blocked version of the Stroop task in which threat-related and neutral words were presented on cards, it was found that high trait-anxious people took longer to name the colour of words when the words themselves were coloured and when colour patches were presented separately from the words (Fox, 1993). However, the magnitude of the Stroop effect was severely decreased when there was a spatial separation between the colour and the words. Subsequent experiments that presented colour patches and words on a computer screen showed that anxious people did not show any Stroop interference when the words were presented at 1.5 degree of visual angle from a to-be-named colour patch. However, this study also failed to replicate the traditional Stroop effect making it difficult to interpret (Fox, 1994, Experiment 1). A similar failure to find enhanced Stroop effects when threat words are separated from a central task was found with a number categorization task (Fox, 1994, Experiment 3). In this study, high and low trait-anxious people had to categorize a centrally located number as odd or even while ignoring spatially displaced words. The presence of threat-related words did not produce an interference effect for the high trait-anxious group, which again was not expected given the prediction of an attentional system that is hypervigilant for threat. However, this study also incorporated a negative priming task, such that participants had to classify a letter string as being a word or a nonword immediately after each trial on the number classification task. It was found that high trait-anxious participants were slower to respond on the lexical decision task if they had just ignored threat-related distractors (on the number classification task) relative to neutral words (Fox, 1994, Experiment 3). This delay was not specific to the trials in which participants had to categorize a threat word on the probe trial, rather it occurred more generally. Thus, a traditional negative priming effect was not found. It seems that ignoring threat-related words did not produce interference immediately but did slow down responses to a subsequent task. This provides some evidence that the distracting words did indeed capture the attention of the high trait-anxious group but were not inhibited perhaps because the time delay was not long enough. It is possible that trait-anxiety is associated with an impaired ability to inhibit threat-related material, which also seems to be a feature of depressive disorders (see Joorman, this volume).

Fox (1993, 1994) proposed that attentional bias in anxiety might only occur when threat-related stimuli have already been detected. In other words, anxiety may be characterized primarily by delays in the *disengagement* of attention from threat-related stimuli rather than to faster shifting of attention toward threat. Much of our research since then has been a follow-up on this hypothesis with different tasks. We must first ask how the results with the dot-probe task fit into this hypothesis? At first sight, the dot-probe literature (see previous section) would seem to suggest that anxious people are indeed shifting attention more quickly to the location of threat. However, if we look carefully at the methods used, this interpretation does not necessarily follow. In most of the dot-probe tasks, word pairs were presented for 500 msec. This gives plenty of time for several attentional shifts between the two locations. What might be happening is that anxious people are shifting attention between the two word locations, and if they happen to notice a threat-related word they then dwell on that word a bit longer than they dwell on a neutral word. This mechanism would explain the faster responses on threat trials. They are not faster because they shift more quickly to a threat location, but rather because they do not disengage as rapidly from a threat location. We tested this hypothesis by conducting a series of experiments using a modified version of Posner's cueing task (Fox et al. 2001; Fox et al., 2002).

These experiments modified the traditional Posner cueing paradigm by presenting threat-related, positively valenced, and neutral items as cues. For example, in one experiment a schematic face was presented either to the right or to the left of fixation, and then a target to be detected was presented in either the same (valid) or the other (invalid) location (see Figure 10.1 for typical valid trial). The schematic faces carried an angry, a happy, or a neutral expression. A strong validity effect was found such that all participants were faster to detect targets when they appeared in valid as opposed to invalid locations. However, there was an interaction between the valence of the cue (angry, happy, neutral) and the anxiety level of the participant (high or low state-anxiety), such that the validity effect was greater for angry cues relative to either happy or neutral cues. The most important finding was that target detection times did not differ according to valence on *valid trials* but only on *invalid trials*. High state-anxious participants were *slower* to detect a target appearing in an invalid location if the cue had been an angry face relative to when the cue was a happy or a neutral expression. This basic pattern of results was found for schematic faces, photographs of real faces, and negative and neutral words (Fox et al., 2001). A typical set of results found with photographs of real faces (Fox, et al., 2001, Experiment 4) is presented in Figure 10.2. We interpreted this general pattern of data as evidence for a delayed disengagement of attention from threat in high-anxious people. It is important to note that the increase in reaction time cannot be attributed solely to a general slowing because of increased arousal and/or anxiety when threat is processed (as may happen in the Stroop task). If this was producing the effect, then a similar slowing would be expected when threat material was presented on *valid* trials. However, this never happened in our studies. Thus, we can be

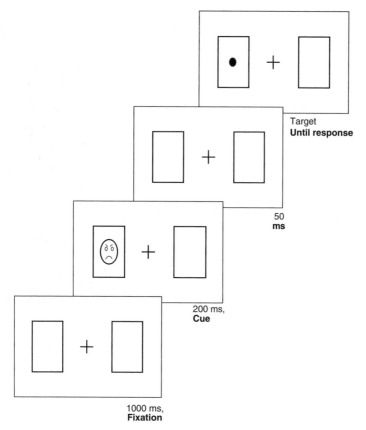

Target
**Until response**

50
**ms**

200 ms,
**Cue**

1000 ms,
**Fixation**

FIGURE 10.1. Example of a valid trial using an "angry" face cue in a modification of the Posner task.

reasonably confident that attentional effects are being measured in this paradigm.

Subsequently, we used the same task but increased the time delay between the cue and the target to examine the effect of valence on the *inhibition of return* (IOR) effect. Posner and Cohen (1984) discovered that cue-onset asynchronies of less than about 300 msec produced *facilitation* (i.e., faster RTs on valid relative to invalid trials). However, when the cue-onset asynchrony was greater than about 500 msec, a reversal took place, such that RTs are now slower on valid trials relative to invalid trials. They called this the IOR effect and argued that it is the result of a mechanism that operates to favour novelty in visual search. The idea is that when a cue appears, attention is automatically drawn to the cue, and then after about 300 msec attention drifts away from the cue location. At that point, it is assumed that attention is inhibited from returning to the cued location.

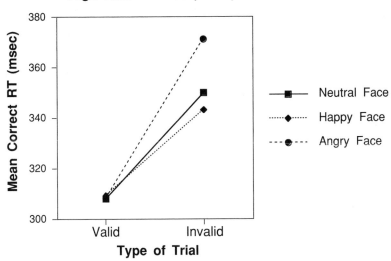

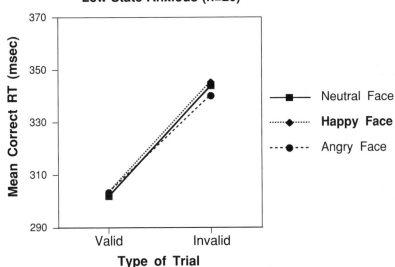

FIGURE 10.2. A typical set of results found with the modified Posner task using facial stimuli varying in emotional valence. As shown, high state-anxious groups take longer to respond to probes following invalid "angry" face cues. This pattern is not seen in the low state-anxious group (see Fox et al., 2001 for further details).

We reasoned that if threat-related stimuli really do hold the attention of anxious people to a greater extent than does neutral stimuli, then using a threat-related cue should *reduce* the magnitude of IOR observed (Fox et al., 2002). We found some evidence for this proposal in that high trait-anxious people showed a reduced IOR effect to angry expressions, relative to neutral expressions, although in some experiments reduced IOR was also found for jumbled faces (Fox et al., 2002, Experiment 2). Nevertheless, given that the jumbled faces were rated as being relatively "threatening," this series of experiments does suggest that the valence of a cue can influence IOR, especially for high trait-anxious participants. Once again, we argued that this was support for the idea that the difference between high- and low-anxious people may reside primarily in the disengage component of attention, rather than in the shifting component.

In summary, several cueing studies using facial expressions have shown no differences on *valid* trials, such that detection times are no faster following threat-related cues relative to happy or neutral cues. Given very fast detection times and possible floor effects, we cannot confidently conclude that threat-related information is drawing attention any faster than neutral cues (Fox et al., 2001). However, a strong conclusion can be drawn that threat-related stimuli are holding the attention of anxious people to a greater extent, given the consistent differences that have been found on *invalid* trials. Similar effects have been found in other laboratories. For example, also using a cueing task, it has been shown that high trait-anxious people take longer to disengage their attention from negative pictures relative to positive pictures. Once again, no valence differences were found on valid trials (Yiend & Mathews, 2001). Derryberry and Reed (2002) recently used their specially modified cueing task (Derryberry & Reed, 1994) in which certain cues were associated with gaining and losing points, respectively. They found that high trait-anxious people were slower to disengage their attention from locations associated with losing points in a game. Thus, taken together it seems that high levels of anxiety are associated with a delay in disengaging attention from threatening facial expressions (Fox et al., 2001, 2002), negative pictures (Yiend & Mathews, 2001), and locations associated with losing points (Derryberry & Reed, 2002).

More recently, we attempted to measure disengagement from threat-related facial expressions more directly. In this task, a photograph of a face is presented at fixation, and after 600 msec, a target letter (X or P) is presented briefly (50 msec) either above, below, to the left, or to the right of the face (see Figure 10.3). In a series of experiments, we found that high trait-anxious people take longer to categorize the target letter if a fearful face is at fixation relative to a sad, happy, or neutral facial expression. In contrast, target categorization times for low trait-anxious participants did not differ across the different face types (Georgiou et al, 2003). We argued that this

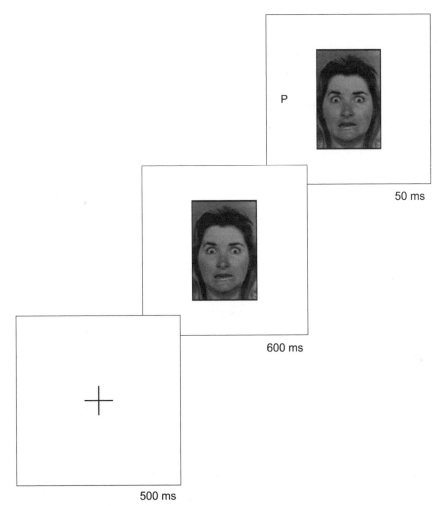

FIGURE 10.3. An example of a trial in a task designed to measure disengagement of attention from faces with varying expressions. This example shows a fearful expression (see Georgiou et al., in press for further details).

pattern of results provides converging evidence that threat-related stimuli hold the attention of high trait-anxious people to a greater extent then for low trait-anxious people. Furthermore, it is supportive of an evolutionary hypothesis in that delayed disengagement in highly anxious individuals is particularly sensitive to the threatening (i.e., fearful facial expression) and not the negative characteristic (i.e., sad facial expression) of a facial expression. This makes intuitive sense as a fearful, as opposed to a sad, facial expression may operate as an early warning cue, alerting others about potential danger in the surrounding environment.

## IMPLICATIONS OF OUR RESEARCH

Our research seems to suggest that attentional bias in anxiety can be characterized by delays in the disengage component of attention. In other words, rather than detecting threat more rapidly, it may be the case that threat stimuli hold the attentional resources of anxious people to a greater extent. This result is consistent with recent theoretical views (e.g., Williams et al., 1997) in showing that attentional processing of threat-related stimuli does differentiate high- and low-anxious participants. However, our work refines the particular component of attention that might be primarily affected. If it is the case that anxious people dwell for longer periods on threat-related stimuli, then we might expect that anxiety should also be characterized by biases in memory for the same material. Williams et al. (1997) argued that the cognitive processes underlying anxiety are compatible with inducing attentional biases but should not induce explicit memory biases for threat-related material. They review a large body of literature suggesting that memory bias in free recall tasks does not indeed generally occur in anxiety. However, in all of the studies reviewed, participants had to analyse words at a relatively deep level (e.g., self-referent encoding). In a recent study, we tested the hypothesis that words encoded at a more shallow level might show a recall bias in anxious individuals (Russo, Fox, Bellinger, & Nguyen-van-Tam, 2001). Russo et al. (2001) found that when participants processed to-be-remembered words at a lexical level (syllable counting) high trait-anxious participants did recall more threat-related words than they did either positive or neutral words. However, when the to-be-remembered words were processed at a semantic level (pleasantness rating), no evidence for a selective memory bias was found. Thus, when words are processed at an incidental level, they seem to show both attentional biases in high trait-anxious participants (Stroop or dot-probe results) and a memory bias (Russo et al., 2001). Although further research is required on these issues, it seems that a tendency to dwell for a longer period on threat-related material may result in both attentional and memory biases. This pattern of results suggests that some modification may be needed to the Williams et al. (1997) theory.

If the delayed disengagement hypothesis is correct, then it is interesting to speculate what implications a relatively short-lived attentional effect (e.g., 20 msec) might generally have on cognitive processing. Our current research addresses exactly this issue. A key working hypothesis is that increased dwell time on threat-related material may be related to increased worry and rumination. The idea is that the delay in disengaging from threat-related stimuli might escalate through the system and result in enhanced memory for this material and increased worry, which is of course a key characteristic of clinical anxiety disorders. An initial study supports this hypothesis in showing that those individuals who demonstrated larger disengage effects (i.e., longer RTs to categorize a peripheral target letter when negative words were presented at fixation, relative to when neutral words were presented at fixation) tended to have higher scores on a measure of worry. This correlational study suggests that the attentional tendency to dwell for a longer period on threat material is related to an increased tendency to worry. We are following up this study by using a more comprehensive range of worry questionnaires and attentional measures. A failure to effectively disengage attentional resources from threatening material, and the consequent enhanced rumination, may have specific effects on executive functions, such as increased pressure on the inhibitory system. As discussed in the chapters by Joorman and Maylor et al. (this volume), inhibitory functioning is crucial to a wide range of executive tasks and may be impaired in normal aging and during depression. It seems that anxiety may also lead to similar deficits in executive functioning. A useful focus for future research would be to examine the similarities and differences in executive functioning across a variety of emotional disorders and aging.

## Author Note

The authors are grateful to Riccardo Russo and Angela Boldini for comments on an earlier draft of this chapter. The work upon which this chapter is based was funded by The Wellcome Trust, to whom we are grateful.

## References

Beck, A. T., & Emery, G. (1985). *Anxiety disorders and phobias: A cognitive perspective.* New York: Basic Books.

Beech, A., Powell, T., McWilliams, J., & Claridge, G. (1989). Evidence of reduced 'cognitive inhibition' in schizophrenia. *British Journal of Psychology, 28,* 109–116.

Bower, G. H. (1981). Mood and memory. *American Psychologist, 36,* 129–148.

Bradley, B. P., Mogg, K., Falla, S. J., & Hamilton, L. R. (1998). Attentional bias for threatening facial expressions in anxiety: Manipulation of stimulus duration. *Cognition and Emotion, 12,* 737–753.

Broadbent, D. E. (1958). *Perception and communication.* Oxford: Pergamon.

Cherry, E. C. (1953). Some experiments on the recognition of speech, with one and with two ears. *Journal of the Acoustical Society of America, 25,* 975–979.

Dalgleish, T. (1995). Performance on the emotional Stroop task in groups of anxious, expert, and control subjects: A comparison of computer and card presentation formats. *Cognition and Emotion, 9,* 341–362.

Derryberry, D., & Reed, M. A. (1994). Temperament and attention: Orienting toward and away from positive and negative signals. *Journal of Personality and Social Psychology, 66,* 1128–1139.

Derryberry, D., & Reed, M. A. (2002). Anxiety-related attentional biases and their regulation by attentional control. *Journal of Abnormal Psychology, 111,* 225–236.

Deutsch, J. A., & Deutsch, D. (1963). Attention: Some theoretical considerations. *Psychological Review, 70,* 80–90.

Ekman, P., & Friesen, W. V. (1975). *Pictures of facial affect.* Palo Alto, CA: Consulting Psychologists Press.

Eysenck, M. W. (1992). *Anxiety: The cognitive perspective.* Hove: Lawrence Erlbaum Associates.

Eysenck, M. W. (1997). *Anxiety: The cognitive perspective: A unified approach.* Hove: Lawrence Erlbaum Associates.

Eysenck, M. W., MacLeod, C., & Mathews, A. (1987). Cognitive functioning and anxiety. *Psychological Research, 49,* 189–195.

Fox, E. (1993). Attentional bias in anxiety: Selective or not? *Behaviour Research and Therapy, 31,* 487–493.

Fox, E. (1994). Attentional bias in anxiety: A defective inhibition hypothesis. *Cognition and Emotion, 8,* 165–195.

Fox, E. (1995). Negative priming from ignored distractors in visual selection: A review. *Psychonomic Bulletin and Review, 2,* 145–173.

Fox, E. (2002). Processing emotional facial expressions: The role of anxiety and awareness. *Cognitive, Affective, and Behavioral Neuroscience, 2,* 52–63.

Fox, E., Russo, R., Bowles, R. J., & Dutton, K. (2001). Do threatening stimuli draw or hold visual attention in sub-clinical anxiety? *Journal of Experimental Psychology: General, 130,* 681–700.

Fox, E., Russo, R., & Dutton, K. (2002). Attentional bias for threat: Evidence for delayed disengagement from emotional faces. *Cognition and Emotion, 16,* 355–379.

Georgiou, G., Bleakley, C., Hayward, J., Russo, R., Dutton, K., Eltiti, S., & Fox, E. (in press). Focusing on fear: Attentional disengagement from emotional faces. *Visual Cognition.*

Hasher, L., Stoltzfus, E. R., Zacks, R. T., & Rympa, B. (1991). Age and inhibition. *Journal of Experimental Psychology: Learning, Memory and Cognition, 17,* 163–169.

Houghton, G., & Tipper, S. P. (1994). A model of inhibitory mechanisms in selective attention. In D. Dagenbach & T. Carr (Eds.), *Inhibitory mechanisms in attention, memory and language.* San Diego, CA: Academic Press.

Lavie, N. (1995). Perceptual load as a necessary condition for selective attention. *Journal of Experimental Psychology: Human Perception and Performance, 21,* 451–468.

Lavie, N., & Fox, E. (2000). The role of perceptual load in negative priming. *Journal of Experimental Psychology: Human Perception and Performance, 26,* 1038–1052.

Lavie, N., & Tsal, Y. (1994). Perceptual load as a major determinant of the locus of selection in visual attention. *Perception and Psychophysics, 56,* 183–197.

MacLeod, C., & Hagan, R. (1992). Individual differences in the selective processing of threatening information, and emotional responses to a stressful life event. *Behaviour Research and Therapy, 30,* 151–161.

MacLeod, C., & Mathews, A. (1988). Anxiety and the allocation of attention to threat. *Quarterly Journal of Experimental Psychology. A, Human Experimental Psychology, 40,* 653–670.

MacLeod, C., Mathews, A., & Tata, P. (1986). Attentional bias in emotional disorders. *Journal of Abnormal Psychology, 95,* 15–20.

MacLeod, C., & Rutherford, E. M. (1992). Anxiety and the selective processing of emotional information: Mediating roles of awareness, trait and state variables, and personal relevance of stimulus materials. *Behaviour Research & Therapy, 30,* 479–491.

Martin, M., Williams, R., & Clark, D. (1991). Does anxiety lead to selective processing of threat-related information? *Behaviour Research and Therapy, 29,* 147–160.

Mathews, A., & Klug, F. (1993). Emotionality and interference with colour-naming in anxiety. *Behaviour Research & Therapy, 31,* 57–62.

Mathews, A., & Mackintosh, B. (1998). A cognitive model of selective processing in anxiety. *Cognitive Therapy and Research, 22,* 539–560.

Mathews, A., & MacLeod, C. (1985). Selective processing of threat cues in anxiety states. *Behaviour Research & Therapy, 23,* 563–569.

Mathews, A., & MacLeod, C. (1986). Discrimination of threat cues without awareness in anxiety states. *Journal of Abnormal Psychology, 98,* 131–138.

Mathews, A., & Sebastian, S. (1993). Suppression of emotional Stroop effects by fear-arousal. *Cognition and Emotion, 7,* 517–530.

May, C. P., Kane, M. J., & Hasher, L. (1995). Determinants of negative priming. *Psychological Bulletin, 118,* 35–54.

McNally, R. J., Amir, N., Louro, C. E., Lukach, B. M., Riemann, B. C., & Calamari, J. E. (1994). Cognitive processing of idiographic emotional information in panic disorder. *Behaviour Research and Therapy, 32,* 119–122.

Mogg, K., & Bradley, B. P. (1998). A cognitive-motivational view analysis of anxiety. *Behaviour Research and Therapy, 36,* 809–848.

Mogg, K., & Bradley, B. P. (1999). Orienting of attention to threatening facial expressions presented under conditions of restricted awareness. *Cognition and Emotion, 13,* 713–740.

Mogg, K., Bradley, B. P., & Hallowell, N. (1994). Attentional bias to threat: Roles of trait anxiety, stressful events, and awareness. *The Quarterly Journal of Experimental Psychology: Human Experimental Psychology, 47A,* 841–864.

Mogg, K., Bradley, B. P., de Bono, J., & Painter. M. (1997). Time course of attentional bias for threat information in non-clinical anxiety. *Behaviour Research and Therapy, 35,* 297–303.

Mogg, K., Bradley, B. P., & Williams, R. (1995). Attentional bias in anxiety and depression: The role of awareness. *British Journal of Clinical Psychology, 34,* 17–36.

Mogg, K., & Marden, B. (1990). Processing of emotional information in anxious subjects. *British Journal of Clinical Psychology, 29,* 227–229.

Mogg, K., Mathews, A., Bird, C., & MacGregor-Morris, R. (1990). Effects of stress and anxiety on the processing of threat stimuli. *Journal of Personality and Social Psychology, 59,* 1230–1237.

Mogg, K., Mathews, A., & Weinman, J. (1989). Selective processing of threat cues in anxiety states: A replication. *Behaviour Research and Therapy, 9,* 104–110.

Moray, N. (1959). Attention in dichotic listening: Affective cues and the influence of instructions. *Quarterly Journal of Experimental Psychology, 11,* 56–60.

Neill, W. T. (1977). Inhibitory and facilitatory processes in selective attention. *Journal of Experimental Psychology: Human Perception and Performance, 3,* 444–450.

Norman, D. A. (1968). Towards a theory of memory and attention. *Psychological Review*, *75*, 522–536.

Posner, M. I., & Petersen, S. E. (1990). The attention system of the human brain. *Annual Review of Neuroscience*, *13*, 25–42.

Posner, M. I. (1980). Orienting of attention. *Quarterly Journal of Experimental Psychology*, *32*, 3–25.

Posner, M. I., & Cohen, Y. (1984). Components of visual orienting. In H. Bouma & D. Bowhuis (Eds.), *Attention and performance, X* (pp. 531–556). Hove, UK: Lawrence Erlbaum Associates Ltd.

Power, M. J., & Dalgleish, T. (1997). *Cognition and emotion: From order to disorder.* Hove: Psychology Press (Erlbaum, UK).

Rapee, R. M. (1991). Generalized anxiety disorder: A review of clinical features and theoretical concepts. *Clinical Psychology Review*, *11*, 419–440.

Richards, A., & French, C. C. (1990). Central versus peripheral presentation of stimuli in an emotional Stroop task. *Anxiety Research*, *3*, 41–49.

Richards, A., & Millwood, B. (1989). Colour-identification of differently valenced words in anxiety. *Cognition and Emotion*, *3*, 171–176.

Riemann, B. C., & McNally, R. J. (1995). Cognitive processing of personally relevant information. *Cognition and Emotion*, *9*, 325–340.

Russo, R., Fox, E., Bellinger, L., & Nguyen-van-Tam, P. (2001). Mood-congruent free recall bias in anxiety. *Cognition and Emotion*, *15*, 419–433.

Spielberger, C. D., Gorsuch, R. L., Lushene, R., Vagg, P. R., & Jacobs, G. A. (1983). *Manual for the state-trait anxiety inventory.* Palo Alto, CA: Consultant Psychologists Press.

Stroop, J. R. (1935). Studies of interference in serial verbal reactions. *Journal of Experimental Psychology*, *18*, 643–662.

Tipper, S. P. (1985). The negative priming effect: Inhibitory effects of ignored primes. *Quarterly Journal of Experimental Psychology*, *37A*, 571–590.

Treisman, A. M. (1960). Contextual cues in selective listening. *Quarterly Journal of Experimental Psychology*, *12*, 242–248.

van den Hout, M., Tenney, N., Huygens, K., Merckelbach, H., & Kindt, M. (1995). Responding to subliminal threat cues is related to trait anxiety and emotional vulnerability: A successful replication of MacLeod and Hagan (1992). *Behaviour Research and Therapy*, *33*, 451–454.

Wilson, E., & MacLeod, C. (2003). Contrasting two accounts of anxiety-linked attentional bias: Selective attention to varying levels of stimulus threat intensity. *Journal of Abnormal Psychology*, *112*, 212–218.

Williams, J. M. G., Mathews, A., & MacLeod, C. (1996). The emotional Stroop task and psychopathology. *Psychological Bulletin*, *120*, 3–24.

Williams, J. M. G., Watts, F. N., MacLeod, C., & Mathews, A. (1988). *Cognitive psychology and emotional disorders.* Chichester: Wiley.

Williams, J. M. G., Watts, F. N., MacLeod, C., & Mathews, A. (1997). *Cognitive psychology and emotional disorders.* Chichester: Wiley.

Yiend, J., & Mathews, A. (2001). Anxiety and attention to threatening pictures. *Quarterly Journal of Experimental Psychology*, *54A*, 665–681.

# 11

# Inhibition, Rumination, and Mood Regulation in Depression

## Jutta Joormann

*The mind seizes hold of something and simply cannot let it go.*
— Winston Churchill

Rumination, as described above by Winston Churchill, is a central, debilitating feature of depressive episodes and of other emotional disorders. Rumination means bringing an idea back to mind over and over again. Originally, the word referred to the way cows and certain other animals eat, storing partially digested food in a stomach called a rumen, bringing that food up later to chew over more thoroughly. Even in the original Latin, however, it took on a vivid figurative meaning, describing the practice of bringing an idea back to mind for further work-over. Many of us mull over important matters in this way, digesting them a little at a time. But in depression, rumination becomes less a deliberate practice of thinking but more an involuntary state of mind, featuring negative, self-deprecating statements and pessimistic ideas about the world and the future. To say to a depressed ruminator, "Just stop thinking about it" – whatever the "it" might be – is not very helpful.

Apart from being a debilitating symptom, rumination has also been linked to a heightened vulnerability for recurring depressive episodes and to prolonged depressive episodes. Therefore, a closer analysis of underlying causes and short-term and long-term consequences of this "symptom" of depression might facilitate our understanding of depressive disorders, ultimately leading to refined treatments and effective prevention.

However, a series of important questions on the relation of rumination and depression remains unanswered. Two of these questions are the central focus of the present chapter: (1) Why does rumination occur? What are the underlying cognitive processes that allow nondepressed people to think over a range of things but to stop thinking and to redirect attention before this process becomes dysfunctional or when other things become more important? Also, along those lines, what are the underlying dysfunctions that prevent these corrective processes from happening in depression? (2) What are the consequences of rumination? How does this "recycling" of thoughts affect cognitive functioning, problem-solving abilities, and mood state?

As outlined in the following pages, rumination, together with other cognitive symptoms of depression, has been explained by deficits in the inhibition of irrelevant information in depression, which might have a negative mood-stabilizing effect and might present a cognitive vulnerability factor for depression. Thus, in trying to understand more about what makes people vulnerable to experiencing depression, this chapter analyzes the relation of inhibition, rumination, and mood regulation. The term "depression" is used here to refer to the broader category of depressive symptoms, dysphoria, and depressive syndrome. Considerable debate within the depression literature has been devoted to the issue of continuity (Coyne & Gotlib, 1983, Gotlib, 1984; Nolen-Hoeksema & Girgus, 1994), which deals with the question of whether mild dysphoria and moderate depressive symptoms differ from the diagnostic category of major depression quantitatively or qualitatively. Dysphoric samples are usually defined through high scores on self-report measures such as the Beck Depression Inventory (BDI; Beck, Steer, & Garbin, 1988) or the Center for Epidemiological Studies Depression Scale (CES-D; Radloff, 1977). In contrast, the assessment of a major depressive episode requires a clinical interview. Although differing results on cognitive tasks have been found when self-report samples and diagnosed samples have been compared (see, for example, Matt, Vazquez, & Campbell, 1992), overall the patterns of results are often very similar (Flett, Vredenburg, & Krames, 1997). In their review paper, Flett et al. (1997) summarized that, although continuities and discontinuities can be observed, the evidence is in general compatible with the continuity hypothesis. Nonetheless, it is important that researchers remain open to the possibility of differential results when studying depressed and dysphoric samples. Thus, whether a given result obtained in one of these samples generalizes to the other sample remains, of course, an empirical question. In this chapter, I review studies that use both the diagnostic category and the self-reported state of dysphoria. Therefore, it is clearly stated if a result described in this chapter was obtained with dysphoric and/or clinically diagnosed depressed participants.

## COGNITIVE PROCESSES IN DEPRESSION

### The Processing of Nonemotional Information: A Generalized Deficit?

Before we examine the relation of rumination and inhibition, it seems helpful to take a closer look at cognitive theories of depression and at findings of differences between depressed and nondepressed participants in cognitive functioning. It is beyond the scope of this chapter to give a detailed and exhaustive review of the findings of over 40 years of research on cognitive processes in depression, especially because other authors have already done this more skillfully (e.g., Williams, Watts, MacLeod, & Mathews, 1997). Instead, some main findings are highlighted in this section, in particular, those findings that give support to the hypothesis that inhibitory functions might be impaired in depression. Also, some questions that have not yet been successfully addressed in the literature are outlined, and directions for future research are discussed.

Two distinct patterns of cognitive correlates of depression and dysphoria are frequently reported: Although depressed and dysphoric people report concentration difficulties and impairments in the recall of neutral stimuli (Burt, Zembar, & Niederehe, 1995), they easily concentrate on negative self-focused thoughts and show enhanced recall of mood-congruent negative memories (Gotlib, Roberts, & Gilboa, 1996; Rusting, 1998). Consequently, there are two separate lines of research on cognitive processes in depression, with only a few attempts in the literature to integrate the findings obtained in these separate lines of empirical study (Ellis & Ashbrook, 1988; Hertel, 1997; Williams et al., 1997). The first line of research is concerned with explaining "cognitive symptoms" of depression, such as concentration difficulties, distractibility, attention deficits, and impaired recall of neutral information. The second line of research is concerned with explaining the biased processing of emotional information.

The main question within the first line of research is whether there is evidence for a generalized cognitive deficit in depression (i.e., a deficit that becomes evident in the processing of neutral, nonemotional information). Indeed, research and clinical practice show that depressed people often complain about concentration difficulties (Watts & Sharrock, 1985), and, consequently, "difficulty concentrating" has been included as a symptom of a major depressive episode in the DSM-IV (Diagnostic and Statistical Manual of Mental Disorders, APA, 1997). Overall, there is a large amount of literature that strongly suggests depression-related impairment in the recall of nonaffective, neutral information (for reviews, see Burt et al., 1995; Johnson & Magaro, 1987; Mathews & MacLeod, 1994). However, it should be cautioned that in the frequently cited meta-analysis by Burt et al. (1995), memory impairments were seen more consistently for inpatients relative to outpatients. Moreover, these kinds of memory impairments were also witnessed in other psychological disorders (e.g. schizophrenia, comorbid substance abuse, and anxiety disorders). Therefore, Burt et al. (1995) suggested that these impairments might be associated with generalized aspects of psychopathology rather than with disorder-specific factors. They further pointed out that, although this result has been noted by various researchers in this area, it has not received enough attention in empirical studies. Moreover, in a series of studies, Hertel and her collaborators (Hertel, 1998;

Hertel & Milan, 1994; Hertel & Rude, 1991) gathered evidence that impairments, when observed at all, are not seen in all aspects of memory but rather are restricted to free recall and controlled components of recognition. Recognition tests typically combine controlled and automatic retrieval processes in that either the controlled consideration of the prior context of the test items, or the automatic experience of familiarity, are used for judgments about prior occurrence. Using Jacoby's process dissociation procedures (Jacoby, 1991) and indirect memory tests, Hertel found the automatic components of recognition to be intact (Hertel, 1998; Hertel & Hardin, 1990; Hertel & Milan, 1994).

These results suggest that this deficit in the recall or recognition of nonemotional information is not as pervasive as one would expect it to be, and, accordingly, these results raise the question of boundary conditions and underlying mechanisms. Studies conducted so far provide evidence that depression and dysphoria are associated with greater memory impairment in contexts in which (1) attention is not constrained by the task (Hertel & Hardin, 1990; Hertel & Rude, 1991), (2) increased cognitive effort is required (Hasher & Zacks, 1979; see also review by Hartlage, Alloy, Vazquez, & Dyckman, 1993), and (3) attention is easily allocated to personal concerns and other thoughts irrelevant to the task (Ellis, Thomas, & Rodriguez, 1984; Seibert & Ellis, 1991).

All of these results support the notion that it is more the controlled, rather than the automatic, aspects of memory that show consistent impairment among depressed and dysphoric individuals. Accordingly, it has been debated whether these impairments are due to limited cognitive capacities on the part of depressed and dysphoric participants. The resource-allocation hypothesis states that depressed participants have deficits in remembering and in engaging in other effortful cognitive procedures because their cognitive capacity is reduced (Ellis & Ashbrook, 1988; Hasher & Zacks, 1979). The general assumption is that there is a limit on the amount of resources available for cognitive operations and that depression either occupies or functionally reduces these resources (Ellis et al., 1984). Deficits should thus become evident in effortful tasks and should only be detectable in effortful, resource-demanding components of memory tasks but not in automatic components.

Although this hypothesis seems to provide an explanation for the obtained results in memory tasks, the resource allocation account has been challenged. In a study that required participants to judge whether a target word fit into a corresponding sentence frame and then tested recall of the target words, Hertel and Rude (1991) were able to eliminate the depressive deficit by providing instructions that focused participants on the task and did not allow mind-wandering. In their "focused" condition, participants were required to keep each word in mind for the duration of the trial. In their "unfocused" condition, however, participants could respond right away and could choose to sustain attention on the task or to think about other matters. Hertel and Rude (1991) found a depressive deficit in the unfocused but not in the focused condition. Accordingly, Hertel argued that depression does not limit the ability to use effortful operations but instead reduces the initiative to use strategies in unconstrained tasks, i.e., tasks that are unstructured and thus profit from the use of special strategies (Hertel, 1997). Therefore, one would not necessarily expect deficits in effortful tasks but rather in unconstrained tasks, no matter how effortful these might be (see also Hertel & Hardin, 1990). Following up on these studies, Hertel (1998) also reported that dysphoric students who had to wait in an unconstrained situation (without being given any instructions regarding what to do during the waiting period) and dysphoric students who were instructed to rate self-focused material designed to invoke rumination, showed comparable recall deficits. However, no deficit was found for dysphoric students who were told what to do during the waiting period (rating self-irrelevant and task-irrelevant material).

These results suggest that, at least with respect to memory deficits, depressed people might have the ability to perform at the level of nondepressed people in structured constrained situations but have problems doing this on their own initiative in unconstrained situations. Moreover, these results show that the elimination of the opportunity to ruminate also eliminated the impairment in the memory task, a result that might explain why unconstrained situations are deficit-provoking for depressed individuals. The preoccupation with task-irrelevant thoughts and rumination seems to interfere with the use of procedures that would otherwise be self-initiated. This is an important finding and, as Hertel (2000) has pointed out, it is time to move beyond the mere assertion that attention is diverted by personal concerns to understand the specific processes that underlie these impairments. Unconstrained situations call for cognitive flexibility and goal-oriented behavior and require attentional control, that is, focal attention to relevant stimuli and inhibition of irrelevant material. Thus, these performance deficits in the recall of neutral information do not seem to reflect a generalized deficit or a lack of resources on the part of depressed subjects but might instead be to the result of inhibitory dysfunctions in the processing of irrelevant information related to depression and dysphoria.

The results obtained for memory tasks might directly suggest deficits in attentional functioning in depression, but memory performance can be affected as much by problems in retrieval as by deficits in encoding. Therefore, to make specific conclusions about attention, one has to consider studies that directly tap attentional processing as independent of retrieval processes as possible. However, research using measures of attentional capacity with less emphasis on retrieval has produced very inconclusive results. Breslow, Kocsis, and Belkin (1980) found differences between depressed and nondepressed participants on the digit span, whereas other studies could not replicate this effect (Gray, Dean, Rattan, & Cramer, 1987; Stromgren, 1977). Other similar studies produced mixed results (Colby & Gotlib, 1988). Channon, Baker, and Robinson (1993) compared depressed participants with controls on a variety of working memory tasks related to attentional resources and found very few differences (i.e., only on the backward digit span). Most of these tasks that involve working memory (e.g., the digit span) involve relative short retention intervals and thus seem to allow a more direct assessment of attentional processes irrespective of retrieval from long-term memory. However, it has been criticized that the relatively slow-paced presentations that are used to ensure perception might allow for chunking and active rehearsal of material (Rokke, Arnell, Koch, & Andrews, 2002). In a more recent study using an attentional blink paradigm that involves rapid serial presentations, significant group differences in performance between moderately to severely dysphoric (BDI over 21) and nondysphoric participants were found but only under demanding dual-tasking conditions (Rokke et al., 2002). Moreover, only nine moderately to severely dysphoric participants were included in this study. Thus, so far, very limited evidence is available to suggest that depressed and dysphoric participants are characterized by an attentional deficit when processing neutral information. Clearly, however, more studies are needed to clarify these results.

To summarize, surprisingly little empirical support has been found so far for depressive deficits in the processing of neutral information. The most promising are results obtained in studies that investigated recall and recognition of emotionally neutral stimuli. Overall, although the literature strongly suggests a depression-related impairment in the recall of neutral information, and although attempts have been made to explain these impairments in terms of deficits in the capacity or allocation of attentional resources in working memory, little direct evidence is available so far that attentional resources are indeed reduced in depression. In summarizing the results obtained to this point, it seems safe to say that the bulk of evidence suggests deficits in the initiation of attentional strategies rather than limited processing capacities. When attention is well controlled by the demands of the task, and does not have to be self-controlled or initiated, no depressive deficits are found, even when the task is resource demanding.

However, this still leaves us with the more important question: Why is the self-controlled focusing of attention so difficult? One answer to this question might be that focusing of attention requires the inhibition of task-irrelevant thoughts. As outlined below, preoccupation with negative task-irrelevant thoughts is a major cognitive feature of depressive episodes. Hertel (1998) showed that an experimental context that eliminated the opportunity to ruminate eliminated the impairments in a memory task. Rumination and negative self-focused thoughts seem to be prepotent responses for depressed individuals, or as Hertel (2004) phrased it, they are "habits of thought." Overriding prepotent responses is the role of inhibitory processes in attention and memory. Inhibitory processes thus allow flexible, goal-oriented, and situationally appropriate behavior. Inhibitory dysfunctions in depression and dysphoria might be responsible for this lack of self-controlled attention to the task at hand. This implies that we have to look at how depressed individuals process emotional information in order to advance our understanding of their difficulties processing neutral information.

### The Processing of Emotional Information

The primary symptom of depression, which also seems more specific to depressive disorders than to concentration difficulties and attention deficits, is sustained negative affect. Again, investigating cognitive processes might be of assistance in understanding this symptom and its role in the etiology and maintenance of depression. As pointed out previously, a first line of research is concerned with the processing of neutral information in depression. However, a second line of research, originating in cognitive theories of emotion, is concerned with explaining the relation of the processing of emotional information and the occurrence of negative affect. Depression is characterized by negative, automatic thoughts about the self, the future, and the world. These cognitive "symptoms" of depression are so prevalent that cognitive theories of depression focus on them in order to explain the onset, maintenance, and recurrence of depressive episodes. In addition, one of the most successful interventions for depression, cognitive – behavioral therapy, focuses interventions on these factors (Beck, 1976), and other models highlight cognitive factors as a possible vulnerability marker (Gotlib & Krasnoperova, 1998; Gotlib & Neubauer, 2000; Ingram, Miranda, & Segal, 1998).

Research on cognitive processes in depression has been guided primarily by Beck's (1976) schema theory of depression and Bower's (1981, 1987) network theory of cognition and emotion. Beck postulates that existing memory representations, or schemata, lead individuals to filter stimuli from the environment such that their attention is directed selectively toward information that is congruent with their schemata. More relevant to depression, Beck theorizes that the schemata of depressed persons include themes of loss, separation, and rejection; consequently, depressed individuals exhibit a systematic bias in their processing of environmental stimuli or information that is relevant to these themes. This bias leads to depressed people attending selectively to negative stimuli in their environment and to depressed people interpreting neutral and ambiguous stimuli in a schema-congruent way. Moreover, this bias is presumed to endure beyond the depressive episode, representing a stable vulnerability factor for depression in formerly depressed individuals.

Bower's (1981, 1987) theory similarly postulates that "associative networks" lead to systematic attentional biases in depressed individuals. These associative networks consist of numerous nodes, each containing specific semantic representations that can be activated by environmental stimuli. The activation of any one node causes the partial activation, or "priming," of all the other nodes within its associative network, through a process of "spreading activation." Consequently, the representations of the primed nodes require less activation for access to occur than do the representations of nonprimed nodes, resulting in an attentional processing advantage for stimuli that are related to these primed representations. Like Beck, Bower also postulates that associative networks are stable constructs; the attentional biases of depressed individuals are expected to endure beyond the depressive episode. Therefore, by adding a few extra assumptions to Bower's model, such as habitually lowered thresholds for activation or habitually strengthened connections between nodes, his model of how mood influences cognitive processes might be used to explain vulnerability to depression. Taken together, Beck and Bower postulate that depressed individuals are characterized by cognitive biases in depression in all aspects of information processing, including perception, attention, memory, and reasoning, which function to facilitate the processing of negatively valenced information. Moreover, because these biases are hypothesized to endure beyond discrete episodes of depression, they should also characterize the functioning of individuals who, although not currently depressed, are vulnerable to experience episodes of depression.

Although these theoretical predictions are straightforward, the empirical results are not as conclusive. In particular, the search for cognitive vulnerability markers (i.e., cognitive factors that predict the onset, maintenance, or recurrence of depressive episodes) is an ongoing focus of depression research. For example, a current controversy in cognitive theories of emotional disorders concerns the existence of attentional biases in depression and dysphoria. Overall, there is strong evidence for biased memory processes in depression (Williams et al., 1997). Biased memory for negative, relative to positive, information represents perhaps the most robust cognitive finding associated with major depression (Blaney, 1986; Matt et al., 1992). In a meta-analysis of studies assessing recall performance of persons with major depression, Matt and colleagues found that this group remembers 10% more negative words than positive words. Nondepressed controls, in contrast, demonstrated a memory bias for positive information in 20 out of 25 studies. In contrast, a number of studies failed to find attentional biases in depression (e.g., MacLeod, Tata & Mathews, 1987; Mogg, Bradley, Williams, & Mathews, 1993). Furthermore, no attentional biases were found in participants who had previously been depressed as compared to participants who had never been depressed (e.g., Gilboa & Gotlib, 1997; Hedlund & Rude, 1995). These results suggest that attentional biases in depression are not as pervasive as suggested by Beck's and Bower's theoretical predictions. Consequently, Williams et al. (1988, 1997) proposed an alternative model, stating that depressed persons are not characterized by biases in attentional functioning but rather by biases in postattentional elaboration. Based on Mandler's distinction between integration (activation) and elaboration, Williams et al. (1988, 1997) suggested that anxiety-congruent biases are located in automatic activation processes, operating at an early orienting stage of processing, prior to awareness, which should be evident in selective attention and priming tasks. In contrast, depressive biases are located in strategic elaboration and therefore would be found in recall tasks but not in selective attention tasks.

Although this formulation seems plausible, it may be premature to conclude that depressed persons are not characterized by an attentional bias. Two recent studies using the dot-probe task, for example, reported selective attention in depression. Interestingly, these biases were found under conditions of long stimuli exposures (Bradley, Mogg, & Lee, 1997; Mogg, Bradley, & Williams, 1995). In the dot-probe task, participants are asked to respond to a probe that replaces one (positive, neutral, or negative) word in a word pair. Allocation of attention to the spatial position of the words is determined from response latencies to the probes. Mogg et al. (1995) reported a mood-congruent bias in depressed participants but only under supraliminal conditions. Likewise, Bradley et al. (1997) reported a mood-congruent bias in the dot-probe task for both induced and naturally occurring dysphoria when stimuli were presented for 500 or 1000 ms but not for briefly presented stimuli (14 ms). Using a dot-probe task with emotional faces instead of words, Gotlib, Krasnoperova, Neubauer, and Joormann (2004) found an attentional bias for negative faces that were presented for 1000 ms in clinically diagnosed depressed participants (Gotlib et al., 2004). According to Bradley et al. (1997), these results suggest that a selective bias for negative information in depression exists but does not operate throughout all aspects of selective attention. Depressed individuals may not automatically orient their attention toward negative information in the environment, but once such information has come into the focus of their attention, they may have greater difficulty in disengaging their attention from it.

These results are consistent with recent research into selective attention, which suggests that selective attention is not a unitary concept and that different components (e.g., orienting vs. maintenance/disengagement) and underlying mechanisms of selective attention have to be separated (LaBerge, 1995; Posner, 1995). Selective attention involves at least two mechanisms: (a) activation of selected, relevant information and (b) active inhibition of unselected, irrelevant information (Hasher & Zacks, 1988; Milliken & Tipper, 1998; Neill, Valdes, & Terry, 1995; Tipper, 1985). The dot-probe findings suggest that depression is not associated with differential initial activation levels of negative, compared to neutral, stimuli representations. Instead, malfunctioning inhibitory mechanisms in the processing of negative stimuli might explain the observed difficulties in disengaging attention from negative material.

To summarize, the aforementioned results strongly suggest that depressed individuals show a memory bias in that they recall negative information more easily than do nondepressed subjects. The results also suggest an attentional bias for negative information but only at long stimuli presentations. Taken together, these results indicate that depression might be characterized by problems in disengaging attention from negative information. This sustained processing of negative information might indeed lead to enhanced elaboration and might thus explain why depressed and dysphoric participants recall negative information so well. Overall, whereas depressed participants do not automatically orient their attention toward negative stimuli in the environment, once negative aspects get into their attentional focus, they have a hard time reorienting their attention. As outlined in the beginning, inhibitory dysfunctions might provide an explanation for these cognitive symptoms. Inhibitory dysfunctions can also be regarded as possible vulnerability markers of depression as they might provide an explanation for the devastating correlate (and possible vulnerability marker) that was presented in the introduction to this chapter: Rumination.

## Ruminative Response Style

A ruminative response style has been defined as one in which individuals focus repetitively on their internal negative emotional state (e.g., depressive symptoms and causes and consequences of these symptoms) without actively making plans or taking steps to relieve their distress. A ruminative response style was proposed as a vulnerability marker of depression (Nolen-Hoeksema, 1991). That is, it was hypothesized that individuals who respond to a dysphoric mood with a ruminative response style are vulnerable to persistent dysphoria and depression. In an extensive program of experimental and correlational studies, Nolen-Hoeksema and colleagues investigated ruminative response styles in depression and dysphoria and analyzed how these response styles exacerbate sad moods and predict future depressive episodes. In an early study on rumination, for example, Morrow and Nolen-Hoeksema (1990) found that, after a negative mood induction, distracting activities alleviated the mood, whereas ruminative, passive responses maintained the negative mood state. Similar results were found with naturally occurring dysphoria (Nolen-Hoeksema & Morrow, 1993). Using a self-report scale, a ruminative response style was found to predict higher levels of dysphoria over time in prospective studies with nonclinical samples, even after controlling for initial differential depression levels (Nolen-Hoeksema & Morrow, 1991; Nolen-Hoeksema, Parker, & Larson, 1994). In a study assessing rumination and mood in 30 consecutive daily measurements, it was found that rumination predicted the duration of dysphoric mood (Nolen-Hoeksema, Morrow, & Frederickson, 1993). Moreover, studies have shown that rumination predicts greater depressive symptoms, predicts the onset of major depressive episodes, and mediates the gender difference in depressive symptoms (Just & Alloy, 1997; Kuehner & Weber, 1999; Nolan, Roberts, & Gotlib, 1998; Nolen-Hoeksema, 2000; Nolen-Hoeksema et al., 1993, Roberts, Gilboa, & Gotlib, 1998). In a recent study, Roberts et al. (1998) presented data showing that elevated levels of rumination were not only found in individuals with current dysphoria, but also in individuals with previous depressive episodes compared to individuals who have never been depressed, although these individuals did not differ on concurrent depressive symptomatology.

According to Nolen-Hoeksema and her collaborators (Nolen-Hoeksema, 1991; Nolen-Hoeksema et al., 1993), what characterizes rumination and differentiates it from negative automatic thoughts is that it is a style of thought rather than just negative content. Thus, rumination is defined by the process of recurring thoughts and ideas described in the beginning of this chapter as a "recycling" of thoughts and not necessarily by the content of these recurring thoughts. Whereas depressive rumination is characterized by negative self-focused thoughts, rumination in an angry or happy mood state features other contents, although the process is similar. In line with this, Roberts et al. (1998) and other researchers criticized that research on rumination relies heavily on self-report measures and that behavioral and information processing measures are needed to assess individual differences in rumination. Also, as outlined in the introduction to this chapter, research that focuses on the underlying cognitive processes and the relation of rumination to biases in memory and attention processes is clearly needed. The majority of studies on rumination are concerned with consequences of ruminative responses. Thus, in general, rumination is induced in one group and distraction in the other group, and researchers study the effect of this manipulation on problem solving, mood states, and memory processes. Although this line of research informs us about the devastating effects of rumination, it is not particularly helpful in determining why it is so difficult for some people to stop thinking and to redirect attention before it becomes dysfunctional and why other people do not find this challenging. Finding an answer to this question might significantly increase our understanding of cognitive processing in depression. As outlined in the following sections, deficits in inhibitory processes might play a central role in the occurrence of ruminative responses.

## WHY DOES RUMINATION OCCUR? THE ROLE OF INHIBITORY PROCESSES

In order to understand the dysfunctional cognitive processes that underlie rumination in depression, it is essential to examine nondepressed people and to analyze the processes that allow people to think over an issue but to stop processing once this thinking becomes dysfunctional or to redirect attention once other information becomes more relevant. Inhibitory processes seem to lie at the heart of this important ability. The environment confronts us with multiple sources of information, events, and objects that can guide our behavior and thoughts. Yet, by necessity, we only respond to some limited subset of these sources. The fundamental question is why we are able to do this? What allows us to attend to a relevant stimulus while ignoring an irrelevant, distracting stimulus, and, more importantly, what happens with the unselected information?

Previous accounts of selective attention stated that the activation resulting from the unselected, irrelevant information just passively decays when it receives no further processing. Thus, selective attention was thought of as being a unitary process, consisting of the enhancement of the processing of the relevant material while the processing of the irrelevant material stops and the associated activation slowly decays. Within this view, differential activation levels of selected versus unselected stimuli representations would account for selective attention. A more recent view of selective attention (LaBerge, 1995; Posner, 1995), however, states that it is not a unitary concept and that it involves at least two processes: the activation of selected, relevant information and the active inhibition of nonselected, irrelevant information (Hasher & Zacks, 1988; Milliken & Tipper, 1998; Neill et al., 1995; Tipper, 1985). Hasher and Zacks (1988) have proposed that this second component, the active inhibition of the processing of irrelevant information, allows us to stop processing irrelevant stimuli. Although it is very straightforward to draw a theoretical distinction between these two positions, it is nevertheless very difficult to generate unequivocal evidence that decides between the two accounts (Anderson & Bjork, 1994; Anderson & Spellman, 1995). However, over the past 15 to 20 years, a number of experimental methodologies have emerged that carry the potential to test these differing predictions because they provide data that cannot be adequately explained by a differential activation account. Some of these designs, such as negative priming (Tipper, 1985) and directed forgetting (Bjork, 1972), are discussed below.

Inhibition processes are suggested to be basic to a range of cognitive tasks including attention, memory, language comprehension, speech production, and problem solving. Inhibition thus seems essential to engaging in goal-directed thought and to maintaining a coherent stream of thought. Along those lines, Hasher and Zacks (1988; Hasher, Zacks, & May, 1999) proposed that the efficient functioning of working memory depends on inhibitory processes that limit the access of information into working memory and update the contents of working memory by removing information that is no longer relevant. They suggested several ways in which inhibitory control of working memory might work. First, inhibition prevents off-goal information from having access to working memory. Off-goal information includes internal thoughts and associations that may be activated along with goal-relevant information. Inhibition also dampens the activation of irrelevant information that accidentally gets into working memory. Second, inhibition reduces the activation of information that was once relevant but now is irrelevant because of a change in goals. Also, inhibition helps to discard thoughts from working memory that were relevant to a previous goal, allowing one to switch attention. Finally, inhibition suppresses the activation of rejected hypotheses, ideas, or interpretations. This function of inhibition prevents attention from returning to discarded ideas. Thus, inhibition helps to have the content of working memory represent current goals. Accordingly, a reduced ability to inhibit irrelevant representations was proposed as a source of low working memory capacity. Engle et al. (Engle, Kane, & Tuholski, 1999) regard inhibition as one aspect of the efficiency of controlled attention, which they equate with working memory capacity. This controlled attention is required for (a) maintaining temporary goals in the face of distraction and interference and (b) blocking, gating, or suppressing distracting events both in perceptual and in memory tasks.

Hasher and Zacks (1988) also outlined consequences that result from inhibitory deficits. First, too much irrelevant information gets into working memory. As a consequence, links between relevant and irrelevant information are created and stored in long-term memory, setting the stage for slow and less accurate retrieval of relevant information and enhanced retrieval of irrelevant information. Second, irrelevant information in working memory is sustained longer. As a consequence, individuals who show an inhibitory deficit are easily distracted by irrelevant information and thoughts. Thus, inhibitory deficits cause cognitive deficits in performance and disrupt a coherent stream of thought. Weakened inhibitory processes were proposed and found in a range of populations, including older adults (Hasher, Stoltzfus, Zacks, & Rympa, 1991), children with attention deficit disorder (Bjorklund & Harnishfeger, 1990), patients with obsessive-compulsive disorder (Enright & Beech, 1990), and patients with schizophrenia (Frith, 1979). As the central function of working memory, malfunctioning inhibitory processes might have severe cognitive and emotional consequences, and rumination may be one of them. These kinds of inhibitory deficits can be linked to the central executive component of working memory (Baddeley, 1986) and have been related to the prefrontal cortex in brain imaging studies (Davidson, 2000). Empirical support for the hypothesis that rumination is related to the executive control component of working memory comes from a recent study by Davis and Nolen-Hoeksema (2000), who reported that ruminators made more errors on the Wisconsin Card Sorting Test (WCST) than nonruminators. The WCST is a widely used measure of executive control and cognitive flexibility.

## How Might Inhibition Be Related to Depression Research?

As outlined above, depression research is concerned with two specific areas of cognitive dysfunction: (a) General distractibility, concentration difficulties, and impaired recall of neutral information, and (b) preferred processing of negative information. Given the consequences of malfunctioning inhibition as outlined by Hasher and Zacks (1988), deficits in the processing of neutral information can easily be explained in terms of inhibitory dysfunctions. Indeed, it was suggested that inhibitory dysfunctions lie at the heart of impaired free recall of neutral information in depression (Hertel, 1997). As outlined previously, Hertel and collaborators reported that impaired memory is most consistently found in situations in which the focus of attention on task-relevant features is not controlled by environmental cues and restrictions but rather needs to be self-initiated. This is the role of inhibitory processes. Thus, because of inhibitory deficit, too much irrelevant information gets into working memory, becomes stored in long-term memory, and interferes with the processing of relevant material. Consequently, retrieval of relevant material is slower and less accurate, and people are more easily distracted by irrelevant material. The less structured the environment, the more it allows irrelevant information to interfere. Accordingly, Hertel (2004) proposed that depressive deficits are caused by two processes: (a) "habits of thought" that lead to the preferred processing of negative information (as is seen in rumination) and (b) lack of cognitive control. Thus, habits of thought interfere under poorly controlled conditions and make it difficult for the depressed person to inhibit and to show cognitive initiative. Inhibition is needed to override the habits of thought, i.e., rumination and other negative thoughts. Nonetheless, it remains unclear why depressed individuals exhibit these negative habits of thought.

Inhibitory dysfunctions, as a general framework, could provide an explanation for the biased processing of emotional information as well, if one more assumption is made: Depression is not characterized by a generalized inhibitory deficit, but rather, this inhibitory deficit is valence-specific. Thus, depressed individuals have trouble inhibiting irrelevant, negative information. If this assumption is made, research on deficits in inhibitory mechanisms of selective attention may provide an explanation for results showing an attentional bias in selective attention tasks under conditions of long stimulus exposure. Further, it may provide an explanation for a range of cognitive symptoms associated with depressive disorders, including rumination and negative automatic thoughts. As outlined above, inhibitory dysfunctions have been linked to rumination (Linville, 1996). Rumination in depression typically features negative thoughts. Consequently, it is not only *too much* irrelevant information that gets into working memory along with goal-relevant information but also, more specifically, *negative* irrelevant information. As a consequence, links are created between relevant and *negative* irrelevant information and stored in long-term memory, setting the stage for slow and less accurate retrieval of relevant and enhanced retrieval of negative irrelevant information. Moreover, negative irrelevant information is not easily discarded from working memory, which might lead to ruminative responses and sustained negative affect. As outlined before, an increased tendency to ruminate on negative information, together with difficulties in distracting oneself from such material, may play an important role in maintaining depressed mood (Nolen-Hoeksema, 1991; Nolen-Hoeksema et al., 1993). Moreover, as has been discussed, a ruminative response style (i.e., a stable tendency to respond to negative life events and negative mood states with ruminative thinking) is considered a vulnerability marker for depressive episodes.

Evidence that individual differences in rumination are related specifically to individual differences in the sustained processing of negative information comes from a recent study using brain imaging. Siegle, Steinhauer, Thase, Stenger, and Carter (2002) examined prolonged elaborative processing of emotional information in depression using functional neuroimaging (fMRI) and found that whereas nondepressed individuals displayed amygdala responses to all stimuli that quickly decayed after offset, depressed individuals in contrast to the controls, displayed sustained amygdala responses to negative words (Siegle et al., 2002). This sustained response lasted throughout the following nonemotional processing trials for depressed participants but not for control participants. Moreover, the difference in sustained amygdala activity to negative and positive words was moderately related to self-reported rumination. In a related study, Siegle, Steinhauer, Carter, Ramel, and Thase (2003) examined the relationship between rumination and pupil dilation, a correlate of cognitive load, in response to emotional and nonemotional information in depression. Depressed individuals showed more sustained pupil dilation in response to stimuli on emotional processing tasks than did nondepressed participants, in particular when confronted with negative personally relevant information. Rumination was also correlated with sustained pupil dilation to negative, personally relevant information. These results are consistent with the idea that rumination might be associated with sustained emotional processing of stimuli.

Taken together, these findings suggest that inhibitory deficits in the processing of negative information not only might be a debilitating symptom of depression, but also might be an important marker of vulnerability to depression. Inhibitory dysfunctions might increase vulnerability as they set the stage for sustained processing of negative information and ruminative responses to negative events and negative mood states. Furthermore, inhibitory dysfunctions might provide the missing link between research concerned with the processing of *neutral* information and research concerned with the processing of *emotional* information (Hertel, 2004). However, it remains unclear whether depression is characterized by a general or by a valence-specific inhibitory deficit.

ASSESSMENT OF INHIBITORY DEFICITS IN DEPRESSION

### Inhibitory Deficits in Depression: Selective Attention Tasks

Active inhibition of irrelevant information is crucial in a range of tasks that require selective attention. The negative priming paradigm (Neill et al., 1995; Tipper, 1985) is an experimental design that makes it possible to distinguish activation from inhibition accounts of selective attention. The *negative priming effect* is defined as a delayed target response latency when the distracter from a previous trial becomes the target on the present trial. Thus, in a negative priming design, participants are asked to respond to a target in the presence of a distracter. For example, participants can be asked to name a word written in red while ignoring a word written in blue that is presented at the same time. Negative priming occurs when, in the following trial, the presented target is identical or related to the previously presented to-be-ignored distracter. In these trials subjects are expected to show a delayed target response latency as compared to trials in which the target and the previously presented distracter are unrelated. The reasoning behind this design is the idea that inhibition of the distracter is activated on the first trial and remains activated on the following trial, delaying the response to a target that is identical to or related to the ignored distracter. Negative priming has been observed in various selective attention tasks, including semantically related distracter-target pairs (e.g., a picture of a dog following an ignored picture of a cat; Tipper, 1985). One of the most prolific areas of research in negative priming was the identification of individual differences that are correlated with the effect. Deficits in negative priming were observed in various subgroups, e.g., in older adults (Hasher et al., 1991), in young children (Tipper, Borque, Anderson, & Brehaut, 1989), and in patients with schizophrenia (Frith, 1979). Such individual differences in negative priming were linked to an inability of these subgroups to inhibit the intrusion of irrelevant information into working memory (Neill et al., 1995). In line with this, Linville (1996) was the first to investigate negative priming in depression. She found that depressed individuals were less likely to inhibit distracting information. Specifically, Linville asked

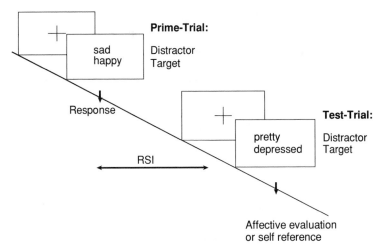

FIGURE 11.1. Design: Negative affective priming. Two consecutive trials, a prime and a test trial, are presented. In each trial, the subject is shown a distracter and a target word and is instructed to respond to the target and to ignore the distracter. The time interval between the participant's response and the presentation of the next pair of words is the so-called Response-Stimulus Interval (RSI). Adapted with permission of Psychology Press Ltd. from Joormann (2004, p. 128, Figure 1). Copyright © 2004 by Psychology Press Ltd., http://www.psypress.co.uk/journals.asp.

participants to complete a modified lexical decision task that required them to inhibit the presence of a distracter (i.e., letter string) while identifying whether a second string is a word. Participants were slower at making these identifications for letter strings that they had been asked to ignore on an earlier trial, thus showing negative priming. Yet, the depressed individuals failed to show this negative priming effect. This is the only published result so far that shows evidence of reduced inhibition in the processing of neutral words in depressed participants. However, as outlined earlier, inhibition deficits might be more prevalent in the processing of emotional information. In particular, the observation of negative automatic thoughts and ruminations on negative information in depression leads to the hypothesis that there is a valence-specific inhibitory deficit in depression: For negative stimuli, inhibition should be selectively reduced.

In a series of studies, I presented a modified negative priming design that allows the assessment of inhibitory processes in the processing of emotional information, i.e., the *negative affective priming* design (NAP, see Figure 11.1; Joormann, 2004). Overall, the paradigm conforms to standard procedures and assumptions from the negative priming literature. However, the stimulus dimension that is supposed to be responsible for the negative priming effect is the stimulus valence. A largely comparable design was proposed by Wentura (1999).

In accordance with standard negative priming designs, the NAP-design consists of consecutive pairs of trials: a prime trial and a test trial. In each trial, two adjectives are presented, i.e., a target and a distracter, along with an instruction to ignore the distracter and to respond to the target. It is important to note that participants are not aware of this separation of trials into prime and test trials. In the negative priming condition, distracters presented in the prime trial (prime-trial distracters) and targets presented in the test trial (test-trial targets) are related by shared valence. In the control condition, prime-trial distracters and test-trial targets are unrelated. Inasmuch as the inhibition of the (valence of) the distracter of the prime trial is still activated, responses to targets of the same valence in the test trial should be delayed. Because the sole function of the prime trial is to manipulate NAP, only responses in the test trials are analyzed. Negative priming is analyzed using a within-subject comparison of negative priming and corresponding control conditions. Also, varying responses can be compared. Participants can be asked to evaluate the valence of the target word (positive vs. negative). Additionally, participants can be asked to evaluate whether the presented target word is self-descriptive. It has been pointed out by several authors that it is important to introduce a self-focus or self-reference in order to find pronounced depressive biases in information processing tasks (e.g., Segal, 1988; Segal & Vella, 1990). The NAP design allows for such a variation.

In a series of studies using this design, it was assumed that the strength of negative priming for emotional words is related to dysphoria and to vulnerability to depression (Joormann, 2004). As outlined before, previous findings suggest that participants with elevated depression scores show reduced inhibition for negative stimuli. Likewise, it was assumed that participants with a history of major depression would show reduced negative priming for negative stimuli relative to participants who have never been depressed. Indeed, this is exactly what was found using valence identification and self-reference versions of the NAP task. An example of the results obtained in these studies is displayed in Figure 11.2.

Positive values represent longer reaction times in the negative priming condition, that is, when the test-trial target valence matched the valence of the prime-trial distracter. Negative values, by contrast, are found if participants responded faster when the test-trial target valence matched the valence of the to-be-ignored distracter. Figure 11.2 shows that delayed responding in the negative priming condition was found for never-depressed participants regardless of target valence. Previously, depressed participants showed a delayed response in the priming condition for positive targets, but they responded faster in the priming condition when negative targets were presented in the test trial. Thus, these participants responded faster when a negative target was presented after a to-be-ignored negative distracter on the previous trial. As predicted, no

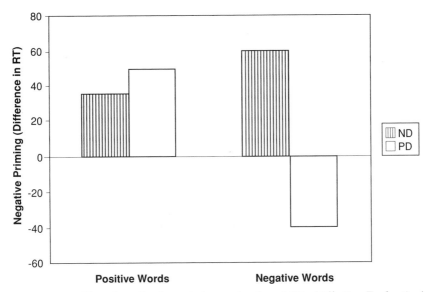

FIGURE 11.2. Negative affective priming and vulnerability (Affective Evaluation). Difference scores of the mean reaction times in the negative priming and corresponding control conditions are presented. A positive value indicates negative priming, a negative value positive priming. PD: Previously depressed participants; ND: Never depressed participants. N = 11 (PD); N = 15 (ND). Adapted with permission of Psychology Press Ltd. from Joormann (2004, p. 138, Figure 3). Copyright © 2004 by Psychology Press Ltd., http://www.psypress.co.uk/journals.asp.

group difference was found for the positive adjectives. The same results as for the previously depressed participants were found for participants with low or high depression scores. These results support the hypothesis that elevated depression scores and vulnerability to depression are related to inhibitory dysfunctions in the processing of negative stimuli.

Taken together, these studies support the hypothesis that inhibitory dysfunctions in the processing of emotional material are related to depressive symptomatology. Furthermore, these results are in line with the hypothesis that depression is related to an inhibitory deficit for negative information. In addition, the results indicate that inhibitory dysfunctions are stable after the remission of the depressive episode and may therefore be a potential vulnerability marker to the disorder.

The present results lend further support to the view that depression is associated with a bias in selective attention to negative information under certain conditions. As Bradley et al. (1997) suggest, it is not the automatic orientation toward negative stimuli that is characteristic of depressive biases. Rather, the disengagement from negative material seems to be specifically problematic in depression. Thus, Williams et al.'s (1997)

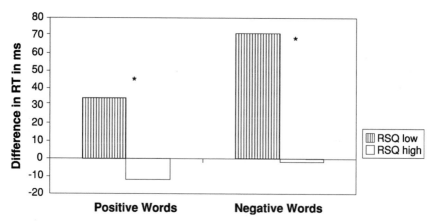

FIGURE 11.3. Negative affective priming and Rumination (self-reference task). Difference scores of the mean reaction times in the negative priming and corresponding control conditions are presented. A positive value shows negative priming, a negative value positive priming. RSQ: Ruminative Response Style Questionnaire. *p < .05

proposal that an attentional bias is not a feature of depression seems to be restricted to the orienting component of selective attention, but it does not apply to the maintenance/disengagement component. Consequently, further insight into the nature of attentional biases and deficits in depression seems to rest on the treatment of selective attention as a process consisting of multiple components and underlying mechanisms. In this respect, it is crucial to undertake a systematic study as to which components of selective attention (e.g., initial shifts in orienting vs. maintenance) are investigated in a particular study. The present results suggest that depression is associated with sustained attention toward negative stimuli resulting from malfunctioning inhibitory processes.

However, throughout the previous sections of this chapter, I advanced the hypothesis that inhibitory deficits are linked to depression via rumination. Thus, the basic idea is that inhibitory deficits set the stage for ruminative responses to negative mood states and negative life events. Therefore, an important question is whether there is evidence that inhibitory processes are directly linked to rumination. In a related study, the NAP task was given to participants who were selected according to their scores on the Response Styles Questionnaire, a frequently used self-report measure of the tendency to ruminate (Nolen-Hoeksema, Larson, & Grayson, 1999). Results showed that participants scoring high on the RSQ showed no negative priming whereas participants scoring low on the RSQ showed negative priming for positive and negative words (see Figure 11.3). This is the first study to show a direct relation of rumination and reduced inhibition (Joormann, 2003a). We should be cautious in interpreting, however, as no study to date has simultaneously included all three variables of interest – depression, rumination and inhibition – at least not with respect to selective attention tasks.

## Inhibitory Deficits in Depression: Memory Tasks

The aforementioned results strongly suggest that depression and inhibitory dysfunctions and rumination and inhibitory dysfunctions in selective attention tasks are related. However, does this evidence for inhibitory dysfunctions reflect mechanisms that are related to selective attention tasks *only* or might the findings result from a more general inhibitory mechanism common to a range of cognitive functions? As outlined above, a consistent finding in cognitive depression research is biased memory processes. It has been suggested that analogous processes might underlie selective retrieval of target items and selective attention to objects in the external environment (Anderson & Spellman, 1995). Thus, attention can be shifted from objects in the external world to objects in the internal world. Anderson and Spellman (1995) refer to instances in which focal awareness is directed to a specific internal representation, the referent of which is no longer in the environment as "conceptually focused selective attention." They further assume that the same mechanisms are at work. The principal difference between attention and selective retrieval is that competition among active representations is conceptually initiated, rather than perceptually initiated, and that the output is a memory rather than a percept. Consequently, if inhibitory dysfunction in depression is found in selective attention tasks, it should also be detectable in memory tasks.

There is a consistent thread of studies within memory research that has addressed the idea of inhibitory dysfunctions. This work is concerned with the phenomenon of directed forgetting. The general idea of directed forgetting studies is to instruct subjects, at some point during the presentation of to-be-remembered (TBR) items, that the items already presented and encoded are now to-be-forgotten and will not be tested later; that is, subjects are directed to forget certain stimuli (Bjork, 1972; Epstein, 1971). At some point, free-recall and recognition of to-be-remembered and to-be-forgotten (TBF) items are tested. In the majority of these studies, the recall of TBF items is usually very low, and recognition level is usually very high. To my knowledge, no study so far has examined directed forgetting effects for neutral material in depressed subjects. However, in a study by Power, Dalgleish, Claudio, Tata, and Kentish (2000) a directed forgetting task with positive and negative words was used to investigate inhibitory dysfunctions in depressed subjects. When control participants and participants with elevated scores on the BDI were given the instruction to make valence judgments about the presented words and to remember

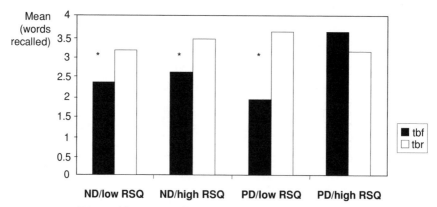

FIGURE 11.4. Directed forgetting effects for negative words. Mean number of words recalled in the to-be-forgotten (tbf) or to-be-remembered (tbr) conditions for never-depressed (ND) or previously depressed (PD) participants who scored high or low on the Ruminative Response Style Questionnaire (RSQ); *p < .05.

them at the same time, both groups showed comparable directed forgetting effects for positive and negative words. However, when participants with elevated depression scores and control participants were asked to rate the presented words in terms of self-descriptiveness, a differential directed forgetting effect was obtained for the control participants in that they recalled more positive than negative words under the "forget" instruction. This positive bias was not found for dysphoric participants. Moreover, in a third study using self-reference judgments and clinically diagnosed depressed participants, Power et al. (2000) showed a facilitation effect for negative words after the "forget" instruction in the depressed group whereas the control subjects, again, showed a positive bias.

In a related directed forgetting study, I used a diagnostic interview to screen out participants who already had experienced a depressive episode at least once in their lifetime but who were not currently depressed. These participants were compared to never-depressed controls, and both groups were further divided according to their current scores on the Response Style Questionnaire (Joormann, 2003b). All participants were asked to make valence judgments about the presented words and to try to remember the words at the same time. Never-depressed participants and previously depressed participants with low rumination scores showed a positive bias comparable to the one reported by Power et al. (2000). Furthermore, with regard to negative words, never-depressed participants and previously depressed participants with low RSQ-scores showed directed forgetting effects. However, previously depressed participants who scored high on the RSQ showed enhanced recall of negative to-be-forgotten items (see Figure 11.4).

In a recent study using a slightly different design, Hertel and Gerstle (2003) found additional evidence for reduced inhibition of negative words in dysphoric students. Hertel and Gerstle (2003) modified a design originally proposed by Anderson and Green (2001). Dysphoric and nondysphoric students learned word pairs, each consisting of a positive or negative adjective and a neutral noun. In subsequent practice trials, subjects practiced either to recall the target word or to suppress (i.e., make an active effort not to think about) the target word when given the adjective as a cue. On the final test, recall for all words was tested. Hertel and Gerstle (2003) found that recall from sets assigned for suppression practice was greater in the dysphoric group, with a tendency toward increased recall of to-be-suppressed negative words. Moreover, the degree of forgetting was significantly correlated with self-report measures of rumination and unwanted thoughts. Again, these results suggest a close relation between self-reported rumination and inhibitory dysfunctions.

These findings are in line with research concerning the role of thought suppression in depression and rumination. Studies indicate that when thought suppression is disrupted, unwanted thoughts enter awareness with greater intensity and frequency than if thought suppression had never been attempted (Wegner, 1994; Wenzlaff & Wegner, 2000). Moreover, it was shown that depressed subjects often try to cope with intruding negative thoughts by trying to suppress them (Wenzlaff, 1993), and further studies have found a correlation between depression and thought suppression (Wegner & Zanakos, 1994; Wenzlaff, Meier, & Salas, 2002). In a recent study, Wenzlaff and Luxton (2003) were able to show that participants who were identified as high thought suppressors and who had experienced high levels of stress reported significant increases in rumination and dysphoria in a 10-week follow-up. These results suggest that the combination of thought suppression efforts and weakened inhibition may result in the recurrence of unwanted negative thoughts, which contributes to the occurrence of ruminative responses in depression.

CONSEQUENCES OF RUMINATION

So far, empirical evidence was summarized that suggests that depression is characterized by inhibitory deficits. The majority of the studies presented suggest that depression and dysphoria are associated with decreased inhibition of negative irrelevant material in attention and memory tasks. Moreover, further evidence was presented that suggests a strong link between inhibitory dysfunctions and the occurrence of rumination. As outlined above, a ruminative response style was identified as a vulnerability marker in that it predicts the recurrence of depressive episodes. In particular, rumination has been linked to the occurrence of mood-congruent recall (Lyubomirsky, Caldwell, & Nolen-Hoeksema, 1998) and to sustained negative affect (Nolen-Hoeksema & Morrow, 1993). In the remainder of this chapter, studies are presented that look at these consequences of rumination in an effort to elucidate why rumination can be considered as increasing the risk of the occurrence of depressive episodes.

Difficulties in disengaging attention from negative stimuli and enhanced mood-congruent recall in response to a negative mood state might have enduring consequences for depressed individuals, resulting in sustained negative affect. It has been suggested that depressed and nondepressed individuals do not differ in the degree to which they become sad but instead differ in the degree to which they are able to repair their mood once they experience sadness (Teasdale, 1983; 1988). Mood repair and mood regulation are important processes that are poorly understood in nonclinical and clinical samples. But research to date suggests that mood repair might have different components: controlled, consciously initiated strategies, and more automatic components. Inhibitory dysfunctions and rumination might especially hinder automatically operating mood-repair processes.

As outlined previously, the results of several studies support the formulation that mood states enhance people's recall of mood-congruent information. However, several investigators have demonstrated the opposite effect; that is, moods can enhance the retrieval of mood-incongruent material (e.g., Erber & Erber, 1994; Parrott & Sabini, 1990). Consequently, it has been suggested that processes of mood regulation and mood repair can modify the mood – memory relationship. When experiencing a negative mood state, people may attempt to regulate their mood by retrieving pleasant thoughts and memories, thereby reducing or even reversing a negative mood-congruency effect (Josephson, Singer, & Salovey, 1996). For example, in his Affect Infusion Model, Forgas (1995) conceptualizes such mood-regulatory processes as a motivated processing strategy. The Affect Infusion Model suggests that mood-congruent processing occurs only during heuristic and substantive processing. During motivated processing, however, mood-incongruent memory may occur. Thus, negative mood-regulation should play a significant role in the production of mood-congruent versus mood-incongruent memory. Accordingly, individual differences, such as depression, that are related to the ability and/or motivation to regulate negative moods should be linked to the occurrence of mood-congruent or mood-incongruent recall. However, few studies have empirically investigated the impact of individual difference variables on mood-congruent and mood-incongruent memory.

In one of the first studies to address these questions, Smith and Petty (1995) investigated the influence of individual differences in self-esteem on mood-congruent versus mood-incongruent recall. In three studies, which included recall of autobiographical memories, they showed that when a negative mood state was induced, participants low in self-esteem recalled mood-congruent memories, but subjects high in self-esteem did not. Moreover, the more negative high self-esteem subjects felt, the more positive were their cognitions. In addition, McFarland and Buehler (1998) presented data suggesting that the relation of mood and memory is dependent on the mood manipulation. In a series of experiments, they showed that participants who were focused on their mood were more likely than participants with less self-focus to recall mood-incongruent memories. Moreover, they assessed individual differences in ruminative tendencies and found that ruminators who were instructed to self-focus reported more negative than positive memories in response to a negative mood induction, whereas nonruminators reported more positive than negative memories. Furthermore, McFarland and Buehler demonstrated that when people adopted a reflective orientation to their mood (e.g., by thinking about why they feel sad or by analyzing recent events to understand their feelings), they were more likely to engage in mood-incongruent recall; whereas when they adopted a ruminative orientation to their mood (e.g., by thinking about how sad they feel), they were more likely to engage in mood-congruent recall. Consistent with these results, Rusting and DeHart (2000) recently demonstrated the occurrence of mood-congruent retrieval when participants stayed focused on events associated with their negative mood; in contrast, when participants engaged in positive reappraisal, mood-incongruent retrieval occurred. Taken together, the results of these studies imply (a) that there are individual difference variables such as self-esteem that affect mood-congruency effects and (b) that self-focus and rumination might impair processes of mood repair and mood regulation.

These results have important implications for depression research. Although most studies of information processing in depression have addressed the etiology and maintenance of this disorder, there are fewer studies concerning recovery from sad moods. Depressed and nondepressed individuals might not differ in the degree to which they become sad but instead might differ in the degree to which they are motivated or able to repair their negative mood, resulting in longer episodes of sadness for depression-prone individuals. Consistent with this formulation, Josephson et al. (1996) found that whereas nondepressed participants asked to recall two memories after a negative mood induction tended to recall more positive second memories in an effort to repair their sad mood, dysphoric participants recalled consecutive negative memories. Moreover, as outlined before, research on rumination in depression suggests that depressed people are especially prone to focus on a temporary negative mood state (e.g., Nolen-Hoeksema, 1991; Nolen-Hoeksema & Morrow, 1993). This response style might strengthen mood-congruency effects and impair mood-repair processes, with a consequent stabilization of the negative mood (Nolen-Hoeksema et al., 1993). Accordingly, studies that explore the effects of self-focus or rumination on autobiographical recall in dysphoria have shown that dysphoric participants who are induced to ruminate engage in enhanced mood-congruent recall (Lyubomirsky et al., 1998; Pyszcynski, Hamilton, Herring, & Greenberg, 1989).

Taken together, this research demonstrates that people who experience a negative mood state sometimes enter into a self-defeating cycle wherein their negative mood primes unpleasant memories, which in turn exacerbate their distress. Sometimes, though, people attempt to break this maladaptive cycle by actively recruiting pleasant memories, thereby repairing their sad mood. For depression research, it is exceedingly important to determine the factors that lead to mood-congruency versus mood repair. Identifying these factors can provide essential clues for improving depression treatment and for preventing relapse. Again, the inhibition of negative irrelevant information might play a crucial role in these processes. The accessibility of mood-incongruent memories might be dependent on the individual's ability to inhibit the mood-congruent memories activated by the sad mood. These processes might operate on a more automatic level and might explain how, usually in nondepressed individuals, sad mood dissipates even though these individuals do not actively take steps to repair their mood. Inasmuch as depressed individuals are not able to inhibit mood-congruent activation, mood-incongruent memories remain less accessible, a process that stabilizes, instead of repairs, negative mood.

In two studies, we sought to examine the notion that dysphoria and rumination are crucial factors in determining whether mood-congruent memory retrieval, as opposed to mood repair, processes occur (Joormann & Siemer, 2004). We tested this idea by simultaneously manipulating both *mood states* and *focus on mood states* in dysphoric and nondysphoric participants and by examining the impact of these manipulations on accessibility of positive and negative autobiographical memories and subsequent mood ratings. In our first study, we focused on the more automatic side of mood-regulation processes. Our main question was whether mood states and mood regulation might directly influence the automatic accessibility of positive and negative autobiographical memories in a way that is consistent with mood repair. We measured the accessibility of positive and negative memories (as indicated by latencies of a key press after recall of a specific negative or positive autobiographical memory in response to a given cue, e.g., "a nice birthday party") after a positive or a negative mood induction in dysphoric or nondysphoric participants who were either asked to ruminate or to distract themselves after the mood induction. Inasmuch as dysphoric participants differ from nondysphoric participants in their spontaneous mood-repair processes, it was hypothesized that mood-congruent versus mood-incongruent accessibility of autobiographical memories is dependent on dysphoria. Overall, after the negative mood induction, mood-incongruency effects were found for the nondysphoric participants, whereas no such effect was found for dysphoric participants.

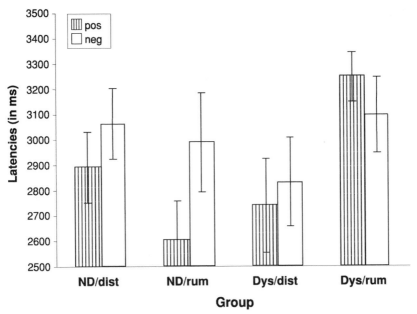

FIGURE 11.5. Mean recall latencies of cued positive (pos) and negative (neg) auto-biographical memories after a negative mood induction and rumination (rum) or distraction (dist) instructions in nondysphoric (ND) and dysphoric (Dys) participants. Adapted with permission of the American Psychological Association from Joormann and Siemer (2004, p. 183, Figure 2). Copyright © 2004 by the American Psychological Association.

Moreover, although a ruminative focus after the negative mood induction was associated with an increased mood-incongruency effect for the nondysphoric participants, a ruminative focus was associated with both prolonged recall latencies for positive memories in dysphoric participants and a tendency toward mood-congruent recall (see Figure 11.5).

Mood ratings further indicated mood improvement after distraction in both groups but no improvement after rumination in the dysphoric group. In addition, after the recall task, mood improved in the nondys-phoric group that ruminated, while mood in the dysphoric group showed an initial slight improvement after the distraction task but deteriorated to postinduction levels after the recall task. Thus, the results of this study show mood-incongruency for nondysphoric participants after a negative mood induction and rumination, whereas no such effect is found for dysphoric participants after rumination.

In our second study, we focused on more effortful mood-repair strategies. It was suggested that mood-congruent biases influence the ease or fluency of remembering, but that mood-incongruent materials can be brought to mind with sufficient persistence (Hertel, 2004). It is unclear, however, if this effortful recall of mood-incongruent memories leads to mood repair. Thus, one could expect that after a negative mood induction, the opportunity to recruit positive memories would alleviate the negative mood. Therefore, in a second study, we wanted to find out what would happen to dysphoric and nondysphoric participant's mood when they were directly instructed to engage in mood-incongruent recall in response to a negative mood induction. Consequently, in the second study, participants only received a negative mood induction and were then directly asked to recall only positive memories. In this study, mood ratings were of primary interest. It was argued that although the first study revealed that dysphoric participants did not show a spontaneous mood-incongruency effect in response to sad mood, this finding does not answer the question of what would happen to their mood if they were directly instructed to recall mood-incongruent memories. The results of this study showed that although dysphoric participants recalled as many specific and positive memories as nondysphoric participants (as indicated by independent rater evaluations), these memories did not affect their mood ratings in the same way. Although nondysphoric participant's mood ratings improved under distraction and under mood-incongruent recall instructions, dysphoric participants did not benefit from the recall of positive memories, whereas distraction seemed to alleviate their sad mood at least temporarily (see Figure 11.6).

Overall, the results are largely consistent with the literature on mood regulation (McFarland & Buehler, 1998; Rusting & DeHart, 2000). Taken together, the results support the notion that mood-incongruent recall is used as a mood-repair strategy in response to a negative mood induction. Typically, however, findings of mood-incongruent recall have been attributed to motivational factors; presumably, participants induced to feel sad were motivated to alleviate their distress by recalling positive events from their lives (Clark & Isen, 1982; Erber & Erber, 1994). In studies on motivated mood repair, positivity of recalled memories or number of positive and negative events recalled is observed as the dependent variable (e.g., Rusting & DeHart, 2000). However, the present results suggest that mood states and mood regulation might additionally influence the more automatic accessibility of positive and negative autobiographical memories, a process that is less susceptible to strategic control. Our results further suggest that it is this component of mood-incongruent recall that seems problematic for dysphoric participants. At this point, one can only speculate that inhibitory deficits might be involved in these differences in accessibility of positive and negative memories after a mood induction. The results of our second study suggest that dysphoric and nondysphoric participants do not differ in their effortful recall of mood-incongruent memories, at least when given the direct instruction to do so and when given enough

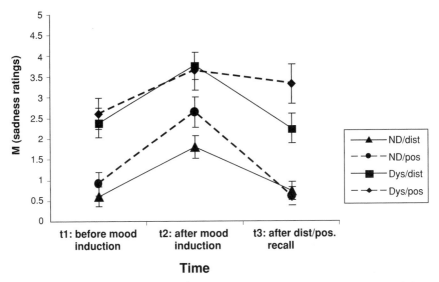

FIGURE 11.6. Mean mood ratings ("sad") after negative mood induction and distraction (dist) or recall of positive autobiographical memories (pos) in dysphoric (Dys) and nondysphoric (ND) participants. Adapted with permission of the American Psychological Association from Joormann and Siemer (2004, p. 185, Figure 4). Copyright © 2004 by the American Psychological Association.

time to do so. However, this effortful recall of mood-incongurent memories does not lead to mood repair in dysphoric participants. These findings are in line with other studies suggesting that the enhanced accessibility of mood-relevant thoughts might interfere with the ability to distract oneself with positive material (Wenzlaff, Wegner, & Roper, 1988). There are several possible mechanisms that may contribute to the dysphoric participant's problems to use effortful recall to repair their negative mood, but the following explanation seems to be the most plausible: Whereas dysphoric participants recalled positive memories, and these positive memories may have triggered initial positive feelings, it is likely that the recall instructions simultaneously triggered a spontaneous ruminative focus in the dysphoric group. Thus, by asking for the effortful recall of a positive autobiographical memory, we induced a self-focus that may have triggered negative rumination in the dysphoric participants. As a result of the ruminative focus, the initial positive feelings triggered by the positive memories were subsequently compared with the current (depressed) feelings. As a consequence, this comparison led to even more negative thoughts and rumination. Thus, recalling a positive event and feeling may have influenced dysphoric participants' mood by way of a contrast effect. Previous research has shown that recalling a negative past can improve current mood if it allows people to perceive self-improvement (e.g., Conway & Ross, 1984). Similarly, recalling a positive past can worsen mood if it suggests deterioration. That is, dysphoric participants may compare their current situation and feeling with those past positive memories and feelings and diagnose a constant decrease in their situation, making them feel worse instead of better. Clearly, further studies are needed to clarify this relationship.

The results do suggest that there are differences between dysphoric and nondysphoric individuals in more automatic mood-regulation processes and in the effectiveness of certain strategies for regulating negative mood and thinking. Whereas dysphoric participants showed at least a temporary mood improvement after distraction, no improvement was observed after rumination or mood-incongruent recall. It is therefore important to note that dysphoric participants are not generally insensitive to mood-regulation strategies. However, dysphoric individuals probably benefit only from a very limited subset of strategies that are effective for nondysphoric individuals. Further research along these lines might afford new insights into possible mechanisms that impair recovery from sad moods in dysphoria and depression.

## SUMMARY AND FUTURE DIRECTIONS

The findings from the studies presented in this chapter imply that inhibitory processes play a central role in depression and that cognitive and affective symptoms might be explained through underlying dysfunctions in inhibitory processes and rumination. Throughout the chapter, however, two recurring themes can be identified that require further empirical study. Although evidence for inhibitory dysfunctions in depression is accumulating, it still remains unclear whether these inhibitory dysfunctions are only seen with regard to emotional material, or if this is a more general dysfunction. Thus, there is still no answer to the question that Hertel (1997) posed so elegantly: "Are distracting thoughts detrimental because they are particularly interesting visitors or because depressed people have trouble showing anyone the door?" (p. 575). In keeping with this, it still remains unclear how the relation between information processing deficits with regard to both neutral material and emotional material should be framed. The central question here remains: Is there a deficit in the processing of neutral information, or are these data easily explained through the prioritization of the processing of self-relevant material, negative material, and rumination? Moreover, it might be of particular interest to extend research on inhibition and rumination to other psychological disorders and/or to include other individual difference variables. It was proposed in this chapter that depression is characterized by an inhibition deficit that is limited to negative information. However, it is easy to think of other disorders, e.g., mania, in which inhibition of positive stimuli might be limited, or anxiety disorders, in which people might encounter difficulties in inhibiting threat-related words. One could even speculate that the underlying processes are similar (i.e., inhibitory deficits), although the content of the thoughts varies and is disorder-specific. Clearly, more research on inhibition using different samples and a variety of experimental designs is needed to get closer to an answer to these kinds of questions.

Another important issue that needs to be addressed more thoroughly pertains to the interface of automatic and strategic processes, both in information processing tasks and in mood regulation. Throughout this chapter, interactions between more automatic and more strategic processes have been highlighted, and although research in this area is still limited, I want to conclude this chapter by summarizing some of the main ideas and by providing an outline of how these processes might be linked to depression and to the vulnerability to experience recurring depressive episodes.

Briefly, as outlined before, Teasdale and other researchers proposed that vulnerable individuals do not differ from nonvulnerable individuals in their initial response to a negative event (e.g., Ingram, 1984; Teasdale, 1988). In both groups, a negative mood state is established consisting of the automatic activation of negative cognitions and memories. However, after a while, mood-regulation or mood-repair processes are activated. For example, as has been shown by research on mood regulation, a short time after a negative mood-induction procedure, mood-incongruency effects can be observed (Erber, 1996; Forgas, Johnson, & Ciarrochi, 1998).

The inhibition of activated mood-congruent memories and cognitions can be seen as an important automatically operating mood-regulation process. In participants who show inhibitory dysfunctions, no automatic mood regulation takes place, although individuals can probably compensate using controlled mood-regulation strategies (e.g., distraction or effortful recall of positive memories). However, when automatic *and* controlled mood-regulation attempts fail, the activation of mood-congruent information is sustained and a ruminative response style is established. As mentioned previously, it is postulated that rumination leads to enhanced recall of negative memories and deficits in recall of neutral or positive information (Hertel, 1998, Lyubomirsky et al., 1998). Also, it was suggested that rumination prolongs negative mood states (e.g., Nolen-Hoeksema et al., 1993). As a consequence, negative cognitions and memories remain highly accessible and negative mood states are maintained.

Therefore, it seems highly promising to further investigate the relation among inhibitory dysfunctions, ruminative responses to negative mood, mood regulation, memory impairments, and depressive vulnerability. Several studies support the hypothesis that in comparison to subjects who have never been depressed, vulnerable subjects react to negative mood with rumination and prolonged negative mood states (Gilboa & Gotlib, 1997; Roberts et al., 1998). Moreover, Nolen-Hoeksema et al. (1993) showed that individuals tend to be consistent in their responses to dysphoric mood over time. This finding suggests that a ruminative response style is a trait-like characteristic of individuals who are vulnerable to prolonged episodes of dysphoric affect. In a recent study, Roberts et al. (1998) presented data showing that elevated levels of rumination were not only found in individuals with current dysphoria but also in individuals with previous depressive episodes compared to individuals who have never been depressed, although these individuals did not differ on concurrent depressive symptomatology. Inhibitory processes might play an important role in explaining such interindividual differences in rumination (Linville, 1996). Nevertheless, studies assessing both factors, rumination and inhibition, are still difficult to find and would provide an important next step in research on vulnerability to depression.

## Author Note

This research was funded by a grant from the German Research Foundation (Deutsche Forschungsgemeinschaft; DFG; JO 399/1-1 and JO 399/1-2). I thank Faith Brozovich, Ian Gotlib, Paula Hertel, Sheri Johnson, Kelly Minor, Wiveka Ramel, Matthias Siemer, and Lisa Talbot for their helpful comments on previous versions of this chapter.

## References

Anderson, M. C., & Bjork, R. A. (1994). Mechanisms of inhibition in long-term memory: A new taxonomy. In D. Dagenbach & T. Carr (Eds.), *Inhibitory processes in attention, memory, and language* (pp. 265–325). San Diego, CA: Academic Press.

Anderson, M. C., & Green, C. (2001). Suppressing unwanted memories by executive control. *Nature, 410,* 366–369.

Anderson, M. C., & Spellman, B. A. (1995). On the status of inhibitory mechanisms in cognition: Memory retrieval as a model case. *Psychological Review, 102,* 68–100.

Baddeley, A. D. (1986). *Working memory.* Oxford: Oxford University Press.

Beck, A. T. (1976). *Cognitive therapy and the emotional disorders.* New York: International Universities Press.

Beck, A. T., Steer, R. A., & Garbin, M. G. (1988). Psychometric properties of the Beck Depression Inventory: Twenty-five years of evaluation. *Clinical Psychology Review, 8,* 77–100.

Bjork, R. A. (1972). Theoretical implications of directed forgetting. In A. W. Melton & E. Martin (Eds.), *Coding processes in human memory.* Washington, DC: Winston.

Bjorklund, D. F., & Harnishfeger, K. K. (1990). The resources construct in cognitive development: Diverse sources of evidence and a theory of inefficient inhibition. *Developmental Review, 10,* 48–71.

Blaney, P. H. (1986). Affect and memory: A review. *Psychological Bulletin, 99,* 229–246.

Bower, G. H. (1981). Mood and memory. *American Psychologist, 36,* 129–148.

Bower, G. H. (1987). Commentary on mood and memory. *Behaviour Research and Therapy, 25,* 443–455.

Bradley, B. P., Mogg, K., & Lee, S. C. (1997). Attentional biases for negative information in induced and naturally occurring dysphoria. *Behaviour Research and Therapy, 35,* 911–927.

Breslow, R., Kocsis, J. H., & Belkin, B. (1980). Memory deficits in depression: Evidence utilizing the Wechsler Memory Scale. *Perceptual and Motor Skills, 51,* 541–542.

Burt, D. B., Zembar, M. J., & Niederehe, G. (1995). Depression and memory impairment: A meta-analysis of the association, its pattern, and specificity. *Psychological Bulletin, 117,* 285–305.

Channon, S., Baker, J. E., & Robertson, M. M. (1993). Working memory in clinical depression: An experimental study. *Psychological Medicine, 23,* 87–91.

Clark, M. S., & Isen, A. M. (1982). Toward understanding the relationship between feeling states and social behaviour. In A. H. Hastorf & A. M. Isen (Eds.), *Cognitive social psychology* (pp. 73–108). New York: Elsevier.

Colby, C. A., & Gotlib, I. H. (1988). Memory deficits in depression. *Cognitive Therapy and Research, 12,* 611–627.

Conway, M., & Ross, M. (1984). Getting what you want by revising what you had. *Journal of Personality & Social Psychology, 47,* 738–748.

Coyne, J. C., & Gotlib, I. H. (1983). The role of cognitions in depression: A critical appraisal. *Psychological Bulletin, 94,* 472–505.

Davidson, R. J. (2000). Affective style, mood, and anxiety disorders: An affective neuroscience approach. In R. J. Davidson (Ed.), *Anxiety, depression, and emotion* (pp. 88–108). New York: Oxford University Press.

Davis, R. N., & Nolen-Hoeksema, S. (2000). Cognitive inflexibility among ruminators and nonruminators. *Cognitive Therapy and Research, 24,* 699–711.

Ellis, H. C., & Ashbrook, P. W. (1988). Resource allocation model of the effects of depressed mood states on memory. In K. Fiedler & J. P. Forgas (Eds.), *Affect, cognition, and social behavior* (pp. 25–43). Göttingen: Hogrefe.

Ellis, H. C., Thomas, R. L., & Rodriguez, I. A. (1984). Emotional mood states and memory: Elaborative encoding, semantic processing, and cognitive effort. *Journal of Experimental Psychology: Learning, Memory, and Cognition, 10,* 470–482.

Engle, R. W., Kane, M. J., & Tuholski, S. W. (1999). Individual differences in working memory capacity and what they tell us about controlled attention, general fluid intelligence, and functions of the prefrontal cortex. In A. Miyake & P. Shah (Eds.), *Models of working memory: Mechanisms of active maintenance and executive control* (pp. 102–134). Cambridge: Cambridge University Press.

Enright, S. J., & Beech, A. R. (1990). Obsessional states: Anxiety disorders or schizotypes? An information processing and personality assessment. *Psychological Medicine, 20,* 621–627.

Epstein, W. (1971). Mechanisms in directed forgetting. In G. H. Bower (Ed.), *The psychology of learning and motivation* (Vol. 6). New York: Academic Press.

Erber, R. (1996). The self-regulation of moods. In L. L. Martin & A. Tesser (Eds.), *Striving and feeling: Interactions among goals, affect, and self-regulation* (pp. 251–275). Mahwah, NJ: Lawrence Erlbaum Associates.

Erber, R., & Erber, M. W. (1994). Beyond mood and social judgment: Mood incongruent recall and mood regulation. *European Journal of Social Psychology Special Issue: Affect in social judgments and cognition, 24,* 79–88.

Flett, G. L., Vredenburg, K., & Krames, L. (1997). The continuity of depression in clinical and nonclinical samples. *Psychological Bulletin, 121,* 395–416.

Forgas, J. P. (1995). Mood and judgment. The affect infusion model (AIM). *Psychological Bulletin, 117,* 39–66.

Forgas, J. P., Johnson, R., & Ciarrochi, J. (1998). Mood management: The role of processing strategies in affect control and affect infusion. In M. Kofta, G. Weary, & G. Sedek (Eds.), *Personal control in action: Cognitive and motivational mechanisms* (pp. 155–195). New York: Plenum Press.

Frith, C. D. (1979). Consciousness, information processing and schizophrenia. *British Journal of Psychiatry, 134,* 225–235.

Gilboa, E., & Gotlib, I. H. (1997). Cognitive biases and affect persistence in previously dysphoric and never-dysphoric individuals. *Cognition and Emotion, 11,* 517–538.

Gotlib, I. H. (1984). Depression and general psychopathology in university students. *Journal of Abnormal Psychology, 93,* 19–30.

Gotlib, I. H., & Krasnoperova, E. (1998). Biased information processing as a vulnerability factor for depression. *Behavior Therapy, 29,* 603–617.

Gotlib, I. H., Krasnoperova, E., Neubauer, D. L., & Joormann, J. (2004). Attentional biases for negative interpersonal stimuli in clinical depression and anxiety. *Journal of Abnormal Psychology, 113,* 386–398.

Gotlib, I. H., & Neubauer, D. L. (2000). Information-processing approaches to the study of cognitive biases in depression. In S. L. Johnson, A. M. Hayes, T. M. Field, N. Schneiderman, & P. M. McCabe (Eds.), *Stress, coping, and depression* (pp. 117–143). Mahwah, NJ: Lawrence Erlbaum Associates.

Gotlib, I. H., Roberts, J. E., & Gilboa, E. (1996). Cognitive interference in depression. In I. G. Sarason, G. R. Pierce, & B. R. Sarason (Eds.), *Cognitive interference: Theories, methods, and findings* (pp. 347–377). Mahwah, NJ: Lawrence Erlbaum Associates.

Gray, J. W., Dean, R. S., Rattan, G., & Cramer, K. M. (1987). Neuropsychological aspects of primary affective depression. *International Journal of Neuroscience, 32,* 911–918.

Hartlage, S., Alloy, L. B., Vazquez, C., & Dykman, B. (1993). Automatic and effortful processing in depression. *Psychological Bulletin, 113,* 247–278.

Hasher, L., Stoltzfus, E. R., Zacks, R. T., & Rypma, B. (1991). Age and inhibition. *Journal of Experimental Psychology: Learning, Memory, and Cognition, 17,* 163–169.

Hasher, L., & Zacks, R. T. (1979). Automatic and effortful processes in memory. *Journal of Experimental Psychology: General, 108,* 356–388.

Hasher, L., & Zacks, R. T. (1988). Working memory, comprehension, and aging: A review and a new view. In G. H. Bower (Ed.), *The psychology of learning and motivation* (Vol. 22, pp. 193–225). San Diego, CA: Academic Press.

Hasher, L., Zacks. R. T., & May, C. P. (1999). Inhibitory control, circadian arousal, and age. In D. Gopher & A. Koriat (Eds.), *Attention and performance* (pp. 653–675). Cambridge, MA: MIT Press.

Hedlund, S., & Rude, S. S. (1995). Evidence of latent depressive schemas in formerly depressed individuals. *Journal of Abnormal Psychology, 104,* 517–525.

Hertel, P. T. (1997). On the contributions of deficient cognitive control to memory impairments in depression. *Cognition and Emotion, 11,* 569–584.

Hertel, P. T. (1998). The relationship between rumination and impaired memory in dysphoric moods. *Journal of Abnormal Psychology, 107,* 166–172.

Hertel, P. T. (2000). The cognitive-initiative account of depression-related impairments in memory. In D. Medin (Ed.), *The psychology of learning and motivation* (Vol. 39, pp. 47–71). New York: Academic Press.

Hertel, P. T. (2004). Memory for emotional and nonemotional events in depression: A question of habit? In D. Reisberg & P. Hertel (Eds.), *Memory and emotion* (pp. 186–216). New York: Oxford University Press.

Hertel, P. T., & Gerstle, M. (2003). Depressive deficits in forgetting. *Psychological Science, 14,* 573–578.

Hertel, P. T., & Hardin, T. S. (1990). Remembering with and without awareness in a depressed mood: Evidence of deficits in initiative. *Journal of Experimental Psychology: General, 119,* 45–59.

Hertel, P. T., & Milan, S. (1994). Depressive deficits in recognition: Dissociation of recollection and familiarity. *Journal of Abnormal Psychology, 103,* 736–742.

Hertel, P. T., & Rude, S. S. (1991). Depressive deficits in memory. Focusing attention improves subsequent recall. *Journal of Experimental Psychology: General, 120,* 301–309.

Ingram, R. E., Miranda, J., & Segal, Z. V. (1998). *Cognitive vulnerability to depression.* New York: Guilford Press.

Jacoby, L. L. (1991). A process dissociation framework: Separating automatic from intentional uses of memory. *Journal of Memory and Language, 30,* 513–541.

Johnson, M. H., & Magaro, P. A. (1987). Effects of mood and severity on memory processes in depression and mania. *Psychological Bulletin, 101,* 28–40.

Joormann, J. (2003a). *The relation of rumination and inhibition: Evidence from a negative priming task.* Manuscript submitted for publication.

Joormann, J. (2003b). *Inhibitory dysfunctions in memory in individuals with a history of major depression.* Manuscript submitted for publication.

Joormann, J. (2004). Attentional bias in dysphoria: The role of inhibitory processes. *Cognition and Emotion, 18,* 125–147.

Joormann, J., & Siemer, M. (2004). Memory accessibility, mood regulation and dysphoria: Difficulties in repairing sad mood with happy memories? *Journal of Abnormal Psychology, 113,* 179–188.

Josephson, B. R., Singer, J. A., & Salovey, P. (1996). Mood regulation and memory: Repairing sad moods with happy memories. *Cognition & Emotion, 10,* 437–444.

Just, N., & Alloy, L. B. (1997). The response styles theory of depression: Tests and an extension of the theory. *Journal of Abnormal Psychology, 106,* 221–229.

Kuehner, C., & Weber, I. (1999). Responses to depression in unipolar depressed patients: An investigation of Nolen-Hoeksema's response styles theory. *Psychological Medicine, 29,* 1323–1333.

LaBerge, D. (1995). *Attentional processing: The brain's art of mindfulness.* Cambridge, MA: Harvard University Press.

Linville, P. (1996). Attention inhibition: Does it underlie ruminative thought? In R. S. Wyer, Jr. (Ed.), *Ruminative thoughts. Advances in social cognition* (Vol. 9, pp. 121–133). Mahwah, NJ: Lawrence Erlbaum Associates.

Lyubomirsky, S., Caldwell, N. D., & Nolen-Hoeksema, S. (1998). Effects of ruminative and distracting responses to depressed mood on retrieval of autobiographical memories. *Journal of Personality & Social Psychology, 75,* 166–177.

MacLeod, C., Tata, P., & Mathews, A. (1987). Perception of emotionally valenced
information in depression. *British Journal of Clinical Psychology, 26,* 67–68.

Mathews, A., & MacLeod, C. (1994). Cognitive approaches to emotion and
emotional disorders. *Annual Review of Psychology, 45,* 25–50.

Matt, G. E., Vazquez, C., & Campbell, W. K. (1992). Mood-congruent recall of affectively toned stimuli: A meta-analytic review. *Clinical Psychology Review, 12,* 227–
255.

McFarland, C., & Buehler, R. (1998). The impact of negative affect on autobiographical memory: The role of self-focused attention to moods. *Journal of Personality &
Social Psychology, 75,* 1424–1440.

Milliken, B., & Tipper, S. P. (1998). Attention and inhibition. In H. Pashler (Ed.),
*Attention* (pp. 191–221). Hove, UK: Psychology Press.

Mogg, K., Bradley, B. P., & Williams, R. (1995). Attentional bias in anxiety and
depression: The role of awareness. *British Journal of Clinical Psychology, 34,* 17–36.

Mogg, K., Bradley, B. P., Williams, R., & Mathews, A. (1993). Subliminal processing
of emotional information in anxiety and depression. *Journal of Abnormal Psychology, 102,* 304–311.

Morrow, J., & Nolen-Hoeksema, S. (1990). Effects of responses to depression on the
remediation of depressive affect. *Journal of Personality and Social Psychology, 58,*
519–527.

Neill, W. T., Valdes, L. A., & Terry, K. M. (1995). Selective attention and the inhibitory
control of cognition. In F. N. Dempster & C. J. Brainerd (Eds.), *Interference and
inhibition in cognition* (pp. 207–261). San Diego, CA: Academic Press.

Nolan, S. A., Roberts, J. E., & Gotlib, I. H. (1998). Neuroticism and ruminative
response style as predictors of change in depressive symptomatology. *Cognitive
Therapy and Research, 22,* 445–455.

Nolen-Hoeksema, S. (1991). Responses to depression and their effects on the duration of depressive episodes. *Journal of Abnormal Psychology, 100,* 569–582.

Nolen-Hoeksema, S. (2000). The role of rumination in depressive disorders and
mixed anxiety/depressive symptoms. *Journal of Abnormal Psychology, 109,* 504–
511.

Nolen-Hoeksema, S., & Girgus, J. S. (1994). The emergence of gender differences in
depression during adolescence. *Psychological Bulletin, 115,* 424–443.

Nolen-Hoeksema, S., Larson, J., & Grayson, C. (1999). Explaining the gender difference in depressive symptoms. *Journal of Personality and Social Psychology, 77,*
1061–1072.

Nolen-Hoeksema, S., & Morrow, J. (1991). A prospective study of depression and
posttraumatic stress symptoms after a natural disaster: The 1989 Loma Prieta
earthquake. *Journal of Personality and Social Psychology, 61,* 115–121.

Nolen-Hoeksema, S., & Morrow, J. (1993). Effects of rumination and distraction on
naturally occurring depressed mood. *Cognition and Emotion, 7,* 561–570.

Nolen-Hoeksema, S., Morrow, J., & Fredrickson, B. L. (1993). Response styles and
the duration of episodes of depressed mood. *Journal of Abnormal Psychology, 102,*
20–28.

Nolen-Hoeksema, S., Parker, L. E., & Larson, J. (1994). Ruminative coping with depressed mood following loss. *Journal of Personality and Social Psychology, 67,* 92–104.

Parrott, W. G., & Sabini, J. (1990). Mood and memory under natural conditions: Evidence for mood incongruent recall. *Journal of Personality & Social Psychology, 59,* 321–336.

Posner, M. I. (1995). Attention in cognitive neuroscience: An overview. In M. S. Gazzaniga (Ed.), *The cognitive neurosciences* (pp. 615–624). Cambridge, MA: MIT Press.

Power, M. J., Dalgleish, T., Claudio, V., Tata, P., & Kentish, J. (2000). The directed forgetting task: Application to emotionally valent material. *Journal of Affective Disorders, 57,* 147–157.

Pyszczynski, T., Hamilton, J. C., Herring, F. H., & Greenberg, J. (1989). Depression, self-focused attention, and the negative memory bias. *Journal of Personality & Social Psychology, 57,* 351–357.

Radloff, L. S. (1977). The CES-D Scale: A new self-report depression scale for research in the general population. *Applied Psychological Measurement, 1,* 385–401.

Roberts, J. E., Gilboa, E., & Gotlib, I. H. (1998). Ruminative response style and vulnerability to episodes of dysphoria: Gender, neuroticism, and episode duration. *Cognitive Therapy and Research, 22,* 401–423.

Rokke, P. D., Arnell, K. M., Koch, M. D., & Andrews, J. T. (2002). Dual-task attention deficits in dysphoric mood. *Journal of Abnormal Psychology, 111,* 370–379.

Rusting, C. L. (1998). Personality, mood, and cognitive processing of emotional information: Three conceptual frameworks. *Psychological Bulletin, 124,* 165–196.

Rusting, C. L., & DeHart, T. (2000). Retrieving positive memories to regulate negative mood: Consequences for mood-congruent memory. *Journal of Personality & Social Psychology, 78,* 737–752.

Segal, Z. V. (1988). Appraisal of the self-schema construct in cognitive models of depression. *Psychological Bulletin, 103,* 147–162.

Segal, Z. V., & Vella, D. D. (1990). Self-schema in major depression: Replication and extension of a priming methodology. Special Issue: Selfhood processes and emotional disorders. *Cognitive Therapy and Research, 14,* 161–176.

Seibert, P. S., & Ellis, H. C. (1991). Irrelevant thoughts, emotional mood states, and cognitive task performance. *Memory and Cognition, 19,* 507–513.

Siegle, G. J., Steinhauer, S. R., Carter, C. S., Ramel, W., & Thase, M. E. (2003). Do the seconds turn into hours? Relationships between sustained pupil dilation in response to emotional information and self-reported rumination. *Cognitive Therapy and Research, 27,* 365–382.

Siegle, G. J., Steinhauer, S. R., Thase, M. E., Stenger, A., & Carter, C. S. (2002). Can't shake that feeling: Event-related fMRI assessment of sustained amygdala activity in response to emotional information in depressed individuals. *Biological Psychiatry, 51,* 693–707.

Smith, S. M., & Petty, R. E. (1995). Personality moderators of mood congruency effects on cognition: The role of self-esteem and negative mood regulation. *Journal of Personality & Social Psychology, 68,* 1092–1107.

Stromgren, L. S. (1977). The influence of depression on memory. *Acta Psychiatrica Scandinavica, 56,* 109–128.

Teasdale, J. D. (1983). Negative thinking in depression: Cause, effect, or reciprocal relationship. *Advances in Behaviour Research and Therapy, 5*, 3–25.

Teasdale, J. D. (1988). Cognitive vulnerability to persistent depression. *Cognition and Emotion, 2*, 247–274.

Tipper, S. P. (1985). The negative priming effect: Inhibitory processes by ignored objects. *Journal of Experimental Psychology, 37*, 571–590.

Tipper, S. P., Bourque, T. A., Anderson, S. H., & Brehaut, J. C. (1989). Mechanisms of attention: A developmental study. *Journal of Experimental Child Psychology, 48*, 353–378.

Watts, F. N., & Sharrock, R. (1985). Description and measurement of concentration problems in depressed patients. *Psychological Medicine, 15*, 317–326.

Wegner, D. M. (1994). Ironic processes of mental control. *Psychological Review, 101*, 34–52.

Wegner, D. M., & Zanakos, S. (1994). Chronic thought suppression. *Journal of Personality, 62*, 615–640.

Wentura, D. (1999). Activation and inhibition of affective information: Evidence for negative priming in the evaluation task. *Cognition and Emotion, 13*, 65–91.

Wenzlaff, R. M. (1993). The mental control of depression: Psychological obstacles to emotional well-being. In D. M. Wegner & J. W. Pennebaker (Eds.), *Handbook of mental control* (pp. 238–257). Englewood Cliffs, NJ: Prentice-Hall.

Wenzlaff, R. M., & Luxton, D. D. (2003). The role of thought suppression in depressive rumination. *Cognitive Therapy and Research, 27*, 293–308.

Wenzlaff, R. M., Meier, J., & Salas, D. M. (2002). Thought suppression and memory biases during and after depressive moods. *Cognition and Emotion, 16*, 403–422.

Wenzlaff, R. M., & Wegner, D. M. (2000). Thought suppression. *Annual Review of Psychology, 51*, 59–91.

Wenzlaff, R. M., Wegner, D. M., & Roper, D. W. (1988). Depression and mental control: The resurgence of unwanted negative thoughts. *Journal of Personality and Social Psychology, 55*, 882–892.

Williams, J. M., Watts, F. N., MacLeod, C., & Mathews, A. (1988). *Cognitive psychology and emotional disorder.* Chichester: Wiley.

Williams, J. M., Watts, F. N., MacLeod, C., & Mathews, A. (1997). *Cognitive psychology and emotional disorder.* Chichester: Wiley.

# 12

# Aging and Inhibitory Processes in Memory, Attentional, and Motor Tasks

Elizabeth A. Maylor, Friederike Schlaghecken, and Derrick G. Watson

The past few years have seen an increasing focus on inhibitory processes in cognition (see Dempster, 1992; Dempster & Brainerd, 1995), especially in their impairment in certain patient populations (e.g., Beech, Powell, McWilliam, & Claridge, 1989; Cohen & Servan-Schreiber, 1992), in their development during childhood (e.g., Harnishfeger, 1995), and in their decline with normal aging (e.g., McDowd, Oseas-Kreger, & Filion, 1995). In this chapter, we briefly describe the inhibition deficit hypothesis of cognitive aging and discuss some logical and methodological issues that have complicated its investigation. We then present three aging studies across the different domains of short-term memory (Maylor & Henson, 2000), visual search (Watson & Maylor, 2002), and motor control (Schlaghecken & Maylor, in press). In each case, it is argued that inhibitory processes are responsible for the effects of interest, namely, the Ranschburg effect (Crowder, 1968; Jahnke, 1969), the preview benefit in visual search (known as visual marking; Watson & Humphreys, 1997), and the negative compatibility effect (Eimer & Schlaghecken, 1998), respectively. What these three effects have in common is that, at some level, they all occur as a result of inhibitory processes that suppress responses to stimuli that are no longer relevant to current goals. The results show mixed support for the inhibition deficit hypothesis of aging, the current status of which is finally discussed in the light of these and other data.

Cognitive aging research in the past has been dominated by "local" explanations, which assume that deficits are localized within particular stages or components of information processing. This approach tends to rely on the Age × Treatment interaction methodology: If the age deficit is greater for a task requiring processes X and Y than for a task requiring only process X, then process Y is supposed to be age sensitive (see Salthouse, 1991, for discussion). However, Age × Treatment interactions are so commonly observed that researchers appear to have identified almost as many age-sensitive processing components as tasks. As Maylor and Rabbitt (1994) commented, "[t]he attempt to analyze cognitive behavior into its constituent elements and then to localize the effect of old age within a particular subset of those elements has led to demonstrations of age deficits at almost every stage of information processing" (p. 224). Moreover, the age-related variance is often substantially shared across different tasks, suggesting that a small number (perhaps just one) of basic mechanisms may be responsible for cognitive aging (Park, 2000; Salthouse, 2000). Consequently, in recent years there has been a shift toward more "global" explanations, in which the effects of aging are attributed to a single factor such as reduced processing speed (see Salthouse, 1996). It is now generally accepted that there are probably both shared (global) and unique (local) effects of old age but that shared effects dominate over unique effects. Our priority as researchers should therefore be to explore shared age-related influences because they explain more of the age-related variance (see chapters in Perfect & Maylor, 2000b, for discussion). One such single-factor explanation of cognitive aging, which has been the subject of much recent research, is the reduced inhibition hypothesis proposed by Hasher and Zacks (1988; see also Hasher, Zacks, & May, 1999).

## INHIBITION DEFICIT HYPOTHESIS OF AGING

Early evidence that older adults are particularly susceptible to interference (e.g., Rabbitt, 1965) led Hasher and Zacks (1988) to suggest that much of what we view as age-related decline in cognition occurs as a result of age-related decline in the efficiency of inhibitory mechanisms. Their theory was originally proposed to explain age differences in working memory capacity, which is "widely thought to be an index of the general capacity available for mental work" (p. 276, Zacks & Hasher, 1997). They identified two consequences of impaired inhibitory processes. First, there is a failure to prevent information that is irrelevant to current goals from entering working memory. For example, studies in which people are asked to read a text while ignoring material interspersed within the target text (e.g., Connelly, Hasher, & Zacks, 1991) or to listen to target speech while ignoring a competing speaker in the background (e.g., Tun, O'Kane, & Wingfield, 2002) show that older adults are more impaired by the distracting information than are young adults. Second, with reduced inhibition, there is also a failure to prevent information from remaining in working memory when no longer relevant to current goals. For example, if an ambiguous word is presented (*bank*) that is then disambiguated by the context (*money*), there is evidence that for older adults, both meanings remain activated (*river bank* and *money bank*), whereas young adults suppress the no-longer-relevant meaning (e.g., Hartman & Hasher, 1991).

A recent update of the inhibitory deficit hypothesis (Hasher et al., 1999) identifies three functions of inhibition (*access, deletion,* and *restraint*) that together control the contents of working memory. The *access* and *deletion* functions correspond to their earlier inhibitory mechanisms of controlling access to working memory by preventing extraneous information from entering working memory and by deleting or suppressing the activation of no-longer-relevant goals or information. Additionally, inhibition is thought to serve a *restraining* function by preventing prepotent candidates for response from controlling thought and action. Evidence for age-related impairments in restraint comes from tasks such as the anti-saccade task (e.g., Nieuwenhuis, Ridderinkhof, de Jong, Kok, & van der Molen, 2000) in which the prepotent response of saccading to a peripheral target has to be intentionally inhibited (see later section on motor control). In summary, the proposal is that "older adults have less inhibitory control over the current contents of working memory than younger adults" (p. 656, Hasher et al., 1999), resulting in working memory that is cluttered up with goal-irrelevant information and easily captured by a dominant response tendency.

SOME PROBLEMS WITH THE INHIBITION DEFICIT HYPOTHESIS

Although the inhibition deficit hypothesis of aging has generated much important and interesting research, there remain a number of controversies surrounding its investigation and status as a viable single-factor theory (see critical reviews by Burke, 1997; McDowd, 1997; see Zacks & Hasher, 1997, for a reply). The inhibition deficit hypothesis has been interpreted, perhaps more broadly than was originally intended, as suggesting that aging impairs all types and levels of inhibitory mechanisms. This assumption possibly accounts for the first main problem for the inhibition deficit hypothesis, which is that the evidence with respect to aging is mixed. For example, in the directed forgetting paradigm, participants are presented with items that they are then either required to remember or to forget. In fact, the final memory test requires the recall of all items. Consistent with the inhibition deficit hypothesis, young adults show a larger difference between "remember" and "forget" items compared with older adults, suggesting that they were more successful in inhibiting the "forget" items than were older adults (e.g., Zacks, Radvansky, & Hasher, 1996). In contrast, no evidence for the inhibition deficit hypothesis has been found from the "inhibition of return" (IOR) effect. This refers to the finding of increased response times to visual targets when they appear at locations to which attention has recently been directed, in comparison with response times to targets at new locations. In other words, IOR is an inhibitory process that acts as a bias against returning one's attention or eyes to recently attended locations or objects in order to promote efficient visual search behavior (see Klein, 2000, for a review). Equivalent IOR effects have been obtained for young and older adults (Faust & Balota, 1997; Hartley & Kieley, 1995; Langley,

Fuentes, Hochhalter, Brandt, & Overmier, 2001), contrary to the reduced inhibition hypothesis. At the very least, such conflicting results "suggest limitations on the generality of inhibitory deficits in healthy aging" (p. 13, Faust & Balota, 1997).

A second complicating issue is that some "inhibitory" phenomena may be explained without inhibition. The obvious example here is the case of negative priming (e.g., Milliken, Joordens, Merikle, & Seiffert, 1998; Neill, 1997). Typically, in a negative priming paradigm, participants are asked to process items while ignoring irrelevant distracting information. If the target on the current trial was the distractor on the previous trial, then responses are slower than to new targets – the negative priming effect. The traditional explanation emphasizes the role of inhibitory processes such that inhibition of a response to the distractor on the previous trial slows down the processing of that item when it subsequently appears as a target (e.g., Neill, 1977; Tipper, 1985; Tipper & Cranston, 1985). Negative priming has often been reported as reduced or absent in older adults in traditional negative priming paradigms (see Verhaeghen & De Meersman, 1998a, for a meta-analysis), which has been taken as support for reduced inhibitory processes in normal aging (e.g., Hasher, Stoltzfus, Zacks, & Rypma, 1991; Tipper, 1991). However, there are alternative explanations for the negative priming effect (see reviews by Fox, 1995; May, Kane, & Hasher, 1995). For example, one explanation is based on episodic retrieval in which the appearance of the target automatically cues the retrieval of the previous processing episode. This contains the information that no response was made to that item, and because this information conflicts with the response required on the current trial, negative priming occurs as a consequence of response competition (see Neill & Valdes, 1992; Neill, Valdes, Terry, & Gorfein, 1992). Thus, age reductions in negative priming could be attributed to well-known deficits in episodic memory rather than to impaired inhibition.[1]

A third problem concerns scaling effects associated with reaction time (RT) measures (see Perfect & Maylor, 2000a; Verhaeghen, Cerella, Bopp, & Basak, this volume; for discussion). This is illustrated with hypothetical data in Figure 12.1. Consider, for example, the classic Stroop task in which participants are asked to name the ink color of a string of Xs as quickly as possible (baseline condition) or to name the ink color of a color word where the ink color conflicts with the color word (interference condition). As illustrated in Figure 12.1, RT is typically longer in the interference condition than in the baseline condition (see MacLeod, 1991, for a review). The Stroop effect can be explained in terms of the interference between two conflicting

---

[1] To complicate this particular issue further, a more recent meta-analysis by Gamboz, Russo, and Fox (2002) concluded that there was no evidence of a significant age difference in the negative priming effect.

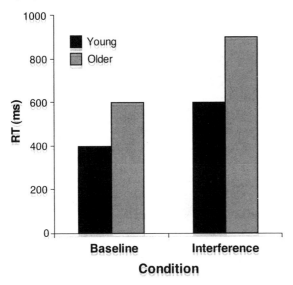

FIGURE 12.1. Hypothetical data from a reaction time (RT) experiment with baseline and interference conditions, which differ only in the absence and presence, respectively, of distracting information. The RT difference between the young and older groups is greater in absolute terms for the interference condition (300 ms) than for the baseline condition (200 ms), leading to the typical Age × Treatment interaction. However, in both conditions, the older group took 1.5 times longer than the young group (proportional slowing).

responses associated with the same input. Thus, one response is elicited by naming the ink color but another response is elicited by reading the word. The response tendency to read the word is relatively automatic; therefore this prepotent response of reading the word must be inhibited in favor of producing the nondominant response of color naming (cf. Hasher et al.'s, 1999, restraint function). Hence, participants are slower in the interference condition than in the baseline condition.

As illustrated in Figure 12.1, older adults are usually slower than young adults in the Stroop task, particularly in the interference condition (see Verhaeghen & De Meersman, 1998b, for examples), leading to an Age × Treatment interaction and the conclusion that older adults are specifically impaired in inhibiting the automatic response of reading the word. However, in a comprehensive review of the evidence on aging and the Stroop effect, Verhaeghen and De Meersman (1998b) noted that generalized slowing theories of aging (e.g., Cerella, 1985, 1990) would also predict a larger interference effect in older adults. In other words, larger age differences would be expected in the interference condition because RTs are slower than in the baseline condition. Indeed, from a meta-analysis of 20 studies, Verhaeghen and De Meersman (1998b) concluded that "the apparent

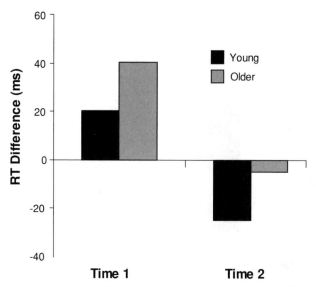

FIGURE 12.2. Hypothetical data from, for example, a negative priming experiment. On the current trial (time 2), responses are slower to targets that were distractors on the previous trial than to new targets (baseline). One interpretation is that on the previous trial, in selecting and responding to the target, the competing distractor was inhibited. If it were possible to probe performance just prior to the onset of this suppression on the previous trial (time 1), responses to distractors would be faster than baseline (hidden activation peak). As illustrated here, data at time 2 suggest greater inhibition for young adults; however, greater initial activation of distractors at time 1 in older adults suggests similar levels of inhibitory control as indicated by the differences between time 1 and time 2.

age-sensitivity of the Stroop interference effect appears to be merely an artifact of general slowing" (p. 120; but see also West & Alain, 2000). Thus, before concluding that any task provides evidence of greater interference (i.e., reduced inhibition) with aging, it is important to demonstrate that the age difference in the interference condition is greater than would be predicted on the basis of generalized slowing.

A fourth complicating factor in the investigation of the inhibition deficit hypothesis was described by Anderson (2002) as the "hidden activation peak" and is illustrated with hypothetical data in Figure 12.2. Differences between baseline and experimental conditions at time 2 would suggest greater inhibitory control in young adults than in older adults. However, it is conceivable that at an earlier point in time, prior to the application of inhibition (time 1), initial activation was greater for older than for young adults (the hidden activation peak). Thus, if inhibitory control were measured instead by the difference between initial facilitation and subsequent inhibition, then young and older adults would not actually differ. Another possibility not shown in Figure 12.2 is that older adults may be slower to apply inhibitory control such that at a later point in time (time 3), older adults could show similar or even greater levels of inhibition than do young adults. The point here is to suggest that it may be misleading to assess inhibitory functioning from a single time sample.

The fifth problem is that irrelevant information may not always be processed by older adults because of perceptual or capacity limitations (see, for example, Maylor & Lavie, 1998). We could therefore be misled into concluding that inhibition was reduced by aging when in fact there simply was no initial activation of the interfering information.

THE PRESENT STUDIES

With the above problems in mind, we now consider three recent aging studies focusing primarily on Hasher et al.'s (1999) delete function – the suppression of no-longer relevant information – across three different domains, to explore the generality of the reduced inhibition hypothesis. In each paradigm, it is argued that there is good evidence that inhibition is involved, although space does not permit exhaustive reviews. Where possible, we have attempted to rule out generalized slowing as an alternative account of the data. Anderson's (2002) recommendations for designs that trace the time course of effects have been followed so that both initial activation and subsequent inhibition are monitored. If we find reduced inhibition in older adults, we can therefore examine whether it can be explained by either increased initial activation (Anderson, 2002) or the absence of activation (Maylor & Lavie, 1998).

### Short-term Memory: The Ranschburg Effect

Reduced efficiency of Hasher and Zacks's (1988) deletion function with aging allows irrelevant information to remain in working memory, leading to increased competition at retrieval. A paradigm that enables this to be readily studied is serially ordered recall from short-term memory. Maylor and Henson (2000) argued that during serial recall, items already recalled from the current list are no longer relevant to the task of recalling the rest of the list and should therefore be inhibited. Such *response suppression*, whereby once an action has been performed it is temporarily inhibited so that it is unlikely to be performed again in the immediate future, is evident across a range of serial behaviors including speech production (MacKay, 1987; Vousden, Brown, & Harley, 2000), typing (Rumelhart & Norman, 1982), goal sequencing (Li, Lindenberger, Rünger, & Frensch, 2000), and serial recall (Duncan & Lewandowsky, in press; Henson, 1998a). Indeed, a crucial feature of recent computational models of serial behavior that provide accurate fits to detailed patterns of human errors is a response suppression component to prevent perseverative responses (e.g., Brown, Preece, & Hulme, 2000; Burgess & Hitch, 1999; Farrell & Lewandowsky, 2002; Henson, 1998b; Lewandowsky, 1999; Page & Norris, 1998).

In serial recall tasks, such short-lived postoutput inhibitory processes are supported by the common observation that repetition errors, where items are erroneously recalled more than once, are relatively infrequent (e.g., Henson, Norris, Page, & Baddeley, 1996). When they do occur, the distance between the repeated outputs is usually quite large (Conrad, 1965). Also consistent with response suppression is the finding of impaired recall of repeated items in comparison with the recall of nonrepeated items (e.g., Crowder, 1968), a phenomenon known as the *Ranschburg effect* (Jahnke, 1969) after the Hungarian psychologist Paul Ranschburg (1870–1945) who discovered the effect and also published on the psychology of aging (see p. 333 of Birren & Schroots, 2000). The Ranschburg effect has been most extensively investigated recently by Henson (1998a), who developed improved methodology and analysis for examining the effects of repeated items on serial recall. For lists with nonadjacent repeated items, he observed *repetition inhibition* (i.e., the Ranschburg effect) such that recall of both repeated items was inferior to the recall of two nonrepeated items at the corresponding serial positions in control lists. This was attributed to the automatic process of response suppression, which not only causes the temporary failure to retrieve an item more than once but also prevents previous responses from coming to mind if guessing is necessary.

Maylor and Henson (2000) therefore proposed the Ranschburg effect as a useful testing ground for Hasher and Zacks's (1988) inhibition deficit hypothesis of aging. Serial recall was expected to be lower overall for older than for young adults (e.g., Maylor, Vousden, & Brown, 1999). However, the interesting prediction was that reduced response suppression in older adults would lead to a reduced Ranschburg effect; that is, older adults would actually be better able to recall repeated items, relative to nonrepeated items, than would young adults.

In Maylor and Henson's (2000) first experiment, there were 36 young adults and 37 older adults, with mean ages of 20 and 72, respectively. Forty-eight experimental lists of six letters were presented to participants on a computer screen at a rate of one letter per second.[2] Immediately following the presentation of each list, participants were required to recall the items in correct serial order by writing their responses in six boxes strictly from left to right. If they were unable to recall an item, they were asked to place a line through the corresponding box. Participants were informed in advance that lists could contain repeated items.

---

[2] This relatively slow rate of presentation ensures that all items are successfully encoded and therefore distinguishes the Ranschburg effect from repetition blindness, which refers to the inability to detect repetitions in rapid serial visual presentation at rates of more than 10 items per second (e.g., Kanwisher, Kim, & Wickens, 1996).

TABLE 12.1. *Composition of List Types in Maylor and Henson's (2000) Ranschburg Experiments*

| List type | Repetition format | Repetition separation | No. of lists |
|---|---|---|---|
| Control | 1 2 3 4 5 6 | n/a | 24 |
| Repetition | 1 R R 4 5 6 | 1 | 3 |
| Repetition | 1 2 R R 5 6 | 1 | 3 |
| Repetition | 1 R 3 R 5 6 | 2 | 3 |
| Repetition | 1 2 R 4 R 6 | 2 | 3 |
| Repetition | 1 R 3 4 R 6 | 3 | 3 |
| Repetition | 1 2 R 4 5 R | 3 | 3 |
| Repetition | R 2 3 4 R 6 | 4 | 3 |
| Repetition | 1 R 3 4 5 R | 4 | 3 |

*Note.* R = repeated item. Thus, *P T D T B V* would be an example of repetition format 1 R 3 R 5 6.

The letters in each list were chosen from the following set of phonologically confusable consonants: *B, D, G, P, T, V.* Our earlier work (Maylor et al., 1999) suggested that six-item lists of phonologically confusable consonants would produce appropriate overall levels of performance in both age groups. Table 12.1 summarizes the composition of the 48 lists: Half were control lists with no repeated items, and half were repetition lists with one repeated item. For repetition lists, the positions of the repeated items varied across lists in eight different formats, with repeated elements between one and four positions apart.

The main dependent measure of interest was the conjoint probability of recalling both repeated elements in repetition lists or both corresponding control elements in control lists, regardless of correct positioning. As expected, overall recall was significantly higher for young (0.78) than for older adults (0.57). Figure 12.3 shows the differences on this measure between repeated and control lists as a function of repetition separation for each age group. Consistent with previous studies of the Ranschburg effect, there was substantial repetition inhibition (i.e., repeated less than control) for nonadjacent repetitions (separations 2–4), attributable to a failure to recall a repeated item more than once. However, it can be seen from Figure 12.3 that, contrary to expectation, this Ranschburg effect was at least as large for older as for young adults, a result that was replicated in Maylor and Henson's (2000) second experiment with 30 young and 29 older adults.

In summary, postoutput response suppression is a fundamental inhibitory mechanism involved in serial behavior, and in short-term memory tasks it is responsible for the Ranschburg effect (see Henson, 1998a). Maylor and Henson (2000) therefore regarded it as analogous to Hasher et al.'s (1999) deletion function, which during retrieval prevents

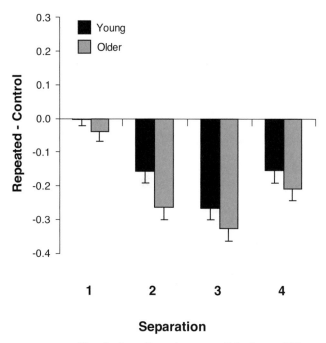

FIGURE 12.3. Results from Experiment 1 of Maylor and Henson (2000) showing the mean differences between the probability of correct recall of both critical elements in repeated and control lists for young and older adults as a function of repetition separation (1–4). Error bars indicate 1 *SE* of the difference.

information from remaining in working memory when no longer relevant to current goals. However, contrary to the reduced inhibition hypothesis, there was no evidence of a reduced Ranschburg effect in older adults, which led Maylor and Henson (2000) to conclude that "the specific process of response suppression during serial recall is not reduced by aging" (p. 657). A similar Ranschburg experiment comparing children aged 7–11 years found no developmental increase in response inhibition, despite substantial improvements in overall recall over this age range (McCormack, Brown, Vousden, & Henson, 2000, Experiment 3). Together, these findings support the view that postoutput response suppression is an inhibitory mechanism that does not follow the predicted rise and fall across the lifespan (e.g., Dempster, 1992). It seems therefore unlikely to play a significant role in accounting for improvement in short-term memory during childhood and decline with aging.

Maylor and Henson (2000) noted the conceptual similarity between postoutput response suppression in serial recall and IOR in visual attention, which both act to avoid perseverations in serial behavior (see also Houghton & Hartley, 1995). They are also similar in being unimpaired by normal aging, thereby challenging the general inhibition deficit hypothesis. However, because both are considered relatively automatic processes (see Henson, 1998a; Taylor & Klein, 1998, respectively), the findings can be reconciled by the suggestion that, whereas controlled inhibitory processes are impaired with aging, automatic inhibitory processes may be preserved (e.g., Kramer, Humphrey, Larish, Logan, & Strayer, 1994; McDowd, 1997). We therefore turn next to an effortful top-down inhibitory mechanism in visual search.

### Visual Search: The Preview Benefit

The visual system is constantly bombarded with more information than can be dealt with at any one time, hence the need to prioritize selection. There might be two ways by which this can be done. One is to actively enhance visible targets, which will be successful only if the information is already present. In contrast, the prioritization of anticipated, newly appearing stimuli could be achieved by actively inhibiting stimuli already visible, which would decrease their competition for selection when the new stimuli arrived. This second process of deprioritization has been termed *visual marking* (Watson & Humphreys, 1997).

Visual marking was demonstrated by Watson and Humphreys (1997) using a modified color-shape conjunction visual search task as illustrated in Figure 12.4a. Participants were required to indicate the presence or absence of a target (a blue H) among a varying number of distractors. In the single-feature condition, the distractors were blue As. Typically, when the target differs from the distractors by the possession of a unique feature, as in this case, then RTs to find the target are not particularly affected by the number of distractors in the display and the target is said to "pop out" (e.g., Treisman & Gelade, 1980). However, if the target is defined by a conjunction of features (i.e., a blue H among blue As and green Hs), then search becomes relatively slow, with RTs increasing more steeply as a function of display size. In addition, the slope for target-absent trials is approximately twice that for target-present trials, consistent with search as serial and self-terminating – on average, only half of the items need to be searched on target-present trials (but see also Humphreys & Müller, 1993; Townsend, 1972).

Watson and Humphreys (1997) contrasted these two baseline conditions (single feature and conjunction) with a preview condition in which one set of distractors (green Hs) was presented for 1000 ms prior to the remaining items (blue As and a blue H if the target was present). Participants were instructed that when the target was present, it would be in the second display. Thus, if the old unwanted information could be successfully ignored, search in this preview condition should be more efficient than when all the items were presented simultaneously (as in the conjunction baseline). In

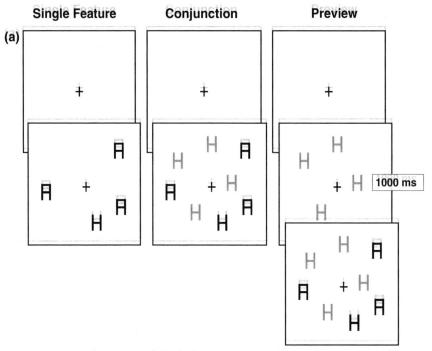

FIGURE 12.4. (a) Examples of single-feature, conjunction, and preview conditions in a typical visual marking experiment in which participants search for a blue H among blue As (single feature) or among blue As and green Hs (conjunction and preview). In the preview condition, the green Hs are presented for 1,000 ms before the appearance of the blue As and blue H (if present). (Blue and green letters are shown here in black and gray, respectively. The screen background and fixation point are shown with black/white reversed.) (b) Mean correct reaction times (RTs) to determine target presence from Watson and Humphreys (1997; Experiment 1) showing similar search rates in the single-feature (14 ms/item) and preview (16 ms/item) conditions but a slower search rate in the conjunction (26 ms/item) condition, indicating that participants were able to ignore the previewed items while searching for the target.

fact, search rate should be equivalent to that of the single-feature condition in which only the blue items from the preview condition were displayed. Figure 12.4b shows the data for target-present trials[3] from Experiment 1 of Watson and Humphreys (1997).[4] In terms of search slopes, the preview

[3] We focus here on target-present trials because when the target is absent, people tend to rely on a number of different strategies and are usually more cautious in responding absent than present (e.g., Chun & Wolfe, 1996).

[4] The data for the single-feature condition are plotted as if there were twice as many items in the display so that if search rate in the preview condition matches that of the single feature baseline, then we can conclude that the previewed items have been excluded from subsequent search.

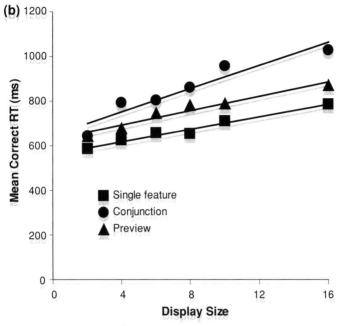

FIGURE 12.4. (*continued*)

condition was indeed as efficient as the single-feature baseline and significantly more efficient than the conjunction baseline (the preview benefit). This ability to exclude the previewed items from the current search, termed visual marking, is an important mechanism for prioritizing and controlling the selection of visual information (see Watson & Humphreys, 1997; Watson, Humphreys, & Olivers, 2003). It can be distinguished from other inhibitory mechanisms, such as the passive inhibition of previously attended objects or locations (i.e., IOR) or the inhibition of previous rejected distractors (i.e., negative priming). Watson and Humphreys (1997) proposed that the preview benefit resulted from the active inhibition of old information, which allows a selection advantage for new stimuli that subsequently appear and is a top-down process that requires the commitment of limited attentional resources (see Humphreys, Watson, & Jolicoeur, 2002; Watson & Humphreys, 1997, 2000, for evidence).

In view of these characteristics, one would expect older adults to show substantial decrements in visual marking tasks. We conducted a series of experiments (Watson & Maylor, 2002) to explore age-related differences in the preview benefit, comparing young and older adults with mean ages of approximately 21 and 71 years, respectively. The first experiment was essentially as already described (see Figure 12.4a), the main difference being that there were fewer display sizes. The results for target-present

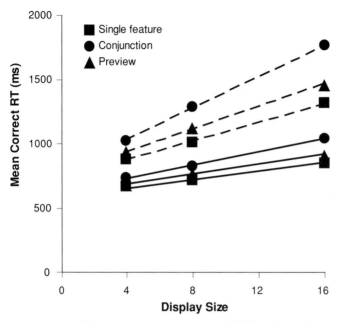

FIGURE 12.5. Mean correct reaction times (RTs) to determine target presence for young (solid lines) and older (dashed lines) adults from Watson and Maylor (2002; Experiment 1). See Figure 12.4a for summary of experimental conditions. Search rates for the single-feature, preview, and conjunction conditions were 12, 14, and 24 ms/item, respectively, for young adults, and 29, 35, and 46 ms/item, respectively, for older adults. For both age groups, the single-feature and preview search rates did not differ but each was faster than the conjunction search rate. Adapted with permission of the American Psychological Association from Watson and Maylor (2002, p. 325, Figure 1). Copyright © 2002 by the American Psychological Association.

trials are shown in Figure 12.5. As expected from previous aging studies (e.g., Humphrey & Kramer, 1997; Plude & Doussard-Roosevelt, 1989), young adults were faster than older adults overall, and their searches were conducted approximately twice as quickly (see Figure 12.5 caption for search rates). Crucially, however, the two age groups did not differ in terms of their ability to visually mark the previewed items as evidenced by the finding that the search rate for the preview condition matched that of the single-feature baseline rather than that of the conjunction baseline for young and older adults alike. Experiment 1 therefore replicated the results from a study of visual marking in old age by Kramer and Atchley (2000), who used different stimuli and much larger display sizes, suggesting that older as well as young adults can successfully ignore at least 15 previewed items. Together, they "provide yet another demonstration of age-related sparing in an inhibitory process" (p. 295, Kramer & Atchley, 2000).

Watson and Humphreys (1997) demonstrated that for stationary stimuli, previewed items are marked by inhibition applied to their locations (see also Olivers, Watson, & Humphreys, 1999; but see also Olivers & Humphreys, 2002, and Braithwaite & Humphreys, 2003, for evidence of feature-based effects with stationary stimuli). Visual marking appears intact in older adults for stationary stimuli, consistent with other work showing preserved location-based inhibitory processes (e.g., Faust & Balota, 1997; Hartley & Kieley, 1995). However, clearly objects in the real world are not always static. Watson and Humphreys (1998) explored displays in which all the items moved linearly down the screen at a constant speed. Their young participants still showed evidence of visual marking; that is, they could successfully ignore the previewed items even though they were continuously moving. However, it was shown that visual marking was not in this case location-based but was instead feature-based; in other words, it operated by the inhibition of a whole feature map (i.e., color; see also Kunar, Humphreys, & Smith, 2003).

In our second experiment (Watson & Maylor, 2002), we compared feature-based visual marking of moving stimuli in young and older adults. The single-feature, conjunction, and preview conditions were as before except that all the stimuli moved continuously down the screen, as illustrated in Figure 12.6a, scrolling back into the top of the display as they reached the bottom. The data for young adults, presented in Figure 12.6b, successfully replicated those of Watson and Humphreys (1998) in showing visual marking of the previewed items. Thus, the preview search rate resembled that of the single-feature rather than the conjunction baseline. In contrast, the older adults showed no evidence of visual marking, with a preview search rate equivalent to that of the conjunction rather than the single-feature baseline. Thus, they were unable to exclude the previewed items from their search of the subsequent display. This experiment therefore demonstrates a clear age-related impairment in feature-based visual marking of moving stimuli.

Feature-based marking of moving stimuli obviously requires there to be a unique feature (in our case, color) that distinguishes between the previewed and new items (see Figure 12.6a). However, if the local spatial relationships, or configuration, among the previewed items remains fixed, then visual marking of moving items can be achieved by grouping them to form a single virtual object (Watson, 2001). Such object-based marking was investigated in our third experiment (Watson & Maylor, 2002) using rotational, rather than linear, motion. This maintained the local spatial relationships among items, but there was now no simple feature distinguishing the old previewed items from the new stimuli. As

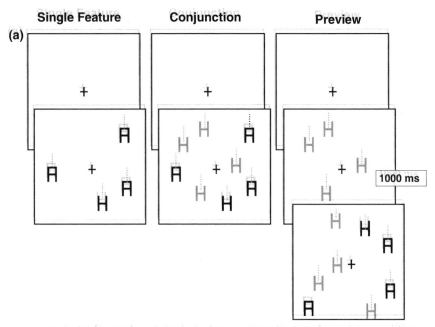

FIGURE 12.6. (a) Examples of single-feature, conjunction, and preview conditions in Experiment 2 of Watson and Maylor (2002), with stimuli (but not the fixation cross) moving linearly down the screen at a speed of 3.8 degrees visual angle per second. When an item reached the bottom of the screen, it gradually disappeared and then reappeared at the top in the same horizontal location. (b) Mean correct reaction times (RTs) to determine target presence for young (solid lines) and older (dashed lines) adults from Watson and Maylor (2002; Experiment 2). Search rates for the single-feature, preview, and conjunction conditions were 15, 19, and 29 ms/item, respectively, for young adults, and 28, 42, and 50 ms/item, respectively, for older adults. For young adults, the single-feature and preview search rates did not differ but each was faster than the conjunction search rate. For older adults, the preview and conjunction search rates did not differ but each was slower than the single-feature search rate. Adapted with permission of the American Psychological Association from Watson and Maylor (2002, p. 328, Figure 2). Copyright © 2002 by the American Psychological Association.

illustrated in Figure 12.7a, the stimuli rotated clockwise around the fixation point in a smooth and continuous fashion. The task was to search for the letter T, with Ls as distractors.[5]

---

[5] The single-feature and conjunction conditions were therefore identical except for display sizes (2, 4, and 8 vs. 4, 8, and 16). In other words, the single feature baseline was also a conjunction search task. We continue to refer to single-feature and conjunction baselines here for consistency with previous experiments.

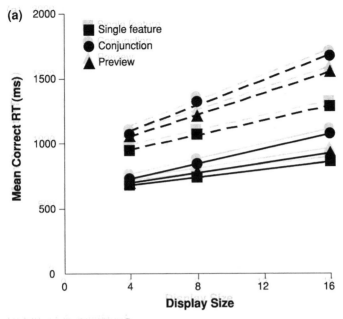

FIGURE 12.6. (*continued*)

The results presented in Figure 12.7b for the young adults replicated those of Watson (2001) in showing a full preview benefit, with the preview search rate matching that of the single-feature and not the conjunction baseline. Older adults, on the other hand, again showed no evidence of a preview benefit, with the preview search rate matching that of the conjunction and not the single-feature baseline. Thus, unlike young adults, older adults were not able to restrict their search to the new items alone in the preview condition.

It appears that whether there was a feature difference between the previewed and new items (Figure 12.6) or whether previewed items could be grouped to form a virtual object (Figure 12.7), there were striking age-related deficits in visual marking of moving stimuli. Can these inhibitory deficits be explained by generalized slowing? They are certainly incompatible with a simple account in which older RTs are a linear transformation of young RTs (e.g., Figure 12.1). This is because there is no linear transformation possible that can convert the young adults' RT data pattern across conditions (i.e., single feature = preview < conjunction) into the older adults' RT data pattern (i.e., single feature < preview = conjunction). Generalized slowing could nevertheless still provide an account on the basis that young adults require approximately 400 ms between the previewed and new items for full visual marking to occur with stationary items (Watson & Humphreys, 1997). Visual marking of moving items may take longer;

**(a) Single Feature          Conjunction          Preview**

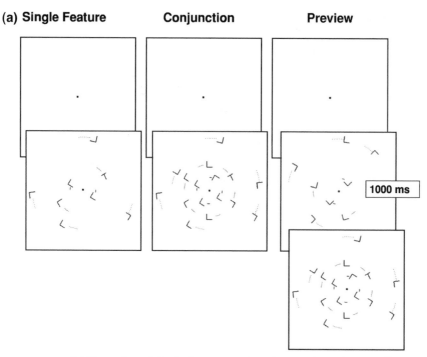

FIGURE 12.7. (a) Examples of single-feature, conjunction, and preview conditions in Experiment 3 of Watson and Maylor (2002), with stimuli (but not the fixation cross) rotating clockwise around virtual concentric rings at a rate of 38 degrees per second. The screen background and stimuli are shown with black/white reversed. Participants searched for a target letter T among distractor letters L, oriented randomly at 0, 90, 180, and 270 degrees. (b) Mean correct reaction times (RTs) to determine target presence for young (solid lines) and older (dashed lines) adults from Watson and Maylor (2002; Experiment 3). Search rates for the single-feature, preview, and conjunction conditions were 14, 17 and 26 ms/item, respectively, for young adults, and 36, 62, and 61 ms/item, respectively, for older adults. For young adults, the single-feature and preview search rates did not differ but each was faster than the conjunction search rate. For older adults, the preview and conjunction search rates did not differ but each was slower than the single-feature search rate. Adapted with permission of the American Psychological Association from Watson and Maylor (2002, p. 332, Figure 3). Copyright © 2002 by the American Psychological Association.

hence, it is possible that whereas a preview display duration of 1000 ms may be sufficient for young adults across all conditions, older adults may require longer than 1,000 ms to mark the previewed items when they are moving.

To examine this possibility of age-related slowing of the time course of visual marking, we conducted a further experiment with older

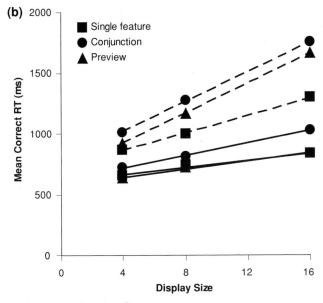

FIGURE 12.7. (*continued*)

participants only (Watson & Maylor, 2002), which was identical to the third experiment with rotating stimuli (see Figure 12.7a) except that the preview duration was increased from 1,000 to 2,000 ms. Despite this additional time, none of the older participants showed any hint of a preview benefit, with mean search slopes of 30 (single feature), 65 (preview), and 56 (conjunction) ms/item. Like the older adults with 1,000 ms preview duration in Figure 12.7b, the preview and conjunction search rates did not differ but each was slower than the single-feature search rate. Consequently, we cannot attribute the age-related deficit in visual marking of moving stimuli to insufficient time to set up and apply marking as a result of generalized slowing.

As noted earlier, it is important to consider whether there are alternative explanations for visual marking that do not involve inhibitory mechanisms. Donk and Theeuwes (2001) recently suggested that the preview benefit might be explained instead in terms of automatic attention capture by the luminance transients (onsets) associated with the appearance of the new items. However, a number of findings argue against this alternative view (see, for example, Watson et al., 2003), including those from the present aging experiments. Kramer, Hahn, Irwin, and Theeuwes (1999) demonstrated that the attentional and oculomotor processes underlying attentional capture by abrupt onsets are unimpaired by old age. If visual marking were due to the prioritization of abrupt onsets, then we would have expected older adults to be able to selectively attend to the abruptly appearing new items, thereby displaying preview benefits. The failure to obtain this result is therefore more in line with an inhibition interpretation than with an attentional capture interpretation of visual marking.

In summary, we have argued that prioritizing the selection of new items in visual search can be achieved through visual marking, that is, the active inhibition of items already present in the visual field (Watson & Humphreys, 1997). Consistent with the inhibition deficit hypothesis of aging, both feature-based and object-based visual marking of moving stimuli were impaired in older adults (Watson & Maylor, 2002, Experiments 2 and 3, respectively). However, there was age-related sparing of location-based visual marking of stationary stimuli (Kramer & Atchley, 2000; Watson & Maylor, 2002, Experiment 1), although it would probably be a mistake to conclude that this would always be the case. Visual marking of stationary stimuli is disrupted in young adults by, for example, the addition of a demanding secondary task such as monitoring digits at fixation (e.g., Humphreys et al., 2002; Watson & Humphreys, 1997). It seems likely, therefore, that visual marking of stationary stimuli with a secondary load would be even more disrupted in older adults than in young adults based on known age-related increases in dual-task costs (e.g., Verhaeghen & Cerella, 2002; Verhaeghen, Steitz, Sliwinski, & Cerella, 2003).

## Motor Control: The Negative Compatibility Effect

Our final case study concerns inhibitory processes in motor control, which is a relatively neglected domain with respect to normal aging. There is, nevertheless, evidence of age-related decline in the ability to voluntarily inhibit prepotent motor responses (cf. Hasher et al.'s, 1999, restraint function). For example, in an antisaccade task in which participants were required to move their eyes in the opposite direction to a peripheral stimulus, Nieuwenhuis et al. (2000) found that older adults were more likely than young adults to saccade toward the cue, and they also took much longer to initiate correct antisaccades. Also, in a "stopping" paradigm in which participants were asked to abort an overt response in the unlikely event that they heard a "stop" signal, Kramer et al. (1994) showed that older adults took disproportionately longer to implement the inhibitory or stopping process in comparison with young adults.

As already noted, it appears from other domains that controlled inhibitory processes (such as required earlier) may be more vulnerable to the adverse effects of aging than automatic inhibitory processes (e.g., McDowd, 1997). We were therefore interested in whether this holds true for the motor domain, that is, whether or not more automatic low-level motor inhibition would be impaired in old age (Schlaghecken & Maylor, in press). To investigate this, we employed a masked prime paradigm (e.g., Eimer & Schlaghecken, 1998; Schlaghecken & Eimer, 2000), which tracks the automatic effects on motor responses of subliminal stimuli. The basic procedure is illustrated in Figure 12.8a. A briefly presented visual stimulus (the prime) is immediately followed by a masking stimulus that renders the prime unavailable to conscious awareness (Eimer & Schlaghecken, 1998, 2002; Schlaghecken & Eimer, 1997) and by a clearly visible target stimulus. Primes and targets can be simple arrows pointing to the left or right, corresponding to the required speeded responses of key presses with the left or right hand, respectively. On each trial, prime and target arrows either point in the same direction (compatible trial), in opposite directions (incompatible trial), or the prime is an unrelated symbol such as an equal sign (neutral trial). Several studies with young adults showed that if the target follows the prime immediately (interstimulus interval [ISI] of 0 ms), behavioral benefits occur on compatible trials, while costs occur on incompatible trials, relative to neutral trials (see Figure 12.8b), demonstrating a positive compatibility effect (PCE; Schlaghecken & Eimer, 1997, 2000). However, if the prime-target ISI is increased to around 100 ms or more, this effect reverses and becomes a negative compatibility effect (NCE), with costs on compatible trials and benefits on incompatible trials (Eimer, 1999; Schlaghecken & Eimer, 2000).

Behavioral and electrophysiological data suggest that the pattern of results illustrated in Figure 12.8b is obtained because the prime, although below the threshold for conscious awareness, initially activates its corresponding motor response (Eimer, 1999; Eimer & Schlaghecken, 1998). If the target is presented immediately after the prime, target-related motor preparation begins during this initial activation phase, hence resulting in behavioral PCEs. However, with longer prime-target ISIs, target-related motor preparation begins at a later stage relative to the initial prime-related activation. Therefore, the motor activation triggered by the masked prime can take its normal time course for longer before target-related activity sets in. Evidence from behavioral and electrophysiological studies of this time course suggests the existence of an automatic self-inhibition process, which actively inhibits the initial prime-induced activation when the sensory evidence for the prime is suddenly removed (Eimer, 1999; Eimer & Schlaghecken, 1998; Schlaghecken & Eimer, 2002). This "emergency brake" mechanism suppresses activation of the initially primed response and allows the alternative response to reach relatively higher activation levels. Consequently, behavioral costs on compatible trials and behavioral benefits on incompatible trials (i.e., NCEs) will be obtained when preparation of the target-related response begins during the self-inhibition phase.

The masked prime paradigm provides an opportunity to begin to address the question of whether more automatic low-level motor inhibition is impaired in old age. We compared eight young and eight older adults, with mean ages of 22 and 76 years, in two masked priming experiments (Schlaghecken & Maylor, in press). An initial pilot study with

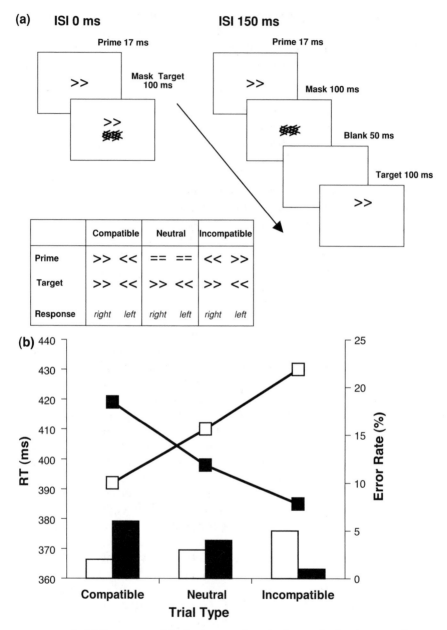

FIGURE 12.8. (a) Summary of the basic procedure in the masked prime paradigm, with prime-target interstimulus intervals (ISIs) of 0 and 150 ms. (b) Typical results from young adults in the masked prime paradigm for reaction times (RTs) and percentage error rates (line and bar graphs, respectively). Open symbols and bars represent 0 ms ISI (positive compatibility effects) and filled symbols and bars represent 150 ms ISI (negative compatibility effects).

parameters based on those employed previously with young participants (e.g., Schlaghecken & Eimer, 2000, 2002) failed to reveal any evidence that the primes had been processed at all by the older adults (presumably a perceptual limitation; see the fifth problem discussed earlier). Prime duration was therefore increased from the typical 17 ms to 33 ms, and stimulus size was larger. On each trial in Experiment 1, a central fixation point was presented for 250 ms followed by a blank screen for 750 ms. The prime was then presented for 33 ms at fixation, followed by a 100 ms mask in the same location. The target was presented for 100 ms either just above or below the central area occupied by the mask. Prime-target ISI was blocked and was either 0 ms or 150 ms. Primes and targets were left- and right-pointing double arrows, with half of the trials compatible (prime and target pointing in the same direction) and half incompatible (prime and target pointing in opposite directions). Participants were required to fixate at the center throughout and to press the left or right response button as quickly as possible according to the direction of the target arrows. With older adults in mind, the interval between target offset and the return of the fixation point was increased slightly from previous experiments to 2,200 ms.

As usual, young adults (mean correct RT = 385 ms) responded more quickly than older adults (mean correct RT = 524 ms), with similar (low) error rates across age groups. Figure 12.9a displays the crucial results of interest, that is, compatibility effects (incompatible – compatible RTs) as a function of ISI. It is clear that despite the slightly altered experimental parameters, the data pattern for young adults of a PCE at 0 ms turning into a NCE at 150 ms successfully replicated those of previous studies (e.g., Schlaghecken & Eimer, 1997, 2000). For older adults, in contrast, there was a PCE at 0 ms but no evidence of a NCE at 150 ms. Although the PCE at 0 ms was numerically larger for older adults, the age difference was not significant. It should also be remembered that because of the overall difference in RT between young and older adults, this small increase with age in the PCE would disappear in terms of proportional RT effects. Thus, we can discount any suggestion of greater early activation in older adults (cf. Anderson's, 2002, hidden activation peak). The age difference at 150 ms, however, was significant suggesting an effect of aging on the self-inhibition component of prime-induced low-level motor control processes.

In our second experiment (Schlaghecken & Maylor, in press), we tested whether early self-inhibition processes as reflected in NCEs in the masked prime task are completely absent or merely follow a slower time course in older adults. The participants from Experiment 1 were therefore asked to return to the laboratory for further testing, on this occasion with prime-target ISIs increased to 300 and 450 ms. Again, the young adults were faster than the older adults (364 vs. 492 ms). The results in terms of compatibility effects are shown in Figure 12.9b. There were no significant effects,

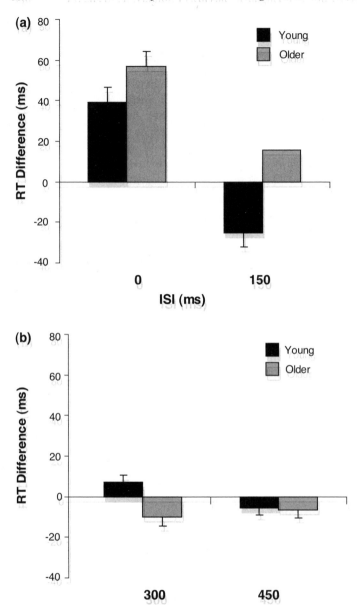

FIGURE 12.9. (a) Mean reaction time (RT) differences (incompatible – compatible), with standard error bars, as a function of interstimulus interval (ISI = 0 and 150 ms) for young and older adults from Experiment 1 of Schlaghecken and Maylor (in press). (b) Mean RT differences (incompatible–compatible), with standard error bars, as a function of ISI (300 and 450 ms) for young and older adults from Experiment 2 of Schlaghecken and Maylor (in press).

although it should be noted that the small NCE for older adults at 300 ms approached significance. Moreover, comparing RTs on incompatible and compatible trials for each individual participant revealed that four of the eight older adults showed reliable NCEs at 300 ms. Thus, for at least some older individuals, there was evidence that the self-inhibition component was delayed relative to young adults, whereas for other older individuals, there was no evidence of NCEs at any ISI.

Schlaghecken and Maylor (in press) concluded that motor activation triggered by subliminal primes via direct perceptuo-motor links is unaffected by old age, as evidenced by older adults' spared PCEs at 0 ms ISI. In contrast, the self-inhibition component of the activation-followed-by-inhibition process triggered by masked primes shows substantial impairment in old age (see Schlaghecken & Maylor, in press, for further analysis and discussion). The study thus extends the inhibition deficit hypothesis of aging to low-level automatic motor inhibition.

## CONCLUSIONS

We have considered here the effects of normal aging on three recent examples of inhibitory processes – associated with short-term memory, prioritization in visual search, and motor control – all requiring the suppression of responses to stimuli no longer relevant to current goals. As others have observed (e.g., Burke, 1997; Kramer et al., 1994; McDowd, 1997), the overall picture emerging is that a general interpretation of the inhibition deficit hypothesis of aging (Hasher & Zacks, 1988; Hasher et al., 1999) is no longer tenable. Thus, the present studies showed no evidence of reduced response suppression with aging in serial recall (Maylor & Henson, 2000), but there were age-related deficits in the visual marking of moving (though not stationary) stimuli (Watson & Maylor, 2002) and in the inhibition of motor responses automatically triggered by subliminal primes (Schlaghecken & Maylor, in press), neither of which could be explained in terms of generalized slowing. The motor control results were also inconsistent with the view (e.g., McDowd, 1997) that automatic inhibitory processes are preserved with aging, whereas controlled inhibitory processes are impaired.

To some extent, such mixed results may seem the inevitable consequence of numerous problems complicating the interpretation of studies of the inhibition deficit hypothesis, some of which were outlined earlier. They may also reflect the possibility that researchers have overextended the use of the term inhibition and that apparently similar inhibitory functions may be quite unrelated (e.g., Friedman & Miyake, 2004) and thus differentially vulnerable to the effects of old age. Similar points were raised in the broader context of executive functioning and its fractionation (see Mayr, Spieler, & Kliegl, 2001; Miyake, Friedman, Emerson, Witzki, & Howerter, 2000; Rabbitt, 1997).

Is it possible then to provide an integrative account of age-related changes in inhibitory processes? For example, a number of researchers (e.g., Dempster, 1992) have suggested that "age-related differences in inhibitory function will be observed to the extent that performance depends on the integrity of the frontal lobes" (p. 493, Kramer et al., 1994). The frontal lobe hypothesis of cognitive aging (West, 1996) derives from evidence that the frontal lobes (traditionally associated with executive functioning) deteriorate disproportionately with normal aging (e.g., Raz, 2000) and that many age-related deficits resemble those exhibited by frontal lobe patients (but see Greenwood, 2000; Perfect, 1997; Reuter-Lorenz, 2000, for discussion). Many inhibitory findings appear consistent with this view – for example, as noted earlier, there is age-related sparing of IOR, which is associated with the superior colliculus and parietal cortex (see Klein, 2000, for a summary), whereas there is age-related impairment in the "stopping" paradigm (see earlier), which involves the frontal lobes (Band & van Boxtel, 1999).

To what extent are the results from the present studies consistent with this frontal approach? Such a question highlights a current practical difficulty in assessing the view, namely, that appropriate evidence to determine the exact brain region(s) responsible for the inhibitory phenomena of interest is not yet available. This certainly applies to the Ranschburg effect. For visual marking, there is preliminary evidence from fMRI to indicate the involvement of superior parietal cortex (precuneus) in the inhibition of stationary stimuli (see Watson et al., 2003, for a summary), but no evidence to date with moving stimuli. Finally, the negative compatibility effect appears to be mediated by subcortical structures, in particular the thalamus and the caudate nucleus of the basal ganglia, and not to involve the frontal lobes (Aron et al., 2003). At first sight, the observed age-related deficit therefore seems contrary to the frontal view. However, loss of neural tissue in old age is not only marked in the frontal lobes but also in the regions to which they connect, namely, the thalamus and the basal ganglia (Raz, 2000).

In summary, it seems that there are probably multiple inhibitory mechanisms subserved by both frontal and nonfrontal regions (see Andrés, 2003; Kok, 1999; Kramer et al., 1994) and that precise predictions of age-related deficits in tasks putatively requiring inhibition will ultimately depend on accurate localization of function together with detailed knowledge of brain aging.

**Author Note**

Some of the research presented in this chapter was supported by Grant R000239180 from the Economic and Social Research Council of Great Britain. The authors are grateful to Liz Blagrove, Lucy Bruce, Nicola Manson, and Liz Pennington for assistance in data collection, and to Michael Anderson, Pilar Andrés, and Rik Henson for helpful discussion.

## References

Andrés, P. (2003). Frontal cortex as the central executive of working memory: Time to revise our view. *Cortex, 39,* 871–895.

Anderson, M. C. (2002). *On measuring inhibitory deficits: Insights from the study of inhibitory processes in human memory.* Paper presented at the Ninth Cognitive Aging Conference, Atlanta, Georgia, April 2002.

Aron, A., Schlaghecken, F., Fletcher, P., Bullmore, E., Eimer, M., Barker, R., Sahakian, B., & Robbins, T. (2003). Inhibition of subliminally primed responses is mediated by the caudate and thalamus: Evidence from fMRI and Huntington's disease. *Brain, 126,* 713–723.

Band, G. P. H., & van Boxtel, G. J. M. (1999). Inhibitory motor control in stop paradigms: Review and reinterpretation of neural mechanisms. *Acta Psychologica, 101,* 179–211.

Beech, A., Powell, T., McWilliam, J., & Claridge, G. (1989). Evidence of reduced "cognitive inhibition" in schizophrenia. *British Journal of Clinical Psychology, 28,* 109–116.

Birren, J. E., & Schroots, J. J. F. (Eds.). (2000). *A history of geropsychology in autobiography.* Washington, DC: American Psychological Association.

Braithwaite, J. J., & Humphreys, G. W. (2003). Inhibition and anticipation in visual search: Evidence from effects of color foreknowledge on preview search. *Perception & Psychophysics, 65,* 213–237.

Brown, G. D. A., Preece, T., & Hulme, C. (2000). Oscillator-based memory for serial order. *Psychological Review, 107,* 127–181.

Burgess, N., & Hitch, G. J. (1999). Memory for serial order: A network model of the phonological loop and its timing. *Psychological Review, 106,* 551–581.

Burke, D. M. (1997). Language, aging, and inhibitory deficit: Evaluation of a theory. *Journal of Gerontology: Psychological Sciences, 52B,* P254–P264.

Cerella, J. (1985). Information processing rates in the elderly. *Psychological Bulletin, 98,* 67–83.

Cerella, J. (1990). Aging and information processing rate. In J. E. Birren & K. W. Schaie (Eds.), *Handbook of the psychology of aging* (3rd ed., pp. 201–221). San Diego, CA: Academic Press.

Chun, M. M., & Wolfe, J. M. (1996). Just say no: How are visual searches terminated when there is no target present? *Cognitive Psychology, 30,* 39–78.

Cohen, J. D., & Servan-Schreiber, D. (1992). Context, cortex, and dopamine: A connectionist approach to behavior and biology in schizophrenia. *Psychological Review, 99,* 45–77.

Connelly, S. L., Hasher, L., & Zacks, R. T. (1991). Age and reading: The impact of distraction. *Psychology and Aging, 6,* 533–541.

Conrad, R. (1965). Order errors in immediate recall of sequences. *Journal of Verbal Learning and Verbal Behavior, 4,* 161–169.

Crowder, R. G. (1968). Intraserial repetition effects in immediate memory. *Journal of Verbal Learning and Verbal Behavior, 7,* 446–451.

Dempster, F. N. (1992). The rise and fall of the inhibitory mechanism: Toward a unified theory of cognitive development and aging. *Developmental Review, 12,* 45–75.

Dempster, F. N., & Brainerd, C. J. (Eds.). (1995). *Interference and inhibition in cognition.* San Diego: Academic Press.

Donk, M., & Theeuwes, J. (2001). Visual marking beside the mark: Prioritizing selection by abrupt onsets. *Perception & Psychophysics, 63,* 891–900.

Duncan, M., & Lewandowsky, S. (in press). The time course of response suppression: No evidence for a gradual release from inhibition. *Memory.*

Eimer, M. (1999). Facilitatory and inhibitory effects of masked prime stimuli on motor activation and behavioural performance. *Acta Psychologica, 101,* 293–313.

Eimer, M., & Schlaghecken, F. (1998). Effects of masked stimuli on motor activation: Behavioral and electrophysiological evidence. *Journal of Experimental Psychology: Human Perception and Performance, 24,* 1737–1747.

Eimer, M. & Schlaghecken, F. (2002). Links between conscious awareness and response inhibition: Evidence from masked priming. *Psychonomic Bulletin & Review, 9,* 514–20.

Farrell, S., & Lewandowsky, S. (2002). An endogenous distributed model of ordering in serial recall. *Psychonomic Bulletin & Review, 9,* 59–79.

Faust, M. E., & Balota, D. A. (1997). Inhibition of return and visuospatial attention in healthy older adults and individuals with dementia of the Alzheimer type. *Neuropsychology, 11,* 13–29.

Fox, E. (1995). Negative priming from ignored distractors in visual selection: A review. *Psychonomic Bulletin & Review, 2,* 145–173.

Friedman, N. P., & Miyake, A. (2004). The relations among inhibition and interference control functions: A latent variable analysis. *Journal of Experimental Psychology: General, 133,* 101–135.

Gamboz, N., Russo, R., & Fox, E. (2002). Age differences and the identity negative priming effect: An updated meta-analysis. *Psychology and Aging, 17,* 525–531.

Greenwood, P. M. (2000). The frontal aging hypothesis evaluated. *Journal of the International Neuropsychological Society, 6,* 705–726.

Harnishfeger, K. K. (1995). The development of cognitive inhibition: Theories, definitions, and research evidence. In F. N. Dempster & C. J. Brainerd (Eds.), *Interference and inhibition in cognition* (pp. 175–204). San Diego: Academic Press.

Hartley, A. A., & Kieley, J. M. (1995). Adult age differences in the inhibition of return of visual attention. *Psychology and Aging, 10,* 670–683.

Hartman, M., & Hasher, L. (1991). Aging and suppression: Memory for previously relevant information. *Psychology and Aging, 6,* 587–594.

Hasher, L., Stoltzfus, E. R., Zacks, R. T., & Rypma, B. (1991). Age and inhibition. *Journal of Experimental Psychology: Learning, Memory, and Cognition, 17,* 163–169.

Hasher, L., & Zacks, R. T. (1988). Working memory, comprehension, and aging: A review and a new view. In G. H. Bower (Ed.), *The psychology of learning and motivation* (Vol. 22, pp. 193–225). New York: Academic Press.

Hasher, L., Zacks, R. T., & May, C. P. (1999). Inhibitory control, circadian arousal, and age. In D. Gopher & A. Koriat (Eds.), *Attention and performance XVII. Cognitive regulation and performance: Interaction of theory and application* (pp. 653–675). Cambridge, MA: MIT Press.

Henson, R. N. A. (1998a). Item repetition in short-term memory: Ranschburg repeated. *Journal of Experimental Psychology: Learning, Memory, and Cognition, 24,* 1162–1181.

Henson, R. N. A. (1998b). Short-term memory for serial order: The start-end model. *Cognitive Psychology, 36*, 73–137.

Henson, R. N. A., Norris, D. G., Page, M. P. A., & Baddeley, A. D. (1996). Unchained memory: Error patterns rule out chaining models of immediate serial recall. *Quarterly Journal of Experimental Psychology, 49A*, 80–115.

Houghton, G., & Hartley, T. (1995). Parallel models of serial behavior: Lashley revisited. *Psyche, 2*(25). Retrieved from the World Wide Web: *http://psyche.cs. monash.edu.au/v2/psyche-2-25-houghton.html*

Humphrey, D. G., & Kramer, A. F. (1997). Age differences in visual search for feature, conjunction, and triple-conjunction targets. *Psychology and Aging, 12*, 704–717.

Humphreys, G. W., & Müller, H. J. (1993). Search via recursive rejection (SERR): A connectionist model of visual search. *Cognitive Psychology, 25*, 43–110.

Humphreys, G. W., Watson, D. G., & Jolicoeur, P. (2002). Fractionating the preview benefit in search: Dual-task decomposition of visual marking by timing and modality. *Journal of Experimental Psychology: Human Perception and Performance, 28*, 640–660.

Jahnke, J. C. (1969). The Ranschburg effect. *Psychological Review, 76*, 592–605.

Kanwisher, N. G., Kim, J. W., & Wickens, T. D. (1996). Signal detection analyses of repetition blindness. *Journal of Experimental Psychology: Human Perception and Performance, 22*, 1249–1260.

Kok, A. (1999). Varieties of inhibition: Manifestations in cognition, event-related potentials and aging. *Acta Psychologica, 101*, 129–158.

Klein, R. M. (2000). Inhibition of return. *Trends in Cognitive Sciences, 4*, 138–147.

Kramer, A. F., & Atchley, P. (2000). Age-related effects in the marking of old objects in visual search. *Psychology and Aging, 15*, 286–296.

Kramer, A. F., Hahn, S., Irwin, D. E., & Theeuwes, J. (1999). Attentional capture and aging: Implications for visual search performance and oculomotor control. *Psychology and Aging, 14*, 135–154.

Kramer, A. F., Humphrey, D. G., Larish, J. F., Logan, G. D., & Strayer, D. L. (1994). Aging and inhibition: Beyond a unitary view of inhibitory processing in attention. *Psychology and Aging, 9*, 491–512.

Kunar, M., Humphreys, G. W., & Smith, K. J. (2003). Visual change with moving displays: More evidence for color feature map inhibition during preview search. *Journal of Experimental Psychology: Human Perception and Performance, 29*, 779–792.

Langley, L. K., Fuentes, L. J., Hochhalter, A. K., Brandt, J., & Overmier, J. B. (2001). Inhibition of return in aging and Alzheimer's disease: Performance as a function of task demands and stimulus timing. *Journal of Clinical and Experimental Neuropsychology, 23*, 431–446.

Lewandowsky, S. (1999). Redintegration and response suppression in serial recall: A dynamic network model. *International Journal of Psychology, 34*, 434–446.

Li, K. Z. H., Lindenberger, U., Rünger, D., & Frensch, P. A. (2000). The role of inhibition in the regulation of sequential action. *Psychological Science, 11*, 343–347.

MacKay, D. G. (1987). *The organization of perception and action*. New York: Springer-Verlag.

MacLeod, C. M. (1991). Half a century of research on the Stroop effect: An integrative review. *Psychological Bulletin, 109,* 163–203.

May, C. P., Kane, M. J., & Hasher, L. (1995). Determinants of negative priming. *Psychological Bulletin, 118,* 35–54.

Maylor, E. A., & Henson, R. N. A. (2000). Aging and the Ranschburg effect: No evidence of reduced response suppression in old age. *Psychology and Aging, 15,* 657–670.

Maylor, E. A., & Lavie, N. (1998). The influence of perceptual load on age differences in selective attention. *Psychology and Aging, 13,* 563–574.

Maylor, E. A., & Rabbitt, P. M. A. (1994). Applying Brinley plots to individuals: Effects of aging on performance distributions in two speeded tasks. *Psychology and Aging, 9,* 224–230.

Maylor, E. A., Vousden, J. I., & Brown, G. D. A. (1999). Adult age differences in memory for serial order: Data and a model. *Psychology and Aging, 14,* 572–594.

Mayr, U., Spieler, D. H., & Kliegl, R. (2001). *Ageing and executive control.* New York: Routledge.

McCormack, T., Brown, G. D. A., Vousden, J. I., & Henson, R. N. A. (2000). The development of serial recall: Implications for short-term memory development. *Journal of Experimental Child Psychology, 76,* 222–252.

McDowd, J. M. (1997). Inhibition in attention and aging. *Journal of Gerontology: Psychological Sciences, 52B,* P265–P273.

McDowd, J. M., Oseas-Kreger, D. M., & Filion, D. L. (1995). Inhibitory processes in cognition and aging. In F. N. Dempster & C. J. Brainerd (Eds.), *Interference and inhibition in cognition* (pp. 363–400). San Diego: Academic Press.

Milliken, B., Joordens, S., Merikle, P. M., & Seiffert, A. E. (1998). Selective attention: A reevaluation of the implications of negative priming. *Psychological Review, 105,* 203–229.

Miyake, A., Friedman, N. P., Emerson, M. J., Witzki, A. H., & Howerter, A. (2000). The unity and diversity of executive functions and their contributions to complex "frontal lobe" tasks: A latent variable analysis. *Cognitive Psychology, 41,* 49–100.

Neill, W. T. (1977). Inhibition and facilitation processes in selective attention. *Journal of Experimental Psychology: Human Perception and Performance, 3,* 444–450.

Neill, W. T. (1997). Episodic retrieval in negative priming and repetition priming. *Journal of Experimental Psychology: Learning, Memory, and Cognition, 23,* 1291–1305.

Neill, W. T., & Valdes, L. A. (1992). Persistence of negative priming: Steady state or decay? *Journal of Experimental Psychology: Learning, Memory, and Cognition, 18,* 565–576.

Neill, W. T., Valdes, L. A., Terry, K. M., & Gorfein, D. S. (1992). Persistence of negative priming: II. Evidence for episodic trace retrieval. *Journal of Experimental Psychology: Learning, Memory, and Cognition, 18,* 993–1000.

Nieuwenhuis, S., Ridderinkhof, K. R., de Jong, R., Kok, A., & van der Molen, M. W. (2000). Inhibitory inefficiency and failures of intention activation: Age-related decline in the control of saccadic eye movements. *Psychology and Aging, 15,* 635–647.

Olivers, C. N. L., & Humphreys, G. W. (2002). When visual marking meets the attentional blink: More evidence for top-down limited-capacity inhibition. *Journal of Experimental Psychology: Human Perception and Performance, 28,* 22–42.

Olivers, C. N. L., Watson, D. G., & Humphreys, G. W. (1999). Visual marking of locations and feature maps: Evidence from within-dimension defined conjunctions. *Quarterly Journal of Experimental Psychology, 52A,* 679–715.

Page, M. P. A., & Norris, D. (1998). The primacy model: A new model of immediate serial recall. *Psychological Review, 105,* 761–781.

Park, D. C. (2000). The basic mechanisms accounting for age-related decline in cognitive function. In D. C. Park & N. Schwarz (Eds.), *Cognitive aging: A primer* (pp. 3–21). Hove, East Sussex: Psychology Press.

Perfect, T. J. (1997). Memory aging as frontal lobe dysfunction. In M. A. Conway (Ed.), *Cognitive Models of Memory* (pp. 315–339). Hove, East Sussex: Psychology Press.

Perfect, T. J., & Maylor, E. A. (2000a). Rejecting the dull hypothesis: The relation between method and theory in cognitive aging research. In T. J. Perfect & E. A. Maylor (Eds.), *Models of cognitive aging* (pp. 1–18). Oxford, UK: Oxford University Press.

Perfect, T. J., & Maylor, E. A. (Eds.). (2000b). *Models of cognitive aging.* Oxford, UK: Oxford University Press.

Plude, D. J., & Doussard-Roosevelt, J. A. (1989). Aging, selective attention, and feature integration. *Psychology and Aging, 4,* 98–105.

Rabbitt, P. M. A. (1965). An age decrement in the ability to ignore irrelevant information. *Journal of Gerontology, 20,* 233–237.

Rabbitt, P. (Ed.). (1997). *Methodology of frontal and executive function.* Hove, East Sussex: Psychology Press.

Raz, N. (2000). Aging of the brain and its impact on cognitive performance: Integration of structural and functional findings. In F. I. M. Craik & T. A. Salthouse (Eds.), *The Handbook of Aging and Cognition* (2nd ed., pp. 1–90). Mahwah, NJ: Lawrence Erlbaum Associates.

Reuter-Lorenz, P. A. (2000). Cognitive neuropsychology of the aging brain. In D. C. Park & N. Schwarz, *Cognitive aging: A primer* (pp. 93–114). Hove, East Sussex: Psychology Press.

Rumelhart, D. E., & Norman, D. (1982). Simulating a skilled typist: A study of skilled cognitive-motor performance. *Cognitive Science, 6,* 1–36.

Salthouse, T. A. (1991). *Theoretical perspectives on cognitive aging.* Hillsdale, NJ: Lawrence Erlbaum Associates.

Salthouse, T. A. (1996). The processing-speed theory of adult age differences in cognition. *Psychological Review, 103,* 403–428.

Salthouse, T. A. (2000). Steps toward the explanation of adult age differences in cognition. In T. J. Perfect & E. A. Maylor (Eds.), *Models of cognitive aging* (pp. 19–49). Oxford, UK: Oxford University Press.

Schlaghecken, F., & Eimer, M. (1997). The influence of subliminally presented primes on response preparation. *Sprache & Kognition, 16,* 166–175.

Schlaghecken, F., & Eimer, M. (2000). A central/peripheral asymmetry in subliminal priming. *Perception & Psychophysics, 62,* 1367–1382.

Schlaghecken, F., & Eimer, M. (2002). Motor activation with and without inhibition: Evidence for a threshold mechanism in motor control. *Perception & Psychophysics, 64,* 148–162.

Schlaghecken, F., & Maylor, E. A. (in press). Motor control in old age: Evidence of impaired low-level inhibition. *Journal of Gerontology: Psychological Sciences.*

Taylor, T. L., & Klein, R. M. (1998). On the causes and effects of inhibition of return. *Psychonomic Bulletin & Review, 5,* 625–643.

Tipper, S. P. (1985). The negative priming effect: Inhibitory effects of ignored primes. *Quarterly Journal of Experimental Psychology, 37A,* 571–590.

Tipper, S. P. (1991). Less attentional selectivity as a result of declining inhibition in older adults. *Bulletin of the Psychonomic Society, 29,* 45–47.

Tipper, S. P., & Cranston, M. (1985). Selective attention and priming: Inhibitory and facilitatory effects of ignored primes. *Quarterly Journal of Experimental Psychology, 37A,* 591–611.

Townsend, J. T. (1972). Some results on the identifiability of parallel and serial processes. *British Journal of Mathematical and Statistical Psychology, 25,* 168–199.

Treisman, A. M., & Gelade, G. (1980). A feature-integration theory of attention. *Cognitive Psychology, 12,* 97–136.

Tun, P. A., O'Kane, G., & Wingfield, A. (2002). Distraction by competing speech in young and older listeners. *Psychology and Aging, 17,* 453–467.

Verhaeghen, P., & Cerella, J. (2002). Aging, executive control, and attention: A review of meta-analyses. *Neuroscience and Biobehavioral Reviews, 26,* 849–857.

Verhaeghen, P., & De Meersman, L. (1998a). Aging and the negative priming effect: A meta-analysis. *Psychology and Aging, 13,* 435–444.

Verhaeghen, P., & De Meersman, L. (1998b). Aging and the Stroop effect: A meta-analysis. *Psychology and Aging, 13,* 120–126.

Verhaeghen, P., Steitz, D. W., Sliwinski, M. J., & Cerella, J. (2003). Aging and dual-task performance: A meta-analysis. *Psychology and Aging, 18,* 443–460.

Vousden, J. I., Brown, G. D. A., & Harley, T. A. (2000). Serial control of phonology: A hierarchical model. *Cognitive Psychology, 41,* 101–175.

Watson, D. G. (2001). Visual marking in moving displays: Feature-based inhibition is not necessary. *Perception & Psychophysics, 63,* 74–84.

Watson, D. G., & Humphreys, G. W. (1997). Visual marking: Prioritizing selection for new objects by top-down attentional inhibition. *Psychological Review, 104,* 90–122.

Watson, D. G., & Humphreys, G. W. (1998). Visual marking of moving objects: A role for top-down feature based inhibition in selection. *Journal of Experimental Psychology: Human Perception and Performance, 24,* 946–962.

Watson, D. G., & Humphreys, G. W. (2000). Visual marking: Evidence for inhibition using a probe-dot paradigm. *Perception & Psychophysics, 62,* 471–481.

Watson, D. G., Humphreys, G. W., & Olivers, C. N. L. (2003). Visual marking: Using time in visual selection. *Trends in Cognitive Sciences, 7,* 180–186.

Watson, D. G., & Maylor, E. A. (2002). Aging and visual marking: Selective deficits for moving stimuli. *Psychology and Aging, 17,* 321–339.

West, R. L. (1996). An application of prefrontal cortex function theory to cognitive aging. *Psychological Bulletin, 120,* 272–292.

West, R., & Alain, C. (2000). Age-related decline in inhibitory control contributes to the increased Stroop effect observed in older adults. *Psychophysiology, 37,* 179–189.

Zacks, R., & Hasher, L. (1997). Cognitive gerontology and attentional inhibition: A reply to Burke and McDowd. *Journal of Gerontology: Psychological Sciences, 52B,* P274–P283.

Zacks, R. T., Radvansky, G., & Hasher, L. (1996). Studies of directed forgetting in older adults. *Journal of Experimental Psychology: Learning, Memory, and Cognition, 22,* 143–156.

# 13

## Impairments of Memory and Reasoning in Patients with Neuropsychiatric Illness

*Disruptions of Dynamic Cognitive Binding?*

James A. Waltz

INTRODUCTION: REPRESENTATION AND PROCESS
IN HIGHER LEVEL COGNITION

Decrements in higher level cognitive abilities are a prevalent feature of dementia associated with psychiatric illnesses, such as schizophrenia and major depression; degenerative neurological disorders, such as Alzheimer's disease and Parkinson's disease; and the normal aging process. The kinds of cognitive deficits that are typically associated with these conditions are fairly well characterized through the wealth of neuropsychological studies dealing with each. However, the task of establishing the link between particular forms of pathophysiology associated with each condition and specific cognitive impairments has proved more difficult. A satisfactory resolution of this issue depends, to a large extent, on the ability to describe what individuals can and cannot do cognitively – what kinds of percepts and concepts they can and cannot represent. I will argue that psychological studies of reasoning have attempted to characterize information processing limitations in two ways: (a) by describing the nature and complexity of percepts and concepts manipulated in reasoning, and (b) by specifying their reliance on working memory, which involves the ability to temporarily store and manipulate pieces of information.

The former approach, I contend, has been used to show that differences in reasoning abilities across cognitive developmental stages or phylogeny, as well as reasoning impairments resulting from brain damage in humans, might be explained by the presence or absence of the ability to represent knowledge structures of a given complexity. It has become apparent in recent years that, in order to capture the flexible nature of human abstract thought, one needs to understand the way in which knowledge, (e.g., representations of concepts) is structured. Fodor and Pylyshyn (1988) describe the nature of human thought as "systematic," which means that concepts do not exist in isolation in the human mind but rather in an interconnected manner that distinguishes between syntactic structures and objects that can participate in those structures. The essence of structure is a kind of symbolic representation called a *relation* (Halford, 1993; Halford, Bain, Maybery, & Andrews, 1996). A *relational representation*, at base, is one that distinguishes roles from their fillers. Representing a relation requires the active binding of a filler to a role – a value to a variable, in other words – which leaves the local representations intact. In other words, a systematic cognitive system has the ability to represent both structures and objects, as well as the ability to arbitrarily bind objects into structures without altering the individual representations of the conceptual structures and objects. The concept "loves," for example, specifies the representation of a relationship between A and B, with A and B being symbols or variables that can take essentially any values. In the simplest form, a relational representation can specify the binding of an object to a concept or category. An example is the proposition *red (car)* where "car" is the filler for the role, "red thing." More complex relations, however, enable the representation of magnitude or functional relationships among objects.

Reasoning of all kinds relies on the systematic representation of relations. Analogical reasoning, which involves the attempt to identify structural similarity between two situations or events, serves as a sort of paradigm case for the representation of structured knowledge. Work by Holyoak and Gentner and colleagues (Gentner, 1983; Gick & Holyoak, 1980; Gick & Holyoak, 1983) showed that analogical reasoning is an important means by which individuals solve problems and acquire new concepts. Specifically, analogical reasoning involves a process of *structure mapping*, in which individuals develop a model of a novel situation, called a target problem, by transferring information from a domain that is better understood, called the source. Thus, analogical reasoning involves the active representation of multiple relational structures and mappings among the elements of these structures (Table 13.1).

An important side effect of the repeated identification of correspondences among representations structures sharing the same relational structure is that the mappings among the shared features of representations structures (i.e., relations) become symbolized. That is to say, a consequence of the performance of mappings among systems, as occurs in analogical reasoning, is the *induction* of abstract relational *schemas*, which are systems of abstract relations describing *classes* of situations, allowing for the application of content-specific rules (Cheng & Holyoak, 1985, 1989). The idea of a schema is similar to that of notions denoted by the terms frame and script, which emerged from the artificial intelligence literature (Minsky, 1975; Schank & Abelson, 1977). An example of a schema is the knowledge that one has regarding behavior in a restaurant, which specifies the customary order of events, roles played by different elements, and actions to be taken when certain conditions obtain. Other theories of reasoning also emphasize

TABLE 13.1. *Analogical Reasoning Involves Actively Representing Systems of Relations: Example of the Solar System and the Atom*

| Base domain | Target domain |
|---|---|
| The Sun attracts the planets of the solar system | The nucleus of the atom attracts the electrons |
| The Sun is larger than the planets | The nucleus of the atom is larger than the electrons |
| The planets revolve around the Sun | The electrons revolve around the nucleus |
| The planets revolve around the Sun because the Sun attracts the planets and the Sun is larger than the planets | The electrons revolve around the nucleus because the nucleus attracts the electrons and the nucleus is larger than the electrons |
| There is life on planet earth | No transfer |

the need to represent abstractions and relationships dynamically – in the construction of mental models (Johnson-Laird, 1983), for example, or in the integration of conditions with production rules in a knowledge base.

If one accepts the premise that human thought can be systematic, an implication is that limitations in higher level cognitive processing arise out of the need to represent relational structures. In order to understand more about how this happens, we need a way of characterizing information processing limitations in terms of the ability to represent structure. Perhaps the most substantial progress in understanding limitations in higher level cognitive processing comes from studies of the reliance of abstract thought on working memory processes. These investigations have helped to answer such questions as: How do working memory limitations relate to limitations in abstract thought? What are the components of working memory systems? How do they interact? Investigations of this subject have revealed, for example, that verbal and visuospatial reasoning place demands on both modality-specific short-term memory stores and modality-independent executive processes. Numerous questions remain open, however, such as how information is represented in working memory and what form executive processes take.

In the next two sections of this chapter, I will assess our present thinking regarding the role of working memory in information processing constraints in human cognition. In particular, I will examine the issue of working memory limitations and the question of how they impact the capacity to represent relational structure (Waltz, Lau, Grewal, & Holyoak, 2000). In the remaining sections of this chapter, I will describe the implications of neuropsychological studies of the role of working memory in reasoning, in terms of what they suggest regarding the effects of brain damage on abstract thought.

It is proposed here that understanding how the brain represents structure is essential for making sense of impairments in abstract thought resulting from neurological and psychiatric illness. Neuropsychiatric illnesses, such as schizophrenia and various forms of dementia, are often associated with impairments in higher level cognition processes, along with deficits in memory and attention. Because these conditions do not involve focal cortical lesions, but rather often involve disruptions of diffuse modulatory systems in the cortex, they are candidates for pharmacological therapy in order to slow or reverse pathological processes. Understanding the nature of abstract thought in these conditions may help us shed light on the nature of information-processing failures and might also be important for understanding the role of neuromodulatory systems in cognition and therapeutic mechanisms.

## THE DEPENDENCE OF ABSTRACT THOUGHT ON WORKING MEMORY

When researchers have attempted to assess processing limitations on reasoning tasks, most commonly they have related them to limitations in working memory. Psychological evidence of a role for working memory in higher level cognition comes mainly from two types of studies: those investigating problem solving performance under conditions of multitasking and those examining correlations between problem-solving performance and some metric of working memory demands. In order to assess the roles of different components of the human working memory system in higher level cognitive processing, Baddeley and colleagues (see Baddeley, 1986, for a review) used a dual-task paradigm, which involved the development of various "distracter" tasks designed to occupy components of the working memory system. For instance, a spatial tracking or tapping task could be used to probe the dependence of a cognitive task on spatial working memory. In some of the seminal work done in this area, Baddeley and Hitch (1974) described how different working memory processes might figure in the computational processes involved in mental arithmetic.

The execution of numerous experiments in which subjects were required to perform cognitive tasks concurrent with various working memory distracter tasks helped to establish clearly the existence of two short-term memory buffers: one for phonological information and one for visuospatial information. Based on these findings, Baddeley (1986) proposed a model of working memory comprising a central executive that mediates between the two short-term memory buffers, which were also called "slave systems." Baddeley's (1986) concept of working memory was the first to incorporate the sort of executive component that distinguishes the concept of working memory from other forms of short-term memory. The idea that the executive component of the working memory system can be dissociated from modality-specific buffers has received additional support in recent years, with other researchers (e.g., Jonides, 1995) arguing that such a model should incorporate additional domain-specific buffers, such as a purely visual buffer and a conceptual buffer.

Several studies in recent years have used the dual-task paradigm to examine specifically the dependence of reasoning on specific subsystems of working memory. Gilhooly and colleagues (Gilhooly, Logie, Wetherick, & Wynn, 1993), for example, found that individuals who were required to perform a syllogistic reasoning task while simultaneously performing a task designed to place demands on the central executive component of working memory (by attempting to generate random digits) showed significant impairment on the reasoning task. Additional studies showed that reducing available working memory resources through multitasking leads to impairments on tasks of propositional reasoning (Klauer, Stegmaier, & Meiser, 1997; Toms, Morris, & Ward, 1993). Together, these results indicate that abstract thought depends on multiple working memory subsystems, including domain-specific stores and domain-general executive processes.

In the past decade, several dual-task studies (Roberts, Hager, & Heron, 1994; Dunbar & Sussman, 1995) demonstrated a role for working memory in cognitive executive function and tried to characterize the working memory demands of tasks, in the same way the studies of Baddeley and colleagues investigated the role of working memory in thinking two decades before. The fact that cognitive executive functions (Roberts et al., 1994; Dunbar & Sussman, 1995) rely on working memory, and that both cognitive executive functions and working memory appear to rely on the same neural substrate (prefrontal cortex), prompts the question of how one can characterize the relationship between relational processing and so-called cognitive executive functions more precisely. The argument that cognitive executive functions depend on a working memory system, which itself includes a central executive module, would appear to be circular and does not really help us understand what cognitive executive processes look like.

Another group of studies used computational analyses of cognitive tasks to ascertain the information processing/working memory demands of tasks *a priori*, as well as correlational analyses to examine the relationships between quantifications of task complexity, or individual working memory capacity, and measures of subjects' performance on these tasks. These methods have been effective in identifying the correspondence between individual working memory capacity in various domains and performance on higher level cognitive tasks, such as language comprehension (Daneman & Carpenter, 1980) and reasoning (Kyllonen & Christal, 1990). In a systematic analysis of cognitive processing in one particular test environment, the Raven Progressive Matrices Test, Carpenter, Just, and Shell (1990) found that the complexity of plans required for solution comprises much of what makes problems difficult. Carpenter and her colleagues found that problem difficulty was influenced by both the number and types of rules that a problem required the test-taker to induce. They argued that action plans for working with memory are limited in the number of representations of subgoals they can concurrently activate.

In examining the relationship between individual differences in working memory capacity and performance of various higher level cognitive tasks, numerous researchers (e.g., Kyllonen & Christal, 1990) concluded that processes of working memory and reasoning are closely intertwined. Engle and associates (see Chapter 2 of this volume; Engle, 2002; Kane & Engle, 2003) found close correspondences between measures of working memory capacity and performance on tasks of controlled attention, such as the Stroop task and the antisaccade task). Studies using the latent-variable approach (Miyake, Friedman, Rettinger, Shah, & Hegarty, 2001; Engle, Tuholski, Laughlin, & Conway, 1999) also provided evidence for a close correspondence among working memory capacity, executive functioning, and what has been called "fluid intelligence," the ability to respond in situations based on dynamic cognitive processes such as inductive inference, rather than accessing "crystallized knowledge" acquired at an earlier time. From these studies, researchers revealed that individual working memory capacity is an excellent predictor of performance on many reasoning tasks, suggesting that reasoning behavior differs from working memory in that reasoning can also rely heavily upon existing knowledge (Kyllonen & Christal, 1990).

## WORKING MEMORY AS A DYNAMIC BINDING PROCESS: PSYCHOLOGICAL EVIDENCE

Studies of the role of working memory in higher level cognition have helped us to understand more about how human beings process information and solve abstract problems. These investigations helped us to learn more about the components of cognitive systems, their capacities, and how they interact. They have told us less, however, about how working memory participates in systematic thought – in the representation of the structure of percepts, concepts, and action plans. This issue, furthermore, relates to questions such as, "How does working memory enable cognitive control?" and "What is the nature of a central executive?" I argue that, in so far as relations are the contents of abstract thought, i.e., that they are the representations about which people reason, they comprise the contents of working memory. What follows from this statement is that quantifying the working memory demands of tasks requires quantifying their complexity in terms of relations. Halford's (1993) taxonomy of cognitive complexity, alluded to earlier, represents one attempt to quantify the information processing demands of a task by describing its relational structure.

In Halford's (1993) system, the level of complexity is defined by the type of memory representations that must be kept in mind in order to generate an appropriate response. The representation of any relation requires a set of bindings, with more complex relational representations requiring more bindings. The lowest level of relational complexity, level 1, defines a role-filler relationship in which the role is an *attribute* of the filler. An example would be a red car, where car fills the role "red thing." A proposition of the second level of relational complexity specifies a *binary relation*, where a role, such as "taller-than," specifies a relationship between two fillers, such as "Fred" and "Phil." Relational representations are significant from a cognitive standpoint in that they allow for the binding of two memory representations of a given level of complexity (such as "Fred" and "Phil") on the basis of some higher order relationship (such as height). A mental representation of the third level of relational complexity makes it possible to define a *system* or a relation between relations. For example, a transitive ordering requires three elements for which the ordering of two pairs constrains the ordering of the third pair. An example would be the inference of the ordering of Fred, Phil, and Sam from tallest to shortest, based on the premises "taller-than (Fred Phil)" and "taller-than (Phil Sam)." The successful inference of the ordering depends on the ability to integrate two relational propositions – to represent a relation between relations, or what is called a *higher order* relation – based on the implications of the concept of transitivity, which takes binary relationships as arguments. The concept of transitivity specifies a relation between binary relations, allowing for the inference of a third pairwise relationship, given two pairwise relationships. It should be noted that, within this framework, purely perceptual representations such as objects, reside within the perceptual hierarchy and are therefore characterized by a relational complexity level of *zero*.

The quantification of relational complexity proposed by Halford (1993) has important implications for quantifying the demands on working memory made by the representation of abstract schemas. Specifically, differing working memory demands may arise because representations at different levels of complexity require the active maintenance of different numbers of variable bindings. In the taxonomy of Halford (1993), an attribute requires a single variable binding, that of a filler (e.g., Fred) to a role (e.g., tall person). The specification of a binary relation, however, requires the maintenance of two variable bindings, for example those binding Fred and John to the roles of "taller-person" and "less-tall person," respectively, in the representation

taller-than (Fred John).

In the case of a system of relations, as is required to be represented in a transitive inference such as the following:

taller-than (Fred John)
taller-than (John Mike)
What is the height relationship between Fred and Mike?

Multiple relations must be bound into a structure, thus specifying six variable bindings (one higher order relation and two lower level relations each specifies two variable bindings). Thus, the difficulty in making inferences of this sort may stem from the number of role-filler bindings required.

The idea that people simultaneously and independently represent relations at multiple levels of complexity is also supported by findings that people identify correspondences among situations based on the similarity of relations among objects and events and that the tendency to use this kind of similarity in the making of inferences can be manipulated separately from the tendency to notice and use object similarity (Holyoak & Koh, 1987; Goldstone, Medin, & Gentner, 1991; Markman & Gentner, 1993). One example is a case in which reasoners are prompted to identify correspondences between two visual scenes: one in which a man is giving groceries to a woman and one in which a woman gives acorns to a squirrel (see Figure 13.1). Markman and Gentner (1993) observed that the tendency of reasoners to identify correspondences based on the similarity of roles played by different elements in relationships could be increased at the expense of their tendency to identify correspondences based on visual/object similarity by prompting subjects to simultaneously find correspondences for all three elements in each scene. Thus, in the case illustrated in Figure 13.1, the instruction to simultaneously find correspondences for all three elements in each scene led more reasoners to identify the man in the first situation as corresponding to the woman in the second situation because they both filled the role of "giver" in the relational system

gives (giver receiver gift).

When prompted only to identify correspondences for individual objects, subjects showed a significantly greater tendency to map the woman in the first scene to the woman in the second scene, based on perceptual attributes.

This result provides convincing evidence for the explicit representation of relations in reasoning, and that these representations can be used apart from lower level features in the identification of similarities among structured knowledge representations, as is required by analogical reasoning.

My colleagues and I (Waltz et al., 2000) directly examined the role of different working memory subsystems in the ability to represent different kinds of relational structures. We asked the question, "Does occupying working memory subsystems under dual-task conditions cause impairment in the ability to 'perceive' relational similarity?" Using a dual-task paradigm, we examined the role of different working memory processes in the performance of tasks dependent on structure mapping, i.e., tasks

(a)

(b)

FIGURE 13.1. Perceiving kinds of similarity. The performance of structure mapping increases the tendency to identify correspondences among situations on the basis of relationships, rather than attributes. Adapted with permission of Elsevier from Markman and Gentner (1993, p. 436, Figure 1). Copyright © 1993 by Elsevier.

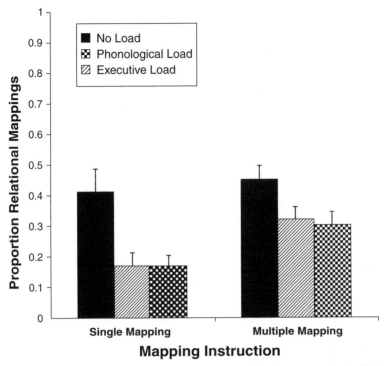

FIGURE 13.2. Effects of secondary tasks on analogical mapping. In both the single-mapping condition (A) and the multiple-mapping condition (B) the performance of a phonological or central executive distracter causes subjects to identify fewer correspondences on the basis of relationships. Adapted with permission of the Psychonomic Society, Inc. from Waltz, Lau, Grewal, and Holyoak (2000, p. 1210, Figure 3). Copyright © 2000 by the Psychonomic Society, Inc.

requiring subjects to perform mappings (to identify correspondences) among situations based on similarity of relationships among objects, rather than just object attributes, such as those described above and illustrated in Figure 13.1.

We found that a secondary task that reduced the availability of either phonological short-term memory resources or executive control resources was sufficient to significantly reduce the tendency of individuals to identify correspondences based on relations (structural similarity; see Figure 13.2). Importantly, subjects who performed the mapping task under dual-task conditions did not make unsystematic errors; rather, they increased their tendency to determine correspondences on the basis of object attributes (surface similarity). These results provide support for the idea that working memory plays an essential role in the online representation of relational structures and may be necessary for the retention of dynamic object-concept bindings. Representing bindings between single objects and their attributes, however, appears to be less susceptible to the effects of reduced working memory resources than representing systems of relations. The active representation of semantic relations in WM seems to involve both phonological storage and executive processes.

In the view of the above-described framework for quantifying relational complexity, the functional role of working memory in relational reasoning is this capacity to actively represent novel bindings between percepts and concepts (systems of relations, in the the case of analogy). There is now a large amount of psychological evidence in support of the idea that binding limitations provide a source of information processing limitations, in terms of both reasoning about concepts and actively representing objects in a given perceptual domain. As Wheeler and Treisman (2002) note, the need to dynamically represent feature bindings likely pertains to both working memory for, and attention to, visual objects. The idea that structured representations of objects comprise at least some of the contents of working memory comes from several sources (Irwin & Andrews, 1996; Luck & Vogel, 1997; Rensink, 2000; Treisman, 1992; Wheeler & Treisman, 2002). These authors have shown that visual working memory is not, or not only, limited in terms of the number of object features but also in terms of the number of objects, possibly independent of the number of features. That is to say: the capacity to actively represent objects may be limited less in terms of the number individual features in a scene and more in terms of the number of bindings of features to objects (or object files). This finding indicates that at least one source of capacity limitations for visual working memory comes from the need to bind object features into structured representations of objects. It also suggests that short-term memory for objects can be impaired either by disrupting temporary stores of features or by interfering with temporary stores of *feature bindings*. A number of studies have shown that short-term memory for objects, in fact, depends heavily upon attention to object features and is extremely susceptible to distraction (Treisman, Sykes, & Gelade, 1977; Stefurak & Boynton, 1986; Isenberg, Nidden, & Marchak, 1990; Simons, 1996; Horowitz & Wolfe, 1998). The idea that at least one source of capacity limitations for visual working memory comes from the need to bind object features into structured representations of *objects* fits extremely well with the framework of Halford, Wilson, and Phillips (1998) and the results of Waltz et al. (2000), in which limitations on information processing capacity stem from the need to represent the structure of *concepts*.

## CHARACTERIZING THE NEURAL BASIS OF RELATIONAL PROCESSING

The results of Waltz et al. (2000) appear to be consistent with the interpretation that the availability of what are often termed "information processing resources" have an effect on the *kinds* of mental representations individuals can form. The finding that the ability to represent complex relational structures can be impaired through limitations in working memory capacity, along with evidence that working memory limitations themselves might be quantified in terms of dynamic bindings, suggests that working memory and relational reasoning might share their neural substrate. Indeed, there is considerable evidence for this idea.

A large number of neuropsychological studies in humans indicate that damage to prefrontal cortex, in particular, has a detrimental effect on tasks involving hypothesis testing, rule-based categorization, planning, and abstract problem solving (e.g., Delis, Squire, Bihrle, & Massman, 1992; Milner & Petrides, 1984; Owen, Downes, Sahakian, Polkey, & Robbins, 1990; Shallice & Burgess, 1991), tasks that might be described in terms of the need to represent and manipulate abstract relations. The evidence from lesion studies in humans that prefrontal cortex plays an essential role in higher level cognition has also received considerable support from functional brain imaging studies in recent years, which have confirmed a role for human prefrontal cortex in many kinds of reasoning (Prabhakaran, Smith, Desmond, Glover, & Gabrieli, 1997; Osherson et al., 1998; Goel, Gold, Kapur, & Houle, 1998).

Many researchers have proposed that the reliance of higher level cognitive processing on prefrontal cortex stems from the role played by prefrontal cortex in working memory function, based on the large amount of evidence indicating that primate prefrontal cortex also figures prominently in the maintenance of information in STM. These results come from both electrophysiological experiments in nonhuman primates and functional brain imaging studies involving human subjects (for reviews, see Fuster, 1995; Goldman-Rakic, 1996; Smith & Jonides, 1997).

In addition to brain lesions, a wide variety of neuropsychiatric conditions can lead to impaired cognitive binding capacity, whether it is in terms of perceptual disturbances, problems of sensorimotor integration, or deficits in long- and/or short-term memory. It is proposed here that one might account for deficits in higher level cognition that might result from neuropsychiatric illness, stress, or advanced age, in terms of the reliance of specific tasks/functions on dynamic binding in the representation of relations. That is to say: one might account for different kinds of binding impairments by understanding the kinds of relational structures that individuals can represent behaviorally and through neuroscientific analyses of cognitive binding, which increase our knowledge of the functional anatomy and neuronal mechanisms underlying binding. In this section, I will discuss how psychological and physiological measures of cognitive binding in working memory might help us to earlier diagnose, monitor treatment, and potentially identify subgroups of patients with degenerative brain disorders affecting higher level cognitive abilities. In a pair of studies, we (Waltz et al., 1999, 2004) sought to determine whether specific kinds of brain damage would affect the particular *kinds* of relational representation that individuals could process. We investigated the specific hypothesis that focal brain degeneration affecting prefrontal cortex would produce a specific impairment in the ability to solve problems requiring the integration of relations into structures.

We specifically examined higher level cognitive function in patients with two degenerative brain disorders: frontotemporal dementia (FTD) and Alzheimer's disease (AD). Frontotemporal dementia is a rare degenerative disorder of uncertain etiology, characterized by relatively focal degeneration of frontal or temporal cortical areas in early stages, after which the degenerative process may subsume large areas of both frontal and temporal cortex either unilaterally or bilaterally. Alzheimer's disease, on the other hand, is the most common cause of dementia and is characterized by global cortical atrophy, resulting in deficits in declarative memory function and other cognitive domains. Although frontal cortical dysfunction is associated with disturbances in executive capacities required for higher level cognitive processing, dysfunction in anterior temporal regions has been linked to deficits in semantic knowledge (Graham & Hodges, 1997; Hodges, Patterson, Oxbury, & Funnell, 1992). Dementia associated with AD is also characterized by a variety of impairments in higher level cognitive abilities. These deficits involve executive capacities (Lafleche & Albert, 1995; Perry & Hodges, 1999 and the ability to identify similarities between objects or concepts (Martin & Fedio, 1983; Pillon, Dubois, Lhermitte, & Agid, 1986; Huber, Shuttleworth, & Freidenberg, 1989) and to comprehend proverbs (Kempler, van Lancker, & Read, 1988). The results of additional studies suggest that individuals with AD experience particular difficulty in what have been termed "generational abilities," an idea closely related to the capacity to perform inductive inference (Cronin-Golomb, Rho, Corkin, & Growdon, 1987) and difficulty in the performance of tasks of cognitive estimation, another form of inference (Goldstein et al., 1996; Mendez, Doss, & Cherrier, 1998; Shallice & Evans, 1978; Smith & Milner, 1984). Furthermore, when one examines more closely memory deficits in AD, ample evidence indicates that, in many cases, short-term memory deficits, in particular, can often be attributed to failures of executive control, rather than impairments in short-term phonological memory (Morris & Baddeley, 1988).

In the first study (Waltz et al., 1999), we tested the hypothesis that prefrontal cortical damage would impair the ability to represent relational structures by examining two subgroups of patients in the early stages of FTD – those for whom the degenerative process began focally in the frontal lobes and those for whom brain dysfunction initiated in the anterior regions of the temporal lobes. It was predicted that the online integration of relations (i.e., the dynamic representation of relations in working memory) would be disrupted by prefrontal cortical damage but not by anterior temporal damage leading to losses in crystallized semantic knowledge.

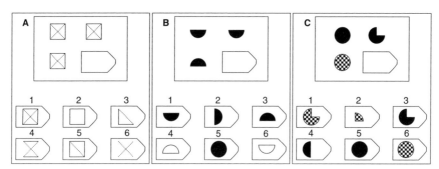

FIGURE 13.3. Sample visuospatial matrix problems. This task required subjects to choose the item from the bottom of the figure that would complete the pattern at the top. (A) A nonrelational problem (relational complexity level 0), requiring only perceptual matching (correct response is choice 1). (B) A one-relation problem (relational complexity level 1), requiring participants to retain the transformation across only one dimension in selecting the correct answer (Choice 3). A two-relation problem, requiring participants to integrate relational transformations across both the horizontal and vertical dimensions in order to make the correct response (Choice 1). Adapted with permission of the Blackwell Publishing from Waltz et al. (1999, p. 121, Figure 2). Copyright © 1999 by the Blackwell Publishing.

We presented two sets of problems, which varied in whether or not they required the integration of relations in the making of inferences, to two subgroups of patients with FTD and controls: visuospatial matrix problems (see Figure 13.3) similar to problems from the Raven Progressive Matrices Test (Raven, 1976), and visually presented transitive inference problems, consisting of sets of propositions describing size relationships of individuals.

We found that patients with focal degeneration of frontal cortex showed systematic impairment in relational reasoning, in that damage to frontal cortex selectively impaired the ability to represent systems of relations online. These patients showed similar patterns of impairment on two distinct relational processing measures: one requiring subjects to *deduce* the correct magnitude relationship among objects from verbal premises and a second requiring subjects to *generate* the appropriate solution to visuospatial analogy problems by *inducing* rules describing the relationships among neighboring objects. Although patients with frontal cortical degeneration showed no impairment on problems not requiring the manipulation of conceptual relations or on problems requiring the manipulation of single conceptual relations in isolation, they performed at chance levels on problems requiring the integration of conceptual relations into structures, relative to controls, and patients with focal anterior temporal cortical degeneration matched closely in terms of age, educational attainment, IQ, and stage of disease. Patients with focal degeneration of frontal cortex demonstrated

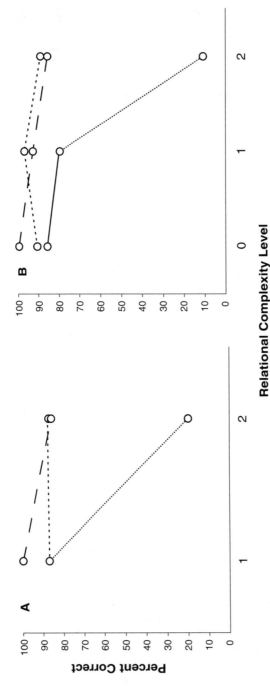

FIGURE 13.4. Effects of brain lesions on relational processing. (A) Results for transitive inference problems from individuals with prefrontal cortical damage (solid line), patients with anterior temporal damage (dotted lines), and normal controls (dashed lines). Standard errors ranged from 8 to 20%. (B) Results for visuospatial matrix problems from participant groups. Legend as in (A). Adapted with permission of the Blackwell Publishing from Waltz et al. (1999, p. 122, Figure 3). Copyright ©1999 by the Blackwell Publishing.

superior performance on tests of declarative memory and semantic knowledge relative to patients with focal anterior temporal cortical degeneration, indicating that these patients did not suffer from a nonspecific dementia affecting almost all aspects of memory and abstract cognition (Figure 13.4).

In a second study, we (Waltz et al., 2004) administered patients with a diagnosis of probable Alzheimer's disease and age- and education-matched control participants the same measures of working memory and reasoning described in the discussion of Waltz et al. (1999), which varied systematically in their relational complexity. Whereas Alzheimer-type dementia is characterized by impairments in higher level cognitive abilities, the extent to which higher level cognitive deficits in AD result from domain-general executive dysfunction is not clear, given that many high-level cognitive tasks require multiple cognitive abilities. Thus, it is important to use tasks in which specific components of executive function can be examined. Furthermore, the neuropathological heterogeneity of patients with AD raises the possibility that executive deficits may be present in only a subset of those patients with mild or moderate AD. Brain imaging investigations (O'Brien, Eagger, Syed, Sahakian, & Levy, 1992; Eberling, Reed, Baker, & Jagust, 1993; Brown et al., 1996) have revealed that a subset of AD patients show reduced activity in frontal cortex associated with impaired executive function. Furthermore, Grady and colleagues (1990) successfully identified four subgroups of AD patients: a temporo–parietal group, a paralimbic group, a left hemisphere group, and a fronto–parietal group, finding that differences among the groups were reflected in cognitive and behavioral measures.

We found that AD patients showed a distinctive pattern of performance on measures of relational reasoning, relative to age- and education-matched control participants, in that they exhibited impairment on problems requiring the integration of multiple relations but not single relations. In contrast, performance of the AD group was relatively good on one-relation problems. When the sample of AD patients was divided into subgroups, based on their relational integration ability, patients who performed poorly on relational integration measures exhibited a marked deficit in performance on three standard measures of executive function, relative to AD patients who showed little or no impairment on relational integration measures. Both patient subgroups performed as well as control participants on problems requiring only the manipulation of single relations in isolation. These results suggest that a subset of patients with AD may resemble frontal patients in terms of deficits in relational reasoning (Waltz et al., 1999). These data also indicate that relational integration tasks may be sensitive to prefrontal cortical dysfunction in AD and may be useful for detecting prefrontal dysfunction in a variety of neurological conditions.

These results were interpreted as indicating that cognitive processes that rely on intact prefrontal cortex (e.g. abstract problem-solving abilities, cognitive executive functions) do so because they require the dynamic representations of relational systems. Developmental and comparative psychological studies provide evidence for a step-wise emergence of relational processing capacities across ontogeny and phylogeny. Results described above suggest that damage to neural substrates underlying relational processing could lead to a step-wise *decrement* in relational processing capacities. The fact that such deficits were particularly prevalent in patients with prefrontal cortical dysfunction suggests that PFC provides an essential neural substrate for the representation of relational structures. The large body of research linking prefrontal cortical function to working memory capacities further underlines the possibility of a close relationship between working memory and the dynamic binding of representations into relational structures. The fact that both relational reasoning and cognitive executive function appear to rely on the same neural substrate fits well with the idea that the dynamic binding of object into relations, and relations into structures, comprises an essential aspect of cognitive executive, and thus working memory, function.

The use of psychological measures that quantify the complexity of problems from neuropsychological tests in terms of relations, as we have done, might provide a means for better understanding the types of problems that cause particular difficulty for individuals with impaired cognitive executive capacities resulting from frontal lobe dysfunction. The use of behavioral measures based on quantifying the relational complexity of problems, accompanied by electrophysiological and cerebral metabolic measures, might be particularly effective in aiding the diagnosis of specific degenerative disorders. Different degenerative disorders have different etiologies and different pharmacological treatments. Therefore, early diagnosis can help in arresting the degenerative process before dementia becomes severe.

## IMPLICATIONS FOR THEORIES OF COGNITIVE EXECUTIVE FUNCTION AND ITS NEURAL BASIS

While psychological evidence points to a role for working memory in cognitive control processes and higher level cognitive faculties, an explanation of *how* working memory fulfills this function – of how working memory enables cognitive control – has remained lacking. The investigations of the human working memory system done by Baddeley and colleagues (see Baddeley, 1986) accomplished much in establishing that various modality-specific short-term memory processes can operate largely independently. One of the main shortcomings of this model, however, is the vagueness with which it specifies the nature of functions of the central executive module of this system. Although there is general agreement on a role for working memory in abstract thought, there is considerable *disagreement* regarding the specific contribution of working memory to abstract thought, as one might expect, because there are many different conceptions of the essential nature of working memory.

Characterizing the contents and capacity limitations of the central executive module of working memory has proven to be a particularly difficult problem, and the central executive has often been treated like a "black box" or "homunculus" in many models of thought. Although many models of working memory and higher level cognitive function include an explicit central executive component, there is still considerable debate as to whether a single central executive module exerts control over cognition. Alternatively, animals may use a number of higher level schemas to exert control over lower level schemas. An explicit central executive is conspicuously absent from man-made cognitive systems engineered based on the two major frameworks of computational models of cognition: production systems and connectionist systems. This lack of an explicit central executive is a feature of both artificial intelligence systems in the domains of engineering and computer science, as well as computational models designed to simulate human cognitive processing in the cognitive psychology tradition. In both of these kinds of systems, actions and outputs are selected through a process of response competition, in which the most highly activated response is selected (based on inputs from a number of sources).

The results of psychological studies of reasoning argue persuasively that human cognition is characterized by a capacity for processing *symbols*. That is, human thinking is typified by the explicit representation of abstract concepts, which can be passed as arguments to schemas or rules for action. To say that symbols can be passed as arguments is to say that they can be bound as fillers to task-relevant roles (i.e., as values to variables), which are specified by conditional rules or action plans. The idea that reasoning involves bindings of values to variables has important implications, potentially, for the discussion of information processing (e.g., working memory) capacity limits. It is proposed here that the consideration of (a) the role of structured knowledge representations in reasoning and (b) the necessity of representing variable bindings dynamically in symbolic processing enables us to make much more specific statements about the nature of cognitive executive processes and their role in abstract thinking (and about the functions of prefrontal cortex), which so often has been linked to cognitive executive function and dysfunction. When one posits that dynamic bindings can be the *contents* of working memory, as well as the source of working memory limitations, one can say that *cognitive executive functions depend on the representation of relational structure, which, in turn, depends on a mechanism for dynamic binding*. In other words, it is argued here that the capacity for dynamic cognitive binding is what makes executive function possible, because it enables the representation of goal hierarchies and the spatiotemporal context in which those goals are to be achieved. I argue that this is a more precise statement than, "Cognitive executive functions depend on working memory, which includes a central executive module."

Dysfunction of prefrontal cortex in humans, as was described above, has most commonly been linked to the emergence of a "dysexecutive syndrome," in which individuals show increased difficulty in suppressing reflexive behaviors and in engaging in complex, goal-directed behaviors. Several theories exist as to what unites tasks and environments in which individuals with frontal lobe lesions exhibit abnormal behavior. For example, higher level cognitive impairments in patients with frontal lobe lesions frequently have been linked to a general inability to inhibit prepotent responses, as is evidenced by the frequency of perseverative errors made by patients with frontal lobe lesions on the Wisconsin Card Sorting Test (WCST); for example, see (Milner, 1963). Difficulty in inhibiting prepotent responses is also evidenced by the poor performance of frontal lobe lesion patients on the Stroop task (Perret, 1974) and on the anti-saccade task (Guitton, Buchtel, & Douglas, 1985). In this framework, an inability to override default responses to stimuli can explain most or all cognitive impairments linked to frontal lobe damage related to abstract problem-solving tasks dependent on reasoning and planning. What is lacking, however, is a more detailed characterization of why and how controlled, flexible, goal-directed behavior breaks down as a consequence of frontal lobe damage, described in terms of how abstract thought is structured and complex action plans are selected. This chapter represents an attempt to answer the question of how working memory systems and their neural substrates participate in *higher level cognition*, arguing that progress in this domain requires a better understanding of how working memory systems and their neural substrates participate in the *representation of structured knowledge*.

The above-described framework from Halford et al. (1998) for quantifying information-processing demands according to relational complexity provides a mechanism for describing "cognitive executive functions" in terms of their relational structure, i.e., their reliance on dynamic binding, which, in turn, allows us to characterize the dependence of cognitive executive functions on working memory in a less circular way. A conception of working memory in which the contents are dynamic bindings might account for the apparent role of working memory in the performance of "executive" tasks requiring the inhibition of prepotent responses and the like. I argue that dynamic binding allows for the representation of action plans as well as the context in which the action must occur, because dynamic binding allows for the representation of relational structures, of which goal hierarchies and spatiotemporal context are special cases. In specific, I will describe examples of how one can describe executive functions in terms of their relational complexity.

Planning has been described by Halford et al. (1998) as depending on relational integration in that goals are special cases of relations; specifically, they are relations that specify a transformation from a start state to a goal state. Thus, the need to represent a relation between a goal and a subordinate subgoal amounts to representing a relation between relations. The idea that human prefrontal cortex is essential for the integration of relations may account for impairments exhibited by PFC lesion patients on measures of planning, such as the Tower of London and Tower of Hanoi tasks. Halford et al. (1998) illustrate how the relational complexity of a plan increases with the number of embedded subgoals. This analysis also shows how a concept of working memory capacity in terms of the complexity of relational representations that can be dynamically constructed, and the number of variable bindings that they specify, is entirely compatible with a notion of working memory capacity in terms of the level of embedding in a goal hierarchy.

Previous formulations, based on production-system models of cognition (e.g., Anderson, 1983; Kimberg & Farah, 1993), have alluded to the idea that knowledge is represented in a propositional and structured manner in working memory, thus allowing for the representation of goal-hierarchies. Other researchers have expressed similar ideas, attributing higher level cognitive impairments in frontal-lobe-lesion patients, especially in terms of planning, to a general problem of goal-neglect (Duncan, Emslie, Williams, Johnson, & Freer, 1996). That is, patients with frontal-lobe lesions are believed to have difficulty keeping an overarching goal in mind when they need to execute a subgoal. Grafman (1994) has also emphasized the structured nature of knowledge representations, describing managerial knowledge units (MKUs) and structured event complexes (SECs), which, he proposes, reside in prefrontal cortex as kinds of schemas. He and his colleagues (Grafman, Sirigu, Spector, & Hendler, 1993) recounted evidence that prefrontal cortical damage leads to a breakdown of structured knowledge representations. A reduced capacity to represent associations among goals in working memory would also result in what Fuster (1989) has termed "loss of set." The idea of preparatory set also relates closely to planning functions, in that preparatory set might correspond to the overarching goal of an action plan. All of the previously mentioned concepts of executive function are fully compatible with the theory of relational complexity proposed by Halford et al. (1998). Describing the nature of relational structures in the mind, however, enables one to account not only for the structure of action, but also for the structure of knowledge in declarative memory.

Neuropsychological studies have revealed that prefrontal cortex figures prominently in declarative memory processes related to both encoding and retrieval. It is of note that many of the memory deficits observed in association with lesions of prefrontal cortex point to an impairment in the ability to represent and encode information in a structured manner. At least three memory functions frequently impaired in PFC lesion patients appear to involve the encoding of structured information: memory for the spatiotemporal context of learning, memory for serial order, and metamemory judgments. The first two of these capacities involve the ability to remember not only a stimulus in isolation, but also, in relation to other items, either those that comprise the context of a learning event or those that precede or follow a stimulus in time. Thus, these memory functions rely upon the ability to both represent and remember the structure of events, both in a particular instance and across time. Metamemory can be viewed as a related capacity, in that it depends on the ability to remember the encoding event.

Finally, it is proposed that those standard neuropsychological tasks that have been deemed "executive" tasks, sensitive to prefrontal cortical damage, are united by the fact that they require the explicit, dynamic representation of variable bindings. Examples of such tasks include the Wisconsin Card Sorting Test, the Stroop task, the similarities subtest of the WAIS-R, the digit span backward subtest of the WAIS-R (but not the digit span forward subtest), and the Trailmaking test (Part B). The idea that PFC is essential for relational integration implies that it should be required for the performance of any task involving the integration of a variable cue with a variable stimulus, regardless of the delay between cue and test. In this framework, the dynamic representation of relational structure makes possible the overriding of a prepotent response, because it involves the recoding of the stimulus as a variable and it enables the establishment of a higher level rule to supersede the dominant stimulus-response association.

In the case of the Stroop task, for example, the dynamic representation of variable stimulus dimensions is necessary to overcome the automatic response of reading when the stimulus is a word. If the stimulus can be dynamically represented as having a variable color and a variable word, then a new response can be associated with a particular binding (e.g., if the instruction is to name the color, then identify the color of the word). Part B of the Trailmaking test requires individuals to alternately follow two incremental series, one alphabetic and one numeric, and thus is similar to the multiple series letter sequences in experiment 1 of this manuscript. The similarities subtest of the WAIS-R is significant in that many items require test-takers to identify *relational* similarities among concepts on the basis of roles played in relational systems. The digit span backwards subtest requires individuals to remember the exact position in which every digit in a string was presented, so that the reverse of the list can be reconstructed. This requires the maintenance of a large number of position-digit bindings.

Recent studies using functional brain imaging techniques and electrophysiological recording techniques have begun to provide more direct evidence for the idea that primate prefrontal cortex plays a critical role in the representation of relations through dynamic binding. Several studies indicate that specific prefrontal areas might be distinguished based on the *kinds* of dynamic bindings that they help to represent. For example, the results of several studies (Koechlin, Basso, Pietrini, Panzer, & Grafman, 1999; Kroger et al., 2002) suggest that frontal polar cortex (Area 10) plays a particularly important role in the representation of relational structures related to concepts and action plans. Koechlin et al. (1999) demonstrated that frontal polar cortex (Area 10) shows increased activation under conditions of multitasking and concluded that this area plays a prominent role in the representation of relations among subgoals in the construction of abstract action plans. More recently, Kroger et al. (2002) provided direct evidence that fMRI activation in frontal polar cortex increases in a stepwise fashion with the relational complexity of visuospatial analogy problems.

Functional brain imaging studies of working memory have also begun to provide direct support for the hypothesis that the essential role of prefrontal cortex in working memory may relate to the need to represent relations/dynamic bindings. D'Esposito et al. (1995), for instance, showed that mid-dorsolateral PFC (Area 46) plays a critical role in the manipulation of information in short-term memory but less of a role in the simple retention or rehearsal of information. More recent studies (Prabhakaran, Narayanan, Zhao, & Gabrieli, 2000; Mitchell, Johnson, Raye, & D'Esposito, 2000; Munk et al., 2002) provided evidence that an area of superior prefrontal cortex plays a particular role in short-term memory for feature conjunctions.

In the past several years, microelectrode recording studies in nonhuman primates have provided evidence that prefrontal cortex in the macaque plays an important role in the representation of feature bindings, concepts, and symbols. Using the delayed matching-to-sample paradigm, Earl Miller and colleagues have shown that neurons in macaque PFC respond selectively to stimuli that occupy particular locations in space (Rao, Rainer, & Miller, 1997) or to particular roles in the task (such as sample or test stimulus; Rainer, Asaad, & Miller, 1998). These results suggest that PFC neurons code not only for stimulus features, but also for bindings among objects and concepts. Subsequent studies have shown that neurons in macaque PFC selectively respond to object categories (such as dog; Freedman, Riesenhuber, Poggio, & Miller, 2002), quantities of objects (Nieder, Freedman, & Miller, 2002), and abstract rules in which objects participate (Wallis, Anderson, & Miller, 2001), independent of the specific sample or cue stimulus.

Although it is doubtful that single neurons code for all possible bindings between features, or for all possible bindings between object and task role (see below), the fact that single neurons *emerge* that selectively respond to bindings suggests that prefrontal cortex at least plays an important role in processing bindings of this sort and in recruiting single neurons to represent the most commonly experienced bindings. The question of how this might happen is itself one of great importance.

## GENERAL CONCLUSIONS: PSYCHOPATHOLOGY, COGNITIVE LIMITATIONS, AND STRESS

Results described above have the potential to add to our understanding of the nature and role dynamic binding in human thought. First, results point to a close relationship between dynamic binding processes in cognition and the functioning of a working memory system, especially in terms of this system's reliance of so-called executive processes. Secondly, neuroscientific analyses indicate that prefrontal cortical areas play an important role in the representation of relational structures in humans. A better understanding of the psychological and neural bases of cognitive binding has important applications in a number of domains, including engineering (for example, in designing hardware and software to recognize objects in the environment) and education (in understanding situation- and individual-specific binding impairments). Potentially, the most vital application of an increased knowledge of cognitive binding mechanisms, however, is in the field of mental health, in the attempt to understand and therapeutically treat cognitive binding deficits that occur as a consequence of neuropsychiatric illness, stress, or advanced age.

The previous sections described examples of impairments of cognitive binding linked to neurologic and psychiatric illness, as well as their neural correlates. In the examples described above, psychopathology is the cause of cognitive limitations. The question of *how* various forms of psychopathology bring about reduced cognitive capacity is obviously a complicated one, but basic neuroscientific research has produced many examples of how abnormal physiological processes associated with neuropsychiatric illness involve processes related to cognitive processes such as memory and attention. Various neuropsychiatric conditions, for example, have been linked to the dysfunction of diffuse neuromodulatory systems, such as those for the substances acetylcholine, dopamine, serotonin, and norepinephrine – neurotransmitters that have also been shown to be critically involved in processes of memory and attention.

As other chapters in this volume make abundantly clear, however, impairments of cognitive binding related to working memory and executive function need not be the product of psychiatric illness; they appear in association with numerous other phenomena, such as aging, stress, and divided attention (see West & Alain, 2000, for a discussion of ERP correlates of attention lapses). Temporary stress and anxiety are well known to acutely influence higher level cognitive functioning (Tohill & Holyoak, 2000; Darke, 1988). Although the binding impairments related to psychiatric illness might be related to chronic brain metabolic and electrophysiological abnormalities, binding impairments resulting from stress or distraction could be because of momentary disturbances of neural mechanisms of cognitive binding.

Furthermore, a considerable body of work demonstrates that stress frequently exacerbates psychopathology (Dohrenwend, 2000). Although stress alone does not cause conditions such as Alzheimer's disease, frontotemporal dementia, schizophrenia, or Parkinson's disease (the expression of which appear to require at least a disposition created by genetic and environmental factors, such as exposure to neurotoxins), stress can influence the expression of psychopathology – the onset and the severity – as well as the therapeutic response to it. In addition, although stress alone likely does not produce neuropsychiatric syndromes, such as those listed above, stressful events often directly precede the first severe expressions of such conditions requiring clinical treatment. Finally, chronic stress does have significant detrimental effects on cognitive abilities, even if it does not result in the emergence of a neuropsychiatric syndrome. The physiological effects of chronic stress can cause irreversible damage to brain structures that play prominent roles of process of memory and attention, such as the hippocampus (McEwan, 1999; Lupien & Lepage, 2001).

The conceptualization of binding impairments related to neuropsychiatric illness has the potential to shed light on cognitive binding deficits that occur as a consequence of aging, stress, and the course of everyday life, because it is possible, even likely, that they have the same neural underpinnings. There are several reasons for believing this. First, stress, anxiety, and mood disorders are known to influence working memory performance (MacLeod & Donnellan, 1993), as well as the activity of the neural circuits upon which working memory is thought to depend. These include both cortical–subcortical pathways and diffuse modulatory systems, such as the dopamine system (Arnsten, 2000; Deutsch & Roth, 1990; Bertolucci-D'Angio, Serrano, Driscoll, & Scatton, 1990). Second, stress (along with neuromodulatory systems in the cortex) is known to modify the motivational state of animals (Weiss & Glazer, 1975; Bowers, Attias, & Amit, 1999) and to influence arousal and attention (Chajut & Algom, 2003; Ellenbogen, Schwartzman, Stewart, & Walker, 2002; Mogg & Bradley, 1999). This is critical in that, as discussed earlier, working memory is a goal-directed process that plays a role in the representation of plans and whose contents are influenced by the focus of attention.

Thus, it is important to understand the interactions among stress, pathophysiology, and cognitive function as a dynamic in terms of the pairwise interactions. We need to understand not only the mechanisms by which forms of pathophysiology lead to cognitive limitations, but also how stress influences these mechanisms. Consequently, we would do well to understand both the effects *and* causes of stress. As other chapters in this volume have emphasized, social psychological phenomena, such as stereotyping and test anxiety, can bring about stress. In this manner, cognitive limitations could participate in a positive feedback circuit that could exacerbate pathophysiological processes and, as a consequence, further worsen cognitive limitations resulting from psychopathology. Understanding the role of stress and anxiety in disrupting abstract thought might require a strategy similar to that required for understanding the role of schizophrenia or Alzheimer's disease in disrupting abstract thought. That is to say, we need to understand the structure of the cognitive processes that are disrupted, the influence of anxiety on action plans and other cognitive representations at the psychological level, and the influence of anxiety on brain structures and processes related to dynamic binding.

## Author Note

Much of the research reported was funded by grants from the John Douglas French Foundation for Alzheimer's Research, the James A. McDonnell Foundation, and a predoctoral National Research Service Award from the National Institutes of Health, Publich Health Service, Department of Health and Human Services. I am grateful to Dr. Barbara Knowlton, Dr. Keith Holyoak, and Dr. Christina Fales for their helpful comments on earlier versions of this manuscript.

## References

Anderson, J. R. (1983). *The architecture of cognition*. Cambridge, MA: Harvard University Press.

Arnsten, A. F. T. (2000). Stress impairs prefrontal cortical function in rats and monkeys: Role of dopamine D1 and norepinephrine alpha-1 receptor mechanisms. In H. B. M. Uylings, C. G. van Eden, J. P. D. de Bruin, M. G. P. Feenstra, & C. M. A. Pennartz (Eds.), *Progress in brain research 126: Cognition, emotion and autonomic responses: The integrative role of the prefrontal cortex and limbic structures* (pp. 183–192). Amsterdam: Elsevier.

Baddeley, A. D. (1986). *Working memory*. Oxford: Oxford University Press.

Baddeley, A. D., & Hitch, G. (1974). Working memory. In G. H. Bower (Ed.), *The psychology of learning and motivation: Advances in research and theory* (Vol. 8). New York: Academic Press.

Bertolucci-D'Angio, M., Serrano, A., Driscoll, P., & Scatton, B. (1990). Involvement of the mesocorticolimbic dopaminergic systems in emotional states. In H. B. M. Uylings, C. G. van Eden, J. P. D. de Bruin, M. A. Corner, & M. G. P. Feenstra (Eds.), *Progress in brain research 85: The prefrontal cortex: Its structure, function, and pathology* (pp. 405–417). Amsterdam: Elsevier.

Bowers, W. J., Attias, E., & Amit, Z. (1999). Stress enhances the response to reward reduction but not food-motivated responding. *Physiology & Behavior, 67,* 777–782.

Brown, D. R. P., Hunter, R., Wyper, D. J., Patterson, J., Kelly, R. C., Montaldi, D., & McCulloch, J. (1996). Longitudinal changes in cognitive function and regional cerebral function in Alzheimer's disease: A SPECT blood flow study. *Journal of Psychiatric Research, 30,* 109–126.

Carpenter, P. A., Just, M. A., & Shell, P. (1990). What one intelligence test measures: A theoretical account of the processing in the Raven Progressive Matrices Test. *Psychological Review, 97*, 404–431.

Chajut, E., & Algom, D. (2003). Selective attention improves under stress: Implications for theories of social cognition. *Journal of Personality & Social Psychology, 85*, 231–248.

Cheng, P. W., & Holyoak, K. J. (1985). Pragmatic reasoning schemas. *Cognitive Psychology, 17*, 391–416.

Cheng, P. W., & Holyoak, K. J. (1989). On the natural selection of reasoning theories. *Cognition, 33*, 285–313.

Cronin-Golomb, A., Rho, W. A., Corkin, S., & Growdon, J. H. (1987). Abstract reasoning in age-related neurological disease. *Journal of Neural Transmission: Supplement, 24*, 79–83.

Daneman, M., & Carpenter, P. A. (1980). Individual differences in working memory and reading. *Journal of Verbal Learning & Verbal Behavior, 19*, 450–466.

Darke, S. (1988). Effects of anxiety on inferential reasoning task performance. *Journal of Personality & Social Psychology, 55*, 499–505.

Delis, D. C., Squire, L. R., Bihrle, A., & Massman, P. (1992). Componential analysis of problem solving ability: Performance of patients with frontal lobe damage and amnesic patients on a new sorting task. *Neuropsychologia, 30*, 683–697.

D'Esposito, M., Detre, J. A., Alsop, D. C., Shin, R. K., Atlas, S., & Grossman, M. (1996). The neural basis of the central executive system of working memory. *Nature, 378*, 279–281.

Deutsch, A. Y., & Roth, R. H. (1990). The determinants of stress-induced activation of the prefrontal cortical dopamine system. In H. B. M. Uylings, C. G. van Eden, J. P. D. de Bruin, M. A. Corner, & M. G. P. Feenstra (Eds.), *Progress in brain research 85: The prefrontal cortex: Its structure, function, and pathology* (pp. 367–403). Amsterdam: Elsevier.

Dohrenwend, B. (2000). The role of adversity and stress in psychopathology: Some evidence and its implications for theory and research. *Journal of Health and Social Behavior, 41*, 1–19.

Dunbar, K., & Sussman, D. (1995). Toward a cognitive account of frontal lobe function: Simulating frontal lobe deficits in normal participants. In J. Grafman, K. J. Holyoak, & F. Boller (Eds.), *Annals of the New York Academy of Sciences, Vol. 769: Structure and functions of the human prefrontal cortex* (pp. 289–304). New York: New York Academy of Sciences.

Duncan, J., Emslie, H., Williams, P., Johnson, R., & Freer, C. (1996). Intelligence and the frontal lobe: The organization of goal-directed behavior. *Cognitive Psychology, 30*, 257–303.

Eberling, J. L., Reed, B. R., Baker, M. G., & Jagust, W. J. (1993). Cognitive correlates of regional cerebral blood flow in Alzheimer's disease. *Archives of Neurology, 50*, 761–766.

Ellenbogen, M. A., Schwartzman, A. E., Stewart, J., & Walker, C.-D. (2002). Stress and selective attention: The interplay of mood, cortisol levels, and emotional information processing. *Psychophysiology, 39*, 723–732.

Engle, R. W. (2002). Working memory capacity as executive attention. *Current Directions in Psychological Science, 11*, 19–23.

Engle, R. W., Tuholski, S. W., Laughlin, J. E., & Conway, A. R. (1999). Working memory, short-term memory, and general fluid intelligence: A latent-variable approach. *Journal of Experimental Psychology: General, 128*, 309–331.

Fodor, J. A., & Pylyshyn, Z. W. (1988). Connectionism and cognitive architecture: A critical analysis. *Cognition, 28*, 3–71.

Freedman, D. J., Riesenhuber, M., Poggio, T., & Miller, E. K. (2002). Categorical representation of visual stimuli in the primate prefrontal cortex. *Science, 291*, 312–316.

Fuster, J. M. (1989). *The prefrontal cortex* (2nd ed.). New York: Raven Press.

Fuster, J. M. (1995). *Memory in the cerebral cortex: An empirical approach to neural networks in the human and nonhuman primate.* Cambridge, MA: MIT Press.

Gentner, D. (1983). Structure-mapping: A theoretical framework for analogy. *Cognitive Science, 7*, 155–170.

Gick, M. L., & Holyoak, K. J. (1980). Analogical problem solving. *Cognitive Psychology, 12*, 306–355.

Gick, M. L., & Holyoak, K. J. (1983). Schema induction and analogical transfer. *Cognitive Psychology, 15*, 1–38.

Gilhooly, K. J., Logie, R. H., Wetherick, N. E., & Wynn, V. (1993). Working memory and strategies in syllogistic-reasoning tasks. *Memory & Cognition, 21*, 115–124.

Goel, V., Gold, B., Kapur, S., & Houle, S. (1998). Neuroanatomical correlates of human reasoning. *Journal of Cognitive Neuroscience, 10*, 293–302.

Goldman-Rakic, P. S. (1996). The prefrontal landscape: implications of functional architecture for understanding human mentation and the central executive. *Philosophical Transactions of the Royal Society of London, Series B, 351*, 1445–1453.

Goldstein, F. C., Green, J., Presley, R., O'Jile, J., Freeman, A., Watts, R., & Green, R. C. (1996). Cognitive estimation in patients with Alzheimer's disease. *Neuropsychiatry, Neuropsychology, & Behavioral Neurology, 9*, 35–42.

Goldstone, R. L., Medin, D. L., & Gentner, D. (1991). Relational similarity and the nonindependence of features in similarity judgments. *Cognitive Psychology, 23*, 222–262.

Grady, C. L., Haxby, J. V., Schapiro, M. B., Gonzalez-Aviles, A., Kumar, A., Ball, M. J., Heston, L., & Rapoport, S. I. (1990). Subgroups in dementia of the Alzheimer type identified using positron emission tomography. *Journal of Neuropsychiatry & Clinical Neurosciences, 2*, 373–384.

Grafman, J. (1994). Neuropsychology of the prefrontal cortex. In D. W. Zaidel (Ed.), *Handbook of perception and cognition: Neuropsychology* (pp. 159–181). San Diego, CA: Academic Press.

Grafman, J., Sirigu, A., Spector, L., & Hendler, J. (1993). Damage to the prefrontal cortex leads to decomposition of structured event complexes. *Journal of Head Trauma Rehabilitation, 8*, 73–87.

Graham, K. S., & Hodges, J. R. (1997). Differentiating the roles of the hippocampal complex and the neocortex in long-term memory storage: Evidence from the study of semantic dementia and Alzheimer's disease. *Neuropsychology, 11*, 77–89.

Guitton, D., Buchtel, H. A., & Douglas, R. M. (1985). Frontal lobe lesions in man cause difficulties in suppressing reflexive glances and in generating goal-directed saccades. *Experimental Brain Research, 58*, 455–472.

Halford, G. S. (1993). *Children's understanding: The development of mental models.* Hillsdale, NJ: Lawrence Erlbaum Associates.

Halford, G. S., Bain, J. D., Maybery, M. T., & Andrews, G. (1996). Induction of relational schemas: Common processes in reasoning and complex learning. *Cognitive Psychology, 35,* 201–245.

Halford, G. S., Wilson, W. H., & Phillips, S. (1998). Processing capacity defined by relational complexity: Implications for comparative, developmental, and cognitive psychology. *Behavioural and Brain Sciences, 21,* 803–831, 860–864.

Hodges, J. R., Patterson, K., Oxbury, S., & Funnell, E. (1992). Semantic dementia: Progressive fluent aphasia with temporal lobe atrophy. *Brain, 115,* 1783–1806.

Holyoak, K. J., & Koh, K. (1987). Surface and similarity in analogical transfer. *Memory and Cognition, 15,* 332–340.

Horowitz, T. S., & Wolfe, J. M. (1998). Visual search has no memory. *Nature, 394,* 575–577.

Huber, S. J., Shuttleworth, E. C., & Freidenberg, D. L. (1989). Neuropsychological differences between the dementias of Alzheimer's and Parkinson's diseases. *Archives of Neurology, 46,* 1287–1291.

Irwin, D. E., & Andrews, R. V. (1996). Integration and accumulation of information across saccadic eye movements. In T. Inui & J. L. McClelland (Eds.), *Attention and performance XVI: Information integration in perception and communication* (pp. 125–155). Cambridge, MA: MIT Press.

Isenberg, L., Nissen, M. J., & Marchak, L. C. (1990). Attentional processing and the independence of color and orientation. *Journal of Experimental Psychology: Human Perception and Performance, 16,* 869–878.

Johnson-Laird, P. N. (1983). *Mental models: Towards a cognitive science of language, inference, and consciousness.* Cambridge, MA: Harvard University Press.

Jonides, J. (1995). Working memory and thinking. In E. E. Smith & D. N. Osherson (Eds.), *An invitation to cognitive science, Vol. 3: Thinking* (2nd ed., pp. 215–266). Cambridge, MA: MIT Press.

Kane, M. J., & Engle, R. W. (2003). Working-memory capacity and the control of attention: The contributions of goal neglect, response competition, and task set to Stroop interference. *Journal of Experimental Psychology: General, 132,* 47–70.

Kempler, D., van Lancker, D., & Read, S. (1988). Proverb and idiom comprehesion in Alzheimer's disease. *Alzheimer's Disease and Associated Disorders, 2,* 38–49.

Kimberg, D. Y., & Farah, M. J. (1993). A unified account of cognitive impairments following frontal lobe damage: The role of working memory in complex, organized behavior. *Journal of Experimental Psychology: General, 122,* 411–428.

Klauer, K. C., Stegmaier, R., & Meiser, T. (1997). Working memory involvement in propositional and spatial reasoning. *Thinking & Reasoning, 3,* 9–48.

Koechlin, E., Basso, G., Pietrini, P., Panzer, S., & Grafman, J. (1999). The role of the anterior prefrontal cortex in human cognition. *Nature, 399,* 148–151.

Kroger, J. K., Sabb, F. W., Fales, C. L., Bookheimer, S. Y., Cohen, M. S., & Holyoak, K. J. (2002). Recruitment of anterior dorsolateral prefrontal cortex in human reasoning: A parametric study of relational complexity. *Cerebral Cortex, 12,* 477–485.

Kyllonen, P. C., & Christal, R. E. (1990). Reasoning ability is (little more than) working-memory capacity? *Intelligence, 14,* 389–433.

Lafleche, G., & Albert, M. S. (1995). Executive function deficits in mild Alzheimer's disease. *Neuropsychology, 9*, 313–320.

Luck, S. J., & Vogel, E. K. (1997). The capacity of visual working memory for features and conjunctions. *Nature, 390*, 279–281.

Lupien, S., & Lepage, M. (2001). Stress, memory, and the hippocampus: can't live with it, can't live without it. *Behavioural Brain Research, 127*, 137–158.

MacLeod, C., & Donnellan, A. M. (1993). Individual differences in anxiety and the restriction of working memory capacity. *Personality & Individual Differences, 15*, 163–173.

Markman, A. B., & Gentner, D. (1993). Structural alignment during similarity comparisons. *Cognitive Psychology, 25*, 431–467.

Martin, A., & Fedio, P. (1983). Word production and comprehension in Alzheimer's disease: The breakdown of semantic knowledge. *Brain & Language, 19*, 124–141.

Mendez, M. F., Doss, R. C., & Cherrier, M. M. (1998). Use of the cognitive estimations test to discriminate frontotemporal dementia from Alzheimer's disease. *Journal of Geriatric Psychiatry & Neurology, 11*, 2–6.

Milner, B. (1963). Effects of different brain lesions on card sorting. *Archives of Neurology, 9*, 90–100.

Milner, B., & Petrides, M. (1984). Behavioural effects of frontal-lobe lesions in man. *Trends in Neuroscience, 7*, 403–407.

Minsky, M. (1975). A framework for representing knowledge. In P. H. Winston (Ed.), *The psychology of computer vision* (pp. 95–128). New York: McGraw-Hill.

Mitchell, K. J., Johnson, M. K., Raye, C. L., & D'Esposito, M. (2000) fMRI evidence of age-related hippocampal dysfunction in feature binding in working memory. *Cognitive Brain Research, 10*, 197–206.

Miyake, A., Friedman, N. P., Rettinger, D. A., Shah, P., & Hegarty, M. (2001). How are visuospatial working memory, executive functioning, and spatial abilities related? A latent-variable analysis. *Journal of Experimental Psychology: General, 130*, 621–640.

Mogg, K., & Bradley, B. P. (1999). Selective attention and anxiety: A cognitive-motivational perspective. In T. Dalgleish & M. J. Power (Eds.), *Handbook of cognition and emotion* (pp. 145–170). New York: Wiley.

Morris, R. G., & Baddeley, A. D. (1988). Primary and working memory functioning in Alzheimer-type dementia. *Journal of Clinical & Experimental Neuropsychology, 10*, 279–296.

Munk, M. H., Linden, D. E. J., Muckli, L., Lanfermann, H., Zanella, F. E., Singer, W., & Goebel, R. (2002). Distributed cortical systems in visual short-term memory revealed by event-related functional magnetic resonance imaging. *Cerebral Cortex, 12*, 866–876.

McEwan, B. S. (1999). Stress and hippocampal plasticity. *Annual Review of Neuroscience, 22*, 105–122.

Nieder, A., Freedman, D. J., & Miller, E. K. (2002). Representation of the quantity of visual items in the primate prefrontal cortex. *Science, 297*, 1708–1711.

O'Brien, J. T., Eagger, S. A., Syed, G. M., Sahakian, B. J., & Levy, R. (1992). A study of regional cerebral blood flow and cognitive performance in Alzheimer's disease. *Journal of Neurology, Neurosurgery & Psychiatry, 55*, 1182–1187.

Osherson, D., Perani, D., Cappa, S., Schnur, T., Grassi, F., & Fazio, F. (1998). Distinct brain loci in deductive versus probabilistic reasoning. *Neuropsychologia, 36,* 369–376.

Owen, A. M., Downes, J. J., Sahakian, B. J., Polkey, C. E., & Robbins, T. W. (1990). Planning and spatial working memory following frontal lobe lesions in man. *Neuropsychologia, 28,* 1021–1034.

Perret, E. (1974). The left frontal lobe of man and the suppression of habitual responses in verbal categorical behaviour. *Neuropsychologia, 12,* 323–330.

Perry, R. J., & Hodges, J. R. (1999). Attention and executive deficits in Alzheimer's disease: A critical review. *Brain, 122,* 383–404.

Pillon, B., Dubois, B., Lhermitte, F., & Agid, Y. (1986). Heterogeneity of cognitive impairment in progressive supranuclear palsy, Parkinson's disease, and Alzheimer's disease. *Neurology, 36,* 1179–1185.

Prabhakaran, V., Narayanan, K., Zhao, Z., & Gabrieli, J. D. E. (2000). Integration of diverse information in working memory within the frontal lobe. *Nature Neuroscience, 3,* 85–90.

Prabhakaran, V., Smith, J. A. L., Desmond, J. E., Glover, G., & Gabrieli, J. D. E. (1997). Neural substrates of fluid reasoning: An fMRI study of neocortical activation during performance of the Raven's Progressive Matrices Test. *Cognitive Psychology, 33,* 43–63.

Rainer, G., Asaad, W. F., & Miller, E. K. (1998). Selective representation of relevant information by neurons in the primate prefrontal cortex. *Nature, 393,* 577–579.

Rao, S. C., Rainer, G., & Miller, E. K (1997). Integration of what and where in the primate prefrontal cortex. *Science, 276,* 821–824.

Raven, J. C. (1976). *Standard progressive matrices: Sets A, B, C, D, & E.* Oxford, UK: Oxford Psychologists Press.

Rensink, R. A. (2000). The dynamic representation of scenes. *Visual Cognition, 7,* 17–42.

Roberts, R. J., Hager, L. D., & Heron, C. (1994). Prefrontal cognitive processes: Working memory and inhibition in the antisaccade task. *Journal of Experimental Psychology: General, 123,* 374–393.

Schank, R., & Abelson, R. (1977). *Scripts, plans, goals, and understanding: An inquiry into human knowledge structures.* Hillsdale, NJ: Lawrence Erlbaum Associates.

Shallice, T., & Burgess, P. (1991). Higher order cognitive impairments and frontal lobe lesions. In H. S. Levin, H. M. Eisenberg, & A. L. Benton (Eds.), *Frontal lobe function and dysfunction* (pp. 125–138). New York: Oxford University Press.

Shallice, T., & Evans, M. E. (1978). The involvement of the frontal lobes in cognitive estimation. *Cortex, 14,* 294–303.

Simons, D. J. (1996). In sight and out of mind: When object representations fail. *Psychological Science, 7,* 301–305.

Smith, E. E., & Jonides, J. (1997). Working memory: A view from neuroimaging. *Cognitive Psychology, 33,* 5–42.

Smith, M. L., & Milner, B. (1984). Differential effects of frontal-lobe lesions on cognitive estimation and spatial memory. *Neuropsychologia, 22,* 697–705.

Stefurak, D. L., & Boynton, R. M. (1986). Independence of memory for categorically different colors and shapes. *Perception & Psychophysics, 39,* 164–174.

Tohill, J. M., & Holyoak, K. J. (2000). The impact of anxiety on analogical reasoning. *Thinking & Reasoning, 6*, 27–40.

Toms, M., Morris, N., & Ward, D. (1993). Working memory and conditional reasoning. *Quarterly Journal of Experimental Psychology: Human Experimental Psychology, 46*, 679–699.

Treisman, A. M. (1992). Perceiving and re-perceiving objects. *American Psychology, 47*, 862–875.

Treisman, A. M., Sykes, M., & Gelade, G. (1977). Selective attention and stimulus integration. In S. Dornic (Ed.), *Attention and performance VI* (pp. 333–361). Hillsdale, NJ: Lawrence Erlbaum Associates.

Wallis, J. D., Anderson, K. C., & Miller, E. K. (2001). Single neurons in prefrontal cortex encode abstract rules. *Nature, 411*, 953–956.

Waltz, J. A., Knowlton, B. J., Holyoak, K. J., Boone, K. B., Back, C., McPherson, S., et al. (2004). Relational integration and executive function in Alzheimer's disease. *Neuropsychology, 18*, 296–305.

Waltz, J. A., Knowlton, B. J., Holyoak, K. J., Boone, K. B., Mishkin, F. S., de Menezes Santos, M., Thomas, C. R., & Miller, B. L. (1999). A system for relational reasoning in human prefrontal cortex. *Psychological Science, 10*, 119–125.

Waltz, J. A., Lau, A., Grewal, S., & Holyoak, K. J. (2000). The role of working memory in analogical reasoning. *Memory & Cognition, 28*, 1205–1212.

Weiss, J. M., & Glazer, H. I. (1975). Effects of acute exposure to stressors on subsequent avoidance–escape behavior. *Psychosomatic Medicine, 37*, 499–521.

West, R., & Alain, C. (2000). Evidence for the transient nature of a neural system supporting goal-directed action. *Cerebral Cortex, 8*, 748–752.

Wheeler, M. E., & Treisman, A. M. (2002). Binding in short-term visual memory. *Journal of Experimental Psychology: General, 131*, 48–64.

# 14

## Generative Reasoning as Influenced by Depression, Aging, Stereotype Threat, and Prejudice

Ulrich von Hecker, Grzegorz Sedek, Kinga
Piber-Dabrowska, and Sylwia Bedynska

This last and interdisciplinary chapter begins with the observation that in many psychological subdisciplines that call themselves "cognitive," there is a continuous debate about the specific nature of the mental limitations across different populations. Research in the *cognitive aging* area focuses on comparisons between older and younger adults in different basic cognitive functions (e.g., attention, working memory) and higher order cognitive functions (e.g., reasoning, comprehension). Research in the *cognitive psychopathology* area centers around similar comparisons and distinctions among emotionally disturbed versus emotionally stable participants. Finally, in the *social cognition* area, cognitive limitations and biases produced by strong prejudice or stereotypes are central issues. Researchers from the previously-mentioned domains often refer to the same psychological mechanisms that might interfere with effective cognitive processing. Just to mention a few, these include lack of motivation or cognitive initiative, limited cognitive resources, inefficient inhibitory mechanisms, or oversimplified strategies of information processing. However, there are very few attempts to directly compare the mechanisms underlying those impairments and limitations across different research domains using the same cognitive tasks.

In this chapter, we describe one of our research projects that aimed to compare the performance of individuals from different populations on the same generative reasoning tasks. The populations included depressed versus nondepressed students, older versus younger adults, students threatened by stereotype versus control students, and finally, students with high versus low levels of ethnic prejudice. We noticed that similar kinds of explanations have been suggested to explain the reduced cognitive performance in some of these groups. We go on to make a case, based on own research data, that those deficits might actually have different origins.

The plan of this chapter is as follows. First, we highlight the importance of generative reasoning as a molar cognitive function in general and describe in more detail the generative linear order paradigm. We then present some major results across four different research domains and look for similarities and differences across this set of findings. We propose that attenuation analysis based on hierarchical regression is a useful tool for assessing the relative strength of group differences and for evaluating the role of basic cognitive processes as potential mediators of the influence of group differences on generative reasoning processes. Finally, we discuss the advantages of crossing the borders of various "cognitive" research domains when comparing different models of processing limitations in reasoning tasks.

## GENERATIVE REASONING AND THE PARADIGM OF LINEAR ORDER CONSTRUCTION

Generative reasoning lies at the core of human higher cognitive functions. It is one of intellect's essential capacities to generate novel representations on the basis of available input information, that is, to go "beyond the information given" (Bruner, 1957). The construction of molar representations, such as mental models, spatial images, or problem solutions, is a typical example of generative reasoning (Halford, 1993; Johnson-Laird, 1983). Generative reasoning is a bottom-up activity, aimed at the creation of new ideas, inferences, instances of a given concept, or some other new or abstract contents that are not explicitly presented in the stimulus information. In text comprehension, generative reasoning is employed to achieve a representation of what the text is about, as opposed to its surface structure (Glenberg & Langston, 1992; Glenberg, Meyer, & Lindem, 1987). In communication, generative reasoning supports online mechanisms such as the understanding of gestures (Emmorey, 2001). In social impression formation, perceivers attempt to infer personality traits from available behavioral information (Bodenhausen, Macrae, & Sherman, 1999). All of these cognitive activities require the flexible allocation of attentional resources to rearrange and combine existing contents in working memory, so that new contents (such as inferences, conclusions, perspectives, or overall representations) become available (see also Hampton, 1997).

Linear order construction is a paradigm that may exemplify our perspective on generative reasoning as a process of integrating piecemeal information. The construction of linear orders from pairwise relational information that implies transitivity has received attention since the early days of cognitive psychology and cognitive developmental psychology (Huttenlocher, 1968; Johnson-Laird, 1972; McGonigle & Chalmers, 1984; Piaget & Inhelder, 1974; Potts, 1972; Rabinowitz, Grant, Howe, & Walsh,

TABLE 14.1. *Pair Arrangements by Difficulty Levels, as Used in Presentation Sequences During the Learning Phase*

| Order No. | Difficulty level | Pair sequence |
|---|---|---|
| 1 | I | AB, BC, CD |
| 2 | | CD, BC, AB |
| 3 | II | BC, CD, AB |
| 4 | | BC, AB, CD |
| 5 | III | AB, CD, BC |
| 6 | | CD, AB, BC |

1994; Sternberg, 1980; Trabasso, Riley, & Wilson, 1975; Tzelgov, Yehene, Kotler, & Alon, 2000).

The experimental procedure was identical for all studies presented in this chapter on subclinical depression, aging, and stereotype threat, with some modifications in the last study on prejudice. Participants were asked in each trial to study three pairs of relations, e.g., "A > B," "B > C," and "C > D," with "A" ... "D" standing for first names, and ">" standing for a relational signifier such as "taller," "older," which was transitive by common sense definition. An integrated mental model representation (Johnson-Laird, 1983) of such a set of pairs would always be a linear order "A > B > C > D." Immediately after presentation of the three pairs, participants were tested on all possible pairs of the order, i.e., AB, BC, CD (adjacent pairs, which had been learned), AC, BD (two-step relations), and AD (end-point relation), by prompting participants with statements in either a correct (e.g., "A > D") or false format (e.g., "D > A") and asking them for a speeded verification.

There were six trials, at three difficulty levels, presented in random order. Difficulty levels were created by arranging different presentation sequences of the three pairs during learning (Mynatt & Smith, 1977). Table 14.1. shows the six different pair arrangements, as grouped into difficulty levels. At level I, a linear mental model can be constructed by simply chaining the three pairs consecutively, making use of the element that is common between two pairs. At level II, chaining is more difficult because individual pairs have to be transposed before the common element can be matched between pairs. At level III, transposition is still necessary, but additionally, the first two pairs cannot be merged at the first attempt. Rather, these two pairs have to be kept in memory as independent units before the chaining can eventually be achieved upon learning the third pair (Mynatt & Smith, 1977). It is easy to see from Table 14.1. that processing demands increase across levels I to III and that demands are particularly

**A**
(studies on depression, aging,
                    stereotype threat)

**B**
(study on prejudice)

Studying phase
(freely paced for participants)

Studying phase
(freely paced for participants)

**Doris is smarter than Carol**
**Brenda is smarter than Alice**
**Alice is smarter than Doris**

**Bogdan is more agressive than Jakub**
**Hans is more aggresive than Jacek**
**Jacek is more aggresive than Bogdan**

Test phase
(freely paced for participants)

Test phase
(freely paced for participants)

Carol smarter than Doris :
    True  or  False ?
    **(adjacent relation)**

Hans is more aggresive than Jacek:      True  or  False ?
    **(adjacent target relation)**

Brenda smarter than Doris:
    True  or  False ?
    **(2-step relation)**

Jakub is more aggressive than Bogdan:  True  or  False ?
    **(adjacent nontarget relation)**

Brenda smarter than Carol:
    True  or  False ?
    **(endpoints relation)**

Bogdan is more aggressive than Hans:    True  or  False ?
    **(2-step target relation)**

Jacek is more aggresive tha Jakub:      True  or  False ?
    **(2-step  nontarget relation)**

**MENTAL ARRAY:**

**Brenda > Alice > Doris > Carol**

**MENTAL ARRAY:**

**Hans > Jacek > Bogdan > Jakub**

FIGURE 14.1. The design of the studies on the depression, cognitive aging, stereotype threat (A; left column), and of the study about prejudice (B; right column).

high on processing the third element in a sequence, because the third element is always the one that allows for a complete chaining of the four persons into a common linear order.

Figure 14.1 (part A) illustrates the procedure for the most difficult linear order. Study time was self-paced, thus allowing the assessment of participants' motivation and of their time allocation patterns. During the test phase, participants were asked about the just-presented *adjacent* pair information (one-step relations; this was used as a measure of memory retrieval and did not constitute a reasoning test per se). They were also asked two questions about to-be-inferred but not presented pair relations, which demanded generative reasoning. The questions about 2-step relations (relations between Brenda and Doris or Alice and Carol) concerned the relations between persons that spanned a distance of two steps on the hypothetical mental array and demanded integration of information from two presented pairs. The questions about relations between endpoint persons (Brenda and Carol) dealt with inferred pairs that spanned the maximum array distance of three steps and demanded integration of information from all three presented pairs.

## LINEAR ORDER REASONING ACROSS DIFFERENT POPULATIONS

In this part we briefly present the main theoretical predictions concerning possible patterns of results for the linear order paradigm, based on previous research on different but conceptually similar tasks in the above-mentioned research domains. In our data, we analyzed study time patterns, accuracy for adjacent relations (thus examining the maintenance function of working memory), and accuracy for generative reasoning (end-point relations). Next, we examined to what extent the obtained group effects on linear order reasoning (end-point relations) might be explained in terms of more elementary motivational or cognitive processes, such as lowered motivation (short study times) or a low level of memory retrieval (poor maintenance of the presented adjacent relations).

Evidence that participants construct a mental model representation about a linear order of the type "A > B > C > D" (">" = "taller") comes from the observation that in the test stage, response times do not increase (or even decrease) and accuracy does not decrease (or even increases), as the distance in the hypothesized mental model increases for queried pairs of elements that were not presented during learning, e.g., AC, BD, or AD. This pattern is referred to as the "distance effect" (Holyoak & Patterson, 1981; Mynatt & Smith, 1977; Potts, 1972; Smith & Foos, 1975; for a recent review, see Leth-Steensen & Marley, 2000). It appears from these results that participants do not simply store the adjacent pairs during learning, but instead they integrate all pairwise information into a unified mental model from which they can easily "read off" the answer to a queried pair. If an individual did not integrate the pairwise pieces of information but used them later during testing to make transitive inferences, decreasing accuracy should be observed as a function of pair distance. This is because the more inferential steps have to be carried out, the more error-prone the overall process will be (Sedek & von Hecker, 2004).

### Subclinical Depression

People in depressed states often experience problems not only in terms of sad mood, lowered motivation, or loss of interest but also at a cognitive level, particularly when dealing with more complex and demanding tasks (for recent reviews, see Ellis, Ottaway, Varner, Becker, & Moore, 1997; Gotlib, Roberts, & Gilboa, 1996; von Hecker, Sedek, & McIntosh, 2000). Areas of documented deficits under depressed mood include the handling of social situations (Marx, Williams, & Claridge, 1992), free recall (Channon, Baker, & Robertson, 1993), concept learning (Smith, Tracy, & Murray, 1993), complex social perception (Conway & Giannopoulos, 1993), and effortful thinking and creativity in general (Ellis & Ashbrook, 1988). Because those areas of impairment appear broadly spread across a range of heterogeneous tasks, it is important to specify more precisely some of the higher order cognitive functions that might account for those deficits associated with ongoing depressed mood. The hypothesis that there may be specific cognitive functions that support the integration of piecemeal information into mental models is strengthened by recent studies from our lab that have identified a reduced ability in the formation of social mental models in depressed participants (von Hecker & Sedek, 1999). Depressed participants in this latter study were less able than nondepressed controls to form accurate representations of groups and cliques in a fictitious social environment. The pattern of findings from this study led us to believe, although we did not directly test this notion, that inference making based on transitivity was one main mechanism to be affected by depressed mood.

The overall set of findings just discussed led us to study the construction of mental models in subclinical depressed mood more systematically, using the linear order construction paradigm as described above, in order to address transitive inference making as a basic mechanism of generative reasoning (for a detailed report, see Sedek & von Hecker, 2004, Experiment 1). College students were classified as subclinically depressed (scores ranging 10 and above) and nondepressed (scores ranging between 0 and 5) using the Beck Depression Inventory (BDI; Beck, 1967). They were tested on the BDI twice at an interval of a week. In order to participate in the study, participants' BDI scores at the second appointment had to fall within the same classification as the first appointment to ensure reliability.

The results of this experiment were clear (see Table 14.2). For the nondepressed group, there was a constant high level of accuracy across analyzed pair distances (adjacent–end-point). This strongly suggests that in this group, participants tended to retrieve their answers from an integrated model, as queries on inferred end point relations (pair distance = 3) were answered with no less accuracy than explicitly learned, adjacent ones (pair distance = 1). On the other hand, in the depressed group, there was a substantial decrease of accuracy from explicitly learned to inferred relations. Following our reasoning outlined above, we concluded from this pattern that depressed individuals did not spontaneously integrate the pairs during learning, but they retrieved the pairs at the time of the query to make transitive inferences at this later point in time. It is of further interest to note that despite the apparent differences in terms of achieved mental model construction, both groups showed strikingly similar behavior during learning. As noted in Table 14.2., overall study times were similar in both groups, that is, slightly, but not significantly longer in the depressed group. As further analyses showed, it took both groups longer to study pairs from more difficult orders than pairs from easier orders, and for both groups this was particularly the case when studying any third pair in the sequence. The observation that both groups apparently exerted similar

TABLE 14.2. *Study Time and Accuracy for the Linear Reasoning Task Across Groups*

| Performance on cognitive task of study groups | Depression | | Aging | | Stereotype threat | | Prejudice | |
|---|---|---|---|---|---|---|---|---|
| | Depressed | Non-depressed | Older adults | Young adults | Stereotype threat | Control students | Prejudiced | Non-prejudiced |
| Study time (s) | $9.39_a$ | $7.48_a$ | $11.93_a$ | $11.44_a$ | $11.29_a$ | $14.87_b$ | $7.12_a$ (t) $6.49_a$ (nt) | $10.01_b$ (t) $9.30_b$ (nt) |
| Accuracy (% correct) Adjacent relations | $90_a$ | $94_a$ | $70_a$ | $92_b$ | $89_a$ | $93_a$ | $90_a$ (t) $79_a$ (nt) | $89_a$ (t) $89_b$ (nt) |
| Inferred relations | $79_a$ | $96_b$ | $74_a$ | $94_b$ | $83_a$ | $97_b$ | $75_a$ (t) $70_a$ (nt) | $81_a$ (t) $86_b$ (nt) |

*Note.* Means with different subscripts for a given research domain (e.g., depressed vs. nondepressed for the Depression domain) differ significantly ($p < .05$). For the Prejudice study, the target pairs or relations are marked as (t), nontarget pairs or relations are marked as (nt).

TABLE 14.3. *Results of Hierarchical Regression Analyses on Generative Reasoning*

| Variable | $R^2$ | $\Delta R^2$ | Percentage attenuated |
|---|---|---|---|
| | Group: Depressed vs. nondepressed | | |
| Group | .156* | | |
| Memory retrieval | .125* | | |
| Group | | .111* | 28.8 |
| | Group: Older adults vs. student control | | |
| Group | .245* | | |
| Memory retrieval | .407* | | |
| Group | | .003 | 98.8 |
| | Group: Stereotype threat vs. control female students | | |
| Group | .134* | | |
| Memory retrieval | .246* | | |
| Group | | .069* | 48.5 |
| | Group: Prejudiced vs. nonprejudiced students (nontarget relations) | | |
| Group | .130* | | |
| Memory retrieval | .100* | | |
| Group | | .072* | 44.6 |

*Note.* The dependent variable was accuracy for end-point relations except for the prejudice study in which the dependent variable was accuracy for two-step relations. The memory retrieval variable was operationalized as accuracy for adjacent (presented) relations. *$p$ <.05.

amounts of effort in their constructive attempts is consistent with earlier findings (von Hecker & Sedek, 1999) that depressed participants, despite engaging in the type of mental activity that is necessary to construct a mental model, are actually not successful in doing so (see also Sedek & Kofta, 1990).

We also made an attempt to assess the effect of depression on accuracy at end-point queries, which is the query that carries the highest demand on generative reasoning, after partialing out the variance associated with successful maintenance of the three learned pairs in working memory (see Salthouse, 1992; Salthouse, Legg, Palmon, & Mitchell, 1990; Salthouse, Mitchell, Skovronek, & Babcock, 1989, for an identical approach in the case of integrative reasoning in different age groups). Maintenance in working memory can be estimated by taking the performance level for adjacent pairs as a proxy, because queries on these pairs directly refer to the stimuli that participants had been learning just immediately prior to the test stage. In a hierarchical regression analysis (see Table 14.3), the initial $R^2$ for the relation between depression status and end-point accuracy of .156 was attenuated by only 28.8% to the value of .111 (still significant) after controlling for performance on adjacent pairs. The attenuation analysis suggests that maintenance in working memory, as measured by memory retrieval (see Table 14.3), did not mediate the effect of depression on generative reasoning accuracy concerning end-points. This hierarchical regression approach is particularly useful in comparing the underlying nature of generative reasoning deficits with respect to the three functions of integration, maintenance, and allocation of attention, as will become clear as we move on.

In the study presented earlier, and in terms of the empirical indices we had defined, depressed participants, unlike nondepressed controls, showed no evidence for model-based memory retrieval, in spite of considerable constructive activity during learning. Instead, depressed individuals seemed to start reasoning from piecemeal information at the moment of being queried. In order to find further evidence for this principal idea, we performed another study (for a detailed report, see Sedek & von Hecker, 2004, Study 3) in which the presentation rate was set to a fixed interval of 5 seconds per relation, while leaving the rest of the methodology unchanged. Research in social cognition has often found that the voluntary allocation of effortful processing resources during a study phase is a crucial factor in producing generative effects of integration, such as in social impression formation (see Hastie, 1980; Srull & Wyer, 1989). Specifically, Bargh and Thein (1985) showed, in a study comparing self-paced and fixed presentation methodologies, that better memory performance for schema-inconsistent information about a person, which is taken to be an indicator of integrative processing and which is usually found using self-paced presentation, disappeared when using fixed presentation. In fact, in the previous study, nondepressed participants' overall high performance levels of between .93 and .95 percent of accurate responses across pair distances could have been due to the high degree of information integration in memory via the generation of a mental model that these participants were able to achieve when they were free to allocate their study time.

Therefore, once participants were prevented from free allocation of their study time, their test performance should decrease to the extent that their retrieval was in fact based on an integrated mental model. The degree of model integration would presumably be lower in a situation where adaptive time allocation was not possible, as it is the case under fixed presentation. On the other hand, if a participant's response to a pair query does not rely on a mental model in the first place, they should not be affected to the same degree by this procedural change. Thus, the hypotheses for this study were straightforward. Because nondepressed participants appeared to base all their responses (i.e., those to adjacent, two-step, and end-point queries) on an integrated linear order, we expected a general impairment for the nondepressed group under these new conditions because their constructive efforts to establish this order during learning would be curtailed. Because, on the other hand, depressed participants appeared to simply store the three pairs and base their later responses on inferential reasoning at the time of the query, we expected the depressed group to replicate their pattern of performance from the previous study. This is exactly what happened in the present experiment. Depressed participants still exhibited the stepwise decrease in performance across pair distance levels, whereas the nondepressed control group showed no such decrease but instead demonstrated a clearly lower overall performance level as compared to the previous study. We had hypothesized that a 5-second limit on presentation times for individual pairs during learning would affect nondepressed control participants more than depressed participants, presumably because the former would attempt to use a more complex strategy (maintenance plus integration) than would the depressed group (only maintenance). Previous research has shown that time restrictions tend to affect those who use more complex strategies more (Engle, 1996). Thus, we conclude for the present study that nondepressed control participants' performance was particularly affected by preventing these participants from integrating the individual adjacent relations into an overall representation in form of a linear order model. Overall, and combined with evidence from the previous experiment, the evidence from this study shows that depressed individuals probably did not spontaneously use generative reasoning for effective retrieval operations.

## Aging

There are specific age-related deficits with complex cognitive tasks, particularly those tasks that have a strong generative component, that is, tasks that require materials to be held in an active state in working memory, while being simultaneously transformed or rearranged (Kliegl, Mayr, & Oberauer, 2000). Whereas older people's problems with working memory have been documented with respect to many tasks in the domains of text comprehension, reasoning, and spatial integration (e.g., Salthouse, 1990; Zabrucky, Moore, & Schultz, 1993; for overviews, see Light, 1996; Craik & Salthouse, 2000; Perfect & Maylor, 2000), the question of in which of the constitutive functions of generative reasoning (i.e., integration, maintenance, or allocation of attention) the source of dysfunction might lie remains. There is reason to believe that the proper "mechanics" of integration as such are not substantially impaired in older age, whereas the observable deficits are mainly driven by problems of maintaining the contents of working memory in an active state. Initial evidence to support this notion comes from Salthouse's work (Salthouse, 1992; Salthouse et al., 1989, 1990), demonstrating that older adults have no problems with complex generative reasoning, such as integrating multiple premises and drawing a conclusion from them, provided the necessary information can be retrieved or held active in working memory. A particular methodological tool used in making this argument was to show a significant attenuation of the statistical influence that age had on reasoning performance, after working memory capacity being taken into account (see Table 14.3). We proceeded in an analogous way in our study (for a detailed report, see Sedek & von Hecker, 2004, Study 2).

The study (17 college students, mean age: 18 years, and 17 older adults, mean age: 71 years) used the same methodology of linear order construction as described in the two foregoing studies. The hypothesis was that if the impairment pattern in the elderly can be explained by maintenance problems, no stepwise decline as a function of pair distance should be observed in their test performance. Rather, performance differences between the two age groups should be visible at all levels and should disappear when maintenance in working memory was accounted for. This is what we found (see Table 14.2 for significant between-group differences for adjacent and end-point relations). Older participants performed worse than younger participants at all levels of pair distance, and the initial $R^2$ for the relation between age group classification and end-point accuracy of .245 (this group difference was the strongest across all described studies) was almost completely reduced to .003 after controlling for the performance on adjacent pairs (see Table 14.3). This suggests that maintenance in working memory was the main factor explaining the effect of age group on generative reasoning accuracy concerning end-points. Framed differently, these results mean that after equalizing both groups with respect to maintenance in working memory, the actual integration performance was unimpaired in the elderly, as compared to the younger group. It also appears unlikely that the elderly's deficit was caused by a lack of attention during the study phase, because there were no group differences in the average study times across all conditions (see Table 14.2).

Within the elderly group there was better performance for more difficult orders, particularly orders 5 and 6, as compared to the easier orders. This effect was not expected, but can be accommodated by current theories on cognitive aging, which warrants a post-hoc explanation. Specifically, older individuals appear to allocate their processing resources in an often more selective and more economic way, engaging in highly demanding cognitive operations, predominantly in those cases where cues in the materials during learning point to a necessity to engage in such operations (e.g., Hess, Bolstad, Woodburn, & Auman, 1999). In a similar vein, the greater difficulty presented by orders 5 and 6, in which two unrelated pairs precede the third pair, could have acted as such a cue, thus triggering the allocation of more attentional resources to the process of memorization during the learning stage. This reasoning is also corroborated by the pattern of study times, showing that elderly participants spent more time than younger participants at studying third pairs in orders 5 and 6 in particular. Again, an explanation of these data in terms of attentional weakness seems not plausible.

## Stereotype Threat

In situations in which a negative stereotype are applicable to a certain social group, members of that group may feel increased anxiety of being seen by others through the lens of that stereotype, thus being confronted with low performance expectations and possibly further diminishing implications (Steele & Aronson, 1995). Recent research following this idea has focused on the mechanisms by which negative stereotypes influence those individuals to whom they potentially apply. Typically, performance effects ascribed to the presence of stereotype threat are demonstrated for domains in which individuals who are potential targets of stereotype threat perform well without this influence. A case in point is the stereotype about women's low abilities in mathematics. In a test situation when this stereotype is made salient to female participants who are normally proficient in math, their performance in a math task typically suffers compared to a control condition in which the stereotype is not made salient (Shih, Pittinsky, & Ambady, 1999). Also, it appears that the skills affected by stereotype threat are particularly generative in nature, for example the generation of suitable alternative strategies in order to solve a math problem (Quinn & Spencer, 2001). On the other hand, if participants are convinced beforehand that, on the grounds of scientific studies, the task at hand does not normally produce gender differences; those adverse performance effects are not visible, even when difficult math problems are used (Spencer, Steele, & Quinn, 1999). The latter finding shows that the impairing effects of stereotype threat are malleable and possibly depend on the operation of social cognitive processes such as attribution and discounting.

Although the more complex cognitive processes associated with the particular ability targeted by the negative stereotype (e.g., math) are most immediately affected, recent research also shows that the cognitive impact of stereotype threat is more general in nature. Schmader and Johns (2003) recently summarized evidence showing that stereotype threat leads to deficits in working memory capacity, as measured by an operation span task (see the detailed discussion about this task in the chapter by Unsworth, Heitz, & Engle, this volume). It therefore seems plausible that the underlying mechanism here is not specifically tied to the target skill (e.g., math ability), but works more broadly through influencing working memory resources at large. We were interested to see to what extent the alteration in psychological state as induced by manipulated stereotype threat would interfere with the construction of linear orders, a task that content-wise has no direct bearing on the particular skill targeted by the stereotype threat manipulation but that reflects generative reasoning in a more general sense (Bedynska, Sedek, & Brzezicka-Rotkiewicz, 2004). Therefore, it would be hypothesized that participants under stereotype threat would show impairments in linear order construction mainly because of a general disruption of working memory functions. On the other hand, based on the research reviewed in the beginning of this section indicating that stereotype threat affects mostly difficult tasks and especially constructive aspects of problem solving (e.g., Quinn & Spencer, 2001), an alternative, more specific prediction might be formulated, which is that stereotype threat, like subclinical depression, impairs the generative aspects of reasoning in particular.

A group of female students, randomly assigned to the stereotype threat versus control conditions, were informed by written instructions about the results of a recent survey indicating that female students usually performed worse than male students in the tests to be taken, which were portrayed as measuring the capacity of logical inference-making (this experimental manipulation was similar to a study by Spencer et al., 1998). The aim of the research, so the instruction explained further, was to examine whether those group differences would also emerge in a different, but similar, type of task (i.e., the linear order task). The students from the control group were informed that the study was part of an international comparative study measuring logical inferences and until now no cross-national differences had been observed. After instructions, all students solved the same linear order problems as in the studies presented above.

As the results showed (see Table 14.2), the stereotype threat condition among female students was associated with impairments in generative reasoning. Participants in this condition exhibited a stepwise decrease in response accuracy as a function of pair distance, such that they answered queries about end-point relations least accurately. On the other hand, female control participants not exposed to stereotype threat showed a slight increase in accuracy from adjacent to end-point relations, as predicted by the mental model view on linear order construction and the literature on the "distance effect" (Leth-Steensen & Marley, 2000). An inspection of study times (see Table 14.2) yielded significant difference between groups and thus also supports an explanation of reasoning deficits in stereotype-threat group in terms of lowered motivation to study the presented materials or explanation in terms of ego-protecting maneuvers (Kofta & Sedek, 1989).

Female participants under stereotype threat manipulation performed worse than did female control participants, and the initial $R^2$ for the relation between group classification and end-point accuracy of .130 was substantially reduced to .07 (however, it was still significant) after controlling for the performance on adjacent pairs (see Table 14.3). This finding suggests that maintenance in working memory was an important factor (but not as crucial as in the research on cognitive aging), explaining the effect of stereotype threat on generative reasoning accuracy concerning end-point relations. However, the stereotype threat manipulation seems to produce a genuine deficit in generative reasoning as well, similar to what was observed in subclinical depression (but see the different results for study time). This pattern of findings partially supports both above predictions about a working memory deficit and a generative reasoning deficit under the stereotype threat manipulation.

## SOCIAL STEREOTYPES AND PREJUDICE

The starting point for the application of the linear order paradigm in the area of social stereotypes and prejudice was the increasing number of studies indicating that using social stereotypes might be an energy-saving and efficient way to process information (Macrae, Milne, & Bodenhausen, 1994a; Sherman, Lee, Bessenoff, & Frost, 1998; for broader reviews, see Fiske, 1998 and Sherman, 2001). Those beneficial aspects of activated stereotypes are especially clear concerning the encoding and representation of stereotype-consistent information, but they might also facilitate encoding of stereotype-inconsistent information (Macrae, Stangor, & Milne, 1994b; Sherman et al., 1998; von Hippel, Sekaquaptewa, & Vargas, 1995).

Macrae and his associates (1994a) were the first to demonstrate in an elegant dual-task paradigm that stereotypes represent an efficient way of information processing, because participants for whom the social stereotypes were activated had more resources for performing a second, unrelated task. We will describe their first experiment in some detail because of its impact on the design of our study and the associated hypotheses. In Macrae et al.'s study, the participants' task was to form an impression of a target person based on trait descriptions (first task). Depending on the group assignment, a category label pertaining to the target stereotype (i.e., skin-head) was either present or absent. Simultaneously, participants monitored some information coming from a tape recorder (second task). They listened to a passage describing basic facts about the geography and economy of Indonesia. The findings showed that participants in the category label condition recalled more stereotype-consistent information than the participants who were not provided with the labels. Additionally, participants in the stereotypic label condition performed better on a multiple choice test on details of the presented facts about Indonesia. This particular finding supported their central prediction:

If stereotypes represent a useful means for economizing condition, then those subjects for whom a stereotype had been activated should have more resources available for the prose-monitoring task.

(Macrae et al., 1994a, p. 40)

Stimulated by this research, we (Piber-Dabrowska & Sedek, 2004) arranged the linear order reasoning task in a way to fit ideally to the predictions based on negative stereotypes toward a specific target group (Germans). The participants were high school students from Warsaw (Poland), classified as negatively prejudiced or not prejudiced toward Germans, using a questionnaire-plus-memory-test procedure developed by Piber-Dabrowska (2000). In line with recent definitions, prejudice was operationalized as a negative evaluation of an individual, based on the group membership of this individual (Crandall & Eshleman, 2003; Fiske, 1998).

In brief, the questionnaire contained a range of synonymous expressions for the traits most often ascribed to the target group. The synonyms varied in valence from negative (e.g., conceited, workaholic) to positive meanings (e.g., self-assured, hard-working). In the first part, participants indicated those expressions that they associated with the target. Next, and unexpectedly, participants had to recall the chosen expressions. Only correctly recalled synonyms were used in the ensuing group classification. Participants were selected as prejudiced when they exclusively recalled synonyms of negative meaning that they had previously associated with Germans. Participants were selected as nonprejudiced when they recalled a mix of moderately positive and negative synonyms of traits they had associated with Germans. Piber-Dabrowska (2000) validated this technique in several studies, using the Implicit Association Test (IAT; Greenwald, McGhee, & Schwartz, 1998). Compared with nonprejudiced participants, prejudiced participants selected in this way showed systematically greater interference in this adapted version of the IAT.

There were three basic modifications in comparison to the standard linear order procedure used in the previous studies (see Figure 14.1, right column). First, there was one single stereotype-target person being used (identified by the German name, e.g., "Hans"), the other three were nontarget persons (identified by Polish first names). Second, the relations among persons were not neutral as in the previous studies, but they expressed the content of six negative stereotypic traits about Germans (e.g., "more aggressive") across the six linear order problems. Third, the position of the target person was always the most extreme one (e.g., Hans is most aggressive) across all linear order tasks; that is, the target person was placed at the position that confirmed the stereotypic view.

Extrapolating directly from the reported research (Macrae et al., 1994a), it might be hypothesized that the experimental situation should demonstrate higher efficiency in the performance of prejudiced participants. Prejudice should facilitate the correct location of the target person at the most extreme negative position on the mental array (that is A, on the mental array A > B > C > D), and consequently, prejudiced individuals should have more resources preserved for the correct location of the other three nontarget persons. The first more general prediction was that the accuracy for target relations (both adjacent and inferred) would be better than for nontarget relations in all participants, because the activation of stereotypic content should facilitate processing information about target objects. Additionally, it was hypothesized that prejudiced individuals should perform at least as well as nonprejudiced participants on the adjacent and inferred target relations. They should outperform nonprejudiced persons on the nontarget relations, because they should have more resources available, especially when processing the more cognitively demanding inferences of wider pair distance.

Interestingly, a completely different set of predictions might be inferred based on classical and novel research on the cognitive consequences of prejudice (for a recent review, see Crandall & Eshleman, 2003). Earlier research is consistent with the notion that prejudice is associated with attentional biases. At the level of signal detection parameters, Dorfman, Keeve, and Saslow (1971) demonstrated that highly anti-Semitic participants had a greater sensitivity than non-anti-Semitic participants when identifying Jews versus non-Jews from facial photographs, which could be explained by greater attention being paid to subtle distinguishing features of those faces. In a more recent study, prejudiced individuals, after perceiving a category label of the prejudiced group, activated stereotypic content about the prejudiced outgroup spontaneously and used this content in subsequent judgments. Nonprejudiced individuals, however, did not do so (Lepore & Brown, 1997), suggesting that prejudice is associated with spontaneous cognitive processing taking place with respect to the targets of prejudice and the relevant information that is available. In an experiment measuring responses at automatic versus controlled levels of processing, participants who were highly prejudiced against Blacks showed a facilitation of the Black stereotype in both these conditions, whereas participants low in prejudice against Blacks showed no such facilitation (Kawakami, Dion, & Dovidio, 1998). The latter result is significant because it appears that not only automatic but also controlled (attention-demanding) strategies are susceptible to the influence of prejudice. From these results, the effects of stereotype-relevant cues should be viewed as potentially interfering, because such cues would direct high-prejudiced individuals' attention away from a generative reasoning task.

Basically, the main prediction from the previous review of prejudice research is that targets of negative stereotypes and prejudices attract special attention, thereby often evoking emotional conflict, or suppression tendencies. In this sense, nontarget elements might be ignored or given less processing. Consequently, memory maintenance and reasoning accuracy for nontarget elements would be diminished. This tendency would be especially evidenced among prejudiced persons because for them, the negative emotions and often fear-laden attentional focus that are evoked by a negative stereotypical target might be especially vivid. In this sense, this prediction is germane to the findings of Fox and her associates (see chapter by Fox & Georgiou in this volume), according to which anxious people were not able to disengange their attentional focus from the threatening object.

We will present and discuss the findings for target and nontarget relations separately, as their patterns were completely different. To symmetrically assess the accuracy for inferred relations, we calculated separate accuracy values concerning 2-step relations for nontarget relations (BD, Jacek vs. Jakub, see Figure 14.1) and for target relations (AC, Hans vs. Bogdan). Additionally, study times and accuracies for adjacent relations were calculated separately for target and nontarget relations.

Prejudiced and nonprejudiced participants did not differ in accuracy for either memory maintenance (target/adjacent relations, see Table 14.2) or for inferred relations (target/2-step relations). However, they differed in their study time pattern. Study times were significantly shorter for prejudiced participants, but their accuracy level for target relations was equivalent to nonprejudiced students. These findings support the first set of predictions, showing that prejudice and negative stereotypes might facilitate processing of stereotypical content. In other words, prejudiced individuals were more efficient – they invested less effort to obtain comparable high accuracy in memory retrieval and linear reasoning about target relations.

However, a completely different story emerged for nontarget relations (see Table 14.2). Prejudiced students were less efficient in accuracy concerning both memory maintenance (nontarget/adjacent relations) and generative reasoning (nontarget/2-step relations). Additionally, and mirroring the results for target pairs, study times were shorter among prejudiced as compared to nonprejudiced participants. It was evident from the attenuation analysis (see Table 14.3) that in contrast to the cognitive aging study, the significantly lowered memory maintenance did not explain the generative reasoning deficit for prejudiced participants. Prejudice still produced a significant impairment of integrative reasoning about a nontarget person when memory retrieval differences were partialled out. The attenuation level obtained here was similar to that observed in our study on stereotype threat.

To conclude, negative stereotypes seem to be effective mental tools when encoding and reasoning about target objects of the particular stereotypical concern. However, stereotypes and prejudice do not seem to have beneficial effects when encoding and reasoning with concerned nontarget objects.

AN INTERIM SUMMARY

To recapitulate, the paradigm used here, that is, the construction of transitive linear orders, allows a number of different perspectives on generative reasoning. First, studying accuracy at testing as a function of pair distance is indicative of whether or not spontaneous integration of piecemeal relations during the learning phase took place. A stepwise decline across levels of pair distance indicates that such spontaneous integration probably did not take place. Second, by conducting attenuation analyses (Salthouse, 1992), we can assess to what degree impairments of this type of integration are accounted for by insufficient maintenance in working memory, or alternatively in cases of no attenuation, what should be considered genuine integrative deficits. Thirdly, the analysis of study times can help clarify participants' strategies of allocating their attention to the materials learned.

In light of these three perspectives, we can now attempt a synopsis of the results across different areas of application that we have so far discussed in this chapter. For mild depression in undergraduate populations (studies 1 and 2), there appears to be a genuine weakness of the integrative function that drives the observed deficits in generative reasoning. Earlier work (von Hecker & Sedek, 1999) has demonstrated analogous effects, as depressed participants showed inferior performance in the construction of a social mental model. Results using different paradigms, such as depressed individuals' difficulties in systematic testing (Smith et al., 1993), their failures to initiate more complex strategies in memory tasks (Hertel & Rude, 1991), or encoding impairments in depression (Channon et al., 1993), may all, at least to a substantial part, be due to a deficit in the online generation of coherent episodic or situation models from incoming pieces of information. Notably, taking working memory maintenance into account did not attenuate the influence of depression on reasoning, nor did the depressed participants show any marked differences in study times, indicating that their allocation of attention was largely the same as in nondepressed students. Moreover, these conclusions were supported by an additional experiment (Sedek & von Hecker, 2004, Study 4) using a measure of working memory (operational span or OSPAN; Turner & Engle, 1989). OSPAN explained a considerable amount of variance in linear integrative reasoning, supporting the existing literature about its strength as the predictor of reasoning accuracy (see chapter by Unsworth et al., this volume). However, depression still remained a significant predictor of linear order reasoning when the impact of OSPAN was partialed out (25% attenuation).

In sharp contrast, study 3 on older versus younger control individuals quite clearly pointed to short-term memory problems as the main cause of the older individuals' impaired generative reasoning. Attenuation in this case was almost complete. In other words, once equalized for the level of maintenance function, older and younger participants exhibited the same performance level with respect to integration. These results were replicated by further study (Sedek & von Hecker, 2004, Study 4) using additional measures of working memory and mental speed. This pattern is interesting in the light of current theories on cognitive deficits in aged people ("simultaneity mechanism," Salthouse, 1996), which emphasize that although some of the initial steps of processing might be executed efficiently, such as initial strategies to store and rehearse the perceived piecemeal relations, the actual contents may become quickly unavailable to further processing because of decay. Thus integration, which comes last in the sequence of cognitive operations in the linear order construction task, would suffer.

The study on stereotype threat demonstrated disruptive effects of the presence of negative stereotypes on generative reasoning, particularly end-point accuracy. This disruption was partially mediated by maintenance problems, as the attenuation analysis revealed. Those maintenance problems are likely due to a general depletion of working memory resources associated with the experience of stereotype threat (Schmader & Johns, 2003). When faced with negative stereotyped expectations, anxiety about underperformance and being unfavorably evaluated constitute a big concern in target individuals (Steele & Aronson, 1995), and as such are likely to absorb a large part of the available attentional resources. It would however appear likely that the ensuing general depletion of attentional resources is not limited to maintenance functions, but also extends to the function of integration, because the statistical relation between stereotype threat and end-point accuracy was only halfway attenuated by maintenance. In light of these findings, it would be informative to carry out further studies that would include both demanding generative reasoning tasks and some measures of working memory capacity as well.

The last study demonstrated that prejudice exerts its impairing influence on generative reasoning substantially, but not entirely, through attentional bias. Interestingly however, those attention-driven maintenance problems did not eliminate the relationship between prejudice and integrative reasoning. It appears likely that the attentional bias that impairs initial strategies of rehearsal and maintenance of those elements that do not contain prejudice-relevant content also impairs the later stage of proper integration. It is of further interest to note that in terms of self-paced study times, although high-prejudiced participants chose much shorter average times than low-prejudiced participants, both groups of participants exhibited a certain attentional bias toward AB, the pair containing prejudice-relevant content.

GENERAL CONCLUSIONS

When looking across the accuracy findings in our four research domains, it is possible to attempt some "ranking" concerning the presence of a genuine generative deficit in integrative reasoning. On the one extreme end of this ranking is subclinical depression. Here, it seems that more elementary memory and attentional processes are preserved, but the more constructive processes (the more abstract cognitive bindings; see the chapter by Waltz, this volume) are impaired. On the other extreme end of this classification is cognitive aging, in which it is obvious that the main problems of older aldults were not the reasoning operations per se but more elementary problems with the maintenance of necessary input information during processing (see also the strong cases about this problem being made by the Oberauer and Verhaeghen et al. chapters in this volume). Intermediary positions on the rank order are taken by the deficits in integrative reasoning shown by participants under stereotype threat and by students who hold negative prejudice (however, in the latter case, the integrative problems are highly selective and concern only nontarget objects). It looks as if in the case of stereotypes and prejudice, maybe paradoxically, the attentional and emotional distractions play a more influential role in lowering reasoning accuracy than they do in the case of subclinical depression. The findings concerning depression confirm the message by McIntosh, Sedek, Fojas, and Brzezicka-Rotkiewicz (this volume), that depression is associated with less efficient strategies of performing more complex cognitive tasks.

Nevertheless, it appears that depression, stereotype threat induction, and, to some extent, high levels of prejudice are associated with some level of genuine integrative deficit that cannot be explained in terms of impaired maintenance in working memory. How would it be possible to elucidate in more detail the nature of those integrative deficits? One way offered by the existing literature is to include additional measures of working memory span (Hambrick & Engle, 2003) or working memory facets (Oberauer, Süß, Wilhelm, & Wittmann, 2003) in research designs dealing with reasoning in different populations. Another way to clarify the issue would be to analyze in more detail the conscious intentions; the representations of tasks, instructions, and goals; and cognitive control attempts in performing more complex procedures (see Carlson & Sohn, 2000; Sohn & Carlson, 1998; see also West & Bowry, and Barch & Braver, this volume).

Overall, the reported research elucidates the fruitfulness of applying one and the same cognitive paradigm to several populations and psychological states with the aim of comparing different models of processing limitations among those populations. We believe that progress in the understanding of resource limitations in a more interdisciplinary sense will depend on the development of paradigms that are specific enough to address elementary as well as more complex functions within working memory but that are at the same time general enough to provide insights into fundamental cognitive capabilities, such as generative reasoning.

## Author Note

The experiments reported and the preparation of this chapter were supported by Polish Committee for Scientific Research grant 5 H01F 013 21 awarded to Grzegorz

Sedek, and by German National Research Foundation grant He 2225 and Economic and Social Research Council grant RES-000-23-0496, both awarded to Ulrich von Hecker. We express thanks to Rhiannon Buck and Sonja Geiger for her helpful comments on a draft of this chapter.

## References

Bargh, S. A., & Thein, R. D. (1985). Individual construct accessibility, person memory, and the recall-judgment-link: The case of information overload. *Journal of Personality and Social Psychology, 49*, 1129–1146.

Beck, A. T. (1967). *Depression: Causes and treatment*. Philadelphia: University of Pennsylvania Press.

Bedynska, S., Sedek, G., & Brzezicka-Rotkiewicz, A. (2004). *The analysis of cognitive impairments among targets of negative stereotype: The integrative reasoning and performance of complex working memory tasks*. Paper presented at the Small Group Meeting of EAESP on Understanding the Academic Underachievement of Low Status Group Members (Paris, France).

Bodenhausen, G. V., Macrae, C. N., & Sherman, J. W. (1999). On the dialectics of discrimination: Dual processes in social stereotyping. In S. Chaiken & Y. Trope (Eds.), *Dual-process theories in social psychology* (pp. 271–290). New York, London: The Guilford Press.

Bruner, J. (1957). On perceptual readiness. *Psychological Review, 64*, 123–152.

Carlson, R. A., & Sohn, M.-H. (2000). Cognitive control of multistep routines: Information processing and conscious intentions. In S. Monsell & J. Driver (Eds.), *Attention and performance XVIII* (pp. 443–464). Cambridge, MA: MIT Press.

Channon, S., Baker, J. E., & Robertson, M. M. (1993). Effects of structure and clustering on recall and recognition memory in clinical depression. *Journal of Abnormal Psychology, 102*, 323–326.

Conway, M., & Giannopoulos, C. (1993). Dysphoria and decision making: Limited information use for evaluations of multiattribute targets. *Journal of Personality and Social Psychology, 64*, 613–623.

Craik, F. I. M., & Salthouse, T. A. (2000). *The handbook of aging and cognition* (2nd ed.). Mahwah, NJ: Lawrence Erlbaum Associates.

Crandall, C. S., & Eshleman, A. (2003). A justification-suppression model of the expression and experience of prejudice. *Psychological Bulletin, 129*, 414–446.

Dorfman, D. D., Keeve, S., & Saslow, C. (1971). Ethnic identification: A signal detection analysis. *Journal of Personality and Social Psychology, 18*, 373–379.

Ellis, H. C., & Ashbrook, P. W. (1988). Resource allocation model of the effects of depressed mood states on memory. In K. Fiedler & J. Forgas (Eds.), *Affect, cognition, and social behaviour* (pp. 25–43), Göttingen, Federal Republic of Germany: Hogrefe.

Ellis, H. C., Ottaway, S. A., Varner, L. J., Becker, A. S., & Moore, B. A. (1997). Emotion, motivation, and text comprehension: The detection of contradictions in passages. *Journal of Experimental Psychology: General, 126*, 131–146.

Emmorey, K. (2001). Space on hand: The exploitation of signing space to illustrate abstract thought. In M. Gattis (Ed.), *Spatial schemas and abstract thought* (pp. 147–174). Cambridge, MA: The MIT Press.

Engle, R. W. (1996). Working memory, and retrieval: An inhibition-resource approach. In J. T. E. Richardson, R. Engle, L. Hasher, R. Logie, E. Stoltzfus, & R. Zacks (Eds.), *Working memory in human cognition* (pp. 89–119). New York: Oxford University Press.

Fiske, S. T. (1998). Stereotyping, prejudice, and discrimination. In D. T. Gilbert, S. T. Fiske, & G. Lindzey (Eds.), *The handbook of social psychology* (4th ed., Vol. 2, pp. 357–411). New York: McGraw-Hill.

Glenberg, A. M., & Langston, W. E. (1992). Comprehension of illustrated text: Pictures help to build mental models. *Journal of Memory and Language, 31,* 129–151.

Glenberg, A. M., Meyer, M., & Lindem, K. (1987). Mental models contribute to foregrounding during text comprehension. *Journal of Memory and Language, 26,* 69–83.

Gotlib, I. H., Roberts, J. E., & Gilboa, E. (1996). Cognitive interference in depression. In I. G. Sarason, G. Pierce, & B. R. Sarason (Eds.), *Cognitive interference. Theories, methods, and findings* (pp. 347–377). Mahwah, NJ: Lawrence Erlbaum Associates.

Greenwald, A. G., McGhee, D. E., & Schwartz, J. L. K. (1998). Measuring individual differences in implicit cognition: The Implicit Association Test. *Journal of Personality and Social Psychology, 74,* 1464–1480.

Halford, G. S. (1993). *Children's understanding. The development of mental models.* Hillsdale, NJ: Lawrence Erlbaum Associates.

Hambrick, D. Z., & Engle, R. W. (2003). The role of working memory in problem solving. In J. E. Davidson & R. J. Sternberg (Eds.), *The psychology of problem solving* (pp. 176–206). Cambridge: Cambridge University Press.

Hampton, J. A. (1997). Emergent attributes in combined concepts. In T. B. Ward, S. M. Smith, & J. Vaid (Eds.), *Creative thought: An investigation of conceptual structures and processes* (pp. 83–110). Washington: APA.

Hastie, R. (1980). Memory for behavioral information that confirms or contradicts a personality impression. In R. Hastie, T. M. Ostrom, E. B. Ebbesen, R. S. Wyer, D. L. Hamilton, & D. E. Carlston (Eds.), *Person Memory: The cognitive basis of social perception* (pp. 155–178). Hillsdale, NJ: Lawrence Erlbaum Associates.

Hertel, P. T., & Rude, S. S. (1991). Depressive deficits in memory: Focusing attention improves subsequent recall. *Journal of Experimental Psychology: General, 120,* 301–309.

Hess, T. M., Bolstad, C. A., Woodburn, S. M., & Auman, C. (1999). Trait diagnosticity versus behavioral consistency as determinants of impression change in adulthood. *Psychology and Aging, 1,* 77–89.

Holyoak, K. J., & Patterson, K. K. (1981). A positional discriminability model of linearorder judgement. *Journal of Experimental Psychology: Human Perception and Performance, 7,* 1283–1302.

Huttenlocher, J. (1968). Constructing spatial images: A strategy in reasoning. *Psychological Review, 75,* 550–560.

Johnson-Laird, P. N. (1972). The three-term series problem. *Cognition, 1,* 57–82.

Johnson-Laird, P. N. (1983). *Mental models: Towards a cognitive science of language, inference and consciousness.* Cambridge, UK: University Press.

Kawakami, K., Dion, K., & Dovidio, J. F. (1998). Racial prejudice and stereotype activation. *Personality and Social Psychology Bulletin, 24,* 407–416.

Kliegl, R., Mayr, U., & Oberauer, K. (2000). Resource limitations and process dissociations in individual differences research. In U. V. Hecker, S. Dutke, & G. Sedek (Eds.), *Generative mental processes and cognitive resources: Integrative research in adaptation and control* (pp. 337–366). Dordrecht: Kluwer Academic Publishers.

Kofta, M., & Sedek, G. (1989). Repeated failure: A source of helplessness, or a factor irrelevant to its emergence? *Journal of Experimental Psychology: General, 118,* 3–12.

Lepore, L., & Brown, R. (1997). Category and stereotype activation: Is prejudice inevitable? *Journal of Personality and Social Psychology, 72,* 275–287.

Leth-Steensen, C., & Marley, A. A. J. (2000). A model or response time effect in symbolic comparison. *Psychological Review, 107,* 62–100.

Light, L. L. (1996). Memory and aging. In E. L. Bjork & R. A. Bjork (Eds.), *Handbook of perception and cognition: Memory* (pp. 443–490). San Diego, CA: Academic Press.

Macrae, C. N., Milne, A. B., & Bodenhausen, G. V. (1994a). Stereotypes as energy-saving devices: A peek inside the cognitive toolbox. *Journal of Personality and Social Psychology, 66,* 37–47.

Macrae, C. N., Stangor, C., & Milne, A. B. (1994b). Activating social stereotypes: A functional analysis. *Journal of Experimental Social Psychology, 30,* 370–389.

Marx, E. M., Williams, J. M. G., & Claridge, G. C. (1992). Depression and social problem solving. *Journal of Abnormal Psychology, 101,* 78–86.

McGonigle, B., & Chalmers, M. (1984). The selective impact of question form and input mode on the symbolic distance effect in children. *Journal of Experimental Child Psychology, 37,* 525–554.

Mynatt, B. T., & Smith, K. H. (1977). Constructive processes in linear order problems revealed by sentence study times. *Journal of Experimental Psychology: Human Learning and Memory, 3,* 357–374.

Oberauer, K., Süß, H.-M., Wilhelm, O., & Wittmann, W. W. (2003). The multiple faces of working memory – storage, processing, supervision, and coordination. *Intelligence, 31,* 167–193.

Perfect, T. J., & Maylor, E. A. (2000). *Models of cognitive aging.* Oxford, UK: Oxford University Press.

Piaget, J., & Inhelder, B. (1974). *The child's construction of quantities: Conservation and atomism.* London: Routledge & Kegan Paul.

Piber-Dabrowska, K. (2000). *Affective processing of information about the out-group: On the relationship between explicit and implicit evaluative associations.* Paper presented at the workshop on Prosocial Behavior, Department of Psychology, University of Cologne, Germany.

Piber-Dabrowska, K., & Sedek, G. (2004). *Prejudice and reasoning about linear orders.* Paper presented at the ESCON Transfer of Knowledge Conference, Lisbon, Portugal.

Potts G. R. (1972). Information processing strategies used in the encoding of linear orderings. *Journal of Verbal Learning and Verbal Behavior, 11,* 727–740.

Quinn, D. M., & Spencer, S. J. (2001). The interference of stereotype threat with women's generation of mathematical problem solving strategies. *Journal of Social Issues, 57,* 55–71.

Rabinowitz, F. M., Grant, M. J., Howe, M. L., & Walsh, C. (1994). Reasoning in middle childhood: A dynamic model of performance on transitive tasks. *Journal of Experimental Child Psychology, 58,* 252–288.

Salthouse, T. A. (1990). Working-memory as a processing resource in cognitive aging. *Developmental Review, 10,* 101–124.

Salthouse, T. A. (1992). Working-memory mediation of adult age differences in integrative reasoning. *Memory and Cognition, 20,* 413–423.

Salthouse, T. A. (1996). The processing-speed theory of adult age differences in cognition. *Psychological Review, 103,* 403–428.

Salthouse, T. A., Legg, S., Palmon, R., & Mitchell, D. (1990). Memory factors in age-related differences in simple reasoning. *Psychology and Aging, 5,* 9–15.

Salthouse, T. A., Mitchell, D. R. D., Skovronek, E., & Babcock, R. L. (1989). Effects of adult age and working memory on reasoning and spatial abilities. *Journal of Experimental Psychology: Learning, Memory, and Cognition, 15,* 507–516.

Schmader, T., & Johns, M. (2003). Converging evidence that stereotype threat reduces working memory capacity. *Journal of Personality and Social Psychology, 85,* 440–452.

Sedek, G., & Kofta, M. (1990). When cognitive exertion does not yield cognitive gain: Toward an informational explanation of learned helplessness. *Journal of Personality and Social Psychology, 58,* 729–743.

Sedek, G., & von Hecker, U. (2004). Effects of subclinical depression and aging on generative reasoning about linear orders: Same or different processing limitations? *Journal of Experimental Psychology: General, 133,* 237–260.

Sherman, J. W. (2001). The dynamic relationship between stereotype efficiency and mental representation. In G. B. Moskowitz (Ed.), *Cognitive social psychology: The Princeton symposium on the legacy and future of social cognition* (pp. 177–190). Mahwah, NJ: Lawrence Erlbaum Associates.

Sherman, J. W., Lee, A. Y., Bessenoff, G. R., & Frost, L. A. (1998). Stereotype efficiency reconsidered: Encoding flexibility under cognitive load. *Journal of Personality and Social Psychology, 75,* 589–606.

Shih, M., Pittinsky, T. L., & Ambady, N. (1999). Stereotype susceptibility: Identity salience and shifts in quantitative performance. *Psychological Science, 10,* 80–83.

Smith, J. D., Tracy, J. I., & Murray, M. J. (1993). Depression and category learning. *Journal of Experimental Psychology: General, 122,* 331–346.

Smith K. H., & Foos, P. W. (1975). Effect of presentation order on the construction of linear orders. *Memory and Cognition, 3,* 614–618.

Sohn, M.-H., & Carlson, R. A. (1998). Procedural frameworks for simple arithmetic skills. *Journal of Experimental Psychology: Learning, Memory, and Cognition, 24,* 1052–1067.

Spencer, S. J., Steele, C. M., & Quinn, D. M. (1999). Stereotype threat and women's math performance. *Journal of Experimental Social Psychology, 35,* 4–28.

Srull, T. K., & Wyer, R. S. (1989). Person memory and judgment. *Psychological Review, 96,* 58–83.

Steele, C. M., & Aronson, J. (1995). Stereotype threat and the intellectual test performance of African American. *Journal of Personality and Social Psychology, 69,* 797–811.

Sternberg, R. J. (1980). Representation and process in linear syllogistic reasoning. *Journal of Experimental Psychology: General, 109,* 119–159.

Trabasso, T., Riley, C. A., & Wilson, E. G. (1975). The representation of linear order and spatial strategies in reasoning: A developmental study. In R. Falmagne

(Ed.), *Reasoning: Representation and process* (pp. 201–229). Hillsdale, NJ: Lawrence Erlbaum Associates.

Turner, M. L., & Engle, R. W. (1989). Is working memory capacity task dependent? *Journal of Memory and Language, 28,* 127–154.

Tzelgov, J., Yehene, V., Kotler, L., & Alon, A. (2000). Automatic comparisons of artificial digits never compared: Learning linear ordering relations. *Journal of Experimental Psychology: Learning, Memory and Cognition, 26,* 103–120.

von Hecker, U., & Sedek, G. (1999). Uncontrollability, depression, and the construction of mental models. *Journal of Personality and Social Psychology, 77,* 833–850.

von Hecker, U., Sedek, G., & McIntosh, D. N. (2000). Impaired systematic, higher order strategies in depression and helplessness: Testing implications of the cognitive exhaustion model. In U. vonHecker, S. Dutke, & G. Sedek (Eds.), *Generative mental processes and cognitive resources: Integrative research on adaptation and control* (pp. 245–275). Dordrecht: Kluwer Academic Publishers.

von Hippel, W., Sekaquapteva, D., & Vargas, P. (1995). On the role of encoding processes in stereotype maintenance. *Advances in Experimental Social Psychology, 27,* 177–254.

Zabrucky, K., Moore, D., & Schultz, N. R., Jr. (1993). Young and older adults' ability to use different standards to evaluate understanding. *Journal of Gerontology: Psychological Sciences, 48,* P238–P244.

# Name Index

# Subject Index

absolute span, 6
abstract reasoning
  schemas in, 347
abstract thought
  interconnectedness of, 346
  knowledge structure and, 346
  in neuropsychiatric illness, 349
  stress, anxiety and, 370
  WM subsystems and, 350
AD. *See* Alzheimer's disease
ADD. *See* Attention Deficit Disorder
additive cost, 168
additive effect, 169
  as multiplicative effect, 169
ADHD. *See* Attention Deficit Hyperactivity
  Disorder
Affect Infusion Model, 298
age
  antisaccade task and, 24
  cognitive control, WM and, 98, 101
  cognitive functioning and, 37
  cognitive performance and, 44
  conflict processing and, 98
  context processing and, 105, 147
  coordination and, 185
  CRN and, 113
  dopamine function and, 101, 147
  ERN and, 112, 113
  generative reasoning and, 386
  goal neglect and, 98
  information inhibition and, 51, 52,
    97
  integration performance and, 387
  intrusion probes and, 61
  motor inhibition and, 333
  processing resources and, 97

  prosaccade task and, 24
  response time and, 163
  selective attention processes and,
    185
  Stroop facilitation effect and, 103
  Stroop interference effect and, 103
  switch costs and, 47
  switch costs, working memory load and,
    65
  task set switching and, 47, 49
  working memory storage and, 65
aging. *See also* cognitive aging
  balance, cognitive function and, 199–208
  cognitive control and, 115, 175, 184
  cognitive deficits in, 346
  conflict processing and, 103–107, 114
  conflict SP and, 107
  coordination and, 171–172
  deficits of, 386–388
  dual-task performance and, 171–172
  error processing and, 114
  executive control and, 173–176
  frontal lobe hypothesis of, 99
  general slowing and, 162–164
  goal maintenance and, 115
  goal neglect and, 107–112, 114,
    115
  inhibition deficit hypothesis of, 314–315
  on inhibitory processes, 337
  lexical v. non-lexical effects of, 171
  on motor control, 335
  neuropsychological effects of, 99
  prefrontal cortex and, 99
  WMC and, 38
aging research
  cognitive psychology and, 185

419